de la Mothe, Cambri

EXILE AND SOCIAL THOUGHT

EXILE AND
SOCIAL THOUGHT

HUNGARIAN INTELLECTUALS
IN GERMANY AND AUSTRIA,
1919–1933

Lee Congdon

PRINCETON UNIVERSITY PRESS

PRINCETON, NEW JERSEY

LIBRARY OF CONGRESS CATALOGING-IN-PUBLICATION DATA

CONGDON, LEE, 1939–

EXILE AND SOCIAL THOUGHT : HUNGARIAN INTELLECTUALS IN
GERMANY AND AUSTRIA, 1919–1933 / BY LEE CONGDON.

P.   CM.

INCLUDES BIBLIOGRAPHICAL REFERENCES AND INDEX.

ISBN 0-691-03159-2

1. INTELLECTUALS—HUNGARY—HISTORY—20TH CENTURY.

2. INTELLECTUALS—GERMANY—HISTORY—20TH CENTURY.

3. INTELLECTUALS—AUSTRIA—HISTORY—20TH CENTURY.

4. HUNGARY—EXILES—HISTORY—20TH CENTURY.

5. GERMANY—EXILES—HISTORY—20TH CENTURY.

6. AUSTRIA—EXILES—HISTORY—20TH CENTURY.

7. SOCIOLOGY—HUNGARY—HISTORY—20TH CENTURY

8. SOCIOLOGY—GERMANY—HISTORY—20TH CENTURY.

9. SOCIOLOGY—AUSTRIA—HISTORY—20TH CENTURY. I. TITLE.

HM213.C55   1991   305.5′52′0943—DC20   90-47718

To Carol, Mitchell, and Colleen

CONTENTS

LIST OF ILLUSTRATIONS

PREFACE

SCHOLARS have devoted a great deal of attention to the intellectual migration from Germany to the United States and England after 1933. Until quite recently, however, not even Budapest historians had studied the 1919 movement of Hungarian social thinkers from their homeland to Germany and Austria. And no one has yet attempted a comprehensive history, perhaps because even the most careful observers of the Weimar era have failed to notice that at almost every turn one meets with a Hungarian emigré. Indeed, it is only a slight exaggeration to say that exiled Hungarians *created* Weimar culture.

This, then, is a historical and critical study of some of the twentieth century's most seminal and influential social theorists. The vast majority of them were men and women of the left, but they were very far from being of one mind. United in opposition to Admiral Miklós Horthy's counterrevolutionary government in Hungary, they disagreed, often violently, about virtually everything else. Even within the three principal camps—communist, avant-garde, and liberal—they regularly engaged in vitriolic polemics.

And yet all of the Communists, among whom Georg Lukács was preeminent, professed allegiance to Soviet Russia and vilified avant-gardists and liberals. The avant-gardists, led by Lajos Kassák, shared a commitment to international modernism, a distrust of communist *parties*, and a contempt for liberalism. The liberals, the least homogeneous and predictable group, often surprised themselves by defending positions informed by a conservative logic. But they all looked to Oszkár Jászi for inspiration and, until 1933 at least, considered themselves to be progressives, more realistic and responsible than Communists and avant-gardists.

In what follows, my principal purpose has been hermeneutical—to interpret a rich corpus of social thought. To that end, I have directed attention to the interrelationship between the ideas these Hungarians entertained, the world in which they lived, and the conditions of their personal existence. The theories they developed were deeply affected by the Great War, the Russian and Hungarian revolutions of 1917–19, and the interwar histories of Germany and Austria. And in an even more literal sense, they were expressions of individual biography. Underlying similarities of outlook derived from a common experience of exile but also, with few exceptions, a common identity as assimilated Jews. Concerning the latter, I must say an introductory word.

Because they supported the national cause during the anti-Habsburg uprising of 1848–49, the Jews of Hungary earned the Magyars' gratitude; in 1849, the revolutionary government enacted a law of Jewish emancipation. Forged in the crucible of a lost war of independence, the act was little more than a gesture of goodwill, but it did constitute a moral commitment on the part of the Magyars, and in the aftermath of the Austro-Hungarian *Ausgleich* (Compromise) of 1867, the Diet enacted a new law. The Magyars assumed that the Jews would assimilate and strengthen the Hungarian nation, and they were not disappointed. By century's end, three-quarters of them had changed nationality, often magyarizing their names and surpassing "pure" Hungarians in their patriotic zeal for the nation and its ruling Liberal Party.

The principals in this study, assimilated Jews who came of age around 1900, had every reason to look forward to a bright future. Secure in their identity, they pursued advanced studies not only in Hungary, but in Germany and Austria as well. Language presented no obstacle because most of them spoke German at home. As a result, they rooted themselves more deeply than their more provincial countrymen in Europe's great bourgeois culture.

At the same time, they lived in a stimulating, and rapidly growing, capital. When Buda and Pest united in 1873, the "new" city of Budapest had a population of some three hundred thousand, making it only Europe's seventeenth largest. By 1900, however, it had climbed to eighth place, with over seven hundred thousand inhabitants. As the Monarchy's second city, moreover, it aspired to be a worthy rival of Vienna, and soon began to transform itself. City fathers saw to the laying out of impressive new thoroughfares such as the *Ringstrasse*, which described a huge arc in Pest, and Andrássy Street, which connected downtown Pest with the City Park. Underneath the latter, they built the continent's first subway. And still they managed to find funds sufficient to construct the Margaret, Franz Josef, and Elizabeth Bridges across the Danube. Everywhere city residents cast their eyes, in fact, they could see new structures rising: the East Railroad Station, the "Fishermen's Bastion," the Opera House, the imposing Parliament building.

This rapid growth produced an urban culture at odds with that rooted in the nobility's county life. It centered in editorial offices and coffeehouses, and framed a liberalism tinged with socialism that challenged the official version. Above all, it was critical, for behind the facade the city erected for the 1896 Millennium—commemorating the Magyars' entry into the Carpathian Basin—its creators discovered a "wasteland" where emigration, suicide, and other social problems testified to a profound malaise. The young Jews in the forefront of the new culture did not hesitate to break with their fathers' social and political conformism. Every bit as patriotic, they believed they could agitate for change without jeopardizing their assimilation.

As the new century opened, however, growing numbers of non-Jewish Magyars, bursting with Millennial pride, came to regard any publicly-voiced dissent from official optimism as "un-Magyar." Patriotism rapidly degenerated into nationalism and stirred the flickering embers of anti-Semitism. Just as incendiary, Jewish immigration continued to increase. Attracted by the opportunities Hungary offered, Jews poured into the country from the east, from

Russia and Galicia. By 1910, 220,000 of them resided in Budapest, or "Judapest" as Austrian anti-Semites called it; they comprised nearly one-fourth of the capital's citizenry. What is more, they were conspicuous in public life. One-fourth to one-half of all physicians, lawyers, and journalists in Hungary were Jewish. Jews dominated banking and commerce even more completely, and as a consequence many who suffered from the disintegrative forces unleashed by the new capitalism channeled their disappointments into racial resentment.

To be sure, the philosemitic government disapproved. In the early 1880s, at the time of a "ritual murder" trial, Minister President Kálmán Tisza reaffirmed his resolve to protect the rights of every citizen and denounced anti-Semitism as injurious to the national honor. But neither he nor his successors could stem the ominous tide, and before long Hungarians, Jewish and non-Jewish, recognized that the problem was no longer merely that of Jewish immigration, but of Jewish assimilation itself. By the time the guns of August 1914 sounded, therefore, the thinkers whose work I have sought to interpret had begun to feel that they might be caught in a process of dissimilation.

Having thus prefaced my interpretive efforts, I wish to add only that I have attempted to accomplish my critical purpose indirectly rather than directly. Hence although I have not concealed my sympathy for the liberals, I have tried to treat each thinker with as much respect as possible. It is one of the failures of our time, I believe, that criticism too often precedes comprehension. As Karl Mannheim argued, we can only engage in meaningful conversation, and debate, when we understand what another intended to say.

ACKNOWLEDGMENTS

ALTHOUGH WRITING is a solitary adventure, even the most monastic of scholars must rely upon the wisdom and kindness of others. In my experience, there were many others, several of whom I would like to thank publicly. Through good times and bad, W. Bruce Lincoln has remained a faithful adviser, example, and friend. At various and sometimes critical stages, I received encouragement from Samuel H. Baron, István Deák, Paul Gottfried, Győző Határ, Árpád Kadárkay, Walter Laqueur, William O. McCagg, Jr., Alasdair MacIntyre, Judith Marcus, Robert A. Nye, Lorenzo Simpson, Zoltán Tarr, and Hans Zeisel. Special thanks are also due to Kári Polányi-Levitt, who spoke to me about her parents (Karl Polányi and Ilona Duczynska), and to the late Paul Ignotus, who recalled a lifetime of encounters with Hungarian intellectuals. During the year that the Institute for Advanced Study in Princeton, N.J., extended its hospitality, Morton White and J. H. Elliott took an inspiriting interest in my researches.

At my home institution, Michael J. Galgano, Chairman of the Department of History, supported my work in countless ways and did everything possible to arrange extended periods of free time. Raymond M. Hyser, Jr., interrupted his own work to instruct me in the use of word processors and to perform some of the more exacting—and mysterious—operations. David Owusu-Ansah lifted my spirits with his sense of humor and dedication to scholarship. And as always, the late David A. Hallman listened to me, as a friend. Among my Budapest colleagues, I am particularly grateful to Éva Gábor, Géza Jeszenszky, György Litván, and J. C. Nyíri. I regret that Miklós Béládi and István Hermann passed away before I could acknowledge their expert advice. Most important, Alex Bandy, Budapest correspondent for the Associated Press, deepened my understanding of Hungarian communism and sacrificed an immense amount of his time to track down and secure needed Hungarian sources. Without his tireless efforts and loyal friendship, I could not have completed this book.

In addition to these colleagues and friends, various institutions have aided my work. Along the way, I enjoyed generous support from the American Council of Learned Societies, the Fulbright-Hays Faculty Research Abroad Program, the International Research and Exchanges Board, James Madison University, and the National Endowment for the Humanities. Archivists and librarians at the Széchenyi National Library, the Ervin Szabó Municipal Library, the Hungarian Academy of Sciences, the Hoover Institution on War, Revolution and Peace, the Joseph Regenstein Library (The University of Chicago), the Firestone and Marquand Libraries (Princeton University), the Library of Congress, the Alderman and Fifke Kimball Libraries (University of

Virginia), and Carrier Library (James Madison University) were invariably competent and courteous.

For allowing me to cite unpublished material I am indebted to Professor David Wiggins of Oxford University (Aurel Kolnai's memoirs) and the Joseph Regenstein Library (Michael Polányi's Papers). For permission to republish material that appeared originally in somewhat different form in *The World and I*, *Georg Lukács: Theory, Culture, and Politics*, and *Georg Lukács—Ersehnte Totalität*, I wish to thank the Washington Times Corporation, Transaction Books, and Germinal Verlag, respectively.

I have indicated my greatest debt in the dedication.

Harrisonburg, Virginia
February 1990

EXILE AND SOCIAL THOUGHT

INTRODUCTION

HUNGARIAN INTELLECTUALS IN WAR

AND REVOLUTION, 1914–1919

Tisza and Ady

COUNT István Tisza greeted with alarm the news that a Bosnian terrorist had assassinated Franz Ferdinand. The son of Kálmán Tisza, who ruled Hungary with an iron hand from 1875 to 1890, the Hungarian Minister President was a man of great personal courage, but he feared for his country because he knew that a European war might release national and social forces inimical to the continued existence of the Habsburg Monarchy. To be sure, his fervent Calvinist faith predisposed him to a pessimistic view of human affairs and, like most of his countrymen, he could not forget Johann Gottfried Herder's "prophecy" that the Magyars might one day drown in the Central European sea of Slavs. Nevertheless, his fears were not unfounded. The unifications of Germany and Italy had stoked the fires of nationalism within the Monarchy just at a time when Magyarization had become the Hungarian government's official policy. Thus, with the notable exceptions of Jews and Germans, the non-Magyar peoples of Hungary had steadfastly refused to assimilate. That was all the more disturbing because the Serbs to the South and the Romanians to the East lived in areas contiguous to already existing national states.

Tisza recognized that history was moving in the direction of unified nation-states. He knew, therefore, that he had his work cut out for him if he was to preserve Hungary's territorial integrity and maintain Magyar supremacy. As he put little faith in the policy of forced Magyarization, he had explored, with indifferent success, the possibility of compromise with the Romanians of Transylvania, the largest national minority. As matters stood, then, Tisza could not but oppose any extension of the highly restrictive franchise that would increase the political power of the non-Magyar peoples. Under mounting pressure to make government more representative, he did permit passage of a bill in 1913, but the new law provided for only a slight increase in the number of voters.[1]

Despite the importance that he attached to Parliamentary control, Tisza perceived that social reform movements also threatened Magyar nationalism. "Two great animating powers inspire human activities," he wrote in 1911, "the divisive social force and the unifying national idea, class interest and common interest, economic egoism and the altruism that aims at national greatness. Both are present in human nature and the struggle between them moves history."[2] As advocates of fundamental social change, the social democrats and "bourgeois radicals" around the sociological journal *Huszadik Század* (*Twentieth Century*) worked against Magyar interests. To offset their growing influence, therefore, Tisza and the conservative writer Ferenc Herczeg founded the *Magyar Figyelő* (*Hungarian Observer*) in 1911.

It was this beleaguered but combative political leader, controversialist, and Magyar nationalist who, in July 1914, represented Hungary in the Austrian councils deciding for or against war. Initially, Tisza opposed the resort to arms for which Conrad von Hötzendorf, chief of the general staff, and Count Leopold Berchtold, Foreign Minister, clamored. For one thing, he feared that the Romanians, presented with an opportunity, would invade Transylvania; for another, he had no wish to acquire Serbian territory and thereby increase the number of Serbs in Hungary. In a larger sense, he reckoned that war, whatever its outcome, might lead to a fatal disruption of the Austro-Hungarian *Ausgleich*.

That historic Compromise had given Hungary home rule without making it necessary to sacrifice the Great Power status that union with Austria afforded. It also guaranteed Magyar supremacy and maintained the social domination of the magnates and gentry. Tisza knew how fragile those arrangements were and he could discover no potential Hungarian gain that would outweigh the risks of war. If, he reasoned, the Russians defeated the Germans, the Monarchy would be destroyed, and if the Germans emerged victorious Hungary would be reduced to playing a minor role in a German-dominated *Mitteleuropa*. Only when Berlin made it clear to Vienna and Budapest that the Reich expected decisive military action against Serbia did Tisza relent.[3]

At 6 p.m. on July 23, Baron Wladimir Giesl, the Monarchy's ambassador in Belgrade, handed an ultimatum to the Serbian government and demanded unconditional acceptance within forty-eight hours. With only fleeting minutes remaining, the Serbian Minister President Nikola Pašić presented the Serbian reply, which, though most conciliatory, was conditional. On July 28, therefore, Berchtold notified the Serbs that a state of war existed between their country and Austria-Hungary; within two weeks, all of Europe's Great Powers were at war.

In general, the European peoples greeted the outbreak of hostilities with enthusiasm. Those who bore direct responsibility for the decision to go to war exuded confidence, at least in public. That was no less true in Hungary, where even Tisza, once committed, did not betray his private doubts. Speaking for the Minister President and *Magyar Figyelő*, Herczeg mused that "if since the Persian Wars there has been any struggle that deserves to be called 'holy,' it is our present war."[4] Gyula Andrássy and Albert Apponyi, Tisza's conservative parliamentary opponents, also defended the call to arms. Gyula Justh and Mihály Károlyi, leaders of the Independence Party's left wing, criticized the Monarchy's foreign policy, particularly its German orientation, but by August 2 they too had come around; *Magyarország* (*Hungary*), the newspaper that espoused their views, characterized the war as a "holy thing."[5] The social democrats, in common with their alleged comrades in other countries, quickly closed ranks behind the national leaders.

Like the responsible politicians and populations at large, the majority of Europe's intellectuals applauded the declarations of war. Among the reasons for their enthusiasm were such personal considerations as a love of adventure, a contempt for bourgeois life, and a weakness for the mystique of violence. Above all, however, Europe's intellectuals saw in the conflict the possibility of ending their felt alienation from their fellows.[6] That was particularly true of the Germans, as György Lukács, the brilliant Hungarian literary critic and philosopher living in Heidelberg, argued in an unpublished essay.[7] The isolation and exaggerated individualism that weighed so heavily on German intellectuals before the war had to end, he maintained; a path to "a new, fraternal community" had to be cleared. By compelling men to become comrades in the face of mortal danger, the war became for intellectuals a catalyst for a return from Gesellschaft to Gemeinschaft, society to community.

Lukács's analysis is consistent with what we know about his friends in the circle gathered around Max Weber. The renowned sociologist's wife Marianne remembered that the coming of war signified "an hour of the greatest solemnity—the hour of depersonalization (Entselbstung), of integration into the community. An ardent love of community spread among people, and they felt powerfully united with one another."[8] Her husband served proudly as a reserve officer and the promising philosopher Emil Lask volunteered for service at the front. For his part, Lukács deplored his friends' susceptibility to the war fever. When Mrs. Weber, whom he much admired, related to him acts of martial heroism, he snapped back, "The better the worse!"[9] Never a pacifist, he insisted that the war was nothing but the quintessential expression of an "age of absolute sinfulness," words he borrowed from Fichte.

Lukács's opposition to the war was, however, the exception rather than the rule among Hungarian intellectuals. Most were every bit as prowar as intellectuals elsewhere, and for many of the same reasons. Moreover, because they had been anti-Russian since the Tsar's military intervention in the 1848–49 revolution, they persuaded themselves that the Monarchy was waging a defensive war. Even writers on the political left such as Ignotus, editor of the modernist literary review *Nyugat* (*West*), novelist Zsigmond Móricz, and poet Gyula Juhász rallied to the national cause.[10] Oszkár Jászi, leader of the bourgeois radicals, was of two minds. One moment he was describing the war as a catastrophe, the next he was speculating about the better future that contemporary agonies might prepare. The war, he allowed, could set the stage for a lasting peace and, at the same time, promote greater economic and cultural integration in Central Europe.[11]

Béla Balázs (born Herbert Bauer), the poet, dramatist, and critic who had forged an intellectual alliance with Lukács in 1908, signaled his support of the war by volunteering for duty. He did so because he viewed the hostilities as a struggle between Germany and France for cultural hegemony. As a former member of Georg Simmel's private seminar and an inveterate champion of German culture, his choice was preordained. French culture was so stagnant, he argued in Nyugat's pages, that young French intellectuals were themselves turning to their Frankish heritage. Men such as André Gide and Romain Rolland looked for inspiration to Balzac and Cézanne, who, though French, did not embody the Latin spirit. They attempted to demonstrate, Balázs wrote, "that Mallarmé's sanguinary obscurity and Claudel's primitive profundity are more truly French because they are not Roman but Frank—of German origin!"[12]

Nor was that all, for, incredible as it seems in retrospect, Balázs believed that the war would foster an internationalist spirit. And if being a Jew helped him to recognize that truth, "then this is the great, proclaimed mission reserved for the Jews."[13] Finally, Balázs longed for community. "Forty million men have now walked into the shadow of death," he told the poet and artist Anna Lesznai. "I want to declare my solidarity with ten million Russians and Serbs and I don't know how many Frenchmen when I share with them a mutual suffering on a common battlefield."[14]

Balázs was the most fervent, but far from the only, Hungarian intellectual to put on a uniform. Béla Zalai, whom Lukács once described as "the only original Hungarian thinker" in the period prior to 1918,[15] answered his country's call and was promptly sent to the Galician front. So was Karl Polányi, who had been the first president of the Galileo Circle, a radical student organization that he helped to found at the University of Budapest. Ferenc Békássy returned from Cambridge in order to follow the colors. A poet and student of history at the University, he was a member of the circle around John Maynard Keynes, Bertrand Russell, and Virginia Woolf. After the war, in fact, Woolf and her husband Leonard published a small edition of his English poems. As a Hungarian poet, Békássy sought the advice of Mihály Babits, twentieth-century Hungary's greatest man of letters.[16] So did another poet-recruit, László Nagy (born László Weisz).

Ironically, all of these men detested Tisza and idolized Endre Ady, Hungary's most gifted modern poet and the war's leading opponent. Perhaps unconsciously they sensed that the personal destinies of those two extraordinary men were somehow intertwined and that, together, they embodied the nation's past and future. That intuitive recognition was first articulated in 1920 by the historian Gyula Szekfű, who in his brilliant, if tendentious, Three Gen-

erations, observed that the difference between Ady and Tisza was not as irreconcilable as that between good and bad. Their destinies, he maintained, exhibited a striking commonality. Though critical of Ady's life and work, Szekfű
conceded that the poet belonged to the nation just as surely as Tisza did. "In
moral worth, two lives as different as heaven and earth, but both are *Magyar*
lives."[17]

Ady himself was fully aware that he was bound to Tisza in subtle as well as
obvious ways. He too had been born to a noble, if impoverished, family and
was heir to a Calvinist heritage. Indeed, he was descended from a long line of
Calvinist ministers on his mother's side. For him as for Tisza, Calvinism was
the Magyar religion—Roman Catholicism being the Habsburg faith—and
Transylvania, the seat of Calvinism, was the most purely Magyar of Hungary's
regions. The difference between them, according to Ady, was that Tisza personified the old Hungary, while he symbolized the new. Whereas the statesman adhered to Calvinism's dogmatic letter, he looked to its rebellious spirit.
While Tisza's Magyarism was narrowly nationalistic and conservative, his was
internationalist, politically democratic, and socially radical. And yet: "Even if
we dislike Tisza, we cannot think of him without warming up our blood. What
a strange, baleful, headstrong, vigorous, and fine man—what a Magyar."[18]

Like Tisza and Hungary, Ady was marked for tragedy. He was already suffering from the effects of tertiary syphilis when the war erupted and, like Tisza,
he was deeply pessimistic about the outcome. His brother Lajos later recalled
his immediate reaction; it might have been Tisza's voice. "Whether we lose or
win the war is all the same: we are finished. If we win, the army, the railways,
the postal service, and perhaps even public administration will be German
within a year."[19] There are echoes of this despair in a poem Ady wrote in April
1915.[20]

> To me comrade it is all the same,
> Whether the wolf or devil devours us.
> We are devoured.
> A bear devours us. That does not matter.
> It is an old and sad story.
> Chance only determines *by whom* we are to be devoured.

Franz Josef's Last Years

Tisza and Ady's pessimism proved to be more in keeping with reality than the
facile optimism to which so many succumbed. At the outset of the war, the
Habsburg army numbered about 1,800,000 men, many of whom had received
insufficient training.[21] This army, like that of the Reich, was asked to conduct
a two-front war, its assignment being to defeat Serbia and, at the same time,

hold off Russia long enough to permit the Germans to conquer France. It would have been a formidable task even if Conrad had been more competent than he was. In the event, the Austrian's inexplicable uncertainty about Russia's intentions and his strategic irresolution contributed mightily to early defeats and staggering losses of life. In the first half year of combat, the Monarchy's army lost three-quarters of a million men.[22]

As if matters were not difficult enough, Italy declared war on Austria-Hungary on May 24, 1915. Yet although a substantial number of the Monarchy's professional soldiers had been killed in action the previous fall, its rebuilt army performed quite creditably, not only against the Italians, but also the Russians. Moreover, on September 6, the government joined Germany in initialing a treaty of alliance with Bulgaria. Together, the three allies attacked Serbia on October 7 and, three days later, entered Belgrade. From Tisza's point of view, the most important aspect of that campaign was the Bulgarian alliance, which was crucial to his hopes of discouraging a Romanian strike into Transylvania.

Despite military successes, however, 1915 witnessed the first stirrings of the antiwar movement in Hungary. The death toll had been catastrophic and there was no end to the bloodletting in sight. Moreover, the initial capital of enthusiasm on the home front was rapidly being spent as privations multiplied. Inspired by the Zimmerwald Conference of September 1915, the Hungarian social democrats began to consider legal methods of promoting peace, but because they feared being charged with disloyalty, they did not advance very far beyond vague declarations. Then too, Tisza showed that he was still very much in command by defeating in Parliament a proposal that would have extended the franchise to any soldier over twenty years of age who was serving in the field.[23]

The Minister President could not, however, keep the lid forever on the cauldron of dissent. Some of the *Nyugat* writers, including Móricz and Juhász, abandoned their original support of the war and began to publish stories and poems that not only reflected their personal disillusionment but dramatized the tragedies that so many Hungarian families were experiencing. The talented Margit Kaffka, wife of Béla Balázs's brother Ervin Bauer, recoiled from the slaughter at the front and gave voice to the frustration and pain that Hungarian women felt. Frigyes Karinthy employed his considerable satirical gifts to ridicule diplomats and military leaders, while at the same time celebrating front-line soldiers who, he knew, would quickly have concluded peace.

Even more important than these antiwar writers was Mihály Babits. Never sympathetic with the Hungarian hawks, Babits was sickened by the terrible loss of life, which he experienced in personal ways. He was badly shaken by the news that, on February 2, 1915, his friend Béla Zalai had succumbed to typhus in the Russian prisoner of war camp at Omsk. Scarcely had he begun to recover from that blow when he received word that Ferenc Békássy had fallen in Bukovina during a successful Austro-Hungarian offensive.

In his anger and grief, Babits organized gatherings of like-minded intellectuals at his home. Jászi attended, along with Karinthy and the literary historian Aladár Schöpflin. Together they began to explore ways in which they might hasten the coming of peace and, at the same time, create a more healthy intellectual atmosphere. To that end, Babits composed a poem that greatly stirred the Hungarian intelligentsia: "Before Easter." In it, he sang of him who would first dare to speak the words: "enough! enough! it is enough!/peace! peace!/ peace! peace now!/let there be an end to it now!"[24]

Meanwhile, Balázs had returned to Hungary from the Serbian front, where he had fallen ill with endocarditis. For a time near death, by summer's end he had recovered and in the fall he was back in Budapest. At about the same time, Lukács, who had originally been classified as unfit for military duty, was reexamined. He would soon learn, he told the German dramatist Paul Ernst, whether or not "the Moloch of Militarism" would devour him.[25] Thanks to his father's connections and a timely letter from Dr. Karl Jaspers, he was again rejected for front-line duty and assigned auxiliary service, first in a military hospital and later in the office of mail censorship. Thus, from October 1915 to July 1916, when he was discharged—again due to his father's intervention—Lukács too was in Budapest.

In December, he and a small group of intellectuals began to meet for discussion on Sunday afternoons, the gathering place being Balázs's Biedermeier apartment on the Buda side of the Danube. It was Balázs, in fact, who conceived the idea of organizing the "Sunday Circle," and after the first few meetings, he was brimming with enthusiasm: "Only *serious* people who are metaphysically disposed are invited. Every new guest is recommended in advance and every member of the group possesses the power of veto."[26] In addition to Balázs and Lukács, the circle included Balázs's wife and principal lover (Edith Hajós and Anna Schlamadinger), and some of Hungary's most promising young thinkers.

Béla Fogarasi was one such individual. A man of varied interests, he worked closely with University of Budapest Professor Bernát Alexander on *Athenaeum* (the official journal of the Hungarian Philosophical Society), lectured regularly to the Sociological Society that Jászi led, and maintained contact with the Bolzano Circle around Jenő Varga. Fogarasi shared Lukács's admiration for Béla Zalai and Emil Lask (another sacrifice to the god of war), and after he began to attend the Sunday afternoon gatherings he fell more and more under the older man's spell.

Even more talented than Fogarasi was a student of philosophy named Karl Mannheim, who had been rejected for military service because of congenital

1. Members of the Sunday Circle. From left to right: Karl Mannheim, Béla Fogarasi, Ernö Lorsy, József Nemes Lampérth, Elza Stephani, Anna Schlamadinger, Edith Hajós, Béla Balázs. Courtesy of the Petőfi Irodalmi Múzeum (Petőfi Museum of Literature), Budapest. Photo by Csaba Gál.

heart problems. He had pursued university studies in Budapest and Berlin and had been particularly impressed by Bernát Alexander and Georg Simmel, the latter having introduced him to the philosophic problem of alienation. Neither Alexander nor Simmel was able, however, completely to capture Mannheim's mind and imagination. Instead, the aspiring philosopher discovered a mentor in Lukács.

These core members of the circle were joined by the aesthetician Arnold Hauser, the art historian Frederick Antal, and three remarkable women: Anna Lesznai, the psychologist Júlia Láng, and the novelist/philosopher Emma Ritoók. In April 1918, the members admitted to their company the aesthetician Lajos Fülep. Among less frequent visitors were the psychologists René Spitz and Géza Révész, the art historian János Wilde, the chemist Michael Polányi, and the pianist-composer Béla Bartók, who once came to play his music for The Wooden Prince.[27]

As the acknowledged leader of the circle, Lukács always chose the subject for discussion. Anna Lesznai remembered that members touched upon a variety of themes—"painting, folklore, history. Most often the conversation turned to love, the philosophy of love."[28] Perhaps it would be more accurate to say that the conversations revolved around religion in the broadest sense of the word. Balázs had only recently converted to Roman Catholicism and, like Lukács, admired the Church Fathers and the medieval mystics—both Christian and Jewish. All of the members of the circle respected Kierkegaard's indifference to dogma and emphasis on the importance of belief.

Dostoevski was even more important than SK. Hauser recalled that he and his friends never discussed politics but regularly explored the great Russian writer's work.[29] Lukács had only recently completed The Theory of the Novel, which had begun as a much longer study of Dostoevski, and like the young people he had imagined for that purpose, he and the other members of the Sunday Circle withdrew from a world at war one day each week. They too attempted "to achieve self-understanding by means of conversations that lead by degrees to the . . . outlook on a Dostoevskian world,"[30] one in which human beings would form a genuine community.

Despite the fact that Lukács and his friends did not concern themselves directly with the war, the titanic confrontation formed the background and the presupposition of their deliberations. Most were inclined to favor Károlyi's pro-Entente position, but Lukács himself never had any use for the West. He later formulated his wartime dilemma in this way: "The Central Powers will probably defeat Russia. That could lead to the downfall of Tsarism: fair enough. There was some likelihood that the West would defeat Germany. If that led to the fall of the Hohenzollerns and Habsburgs, I would be equally pleased. But then the question arose: Who would save us from Western Civilization" or "Western democracy?"[31] In 1914–15, he believed, Western Civilization had failed the test and he therefore enjoined members of the Sunday Circle to look to the East for signs of hope. He had in mind the Russia of Dostoevski and Tolstoi, a Russia that could only be viewed through the prism of a utopian imagination.

At about the same time that Balázs and Lukács organized the Sunday Circle, Lajos Kassák formed a more radical antiwar group. Born in Érsekújvár (now in Czechoslovakia) in 1887, Kassák was the offspring of poor parents. A school dropout, he went to Budapest to find employment and eked out a living as an ironworker. In due course he joined the Social Democratic Party and moved in with Jolán Simon, an intelligent and talented woman whom he married. Restless and rebellious by nature, Kassák participated in strikes and pored over party literature. Soon, however, he was reading Ady and other Nyugat poets and trying his own hand. These initial efforts were rather pale imitations of the work he discovered in Nyugat's pages, but even at that he managed to place a few of them in lesser newspapers and reviews.

In April 1909, on an impulse, Kassák and a friend named Gödrös decided to make a pilgrimage to Paris. With little money and only the clothes on their backs, they boarded a Danube boat for Pozsony (Bratislava). From there, they set out on foot. In Stuttgart, they split when Kassák met a new companion, another Hungarian and published writer called Emil Szittya. An anarchist, Szittya was to exercise a lasting influence on Kassák's thinking.[32] Continuing on, the two men arrived at their destination in October.

In his extraordinary autobiography, One Man's Life, Kassák lamented the fact that he had seen and done little during the two months he spent in the French capital, but later, with the advantage of hindsight, he remembered that he had visited museums and coffee houses, where he took in the Parisian atmosphere. For the first time, too, he heard the magical names of Cendrars, Apollinaire, Rodin, Picasso, and Henri Rousseau. For the young autodidact, it was better than a university education, and he returned home in possession of a new and clearer sense of his own identity.

Although, for example, he got on well with *Nyugat*'s working editor Ernő Osvát, Kassák now knew that he could never truly be one of the journal's own. There was in him, to be sure, a certain resentment toward those who were well born and educated, and who knew nothing of physical labor. He did not try to conceal his contempt for *Nyugat* writers, including Lukács and Balázs who were never members of the journal's inner circle. And even Ady left him cold. "He was not a socialist," Kassák once observed, "but a Hungarian aristocrat with wounded pride."[33] In addition to this *ressentiment*, however, Kassák recognized that he could make his literary mark only by writing about the life and world that he knew at firsthand and by approaching literature as a worker, or as he liked to say, a "craftsman."

By the time the war broke out, Kassák was an isolated figure in Hungarian cultural life. Even more so after he broke with the social democrats over their support of the war effort. Quite naturally, then, he was attracted to those writers and artists in other countries who espoused cultural internationalism and who, as a result, tended to be vocal opponents of the war. His interest soared when a friend provided him with rough translations of poems by Iwan Goll and Ludwig Rubiner, and showed him a copy of Franz Pfemfert's left-wing expressionist review *Die Aktion*. These, Kassák believed, were men with whom he could make common cause. "Our isolation," he wrote years later, "related only to Hungary. In foreign countries we already had comrades, in art as well as in politics."[34]

From the beginning, in fact, Kassák conceived of art, politics, and society as one. He despised the *l'art pour l'art* that some *Nyugat* writers championed and he could not be satisfied with a politics based upon historical experience, patient compromise, and national interest. He believed that the true aim of politics, as of art, was to create new men who realized their individuality only by identifying with members of all social classes and nationalities; Kassák later called these new men "collective individuals." In order to prepare the way for the inner, moral revolution he envisioned and to campaign against the war more effectively, Kassák resolved to create his own journal.

Although money was a problem, he and his closest friends dug into their own pockets and published the first number of *A Tett* (*Action*) on November 1, 1915. Kassák served as editor of this combative "literary, artistic, and social review," which aspired to be something of a cross between *Die Aktion* and Herwarth Walden's *Der Sturm*. Among his fellow workers and contributors were such young Turks as Aladár Komját, Mátyás György, József Lengyel, and János Mácza. Béla Uitz was the best known painter. Together these firebrands contrived to attack virtually everyone in Hungary: government leaders, reformist social democrats, *Nyugat* writers. Their central obsessions, however, were the war and the postwar creation of the "new man."

By design, Kassák did not offer A *Tett*'s readers a programmatic statement until the tenth number (March 20, 1916). After denouncing the horrors of war, he proclaimed that the makers of the new literature bore the solemn responsibility for forming the coming generation. To that end they had to maintain contact with progressive economic and political movements and free themselves from all conventional ideas and technical restraints. He refused to identify this new literature with any existing "ism," and he singled out Italian futurism for particular censure. The futurists, he complained, had sung the praises of war.[35]

From the beginning, the censors regarded A *Tett* with suspicion. For some reason, they judged Péter Dobrovits's illustration, *Lamentation Over the Dead Christ*, to be offensive to religious sensibility, and prohibited street sales of the review. When, in October 1916, Kassák put together an "International Number," they banned any further publication on the grounds that A *Tett* contained material detrimental to the war effort. The number included work by foreigners—Kandinsky, Verhaeren, Bernard Shaw—whose countries were at war with Hungary.

The government had good reason to be edgy. Despite victories in 1915, 1916 was a critical year for the Monarchy. The Russians, under the command of General A. A. Brusilov, launched an offensive that was halted only with the aid of German reinforcements. Austria-Hungary lost 750,000 men, 380,000 of whom were taken prisoner. To make matters worse, Romania entered the war as an ally of the Entente powers on August 27, and almost immediately three Romanian armies moved into Transylvania. All along this had been Tisza's—and Ady's—greatest fear. On receiving news of the attack, opposition leaders in the Hungarian Parliament demanded Tisza's resignation, while Károlyi insisted that Hungarian troops on other fronts be recalled and sent to Transylvania.[36] Once again, however, the Germans arrived in time and pushed the Romanians back. By the end of the year, in fact, they had occupied Bucharest.

Together with increasing hardship on the home front, the military setbacks and the mounting death tolls added greatly to Tisza's burden. In Parliament, Andrássy and Apponyi now favored some kind of suffrage reform and Károlyi was demanding that Hungary break with the Germans, sign a separate peace, and adopt a pro-Entente orientation. On July 9, 1916, he resigned from the Independence party in order to form the United Party of Independence and 1848, which while it opposed a war of annexation, sought a peace that would guarantee Hungary's territorial integrity. It championed universal suffrage and democratic social policies, but favored the prewar status quo with respect to the nationalities problem.

The Károlyi Party, as it was popularly known, did not exercise power sufficient to influence Hungarian policy in a decisive manner. As a result, intellectuals continued to direct the growing antiwar movement. Babits dedicated more of his time and effort to the cause of peace. Soon, Aladár Schöpflin put him in touch with Ervin Szabó, head librarian at the Municipal Library and father of Hungarian Marxism. These two very different men forged a close friendship and together with Jászi, met regularly to discuss the war.[37]

Meanwhile, the members of the Sunday Circle marked time because, after his discharge from the army in July 1916, Lukács had returned to Heidelberg to begin work on his *Aesthetics*. The more publicly active Kassák, on the other hand, founded a new journal called *Ma* (*Today*). "1916. October," he wrote in *One Man's Life*. "Millions of the dead lie everywhere beneath the ground. But we live, because we were born for life and we want to live."[38] This great review, which repeatedly invoked the primacy of life, was to become the voice of the Hungarian avant-garde, the center of a movement that was to produce a profound and lasting impact not only on Hungarian literature, but on modern European culture generally. "We do not," Kassák wrote, "want to remain in the sphere of the printed word, as *Nyugat* does."[39] Rather, he projected drama and poetry matinées, art exhibitions, and contacts with avant-garde composers.

Six days after the first number of *Ma* appeared, Franz Josef died. This was an event of enormous significance for Austria-Hungary and its peoples, for the melancholy old man had ruled since 1848 and, in the course of time, become closely identified with the monarchy; his death seemed to presage the empire's demise. Sensing this, Karl, the new Emperor-King, began a frantic search for peace that inspired new hope in intellectual circles. His Foreign Minister, Tisza's friend Count István Burián, made this entry in his diary on November 25: "Long conversation with the ruler. He wants to speed the drive for peace against German procrastination."[40] But for the Habsburgs, it was late in the day.

The Russian Revolutions

After the death of Franz Josef, Tisza's position steadily weakened. More and more Hungarians had come to believe that the Minister President had visited the war upon them and stood in the way of a negotiated peace. The King himself seems to have held this view and attempted to pressure the recalcitrant Calvinist to make concessions on the volatile suffrage issue.[41] Precisely on that question, however, Tisza was immovable. So much so that even Count Burián finally became exasperated; the time, he concluded, was past when the government could maintain the restricted franchise. Despite his efforts to mediate between King and Minister President, matters came to a head in the spring of 1917. On May 23, Tisza submitted his resignation upon the King's request, and on June 15 the inexperienced Count Móric Esterházy formed a new cabinet, pledged to suffrage reform.

Almost as if his fortunes were linked directly to those of Tisza, Ady had, by 1917, sunk into the deepest despair. His syphilitic condition steadily worsened, and he was in and out of sanitariums. His chronic insomnia denied him needed rest, and he had barely enough money to live. It is unlikely that he would have been able to go on without his "Csinszka,"[42] Berta Boncza. Csinszka began writing to Ady in the fall of 1911, but the poet took little note of her until after he had broken off his long relationship with Adél Brüll (the "Léda" of his love poems) the following year. There were several lovers after Léda, but Csinszka's earnest love and refreshing innocence moved Ady most deeply. He wrote to her often and soon proposed marriage.

Ironically, Csinszka's father was a prominent figure in official circles and Tisza's close friend. He was therefore horrified to learn of his daughter's involvement with Tisza's archenemy. In a daring attempt to secure Boncza's blessing, Ady wrote to Tisza, asking that he use his good offices to promote the marriage; he received a curt reply from the Minister President's secretary describing the time-consuming burdens of public office. In the end, however, Csinszka triumphed over her father's objections, and she and Ady married in the spring of 1915. For the rest of the war, they lived at the Boncza family castle at Csucsa in Transylvania, and the Ady family home at Érmindszent. In his solitude, the poet mourned the destruction of his prewar hopes for Hungary's national regeneration:

> Everything we believed in is lost,
> Lost, lost;
> Fortunate and happy
> Is he who is unhappy only for himself.[43]

In 1917, he wrote "Remembrance of a Summer's Night," one of the greatest poems inspired by the war in any language. The haunting refrain, "it was a strange, strange summer night" (when he received news of the war's outbreak), is redolent of a lost world.

Two political issues were then paramount for the beleaguered Hungarian government: universal suffrage and peace. Esterházy quickly broke under the strain of dealing with those problems and, citing reasons of health, resigned on August 19. The following day, Sándor Wekerle assumed the responsibilities of Minister President. Of German descent, Wekerle was almost seventy years of age and had many years of government service to his credit. At first, he affected to share his predecessor's commitment to suffrage reform and proposed a reduction of the age limit from thirty to twenty-four, unconditional franchise for war veterans, and a redistribution of electoral districts.[44]

Tisza, who still wielded considerable power behind the scenes, opposed the measure, thus dooming it from the beginning. Wekerle did attempt to engineer some sort of compromise, but he acted half-heartedly, not relishing the prospect of challenging Tisza. In the end, Parliament passed a new suffrage bill on July 19, 1918, but the number of voters rose only to about 13 percent of the total population. Tisza exalted: "Only a small but vocal minority and not the overwhelming majority of the Hungarian nation demands universal suffrage."[45]

The search for peace was, if anything, more frustrating. Before the King dismissed Tisza, he and Count Ottokar Czernin, who had replaced Burián as Foreign Minister on December 22, 1916, made it clear to the Germans that the monarchy was at the point of exhaustion. Subsequently, they suggested that Germany make territorial concessions in the west in exchange for an extended empire in the east that would include much of Galicia.[46] At the same time, they sent out peace feelers to the Allies. Unfortunately, these efforts came to naught because of Italian ambitions and the monarchy's continued determination to maintain its territorial integrity.

The war dragged on. In the summer of 1917, the Russians began a new offensive which was all the more surprising for having been ordered by the Kerensky government that had taken over after the February Revolution had toppled the Romanovs. On July 1, following three days of heavy bombardment, General Brusilov struck in the direction of Lemberg. His troops quickly broke through the Austro-Hungarian lines, but on July 19 the monarchy's forces counterattacked and forced a retreat. On July 8 General Lavr Kornilov's army broke through south of the Dniester River, but the Germans and Austro-Hungarians quickly checked that drive as well. The scenario was much the same on the Romanian front, where the Russians and Romanians attacked jointly on July 22. After a twenty kilometer advance, the attack stalled and when General August von Mackensen counterattacked, the aggressors were obliged to retreat.[47]

Having defended themselves against the Entente attacks, the Central Powers went over to the offensive. In September they captured Riga and attacked in Eastern Galicia and Bukovina, driving the Russians back. The following month, they assembled fourteen divisions against Italy's four at Caporetto; on the 24th, they began the twelfth battle of the Isonzo with a bombardment. By November 10, they succeeded in driving the Italian forces back all the way to the Piave River, an overwhelming victory that all but put Italy out of the war.

The Central Powers' campaign in the east was given an even greater boost when, after the bolshevik seizure of power in October, Russia withdrew from the war. At Lenin's insistence, the new revolutionary government signed the Treaty of Brest-Litovsk on March 3, 1918, and two days later the Central Powers concluded a preliminary peace with Romania that was finalized on May 7. These successes encouraged the Germans to press on in the west, while the leaders of the monarchy continued to argue for a compromise peace. Unable to persuade their ally, they had little choice but to begin a new offensive against Italy. On June 15, the Austro-Hungarian army commenced an operation along the Piave River that the Italians repulsed with help from the

French and British. The monarchy's casualties numbered 142,000. After this defeat, mutinies and mass desertions increased in frequency.[48]

In the fall of 1918, General Franchet d'Esperey led French and Serbian troops in a Balkan offensive. He quickly forced the Bulgarian government to sign an armistice agreement, after which Burián concluded that the monarchy could not continue the struggle. Wekerle agreed, but he still insisted that Austria-Hungary's territorial integrity be preserved. Both men now hoped to achieve peace on the basis of Woodrow Wilson's Fourteen Points, even while the monarchy was collapsing around them. By the middle of October, the leaders of the nationalities were no longer willing to obey Vienna and Budapest. In a desperate effort to stave off the inevitable, the Emperor-King issued a manifesto (October 16) that made of Austria (but *not* Hungary) a federal state. Events, however, had overtaken any such solution.

On the same day that Karl issued his manifesto, Károlyi made a Parliamentary speech in which he demanded that power be given to those who would chart a new domestic and international course. A member of his party, János Hock, then read a list of demands that included calling Hungarian soldiers home to defend the country's frontiers, initiating democratic reforms, and settling the nationality question in a Wilsonian spirit. With a perfectly straight face, Wekerle replied that Wilsonian principles were consistent with Hungary's inherited traditions. But with pressure mounting, he resigned on October 23.

While Andrássy, Apponyi, Tisza, and the King deliberated about the formation of a new government, members of the left-wing parties—Independence, Radical, and Social Democratic—constituted themselves the Hungarian National Council. As the name suggests, the Council considered itself to be the true representative of the Hungarian nation, a claim that was clearly revolutionary in character. On October 26, the Council made public the twelve-point program that Jászi had written. It called for a new government, an independent Hungary, an immediate end to the war, an end to the German alliance, new elections on the basis of universal suffrage and the secret ballot, and a nationality policy that would be Wilsonian without endangering Hungary's territorial integrity.[49] Károlyi was the Council's President.

Károlyi's name had by then become synonymous with peace and democracy, for the war had driven this decent though not overly competent man steadily to the left. In November 1917, he and Jászi had attended the Bern conference of the League of Lasting Peace, where they discussed at length the latter's conception of a federated Austria-Hungary. Károlyi was completely won over, though he was moved as much by Jászi's character as his ideas. "What gives him /Jászi/ a quite special place among Hungarian politicians," Károlyi later wrote, "is his rare moral courage. Only Justh in our camp and only Tisza in the opposite camp possessed this quality in equal measure with Jászi."[50]

Like Károlyi, Jászi had done some rethinking. For a time, he had favored a democratic and antinationalist version of Friedrich Naumann's *Mitteleuropa* plan—according to which Germany and Austria-Hungary would establish a customs union and close political alliance. But after the first Russian Revolution of 1917 ended Tsarist rule, he adopted the pro-Entente position long advocated by Károlyi. As a result, he began to advance the idea of a United States of Danubia. According to his plan, five nationalities would possess political autonomy within the context of the monarchy: Magyar, German, Polish, Czech, and Serbo-Croatian.[51] Each of those nationalities, he argued, possessed the territory, population, and historical consciousness requisite for autonomy. Moreover, they would be bound, in consideration of the fate of their ethnic brothers in other states, to protect the rights of minorities within their frontiers.

At the time Jászi developed this plan, he was meeting regularly, sometimes throughout the day, with Babits and Szabó. Each of these men radiated a moral strength that exerted a formative influence on two generations of Hungarian intellectuals. According to Károlyi, "all progressive young intellectuals were /Jászi's/ devoted and enthusiastic followers." He exercised over them "an influence like that of Masaryk over the young Czechs."[52] One of his most faithful followers, Karl Polányi, compared Jászi to István Széchenyi, the nineteenth-century aristocrat who labored ceaselessly for Hungary's national and moral regeneration.[53] Like Széchenyi, Jászi was a reformer who opposed violent revolution. The Radical party he founded in 1914 steadfastly eschewed the use of brutal means to achieve its ends.

Though less of a public figure than Jászi, Babits also exerted a powerful influence on Hungarian intellectuals of his and the younger generation. We have seen that Ferenc Békássy sought his counsel and friendship. So did the philosopher Vilmos Szilasi, who in 1910 gave Babits a copy of his book on Plato. And during the early months of 1918, László Nagy sent postcards to Babits on which he had penciled some striking sketches. By the end of the year, the young man was signing his correspondence "László Moholy-Nagy"[54] and, having returned from the front, he reported to Babits that "somehow I must secure my livelihood (because for the time being I cannot live off painting), so I have become a newspaperman. Thus, once again I am trying my hand at poetry. Please, dear teacher, accept them with my esteem."[55]

Like Babits, Szabó was a private person. Never very healthy, he cherished books and the quiet of the libraries in which he earned his living. Always sensitive to moral issues, he turned increasingly in his last years to the moral foundations of his radical political convictions. Although he was stirred by the Russian Revolutions, he soon began to question the legitimacy of unfettered class struggle. According to Jászi, he spoke bitterly of the "moral defects of Russian bolshevism."[56] That is not surprising, for he always emphasized the importance of moral renewal. New laws and economic policies were needed, he once observed, "but as the English say: not measures: men—above all we need men, different, better, more perfect men."[57]

Precisely, Jászi wrote, because of this moral sense, Szabó "exerted an almost magical influence on idealistic youth and on women."[58] The remarkable Ilona Duczynska was a case in point. Duczynska was the daughter of Helén Békássy and a ne'er-do-well railroad official of noble Polish descent. In 1904, her father emigrated to the United States, where he soon died. This loss marked her for life. Though well cared for, her mother and she were always treated as poor relations, in part because the Békássy family belonged to the gentry and had opposed the marriage. This experience of humiliation and loneliness was soon enough transmuted into a hatred of the upper classes and a combative temperament. At ten years of age, Duczynska knew already that she would always stand "against the world."[59]

Early on, young Ilona adopted her missing father's atheism, anarchism, and fervent belief in the natural sciences. In his library she discovered the latest scientific works as well as books—such as Ernst Haeckel's *The Riddle of the Universe*—that sought to establish science in the place once occupied by religion. Small wonder, then, that she was attracted to the nihilist student Bazarov in Turgenev's *Fathers and Sons*. Before long she was reading all of the Russian writers, finding in them a new world and a messianic spirit.

With one of her relatives, however, she could discuss her longings and enthusiasms—her cousin Ferenc Békássy. A recent biographer suggests that Duczynska may have been in love with the ill-fated poet,[60] but there is no doubt that he reinforced her idealism, even though he himself possessed a conservative temperament. When the war broke out and the Socialists disappointed her, as they did so many others, she needed his companionship even more. She was pleased to receive his letters from officers' training school. In one he wrote: "Perhaps your plans are more beautiful than mine. If only I could believe that it is possible to improve the human condition!"[61] Seven months later he was killed in action.

Duczynska might have succumbed to bitterness and despair had she not, at about the same time, met Szabó at her aunt's home. Something of a parlor liberal, the aunt introduced the Hungarian radical by telling her niece that she could now "see the other Hungary." Instead, Duczynska saw the likeness of her missing father: "His Nietzsche-like head resembled that of my father, as did his rebellious spirit and his idealistic anarchism."[62] Near the end of her long life, she still remembered the profound impression Szabó made. "Finally I became convinced that I was not crazy and that there were other serious socialists."[63] Renewed in spirit, she traveled to Zürich to begin studies at the Polytechnical University where her father had once hoped to enroll.

The Swiss city was then a center for European and Russian emigrés and Duczynska always remembered seeing Lenin working in the library. Though she performed well in school, she was far more interested in the Zimmerwald

Conference and the ideas of the Polish revolutionary Henrik Lauer, a teaching assistant at the university. Lauer encouraged Duczynska's radicalism until one day, in the same month that the Tsar's government collapsed, she announced her intention to return to Hungary to do something to help end the war. Still recovering from tuberculosis, she met first with Angelica Balabanova at the secretariat of the International Socialist Committee and obtained a copy of the Zimmerwald antiwar manifesto that was addressed to workers and soldiers. After a brief stopover in Vienna, she arrived in Budapest in late April 1917: "I was 20, tuberculer, and rather unconversant with Marxism."[64]

Duczynska was not, however, unconversant with handguns. In Switzerland, she had practiced until she could acquit herself quite well. Years later, she still could not say why she had taught herself to use firearms, but she believed that she intended to imitate the Russian terrorists who called their organization "The People's Will." More likely, as she herself once speculated, this interest could be traced back to her childhood desire to target shoot as her father had done.[65] At any rate, one day, at the home of the radical dentist József Madzsar, Duczynska chanced upon a browning revolver and, almost without thinking, thrust it into her pocket.

It was May and Hungarian newspapers were filled with stories about the Austrian Socialist Friedrich Adler, who was about to be placed on trial for having assassinated Karl Stürgkh, Minister President in Vienna. In like manner, Duczynska decided that she would rid Hungary of István Tisza. She went to Szabó with her plan and, according to her account, he supported the idea in principle. Only recently, to be sure, he had described the Hungarian leader as "mankind's danger," but as the most distinguished student of his life has remarked, he always refused to sanction evil means to achieve good.[66] Moreover, Duczynska, who related this story for the first time late in life, had a habit of recasting people in her own radical image. She claimed, at any rate, that he raised only a practical objection, namely that the Hungarian people might view her as an agent of the Entente.

In order to dispel that suspicion, he recommended that she identify herself with some Hungarian group, sending her to the Galileo Circle because by then she had matriculated in the University of Budapest's liberal arts faculty. To her chagrin, however, Tisza soon resigned. Dejectedly she returned Madzsar's handgun to the drawer of his desk. As she told it, Szabó expressed his sympathy and observed bitterly that Tisza would now direct Hungary's affairs from the background without having any longer to be a politically visible symbol of the war. More likely, he was relieved that the headstrong young woman did not carry the logic of some of his ideas to its murderous conclusion.

Duczynska's identification with the Galileo Circle was largely formal, since she disliked what she regarded as its ivory tower, apolitical, atmosphere. To be sure, beginning late in 1917, members of the Circle did advocate publicly a negotiated peace, but under the influence of Jászi and Polányi they eschewed violent action. That being the case, Duczynska, along with her lover Tivadar

Sugár, Miklós Sisa (then the Circle's president), and Árpád Haas formed their own group within the Circle, one committed to illegal action. Never more than twelve in number, they styled themselves "revolutionary socialists," sought Szabó's advice, and plotted to organize demonstrations and circulate antiwar leaflets to soldiers. Szabó lent them moral support and recommended contacts with workers uncontaminated by close association with Socialist trade union officials, but he refused to countenance street demonstrations. The radical young people pressed ahead nevertheless. From Russian bolsheviks living in Budapest, they learned the art of clandestine printing and began to prepare leaflets. In due course, Duczynska managed to throw a bundle of copies over the wall of a military barracks.

Perhaps on the strength of information received from an insider, police arrested Duczynska and her friends in January. In June the government accused them formally of having prepared and disseminated leaflets designed to demoralize the Austro-Hungarian army, and in September they appeared in court to answer the charges. From the first, Duczynska and Sugár (who later disappeared during Stalin's purges) were the most outspoken defendants. Rather disingenuously, she maintained that she regarded her mission as one of enlightenment, not agitation. He argued cleverly that they were merely popularizing views—a peace without annexations or reparations—that Count Czernin himself espoused. For all their chutzpah, however, the court sentenced Duczynska to two years in jail, Sugár to three.[67]

With their leaders under lock and key, the revolutionary socialists regrouped. Ottó Korvin (Klein), a bank employee and brother of one of the defendants, assumed the leadership. Never having been a member of the Duczynska-Sugár group, he was an ideal—because unknown—choice to succeed the jailed leaders. Like his predecessors, he and his followers sought Szabó's guidance, but the tireless librarian was by then mortally ill and, in any event, harbored doubts about their fanatical radicalism.

Korvin maintained far fewer scruples, witness his revival of the idea of assassinating Tisza. After some discussion, the lot fell to János Lékai (Jakab Leitner), who was consumptive and not expected to live. Korvin had to explain to him the use of a revolver, after which he took up a position near one of the Parliament building's exits. The date was October 16. When Tisza appeared, Lékai aimed and tried in vain to fire. Before he could release the trigger he had mistakenly locked, the Minister President's chauffer restrained him. Despite Lékai's failure, however, Korvin and his followers continued their efforts to end the war and bring bolshevism to Hungary. Indeed, through his friend Ernő Seidler, Szabó's cousin, Korvin met Béla Kun, who had become a bolshevik during the time he was a Russian prisoner of war. Along with left-wing Socialists and Kun and other converted war prisoners, Korvin's "revolutionary socialists" organized the Hungarian Communist Party on November 24, 1918.

Whether or not Szabó, had he not succumbed to the Spanish influenza in late September, would have joined the Hungarian bolsheviks must remain a moot question. Jászi, who knew him as well as anyone, believed that in the end he would have given in to the temptation, though the fact that his moral sensibility almost always prevailed over his eclectic syndicalist/Marxist ideas might suggest otherwise. The question may not seem important, but Jászi rightly recognized that the war and the Russian Revolutions were driving even the most apolitical and morally literate Hungarian intellectuals toward the revolutionary left. Lukács, who once described Szabó as "the spiritual/intellectual father of us all,"[68] was a case in point.

He was still in Heidelberg when, early in 1917, the members of the Sunday Circle formulated plans to establish a Free School of the Humanistic Sciences, somewhat in the manner of the Free School of the Sociological Society that Jászi organized in 1906. Unlike Jászi's school, which was informed by positivism, their school was to be inspired by neo-idealism. After Balázs secured classrooms on the premises of the National Pedagogical Institute, he scheduled the first lectures and seminars for the months of March to June 1917.

Despite a high level of sophistication, the Free School achieved a considerable success. Lectures attracted as many as seventy students, among whom were the most gifted young men and women in Hungary. Obviously pleased, Balázs recorded his evaluation of the first semester's work in his diary: "Fogarasi's lectures on the theory of philosophic thought were first rate. Hauser's on aesthetics after Kant less able, but he had done an impressive amount of work. Antal's lectures were a bit weak, but Mannheim's on the logic of epistemology were excellent, exciting, and rich; the first appearance of an important philosopher of the future. Gyuri /Lukács/ also arrived, and although he improvised the ethical lectures, they were still paramount in importance.... What a splendid lecturer Gyuri is! An ideal professor. Everyone who heard him could sense that a new heroic age was dawning for philosophy."[69]

The Free School's second semester began in February 1918. Preparatory to its opening, Mannheim delivered a programmatic lecture entitled "Soul and Culture," in which he elucidated the school's central preoccupation: the problem of alienation. "We are many and we live apart," he told his audience, "divorced from one another, longing for one another, but unable to draw near to one another. But it is not only the other who is out of our reach, but we ourselves as well."[70]

Because modern man's soul (his essential self) had become alienated from his culture (the soul's objectivization), Mannheim explained, he and his colleagues had undertaken the task of cultural criticism, the analysis of the structure of each cultural form.[71] "Last /semester/ we assayed to analyze the fundamentals and structures peculiar to ethics, aesthetics, epistemology, philosophy, and art."[72] The faculty hoped, Mannheim continued, to further this effort during the semester to come, and as a result of such analysis, he held out the prospect of a new culture, the forms of which would express more authentically the soul's new experiences. Such a culture alone could overcome human alienation.

In the most general sense, Lukács identified himself with Mannheim's remarks, because he agreed that the alienation problem was central to the crisis of culture. He and Mannheim both believed that the "forms" of contemporary life had become divorced from human spiritual experience. Nevertheless, there was a fundamental difference between the two men. Lukács was searching for a utopian world beyond life's forms, including its *social* forms. Like Balázs, he hoped to discover a path that would lead to a world in which "naked souls" might meet directly, without the mediation of their social identities.

Mannheim, on the other hand, never entertained any sympathy for utopianism. He maintained that it had become evident, even before the war, that the forms of cultural expression—religion, ethics, art, politics, society—had begun to develop autonomously, in accordance with their own laws and without reference to the soul's ever maturing self-consciousness. Soul and culture, that is, were becoming ever more alienated. As Europeans became aware of this alienation, they attempted to reach beyond the forms, with the result that they created an even more desperate state of affairs. In art, expressionists and futurists—he did not mention the *Ma*-ists by name—sought to destroy all forms, while in religion, latter-day mystics searched for immediate union with God, rejecting the church's mediation. Those efforts, according to Mannheim, could not be successful, " because true freedom from form is not humanly possible."[73] Nor was it desirable, because men could confront their souls only through cultural forms.

Mannheim was not alone in his opposition to some of the views that Lukács, Balázs, and Fogarasi espoused. Lajos Fülep, Emma Ritoók, and, to a lesser degree, Anna Lesznai were also independently minded and incisive critics. Yet all of them recognized that they had enough in common with Lukács to make possible their cooperation at the Free School.

Unfortunately, we know relatively little about the second semester, for postwar events soon overtook the Free School of the Humanistic Sciences. Despite its brief existence, however, one can scarcely exaggerate its importance to *European* intellectual history. Lukács, Balázs, Mannheim, Hauser, Antal, Fogarasi, Michael Polányi, Charles de Tolnay; even this partial list of names suffices to indicate the scope and significance of its work. Perhaps Tolnay summed up the school's ideals and achievements as well as anyone: "In opposition to the scholarship for scholarship's sake characteristic of Hungarian and Western universities, the Free School set a new objective for scholarly work. Knowledge would no longer be an end in itself, but rather a road to the soul's self-fulfillment. . . . Within this circle of young people of learning, a spiritual community took form. For the first time in modern Hungarian spiritual life, there was realized . . . the most fervent desire of every contemporary scholar and human being: the rediscovery of community."[74]

On a more theoretical level, the leaders of the Free School awakened in Hungarian intellectuals a new interest in philosophic idealism. In his review of the published version of *Soul and Culture*, for example, Jászi praised

Mannheim and his colleagues for opposing positivism and historical materialism.[75] On March 5, 1918, Béla Fogarasi delivered a lecture entitled "Conservative and Progressive Idealism"[76] to a joint meeting of the Sociological Society and the Sunday Circle. Dedicated to the latter, the address and subsequent discussion signaled a new reciprocity between radical politics and philosophic idealism.

Fogarasi was the right lecturer for so auspicious an occasion, for although he was closely identified with Lukács and the Sunday Circle, he continued to be active in the Sociological Society, to which he spoke often on the history of philosophy. No one was in a better position to refute the view according to which there existed a necessary correlation between positivism and progressive politics. Because they assumed a preestablished harmony between progressive desiderata and evolutionary transmutations, positivists put their trust in a deterministic law of development—and ended by espousing Realpolitik. Ought collapsed into is, and end goals were soon abandoned for present realities. Nowhere, Fogarasi observed, was that unhappy marriage of progressive politics and determinism more problematic than in Marxist circles.

Progressive politics, Fogarasi insisted, could not build on the shifting sands of natural science, but only on the rock of an idealism that, by recognizing the absolute validity of logical truths, ethical imperatives, and aesthetic values, upheld the independence of norms vis-à-vis Being and historical fortune. To be sure, not every idealism was conducive to progressive politics; metaphysical and aesthetic idealism—that of the Romantics, the later Schelling, and Hegel—gravitated toward conservatism. But the ethical idealism of Kant and Fichte *was* progressive: democratic and socialist. The Königsberg philosopher first formulated that idealism when he stressed the dualism of *Sein* and *Sollen*, what is and what ought to be.

But here, according to Fogarasi, a problem arose, because the categorical imperative recognized no norms of content. On the basis of what ethical postulate of content, he asked rhetorically, could he and his friends demand democracy and equality? The answer, he replied, could be deduced from the Kantian-Fichtean concept of dignity (*Würdigkeit*). The dignity of men and women derived from their responsibility, and only democracy and socialism could create a world in which they were in a position to accept full responsibility for their actions. Fogarasi cautioned, finally, not to confuse *political* with *ethical* ends. Neither democracy nor socialism could summon into existence the true end of ethics—love and brotherhood beyond Kant's ethic of responsibility. The ethical transformation of human beings could transform completely the political situation, but the reverse could never be true.

Following Fogarasi's lecture, the Sociological Society convened on three occasions to debate his theses. Lukács's comments were particularly important,[77] for he insisted even more forcefully than Fogarasi that what was crucial to progressive action was the specific morality, not the metaphysical theory, on which that action was based. In concert with his protegé, he made a sharp distinction between ethics and politics. Ethical action, he argued, was directed toward the inner transformation of men and women such that the intention of their actions conformed to ethical norms. Political action, on the other hand, aimed at the creation, preservation, or transformation of institutions.

Lukács preferred ethical *action directe*, because such action aimed at the transformation of men's souls without the mediation of politics or institutions. If recourse was had to the latter, they had to serve the ethical goal, for the moment they became ends in themselves, they fell from the sphere of value to that of the merely existent; Lukács instanced German socialism before and during the war. In opposition to that "conservative" fall from grace, "the permanent revolution of ethical idealism opposes existence /institutions/ as existence, as that which is of no value to the ethical ideal, and because it is a permanent revolution, because it is an absolute revolution, it can determine the direction of the never-coming-to-rest, never-stagnating development and regulate its movement."[78]

Lukács's contribution to the discussion highlighted the utopian impulses that informed Fogarasi's lecture and reflected his own interest in anarchosyndicalism. He had, in fact, been reading Georges Sorel, to whose work he had been introduced by Szabó, who was also a discussant. The ailing Socialist librarian cautioned against ignoring "objective" factors, since they provided and delimited the possibilities of moral action. But he too laid emphasis on "subjective" factors. If objective development failed to measure up morally, men had to struggle against it and chart a new direction. That was possible because the mind/spirit "is also an independent force that exerts an influence on society, just as society does on it." A struggle then ensued and there was no guarantee that a new development would triumph over the old. "But a moral man would rather perish than be untrue to his spirit, ideals, and categorical imperatives."[79]

In his closing remarks, Fogarasi observed that "with respect to the question of the relationship between politics and morality, I accept /Szabó's/conclusions without reservation."[80] He expressed his satisfaction that the mutual indifference between philosophy and politics had finally come to an end and that the way had been prepared for a new radicalism. What he did not know then was that he, Lukács, and other Hungarians would proclaim that new philosophical politics only in exile.

At the same time that the Sociological Society and the Sunday Circle deliberated, the Hungarian avant-garde was preparing a moral revolution that would create a "new man," the collective individual. That revolution was to be made by a new and radical art and it would be far more important than any political revolution. The prophet of the revolution was Kassák who, with his black shirt and long hair, cut an anarchistic figure in Hungarian intellectual circles. During 1917–18, Kassák published books, organized art exhibits, and sponsored poetry readings. In *Ma*, he featured unconventional artists such as János Máttis Teutsch, József Nemes Lampérth, and Sándor Bortnyik. He even published original scores by Bartók. In an effort to lend *Ma* an international flavor, he reproduced drawings and paintings by Picasso, Max Pechstein, and Franz Marc.

Taken all in all, *Ma* was a fascinating, if uneven, review. Yet despite Kassák's authoritarian personality, he could not impose his will without challenge. Some members of the circle, such as Máttis Teutsch and Nemes Lampérth—a veteran with mental problems—were apolitical radicals, while others were critical of Kassák's unwillingness to engage in active politics. One of the latter was János Lékai, who subsequently made the attempt on Tisza's life. Another was József Révai, a poet whom Kassák judged to be effeminate. Still another was József Lengyel, who, like Lékai, had come under Korvin's spell. Tensions within the *Ma* Circle increased after the bolshevik revolution when, according to Lengyel, "four of us: György, Komját, Révai, and I no longer wished to continue on the path to what was merely a revolution of forms. . . . At that time, we regarded poetry as a means that had to be subordinate to the revolutionary end."[81] They demanded that they be admitted to an editorial board that would replace Kassák, but the latter dismissed the idea out of hand. The four rebels then took their leave, announcing their intention to publish a journal called *1917*.

Although the censors proscribed *1917* before the first issue appeared, the editors had already drafted a programmatic statement that emphasized the significance of the Russian Revolution. "We want to socialize literature in its very essence, to fill it with social content, to revolutionize it aesthetically in content and form. Let the new literature be the awakener of social revolution, and not a social narcotic. We want to destroy everything in scholarship and literature that stands in the way of the 1917 idea."[82] The battle in Hungary between revolutionary modernism and party art was now joined. In January 1919, *1917* resurfaced as *Internationale*, the theoretical journal of the Hungarian Communist Party.

During the final two years of war, Hungarian intellectuals stepped up their opposition and, at the same time, began to project revolutionary futures for their country. Having witnessed the revolutions in Russia, their despair gave place to extravagant, if desperate, hope. Perhaps only Ady grasped the magnitude of the impending national disaster. In the fall of 1918 Csinszka brought her husband to their Budapest apartment. His health had deteriorated so much that he rarely left his room. He became more and more despondent as it became obvious that Hungary had lost the war and soon would be at the mercy of the victors. Knowing full well that cries of revenge were already in the air, Ady pleaded with his country's conquerors not to "ride roughshod over our poor and beautiful heart." The Magyars were "woeful and ill-starred" people upon whom evil men had visited the war:

> We were the earth's fool,
> Poor vitiated Magyars,
> And now you conquerors, come!
> Greetings to the victor.[83]

On the inside cover of his beloved Bible, he wrote with trembling hand: "Eli, Eli lama sabachthani. October 23, 1918."[84] He had little time remaining.

Tisza had even less. Out of office and fifty-six years of age, he volunteered for frontline duty late in 1917. For the next year, he served as a colonel of the hussars, though he saw little action. After returning to Parliament, he let slip on October 17 the sober truth that Austria-Hungary had lost the war. Shaken and aware that his life was in danger, Tisza refused to flee. He, his wife, and niece took up residence in a Pest villa that was all but unguarded. On October 31, military vehicles pulled up in front. Men in field uniforms jumped out and three of them entered the building. Tisza emerged with gun in hand, but, seeing that he was outnumbered, lowered his arm. After a brief battle of words, the team of assassins gunned down the man who had come to symbolize the war.[85] Although many men eventually came under suspicion and one, the Socialist journalist Pál Kéri, was later convicted, the assassins' identities remain uncertain. What is certain is that Tisza and Ady were spared the postwar agonies of the country both loved so well.

The Democratic Republic

On the day self-appointed executioners assassinated Tisza, King Karl named Károlyi Minister President. Only two days before, the young sovereign had chosen Count János Hadik to succeed Wekerle. But the size of the pro-Károlyi crowds that filled the capital's streets and the occupation by revolutionary soldiers of key public buildings persuaded him to make the change. By then, most Hungarians believed that Károlyi was the only man capable of saving the nation. Moreover, they saw in the democratic convert "the personification of those hopes for which /Jászi/ had fought for two decades in his speeches and writings."[86] On learning of his appointment, therefore, they sang and yelled, "long live Count Mihály Károlyi, the People's leader." Soldiers and workers seemed to be everywhere and they soon released Lékai, Duczynska, and Sugár from prison.

Because the King had nominated a man who headed the extra-legal National Council, October 31 marked the victory of the "October" or "Aster" Revolution.[87] If General Géza Lukachich, the military commander in Budapest, had had his way he would have contested the revolution, but with the war lost he could no longer rely on his troops. More important, the King ordered him to avoid bloodshed. The revolution was marred only by the murder of Tisza. Yet that act of violence was enough to make Jászi uneasy. "The blood council is not in keeping with our mission," he said. The assassination "profanes our unblemished revolution."[88]

All the same, the Radical leader accepted the "nationalities" portfolio in the Károlyi government and urged his colleagues—members of the Radical, Social Democratic, and Independence parties—to institute without delay a wide-ranging program of reforms. First, however, there was the matter of Hungary's relationship with Austria. Agitation for a republic was such that Archduke Josef himself advised the King to release Károlyi from the oath he had dutifully sworn to the crown. Reluctantly, Karl yielded on November 1 and on November 13 he renounced his own claims and signaled his readiness to recognize whatever form of government the National Council might choose. Three days later, János Hock, who had succeeded Károlyi as President of the National Council, proclaimed "The People's Republic of Hungary" to exuberant crowds in front of the Parliament building.

Among the intellectuals there was more than one reaction to the revolution. Babits was cautiously sympathetic, but elected to restrict himself to literary and educational work. Jászi was of course fully committed to the Károlyi government's goals, but he was not blind to the new Hungary's problems and dangers. He no longer believed, for example, that the country's territorial integrity could be preserved by granting autonomy and democratic rights to the nationalities. Indeed, he knew that the Sabor, the Croatian assembly, had already declared Croatia's secession and that the Slovaks had quickly followed suit. He attempted to negotiate with the Romanians, but to no avail.[89] His policy as Minister of Nationalities, he later insisted, "was directed to the future rather than the present. . . . I worked to preserve for the future the conception of a free Hungary living at peace in a confederation of Danubian peoples."[90]

Certainly Jászi had every reason to be pessimistic. Czech, Romanian, and South Slav troops had begun to violate the demarcation lines established by the territorially punitive Belgrade Armistice of November 13. These military forays were clearly designed to produce a territorial fait accompli before the peace negotiations got under way in Paris. To the Hungarians' chagrin, neither General Franchet d'Esperey, the Entente commander in the Balkans, nor Lieutenant Colonel Vyx, Allied representative in Budapest, evidenced the least sympathy for Hungary. It had become obvious, in fact, that they were in no mood to distinguish between Károlyi and Tisza; nor would it have mattered if they had been, for the Allies had already committed themselves to the dismemberment of the crown lands.

As this bitter truth began to sink in, public confidence in the government wavered. Forces on the political right and left began to gather as increasing numbers of Hungarians cast Károlyi in Kerensky's role. More than any other oppositional force, the Hungarian Communist Party stood ready in the wings, waiting to move to center stage the moment the government faltered. The party's confidence was not surprising; four great empires had fallen and the possibilities of creating a radically new world suddenly seemed very real. Because, therefore, a soviet republic was the most likely alternative to Károlyi's democratic republic, the Galileo Circle's journal *Szabadgondolat* (*Free Thought*) devoted its December 1918 issue to bolshevism.

In his contribution,[91] Jászi registered his opposition to all dictatorships as antithetical to democracy and morality. Nor would he accept the bolsheviks' argument that the dictatorship marked a transitional stage that would *necessarily* give way to a stateless and classless society. In his view, a correct social theory had to allow for the independent contributions of man's intellectual powers. If, as he believed, social and political development was not automatic, there could be no rational ground for assuming that the dictatorship would dissolve itself. Thus, in the end, Jászi rejected bolshevism because of his profound moral sensibility and his conviction that in the final analysis men made their own history. Not the class struggle, but reason and moral consciousness had to lead human beings to create a better world.

As editor of *Szabadgondolat* and a longtime friend, Karl Polányi also invited Lukács to contribute to the debate on bolshevism. At the time, the Sunday Circle leader was still sorting out his reactions to the October Revolution. His initial response had been favorable. Yet he never regarded a democratic republic as the final goal. Eleven days after Károlyi assumed power, he distilled the utopian essence of his "ethical idealism" as a warning to his countrymen.

> But let us never forget that in the achievement of the republic, the revolution has only begun, not ended. The republic is today the beautiful symbol of the new order, the new Hungary that all of us are awaiting, but it is only a means and a symbol and everything will be lost if we permit it to become an end in itself. . . .
> The history of every revolution exhibits this evolution. Those political institutions, the creation of which was necessary for the sake of an economic and social transformation, become ends in themselves, eclipsing that for which we first looked to them; indeed, they turn against it. This transformation of political aims into ends in themselves always signifies the end of revolutions and the victory of reaction.[92]

For his contribution to *Szabadgondolat*, Lukács chose the title "Bolshevism as a Moral Problem." The problem to which he referred hinged on the issue of democracy. Was democracy an integral part of socialism or merely a tactic, useful until the proletariat assumed power? In order to clarify the question, Lukács pointed to the contradiction between Marx's sociological method and utopian vision of the classless society. On the one hand, the German had claimed that class struggle was the motive force of historical development; on the other, he had asserted that the proletariat's victory over its class enemy, the bourgeoisie, would bring oppression to an end. Yet, viewed as sociological necessity, the victory of the proletariat signified nothing more than the ascendancy of new oppressors. If Marx had indeed discovered the propelling force of history, one would be forced to accept evil as evil, oppression as oppression.

If bolshevism's confidence in the messianic mission of the proletariat could not be justified by reference to its understanding of historical process, it could only rest on faith.

> Bolshevism rests on the metaphysical assumption that good can issue from evil, that it is possible, as Razumikhin says in Crime and Punishment, to lie our way through to the truth. The present writer is not able to share this faith and therefore he sees at the root of the bolshevik position an irresolvable moral dilemma. Democracy in his view requires only superhuman self-abnegation and self-sacrifice from those who consciously and honestly wish to persevere to the end, but this, if perhaps it necessitates superhuman strength, is not in essence an insoluble question as is bolshevism's moral problem.[93]

In the same month that this article appeared, Lukács, accompanied by Fogarasi, joined the Hungarian Communist Party. Although he did not then become a Party member, Balázs also identified himself with the Communist movement. Without mentioning the fact that the University of Heidelberg had rejected his application for Habilitation as Privatdozent on December 7, Lukács attempted to explain the reasons for his sudden volte face in "Tactics and Ethics,"[94] an essay he wrote late in December 1918 or early in January 1919. He did not deny the terrible moral responsibility of those who employed terror or other immoral means, but he insisted that they were not alone morally culpable. All who took sides with communism's opponents had to shoulder responsibility for lives lost due to imperialistic wars and class oppression.

Lukács's conviction that there was no escape for those who wished to preserve their moral purity in the age of absolute sinfulness enabled him to overcome his eleventh-hour scruples concerning the resort to terror. All men and women, he had persuaded himself, were caught in the tragic dilemma of having to choose between the purposeful and ephemeral violence of the revolution and the meaningless and never ceasing violence of the old world. And the choice was not an arbitrary one, for there existed a standard for judging the lesser evil that Lukács called "sacrifice."

> Murder is not permitted; murder is an unconditional and unforgivable sin, but it is inescapably necessary. It is not permitted, but it must be done. And in a different place in his fiction, Savinkov[95] sees not the justification of his act (that is impossible), but its deepest moral root in that he sacrifices not only his life, but also his purity, morality, even his soul for his brothers. In other words, only that

man's murderous act can be—tragically—moral, who knows that murder is not permitted under any circumstances. Or let us express this idea that belongs to the ultimate human tragedy in the unsurpassably beautiful words of /Friedrich/ Hebbel's Judith: "And if God has placed sin between me and the deed required of me—who am I that I should be able to evade it?"

Those members of the Sunday Circle who remained uncommitted to communism received the news of Lukács's party allegiance with stunned disbelief. Anna Lesznai remembered that his "conversion took place in the interval between two Sundays: Saul became Paul."[96] Enemies were plainly suspicious. József Lengyel, the Ma dissident and no-nonsense materialist, never reconciled himself to the presence in the party of the "ethical ones." Though antimilitarists, they had not, Lengyel charged, struggled actively against the war and in Szabadgondolat Lukács had rejected violent revolution on grounds of conscience.[97]

Kassák was openly cynical. He described a meeting of the Vörös Újság (Red Gazette) editorial staff late in 1918, at the time of Lukács's co-optation. "I was a little surprised that Lukács had undertaken this work, he who a few days earlier had published an article in Szabadgondolat in which he wrote with philosophic emphasis that the Communist movement had no ethical base and was therefore inadequate for the creation of a new world. The day before yesterday he wrote this, but today he sits at the table of the Vörös Újság editorial staff."[98]

Kassák's own attitude toward bolshevism and the Hungarian Communist Party was, however, no less problematic. He sympathized with the aims of the Communist movement and refused to rule out the use of terror. Yet he declined to join the party and criticized those, such as Révai, Komját, György, and Lengyel, who did. Once, after having heard Béla Kun speak, he approached the party chief to declare his readiness to serve: "I believe that the movement has need of me and I am in it body and soul." Kun replied icily: "The communist movement is the communist party!"[99] Stung by those words, Kassák would not reconsider. In the pages of Ma, he insisted that revolutionary art was of primary importance, for it alone could create a new world in the realm of the imagination. In his view, art had to create in men and women a new sensibility, a new way of seeing the world such that the old visions no longer defined the limits and strategies of change.

Speaking for Kassák and the Ma Circle, Sándor Barta and Árpád Szélpál (Schwartz) elaborated. The former, soon to become Kassák's brother-in-law, used the occasion of an attack on the schismatics—Lengyel, Révai, et al.—to observe that the revolution had to be made in the minds of men before it could be made in daily life.[100] The latter maintained that the true artist never accepted as given a party program; rather, he created a program for himself and others. Since that program could never be final, the artist had always to create anew, to be dissatisfied with what exists. Any art that ceased to be restless, that became conservative, was no longer art. "Party art" was actually a contradiction in terms. Parties drafted programs and in that very act they destroyed movements and dictated to artists. In the final analysis, there was no difference between conservative and revolutionary parties.[101]

For Kassák and his circle, then, the revolution was permanent and took place primarily in the realms of mind and spirit. In the main, they accepted the Communists' economic and social programs, but they were not much interested in the details. As artists, they saw it as their responsibility to make it possible for men and women to envision a world that was completely distinct from the world of the past and the present. Theirs, in short, was a project at once ill-defined and utopian. Insofar as they had any political hero, it was Szabó, who was himself a bundle of contradictions—Marxist and syndicalist, reformer and revolutionary, pacifist and counselor to terrorists, Socialist and antiparty radical. Of the fallen leader, Kassák wrote with unaccustomed humility: "/He/ was a model always one step ahead of us, someone who taught us, and from whom we learned with confidence."[102]

It is a measure of Szabó's own theoretical confusion that the leaders of the October Revolution also found much to admire in him. For *that* revolution, Kassák had little use. He was appalled by the euphoria that attended Károlyi's accession to power and skeptical about the new government's aims. "This revolution is not going to stop with Károlyi and his followers. I am glad that it has come, but I do not believe that this is the revolution for which we worked."[103] In November, *Ma* issued a special number in which Kassák proclaimed his commitment to a *soviet* republic.

Kassák's opposition to the new government only increased when, at Jászi's urging, Károlyi appointed a delegation to convey official greetings to Ady, who then lay mortally ill. That only went to show, the avant-garde leader believed, that the October Revolution marked the end of the old epoch, not the beginning of the new. When Ady died the morning of January 27, 1919, Kassák eulogized him as the last representative of a political and artistic era that had opened in Hungary in 1848, with the anti-Habsburg revolution and its bard Sándor Petőfi. As Ady was not "the new world's new man," he could not serve as an inspiration to Hungarians living in an age that demanded a new Petőfi, a poet who possessed an *active* temperament.[104]

Kassák's obituary was self-serving enough, there being no doubt that he had cast himself in the role of the new Petőfi. Yet he also knew that the Károlyi regime was in deep trouble. To be sure, the government had made strenuous efforts to implement its democratic program. On November 16, for example, it issued a Bill of Rights that included a new voting law extending the franchise to all men over twenty-one and all women over twenty-four years of age. It had also placed tax reform on the agenda. In fact, Pál Szende, a Radical party member close to Károlyi and Jászi, promoted the idea of a progressive inheritance tax. Unfortunately for Károlyi, land reform, the most important aspect of the government's program, was slow in coming, in part because of the complexities involved. That procrastination exasperated Jászi, and in a letter of December 10, he resigned from office. The government, he told Károlyi, lacked the determination to save Hungary from the forces of reaction and the advocates of violent revolution.[105]

One month later, Károlyi assumed the office of President, and Dénes Berinkey, an expert on international law whom Károlyi hoped would unite the heterogeneous elements of his coalition, formed a government dominated by the Social Democrats. This shift to the left did not, of course, satisfy the Communists, who continued to make inflammatory speeches and organize demonstrations. Though exceedingly dangerous to him, Károlyi refused to silence his opponents lest he appear to be denying the freedom of speech he had always championed.

On February 16, the government finally passed a Land Reform Bill that divided all properties greater than seven hundred acres. Priority in the distribution of land was to be given to poor farm hands, laborers, and war veterans.[106] In the end, however, the only instance of land partition carried out by the government was Károlyi's distribution of his own estates. The Communists were no help here either because they opposed any increase in the class of small holders and were ideologically committed to collectivization.

As if Károlyi did not have trouble enough, the Association of the Unemployed organized, on February 20, a Communist-sponsored demonstration in front of the editorial offices of Népszava (Voice of the People), the Social Democratic paper. Fearing violence, the socialists had asked for police protection, and as usual in such cases, someone fired a shot. By the time the shooting was over, four policemen lay dead, and on the following day the authorities rounded up Communist leaders. After these arrests, overzealous police officers beat Kun, on one occasion in the presence of a newspaper journalist, who reported the attack the next day, February 22. A wave of sympathy for the bolsheviks swept over the capital.

With Kun and the members of the Central Committee in jail, the party organized (or activated) a new Central Committee; chaired by Tibor Szamuely, a former prisoner of war in Russia, it numbered Lukács among its members. From this position of authority, the convert attacked the Socialists for their part in the police crackdown. There could no longer be any doubt, Lukács believed, that the Socialists feared the proletarian revolution as much as any bourgeois leader. Having denounced bolshevik violence in the name of law and order, they did not scruple to sanction police brutality.

In a lecture delivered on the day of the demonstration, Kassák also criticized the Socialists and, by clear implication, the Károlyi government. For the first time, he affixed the expressionist label "activism" to the avant-garde movement he led. He then proceeded to compare social democracy unfavorably with communism. Avoiding any direct mention of Hungary, he denounced Kerensky (read Károlyi) for the demagogic and compromising politics he pursued in Russia and he signaled his approval of Lenin's seizure of power and the bolshevik dictatorship.[107]

Had he stopped there, Kun might have been gratified, but once again Kassák chose to make explicit the difference between communism in its party incarnation and activism, because he insisted that economic and political revolution could not be equated with a revolution that had as its aim universal life. After the liberation of the body must come that of the soul. And the means to that revolutionary end could never be politics, but only art. That, he wrote, was the lesson of *Russia*'s October Revolution. The Russian working class had not been noticeably worse off than its counterparts in Western Europe; hence, one could not seek bolshevism's roots in economic conditions alone, but only in the moral revolution that had already begun to transform Russian souls. That revolution was not instigated by political leaders, but by writers and artists who provided their countrymen with a radically new vision of the world. Just so, the Hungarian activists regarded it as their responsibility to produce an art that would in turn create a new and morally superior man.

By following the Russian example, the activists turned away from Western Europe, where they believed artists, with few exceptions, had not yet recognized their revolutionary calling. To be sure, the exponents of futurism, expressionism, and cubism had begun an unselfconscious, anarchist revolution that aimed at destroying bourgeois culture's antiquated forms, but they did not yet understand, as Kassák and the activists did, that they had also to *build* anew. To do so would require that they live a life of action and proclaim through their work the permanent revolution of morality.

While Kassák announced these vague but extravagant aims, things were going from bad to worse for Károlyi and his government. Embarrassed by the mistreatment of Kun, Károlyi received from Lenin a telegram advising him of the arrest in Moscow of the Hungarian Red Cross Mission and reminding him that many Hungarian officers remained in Russian prisoner of war camps. Lenin warned him, therefore, to protect the Hungarian Communists. Károlyi quickly called a meeting of his cabinet, subsequent to which he ordered the release of twenty-nine Communists, dropped charges of incitement to murder against the others, and directed that prisoners be treated in a civilized manner.[108]

As a result of this affair, increased fear of counterrevolution, and impatience with Allied unfriendliness, left-wing Socialists began to explore the possibility of a reconciliation with the Communists. In fact, Jenő Varga, Jenő Landler, and József Pogány had already decided that bolshevism represented authentic socialism. Negotiations with Kun began while he was still incarcerated and continued into March. On the 20th, Lieutenant Colonel Vyx presented the infamous "ultimatum" to Károlyi that administered the coup de grace to the democratic republic and led directly to the formation of the Soviet Republic.

The ultimatum was a result of the insensitivity and miscalculation that characterized much of postwar diplomacy. Under its terms, the armistice line between Hungary and Romania that had previously been agreed upon in Belgrade would be moved forty-five miles closer to Budapest. Debrecen and Szeged, unambiguously Hungarian cities, were to be included in the neutral zone. Further, when Vyx handed the note to Károlyi, he informed him that Hungarian troop withdrawal had to begin by March 23 and be completed within ten days. Most disheartening for the Hungarians was the Frenchman's suggestion that the new line should be regarded as a definite political frontier.[109]

Cognizant of the fact that no government that agreed to such demands could survive, Károlyi rejected the ultimatum and charged the Social Democrats, in conjunction with the Communists, with the formation of a new government. Pursuant to that end, Sándor Juhász-Nagy, the Minister of Justice, ordered the release of Kun and the remaining Communist prisoners. Meanwhile, however, the Socialists, recognizing the increasing popularity of the Communists and hoping for assistance from Soviet Russia, had concluded an agreement with their former enemies to amalgamate their parties and to form a Soviet rather than a Social Democratic government.

On March 21, the Socialist members of the existing government proclaimed the Dictatorship of the Proletariat and asked Károlyi to resign power to the "Hungarian workers." Although he refused, *Népszava* published a letter of resignation over his forged signature.[110] As one Socialist leader put it: "The imperialists of the Entente took democracy and national self-determination as their slogans, but since victory they have acted differently. Our hope for peace was destroyed by the ukase from Colonel Vyx. There is no longer any doubt that those gentlemen in Paris wish to give us an imperialist peace. . . . From now on we must look to the east for justice, as it has been denied to us in the west."[111]

The Soviet Republic

Károlyi's western (Wilsonian) policy had failed to protect Hungary's territorial integrity. Desperate and believing themselves to have been betrayed, Hungarians, even many who were anti-Communists, now fastened their hopes on Kun's eastern (Leninist) policy. Like Károlyi, Kun formed a coalition government, and again the dominant partner was the older and far better organized Social Democratic party. This time, however, the party's left replaced its right/center and its partner was the Communist rather than the Radical party.

Eager to present a united front, the Communists and Social Democrats merged as the Hungarian Party of Socialist-Communist Workers. According to the "documents of unity" signed in the Budapest City Prison on March 21, the two parties would "jointly participate in the leadership of the new party and the government." Moreover, "in order to ensure the complete authority of the proletariat and to /make a stand against/ Entente imperialism, the fullest and closest military and spiritual alliance must be concluded with the Russian Soviet government."[112]

Despite this show of oneness, Socialists and Communists continued to harbor mutual suspicions. The composition of the new Revolutionary Governing Council was the first major problem. Kun was the only Communist among twelve people's commissars, but as Commissar of Foreign Affairs, he was the real leader of the Soviet Republic, nothing being more important than the effort to enlist Soviet Russia in the struggle for Hungarian national interests. Seven of the twenty-one deputy people's commissars were Communists, and Lukács was to serve under Zsigmond Kunfi as Deputy People's Commissar of Public Education. In less than one month, however, the government abolished the distinction between full and deputy commissar and in many commissariats the Communists were in de facto control. From the first, indeed, Lukács dictated cultural policies.[113]

Like Weimar culture, Hungarian culture during the Soviet Republic "was the creation of outsiders, propelled by history into the inside, for a short, dizzying, fragile moment."[114] Years later, Lukács still recalled with pride how thoroughly his Commissariat cleaned house, dismissing old regime officials and suspending all "bourgeois" papers and journals. At the same time, he made a series of impressive appointments. Early in April, he announced that new lecture series would enliven the University of Budapest's life: József Révai— "Cicero"; Karl Mannheim—"Philosophy of Culture"; Mihály Babits—"Ady Seminar"; Lajos Fülep—"Dante: Vita Nuova"; Frederick Antal—"Modern Painting: Folk Art"; and Béla Fogarasi—"The Philosophic Foundations of the Humanistic Sciences."[115]

It was Fogarasi, speaking in his capacity as director of the new Marx-Engels Workers' University, who expressed regret that socialism had previously neglected philosophy and identified itself with the natural sciences. That, he said, was about to change. For if, as Engels had written, the proletariat was humanity's heart, philosophy was its head.[116]

The day after Fogarasi spoke, Lukács announced several University appointments: Babits—Modern Hungarian Literature and World Literature; Fülep—Italian Language and Literature; and Gyula Szekfű—Historical Auxiliary Sciences. On May 11, he named to the faculty of Budapest's Secondary-School Teacher-Training College Mannheim (Philosophy), Hauser (Literary Theory), and György Pólya (Mathematics). To the Writers Directory he appointed himself (President), Balázs, Fülep, Kassák, and Komját.[117] To the

Committee for the Communization of Theaters he named, among others, Balázs and Kassák.

To the Musical Arts Directory, Lukács appointed Bartók, Zoltán Kodály, and Ernő Dohnányi. Although he regarded Dohnányi as a political opportunist and was cool toward Kodály, he greatly respected Bartók. "For our generation," he recalled later, "it was not only the Waldbauer Quartet's first concerts that constituted a great experience, but also—above all—*The Wooden Prince*, in which, really for the first time in Hungary, serious art took up seriously the problem of alienation."[118] Despite many plans, however, the Music Directory effected little change because, according to Bartók, "the political atmosphere is too troubled. It is impossible to work well and soundly."[119]

These appointments included many noncommunists who considered their work to be a national contribution, and who were attracted by Lukács's program. Even Jászi could write that "under the direction of George Lukács, the policy of the dictators in regard to education and art was certainly distinguished by many great ideals."[120] To be more precise, Lukács's policy was guided by his determination to end human alienation; the new culture was to be the connecting link between human beings. In that sense, politics was "only the means, culture the goal."[121] His was, in fact, a decidedly utopian program designed to create "new men" who would live together in freedom and harmony without the mediation of social institutions.

In the effort to translate his otherworldly goal into reality, Lukács focused his attention on cultural realms that had always fascinated him—drama and fairy tales. Initially, he nationalized all of Budapest's theaters in order "to open the places of culture to the proletariat, the workers: our theaters will no longer be the monopoly of the wealthy."[122] According to Balázs, the Commissariat would revise the repertoire of plays to include only the greatest works of world literature, and build new theaters, including one devoted to experimental works. It would provide opportunities for talented actors and direct leading companies to perform in provincial cities.[123]

If the drama was the most important educational art in the struggle to forge a world free of alienation, the fairy tale was a close second. "As a result of the provisions of the Commissariat of Public Education," Vörös Újság reported on April 17, "120,000 proletarian children today heard fairy tales in every school and children's hospital in Budapest."[124] According to Lukács and Balázs's plan, "fairy tale afternoons" would continue throughout the summer, in parks and theaters. In a published defense of that policy, Balázs asserted that the new economic order was merely a means, the ultimate goal was "the new man, whose name today is still child." Unfortunately, many Communists failed to understand how fairy tales contributed to the achievement of that goal; they insisted that children be taught "reality," rather than fantasy.

Such a policy would be shortsighted, Balázs warned, because children could understand the world only through the medium of fairy tales. In them they encountered a world "in which everything is possible for everyone in accord with inner worth, where the characters change not only their class, but also their form and their life. Such a world is more communist than our communism. We abolished only the differences between human classes; with the possibility provided by enchantment, the fairy tale erased the border between animal/vegetable and human being, between every existing and non-existing being. The communist Weltanschauung of fairy tales is far more profound, even in its most naive forms, than that of consciously socialist poetry."[125]

These arguments and policies did not go unchallenged. Although, for example, Lukács and Balázs insisted that they recognized no official literature, not everyone was convinced, and on April 15, Pál Kéri attacked the Commissariat's literary policies in the social democratic weekly *Az Ember* (*Man*). According to Kéri, Lukács and Balázs had cast their lot with Kassák and the *Ma* Circle, which Kéri portrayed as a hopelessly muddled group of incompetents and philistines. He described Balázs as a journalist at best, and Lukács as a wealthy eccentric.

The following day, *Vörös Újság* charged Kéri with "cultural counterrevolution." Ferenc Göndör, editor of *Az Ember*, came to Kéri's defense and renewed the assault on Kassák and Balázs—but not Lukács. In reply to both Kéri and Göndör, József Révai pointed out that "the *official* cultural program of the Commissariat of Public Education has not to this day been announced." Finally, in a carefully worded essay, Lukács assayed to set the record straight. *Ma* was not and never would be the Commissariat's official organ. He regarded the writers and artists around the journal as no better, and no worse, than any other well-intentioned group. What was more, he did not intend to promote officially *any* literary trend, because a Communist cultural program distinguished only between good and bad literature. Not surprisingly, the united party stood behind Lukács's disclaimer and ordered *Az Ember* to cease publication.[126]

Kéri and Göndör might have been forgiven for their confusion. Kassák and the *Ma*-ists certainly behaved as though they exemplified Communist literature, and on matters such as the new culture, the moral revolution, and the "new man," they often sounded very much like Lukács and Balázs. Only four days after the proclamation of the Soviet Republic, they issued a public statement of their aims. Parallel with the economic revolution, they announced their intention to lead a Communist cultural revolution that would be moral in essence and would make possible for the "new man" a free and "monumental" life. Among the activist painters who signed the proclamation was László Moholy-Nagy.[127]

Although that was the only occasion, prior to his emigration, that Moholy identified himself publicly with the *Ma* Circle, he later observed that "the decisively important movement of the *Ma* set the standard of my work. The debates and conversations I had with Uitz and Nemes Lampérth helped to clarify my errors and to make up my half-thoughts."[128] He was also intrigued by Kassák's idea that the true revolution was moral and cultural and that its goal was the creation of the new man. Thus, he was grateful to his friend, the critic Iván Hevesy, for introducing him to members of the Circle.

A contributor to Ma, Hevesy shared many of Kassák's enthusiasms, especially that for posters.[129] Although he knew little about such pioneers of poster art as Jules Chéret and Henri de Toulouse-Lautrec, Kassák did know about the expressionists and their work. He noted that the poster was always born under the sign of radicalism, always bursting with agitational energies. More completely than any other art form, it fulfilled the requirements of a century that was urban and socially conscious, one in which the rhythm of life had quickened immeasurably. There could be no turning back, Kassák insisted; "he who works in this century, who wishes to transmit this century's character, must be a man of his time not only in his work and his blood, but in every fiber of his being." To be a successful poster artist he would have to be filled with faith and engaged in the struggle for a new world.

During the 133 days of the Soviet Republic's existence, Hungarians had an opportunity to catch a glimpse of that faith in publicly displayed posters and prints by Uitz, Bortnyik, Nemes Lampérth, and other Ma artists. They could also attend Ma-sponsored "Propaganda Evenings" and "Propaganda Matinées," during which members of the Circle read their poetry and musicians performed new music, often by Bartók. On occasion, Kassák organized "International Propaganda Evenings," when he and his friends read translations of foreign poets. All of this activity had as its purpose not so much the defense of the Soviet Republic, as the propagation of permanent revolution.

In view of Lukács's distaste for the avant-garde, it is a wonder that he did not silence Ma early on. He seems, however, to have viewed Kassák and his followers as useful, if unreliable, allies in the struggle to create a new culture. In April, as we have seen, he refused to condemn them, even as he made clear that Ma was not the Commissariat's official voice. By June, however, the Republic was in deep trouble and neither Lukács nor Kun had much patience left. For one thing, the economy was in a shambles. At a meeting of June 16, Jenő Varga, the republic's principal economic adviser, conceded that labor production had fallen precipitously. He attributed this melancholy circumstance to three factors: the absence of any labor discipline; the ruinous effect of time wages; and the regrettable fact that "men have not yet attained the higher type of Socialist mentality which will be the starting point of the coming generation."[130]

As pressing as economic problems were, however, the republic faced even greater military difficulties. On April 16, Romania had launched an offensive against Hungary, and although there is no evidence to suggest that the Big Three ordered the attack, the Hungarians had reason to be suspicious. Only a week or so prior to the assault, Kun had rejected Allied General Jan Smuts's proposal for a new demarcation line, somewhat more favorable to Hungary. Worried that the Allies might offer further concessions, the Romanians advanced to the Tisza River and even crossed it at several points.

As the Fifth Division's political commissar, Lukács was at the front with the commander, Tibor Sárói Szabó, a hussar turned Communist. When one of the three Hungarian battalions fled before the advancing Romanians, the two men agreed to execute eight Red Army soldiers as an example to the rest. With this draconian measure, Lukács boasted at the time, he had helped to turn the tide.[131] More likely, Allied intervention saved the day. In a meeting with Ionel Bratianu in Paris, Clemenceau ordered that the Romanian advance be halted.

Romania was not, however, Hungary's only enemy, for on April 26 Czechoslovak troops crossed the military demarcation line in the north. Knowing that the republic's fate hung in the balance, the Hungarian leaders ordered a counter-offensive in the second half of May. By then, Lukács and the Fifth Division had moved north. Though the commissar later spoke highly of the Red Army, he conceded that many peasant-soldiers hated the Kun government because it had not, like Lenin's regime, divided the land. In a major tactical blunder, Kun had refused to partition the *latifundia*, turning them instead into state concerns, in most cases with the former owners as managers. The peasant-soldiers had remained loyal to the Soviet Republic only because of national feeling. "This army," Lukács admitted, "was essentially a Hungarian army. It defended /Hungary/ against foreign attacks."[132]

In large measure because of the soldiers' national feeling, the Red Army not only halted the Czechoslovak advance but occupied more than one-third of Slovakia and arranged for the proclamation of the "Slovak Soviet Republic." Desperate, Eduard Beneš appealed to Paris for assistance, and, on June 8 and 13, Clemenceau forwarded ultimata to Kun. In the latter note, the French leader demanded that the Red Army withdraw from Slovakia. "If the Allies and Associated Governments are not informed by their representatives on the spot within four days from midday on June 14, 1919, that this operation is being effectively carried out, they will hold themselves free to advance on Budapest and to take such other steps as may seem desirable to secure a just and speedy peace."[133]

Faced with such a threat and problems of "internal disorganization," Kun acquiesced, although he and his comrades, Lukács excluded, were pleased to think of their capitulation as akin to Russia's acceptance of Brest-Litovsk. Before the end of June, Hungarian troops had abandoned Slovakia and the Slovak Soviet Republic had collapsed. This was undoubtedly Kun's greatest mistake. So long as his government satisfied the Hungarians' national feeling, he could rely on widespread support, but the moment it became clear that he could not, or would not, defend Hungary's vital interests, his dictatorship lost all raison d'être. Indeed, the retreat provoked the resignation of several leading officers, including Colonel Aurél Stromfeld, the outstanding Chief of the General Staff.

In the midst of those critical and nerve-shattering events, the party held a congress that was punctuated by controversy, not least concerning the republic's cultural life. In a courageous speech given on opening day, Kunfi bemoaned the government's repeated resort to coercion. "In my judgment," he said, "scholarly, literary, and artistic life cannot develop without *a certain atmosphere of freedom.*" Under the dictatorship, an intellectual paralysis had gripped Hungarian writers and thinkers, a situation that could only be improved by expanding the perimeters of liberty.[134]

The following day, Lukács and Kun answered Kunfi's charges. As cultural tsar, the former proclaimed his willingness to tolerate criticism, but only of a certain kind. Freedom would not be extended to those who might arouse counterrevolutionary feelings in workers who had not yet achieved a fully developed revolutionary consciousness. For his part, Kun maintained that any cultural problem the republic might have was the result of intellectual poverty, not dictatorial methods. He expressed confidence that the proletariat would soon produce a culture worthy of it. Quite gratuitously, he then added: "There is no doubt that *this* /efflorescence/ *is not represented by the literature of Ma, which is the product of bourgeois decadence.*"[135]

In the next number of *Ma*, Kassák addressed an open "letter to Béla Kun in the name of art,"[136] in which he rehearsed for Kun's benefit the history of the activist movement, beginning with *A Tett*'s antiwar campaign and official suppression. While Kun was taking part in the *Russian* civil war, the *Ma*-ists were already agitating for communism in Hungary. True, they had not joined the Hungarian Communist party, but that was because they were fighting for the final goal—"the absolute man"—that by its very nature could never be reached, precisely because that man's "only life form is revolutionary action." The new man, that is, could only be realized in the continuous act of realization. Or as a leading student of the avant-garde once put it: the movement often "takes shape and agitates for no other end than its own self, out of the sheer joy of dynamism, a taste for action, a sportive enthusiasm, and the emotional fascination of adventure."[137]

Harried on all sides and recognizing the contingent nature of avant-garde loyalty, Kun elected not to continue the debate. After the appearance in July of one more issue of *Ma*, the government banned further publication. Moreover, it insisted that Kassák take a four-week sick leave at Keszthely, near Lake Balaton.

By the time Kassák left Budapest, Kun had his back to the wall. Clemenceau, in his note of June 13, had promised him that "the Romanian troops will be withdrawn from Hungarian territory as soon as the Hungarian troops have evacuated Czechoslovakia."[138] The Romanians, however, refused to honor that pledge and their troops remained at the Tisza River. The Allies did upbraid the Romanian government, but they took no steps to enforce compliance, and on July 10, Hungary's Revolutionary Governing Council decided on a new offensive against the Romanian army. Despite the risks that such an attack entailed, Hungarian forces initiated hostilities on July 21.[139] Kun had few alternatives left. Having withdrawn from Czechoslovakia, he had alienated Hungarian national sensibilities, and without nationalist support, he knew that his days were numbered. The Romanian campaign was thus a desperate gamble not merely to win territory but, more important, support at home. In the event, Kun lost, for the attack failed to dislodge the Romanians. Worse, the enemy went over to the offensive.

When news of the Red Army's failure and disorganization reached Budapest, the government sent Lukács to rejoin the Fifth Division, then fighting in the area between the Danube and Tisza rivers.[140] His assignment was to restore the division's battle-readiness, a mission that he later conceded had "ended in complete failure." On his arrival, he discovered that "there was complete panic" among the soldiers; no one any longer believed that victory was possible. Everyone was convinced that the Romanians would take Budapest and that the Soviet Republic was doomed. And they were not mistaken. On August 1, the day Lukács returned from the front, the government collapsed.

PART ONE

THE COMMUNISTS

ONE

GEORG LUKÁCS:

THE ROAD TO LENIN

The Lure of Politics

AFTER RESIGNING in favor of a caretaker trade-union government, the Soviet Republic's leaders left for Austria aboard a train protected by the Italian military mission. Lukács did not accompany them because Kun had instructed him and Ottó Korvin, the Republic's security chief, to stay behind and organize an underground movement aimed at reestablishing communist rule. It was a hopeless and dangerous mission. Lukács had all he could do just to escape detection. At great personal risk, Béla Zalai's widow, Olga Máté, hid him in her attic during daylight hours. When, on August 7, Lukács learned that the police had apprehended Korvin, he contemplated suicide, but finally concluded that "a member of the Central Committee must set the example."[1] On September 1, Karl Mannheim, the sculptor Márk Vedres, and others arranged for him to pose as the chauffeur for a German officer traveling to Vienna. Since Lukács did not know how to drive, his friends bound up his arm so that he could claim to have had an accident en route, and thus account for the fact that the officer was at the wheel.

By late summer of 1919, Vienna was no longer a proud and prosperous imperial capital. More than one hundred thousand Viennese were out of work, and even those who could put food on the table looked forward to a particularly uncertain future. Under the circumstances, Karl Renner's government did not welcome the Hungarian Soviet Republic's fugitive leaders. Authorities permitted the Social Democrats to settle in Austria, but arrested most of the Communists. They detained Lukács, a noted scholar, only briefly, but kept him under surveillance. On September 6, István Friedrich's new, nonsocialist government demanded that Kun and eight others be extradited. Lukács's name did not appear on the list because the Hungarians believed that he was still in Hungary. In Vienna, his life depended upon Austrian willingness to grant him political asylum.

In an effort to forestall Lukács's extradition, two friends, Franz Baumgarten and Bruno Steinbach,[2] drafted an appeal that appeared in the *Berliner Tageblatt* on November 12, 1919.

Not Georg von Lukács the politician, but the man and thinker ought to be vindi-
cated. Once he gave up the allurements of the pampered life that were his by
birth for the office of responsible, solitary thought. When he applied himself to
politics, he sacrificed what was most dear to him—his freedom as a thinker—for
the reformer's work he intended to accomplish. The Hungarian government demands his extradition from Austria. . . . He is said to have instigated the murder
of political opponents, but only blind hate can believe the accusation. Lukács's
salvation is no party matter. All who have come to know personally his human
purity and who admire the high spirituality of his philosophic-aesthetic books are
duty bound to protest the extradition.

The statement was signed by Baumgarten, Richard Beer-Hofmann, Richard
Dehmel, Paul Ernst, Bruno Frank, Maximilian Harden, Alfred Kerr, Heinrich
Mann, Thomas Mann, Emil Praetorius, and Karl Scheffler.[3]

Ernst Bloch added his voice to the chorus of protest in the December issue
of *Die weissen Blätter*. He branded charges that Lukács was a murderer as infamous lies, praised his friend's philosophic gift, and predicted that he would
travel to the end the theoretical journey begun by Tolstoi and Dostoevski.[4]
Max Weber made no public appeal, but he did send a telegram to the Hungarian Ministry of Justice, warning officials that Hungary's reputation would be
damaged if they prosecuted Lukács.[5]

Aware that the extradition of Lukács and the other Hungarian Communists
would be tantamount to a death sentence and concerned about Austrian citizens still in Russia, the Austrian government decided not to accede to the
Hungarian demand. Nevertheless, Lukács's initial Austrian permit was valid
for only six months, and it is hardly surprising that he presented "the most
heart-rending spectacle; deathly pale, haggard, nervous, and disconsolate. He
. . . walks about with a revolver in his pocket, because he has reason to fear
that they will abduct him."[6]

Balázs was even more nervous, and confessed to his diary that he was avoiding Lukács because he did not want to compromise himself in the eyes of the
authorities. Nor did he want to have anything to do with emigré politics: "The
truth is that I do not wish to take part any longer in politics, just as I did not
take part in them before, because they are not my concern. Communism is my
religion, not my politics, and from now on I want only to be an artist and
nothing more!"[7]

Lukács, on the other hand, elected to engage in political work—organizational and theoretical. For that and other reasons, the intellectual alliance
that he and Balázs had forged before the war came to an end. In his diary, the
latter wrote a fitting epitaph:

It seems that one must choose whether one writes or lives one's ethic, just as the
philosopher of religion reckons with but does not live God. If this is true, then it
seems that György Lukács, out of integrity and moral imperative, is going to live

his life to the very end in untruth, because Lukács the conspiratorial, active politician and revolutionary is assuming a *mask*, /is living in/ untruth; it is not his metaphysically rooted mission. He was born a quiet scholar, a lonely sage, a seer of things eternal; not, however, to search for stolen party funds in spacious coffee-houses, to keep an eye on the daily stream of ephemeral politics, or to strive to influence the masses—he who *is not speaking* his own *language* if more than ten people understand. His is a terrible banishment; he is truly homeless because he has lost his home. Of course, the question is: What is more important, purity or the truth? He lives an inauthentic life out of purity (he does not live his own life). He commits a metaphysical sin, but it is not given to us either to intervene in the decision of a man of such profound ethical worth or to judge him. Who knows what kind of reasons he has.[8]

Lukács's father also hoped that his son's political involvement would prove to be a passing aberration. In a letter of 1920, he appealed to the dramatist Paul Ernst to do what he could "to rescue him from accursed politics" and to guide him back to scholarship. He must, the elder Lukács wrote, return to Heidelberg.[9] There was little, however, that Ernst could do, for if Lukács did not listen to Balázs, he was wholly deaf to entreaties from Ernst or his father. He turned instead to the one person who seemed to understand him—Gertrúd Bortstieber.

In the spring of 1917, when he delivered his Free School lectures on ethics, Lukács renewed his acquaintance with Bortstieber. Many years earlier his sister Mici had introduced them, but their paths soon diverged. She married the mathematician Imre Jánossy and bore him two sons. An economist by training, she united "in her person the qualities of great practical wisdom and sense of realism with an irrepressibly serene outlook on life and a radiating warmth of character."[10] In the last year of his life, Lukács remembered this woman, who became his second wife, with love and gratitude: "The beginning of the new bond: obscure, but the feeling that, finally, for the first time in my life, love, completion, solid basis for life (examination of thought), not opposition. . . . I don't know whether the inner metamorphosis of my thought (1917–19) would have occurred without the help of this examination."[11] As those who were closest to Lukács during his last years have testified repeatedly, it was Gertrúd Bortstieber's "unique personality, a combination of traits of a *grande dame* of the Enlightenment and a plebeian heroine in a Gottfried Keller novella, that taught him to appreciate the 'ordinary life' he had formerly despised."[12]

Early in 1920, following her husband's death, the widow Jánossy and her sons went to live with her sister in Hütteldorf, near Vienna; before long, Lukács joined them. Later, he and Gertrúd moved to Vienna's eighth district and had a daughter of their own, although they did not marry immediately for fear that she might lose her widow's pension. This family life, which he had

2. Georg and Gertrúd Lukács on an outing near Vienna, 1927. Courtesy of the Magyar Tudományos Akadémia Filozófiai Intézet Lukács Archívum és Könyvtár (Lukács Archives and Library, Institute of Philosophy, Hungarian Academy of Sciences), Budapest.

3. Georg Lukács in the 1920s. Courtesy of the Lukács Archives and Library, Budapest.

never before known, made it necessary for Lukács to come to terms daily with "specific human reality."[13] Indeed, his life with Gertrúd created in him a new, and far more affirmative attitude toward reality.

Lukács's friendship with Jenő Landler only deepened his new appreciation for reality. A Social Democrat turned Communist whom he had come to know during the final days of the Soviet Republic, Landler always "endeavored to derive the political and organizational tasks of the Hungarian communist movement from the concrete problems of Hungary's concrete situation."[14] His ability to discern political possibilities at any given moment contributed much to Lukács's growing suspicion of left-wing communism.

Lukács had not been in Vienna for long when the emigré Communists had a falling out. In part the issue was Kun, an arrogant and dictatorial man with whom Lukács had never been on good terms. The Russian revolutionary Victor Serge remembered that to Lukács and others, Kun "was a remarkably odious figure. He was the incarnation of intellectual inadequacy, uncertainty of will, and authoritarian corruption."[15] On his arrival in Vienna, Kun had been taken into custody and placed under house arrest at Karlstein near the Czech border, because officials could not guarantee his safety in the capital. Due to the fact that the building in which he was detained could not be adequately heated, Kun threatened a hunger strike; thus, on February 7, 1920, he was taken to Stockerau near Vienna, where he occupied the local hospital's empty psychiatric ward. A few days later, he joined some of his comrades at Vienna's Steinhof Institute for Neurology.[16] Eager to be rid of him, the Austrians agreed to a Soviet proposal that he be sent to Russia, and, on August 11, he reached Petrograd. Physically removed from the Viennese emigration, Kun could not prevent the organization of an intraparty opposition.

The issues that occasioned the Party's split into factions were not, of course, merely personal; from his new place of exile in Moscow, Kun wished to continue to control the Hungarian Communist movement. Landler, on the other hand, insisted that the emigration, cut off as it was from Hungarian reality, ought to act in support of the movement in Hungary. Thus, while Kun hatched ambitious plots to reestablish the Soviet Republic, Landler fixed his eyes on the Party's real, and decidedly limited, possibilities. His was not a counsel of despair, but of patience and commitment to small but steady efforts to regain the initiative.

Matters came to a head in the fall of 1921 when Kun, embarrassed by the failure of his revolutionary "March Action" in Germany, demanded that the Communists living in Hungary refuse any longer to pay the Social Democratic party dues included in trade union assessments. Outraged, Landler argued that such a refusal would preclude further legal work in Hungary. He was convinced that the Communists, whose party was outlawed, had no choice but to work within—and attempt to gain control of—trade unions and the legal Social Democratic party. From the first, Lukács sided with Landler.

Utopia and Bureaucracy

Against this background of factional struggles, Lukács began to work out in print his conception of Marxism and proposals for political action. Between 1920 and 1922, he published numerous essays in the Hungarian-language *Proletár* (*Proletarian*) and the German-language *Kommunismus*. Taken together, those theoretical explorations constituted a defense of the Communist party as that organization capable of steering a course between the Scylla of utopia and the Charybdis of bureaucracy.

By 1920, utopia was anathema to Lukács. "Genuine revolutionaries," he wrote in *Kommunismus*, "above all Lenin, distinguish themselves from petit-bourgeois utopianism by their want of illusion."[17] The greatest illusion of all, he believed, was that to which he himself had earlier succumbed: that the new world could be brought into being at one stroke. "This transition from 'necessity' to 'freedom,' " he had become convinced, "cannot under any circumstances be a once-for-all, sudden, and unmediated act, but only a *process*."[18] He was now a "realist," a historical rather than an abstract thinker.

Contemptuous of his ideological opponents, Lukács accepted criticism from only one man—Lenin, the consummate revolutionary realist whose *theoretical* work came as a revelation. We know that because of an essay entitled "On the Question of Parliamentarianism"[19] that the Hungarian published early in 1920. Inspired by the contemporary debate in Communist circles throughout Europe, he attacked those who advocated parliamentary participation. As bourgeois institutions, he argued, parliaments could serve only to undermine true revolutionary action, as represented by genuine "workers' councils" (soviets). To his dismay, Lenin was displeased: "G. L.'s article is very left-wing and very poor. Its Marxism is purely verbal; . . . it gives no concrete analysis of precise and definite historical situations; it takes no account of what is more essential (the need to take over and to learn to take over, all fields of work and all institutions in which the bourgeoisie exerts its influence over the masses, etc.)."[20]

Lenin had made "left-wing" communism one of his central concerns, witness his famous treatise, *Left-Wing Communism—An Infantile Disorder*. While the goal of communism did not change, he wrote, the path to that goal was never the same. The refusal, "on principle," to participate in bourgeois parliaments reflected an abstract, undialectical, and unhistorical understanding. Although Communists recognized that parliamentarianism would give place to soviets, only the rash concluded that parliaments were no longer political realities with which to reckon. Communists had to destroy parliamentarianism from *within* parliaments; they had to cooperate with parliamentary parties in order to *subvert* parliamentary government.[21]

Impressed by Lenin's reasoning, Lukács was embarrassed to discover that he had not completely freed himself from utopianism. At the same time that he embraced the bolshevik leader's position, however, he continued to affirm his faith in the proletariat's messianic mission, for to lose all sight of utopia, he believed, would be to encourage the growth of bureaucracy and a bureaucratic mentality. Recalling Max Weber's work and his old fears of institutional forms alienated from life, Lukács attacked bureaucratization within the Communist movement with all the means at his command.

The old parties, he wrote, were compromise collectivities of heterogeneous individuals. Consequently, they rapidly became bureaucratized, generating an aristocracy of party officials cut off from the masses. Precisely because of the bureaucratic character of the old parties, many revolutionaries had turned to syndicalism. But the parties were not alone guilty. The Second International itself possessed only a bureaucratic unity. There was no greater danger to the Communist party and the Third International than bureaucratization, and in Lukács's judgment, the Central Committee of the Hungarian Communist Party headed by Kun had already (by 1922) degenerated into an "empty bureaucracy."[22]

Lukács maintained that the Russian Communist party had succumbed neither to utopianism nor to bureaucratization; it constituted a *tertium datur*. It was, to be sure, an "organization," but one wholly unlike bureaucratic organizations. For the Communist party, "organization is not the prerequisite of action, but rather a constant interplay of prerequisite and result *during* action. Indeed, if one of these two aspects predominates, organization ought to be understood as result rather than as prerequisite."[23] The Communist party was not simply a means to an end—the revolution; it was an end in itself. The seizure of power was an important step in the building of communism, but it was only *one* step. The Party and the revolution were dialectically related; without the Party there could be no revolution, and without the revolution the Party would remain the home of a minority.

The Party was an end in itself, "the first incarnation of the realm of freedom. In it, the spirit of brotherhood, of true solidarity, of willingness and ability to sacrifice ought first to prevail." Lukács had persuaded himself that the Party was the *Gemeinschaft* for which he had searched so long. Prophetically, he warned that if the Party should fail to constitute itself a true community, the seizure of power would simply substitute one oppressor for another; bureaucracy and corruption would not disappear. But if, as Lukács believed, the Party became a *Gemeinschaft*, it could act as "the educator of humanity to freedom and self-discipline."[24]

To be "educated," in Lukács's new terminology, was to be class conscious, and proletarian class consciousness was the realization of human solidarity because the proletariat was the universal class, which could not free itself without at the same time liberating all men. Such education was not simply or even primarily the result of propaganda, but of action. A "unity of the deed" could be forged even if a particular action failed to achieve its aim. "The proletariat," Lukács wrote, "can constitute itself a class only in actual class struggle."[25] When the proletariat was fully conscious and in possession of political power, Lukács believed that community would become a reality for all men and women.

Toward a Marxist Theory of Literature

As we have seen, Lukács was preoccupied with politics during the years 1920–22, yet he did not set literary-cultural questions completely aside. It is true that Balázs complained to his diary on October 26, 1920 that Lukács alone could reunite the members of the Sunday Circle, but "he does not now have time because he is fashioning world revolution." But a mere three months later, he reported that the Circle had reorganized, even if it met on Mondays in the chilly atelier of the Hungarian sculptor, Béni Ferenczy. In addition to Balázs and Lukács, the members included Révai, Lukács's first wife Ljena Grabenko, Fogarasi, the illustrator Tibor Gergely, Edith Hajós, Anna Schlamadinger, and Anna Lesznai. "Ah, once again we are together," Balázs cooed, and "not even the world revolution will break up this sect."[26]

Soon other Hungarian emigrés joined the Circle: Charles de Tolnay, László Radványi, Andor Gábor, Ervin Sinkó, and György Káldor. From time to time, the Austrian writer Maria Lazar and the composer Hanns Eisler also visited. In the fall of 1921, Mannheim and Hauser contacted Balázs and Lukács, who refused to receive them. "This return of theirs is probably related to the fact that the world revolution is being deferred to an ever more remote future. As a result, the Circle's commitment to serious action cannot for the time being be a topic of discussion. Consequently, it is now less dangerous to be around us."[27]

Much had changed since Budapest days. The subjects of discussion were not very different, but members now approached them from a Communist perspective. The major problem was that of the individualistic ethic that "led us to give ourselves to a movement that excludes this individualistic ethic. For humanity, two lines of development are relevant: the evolution of classes and of individual souls. They may travel on completely distinct paths and intersect with each other in us, but they remain two in number. Under these circumstances, to renounce our ethic will be the 'most ethical' of our acts."[28]

This decision to merge one's individuality with a class was, as Sinkó later observed, a modern version of the "unio mystica" with God. In the past, people had attempted to escape their problems and sorrows, their isolation, by escaping from this world. Those living in the present, however, knew only this world and feared the abyss of nothingness. Thus, in order to obtain freedom from the self, they escaped to an impersonal unity with the masses.[29]

The members of the reconstituted Sunday Circle also discussed Communist art and literature. At the time, artistic and literary questions had not yet been answered in Soviet Russia, where A. V. Lunacharski directed the Commissariat of Enlightenment in a relatively liberal spirit. True, Lenin despised the avant-garde. But in the early 1920s, it was not yet clear that "realism" would become the official artistic mode, and the Hungarian emigrés in Vienna spent hours arguing about expressionism and activism, Kassák and Ma, and the "proletarian art" to come. Balázs, Lukács, and their friends denied that the avant-garde represented the wave of the Communist future, for they had finally concluded that Kassák and his followers were nihilists who wished to sever all connection with the past. To reject the progressive traditions of literature was, they believed, to destroy the roots of a profound, traditionally grounded, Communist literature.

In a series of essays that he published in Die Rote Fahne, an organ of the German Communist Party, Lukács formulated his new ideas concerning literature. Taken together, those explorations constituted a revised version of his first book, History of the Evolution of the Modern Drama, in which he tried to account for the rise and decline of tragic ages. A tragic age, he had concluded, was "the heroic age of a class's decline."[30] The decline of the bourgeoisie made possible a rebirth of the tragic spirit and hence of the tragic drama. In the Rote Fahne essays, he employed the same historical/sociological theory, but by then he was more interested in the literature inspired by a class on the rise, one that conceived of the causes of its difficulties as temporary and hence subject to change. That class was the proletariat. But since an authentic "proletarian" literature had not yet emerged, Lukács focused his attention on writers whose work reflected the optimistic, self-confident strivings of the bourgeoisie during the late eighteenth and early nineteenth centuries.

Balzac was one of the greatest of those writers. During the second half of the nineteenth century, his fame, Lukács noted,[31] had been eclipsed by that of Flaubert, Zola, Daudet, and Maupassant, a turn of events that was not accidental, because behind it were social changes and hence changes in bourgeois ideology. Despite consciously reactionary views, Balzac gave literary expression to the rising bourgeoisie. Unlike the disillusioned, resigned writers of the declining bourgeoisie (late nineteenth century), he not only portrayed human passions and analyzed them psychologically, he also understood them in their relationship to the whole of social life. After 1848, when the decline of the bourgeoisie began, Balzac's work no longer corresponded to the class-dictated spirit of the age.

The Balzac essay revealed the grounds for Lukács's notorious insensitivity to modern literature. In his view, bourgeois writers of the post-1848 period could, at best, hold up a mirror to the decline of their class; at worst, they contributed to the decay. Perceiving reality to be immediately given and fundamentally unalterable, they succeeded only in presenting endless variations on the theme of despair. For them, the tragedy of human alienation, the central tragedy of the bourgeois age, was inescapable. The class standpoint of the bourgeoisie made impossible any recognition that Being was social and that reality was constituted by a series of mediations, potentialities in the process of actualization.

A similar failure of recognition led Lukács to bid farewell to the literary hero of his utopian years, Feodor Dostoevski. In his most important literary essay of the early 1920s—"Stavrogin's Confession"[32]—he charged that the Russian genius had ignored the social roots of human problems, viewing them instead as *individual* failures. In accord with his utopian disposition, Dostoevski held "that the redeeming principle for every need in the pure human relationships of men to one another is to be found in the recognition and love of the human essence in every man, in love and in goodness." That attempt to translate social Being into pure spirituality could not but run aground, because the problem of human alienation would yield only to fundamental economic and social change. Men's relationships with other men were always determined by the existing social order in its totality.

It followed, Lukács believed, that Marxist literary criticism could not be satisfied with purely aesthetic judgments. In that respect, he wrote in *Die Rote Fahne*, there was much to be learned from radical Russian critics such as Belinski, Dobrolyubov, and Pisarev, all of whom approached works of literature as parts of a social totality. Belinski, especially, "viewed and judged every work of art in its relationship to reality, to the totality of the life of Russian society." For the Russian critics there was, in fact, no distinction between aesthetic and social judgment; literary criticism and ideological class struggle were one.[33]

It is not surprising that Lukács felt an affinity for Belinski, for it was that consumptive and combative man who transmitted the doctrines of German idealism to the tradition of Russian criticism. Like Lukács, he and the members of his generation of radicals lived in the aftermath of a failed revolution, the Decembrist uprising of 1825. They too confronted a "counterrevolutionary" regime—that of Nicholas I—and they too looked to Germany for a new philosophy. They believed their problem was similar to that which German thinkers encountered in the wake of the French Revolution. The reaction to that event, though a European phenomenon, had been especially acute in Germany. Never completely at ease with French rationalism, German thinkers attempted to transform Enlightenment thought (the inspiration of those among the Decembrists who were philosophically inclined) into a more coherent and less vulgar formulation.

Although Schelling and Schiller exerted an influence on the members of Belinski's generation, Hegel became their lodestar. Influenced by Nicholas Stankevich and members of his circle such as Michael Bakunin, Belinski became a Hegelian, at first of the right. In 1839 or 1840, he wrote to Bakunin about his Hegelian reconciliation with reality: "I look upon reality, which I used to hold in such contempt, and tremble with mystic joy, recognizing its rationality, realising that nothing of it may be rejected, nothing in it may be condemned or spurned."[34] By 1841, however, Belinski had abandoned Right Hegelianism, largely because of his hunger for action and social transformation. Yet he did not turn his back on Hegel. "Grown to sturdy manhood," he wrote in 1842, "philosophy is now returning to life, from the maddening noise of which it was once forced into retirement to cognize itself in solitude and quiet. The beginning of this beneficent reconciliation between philosophy and practice was achieved on the left side of present-day Hegelianism."[35]

Lukács knew that Belinski possessed only a rudimentary knowledge of Hegel and that he subscribed to a rather crude materialism, but as he later pointed out, the Russian always "retained the great historical perspectives of the Hegelian dialectic." For the remainder of his life, Lukács criticized literature within the methodological tradition established by Belinski and other radical Russian critics.[36] Like them, he believed that the true value of a literary work consisted of its ability to lay bare the structure of society. Dobrolyubov's famous critique of Turgenev's On the Eve served as a case in point. There the Russian eschewed any aesthetic analysis of the novel, examining "only its form, as a prototype of society, and its events and actions in so far as they were characteristic for that society."[37]

Dialectical Dogmatics

Despite these initial investigations, Lukács did not work out a Marxist theory of literature in any detail because he was channeling most of his energy into emigré polemics and a theory of practice. When he and the members of the reconstituted Sunday Circle were not discussing moral and literary questions, they exchanged views concerning the Soviet Republic's fall and the imperatives of Hungarian politics. For the government in their homeland they had, of course, no use whatever. Lukács could be particularly vituperative, especially when he recalled the execution, late in 1919, of Ottó Korvin.[38] The formation, in 1922, of Count István Bethlen's authoritarian, but capable and decent, government did not lessen his hostility, even though the new leader brought to heel the anti-Semitic officers who had instigated a White Terror.

For other emigré groups, Lukács and the Communists reserved a similar contempt. They set themselves against not only Kassák and the Ma Circle, but Jászi and the liberal Socialists gathered around the Bécsi Magyar Újság (Hungarian Newspaper of Vienna). Because of Lukács's disdain for Jászi, he left the antiliberal polemics to Andor Gábor, a member of the Sunday Circle who had tried to make a name for himself as a playwright for Erwin Piscator's newly organized Proletarian Theater in Berlin. On opening night, October 14, 1920, Piscator staged three agitprop (agitation and propaganda) plays, one of which was Gábor's *At the Gate*, an exposé of concentration camps in his homeland.[39] The play shared billing with *The Cripple* by "Julius Haidvogel" (Karl August Wittfogel) and *Russia's Day* by Lajos Barta, another Hungarian emigré.

As Piscator himself pointed out, his " 'plays' were appeals and were intended to have an effect on current events, to be a form of 'political activity.' "[40] Certainly he provided the exiled Hungarians with an opportunity to vent their spleens. At the same time, their "plays" helped to establish agitprop as a genre and to prepare the way for Bertolt Brecht's "epic theater." Last, but not least, they pioneered that defense of Soviet Russia that became the hallmark of communist propaganda for more than two decades. In *Russia's Day*, world revolution is far less important than the integrity of Russia's frontiers.

Fate decreed that the Proletarian Theater be short-lived; it gave its final performance on April 21, 1921. Thus, Gábor's play, *The Wife Comes Home*, was never performed. For the time being, then, the Hungarian had been obliged to join forces with some of the non-Communist opponents of Regent Miklós Horthy's regime. Indeed, he had been willing, initially, to write for the *Bécsi Magyar Újság*, even though Jászi was the paper's guiding spirit. According to Gábor, he and Jászi agreed to set aside their political differences in order to make common cause against Horthy.[41]

The pact had been tenuous at best and did not long survive. Jászi could not, in good conscience, remain silent concerning Communist provocations. By attacking the Hungarian Communist Party in the pages of the *Bécsi Magyar Újság*, he quickly forced Gábor to end their association. Almost immediately, the latter began a campaign of vilification that was all the more effective because of his gift for sarcasm. In 1924, the AMA Verlag of Vienna, the Communist party press, issued Gábor's book, which bore the curious title *And Here Comes Oszkár Jászi, Who Devours Marx and Lenin*. To make Jászi appear ridiculous, Gábor charged that the Radical leader was an anti-Marxist without understanding Marxism.[42] As if he himself were a serious student of Marx and Marxism.

It was not with Gábor, but with Béla Fogarasi that Lukács discussed complex theoretical problems of Marxism. Not an original thinker, Fogarasi was an intelligent and well-read man. As early as December 1915, he lectured to the Hungarian Philosophical Society on historical materialism.[43] Informed by the work of Dilthey, Windelband, and Rickert, the lecture was critical of economic determinism, which, according to Fogarasi, was only another form of metaphysical dogmatism. "The relationship of historical materialism to Hegelianism," he said, "was of decisive importance to its development." For those who wished to understand Marx, philosophy was at least as important as economics; indeed, Fogarasi insisted that, for Marx, economic and intellectual factors were joined in "indissoluble connection."

We recall that in his lecture, "Conservative and Progressive Idealism," Fogarasi had heralded the new unity of philosophy and politics. Soon after that he joined the Communist party. He worked under Lukács's direction for the Soviet Republic, and, in Vienna, continued to follow Lukács's philosophic leads. Thus it was that in 1922 he published his *Introduction to Marxist Philosophy*.[44] Acknowledging his debt to Lukács, Fogarasi presented there a clearly-stated précis of the soon to be published *History and Class Consciousness*. Like Lukács, he emphasized the *philosophical* relevance of Marxism and attempted to dispel the notion that Marx was a positivist. But let us allow the master to speak for himself.

In 1923, Lukács published *History and Class Consciousness: Studies in Marxist Dialectics*, a collection of eight essays he dedicated to Gertrúd Bortstieber. In this brilliant volume he proposed a solution to the problem of alienation with which he had wrestled personally and publicly from his earliest years. "For the first time since Marx," he recalled with pride in 1967, "alienation is treated as the central question of the revolutionary critique of capitalism."[45] It was capitalism that had transformed *relations between men*—which, according to Lukács, defined the conditions of human life and history—into impersonal things or economic commodities. The solution to this problem of alienation, or "reification," could be found only with the aid of the Marxist, or dialectical, method; hence, "if these essays offer the beginning or merely the occasion for a genuinely fruitful discussion of the dialectical method, a discussion that brings to general consciousness again the essence of the method, they will have fulfilled their function completely."[46]

In "What is Orthodox Marxism?" Lukács identified orthodoxy with the dialectical method as it applied to history, but not, as Engels had maintained, to nature, which men could only grasp contemplatively.[47] In that way he rejected the Second International's reduction of Marx's teachings to the science of economic determinism. Although scientific Marxists also paid lip service to the historical point of view, few of them acknowledged the Hegelian character of Marx's thought and fewer still understood fully that correct Marxist thinking entailed a concept of historical totality that placed immediately given "facts" into temporal context. Properly understood, Marxism was not a description of what is or a dream of what might be; it was the self-knowledge of what is in the process of becoming. In other words, it was the unity of is and ought.[48]

In "The Changing Function of Historical Materialism," Lukács boldly applied the historical/dialectical method to historical materialism itself. As an ideology, he maintained, historical materialism was not relative; it was absolutely valid within a capitalist social order. It was, in fact, capitalist society's self-knowledge. Yet by clinging to the deterministic form of historical materialism at a time when capitalism had entered a period of mortal crisis, scientific Marxists only conspired to prolong the capitalist era. To deny the necessity of acts of violence in favor of patient waiting on the immanent laws of economics was, Lukács argued, to remain passive in the face of a revolutionary situation.

He therefore invited Marxists to reinterpret historical materialism in accordance with the demands of a changing historical reality. Before their very eyes, the necessity of the objective economic process was being transformed into the freedom of the subjective human will, which was only another way of saying that historical evolution was becoming *conscious*. Viewed dialectically, necessity and freedom were identical, for the passage from the realm of necessity to the realm of freedom corresponded to the increasing consciousness of the proletariat, the class which was alone capable of perceiving history's subject-object identity because it *was* the subject as well as the object of history. Proletarian understanding and proletarian action were both aspects of a single historical reality in the process of being created. That is to say, the proletariat understood the world only in the act of changing it. All distinction between theory and practice dissolved as soon as it became apparent that true theory was practice.[49]

If Lukács was right, the fate of the revolution depended upon the class consciousness of the proletariat. Only that class's conscious deeds could lead mankind along the path to freedom. Lukács emphasized that the consciousness of individuals, no matter how great the individuals might be, could not affect the course of history decisively. Classes, not individuals, made history. Proletarian class consciousness could not, therefore, be equated with the sum of the empirical consciousnesses of individual proletarians. The class consciousness of the proletariat was that which it would be—Lukács spoke of its "objective possibility"[50]—if it were fully *conscious* of its, and hence humanity's, true interests and historic mission. Until consciousness arrived at that point, it could only be *imputed* to the proletariat, as Lenin had maintained in *What Is To Be Done?*[51]

That was an important point, for with the positing of an ideal consciousness known only to the initiated, Lukács was preparing the ideological ground for tyranny. Indeed, he hastened to identify the Communist party as the contemporary form taken by proletarian class consciousness. The Party alone, therefore, was in a position to impute consciousness to the proletariat. In plain language, the Party arrogated to itself the right to coerce workers for their own, and history's, good. The Party was not merely a means to the proletarian revolution, but an end in itself, the source of further human freedom. When all men and women were members of the Party, that realm would be fully realized.[52]

As the incarnation of proletarian class consciousness, the Party was not only the creator/interpreter of historical truth, but of historical morality. In fact, the two were identical. "Class consciousness," Lukács wrote, "is the 'ethics' of the proletariat, the unity of its theory and its practice, the point at which the economic necessity of its struggle for liberation changes dialectically into freedom. Because the Party is understood as the historical form and as the active bearer of class consciousness, it becomes at the same time the bearer of the ethics of the fighting proletariat."[53] What that meant was that the dialectical advance of history was ethical by definition because its goal— a community of free men and women—was the highest ethical ideal. Lukács insisted, however, that that goal was not something "above" or "beyond" history, but a process in time.

"Reification and the Consciousness of the Proletariat,"[54] was the most important essay in *History and Class Consciousness*. Lukács entitled the first section of the piece "The Phenomenon of Reification (*Verdinglichung*)," which he understood as a synonym for "alienation" (*Entfremdung*).[55] The central structural problem of capitalist society was, he began, that of commodities, because commodity structure, regarded as a thing, concealed the true structure of society, i.e., *the relations between men*. With the advent of capitalism, those human relations designed to guarantee a mutual supply of human necessities became impersonally "economic" in the modern sense—material things which served a mechanism that had become an end in itself.

This *objectification* or reification of authentic human relationships was *the* distinguishing characteristic of capitalist society. Rather than serving human beings, the economic order mastered them, forcing them to act "rationally," in keeping with the rationalization necessary for the maximization of economic efficiency. No longer fully human, men were defined by the role they played in the economic order, and as that role became more specialized, man's alienation from his fellows became more complete. What is more, this economically created isolation became the paradigm for all social relations under capitalism—the economically organized society *par excellence*. Worse, with the passing of time, the reified world of capitalism came to be regarded as the "natural" and eternal order of things, and men forgot that they were men. Human consciousness itself became reified. "The transformation of the commodity relation into a thing of 'ghostly objectivity' . . . stamps its structure on the entire consciousness of man."[56]

In section two, "The Antinomies of Bourgeois Thought," Lukács attempted a critique of modern philosophy based upon his analysis of the reified world dominated by the bourgeoisie. "Modern critical philosophy," he maintained, "originated in the reified structure of consciousness."[57] The alienated consciousness of man in bourgeois society necessitated a philosophy characterized by unresolved antinomies, and as a result even the greatest philosophies of the bourgeois era—those of Kant, Fichte, and Hegel—were antinomic to the core.

Kant's famous distinction between phenomena and noumena, his insistence that the "thing-in-itself" could never be known, simply pointed up for

Lukács the dilemma of bourgeois thought. On the one hand, Kant sought a rational system that was unified and complete, while on the other, due to his reified consciousness, he could not discover a means by which the thing-in-itself could be subjected to the categories of the understanding. Great as he was, therefore, the Königsberg philosopher failed to erect a system capable of grasping reality as a totality. "The 'eternal, brazen' regularity of natural events and the pure inner freedom of individual, moral praxis appear at the conclusion of the *Critique of Practical Reason* as irreconcilably separated, but at the same time—in their separation—the unchangeably given foundations of human existence."[58] Kant's true greatness, according to Lukács, was to have articulated clearly the philosophic antinomies of bourgeois thought and resisted any effort to resolve them dogmatically.

In the philosophy of Hegel, bourgeois thought came closest to overcoming Kant's antinomies. Indeed, Hegel pointed the way out of the dilemma, because in place of formal rationalism, he substituted dialectics. In place of two worlds—phenomenal and noumenal—he posited one, the historical. And he believed that that world could be grasped as a concrete totality. But despite Hegel's great philosophic advances, he had been unable to take the last step—the correct identification of the *subject* of the historical process. The antinomic structure of bourgeois existence invaded and distorted even his consciousness, and, on the edge of the final discovery, he retreated to idealistic metaphysics, positing the "World Spirit," which, as pure subject, lay beyond history. Working its way through time, the World Spirit achieved full self-consciousness at the stage of "Absolute Spirit"—art, religion, and philosophy. For Lukács, this was nothing but sophisticated mythmaking, the inescapable limit imposed on the brilliant but reified consciousness of a thinker unable to transcend the standpoint of the bourgeoisie.

In section three, "The Standpoint of the Proletariat," Lukács argued that it was only from the standpoint of the proletariat that the veil of the reified commodity structure of the bourgeois world could be lifted to reveal the authentic world and the relations between men. Since all thinking was defined by the existence of the relevant class, bourgeois thinkers had to view the world in its *immediacy*; for them, reality was immediately given, natural, the unalterable object of contemplation. They could not regard the world and the social order as anything but the sum of eternal, isolated "facts." Were they to abandon abstract, formal rationality, they would have to recognize that bourgeois class dominance was a temporal, not an eternal, phenomenon. To be sure, the best bourgeois thinkers were not willfully and cynically obtuse, but they possessed a consciousness that distorted ultimate reality in the interest of their class.

The privileged epistemological standpoint of the proletariat was also a function of class interest. Precisely because it was not in that class's interest to view reality in its factual immediacy, it was capable of achieving a *mediated* view for which facts derived their meaning from their relation to the whole, or the totality, of history. What for bourgeois thinkers were static, isolated "things" were for the proletariat dynamic aspects of processes, immanent tendencies and possibilities. Rightly understood, reality *was* not, it *became*; hence, the proper cognitive relationship to reality was not contemplation, but action. "The philosophers have only *interpreted* the world, in various ways," Marx had written. "The point, however, is to *change* it."

Thus Lukács's Marxism. At a distance of more than half a century, its lineaments stand out in sharp relief. To begin with, *History and Class Consciousness* is not a work of philosophy, but the systematization and explication of a faith. Just as a Christian dogmatics constitutes an effort to elucidate the truths and implications of a prior commitment, so Lukács's Marxism is a rendering of that political faith to which he had converted in 1918. It is therefore invulnerable to external criticism or argument.[59] No evidence can be adduced to disprove the dogma, which is internally consistent and self-certifying. We can know the truth, according to Lukács, by adopting the standpoint of the proletariat, which can be done only by participating actively in the communist movement. Those who remain outside the Party cannot possibly know the truth, because it is nothing but the self-awareness of the movement.

But how do we know that the standpoint of the proletariat is privileged? Because, Lukács replies, Marxism tells us so as the class consciousness of the proletariat. To the objection that the proletariat has often been misled or mistaken, Lukács answers that authentic proletarian class consciousness is an ideal, not an empirical and hence verifiable, consciousness. Only the Party, as the custodian of authentic class consciousness, possesses the truth, which, being dialectical, repeatedly twists and turns. And how do we know that the Party expresses the authentic will of the proletariat? Again, because Marxism tells us so. The argument is, and must be, circular, or else evidence could count against it.

Nor is this the final article of belief. If we accept the privileged character of the proletarian, and hence the Party, standpoint, we must also assent to the claim that that standpoint permits an undistorted view of the truth as it is progressively revealed/created in time; thus, however contradictory and problematic its advance, history does ultimately move in a progressive direction. Lukács's Marxism is, in fact, a theodicy, for if he meant to say only that progress is possible, he would have been obliged to concede that history does not *by its nature* create truth. But that concession would be to give away the game. It could then be argued that terror resulted from human cruelty and was not a necessary moment in the actualization of human freedom.

Nor is the problem skirted by arguing, as Lukács did, that utopia is not some future state, but an endless, progressive becoming, in which means and ends are one. That is only another way of saying that there are no ends and that crimes committed in the name of Marxism are, rightly understood, aspects of freedom. "The dialectic miracle," Albert Camus once wrote, "is the decision to call total servitude freedom."[60]

Lukács's Marxism is enormously stimulating, but the claim made by Western Marxists, that History and Class Consciousness represents an alternative to Soviet Marxism, cannot be taken seriously. As the late Morris Watnick astutely observed, Lukács's argument "is unmistakably Leninist to the core, if by Leninism we mean an attempt to force the pace of the dialectic of history as Marx had foreseen it, and a doctrine which entrusts this act of premeditated history to the consciousness of a party elite."[61] Indeed Lukács offered a more impressive defense of the omniscience of the Party than Lenin himself was able to do.

The Lukács Debate

In the same year that Lukács published History and Class Consciousness, German Communist and law professor Karl Korsch contributed an essay entitled "Marxism and Philosophy" to the Archiv für die Geschichte des Sozialismus und der Arbeiterbewegung. In a postscript that he added just prior to publication, Korsch took note of Lukács's work and expressed his fundamental agreement.[62] Indeed, with this essay, Korsch became an honorary member of the evolving school of Hungarian Marxism. Like Lukács, he dismissed the scientific Marxism of the Second International and maintained that Marx's writings were deeply rooted in Hegel's philosophy. It was from Hegel that Marx had learned that philosophy was the expression of its age. And just as German idealism had been the theoretical expression of the bourgeois revolutionary movement, so Marxism was that of a proletarian revolutionary force.[63] Pushing the parallel even further, Korsch concluded that just as the revolutionary proletariat had developed out of the revolutionary bourgeoisie, so too Marxism had developed out of Hegelianism.

Like Lukács again, Korsch emphasized the dialectical character of Marxism, which could not be divided into a theory and a practice because for it the two were inseparable. Hence, one literally could not be a theoretical Marxist and a reformist. Those who believed such an unnatural union to be possible deceived themselves, for Marxism could only be understood aright from within the revolutionary movement of the proletariat. In fact, on Korsch's view, "truth" could be predicated only of ideas that served the cause of the progressive class by making it conscious of its tasks, validating its historic vision, and contributing to its revolutionary practice. In the end, then, his Marxism, like Lukács's construction, was less a philosophic system than the spelling out of a faith.

Although "Marxism and Philosophy" was not nearly as sophisticated as *History and Class Consciousness*, it too laid particular stress on the revolutionary importance of human—that is, class—will. Ideas were not simply elements of a superstructure, but exercised a reciprocal influence on the socioeconomic order. They were essential weapons in the war on bourgeois society. Lukács agreed but did not discuss Korsch's work in print. Welcoming the German to the Hungarian Marxist camp was Béla Fogarasi, who eagerly accepted Korsch's invitation to review the book version of *Marxism and Philosophy* for the communist journal *Die Internationale*.[64]

In his 1918 lecture on idealism, Fogarasi had called for an end to the mutual indifference between philosophy and politics and he was therefore quick to praise Korsch for clarifying "the relationship between philosophy and the proletarian social revolution." The German was right to remind Marxists that Hegel had recognized the relationship between philosophy and reality at a time when the bourgeoisie was still a revolutionary class. Only when it ceased to be so, after 1848, did a separation occur in the realm of thought between ideal and real historical factors. This did not signal philosophy's decomposition, but rather its transition from the ideological tool of the bourgeoisie to an instrument of the proletariat. "Marxism," he concluded with Korsch, "stands in precisely the same relationship to German idealism as the proletarian movement does to the movement of the revolutionary bourgeoisie."

Fogarasi was not the only Hungarian Marxist to hail Korsch's study. The prestigious *Archiv für Sozialwissenschaft und Sozialpolitik* printed a review of *Marxism and Philosophy* by László Radványi, one of the Sunday Circle's "Knaben" ("young lads") before he moved to Heidelberg to study under Karl Jaspers and Emil Lederer, the latter an editor of the *Archiv*. It was there that he met Anna Seghers (Netty Reiling), the future Communist novelist who was then pursuing studies in philosophy and art history. After their marriage in 1925, the couple moved on to Berlin, where, shortly after he published his review of *Marxism and Philosophy*—which Korsch described as "thorough and penetrating"[65]—Radványi changed his name to Johann-Lorenz Schmidt.

Like Fogarasi, Radványi came to praise Korsch, and, by implication, Lukács. After rehearsing the German's argument, he emphasized that "the material world and the world of consciousness form a connected whole, in which they are reciprocally conditioned." Thus, he concluded, authentic Marxism was not a form of "pan-economism," for which the economic sphere alone was real. Marxism also recognized a spiritual side of reality that shaped social life.[66]

Clearly, the Hungarian Marxists—Lukács, Fogarasi, Radványi—had little use for the positivism they identified with the Second International. All of them had come to Marxism by way of philosophy and the *Geisteswissenschaften* rather than positivism and the *Naturwissenschaften*. Their great discovery had been, as Fogarasi had argued in 1918, that there were "progressive" as well as "conservative" forms of idealism. In the beginning, they looked to Kant and, even more, to Fichte, but in the end they turned to Hegel. Equally important perhaps, they had lived in the Hungarian Soviet Republic, which, though it failed, had survived for a time. Hence their confidence in human will and their impatience with the pace of history was greater than that of those who lived in countries where reformism had been more successful.

This also applied to another Hungarian exile, József Révai, the former Maist who in the early 1920s was both a Lukácsian and a proponent of Hegelian Marxism. A contributor to various communist journals, Révai reviewed *History and Class Consciousness* twice. In *Die Rote Fahne* he praised Lukács for having challenged revisionism's Kantianism and naturalistic materialism and for rejecting the dialectic of nature. "The true home of the dialectic," he wrote, "is society and history."[67] His expansive review in the *Archiv für die Geschichte des Sozialismus und der Arbeiterbewegung*[68] defended the Hungarian Marxist position—while unwittingly undermining it.

Révai began harmlessly enough. He pointed out that the question of the Marxist dialectic was synonymous with that of the relationship between Marx and Hegel. Like Lukács, Korsch, Fogarasi, and Radványi, he criticized the theorists of the Second International for their efforts to make of Marxism a monistic science. Engels, he contended, had failed to appreciate the dialectical relationship between Being and thought. Recognizing these failures, Lukács had made the first systematic attempt to elucidate the Hegelian dialectic inherent in Marxism. This was extremely important because, according to Révai, reality could only be grasped as a totality, not as a set of isolated facts. He also extolled his mentor for rejecting the dialectic of nature, which Marxists had adopted as a consequence of their excessive reverence for natural science.

Révai then proceeded to prepare the ground for his "critical observations." According to Lukács, he wrote, Marx had advanced beyond Hegel by rejecting the idea that history could be observed only as a completed process and hence only contemplatively. Marx had denied the truth of Hegel's famous words in *The Philosophy of Right*: "When philosophy paints its grey on grey, then has a shape of life grown old. And by this grey on grey it can only be understood, not rejuvenated. The owl of Minerva spreads its wings only with the falling of the dusk." For Marx, of course, this was one more effort to understand rather than change the world. In response, he incorporated the future, understood as a reality already inherent and active in the present, into the sphere of a revolutionary dialectic.

Precisely here Révai took issue with Marx and Lukács. The contemplation they imputed to Hegel was, he argued, more properly attributed to Kant. It was Kant who recognized law-regulated processes that, viewed from within, could never yield a grasp of history as totality. Hegel had indeed, as Lukács suggested, contemplated a completed process whose meaning had already become evident. Moreover, this Hegelian viewpoint became incorporated into Marxism, which taught that the realm of necessity was advancing dialectically toward the realm of freedom. Paradoxically, this knowledge of history's process had become possible only from the vantage point of its conclusion or realization. "Marxism is the post hoc consciousness of a historical period /yet to come/ that is methodologically already thought of as completed." In short, according to Révai, "the kinship between Hegel and Marx is even greater" than Lukács suggested.

In this ingenuous review-essay, Révai let the cat out of the bag. Unlike Lukács, who attempted to disguise the dogmatic character of Marxism, he insisted that Marxists had to believe that they already knew the contours of the future. The new, fully realized, "man" of the communist future Révai described as "an unavoidable conceptual mythology" based upon the proletariat's reconstruction of reality. If Révai believed this argument could persuade anyone outside the communist movement, he was mistaken. One cannot validate a myth by making an appeal to its authority. What he did do was to expose with startling candor Marxism's dogmatic essence.

Révai was not the only friendly critic to make Lukács wince. Ernst Bloch devoted an essay entitled "Actuality and Utopia" to History and Class Consciousness.[69] Bloch had met Lukács before the war, when both men were members of Georg Simmel's private seminar, and he had exerted a considerable influence on the Hungarian. Before he encountered Bloch, Lukács later recalled, he had inclined toward the fashionable Neo-Kantianism of the day. In Bloch, "I saw someone who philosophized as if that philosophy did not exist. I saw that it was possible to philosophize in the manner of Aristotle or Hegel."[70] Together, the two men took up residence in Heidelberg, where they became the most assertive members of the circle around Max Weber.

Bloch was particularly intrigued by the relationship between utopia and Lukács's conception of actuality. Should his friend's rejection of utopianism be taken at face value? In the final analysis, Bloch did not think so. Lukács's emphasis on the present (das Jetzt) by no means signaled an indifference to the future, the only period of time that ever interested Bloch. On the contrary, the dialectical concept of the present as Becoming made it possible to uncover existing tendencies that could lead to the creation of the future. The present, according to this view, was not constituted by empirical facts but by the higher reality of developmental trends. Utopia was not an ought that stood outside the historical process, but a reality on its way to realization. "The proletariat," Bloch wrote, paraphrasing Marx, "has no ideals to realize, but only a new society to erect in freedom."

Lukács must have been chagrined to learn that in Bloch's judgment the central theme of History and Class Consciousness harmonized with that of the

German's own *Spirit of Utopia*. That was because "actuality and utopia are not antitheses, but, on the contrary, the present is really ultimately the only theme of utopia." The present, though, was to be understood as already pregnant with the future. Bloch concluded by citing Marx's judgment that "the world has long possessed the dream of that which it must only become conscious in order to possess in reality."[71]

Bloch must have known that his discussion of the utopian core of *History and Class Consciousness* would not please Lukács. Certainly he knew that the book would not be well received in the Soviet Union. "The Russians," he wrote, "who act philosophically after a fashion, but think like uneducated dogs, will even smell garbage in it."[72] He was more right than he knew, for in the July 25, 1924 issue of *Pravda*, the Soviet philosopher Ivan Luppol published an attack on Lukács and his "followers," Korsch, Fogarasi, and Révai. He accused them, quite accurately, of rejecting philosophical materialism and the dialectic of nature.[73]

Luppol's attack was but a rivulet in what would soon be a torrent of criticism. It was, in fact, little more than a codicil to a scathing attack on Lukács that Abram Deborin, Luppol's teacher, published in the Vienna-based *Arbeiter-Literatur*.[74] A former Menshevik and follower of Georgi Plekhanov, Deborin himself had been profoundly influenced by Hegel. Indeed, he was shortly to become the leader of the so-called Dialecticians, who waged— and by 1929 won—an ideological war against the Mechanists, who maintained that science had rendered philosophy superfluous. Nevertheless, Deborin adopted a tone of superiority and righteous indignation while condemning Lukács for his idealist heresies and his effort to play a sophisticated Marx off against a simple-minded Engels, a particularly touchy matter in light of Lenin's dependence upon Engels's writings. The Hungarian and his followers—Deborin mentioned Korsch, Fogarasi, and Révai by name—represented a "new current" in Marxism that could not safely be ignored.

Deborin claimed to be appalled by Lukács's rejection of the dialectic of nature, which he saw as a logical consequence of the rejection of materialism. After all, he wrote, "from the standpoint of dialectical materialism, nature is dialectical in itself." This, Deborin said, was not only the view of Engels, but also of Marx, for the two men had always worked in the closest possible association. Between them there had never been any fundamental disagreement. Only "an idealist from head to foot," would argue to the contrary.[75] The archimedean point of Lukács's idealism, Deborin pointed out, was his identification of subject and object, of thought and Being. In such a view, thought was as important as material existence, a heresy that Lenin had condemned in *Materialism and Empirio-Criticism*.

Lukács and the other Hungarian Marxists stood accused of being idealists in a movement that had come to accept an extremely naive form of materialism. But there was even more to it than that. For Marxism in general and Leninism in particular, ideas have always been regarded as weapons in the struggle for power. The Soviet leaders, very much including Stalin who was soon to consolidate his position as Lenin's successor, were interested not in arguments, but in obedience. Leninism had become the emblem of authority and legitimacy and they its rightful guardians. Any deviation from the orthodoxy that *they* prescribed carried with it political implications and dangers. As the self-proclaimed heirs of Marx, Engels, and Lenin, they could not admit that a handful of Hungarians possessed a deeper and more perfect understanding of the masters than they. To do so would be to confer upon *them* a claim to the leadership of the Communist movement. Deborin's attack, then, must be read as a political rather than a philosophical document, for what was at stake was discipline and submission to Moscow. *History and Class Consciousness* stood out as a symbol of rebellion and indiscipline. It was for that reason, rather than for any philosophical error, that the book came under attack.

What was true of Deborin's essay applied also to László Rudas's rambling polemic in the same journal.[76] A Hungarian emigré, Rudas had initially sided with the Landler faction in Vienna and had popularized Lukács's views. In 1922, however, he took up residence in the Soviet Union and began work at the Marx-Engels Institute. With an eye to his political future, he joined the Kun faction and, as proof of his conversion, leveled an attack on Lukács, the chief ideologist in the Landler camp. Like Deborin, Rudas charged his countryman with the sin of idealism, an evil to which he was said to have inclined as a result of his Heidelberg associations with Weber, Lask, and Heinrich Rickert. Although Lukács had broken with his social past, he had been unable, according to Rudas, to free himself from the yoke of idealism. As a result, he even had the temerity to criticize Engels.

Once again the major issue was the dialectic of nature. Rudas, following Deborin, was at pains to show that Marx and Engels worked together as one and that the former, no less than the latter, had refused to limit the dialectic to society. Since, as an idealist, Lukács could not accept the dialectic of nature, he fell into the error of arguing that theory alone could make the revolution. Rising to the full height of indignation, Rudas characterized such a view as "mystical." Marx, he assured his readers, had always maintained that the material course of history and society determined theory. Hence, it was Engels the materialist, not Lukács the idealist, who spoke for orthodox Marxism.

It was no accident that Rudas and Deborin's charges ran parallel. In both cases the principal aim was to weaken that Communist faction that was most independent of Moscow. Lukács himself never entertained any doubts about this. "All of those in Kun's camp," he recalled late in life, "considered it to be their duty to attack the work."[77] It was, in fact, their responsibility to prepare the way for the official anathema that Zinoviev, Kun's closest ally in the Soviet Union, pronounced in the course of an address to the Third International's Fifth World Congress on June 19, 1924:

Comrade Graziadei in Italy published a book containing a reprint of articles attacking Marxism which he wrote when he was a Social Democratic revisionist. This theoretical revisionism cannot be allowed to pass with impunity. Neither will we tolerate our Hungarian Comrade Lukács doing the same thing in the domain of philosophy and sociology. I have received a letter from Comrade Rudas, one of the leaders of this faction. He explains that he intended to oppose Lukács, but the faction forbade him to do so; thereupon he left the faction because he could not see Marxism watered down. Well done, Rudas! We have a similar tendency in the German party. Comrade Graziadei is a professor. Korsch is also a professor—(interruption from the floor: "Lukács is a professor, too!"). If we get a few more of these professors spinning out their Marxist theories we shall be lost. We cannot tolerate such theoretical revisionism in our Communist International.[78]

In the immediate aftermath of Zinoviev's attack, Lukács remained silent, submitting quietly to Party discipline. Ousted from the Central Committee of the Hungarian Communist Party, he refused, until the 1960s, to permit the republication of *History and Class Consciousness*. This was not to be the last time that he bent his knee before the Party's altar. Yet it would be a mistake to think of this surrender as an act of cowardice and opportunism. Lukács himself had supplied the justification for his submission. He had written a book "that hypostasised the party as the institutionalised will and expression of proletarian class consciousness and thereby endowed it with a superior view of 'total' reality. In other words, /*History and Class Consciousness*/ contains a built-in veto, as it were, of its own defense against party criticism, thus giving Lukács' silence at the time a melancholy consistency all its own."[79]

The Non-Communist Reception of an Indexed Book

Although the Party had placed it on the index, *History and Class Consciousness* exerted a widespread influence. Because it articulated a new Marxism, it attracted those for whom automatic Marxism was as dead as the Second International. During the summer of 1922, before the critical storm broke, Lukács had taken part in the First Marxist Work Week, which met in Ilmenau, Thuringia. The inspiration for the gathering, according to its wealthy organizer Felix J. Weil, was the "hope that the different trends in Marxism, if afforded an opportunity of talking it out together, could arrive at a 'true' or 'pure' Marxism."[80] In addition to Lukács, the participants included Korsch, Fogarasi, Wittfogel, Richard Sorge, and Friedrich Pollock.

With the encouragement of friends at the University of Frankfurt, Weil soon began to think in terms of a permanent institute devoted to the reconstruction of Marxism. As a result of his efforts, the *Institut für Sozialforschung* was organized in February 1923; its first active director was Carl Grünberg, an Austro-Marxist who edited the *Archiv für die Geschichte des Sozialismus und der Arbeiterbewegung*. Grünberg suffered a stroke in 1927, but continued on for two more years, when, at age sixty-nine, he relinquished the reins to Max Horkheimer.

Like Lukács and the Hungarian Marxists, Horkheimer and the other members of the Institute received their philosophical training outside the Marxist tradition. Thus, they had no interest in a Marxism that meant little more than economic determinism; from the first, indeed, they were "very much taken with the notions of reification and commodity fetishism which Lukács had done so much to revive."[81] And if they did not accept the privileged standpoint of the proletariat or the dogmas of the Party, they were as eager as Lukács was to unveil the ideological character of bourgeois thought and culture. Obsessed with the negative aspects of modern society but reluctant to submit to Communist authority, they never offered an alternative that went much beyond vague talk of "emancipation" or "liberation." Nevertheless, they helped to keep many Lukácsian ideas alive.

One of the Institute's future associates, Herbert Marcuse, held a typically unsettled view of Lukács's book. He admired the Hungarian's contribution to the revitalization of Marxism, but dismissed the concept of a "correct" class consciousness. This same man wrote his first book, *Hegel's Ontology and the Foundation of a Theory of Historicity*, under the spell of his Freiburg mentor, Martin Heidegger. That he drew inspiration from both Lukács and Heidegger might have suggested an affinity between *History and Class Consciousness* and *Sein und Zeit* (*Being and Time*), Heidegger's epoch-making work of 1927, but only when Lucien Goldmann appeared on the philosophic scene after World War II did the idea gain currency.

That Heidegger knew of Lukács's work now seems certain. Throughout the early 1920s, he had regular conversations with Vilmos (Wilhelm) Szilasi, the Hungarian-born philosopher who was living in Freiburg. When *Being and Time* appeared, Szilasi wrote to Mihály Babits: "Recently, there appeared a book—*Sein und Zeit*—by my friend Heidegger, whom you know. It is a metaphysical work that moves in a precisely similar direction and belongs to the same tendency as my logical investigations. In my judgment, the book is a masterpiece."[82] The respect was mutual and, upon succeeding Husserl at Freiburg in 1928, Heidegger invited Szilasi to serve as guest professor continuously from 1928 to 1933. During the years before and after the appearance of *Being and Time*, Szilasi must certainly have had occasion to discuss Lukács's work with Heidegger.

In any event, *Being and Time* played a critical role in guaranteeing *History and Class Consciousness*'s lasting fame. Indeed, had it not been for Heidegger, Lukács's heresy might have remained a mere episode in the history of Marxism-Leninism. Rejected by official communism and subsequently repudiated by its author, *History and Class Consciousness* was embraced by only a small group of Hegelian Marxists, most of whom were Lukács's Hungarian comrades. In the end, many of them, Fogarasi and Révai included, turned their back on the book and its author. Outside of the Communist movement, few were impressed or even much interested in Lukács's analysis of proletarian class consciousness. What they *were* interested in, largely as a result of Heidegger's widely-discussed magnum opus, was the existential character of Lukács's ideas.

It is instructive in this regard to compare two discussions of *History and Class Consciousness*, both written by the socialist philosopher Siegfried Marck. In 1924, Marck reviewed Lukács's book for the social democratic journal *Die Gesellschaft*.[83] After identifying Lukács as a "new communist" akin to the young Marx, he charged him with having proposed a materialistic-activistic metaphysics and defended a mythological class consciousness. In the dogmatic attempt to absolutize the proletariat, Lukács had contrived only to put that class in place of Hegel's World Spirit. Moreover, this new dogmatism, because of the concept of "imputed" class consciousness, could be employed as a theoretical justification for the dictatorship of the Communist party.

In 1929, two years after *Being and Time* appeared, Marck devoted several pages of his *Dialectic in Contemporary Philosophy* to Lukács's "historical dialectics" as part of a broader examination of the "Existential Dialectic." He was still critical of an ideal class consciousness, but he had come to regard Lukács's work as an important contribution to existential thought. *History and Class Consciousness* constituted a dialectical existential philosophy based upon human action and existence. Like Heidegger, Lukács rejected not only all formal rationalism, but any form of Platonism, with its contemplative interest in an unchanging, transcendent, reality. His world, like Heidegger's, was radically historical. He viewed the task of thought as the furnishing of a set of categories that clarified for men the bases of their existence and of their mutual relationships. "The categories function, to use Heidegger's term, as 'existentials'; to be sure, as social existentials."[84]

Marck knew that for Heidegger "existentials" were what categories were to "ontic" inquiries—a priori conditions, necessary ways in which *Dasein* is aware of itself. "Being-in-the-world" was, for example, an "existential" because, Heidegger argued, before we can study the world as a collectivity of objects—that is, scientifically—we must already be aware of ourselves as beings who have a world which is "ready-at-hand" (*zuhanden*), available for our use. Another of the ways in which *Dasein* is aware of itself is as historical, as stretching along between birth and death; hence, historicality (*Geschichtlichkeit*) is also an existential.[85] Other existentials—and Heidegger did not intend the list to be complete—included care (*Sorge*), anxiety (*Angst*), being-unto-death (*Sein-zum-Tode*), alienation (*Entfremdung*), guilt (*Schuld*), and resolve (*Entschlossenheit*). By granting priority to the existentials, that is to *Dasein's* preconceptual awareness of its existence, Heidegger sought to undercut the subject-object dichotomy. He had also, by refusing to interpret *Dasein* primarily as a thing, object, or substance in nature and by insisting on the ontological priority of lived experience in time, uncovered its fundamental historicity.

To Marck, Lukács's rejection of the subject-object dichotomy, emphasis on the historicity of human existence, and attempt to uncover a more immediate world beneath the reified world of the bourgeoisie took on a new meaning. In concert with Heidegger, the Hungarian seemed to Marck to have elaborated an "existential rationalism." In that new light, the revolutionary character of Lukács's thinking consisted not so much in his theory of proletarian class consciousness, but in his radical positing of "the decisive question between Platonism and existential thought, between philosophy and practical theory."[86]

It was, finally, fittingly ironic that Thomas Mann, the master ironist who had not even read *History and Class Consciousness*,[87] understood and interpreted the book's message better than anyone. That was possible because he had previously formed a profound impression of its author's personality, a success all the more astonishing in view of the fact that he had met Lukács only once, in Vienna on January 17, 1922. He was then on the final leg of a lecture tour that had taken him to Budapest, where Lukács's father had served as his host.

On that winter's night in Mann's Vienna hotel room, Lukács expounded his newest theories concerning the contemporary function of art, studiously avoiding any discussion of politics. "As long as he spoke," Mann later recalled, "he was right," but afterward the German's only impression was that of an "almost uncanny abstraction."[88] Even as he attended to Lukács's perfervid discourse, however, Mann formed a physical and spiritual image of a personality. He observed and listened to the Hungarian for no more than an hour, but that, according to his wife, "was the remarkable thing about him: he got a complete picture of a person immediately."[89]

So much is true. And yet by the time they met, Mann had already formed rather distinct impressions of Lukács from his early, nonpolitical, writings. He was, for example, among the first to praise *Die Seele und die Formen* (1911), from which, indeed, he gained partial inspiration for *Death in Venice*.[90] Furthermore, he had long been intrigued by Jewish intellectuals, who crop up repeatedly in his novels and stories, those that antedate as well as those that succeed *The Magic Mountain*.[91]

Less than five months after meeting Lukács, Mann informed a friend that "Leo Naphta, a half-Jewish pupil of the Jesuits with crass views, has suddenly appeared and continually engages Settembrini in pointed debate."[92] He referred to his work-in-progress, *The Magic Mountain*, which he had begun in 1912 only to set aside during the war. In the early stages of that powerful novel, Mann introduced Ludovico Settembrini, a liberal humanist and partisan of "progress" who represents a point of view closely akin to that of the *Zivilizationsliterat*—in reality, Heinrich Mann—whom Mann castigated in his wartime *Reflections of a Non-Political Man* and who quickly becomes Hans Castorp's spiritual counselor and guide. Settembrini's authority remains unchallenged until Naphta appears on the scene. When the tuberculer Jesuit first meets Hans Castorp, he resides at the home of a ladies' tailor named "Lukaçek." Physically, he resembles Lukács and, more important, he is, like Lukács, an alarmingly cunning defender of communism and terror.

To Settembrini's horror, Naphta pours contempt upon bourgeois humanism with its interminable chatter about progress, science, and democracy. Having himself escaped from bourgeois individualism by entering the Jesuits' militant community, he prophesies a great sacramental shedding of blood, after which the world will be purified. The executor of History's will shall be the proletariat: "The proletariat has taken up the work of Gregory /the Great/, his holy zeal is in it; and as little as he, may it withhold its hand from blood. Its task is to strike terror into the world and thus to achieve the redemptive goal of a filial relationship to God, without political states or social classes."[93]

Brilliantly and remarkably, Mann had perceived the religious character of Lukács's thinking and hence he intuited the burden of *History and Class Consciousness*. The Marxist convert's book, he knew, could only be the explication of a dogma. In reply to Settembrini's defense of pure knowledge, Naphta/ Lukács proclaims his credo: "Good friend, there is no such thing as pure knowledge. The legitimacy of the Church's philosophy, which can be summed up in Augustine's tenet 'I believe so that I may understand,' is absolutely incontestable. Faith is the organ of knowledge; the intellect is secondary."[94]

Romantic Realism

In the midst of the controversy that swirled around *History and Class Consciousness*, Lenin died. Within a few weeks of his passing, the Verlag der Arbeiterbuchhandlung (Vienna) published Lukács's *Lenin: A Study of the Unity of His Thought*, a pioneering attempt to establish the bolshevik leader's importance as a theorist and a declaration of discipleship. If it did nothing else, that slender volume dispelled any notion that the author had recanted his Hegelian heresies. The core of Lenin's thought, he wrote, was the actuality of the revolution, which meant "treating each particular question of the day in concrete association with the socio-historic whole, as moments in the liberation of the proletariat." Critical of utopianism, Lenin was a realist, but one who knew that there was always "something more real and therefore more important than *isolated* facts or tendencies: *the reality of the total process*, the totality of social development." That reality was manifest to those who had eyes to see. The bourgeoisie, living in the age of the proletariat's rise, had ceased to be a revolutionary class, and in an effort to prevent or forestall its loss of power, it had forged an alliance with the defeated feudal-absolutist class. As a result of that devil's pact, suggested to Lukács by Hungary's semi-feudal condition, the proletariat's initial task was to effect the full realization of the bourgeoisie's historical tasks.[95]

Lukács quickly added that the revolution in the making was not purely bourgeois. The "real revolution is the dialectical transformation of the bourgeois revolution into the proletarian revolution."[96] The proletariat was the legatee of the *revolutionary* bourgeoisie. It followed from this that the privileged standpoint of the proletariat could not be separated absolutely from that of the revolutionary bourgeoisie and that therefore the proletariat should attend to the history and literature of its revolutionary forebear.

Inspired by Lenin's emphasis on the concrete, Lukács threw himself into Hungarian Communist politics with renewed vigor. Throughout 1924, he worked closely with Landler on a plan to create the Socialist Workers' Party of Hungary. The illegal Hungarian Communist Party would direct the new, and legal, party. Although the Kun faction opposed the plan, the Fifth Congress of the Comintern gave it official approval. Along with Landler and Révai, Lukács formulated a program and, on April 14, 1925, the party was formally constituted. Its central slogan was "the republic,"[97] the idea being that before the proletarian dictatorship could be placed on the political agenda, the bourgeois revolution would have to be completed.

Lukács's absorption in Hungarian political realities awakened in him an unwonted interest in his country's past. In reexamining Hungarian history, he focused his attention on the abortive 1848–49 Revolution, Hungary's would-be equivalent of the French (bourgeois) Revolution. Perhaps, he reasoned, he could discover the causes of the Soviet Republic's fall in that earlier failure.

Lukács's conception of that epochal event was strongly influenced by Ervin Szabó's *Social and Party Struggles in the 1848–49 Hungarian Revolution* (1921), a work that attributed the revolution's failure to its conservative social character. Because Kossuth had moved steadily to the political right, he had frustrated a democratic revolution. Szabó therefore lionized Petőfi and the publicist Mihály Táncsics, both of whom looked to the French Revolution's most radical moments.[98] Lukács also held Petőfi and Táncsics in high regard, but he was not nearly so critical of Kossuth. Perhaps, he reflected, the revolution had been tragically premature.

It may be that Lukács was reacting to the tendency in official Hungarian circles to compare Kossuth unfavorably with conservative figures such as István Széchenyi and Ferenc Deák. In a 1928 review that he wrote of Count Kunó Klebelsberg's *Neo-Nationalism*, he complained because Hungary's Minister of Education denigrated Kossuth's achievement. "The fundamental thesis of neo-nationalism's historical view is that 1848 is only a historical memory, without significance or promise for contemporary development. It is a dead end. After abandoning it, it was possible only to return to the sole correct path, that of Széchenyi and Deák, of evolution."[99] According to Lukács's new theory, the historical task was to *complete* the 1848 Revolution and then, almost imperceptibly, to pass on to the revolution of the proletariat.

Lukács's favorable assessment of 1848 went hand in hand with his uncompromising hostility to 1867, the year of the *Ausgleich*. If 1848 was a historical tragedy, 1867 constituted a conscious political maneuver, a class compromise between the gentry (acting in lieu of Hungary's small bourgeoisie) and the magnates.[100] As a result of the gentry's abandonment of the unfulfilled tasks of the bourgeois revolution, Dualist Hungary witnessed a social and political degeneration that could only be reversed by the proletariat, the class that could assume the authentic bourgeois revolutionary heritage.

As always, Lukács's political and historical conception exerted a decisive influence on his literary judgments. Indeed, in Hungarian-language journals of the late 1920s, he offered a remarkably consistent and resolutely political critique of modern Hungarian literature, endeavoring in the process to identify an authentic tradition of revolt. Following Szabó, he acclaimed Petőfi's plebeian politics and revolutionary poetry while characterizing the second half of the nineteenth century as an age of epigones and second-rate apologists for the *Ausgleich*. Only after the turn of the century, he argued, did a worthy successor to Petőfi appear: Endre Ady.

Lukács had always admired Ady and he reacted sharply against the attempt by contemporary Hungarian cultural leaders to co-opt the poet for a conservative national renascence. It is, however, far from clear that he had the best case, for if there is no doubt concerning Ady's radical social and political views, his lasting significance is due to his complete identification with the Hungarian nation and its history. Furthermore, it is misleading to assert, as Lukács did, that Ady's "thought and poetry was not, in its essence, Romantic."[101] Indeed, Lukács's praise for Petőfi and Ady constituted evidence that his own romanticism was not, as he insisted, a thing of the past.

It is well to bear this in mind when examining Lukács's closely argued attacks on forms of socialism that competed with Leninist realism for the allegiance of the proletariat and the intelligentsia. In his most famous essays of the decade, on Ferdinand Lassalle and Moses Hess, he attempted to exorcise forever his own youthful utopian romanticism by identifying it with bourgeois class consciousness in the age of bourgeois decline. Yet by retracing his spiritual and intellectual pilgrimage from Fichtean utopianism to Hegelian dialectics, he merely contrived to chart a course from one form of romanticism to another. For if it is true, as one distinguished scholar has argued, that "Romantic philosophy is ... primarily a metaphysics of integration, of which the key principle is that of the 'reconciliation,' or synthesis, of whatever is divided, opposed, and conflicting,"[102] Hegel was the quintessential Romantic. Just so, Lukács's Hegelian Marxism was Romantic in its abstract schema as well as in its idealist conception of reality.

Lukács had a few kind things to say of Lassalle, because the flamboyant social democratic leader himself admired Hegel. All the more unfortunate then, according to Lukács, that Lassalle turned to Fichte's activism in an effort to transform the Hegelian dialectic into a philosophy of revolution. That was a profound error, for although Fichte possessed a more revolutionary disposition than Hegel did, that disposition was utopian. For him, the present constituted the third of five world-historical ages—the age of absolute sinfulness; as such, it was negative through and through. The final two ages, described by Fichte in *Characteristics of the Present Age*, constituted the utopian future and were to witness the realization of that formal "ought" that had for so long stood over against reality—the "is." But precisely *how* was history to pass from one age to the next? How was utopia to be achieved? Here, Lukács believed, Fichte's philosophy of history revealed its Achilles heel.[103]

If, Lukács reasoned, Hegel's "reconciliation with reality" ultimately became reactionary in politics and contemplative in philosophy, it yet made possible an understanding of the connection between logical categories and the structural forms of bourgeois society. By rejecting the utopian ought and focusing philosophy on the understanding of the present, grasped dialectically, Hegel had pointed to the only way of knowing that which was alone knowable about the future—the tendencies in the present that impel history forward.

By correcting Hegel with Fichte, Lassalle unwittingly fell into the trap of reading history as the record of absolute disjunctions and fundamental antinomies; thus, contrary to his intention, he regarded what is as immediately given and what ought to be as totally other. The very antinomic structure of his thinking betrayed its essentially bourgeois character. Perhaps most damaging, that structure made it necessary for Lassalle to regard the bourgeois and proletarian revolutions as completely distinct phenomena, blinding him to the fact that they were related moments of a single process. Naturally, then, he failed to recognize that in the present age, the proletariat had inherited the task of completing the bourgeois revolution, before the latter passed dialectically on. In the final analysis, Lassalle could be nothing more than the theorist of the bourgeois revolution, the age of which had past.[104]

Lukács dealt with similar themes in an essay on Moses Hess, that fascinating precursor of Zionism who was Lassalle's chief organizer in the Rhineland. Once again he discussed the relationship of the bourgeois to the proletarian revolution and rejected the Fichtean views he himself had espoused during the war. Like Lassalle, he insisted, Hess attempted to impart to Hegelianism a Fichtean cast, thus obscuring Hegel's "splendid realism," his recognition that the present derived its distinctive character from what it was and would be. The present *always* pointed dialectically beyond itself. Hence, "reconciliation with reality" did not imply an affirmation of the world *immediately present*, but of the world to come that was already a living potentiality. Even if, Lukács continued, the pull of Hegel's bourgeois consciousness led him to permit the present to lose its inner dynamic, his *method* was not thereby discredited. After reverting to Fichte, Hess had to condemn the alienated present from an abstract, moral point of view—a quintessentially bourgeois standpoint.[105]

In the age of the proletarian revolution the proletariat possessed the only correct standpoint, for from it one could see that reality was not completely negative, that its progressive possibilities could be realized by critical, practical activity. That was an extremely important point with respect to the question of alienation, for Lukács believed that alienation was overcome in the active struggle to overcome it.[106] As the Party led that struggle, it constituted itself an ever expanding Gemeinschaft.

Now since alienation was rooted in the very social, and hence economic, structure of bourgeois capitalist society, a critique of political economy, such as Marx had carried out, was at the same time a critique of alienation and a pivotal moment in the process that is the overcoming of alienation. In short, Marx had surpassed Hegel by adopting the standpoint of the proletariat and substituting a materialistic for an idealistic dialectic.[107] Yet even here he did not greatly outstrip Hegel, for in many respects, Lukács maintained, the author of the Phenomenology had advanced "in the direction of materialism."[108]

Lukács did not restrict his critique of the utopian left to political thinkers; he attacked the literary avant-garde with equal vehemence. During the Soviet Republic, he had named Kassák to the Writers Directory, but even then he perceived in the avant-garde an avatar of utopianism. By insisting on a complete break with bourgeois culture, the avant-garde could not transcend a rigid dualism, and by refusing to connect itself with the progressive national literary tradition, it sentenced itself to irrelevancy. Although he did not say so at the time, Lukács agreed with Kun, when, in 1919, the Soviet Republic's leader characterized the literature of Ma as "the product of bourgeois decadence."

Lukács's literary-cultural theory thus paralleled his political conception. Just as he admitted of no absolute disjunction between bourgeois and proletarian revolutions, so he refused to sanction any between bourgeois and proletarian cultures. At the existing stage of historical progress, the culture of the revolutionary bourgeoisie continued to be relevant because it constituted the only soil in which the proletarian culture could grow. All attempts to create a new culture at a stroke were as futile and undialectical as all efforts to bring heaven to earth in a single apocalyptic moment.

That idea was of enormous significance for Lukács's critical career and for Marxist theory in general, for it insisted that in culture as well as in politics, Marxism was the inheritor, rather than the destroyer, of what was best in the Western tradition. Indeed, it was precisely Lukács's "sense for continuity and tradition" that so attracted Thomas Mann[109] and many other non-Marxists. It also led to a seeming contradiction—a revolutionary with conservative literary/cultural tastes, a Communist for whom the literary past, or at least an important segment of it, was very much alive. That never disturbed Lukács however, for he recalled what Mann had written in 1922. By then a convert to the Weimar Republic, the German argued that radical politics could, and indeed should, go hand in hand with cultural tradition. Germany, he maintained, would not realize its proper destiny until "Karl Marx has read Friedrich Hölderlin."[110]

So much for revolutionary bourgeois culture, but what of *proletarian* culture? Lukács attempted to answer that question in a pivotal essay of 1926: "*L'art pour l'art* and Proletarian Literature." There he reflected upon the tragedy of writers living in late, declining, bourgeois society. Since they viewed reality in its immediacy, they could not perceive life's deeper possibilities, particularly with respect to the authentic relationship of men to one another, always, for Lukács, "the subject matter of literature." Those who did not attempt to escape reality altogether by means of form experiments (*l'art pour l'art*) often opted for a "didactic art," conjuring up "abstract-Romantic utopias" or providing glimpses of life in its brute, surface immediacy.[111]

Lukács identified all of these literary trends with romanticism, but he had in mind a romanticism of despair and blind revolt; what, in 1907, he had called romanticism *à rebours*. At that time, he observed that the romanticism of Baudelaire, Flaubert, and Ibsen differed markedly from that of the early nineteenth-century writers. Whereas the latter retained faith in man and the world, the former had lost their faith and become bitterly disillusioned. They despised their own time, but felt themselves to be impotent in the face of it. Hence, they turned from life, fearing disappointment; Romantic sensibility was rechanneled. Instead of belief, there was radical doubt about everything.[112]

Precisely that turn from life, that "sympathy with death" defined the sensibility of the young Thomas Mann, the author of *Buddenbrooks*. Only after the war, when he shuddered at the increasingly nihilistic politics practiced by the enemies of the Weimar Republic, did Mann eschew romanticism *à rebours*. In 1922, he surprised many by defending the new order and arguing that true romanticism led *through* sympathy with death to affirmation of life. That idea was also to be central to *The Magic Mountain*. In the celebrated "Snow" section, Hans Castorp learns the lesson that Mann himself had learned: death must never be permitted to have dominion over man's thoughts.[113] Naturally enough, then, Lukács exempted Mann from his critique of latter-day bourgeois writers.

He was even less critical of Leo Tolstoi. "There are," he observed, "other great writers who criticized sharply the existing social order (Flaubert, Turgenev, Ibsen), but they called attention only to the consequences of the basic arrangements, while Tolstoi always points to the basis itself. . . . He does not take as his point of departure the inner spiritual problems of his characters, but rather he regards the inner spiritual problems that afflict protagonists as the result of material conditions."[114] Despite Tolstoi's explicit and reactionary program, that insight lent his work a profound and lasting significance.

Lukács's celebration of Tolstoi may seem at first glance to pose a problem, for there is no doubt that his literary criticism was structured by a very schematic historical periodization that owed a great deal to the course of Hungarian history. The proletariat's authentic heritage was that bequeathed to it by the rising bourgeoisie, a class that was revolutionary vis-à-vis the feudal order and therefore historically prescient prior to 1848. After that tumultuous year, the bourgeoisie betrayed its democratic calling and entered its period of compromise and decline. As a consequence, the literature of the period could only reflect that decadence, whether it took the form of naturalism, *l'art pour l'art*, or the avant-garde. How then could Lukács account for Tolstoi's success? The answer he gave was that Tolstoi's Russia was still in its precapitalist phase; retarded development offered him the kind of literary/ideological possibilities that had been available to bourgeois Western European writers before 1848.

But what, finally, of proletarian literature? On this question Lukács said little in the mid-1920s. Indeed, it could not have seemed very pressing in the central and eastern European context of retarded development. What could the proletarian revolution offer the development of art, he asked rhetorically at the time. "Very little," came the reply, because the age of the proletarian revolution was still very much in its initial stages. In an obvious lecture to himself, he wrote that "the mighty upheaval that we are experiencing, that the revolutionary proletariat is carrying out, revolutionizes—in the first instance—the *immediate-sensuous* reality (the subject matter and form of literature) less than one would believe at a superficial glance. This explains the 'disillusionment' with the Russian Revolution of those intellectuals who expected from it the immediate solution to their special existential problems."[115] All the more reason, then, to focus attention on the literature of the great age of the revolutionary bourgeoisie, a literature that was more relevant to the existing stage of historical development.

One should read Lukács's famous "Blum Theses" in conjunction with the literary theory he worked out in the 1920s as well as with the contemporary Comintern line. Prepared for the Hungarian Communist Party's Second Congress, the Theses took up where the Sixth Congress of the Comintern (July 17–September 1, 1928) had left off. That Congress took the position that the international proletarian revolution consisted "of a series of processes, differing in character and in time: purely proletarian revolutions; revolutions of a bourgeois-democratic type which turn into proletarian revolutions; wars of national liberation, or colonial revolutions." In countries such as Hungary, where capitalist development remained at a medium level, it maintained that a transitional stage would very likely precede the proletarian revolution. That stage, identified as the "democratic dictatorship of the proletariat and peasantry," would then transform itself, more or less rapidly, into an unalloyed dictatorship of the proletariat.[116]

Not surprisingly then, Blum/Lukács took the position that the principal problem confronting the Hungarian Communist Party was the Bethlen government's betrayal and liquidation of bourgeois democracy and the Social Democratic party's unprincipled collaboration. In view of that situation, the Party's immediate task should be to lead the struggle for the full realization of bourgeois democracy. That could best be accomplished by establishing a democratic dictatorship of the proletariat and the peasantry, the very solution the Comintern had proposed, as a "mediation" or transitional phase on the road to proletarian power.[117] However paradoxical, the proletariat had to engage in a struggle against the bourgeoisie in order to complete the latter class's Jacobin tasks. That was so because the bourgeoisie had betrayed its own best self, succumbing to reaction and, increasingly, to fascism.

Lukács emphasized the peculiarity of Hungarian development, which combined the old feudal form of land distribution with a relatively developed form of capitalism. That unholy alliance between land owners and capitalists had to be confronted by an alliance of the proletariat and the peasantry, taking its stand on a program of full democracy. Thus, Lukács held that the full realization of bourgeois democracy was the proper goal of the Communist party in underdeveloped countries as well as in developed capitalist states. The latter had turned their backs on bourgeois democracy, however much they preserved its forms; the former had not yet placed democracy on the agenda. In both cases, the responsibility for bourgeois democracy devolved on the proletariat and its Party.

At first, Kun accepted Lukács's Theses with but minor criticisms. To him they seemed to be in keeping with the Sixth Congress of the Comintern's recent assessment of the Hungarian situation. On February 28, 1929, however, Comintern official D. Z. Manuilski fired off a letter to Kun that prompted a reversal. The Russian pronounced the Theses too lengthy and in need of "restructuring." The Hungarian leaders, he said, should not forget that the Communist movement had entered its "Third Period" of activity since the war's end. After the relative stabilization of capitalism about 1924, crisis and revolution were again on the agenda. Fascism had emerged and the proletariat was once again becoming militant. Hence, Blum/Lukács's call for a "democratic" rather than a proletarian dictatorship was untimely. It should never be forgotten, Manuilski concluded, that Hungary had already experienced proletarian dictatorship and that history never made backward jumps.[118]

Immediately, Kun and Révai forwarded an encoded telegram to the Party's Foreign Committee in Vienna ordering that the Blum Theses not be disseminated. Landler having died in 1928, nothing could be done to save them. Seeing the handwriting on the wall, Lukács wrote a letter to the Central Committee in which he repudiated his handiwork, an act of "self-criticism" that he subsequently described as insincere. In this letter he claimed to understand that the next Hungarian revolution could not be less than the first, that after a proletarian dictatorship a democratic dictatorship was impossible.[119] After his defeat, he withdrew from active politics to concentrate his energies on Marxist aesthetics and literary criticism.

It is only reasonable to ask why Lukács exercised self-criticism when he believed that he was right. By his account, he did so because he knew that the German Party had expelled Korsch in 1926 and he did not wish to give Kun an opportunity to excommunicate him, thus removing him from the struggle against fascism. But there was more to it than that. For Lukács the Party was a microcosm of a new, emerging social order, a totality within which human beings, no longer subject to the atomizing effects of capitalist society, could meet at last. One is reminded of the Hungarian proverb: "Outside of Hungary there is no life; and if there is, it is unlike it" (*Extra Hungariam non est vita; Aut si vita, non est ita*). For "Hungary," Lukács, the political and existential exile, substituted "the Party."

At the Party's behest, Lukács returned to Hungary for three months, during which time he directed underground work; back in Vienna, he learned that the Austrian government was preparing to expel him. He made every effort to prevent this, including a request for a glandular operation. In a well-known letter to the Austrian Chancellor, Ignaz Seipel, Thomas Mann interceded on his behalf. But in the end, the government issued an expulsion order, and Lukács went to the Soviet Union, where he lived and worked from late 1929 to summer 1931.

Moscow Interlude

Lukács had been in Moscow briefly in 1921, when he was one of the Hungarian Communist Party's representatives at the Comintern's Third Congress. At that time, Lenin was at the helm, the Civil War was over, and many anticipated the world revolution. When he returned eight years later, Lenin was dead, Stalin wielded absolute power, and "socialism in one country" was official doctrine. The state was waging war on the peasants in its determination to collectivize agriculture and thus to increase the slave labor supply in the factories. The Gulag Archipelago was already mapped out and the long, dark night of terror had descended. It is well to keep this in mind when considering Lukács's Moscow writings.

In his recorded recollections of his first extended stay in the Soviet Union, Lukács did not speak of such fearsome things. Instead, he emphasized his good fortune with respect to theoretical matters. On arrival, he recalled, he was assigned to the Marx-Engels (from 1931, the Marx-Engels-Lenin) Institute, then under the able direction of David Ryazanov, who possessed an encyclopedic knowledge of Marx's writings. On meeting Lukács, Ryazanov, who like so many others was to perish in the purges, joked that the Hungarian had been "Cominterned," that is, put out to nonpolitical pasture.[120] Often, indeed, the Comintern placed those whose views were not in vogue at the Institute. Lukács was not disturbed by this and looked forward to a period of quiet research and reflection. When, however, Ryazanov showed him Marx's unpublished *Economic-Philosophic Manuscripts*, he was stunned.

Published in 1932, those manuscripts created a sensation in Marxist circles, above all because they testified to the young Marx's profound interest in the problem of alienation. On reading them, Lukács was gratified to have confirmed his claim in *History and Class Consciousness* that that problem was central to Marxism. At the same time, however, he was dismayed to learn that Marx rejected the equation of alienation (*Entfremdung*) with objectification (*Vergegenständlichung*) that *History and Class Consciousness* had assumed.[121]

In the three manuscripts that Marx wrote in Paris between April and August 1844, he attempted to work out his criticisms of Hegel and the classical economists Smith, Ricardo, and Say. For all their insights, he argued, those thinkers had not understood, much less prescribed a cure for, the alienation of man under capitalism. That was because they failed to grasp the *economic* cause of that estrangement. In the capitalist system man was alienated from himself and thus from other men because his labor, or productive life, by means of which alone he could objectify and realize his "species essence" ("*Gattungswesen*"), was not, as it should be, an end in itself, but merely a means to sustain his existence. Unable to realize his own species essence, he could not recognize his oneness with others.[122]

What particularly struck Lukács about this was Marx's insistence that objectification was not bad in and of itself, but was necessary for man's self-realization. "The object of labor," Marx had written, "is . . . the *objectification of man's species life*"; man contemplates his essential self in the world he has created.[123] Alienated labor ("*entfremdete Arbeit*"), labor that was no longer his own, separated man from the only means he had at his disposal *to become what he was by nature*—a creatively productive being. On reading this, Lukács concluded that Marx was right: objectification was value free. Only when objectified forms acquired functions that "bring the essence /Wesen/ of man into opposition with his existence /Sein/," could one speak of alienation.[124]

Marx went on to praise Hegel for his grasp of labor as the essence of man, but argued—mistakenly—that he had fallen into the trap of identifying alienation with objectivity.[125] Hence, for him, the overcoming of alienation necessarily entailed the annulment of objectivity as well. But then man could only be regarded as "a *non-objective, spiritual* essence," a self-consciousness.[126] Lukács was shaken when he read this, because he judged that *History and Class Consciousness*, with its undisguised distrust of all institutional forms and its predilection for formless human community, was vulnerable to the same critique. If the object existed only as an alienation (*Entäusserung*) from self-consciousness, its return to the subject would signal the end of objective reality, and thus of reality generally. The conclusion seemed inescapable: *History and Class Consciousness* was far more idealist and Hegelian in conception than he had imagined. He would have to begin anew from a properly Marxist—that is, materialist—standpoint.[127] What is more, he would have to regard *some* social institutions as necessary and not evil by nature. In the Soviet Union they did not, after all, evidence any sign of disappearing.

But the identification of alienation with objectification was not the only error Lukács now thought that he perceived in *History and Class Consciousness*. Ágnes Heller remembers that in later years he often remarked to her and others "how crucial the reading of the *Paris Manuscripts* was for his self-criticism: the discovery of the concept of human species and of the central role, in Marx, of 'species essence' (*Gattungswesen*) was a great intellectual shock for him. 'Class' cannot take the place of 'species'—that was how he now came to conceive Marx's position—but it was just such a substitution that had characterized *History and Class Consciousness*."[128] For too long, Lukács had emphasized the social and historical category of class to the exclusion of the natural category of species.

He had now changed his mind about basic categories. Nature, the objective material world, was prior to all social relationships. The dialectic of *nature* was therefore crucial. Moreover, the goal of history was not, as he had formerly believed, the withering away of all formal structures, but rather the unity, within social forms, of each individual with the essence, or nature, of the human species. According to such a revised formulation, species essence would be *discovered* in its many objectifications once labor was truly free. Marxism was not, then, to be understood primarily as a theory of revolutionary praxis, but as a universal and systematic philosophy of nature, including human nature. The extreme subjectivism of *History and Class Consciousness* would have to be replaced by a greater attention to "objective reality," which was not something to be created, but realized.

It is important to emphasize the genuine character of this change in Lukács's views not only because, as we have seen, he sometimes made insincere recantations, but because he had here accepted the foundations for what was to become his final theoretical position. As a result of his new conviction that *History and Class Consciousness* was fundamentally flawed and of his growing recognition that he could not be faithful to Leninism or useful to the Communist party of the Soviet Union if he did not distance himself from even the suspicion of idealism, he now committed himself to two ideas he had previously rejected: the dialectics of nature and the "theory of reflection." He made this commitment public in his famous essay of 1933, "My Road to Marx," and in the 1934 lecture that he delivered to members of the Soviet Academy of Sciences, assembled to commemorate the twenty-fifth anniversary of the publication of *Materialism and Empirio-Criticism*. "My battle against the theory of reflection and the Marx-Engels conception of the dialectic of nature was," he said on that occasion, "a typical manifestation of that 'subterranean idealism' " that Lenin had condemned in his major work of philosophy.[129] He was, after all, guilty of the sins with which Deborin and Rudas had charged him a decade before.

That being said, it is instructive to point out that this dramatic and genuine change of mind corresponded nicely with Stalin's December 9, 1930 attack on Deborin and his followers for their "Menshevist /that is, social democratic/ idealism." He and Lenin, rather than Plekhanov and Deborin, were Marx's true philosophical heirs. The worm had turned and Deborin was now accused of that which he had accused Lukács. Of course Stalin's attack was not really philosophic in character; it was part of the Comintern's assault on social democracy, triggered by the entry in 1929 of pro-French Social Democrats into the German government. Thus, he declared the Social Democrats to be "social fascists" and enemies of Marxism.

Lukács later maintained that Stalin's attack had played "a very positive role" in his theoretical development.[130] The attack on Plekhanov inspired him to attack representative social democratic theorists such as Lassalle and Franz Mehring. In this, politics and personal safety were undoubtedly important; after having had to repudiate the Blum Theses, Lukács was not elected to the Hungarian Communist Party's Central Committee. In danger of expulsion from the movement or worse, he hastened to join the attack on Deborin and the Social Democrats and to repudiate idealism. As the most knowledgeable student of these years has observed, Lukács's rejection of idealism was not simply the result of reading Marx's Paris manuscripts.[131]

Lukács did not spell out the full implications of his new insights until the late 1930s, when he wrote *The Young Hegel: Studies in the Relations between Dialectics and Economics*, a book he dedicated to Mikhail Alexandrovitch Lifshitz "in devotion and friendship." He met Lifshitz at the Marx-Engels Institute in 1930 and quickly formed what was to be a lifelong friendship. Indeed, since the death in 1911 of Leó Popper, the only close friend of his youth, Lifshitz was the first with whom Lukács lived "in true friendship" and "spiritual community." In a letter he wrote to the Russian in 1970, the year before he died, Lukács recalled their first meeting: "I always remember with great pleasure making your acquaintance in 1930. It was the first and still the only time in the course of my long life that I came into contact with a scholar much younger than I without having so much as the thought of a teacher-student relationship arise."[132]

Born in 1905, Lifshitz was twenty years Lukács's junior. Attracted to the arts, he studied in the early 1920s at the VKHUTEMAS (Higher Technical Art Workshop), an avant-garde art school. Very soon, however, he began to entertain second thoughts about modernism. "His conception," Lukács later recalled, "became conservative through and through."[133] At the Institute Lifshitz teamed with Franz Schiller to collect Marx and Engels's scattered writings on aesthetics, part of an ongoing project of identifying and publishing important Marxist sources. Lukács and Lifshitz discussed at length a wide range of questions—political, historical, and aesthetic. As a consequence, they determined to provide Marxism with a systematic aesthetics. Previous efforts by social democratic disciples such as Mehring and Plekhanov they considered to be excessively dependent upon one or another bourgeois philosophy. Marxism was not, in their view, a social-economic theory to which other things could be added on; it was a universal Weltanschauung. Years later, Lukács proudly claimed that he and Lifshitz had been the first to speak of a specific Marxist aesthetics as an organic part of the general Marxist system.

Berlin

The Comintern's decision to send Lukács to Berlin was not made without careful consideration.[134] By the summer of 1931, Germany was in the throes of a severe and ever deepening depression; but despite the growing Nazi threat, the German Communist Party (KPD) viewed its immediate prospects with optimism. Party hopes continued to soar as Chancellor Heinrich Brüning's policy of stringent economy and deflation, prompted by vivid memories of the 1923 inflation, did little to alleviate the crisis and less to project a long-term solution. Almost five million workers were unemployed and millions more faced an uncertain future. So great, in fact, was the number of those out of work that the Marxist Workers' School (*Marxistische Arbeiterschule*, or MASCH), which attempted to capitalize on the government's problems, did not hesitate to schedule morning classes in the Karl-Liebknecht Haus, the KPD's Berlin headquarters. Recalling the days in Hungary when he helped organize the Thália Theater's workers performances and lectured to worker-students at the Free School of the Sociological Society, Lukács placed himself at the disposal of MASCH's founder and director, Johann-Lorenz Schmidt, whom he knew as László Radványi.

As early as the fall of 1925, Radványi had begun to arrange weekly lectures in the attic of the Karl-Liebknecht Haus. So impressed with the results was the KPD's Central Committee, that it authorized him to expand his efforts, and the following fall the school began its official existence. Open to all who paid a modest fee, MASCH was committed to Marxist-Leninist doctrine and propagated whatever the KPD political line happened to be. Its Communist outlook notwithstanding, the school embodied, according to Radványi, the spirit of the Sunday Circle and the Free School of the Humanistic Sciences.[135]

In the beginning, MASCH offered classes in political economy, history, dialectical materialism, and the Leninist theory of imperialism. Soon, however, Radványi added courses on "socialist construction" in the USSR and the history of the German and international workers' movement; they became regular offerings, designed to convince the unemployed that their plight was bound up with the capitalist system. With each new trimester, Radványi arranged additional courses—on militarism, fascism, trade union problems, education, working-class youth, proletarian literature, and the press. Eventually, MASCH boasted of courses in 31 different areas, including physics, chemistry, biology, mathematics, and foreign languages, especially Russian.

By the time Lukács arrived, MASCH was conducting extension classes not only in suburbs and towns near Berlin, but in some thirty other German cities, Amsterdam, Zürich, and Vienna. Radványi later estimated the total number of students in all of MASCH's branches to be thirty thousand. The figure is almost certainly too high,[136] but the school's overall impact was far from being negligible. In fact as time passed, Radványi scheduled advanced courses for workers, university students, and intellectuals. That did not present any staffing problem, for he had recruited some remarkable teachers to join those, such as Hermann Duncker, whose principal credential was Party loyalty. During the first trimester of the 1931–32 school year, for example, Albert Einstein lectured on relativity theory. One who attended has left a vivid account of the great scientist's encounter with working-class comrades:

> I cannot say that his performance on this occasion was memorable . . . but even less edifying was the behavior of the audience. Strong in their Marxist schooling, the Communist workers boldly got up and told Einstein that his thinking was not sufficiently dialectical and that relativity was a bourgeois concept. It was then that he showed his great humanity. He patiently tried to correct what he said must be misunderstandings and endeavored to find merit in the most naive arguments. He was less indulgent with some Communist intellectuals whose harassments he obviously was not experiencing for the first time.[137]

Those who stood farther to the political left undoubtedly fared better. Thanks to Radványi's efforts, Ludwig Renn and Egon Erwin Kisch lectured on literature and journalism, Erwin Piscator on theater, John Heartfield on art, Hanns Eisler on music, and Walter Gropius and Bruno Taut on architecture. From the Hungarian emigration, Gábor and Fogarasi offered their services. Using the name "Hans Keller," Lukács organized a series of lectures on "Selected Questions Concerning Marxist Literary Criticism." Subsequently he proposed to lecture on a wide range of topics: "Marxist Literary History"; "The Literature of the French Revolution"; "Principal Currents in Modern Bourgeois Literature"; "War Literature"; and "Fascist and Social-Fascist Literature." We know too that in late 1931–early 1932, he elaborated publicly on the theme "Hegel-Marx-Lenin."[138] Gertrúd Lukács ("Anna Keller") taught an introduction to political economy.

Lukács did not restrict his activities to the work with MASCH. His principal assignment, in fact, was to give ideological direction to the League of Proletarian-Revolutionary Writers that representatives of various groups of Communist authors and "worker-correspondents"—workers who contributed reports to KPD publications—had organized on October 19, 1928 with the support of Moscow's International Alliance of Revolutionary Writers.[139] The following summer the League's executive committee, chaired by Johannes R. Becher, an expressionist poet turned Communist, formulated plans to publish a monthly journal, Die Linkskurve. Here too, Moscow supplied the necessary funds; at the behest of the Comintern, the International Bureau for Revolutionary Literature channeled money to the editors. The chief of the Bureau was Béla Illés, another Hungarian emigré who had left Vienna for Moscow in 1923.

The first issue of Die Linkskurve appeared in August 1929; in addition to Becher and Kurt Kläber, one of its principal editors was Andor Gábor, who had arrived in Berlin early in 1926. In the pages of the new review, the Hungarian criticized writers on the non-Communist left and Communist writers who showed even the slightest sign of independence. At the same time, he placed himself foursquare against the literary avant-garde: "When I see a magazine in which the type is revolutionized, the names of authors printed vertically instead of horizontally, 'henri barbusse' instead of 'Henri Barbusse,' I suspect that what lies behind the revolutionary type is not very revolutionary."[140] Clearly, Gábor and his Moscow sponsors rejected the idea that avant-garde theory and practice represented communism in art.

In Gábor's view, avant-garde art and literature were bourgeois through and through. A truly proletarian literature had to be placed in the hands of writers recruited from the ranks of the working class.[141] It was an argument he soon had reason to regret, because in Moscow it sounded too much like a revival of the "Proletcult," formed shortly before the October Revolution. The Proletarian Cultural and Educational Organization purposed to encourage the creation of a proletarian culture that would replace the bourgeois culture soon to disappear. Led by Aleksandr A. Bogdanov and others, the Proletcult organized literary studios and published numerous periodicals. From the first, however, the Communist party was alarmed by Bogdanov's insistence that the organization be free of political control. In October 1920, Lenin, who disliked Bogdanov and viewed with suspicion any independent power base, compelled the group to function as a subordinate body within the Commissariat of Education.[142]

On the theoretical level, Lenin objected to the Proletcult's indifference to the heritage of bourgeois thought and culture. Whatever form the new culture eventually took, it would, he insisted, have to develop out of the best models and traditions of bourgeois culture. It was to Lenin's authority that Josef Lenz, a leading KPD functionary, appealed in the March 1930 number of Die Linkskurve. Against Gábor, he argued that the development of proletarian literature could proceed only from a collaborative effort on the part of workers and intellectuals, an effort that entailed the assimilation of bourgeois literature.[143]

There can be no doubt that Lenz, who was close to Party leader Ernst Thälmann, wrote that article under Moscow's instructions, transmitted, in all probability, by Illés, who was in Berlin early in 1930 for conversations with Thälmann and Becher. Illés informed the Germans of the official line in Moscow, that represented by RAPP, the Russian Association of Proletarian Writers. The inquisitorial leaders of RAPP—Leopold Averbakh, Vladimir Ermilov, Aleksandr Fadeev, and Yuri Libedinskii—were not workers, and insisted, in Averbakh's words, that "proletarian art is not a form of art which must necessarily be created by a proletarian."[144]

Nor was that all. If bourgeois writers could create proletarian art, they could also learn from the best elements of bourgeois culture, particularly the classics of realism. In this, the members of RAPP could appeal to Engels's well-known admiration for Balzac and Marx's insistence that Shakespearean realism was preferable to Schillerian idealism. Indeed, in 1929 Fadeev published an article entitled "Down with Schiller!" that proclaimed the official RAPP position that proletarian writers had the most to learn from realists such as Stendhal, Balzac, and Tolstoi. Remembering Lenin's enthusiasms, Fadeev and his colleagues displayed a special reverence for the author of *War and Peace*.[145]

Since Gábor had published an article that revealed him to be a "left oppositionist," he was dropped from the editorial committee in favor of Hans Marchwitza, a former miner and worker-correspondent. More important than this change, however, was the addition to the committee of Karl August Wittfogel who, unlike most members of the League, had studied philosophy and aesthetics. Thus, he could provide the League with a Marxist theory of literature; over the next year, he published a series of articles under the title "On the Question of a Marxist Aesthetics." In keeping with Lenz's demand that Marxists assimilate their bourgeois heritage, Wittfogel, like Marx and Lukács, focused his attention on Hegel. "The Hegelian philosophy," he wrote, "was the last, most profound, most comprehensive expression of bourgeois philosophy."[146]

In part because of Wittfogel's philosophic sophistication, his articles failed to elicit a theoretical response. Moreover, his bourgeois origins and obvious indifference to worker-correspondents provoked the "left opposition" to launch an attack on the new line. Undoubtedly, this opposition was emboldened by the "left opposition" in the Soviet Union, the so-called Litfront (Literary Front). Led by poets Aleksandr Bezymenskii and Semen Rodov, critic A. Zonin, and theorist Georgy Gorbachev, the Litfront stood opposed to RAPP's espousal of realism and the bourgeois heritage. Instead, it campaigned for a utilitarian literature that would focus on contemporary themes and speak directly to the masses.

As early as October 1930, Becher wrote to Illés concerning the League's "ultraleft factional struggles." It is worth noting that most of those who constituted the "left opposition" were Hungarians: Alfréd Durus (Kemény), who had abandoned the avant-garde to become a critic for *Die Rote Fahne*; Karl

Báró-Rosinger (Andor Réz), a journalist active in the worker-correspondent movement; and Aladár Komját, the group's spokesman. As we have seen, Komját had broken with *Ma* in 1917 and founded *1917/Internationale*. As a member of the Writers Directory during the Soviet Republic, he had opposed both Kassák and Lukács and championed a "proletarian *Kulturpolitik*."[147]

Komját and his group seized the initiative during the summer of 1931, presenting a draft of a new program for the League. Coauthored by Réz, it resurrected the idea that workers must themselves take the lead in the creation of a genuine proletarian literature. Under attack, the weak-kneed Becher all but capitulated. Gábor, despite his former "left" views, did not join Komját's group, allying himself instead with the wavering Becher, Wittfogel, and the much maligned responsible editor, Otto Biha. He did so because of Lukács's arrival in Berlin.

Acting on instructions from Moscow as well as conviction, Lukács rallied the League leadership against the Komját group's program. In all probability, Becher drafted the alternative program that Lukács, Wittfogel, and Gábor emended. This counterdraft emphasized the necessity of theoretical elucidation and insisted that agitation and propaganda were not enough. It called for the creation of a "great bolshevik artwork" that would reveal the developmental tendencies in the present and be rooted in the cultural heritage bequeathed by the bourgeoisie's revolutionary period.[148]

While this behind-the-scenes struggle was going on, Lukács prepared to advance RAPP ideas in the pages of *Die Linkskurve*; he did not know that the Soviet organization would soon fall from grace. In November 1931, he published a critique of two novels by Willi Bredel, a former lathe operator.[149] After a few flattering comments, he took the aspiring author to task for his Proletcult tendencies. To begin with, Bredel's characters were mere stereotypes, not "living men" who change and develop over time. "For the living man" was the most important RAPP slogan, designed to combat the crude tendentiousness of the Proletcult by championing a kind of psychological realism.

Lukács also attacked Bredel's use of language, in particular his reliance on *Reportage* (journalistic reports). Even casual conversations between workers, he pointed out, sounded stilted and lifeless. As a consequence, Bredel forfeited all sense of reality. This criticism too derived from RAPP ideology, according to which Proletcult products were little more than "newspaper reportage in the form of belles-lettres."[150]

Lukács concluded that Bredel's problem was not simply one of technique or style. He failed above all because he had not applied the materialist dialectic to literature. He did indeed portray the upward course of the revolutionary movement, but failed to depict the obstacles and setbacks. Hence his readers learned nothing about the process of dialectical advance. They were presented with the rigid appearance of things, followed by sudden and seemingly inexplicable changes. Again, Lukács repeated ideas he heard from the RAPP theoreticians in the Soviet Union. They had called upon Communist writers to lay bare the conflicts and contradictions within the living man and to "understand these contradictions as part of a 'dialectical' process of development." The "living man" slogan represented "the *dialectical* aspect of /the/ dialectical-materialist method."[151]

Although Bredel accepted Lukács's criticisms without demur, one Otto Gotsche took up the cudgels on his behalf. He reported that workers with whom he had spoken liked the novels and challenged Lukács to do better before being critical. In his rejoinder,[152] Lukács dismissed the notion that criticism was invalid so long as the critic himself could not produce better creative works. At the same time, he availed himself of the opportunity to identify his critical outlook with Averbakh's. "A Russian worker," he wrote, "would open his eyes in surprise if he were expected to demand better novels, short stories, poems, etc., from Comrade Averbakh, before the latter might presume to criticize such works." Criticism had its own, distinctive role to play in the proletarian-revolutionary literary movement: to discover and elucidate, by applying the materialist dialectic to literature, those creative methods that corresponded best to the problems of the class struggle at a given time.

Lukács presented the RAPP position with force and conviction because he genuinely shared it. Even more deeply than Averbakh and his allies, he believed that realism was the genre most consistent with Marxism's materialist dialectic. In his view, Bredel's reportage technique was a crude form of naturalism that "fetishized" and eternalized reality. Only a subtle, dialectical presentation of the world could reveal its developmental, processlike character, and hence overcome the notion that reality was static and fundamental change impossible.

In "Tendency or Partisanship?"[153] Lukács returned to that theme. He employed the word "tendency" (*Tendenz*) in the way German radicals had long used it—as an ought or ideal that the creative writer counterposed to reality. It was only natural, according to Lukács, that radical writers should propagate a vision of a better world since they believed the only alternative to be some sort of "pure art" interested only in perfecting aesthetic forms. But that, Lukács argued, was a false dilemma because it presupposed the independence of aesthetics from social reality. From that point of view, the introduction of social or political demands had to seem foreign to the very nature of art.

Properly understood, aesthetics constituted an integral part of the universal Weltanschauung that was dialectical materialism. "Pure art" did not and could not exist, because products of the imagination were inextricably intertwined with social reality. As a, or rather *the*, theory of social reality, Marxism was by its very nature an aesthetic. Hence it was unnecessary, even logically impossible, to import from *outside* of literature some abstract, wished-for "ought." Reality was dialectical, a process of becoming. The proletarian-revolutionary writers needed only, then, to depict reality as it truly was in order at the same time to lay bare the developmental tendencies that were always and ever present.

One could not know in advance the nature of the society to come, but Lukács never doubted that a much better social order *was* in the making. That was so because he was "partisan," loyal to the proletariat as the contemporary bearer of historical progress. That partisanship which Lukács commended to proletarian-revolutionary writers was different from subjective tendency that stood outside of objective, dialectical reality. Partisanship provided a perspective from which reality as dialectical development could clearly be contemplated. Among the immediate tasks of the Communist movement, the abandonment of *Tendenz* literature was of the first order of importance.

Lukács returned to the attack on journalistic reportage in an extended critique of Ernst Ottwalt's novel, *Denn sie wissen, was sie tun: Ein deutscher Justiz-Roman* (1931),[154] an attempt to expose, by reporting actual cases, what the author, a member of the League, regarded as the unjust, bourgeois character of the Weimar legal system. Once again, Lukács insisted that exposés of isolated wrongs had the unintended effect of "fetishizing" them, making them appear to be "things" against which one could do nothing but express moral outrage. Failing to apply the materialist dialectic to quotidian data, Ottwalt and others who employed the same technique obscured the driving forces of reality's processlike character.

In opposition to journalistic reportage, Lukács advocated "construction" or "formation" (*Gestaltung*). Only by giving form to the total process that is reality could a creative writer uncover the fetishism of the economic and social forms of capitalist society in order to reveal authentic reality—"the (class) relations between human beings." Ottwalt should have presented Weimar's judicial system as a single moment in an ongoing process of development.

To illustrate his theses, Lukács compared Ottwalt's novel to Tolstoi's *Resurrection*. Although both books attempted to discredit existing judicial systems, they employed fundamentally different creative methods: Ottwalt that of reportage, Tolstoi that of "formation." Hence the Russian's superiority was not simply a result of the fact that he possessed more talent. "Tolstoi is the greater writer because he puts the question more comprehensively, universally, materialistically, and dialectically than Ottwalt does. The administration of the law is for Tolstoi a part of the total process."

If Ottwalt objected to being described as un-Tolstoian, he did not say so. For one thing, he worked consciously in accord with theories espoused by an anti-RAPP group that flourished between 1923 and 1929: the Left Front of Arts (LEF). This group considered itself to be the only authentic representative of revolutionary art and counted among its members such well-known figures as Vladimir Mayakovsky, Sergey Tretyakov, and Osip Brik. An offspring of Russian futurism, LEF admired technology and no-nonsense rationalism. Its members, convinced that the bolsheviks were building a new and truly rational world, held that writers could do their part by producing a "literature of fact" based upon newspaper reports, historical records, and various other sorts of data. The literary heritage, they argued, was completely irrelevant.[155]

Tretyakov brought this message to Berlin in 1931. In a widely discussed public lecture of that year, he gave an account of his experiences on a collective farm and argued that the time had come to advance beyond the necessary stage of reportage to direct participation in the building of socialism. Inspired by this lecture and by his association with Bertolt Brecht, Ottwalt rejected Lukács's criticism. In his view, literature's task was to hasten the immediate and total transformation of reality. Hence the proletariat, as the revolutionary class, had necessarily to prefer "facts" to literary forms, a progressive proletarian literature to a reactionary classical realism.[156]

In his rejoinder,[157] Lukács leveled an attack on modernism he never repudiated. That he wished above all to combat the influence of Brecht's theory and practice is clear from the Ottwalt quote he singled out for particular censure: "For the goal of these /older/ works is the shaping, the striving for a self-contained artwork that is static and complete in itself, and before which the reader is automatically transformed into an epicure, drawing no conclusions and being satisfied with what is given, with the emotional stimulation and the placid satisfaction of having read a good book."

That, as Lukács observed, corresponded exactly to Brecht's views, particularly with respect to the distinction between the old dramatic (or "Aristotelian") and the new "epic" theater. According to the controversial playwright, the old theater was one of illusion in which actors became or attempted to become the characters they portrayed, thus seducing spectators into believing that what they were seeing was reality. In the epic theater, on the other hand, actors consciously resisted the temptation to become the characters they played, striving instead to *tell about* the character, in part by repeating his actions; as if to say, "this is how he did it." At the same time, the spectators never forgot that they were sitting in a theater, listening to an account of past events—just as people once listened to songs and stories (epic recreations) of great heroes of the past.

Brecht called this the *Verfremdungseffekt*, the alienation effect. By creating this effect, he hoped to make of the theater a lecture hall where actors and spectators, detached from the action, would be encouraged to think about the evils of bourgeois society. "The essential point of the epic theatre," he wrote in 1927, "is perhaps that it appeals less to the feelings than to the spectator's reason. Instead of sharing an experience the spectator must come to grips with things."[158]

The source of Ottwalt and Brecht's errors, according to Lukács, was their total rejection of the revolutionary heritage. Having forgotten that Engels spoke of the German workers' movement as the heir of classical German philosophy and that Marx acknowledged his debt to classical philosophy and economics, they insisted that proletarian literature, and proletarian culture in general, "arise out of nothing without connection with the past." This was precisely what Lenin had denounced in the Proletcult. Unlike Ottwalt and Brecht, the bolshevik leader recognized that "cut off from the great current of revolutionary development and tradition, it /the new proletarian culture/feeds on the degenerate ideological products of the declining bourgeoisie."[159]

Lukács's position, worked out in the late 1920s, was simple and ingenious. On the basis of it, he explained far better than Marx had why past works remained alive for the proletarian movement. Such works portrayed a society in process, one in which a revolutionary class was on the rise. Of particular importance, of course, was that part of the heritage that was most immediate—the great realist works that portrayed objectively the rise of the revolutionary bourgeoisie. It was with that heritage that the new proletarian culture had to connect if it wished to be authentic.

On that view, modernist experiments that repudiated the entire cultural past were doomed to failure. Although they pretended to be creations ex nihilo, they were in fact unconscious manifestations of bourgeois decadence. By failing to appropriate their rightful heritage, modernist artists such as Brecht and Ottwalt could do nothing but reflect the decay that surrounded them. In that sense, their work differed little from expressionism and the "neue Sachlichkeit," which, whatever their revolutionary pretensions, were both late bourgeois in essence and therefore unable to portray the totality of reality and the objective driving forces of the proletarian revolution.

Not until Gyula Háy exploded on the German scene late in 1932 did Lukács discover a rival to Brecht whom he could admire and champion. Like so many of the Hungarian emigrés, Háy descended from Jewish forebears and turned bolshevik during the war. After the formation of the Soviet Republic, he secured a minor position as a propagandist in the People's Commissariat of Public Education, over which Lukács presided. In 1919, he emigrated to Germany, where he eked out an existence as a stage designer, before returning home at the end of 1923, after Bethlen had restored order and legality. There he married, but, unable to find work in a country flooded with refugees from the successor states, he emigrated to Germany once again, only to encounter the great inflation. Again he returned to Hungary, where he published his first articles, reviews, and short stories.

Háy's ambition did not, however, find sufficient scope in his homeland and he began to long for the excitement and opportunity that Berlin offered. When, one day in 1929, he heard the irresistible score of Brecht and Weill's Threepenny Opera, he resolved to return to the German capital to make a name for himself as a playwright and "to change the existing social order."[160] Even as he made that decision, he played with the idea of a historical drama about the Emperor Sigismund and the Czech Reformer, John Huss.

Háy completed that drama in the spring of 1932, at about the time he met Brecht, with whom he disagreed about the "alienation effect." For the Hungarian, the transformation of the actor into the character he was playing always constituted a "holy moment." The difference of conception must have been clear to those who attended the first performance of *Sigismund* in Breslau on October 15, 1932. By then Max Reinhardt's Deutsche Theater had secured the Berlin rights, changing the title to *God, Emperor and Peasant*, and casting such stellar and politically committed actors as Fritz Kortner and Erwin Kalser. Karl Heinz Martin would direct.

In preparation for writing the play, Háy carried out extensive research on the late fourteenth and early fifteenth centuries, the time of the Church's Great Schism (1378–1417) and of Huss's rise to prominence. Like so many Marxists, he was fascinated by the revolutionary character of medieval religious movements, seeing in them precursors of modern communism. At the same time, he wished to write a tragedy that was historical, rather than personal, one that would dramatize the collision of opposing social forces. Thus, he hit upon the idea of setting the play in the time of Sigismund (1368–1437), the son of Charles IV, who became Holy Roman Emperor.

Betrothed to the eldest daughter of Louis the Great, King of Poland and Hungary, Sigismund received his education at the Hungarian court and became thoroughly Magyarized. He married the sickly Maria in 1385 and became King of Hungary two years later, though it was some years before he secured unchallenged recognition. That hard won victory did not last long, however, because he soon suffered military defeat at the hands of the Turks and was deprived of his authority in Hungary. On his return in 1401, he discovered that he had many enemies among the nobles and was briefly imprisoned. As Háy's play opens, the widowed Sigismund is a prisoner in the castle at Siklós, where leading Hungarian nobles demand that he abdicate. In that way, Háy sought to show that the King had run afoul of the nobility because of his efforts to create a modern centralized, or in Marxist terms a bourgeois, state.

In a wonderfully crafted scene, Sigismund wins the rebellious nobles over to his side by appealing to their self-interest. He reminds them that they live in a time of "colossal events" and great opportunity. "Where there is no Emperor, the path is clear to the imperial throne. Where two popes tussle, the moment for world power, for gaining ascendency over the Church, has come." So long as there are two popes, one must serve the Emperor or else confront new churches and religions. The nobles profess to be shocked, but are in fact intrigued. Sigismund appeals next to their ego and, at the same time, their lust for power and influence: "When will you again be offered an opportunity to create a Roman Emperor out of nothing." Finally convinced, the nobles agree to work for Sigismund's election.[161]

After further struggles, Sigismund was elected in 1410. Four years later, he secured agreement from Pope John XXIII, the third and latest claimant to the Holy See, to convene a council at Constance, the principal object of which was to be the restoration of Church unity. Yet, increasing unrest in Bohemia dictates that serious attention be paid to John Huss as well. Although he possessed a safe-conduct from Sigismund, Church officials took the Czech Reformer into custody upon his arrival at the Council. Here Háy picked up the story, dramatically presenting Constance as the scene of endless intrigue and worldly ambition, the meeting place of nobles, princes of the Church, Emperor, Pope, and Reformer. But the dramatist left no doubt that the remainder of the play would focus on Sigismund's dealings with Huss.

The Emperor's second wife Barbara has studied Huss's writings. Greatly impressed, she urges her husband to visit the scholarly and recalcitrant prisoner. The ensuing scene, the most important in the drama, opens as Huss and the doctor sent by Sigismund are talking. The Czech knows that his fate has been sealed, despite the physician's assurances that the Emperor will save him. "The Emperor is an Emperor," he says, "and an Emperor can as little be for Huss as a Czech peasant or burgher can be against Huss." Huss sees what Sigismund cannot see and what Háy wanted theatergoers to understand: not individual intentions, but the social identity of historical agents, determine events. Wherever Sigismund's personal sympathies lay, he had, in the end, to act in the interest of the ruling classes.[162]

When the Emperor enters the prison, he expresses regret that he cannot set Huss free. The Empress sympathizes even more, and tells the Czech that she wishes to help establish a mutual trust. To her surprise, Huss will have none of it. "I am a son of peasants from /the market village of/ Hussinecz," he says with pride. "I view the world from below. And seen from below, all rulers in world history are alike." Sigismund protests: "Don't you think that I am strong enough to accomplish what I wish?" Huss replies calmly: "I think you are strong enough never to wish anything that you cannot accomplish."[163]

At this point Huss begins to sound more and more like a modern social revolutionary. The Emperor had come, he says, because he sensed a threat from new and gathering forces. To stand in the way of those forces, he warns, is to invite greater violence and bloodshed. The Empress protests that she had read in his books about love for one's fellow men, but Huss answers back coolly that "love" that shrinks from bloodshed is an empty word. For Háy's purposes, it mattered little that Huss would not have said this. He knew that the Taborites, those most extreme of the Reformer's followers, were brutal and fanatical.

Genuinely moved by Huss's conviction and outspoken opposition to the medieval church, Sigismund believes that he and the Czech might become allies. Both men, the Empress adds convincingly, seek to end the unscrupulous rule of avaricious priests and witness the victory of burghers and peasants.

Warming to the idea, Sigismund suggests that Constantine saved the Roman Empire by making Christianity, the religion of a heretical minority, the state religion. Why could he not do the same by adopting Huss's faith?

But Huss steadfastly refuses to credit the idea of an alliance. Constantine's decision, he says, signaled the beginning of imperial decline. It could not have been otherwise, for all rulers, "good" and "bad," are finally alike. And because Sigismund is a ruler, he can never make common cause with the peasantry. Even if he were to save the Reformer's life, it would be no more than a temporary reprieve. Martyrdom alone could keep his name alive for those who would come after. In one of Háy's few major historical distortions, he has Huss dismiss any talk of hope for the afterlife: "True martyrdom rests on an unshakable belief in a communal life in the here and now on earth." As Sigismund turns to leave, Huss tells him again that he cannot and will not save him.[164]

The play's final scene opens in Prague, where nobles sympathetic to Huss have just arrived. They attempt to persuade the Hussites of Sigismund's sympathy. But John Žiška, the fearsome Taborite commander repeats what Huss had said—the Emperor dare not help them. The Empress enters, having been sent by her husband to obtain money from his brother, the Bohemian King Wenceslaus. She renounces her own and her husband's past and promises a new and revolutionary beginning. Žiška only sneers and tells her to return to Constance to call the poor to arms. With that, her hopes of an alliance with the Hussites end; the Hussite Wars are about to begin.

In Constance, Sigismund learns of the Hussite rebellion and quickly comes to terms with the nobility and the Cardinals and Bishops of the Church. He knows, at last, that his own fate depends upon their support; nothing else any longer matters. When, therefore, Cardinal Zarabella probes to find out his attitude regarding the prosecution of Huss, he says he has never raised any objection to the council's plans. "He /Huss/ was right," he sadly tells his wife. "I cannot save him and I will not be able to save him."[165] The tragedy is complete, at least if one is on the side of revolution.

God, Emperor and Peasant's opening night was a great success, but on the third evening youths claiming that they objected to Háy's portrayal of Pope John XXIII repeatedly interrupted. The playwright was skeptical. "Admittedly," he wrote years later, "my political outlook was simple and naive but . . . I found it hard to believe that young Christians should find anything to object to in the artistic representation of a medieval anti-pope whom the Church itself had rejected at the time."[166] The fourth evening, the protesters revealed themselves to be Nazis. Indeed, Germania, the official organ of the Catholic Center Party, conceded reluctantly that the play was faithful to history. Nevertheless, with pressure mounting, the government prohibited further performances on December 29. Háy considered himself to be the moral victor.

Lukács agreed. With God, Emperor and Peasant, he wrote enthusiastically, Háy had taken "a giant step away from a stage that was merely propagandistic toward genuine drama." He dramatized those great conflicts of historical forces that produce antagonistic and socially significant relationships between human beings. He portrayed Sigismund as the representative of the rising bourgeoisie, a man who wished to destroy the feudalistic power of nobles and clergy and to create a modern, centralized (bourgeois) state. But Huss and the specter of mass revolution forced the ruler to make his peace with the nobility, secular and spiritual. Herein lay not merely his, but German history's, tragedy. His betrayal of Huss, as Háy had emphasized, was inevitable for *historical*, rather than personal reasons.[167]

Lukács's analysis was astute, for that was surely the way Háy intended the drama to be understood. It is likely, in fact, that he hit upon the idea for the tragedy while thinking about the Hungarian Communist criticism of the *Ausgleich*: that it represented a devil's pact between the gentry (Hungary's substitute bourgeoisie) and the magnates to forestall plebeian revolution. The KPD's attacks on the Social Democrats as "social fascists" only reinforced the idea. The Socialists, fearing the Communists and the "people," allied themselves with members of the old ruling class—the Junkers, the military, and the capitalists.

Although all of this depended on revolutionary faith and a narrowly ideological interpretation of the past, Háy did handle the historical material with consummate dramatic skill. *God, Emperor and Peasant* towers above agitprop vulgarity and compares favorably with the best efforts of Brecht, whom Arthur Koestler rightly described as Háy's "only rival of comparable stature among playwrights of the European left."[168]

Brecht, naturally enough, disliked Háy's plays. And it was not long before he took up Lukács's challenge, even though he was not in the Hungarian's class when it came to theoretical rigor. Nor, of course, was the unfortunate Ottwalt, who, after collaborating with Brecht on the script for the Communist film *Kuhle Wampe*, emigrated in 1933. After sojourns in Denmark and Czechoslovakia, he settled in Moscow, where, after his arrest in 1936, he— like his friend Tretyakov—disappeared without a trace. Only after World War II did Soviet officials notify his wife that he had perished in 1943 as a slave laborer in Archangel.

It would be unjust to hold Lukács responsible for Ottwalt's unhappy fate. Nevertheless, his Berlin writings testify to his total allegiance to Stalin and the Soviet Union. True, he shared RAPP's literary views, but he also lent his name to the notion that Socialists were Social Fascists, and to outrageous untruths about life in the USSR. In a *Linkskurve* article on George Bernard Shaw's trip to Russia in 1931, for example, he praised the playwright for recognizing "that 'forced labor' and 'G.P.U. terror' are stupid and vile lies."[169]

Like so many Western intellectuals, Shaw was an easy mark. Lukács, on the other hand, was not naive and had experienced life in the Soviet Union. He knew the truth. Why then did he not protest? In part, no doubt, because of fear. But he also put theoretical reasons on display in an essay published in *Der Marxist*, MASCH's journal of ideas: "Goethe and the Dialectic."[170] In many ways, that pivotal essay summed up Lukács's conversion from idealism to materialism. In it, he identified the development of an idealist dialectic as the central theoretical problem of the classical, bourgeois, epoch of German philosophy and literature. The greatest German thinkers, he argued, concerned themselves above all with the resolution of contradictions. Some, like Kant— of the *Critique of Pure Reason*—were prepared to live in a world in which the antinomies defined the limits of human knowledge, but most attempted to discover a means of unification. Unfortunately, they sought unity in God or some transcendent sphere, leaving materialism of any sort behind.

Precisely here Goethe became relevant, for because of his interest in natural philosophy he was attracted to pantheism and thus reopened the way to materialism. And that was true not only of his scientific work, but of his literary achievement as well. "In a literary sense, Goethe advocated—with occasional waverings—a realistic line. He wanted thus to keep at a distance the claims of literary idealism (Schiller, Romanticism)." That, according to Lukács, was to the good, even though Goethe stopped short of a thoroughgoing materialism. He came at last to occupy middle ground between naturalism and idealism. Philosophically, to be sure, he gravitated toward the late Kant (of the *Critique of Judgment*) and Schelling; yet his instinct for a materialistically colored empiricism and his determination to remain close to primal phenomena prevented him from succumbing completely to the idealist seduction.

But what of Goethe's relationship to Hegel, the greatest of bourgeois thinkers? On the one hand, Lukács maintained, the author of *Faust* was more materialistic than the philosopher; on the other, he never appreciated the full significance of Hegel's dialectic. In a real sense, then, Goethe and Hegel had come to represent for Lukács Marxism's two fundamental aspects—materialism and dialectics.

Of the two, dialectics was still more important. Goethe, Lukács pointed out, rejected the French Revolution. Hence, for him Napoleon was the Revolution's conqueror, not its *heir*. Hegel, on the other hand, regarded the Revolution as a necessary moment in history's development. And so was the heir of the Revolution—Napoleon. That at least was what Lukács argued two years later: "The world historical significance of Hegel's accommodation consists precisely in the fact that he grasped . . . the revolutionary development of the bourgeoisie as a unitary process, one in which the revolutionary Terror as well as Thermidor and Napoleon were only necessary phases."[171]

By the early 1930s Lukács had cast himself consciously in the role of the new Hegel, for like the German philosopher he lived in an age of revolution. And just as the French Revolution and the "bourgeois-revolutionary" philosophy of the Enlightenment exerted a decisive influence on Hegel, so the Russian Revolution and the proletarian-revolutionary philosophy of Marx changed his life. It was natural for him, therefore, to compare the postwar counterrevolution with the French Thermidor. And if a new Napoleon—Joseph Stalin—had consolidated his power in the home of the revolution, Lukács was prepared, as Hegel had been, to reconcile himself to tyranny. For him, Stalinism was a necessary moment in the actualization of the bolshevik revolution.

On April 23, 1932, the Central Committee of the CPSU liquidated RAPP, in part because its leaders resisted the Party's determination to use literature as an instrument of propaganda for the Five-Year Plan. Five years later, the Soviet government launched a concerted attack on the RAPP leaders, including Averbakh, whose brother-in-law Gemrikh Yagoda, former head of the G.P.U., was executed the following year. The charges—that Averbakh and his colleagues were "Trotskyites" and "traitors"—were ridiculous. Nevertheless, the RAPP leader paid for his "crimes" with his life. Writing in 1943 Alexei Tolstoi wrote an epitaph—Soviet style—for RAPP: "In the activity of RAPP there was (in addition to ignorance and Russian nihilism) the direct work of fascist agents who had crept into literature."[172] Not to be outdone, Lukács subsequently (1941; 1957) claimed that he had "always stood in opposition" to RAPP and had participated in the struggle against its tenets.[173]

In January 1933, Hindenburg appointed Hitler Chancellor of Germany and, two weeks after the Reichstag fire of February 27, Lukács returned to the Soviet Union by way of Prague. About a year into his second, and far longer, sojourn there, he spoke to the Philosophical Institute of the Communist Academy concerning "The Significance of *Materialism and Empirio-Criticism* in the Bolshevizing of the Communist Parties." That important address was on the one hand an exercise in self-criticism and a public submission to Party discipline; on the other hand, it summed up Lukács's philosophic allegiance to dialectical materialism as Engels and Lenin understood and propagated it. He was never to waver in that allegiance because for him idealism and materialism were no longer simply epistemologies or general philosophical standpoints; they were ideological expressions of the only alternatives remaining to mankind: fascism and bolshevism. *Tertium non datur.*

Lukács announced the principal thesis of his address in his opening sentences: *Materialism and Empirio-Criticism* was not merely a critique of Ernst Mach's peculiar formulation of idealism but an attack on idealism *tout court.* Lenin's genius was to have sensed even before the war that idealism, as the philosophy of the imperialist bourgeoisie, was steadily becoming what it had always been in essence: the ideology of fascism. Just as he did years later in *The Destruction of Reason*, Lukács identified without exception *all* those who rejected materialism as precursors of Nazi "philosophers" such as Alfred Bäumler and Alfred Rosenberg.[174]

Operating with that sole criterion, Lukács exonerated very few thinkers. In fact, his roster of the guilty reads like a who's who of late nineteenth-century intellectual history: Mach, Dilthey, Rickert, Simmel, Bergson, Nietzsche. Nor did Lukács miss the opportunity to castigate Social Democrats; he denounced Max and Friedrich Adler, Siegfried Marck, and Eduard Bernstein, as well as those whom he described as "Western Communists"—Anton Pannekoek, Hermann Gorter, Ruth Fischer, and Karl Korsch. Despite their many and obvious differences, all, Lukács insisted, had committed the sin of idealism.

And so had he. Idealist philosophies, he confessed, had determined his own youthful intellectual career. To his everlasting shame, he had been a student of Simmel and Weber, a defender of the *Geisteswissenschaften*, and a disciple of Sorel. As a Party neophyte he had written *History and Class Consciousness*, a "philosophical summing up" of those several influences. In that heretical volume, he had unintentionally given aid to the enemy by waging war on the reflection theory of knowledge and the dialectic of nature. Only after immersing himself in Party work and reading Lenin and Stalin had he begun to free himself from idealism's shackles. At last, during his 1929–31 stay in the Soviet Union, he completed his education, thanks to the "philosophical argument" between Stalin (the Leninist) and Deborin (the Plekhanovite).[175]

In 1934, Soviet Russia was a dangerous place, not least for foreign Communists. Many, including Hungarians, disappeared without a trace. Lukács was not indifferent to his fate. Nevertheless, it would be a mistake to treat his recantation as though it constituted nothing more than a cowardly capitulation. Lukács believed every word he uttered, not only in 1934 but until the end of his days.[176] He had become an orthodox Leninist and a defender of dialectical materialism, in part because he was the kind of man for whom commitment to a faith entailed strict obedience and total submission, in part because he had come to believe that German thought (idealism) in the age of the declining bourgeoisie was necessarily decadent and had helped to prepare the way for Nazism.

Those whom Lukács had once revered now stood condemned as pseudo–John the Baptists for an anti-Christ who was both anti-Communist and anti-Semitic. He himself, insofar as he had shared their weakness for idealism was anything but innocent. Because of what Lenin would have termed its subterranean idealism, *History and Class Consciousness* had played a role, however small, in preparing a fertile soil for Nazi propaganda. Thus, just as he sought throughout his mature life to redeem himself for having driven his first love, Irma Seidler, to suicide, so he struggled from 1933 on to make good his imagined complicity in Hitler's success. Indeed, the burden of guilt that he continued to bear was the inverse side of his unswerving fidelity to Lenin, dialectical materialism, and the Communist party.

TWO

BÉLA BALÁZS:

THE ROAD TO THE PARTY

Vienna: Literary Communism

"I KNOW that we are headed for a better life," Anna Schlamadinger Balázs remarked, with forced conviction, on her and her new husband's way into exile.[1] It was November 1919 and she and Balázs huddled together on board a Danube steamer making its way from Budapest to Vienna. Sporting a false mustache, sideburns, and a pince-nez, Balázs carried his brother Ervin's identification papers and money he had received from Júlia Láng. Before fleeing to Austria, Béla Kun had entrusted friendly non-Communists, including Láng, with funds to aid comrades in need.

The nervewracking trip passed without incident, and as soon as the Balázses reached safety, they were joined by Edith Hajós, Balázs's ex-wife, who arrived from Soviet Russia to lend a hand. Balázs, who was nothing if not catholic in his attentions, was so overcome with emotion that he expressed his readiness to remarry her—without ending his recently contracted marriage to Anna. Edith, however, was eager to return to her Russian lover, and as the Balázses settled in Reichenau near Vienna, she prepared to leave.

Balázs knew that his status as a revolutionary in exile was a precarious one. That is why he moved to Reichenau and maintained his distance from Lukács, who was well known to the Austrian authorities, and why he chose to eschew everyday politics. To be sure, he sympathized with Landler's Vienna-based faction, but he was not particularly disappointed when the Party rejected his application for membership. In part that was because he believed he could accomplish more by writing as an "independent" for "bourgeois" journals; but he also knew that Lukács opposed his candidacy on the grounds that he was incapable of total commitment. Nevertheless, he paid Party dues and considered himself to be a communist. In fact, he looked forward to the prospect of serving his "religion"—as he preferred to call it—as a writer. That he did, although it was to be some time before he disentangled his dedication from his pressing need to earn a living and his ambition to achieve a literary success on a European scale.

There was something exhilarating and liberating about entering the world of German culture, and Balázs was more fortunate than some of his fellow exiles because he could write in German without difficulty. He was therefore eager to establish contacts with German-language publishers and journal editors, not only in the hope of publishing in German some of his recent Hungarian work, but also with an eye toward securing a steady income from occasional pieces. Anna secured a secretarial position at *Bécsi Magyar Újság*, but her salary was not nearly enough to support them. In a gesture of goodwill, Lukács wrote to Martin Buber, asking that he help introduce Balázs around German literary circles.[2] Fogarasi, who had gone on to Berlin to accept an editorial position at *Die Rote Fahne*, invited him to submit articles.

On his own initiative, Balázs befriended the working-class novelist Leonhard Frank and, more important, Robert Musil, who did what he could to help. He also met Helene Weigel, the actress who later married Bertolt Brecht, and Hanns Eisler, the leftist composer who had studied with Schönberg. And in 1922, he began to attend and take an active part in meetings of the Vienna branch of the *Clarté* movement. He had, to be sure, never read a single work by Henri Barbusse or Romain Rolland, the Paris-based group's leading lights, but he approved of *Clarté*'s pro-Communist internationalism. Just as important, he saw it as a place to make valuable contacts with likeminded intellectuals.

Nor did Balázs ignore the Hungarian Communists. On the contrary, he lectured often to emigré groups; in the fall of 1920, for example, he held a weekly seminar on Ady for Hungarian workers. Moreover, he published widely in journals in Vienna and elsewhere in East Central Europe: *Bécsi Magyar Újság*, *Új Világ* (*New World*), *Tűz* (*Fire*), *Kassai Munkás* (*Kassa Worker*), *Diogenes*, and others. Like most Hungarian intellectuals living in and around Vienna, he frequented coffeehouses, where he exchanged ideas about literature, art, and politics. He was particularly fond of the Stöckl, a den of rumor and intrigue where Hungarians and other exiles gathered regularly. There he went almost daily to agitate on behalf of communism's "literary politics."[3]

Despite this feverish activity and a commitment to internationalism, however, Balázs did not feel at home. "It is true," he confided to his diary, "that I proclaimed the synthesis of the nations, the European man. . . . It is true that I always felt my deepest metaphysical roots to be beyond *every* race and nation and I knew myself to be a wanderer, solitary. . . . It is true that according to my biological lineage, I am a Jew; thus, there is no more Turanian blood in me than there was in Sándor Petőfi. . . .[4] And yet, what hurts? Why *do I feel* myself to be an exile?"[5]

During that first melancholy Christmas in Austria, Balázs wrote a poetic song of exile that expressed the spiritual pain he was experiencing. "Don't look back my poor friend," he began, "We have already crossed seven frontiers/Mist before us, mist behind us/Who knows where we are headed."[6] As the poem suggested, exile deepened Balázs's loneliness and his longing for a community of souls. We have seen that longing manifested during the first days of war in 1914, but his sense of alienation reached back to his youth in the southern city of Szeged. Not only did his father die at an early age, but the young Balázs (then Herbert Bauer) was acutely conscious of being Jewish; all the more so because of his burning ambition to be accepted by the Hungarian people. That, certainly, was one reason he adopted the nom de plume "Béla Balázs." Even late in life, he remembered his desire and early sorrow: "That I was excluded from one community without belonging to another, that in my early childhood I stood outside of every denomination and every community as an isolated, lonely individual, this determined my conduct and my fate throughout my entire life."[7]

Almost as early, Balázs regarded the problematic relationship between men and women as emblematic of the alienation that defined the human condition. That too was a consequence of personal experience. Meeting a woman always stirred in him a mixture of fantasy, desire, hope, and philosophic reflection. The women he encountered obviously sensed and were excited by that response, for most found him to be irresistible. And yet, no matter how many sexual conquests he made—and they were many indeed—he never experienced the intimacy of soul, the oneness, for which he longed. Thus he continued the search in exile. Almost as soon as he arrived in Vienna, a friend introduced him to the Danish novelist/playwright Karin Michaelis, and he quickly added her name to his list of lovers. But to his genuine surprise and consternation, jealousy immediately raised its head; the unusually "understanding" Anna threatened to leave him to join Edith in Russia. Shaken by the prospect of losing her, Balázs arranged to spend a week with Karin, after which he resolved to end the affair.

It was during that farewell week that Karin suggested that they combine their talents to write a novel about a woman who "borrows" another's husband for a period of a month. The lovers would keep diaries about their brief and unconventional life together. When they emerged at the end of the week, Balázs and Michaelis plunged into the work with enthusiasm, often writing for as long as fourteen hours at a stretch. By the time they finished, Karin had satisfied herself that she had poured her very life into it. Balázs regarded it as a fitting monument to his many lovers, "a document of guilt feelings and hortatory admonitions."[8] *Beyond the Body: The Diary of a Man and a Woman* appeared in Hungarian in 1920.

In that book, Balázs placed the emphasis on a meeting of souls "beyond the body."[9] And not for reasons of discretion; he had discovered sex to be a pleasurable and necessary pastime, but one quite irrelevant to the soul's effort to unite with another. His body seemed completely soulless. "My spiritual life," he wrote in his diary, "is autonomous, isolated from my erotic life. I, the most sensuous of men, regulate my life purely in accord with the pull of spiritual attractions, which have nothing to do with my sexuality."[10] The purpose of life was not to compile the longest list of female conquests, but to create a world in which one's soul felt at home with itself and others. Precisely there was where communism came in. It was not, for Balázs, a sociological method or a political agenda, but a means by which the soul would finally be set free and human alienation be overcome. It was, that is, the modern world's religion. To his old friend Anna Lesznai, he wrote in 1921: "Everything depends on our spiritualizing communism into a religion. That is our mission. There are so many today with hungry hearts; more than ever before."[11]

In order to carry out that mission, Balázs hoped to articulate a literary vision of a new and more perfect reality—a vision of utopia. The transforming power of such a vision was to contribute to the making of a transpolitical and "indirect" revolution. There existed, he told one audience, utopian visions more authentically "real" than mere empirical reality. That which most men thought of as reality was in fact an unnatural state of loneliness and alienation, so much so that those who could see with the soul's eyes often *chose* a life of extreme isolation as a gesture of rebellion and faith. Out of the most profound depths of alienation they hoped to discover the way to a new beginning.[12]

Balázs regarded this loneliness, whether self-imposed or not, as the essence of the tragic drama. That is why, as a young man, he had written a number of tragedies as well as a theoretical work with the arresting title *Death Aesthetics*. The artist, he claimed in that work, was distinguished by his ability to penetrate behind the world of appearances and to catch sight of *the* life, "the *Ding an sich* life." Art was consciousness of noumenal life, but that consciousness was possible only because of man's finitude, his knowledge that his *phenomenal* life would end. "If we were immortal, we would not know that we were alive. In that case, neither the concept nor even the beautiful word 'life' would be conceivable. Only through death is the consciousness of life possible. Death makes it possible for us to recognize life as a wonderful event. '*Der Tod ist der Musaget der Philosophie*,' Schopenhauer says. We can only catch sight of that which has boundaries."[13] By setting boundaries to life, death directed attention away from quotidian existence toward noumenal (essential) life, life as *formed*.

If art was that consciousness of essential life made possible by human finitude, the crown of art, Balázs went on to say, was tragedy, in which life was given form not only by death but by fate as well.[14] By excluding what was merely accidental, fate focused attention on what was essential. In *The Theory of the Drama* (1922), Balázs advanced a similar argument. Tragedy was the most perfect literary genre and human finitude the essence of man's tragic destiny. Now, however, he added an unexpected, and hopeful, twist. Death, he now believed, was not merely the boundary of life, but the *frontier* beyond which lay some form of transcendence. Tragedy and loneliness were characteristic only of *empirical* life; behind every death, "we—tragedy's Dionysian chorus—hear the music of a victorious eternal reality, the *still* living life."[15]

This interest in drama as the playing out of human alienation had first attracted Balázs to Dostoevski, whose novels possessed a dramatic structure.

Taking his cue from the young Lukács, he believed that in the great Russian's work "naked souls" met beyond alienating social identity. Dostoevski was thus a utopian, the prophet of a new world. Whatever his reactionary political views might have been, Balázs wrote in exile, Dostoevski unveiled for his readers a "profound reality" that could not be discerned merely by observing the surface of everyday life. He shocked many of his readers only because modern men and women were so blind to true reality that they regarded it as something fantastic.[16]

Balázs resolved to continue working in the Dostoevskian tradition, not, in the first instance, as a novelist of ideas, but as a creator of fairy tales "dense with reality." Those fables would be utopian in essence, would transport men and women from the given to a new world. "It is no accident that I am a fabulist," he told his diary. "My truth is not yet reality. Claudel is also isolated from reality, his similes and images create his peculiar atmosphere. They sever every one of his characters and every one of his words from contemporary reality—but not from the eternal reality!"[17]

We have already seen that Balázs was the leading exponent of fairy tales for children—and adults for that matter—during the Hungarian Soviet Republic's brief existence. The world of fairy tales, he had written then, "is more communist than our communism." Thus it was that he was intrigued when, early in 1922, his friend and patron Genia Schwarzwald brought him twenty grotesque water colors painted in an affected Chinese style. The artist, Mariette Lydis, was a Greek heiress who had already located a publisher, but who needed an accompanying text in the form of matching fables. In order to produce the book by Christmas, the publisher asked to have the stories in hand within three weeks. After some financial haggling, Balázs accepted the assignment and, having perused a volume of Chinese fables to get a feel for the "jargon," set to work. The result was The Mantle of Dreams (1922).

Although he wrote under pressure of time, Balázs produced sixteen fables to accompany Lydis's drawings. Not surprisingly, he stuck to his favorite theme—human alienation. In the title story,[18] he told of the Emperor Ming-Huang and his beautiful wife Näi-Fe. The Empress possessed a soul that sustained itself on dreams; even in her husband's arms, therefore, her soul was far distant. One night she dreamed that the Emperor was wearing a magnificent coat on which someone had embroidered the images of her dreams. When she awoke, she told her husband that he must wear such a coat or else forfeit her love. But that was not all. When he wore the coat, Näi-Fe's soul longed for the Emperor in such a way that she and he were truly one, so much so that physical union could only break the spell. Without the coat, the Emperor could enjoy his wife's body, but could never touch her soul. Preferring a chaste but profound union, Ming-Huang wore the mantle of dreams from thence forth.

In "The Parasols,"[19] Balázs expressed again his utopian longing to unite his soul with that of another. Yang-Tsu is a peddler who envies the rich and quarrels with his wife to such an extent that they are alienated from each other. She blames the heat of the sun for her husband's fierce anger and suggests that he purchase a parasol. He agrees and in due course encounters a man who sells parasols, on the underside of which are painted various skies. After trying many of these beautiful parasols, Yang-Tsu opens one with an autumn evening sky, across which wild geese fly. Immediately his heart is gripped by "a longing for an unknown, unreachable distant place." Once again he passes through the streets, observing the splendors of the world, but no longer do they agitate his soul, for his gaze follows the wild geese to the far places of the imagination. When he returns home, he and his wife are at peace with each other, their souls united in a common longing for a better world.

In the final fable, "The Victor,"[20] Balázs told the story of a warrior, Du-Dsi-Tsun, who pines for the warm love of a woman. On learning that the King plans to give his three daughters in marriage to the victors in three tests of strength, he hastens to the court. Three times he engages in combat and three times he is victorious. But after each conquest, the daughter in question gives herself to the defeated, whose *soul* is in greater need. Cursing his physical prowess, Du-Dsi-Tsun hangs himself.

In these fables, Balázs suggested that men could only unite with women in the utopian world of dreams and longing. He was careful to show that sexual union was not only not enough, but that it actually stood in the way of a union of souls. That explains why several tales revolve around friendship. Friends of the same sex could achieve a meeting of souls precisely because they were not sexual partners. In "The Opium Smokers,"[21] for example, two friends—Hu-Fu and Tschen-Hu—are deaf and dumb; they lack the bridge of words and yet desire to be one. One day they happen upon some money and enter an opium den where they seek and find each other in the garden of dreams. "For there, no words are needed." Soon their identity is complete: "Hu-Fu became Tschen-Hu and Tschen-Hu became Hu-Fu." At last, they knew unspeakable happiness. Clearly, Balázs had begun to explore the possibility that language stood in the way of a more immediate communication between souls.

Much of this was lost on Balázs's readers, most of whom were content simply to marvel at his creativity. That certainly was true of Thomas Mann, who gave the book a glowing review in the *Neue Freie Presse*.[22] Mann, to whom Lukács had introduced Balázs's work, expressed his amazement at the Hungarian's ability to invent fables on the spur of the moment. And to do so with poetic skill and metaphysical insight. He concluded by urging readers to experience for themselves the book's rare beauty—high praise from Germany's greatest writer. Small wonder, then, that Balázs noted with pride the electrifying effect the review had on the Hungarians who frequented the Stöckl coffeehouse.[23]

Still, Balázs was after more than critical success and he returned once again to the alienation theme in a little book entitled *The Fantasy Guidebook: A Baedeker of the Soul for Summer Travelers* (1925). Here he took up the great symbol of his early work: the wanderer. Years before, he had chosen *The Wan-derer Sings* as the title of his first collection of verse, the burden of which, Lukács argued at the time, was the "tragedy of love," the inability of men and women to reach out to one another.[24] He had also made a wanderer of the protagonist of his first tragic drama, *Doctor Margit Szélpál*, the story of a village girl who wins her doctorate in Berlin only to discover that she is no longer at home anywhere. In the end, she leaves her uneducated husband *and* her profession to roam the world.

Balázs did not return to the wanderer symbol in his *Baedeker* merely for literary effect. If he was no longer resigned to the tragedy of alienation, he still saw himself as a wandering soul searching for a home in a utopian world to come. Thus, he spoke from the heart when he wrote that homesickness was "the deepest and sweetest of all experiences." It was itself a kind of home.[25] And in the series of Neo-Romantic reflections that make up the book, he focused on a number of experiences that human beings often take for granted: nights in a train, morning in bed, the stillness of the forest, the peculiar society of semi-naked people at a swimming pool.

Concerning the latter, Balázs mused that in the society of the dressed, people were closely identified with their class, as it was reflected in the clothes they wore. At the pool, however, they were more truly themselves because semi-nakedness forced them to set aside the soul's masks. It followed, accord-ing to Balázs, that those for whom "summer acquaintanceships" were fleeting and unimportant, because socially inconsequential, were victims and uphold-ers of the alienated bourgeois order. "For this group of people, a person's sig-nificance was defined only by his social position and nothing more."[26]

Balázs reserved his praise for those whose most decisive relationships were formed during summer travels—that is to say, were fleeting. They looked for-ward to making new friends and encountering new lovers on holiday because they knew that they would be men and women stripped of their accidental qualities. It was a provocative and interesting claim, though one might re-spond that the meeting—sexual or platonic—of strangers is inauthentic pre-cisely because selfhood depends upon knowledge of the past, including one's experience in society. Not knowing each other's pasts, strangers can never truly meet as human beings.

Be that as it may, Balázs attempted to identify those things that brought human beings together. Central to that project was his meditation on silence, which, he argued, united men in ways that sound could not, because "there are innumerable sounds, but only one silence." While some sounds seemed strange, humans recognized every silence; indeed, silence awakened in them memories of past silences and reminded them that they shared something precious with all others—past, present, and future. "If you hear silence in a forest, it is the same silence that others hear in other forests or on lonely summits. Thus you are all united, one with another."[27]

The idea that informed Balázs's *Baedeker*, then, was classically Neo-Platonic and Romantic: there exists a primal unity behind divided appearances and that unity must be recaptured in its plentitude. "All evil and wickedness is isolating," Novalis once wrote, "it is the principle of separation."[28] Balázs believed that to be true and he was therefore intent on creating in men and women a desire for those things that separate them least. Thus, just as he preferred silence to noise, so he elevated night above day. As the sun sinks, things shed their peculiar masks and begin to recognize that "they are all brothers and sisters of one substance."[29]

Balázs gave fullest expression to his longing for reunion with others and with his essential self in his meditation on "Recollection." There he described the experience of wandering through fields outside the city. Although, he wrote, he had set out without any destination in mind, he suddenly felt that he had arrived, that he was at home. In a symbolic sense, he had come to himself and he felt as though he were the first man on the first day in human history; "and the primal beginning reflects the final end." He might better have said that the return to the primal beginning *was* the final end. Nature had remained the same, while time, which had covered up the truth, suddenly became as transparent as a mountain lake. Human beings, Balázs meant to say, must finally see through history to nature, but first they must follow its only partially charted course. "Travel and wandering," that is, "are allegories of human destiny in general."[30]

Balázs's conviction that communism would lead men back to their true nature and resolve the problem of alienation was reinforced by the discussions he participated in at the reorganized Sunday Circle and by the example of other Communists. He was particularly moved when the government in Budapest hanged Ottó Korvin. In a memorial poem, he praised Korvin as a hero whose life would inspire future struggles.[31] Nor had he ceased to learn from Lukács, despite a growing, and mutual, personal coolness that had its roots in the past. It was after an affair with Balázs that Irma Seidler had committed suicide in 1911, and Lukács never forgot or forgave his intellectual ally.[32]

Nevertheless, because it focused on the problem of alienation, or reification, Balázs recommended *History and Class Consciousness* in connection with the important essay that he published in 1923 under the title "On Lyric Sensibility." There he took up the question of the loneliness that characterized modern lyric poetry. In the Middle Ages the alienation of the soul, or subject, from nature, its true object, was mitigated by the fact that the former believed it had a home in heaven. Thus, it was only with the decline of the religious world view and the development of capitalist society that the individualistic consciousness (the lonely soul) made its historic appearance; and with it, the poetics of loneliness.[33]

That modern sensibility could be traced to Rousseau, the quintessential outsider. He and the Romantics who followed him rose up in revolt against soulless, reified society and sought to reestablish contact with nature, which henceforth became the *symbol* of utopia, a new—long lost—home. "The soul's home is elsewhere. This is the basic formula of Romanticism."[34] In attempting to envision this natural home, the Romantics projected in their poetry lands of dreams, golden ages, fairy lands, and sometimes an imaginary East. Their visions, based as they were on a longing for true, as opposed to alienated second, nature, were therefore closer to them than any distant heaven; but the Romantics did not discover the road that would lead back to nature.

With Goethe, Balázs continued, came the modern turn toward an extreme subjectivity. The German genius did not regard nature as a nearby utopian land, but took it to be identical with himself. One might think then that he had ended loneliness by making the soul and nature, subject and object, one. But the problem, Balázs wrote, was that there were two ways in which the soul could become one with nature; either it could become its own, unreified, nature—or nature could become it. Goethe chose the latter course and swallowed nature up into his reified soul. If there was no longer a dualism of subject and object, that was only because there was no object: "*the soul now stood completely alone, because it no longer recognized an independently living, objective reality.*"[35]

At that point in his argument, Balázs chose to settle accounts with Kassák and avant-garde modernism. The difficulty, as he saw it, was that avant-garde poets such as Kassák, Whitman, Cendrars, and Marinetti were Goethe's decadent heirs. They had lost all sense of objective reality and, along with avant-garde painters, contrived to bring modern culture to its reified, subjective end—an idea suggested to him by Viennese culture. Gone were the common themes that medieval faith and Renaissance culture had made available to art. Instead, futurists, expressionists, dadaists, and activists offered meaningless collections of words for purely acoustic effect. "This art refuses to recognize not only a common reality, but even common concepts and a common language. Here every bridge from person to person has been destroyed."[36] Lacking any objective reality, the subject was not merely lonely, it was nothing—a pure nihilism.

Balázs concluded by considering how it was that the true poet's words could point to something that lay beyond language. How could a poet name something that had not yet come into existence? How could he or she put the ineffable into words? The answer, he wrote, was that the poet had to make the reader *hear* what was not said specifically. It thus fell to the reader to complete the communication, thereby making the reading of a poem a cooperative, *social* endeavor. Language, Balázs suggested, was less reliable than silence as a means of human communication. By the time he had revised this essay—he had written an earlier draft in 1917—Balázs had begun to evince an interest in the silent film, both as a new form of art and as a means by which communism's alleged struggle to end alienation might be lent significant support.

Vienna: Visual Communism

Balázs's entry into the film world came almost by accident. As a habitué of the Café Filmhof, he often joined the company of Hungarian filmmakers and actors who, like him, had fled the counterrevolution. Among those able and ambitious men were several destined to achieve international recognition: Alexander Korda (b. Sándor Kellner), Michael Curtiz (b. Mihály Kertész), Lajos Biró, and Béla Lugosi (b. Béla Blaskó). Curtiz and Korda, in particular, had been prime movers in the promising Hungarian film industry. The former obtained his start as a stage actor and directed the first Hungarian film, *Today and Tomorrow*, in 1912. The following year he traveled to Denmark to study Danish filmmaking and may well have been instrumental in arranging the visit to Budapest of the celebrated actress Asta Nielsen and her director husband Urban Gad. Curtiz went on to make thirty-seven more films in his homeland before signing a contract that took him to Vienna in the spring of 1918.[37]

Even more important that Curtiz was the flamboyant Sándor Korda. The son of a retired sergeant of the hussars, Korda arrived in the Hungarian capital in 1908 and, with help from a friend, landed a job in the editorial offices of *Független Magyarország* (*Independent Hungary*), a liberal daily. After he began to publish stories and articles, he met Biró, a writer connected with Jászi and with Mór Ungerleider, cofounder of Projectograph, the first Hungarian motion picture company. Ungerleider hired Korda to oversee publicity for the company, a position that left him sufficient time to launch Hungary's first film journal, the weekly *Pesti Mozi* (*Budapest Cinema*), in 1912.[38]

Almost intuitively, Korda recognized that he could win fame and fortune in the fledgling industry. When the war began in 1914 and the incoming flow of foreign films all but halted, the actor Gyula Zilahy engaged the dynamic young man to help him direct Hungarian films. So successful was he that the enterprising Jenő Janovics hired him to assume direction of the Corvin Studio in Kolozsvár. The following year, 1917, Korda and a friend bought Janovics out and moved Corvin to Budapest; by the time the war ended, he had nineteen films to his credit and was editor of *Mozihét* (*Cinema Week*).

At that time, Korda held vaguely leftist views, but he was more interested in his own prospects than in ideological causes. He sided, for example, with the Károlyi government in its effort to nationalize the film industry, but only because the democratic Count was determined to break the stranglehold that distributors then had on producers. Like many non-Communist intellectuals, Korda later served the Soviet Republic, heading up the film directory's department of film production. Three films that he directed were released during the months that Kun retained power.

Due to that work and his Jewish birth, Korda was briefly detained after the revolutionary government collapsed and, fearing a worse fate, he emigrated to

Vienna in the autumn of 1919. There, quite brazenly in view of the fact that he had little hard currency, he checked into a luxurious hotel and sat back, waiting for something to develop. Such chutzpah did not go unrewarded, for before long Count Alexander Kolowrat-Krokowsky, an Austrian nobleman interested in film, contacted him. Together these unlikely partners planned Korda's first German film, *Seine Majestät das Bettelkind*. Once more, the Hungarian was off and running.[39]

Korda knew that sooner or later he would have to go on to Berlin, the hub of the German film world. But before leaving Vienna in January 1923, he approached Balázs about the possibility of artistic collaboration. Brimming with enthusiasm, the latter dashed off two scenarios. Nothing came of them, however, because Balázs had displayed something less than full appreciation for Mrs. Korda's talents as an actress. Nevertheless, his efforts had not been utterly in vain. He deepened his understanding of film technique and of direction. At the same time, he concluded that there was big money to be made. It was unthinkable, he told his diary, that his talent should be wasted. "I want to prepare the great mass drama of the future. This is my mission!"[40]

In fact, Balázs had already achieved a measure of success as a film script writer. Early in 1922, Karl Polányi introduced him to Egon Szécsi, a Hungarian who was looking for someone to rewrite an existing scenario about the deposed Habsburg Emperor Karl's abortive effort to reclaim the Hungarian throne from Regent Horthy the previous year. Szécsi wanted the job done within twenty-four hours, and offered a substantial fee. Balázs accepted the challenge and wrote "Habsburg's Fortune and Fall." He helped direct the film, although he was not able to exercise decisive artistic control. Indeed, he had twice to rework the script and to endure Hans Otto Löwenstein's insensitive direction.[41] He scarcely recognized his work when Löwenstein finally released the film under the title *Emperor Karl*.

Despite that disillusioning experience, Balázs was quick to accept another assignment from Löwenstein because he continued to think of film work primarily as a means to earn a good bit of money without having to invest much time. Löwenstein released this film in July 1922 under the title *The Stranger from Russia*, and once again Balázs thought the job completely "botched." That fall he wrote another script for Löwenstein and one for the production firm "Sun-Film," but neither was filmed. During his last three years in Vienna, 1923–26, he authored, or coauthored, two other scenarios, one of which— *Modern Marriages*—Löwenstein directed and released. According to one reviewer, the film depicted "the sometimes secret, sometimes open, sometimes imperceptible, sometimes fierce battle of the sexes within legitimate boundaries."[42]

But if Balázs produced relatively few scenarios in the Austrian capital, he wrote a substantial number of film reviews and articles. At first he contributed pieces to *Bécsi Magyar Újság* and *Die Rote Fahne*, but toward the end of 1922, he had a stroke of good luck: He became the regular film critic for Der Tag, a new Viennese newspaper that the banker and speculator Sigmund Bosel launched on November 25. Although Bosel's interests were primarily economic, he permitted his editors, Maximilian Schreier and Josef Koller, to adopt a left-liberal political stance and recruit as many talented writers as possible. Soon Der Tag was publishing work by such established figures as Alfred Polgar, Max Brod, and Robert Musil.

According to Anna Balázs, the editors informed her husband that they would hire him as a regular contributor if he could come up with an original idea. He immediately suggested that he establish a column devoted to film. The editors liked the idea and Balázs published his first "Film Reporter" article on December 1. In it, he wondered out loud why, until then, there had been no such column in Vienna. After all, he observed, "the cinema has become the art, poetry, the imagination of the people." He pointed out that there were 180 movie theaters in the city, each with a seating capacity of some 450. If these houses were three-quarters filled during each of three performances, close to two hundred thousand Viennese saw a movie every day. Without doubt, the cinema had become "for urban populations throughout the world what folk songs and folk tales once were."[43]

The implications, according to Balázs, were staggering. In a passage worthy of Marshall McLuhan, he compared the birth of the new art with the invention of the printing press. Books had once replaced medieval cathedrals as the bearers of the folk spirit. "From a visible spirit there came to be a legible spirit, from a visual culture an abstract culture." That abstract, verbal culture transformed society. In the twentieth century once again, a machine, the cinematograph, was bringing new spiritual forms into play. Men and women were beginning to relearn a language long forgotten—the international language of mimic expression. Behind that language lay a spirit and a sensibility that had been stifled for far too long. "Do we," he concluded rhetorically, "stand at the beginning of a new visual culture?"[44]

Balázs was not, to be sure, the first writer to take films seriously. The American poet Vachel Lindsay devoted a not very penetrating study of 1915 to "the art of the moving pictures" and the Kantian philosopher Hugo Munsterberg published The Photoplay: A Psychological Study in 1916. Nevertheless, Balázs was the first to work out a fully developed theory of the new art, despite the fact that he could not always see epoch-making films in Vienna's rather provincial theaters. He did view D. W. Griffith's Intolerance early in 1923, but he saw The Birth of a Nation—which he denounced because of Griffith's depiction of Blacks—only in 1925. Moreover, he was constantly exasperated by the fact that censors and theater managers often edited films—badly.

The films that Balázs did view, he judged strictly in accord with his evolving theory. From the first, he focused attention on actors such as Asta Nielsen, Emil Jannings, and, especially, Charlie Chaplin, with whom he empathized as "a singular wanderer among strange people, lonely and misunderstood."[45] All, he believed, revealed their souls to filmgoers. Asta Nielsen's eroticism, he wrote, was so filled with her soul that one could "see" it at work even though she was fully dressed. Jannings could communicate more about his spiritual state with facial expressions than good writers could with hundreds of words. Chaplin filled the things of the world with his life's blood; his relationship to them was never one of mere observation but of identification.[46] Balázs was convinced, that is, that the silent film provided those great artists with an opportunity to unite soul and body in a way that verbal abstractions made impossible.

That was true because the soul could more easily fill the body than it could words. In part that was due to the fact that words came to us with their meanings ready made; they could not, therefore, express *particular* feelings with any exactitude. Facial expression, on the other hand, was inexhaustible and concrete. The face was a transparent mask through which we could make out something hidden—a *natural* physiognomy. In the changing distance between that hidden face and its mask we could define a person's character and measure his or her self-alienation. But that was not all. Beneath the true, natural face we could sometimes catch sight of the soul that sought to realize itself by *transforming* nature. Balázs referred here to what he took to be the universal human longing for utopia—the desire to be other than we are. Those who possessed the ability to read faces could, he believed, penetrate behind masks not only to what humans were, but to what they wished to be.[47]

Balázs could only touch on theoretical questions such as these in the brief reviews he wrote for *Der Tag*, but by January 1924, he had completed a book on film that was to make him famous overnight: *The Visible Man, or Film Culture*. In a real sense, this book contained Balázs's vision of the new, unalienated culture for which he and his colleagues at Budapest's Free School of the Humanistic Sciences had been searching. Indeed, he began the book by repeating what he had written in his initial *Der Tag* column about the printing press, the cinematograph, and the rebirth of visual culture. "Rebirth" because as Johan Huizinga wrote at almost precisely the same time, "one of the fundamental traits of the mind of the declining Middle Ages is the predominance of the sense of sight"; though he added that it was a predominance "closely connected with the atrophy of thought."[48]

The man who lived in a visual culture, Balázs contended, expressed in his face and movements profound facets of his soul that words could never reveal. His soul was literally *visible in his body*. Since the invention of the printing press, language had constituted the principal, albeit shaky, bridge between human beings. "The soul has gathered and crystallized in the word. The body, however, has become destitute: without soul and empty." Balázs was here making a personal confession as much as a philosophic claim. The new visual culture of the film was the agent of utopia. It would respiritualize nature—

bodies as well as things. Moreover, it would be founded on an *international* language of expression and movement that would finally end man's imprisonment in a particular language. At last, men and women of all nations could meet as naked and intelligible souls and human alienation would be overcome.[49]

But even if all of that were true, what had it to do with communism or Marxist theory? The question obviously troubled Balázs because in *The Visible Man*'s final pages he added a section entitled "Weltanschauung," in which he summoned a deus ex machina to save the Marxist day. The fact was, he wrote, that contemporary culture's dematerialized, abstract character was rooted in capitalism. The invention of the printing press had indeed marked the transformation of a visual into a conceptual culture, but it had done so only because the economically dictated development of spirit was already moving in the direction of ever greater abstraction. "The culture of the printing press only accelerated 'reification,' as Karl Marx called the process of that abstraction." Film, Balázs concluded, conflicted with the spiritual atmosphere of capitalist culture. Yet by itself, it could no more transform culture than the printing press alone could in its time. Film would only create a culture corresponding to its immanent possibilities if the general development of the surrounding social/economic world created the requisite spiritual atmosphere.[50]

Marxists might be forgiven for not being impressed by this eleventh-hour bow to orthodoxy. Far from being integral to the theory, it added nothing of substance. The entire burden of Balázs's argument had been that the logic of technological sophistication and the pain of alienation were driving men inexorably on to the new visual culture. The revolution would not, therefore, be direct and political, but indirect and cultural. Yet even more striking than Balázs's indifference to social and economic matters was his un-Marxist failure to treat man as a historical being. Without language, after all, there would be no past and without the past there would be no self—merely a body. True, the loss of historical consciousness might end alienation, but only at the cost of our humanity. We would be reduced to little more than natural existence, for nothing distinguishes us from animals so much as our possession of language.

Still, there was something to be said in Balázs's favor. He was right, for example, to recognize that film, at its best, was an art form, that the problem of human alienation was of fundamental significance, and that there was more to being human than the ability to reason. Moreover, he offered, for the first time, a coherent dramaturgy of the film that emphasized the new art's independence from literature and focused on an expressionist aesthetics of physiognomy. Balázs referred not only to human physiognomy, but also to that of nonhuman things. The latter, in fact, assumed new meaning and a certain equality, because in film humans too were dumb. Balázs emphasized that humans were not simply *silent*, because he believed that the movement of the lips was one of the most expressive of acts.[51]

But above all, Balázs spoke of the human face and its ability to express poetically the soul's innermost secrets. His film aesthetics was thus quintessentially lyrical and modernist in its rejection of meanings that could be translated into prose statements. In his view, film possessed no more "content"—in the traditional literary sense—than symbolist poetry. At its best it attempted not to narrate—or not *primarily* to narrate—a story but to summon up meanings, or dimensions, of the soul that were verbally ineffable, yet somehow immediately *visible* on the faces of actors and actresses. Balázs described, for example, how the French actress Suzanne Després managed, solely by means of facial expression, to *show* us hope, anxiety, joy, compassion, grief, courage, faith, and despair—all in a film that told a banal story about a woman and her dying child. "On this face," he wrote, "the real drama was played out, the essential content of the film. The 'story' merely occasioned it."[52]

It followed that the most important aspect of the director's vision was not his choice of stories, but his casting of parts. Film was not epical, but lyrical, not a story but the expression of feelings. And that expression was more profound than that of words because it was unbroken in its multiple transformations. In fact, the human face could exhibit several emotions simultaneously. In *Alles für Geld*, Emil Jannings's face was at once criminally cunning and naively sympathetic, for what one saw beneath the look of evil was the possibility of good. Thus, one was not surprised when, at the film's end, Jannings's soul finally triumphed.[53]

In view of the emphasis that Balázs placed on facial expression, it was only natural that he should hail the close-up as the most important technical achievement—and poetry—of film art. Not that that was an ideosyncratic view. The Austrian-born American director and actor Erich von Stroheim once told an interviewer that he often worked "day and night, without food, without sleeping sometimes, to have every detail perfect, even to descriptions of how facial expressions should change."[54] Whereas on the stage even the most important face was only one element in the drama, Balázs recognized that in the film a close-up of a face could itself *be* the drama. Here, at last, the lineaments of the soul were open to scrutiny.

Close-ups of the eyes, in particular, radiated more of the soul than the entire body. With such close-ups, he wrote, "it is possible to provide a subjective picture of the world and, in spite of the camera's objectivity, to exhibit the world in the hue of a temperament, in the illumination of an emotion: a projected, an objectivized lyric."[55] Just as he had in his essay on lyric sensibility, Balázs rejected pure subjectivity in favor of the union of subjective and objective—the intellectual expression of his own existential longing to achieve a unity of self and a oneness with others.

In a particularly fascinating section of *The Visible Man*, Balázs analyzed the "face of things" as a symbol of meaning. The things of this world were not, he argued, simply tools that man employed to some end. They possessed an autonomy, a soul, a *face* of their own. More than any other form of art, the film was called upon to show forth this face of things. And not merely landscapes; it also bore responsibility for showing us the face of factory machinery, however fantastic and phantomlike working conditions were under capitalism. In his film *Explosion*, for example, Karl Grune portrayed "the demonic physiognomy" of things in a contemporary coal mine. It was precisely against the demonic and foreign things of capitalist civilization, according to Balázs, that Chaplin, the "little tramp," struggled. That struggle was as sobering as it was amusing, for Chaplin represented the natural man in the midst of a "reified" world. Despite his defeats and frustrations, he seemed destined to win because he had right on his side.[56]

Thus *The Visible Man*. The book, which was eventually translated into eleven languages, established Balázs as Europe's leading theorist of the film. Robert Musil spoke of his "exceptional talent" and Alfred Polgar described him as the "evangelist of the new art." According to Leopold Jessner, the book offered "a scientific taxonomy." Karl Grune was sure it signaled the first step toward "a universal dramaturgy of the film."[57] Russians such as Kuleshov, Pudovkin, and Eisenstein read the Russian translation, published in 1925, with great interest. Indeed, almost everyone who counted in the world of film read the book and followed with fresh interest Balázs's reviews in *Der Tag* and his longer, more theoretical, essays in the Berlin-based journal *Die Filmtechnik*. In those extensive writings, he returned again and again to the thematic territory he had staked out in *The Visible Man*.

One of his most memorable pieces dealt with Lillian Gish. It was her performance, especially, that impressed Balázs when he saw Griffith's last masterpiece, *Broken Blossoms*, early in 1924. Based on a story with the regrettable title "The Chink and the Child," the film concerned a waif from the London slums whose father brutally mistreats her. She finds sanctuary in the chaste love of a Chinese boy, but when the father learns of it, he beats her to death. Stricken with grief, the boy kills the father before taking his own life. Balázs titled his review "The Great Sonnet of Anguish" because he believed the film's true subject, as opposed to the primitive plot, to be "the perfect expression of horror." Lillian Gish lent her character's personal suffering a cosmic significance, largely by means of facial expressions; in her countenance, filmgoers could *see* anguish. Of the famous scene in which Miss Gish, standing before a mirror, attempted to counterfeit a smile by propping up the corners of her mouth with her fingers, Balázs observed with insight that "no weeping face in the world can be so mournful as this smile of Lillian Gish."[58]

Not long after he wrote those words, Balázs visited Berlin, where he wished to take up residence in order to be closer to the center of the German film industry. When, early in 1926, Sigmund Bosel declared bankruptcy and sold controlling interest in *Der Tag*, Balázs knew that his days at the newspaper were numbered. Almost immediately, in fact, he came into conflict with the

new, less liberal, owners. On April 7, he published a review of Romain Rolland's play about the French Revolution, in which he attacked the French
writer for having portrayed members of the "proletariat" as enemies of all that
was good and beautiful. Letters of protest poured in and the new owners decided to hand Balázs his walking papers, along with a year's salary. Free to
move on to Berlin, he accepted the German Cameramen's Club's invitation
to lecture. On his arrival in the German capital, Alexander Korda entrusted
him with responsibility for a film scenario.[59]

Berlin: Film Theory and Practice

When Balázs arrived in May 1926, Berlin was a vibrant city of four million and
the home of the first modern culture. The spring air was charged with an
artistic and political electricity that energized a seemingly endless series of
experiments in virtually every cultural field, particularly those, such as the
film, that could contribute to the missionary effort to bring art, and a political
message, to the masses. No wonder, then, that as a Marxist and the author of
the first theory of film, Balázs was hailed as a prophet. *Film-Kurier* and *Die
Literarische Welt* reported on the lecture that he delivered to spellbound members of the German Cameramen's Club on June 9. *Die Filmtechnik* and the
Soviet journal *Kino* published Balázs's remarks in their entirety.

Balázs used the occasion to indicate the direction he believed film had to
move if it wished to give the world works that would rank with *Faust*, the
Ninth Symphony, and the "Moses." In the past—and this was just as true of
The Visible Man's author—critics had focused their attention on film actors
and directors. As a result, according to Balázs, they had failed to appreciate
fully the role that cameramen played. Those unheralded artists understood
better than others that photography could be *productive* as well as reproduc-
tive, that carefully planned shots could express the soul. They knew that artistic photographs possessed a symbolic significance that transcended their representational character.

To illustrate his point, Balázs cited two scenes from Sergei Eisenstein's
Battleship Potemkin (1925), which, despite its special pleading, was one of the
finest of contemporary films. In the first, he pointed out, the people of Odessa
express their jubilation at the sailors' mutiny, while sailboats bring food to the
ship. With the aid of skillful photography, however, one could see more than
that narrative line; one perceived the sails as a group countenance that expressed more happiness and hope than the face of even the greatest actor. The
scene, in other words, was the purest poetry. And so was that in which the
camera looked down on the sailboats from the ship's deck. They lower their
sails so that they can come to rest, but thanks to the cameraman's poetic
vision, the audience understands the sails to be saluting the heroic sailors.

What was important here was that subjective meanings possessed objective correlates; they did not derive from pictures meaningless in themselves.[60]

Eisenstein took issue with Balázs's interpretation. In the pages of *Kino*, he wrote of his regard for the Hungarian as a film authority, but rejected his argument about the central importance of setting shots. In the temperamental filmmaker's view, montage—the creative editing or "collision" of independent shots—constituted the major element in film art.[61] Rather than continue the discussion, Balázs elected to show in practice what he preached in theory. He accepted Korda's assignment to write a scenario for *Madam Doesn't Want Children*, starring Maria Corda and Harry Liedtke, who appeared often in Ernst Lubitsch's sophisticated comedies. For the first time, he would be working with Karl Freund, the brilliant cinematographer who had directed photography for such distinguished films as F. W. Murnau's *Der letzte Mann* (1924) and Fritz Lang's *Metropolis* (1926).

As Korda was about to leave Germany for Hollywood, Freund had to shoot the entire film in thirteen days. Balázs was disappointed with the result, though the film achieved a box-office success. More surprising, *Der Montag Morgen, Deutsche Filmwoche, Berliner Tageblatt*, and *Film-Kurier* praised it as one of the best German productions of 1926 and one of the few good German comedies.[62] Even the humorless *Rote Fahne*, though careful to remind readers of the difference between the frivolous Elyane (Maria Corda) and working-class wives, judged the film to be an amusing parody.[63] Years later, during his exile in the Soviet Union, Balázs was himself amused to find that the film was enjoying a successful run there.

But if Balázs was unhappy with *Madam*, he was proud of the scenario he wrote for *The Adventures of a Ten-Mark Note* (1926), a Fox-Europe film that Berthold Viertel directed and Freund shot. No print of the film has survived, but Balázs described "the story" as follows:

> The ostensible central hero was a ten-mark banknote, which as it passed from hand to hand, was the cause of all the adventures recorded in the film. The other characters changed in every scene. The events were in casual connection with each other but the human characters moved past each other as in a mist, unaware of each other and not even suspecting that their actions decided the fate of the others. The ten-mark banknote was the only thread that held the scenes together.[64]

The film did not, then, constitute a narrative in the literary sense of the word. Nor was that Balázs's intention, for he wanted to "move toward a new dimension" appropriate to film alone. He hoped, that is, to infuse the unrelated events with the kind of evocative power that a great poem or piece of music might possess. That goal stands out clearly in the scene that the *Berliner Tageblatt* printed on October 16, 1926. Seeing that an old and sick factory worker could no longer produce, the foreman orders him to pick up his pay and leave. The old man begs to stay on, but the foreman cannot be moved. The cashier, "a calculating machine with a human mask," counts out the final wage, including the ten-mark banknote.[65]

Consistent with Balázs's theory, this objective event possessed a deeper, symbolic meaning: under capitalism a ruthless, impersonal cash nexus characterizes the relationships between human beings. Some, though not all, contemporary critics recognized this meaning. Leo Lania, with whom Balázs later collaborated, wrote that the film focused on the "lack of connection among modern city dwellers." And Rudolf Schwarzkopf, president of the "People's League for Film Art," insightfully described the film in the radical journal *Film und Volk* (April 1928): "It shows the essence—the curse of money—in a capitalist economy. It shows how money destroys the relation between man and man; how it poisons and corrupts every good and pure relationship."[66]

The success of *The Adventures of a Ten-Mark Note* encouraged Balázs to believe that he could write scenarios that were artistically inventive as well as socially significant. Thus, in 1927 he turned out scripts for four new films, the first of which, *One Plus One Makes Three*, was a modest success. Hermann Kosterlitz, who as Henry Koster later became a Hollywood director, coscripted this comedy about two bohemians, one of whom stands to inherit a large sum of money if only he does not marry. Willi Münzenberg's pro-Communist Prometheus Firm, with which Balázs maintained good relations, produced the film. By then UFA (*Universum Film Aktiengesellschaft*), Germany's largest producer and distributor of films, viewed the Hungarian Marxist with suspicion.

Established by government decree in 1917, UFA aimed originally to carry out the propaganda mandate that General Ludendorff had given it. When the war ended, the government sold its shares and the conglomerate passed completely into private hands. In 1927, Alfred Hugenberg, leader of the German Nationalist Party, purchased controlling interest. Increasingly concerned about left-wing propaganda, the company's censors made drastic cuts in Balázs's script for *Grand Hotel*, a film ostensibly about a female medical student's love for a poor scholar. Like *Doctor Margit Szélpál*, Balázs based the story on his own experiences as a student in Berlin. But as with all his films, he intended a deeper, symbolic meaning as well. The student works as a maid in an elegant hotel in order to earn money for her education. There she comes into contact with an odd assortment of anarchists, swindlers, diplomats, and others who are supposed to reflect the character of capitalist society.

On the September day that the film premiered in Berlin's Mozartsaal, Balázs published one of the censored scenes in *Film-Kurier*. On the evidence of that publication, UFA representatives knew their business. Outside the hotel, a blind man and a down-and-out young woman beg for money. There is to be a masked ball in the hotel and the arriving guests mistake the beggars' rags for costumes. They usher the bewildered pair into the ballroom, where several men lift the poor girl onto the champagne table and insist that she drink a glass. Confused and fearful, she cries out that she is hungry, but the men only laugh and applaud her "act." Finally, they force her to drink the champagne.[67]

Whether or not this unhappy experience with the censors caused Balázs unconsciously to trim his radical sails is uncertain. What is not in doubt is that his next two films, *The Miss with the Five Zeros* and *Doña Juana*, were disasters. Of the first, one critic observed: "More than two souls live in his /Balázs's/ breast. He is a hope. He campaigns . . . for the present generation . . . but what do we see today? An inhibited adept and purveyor of kitsch." Even worse, Paul Czinner, who coscripted and directed *Doña Juana*, turned it into a simple vehicle for his wife, Elisabeth Bergner. So embarrassed was Balázs that on the day the film premiered he published a statement in *Film-Kurier* to the effect that his collaboration had been limited to preliminary work on the scenario. And he followed that up with a newspaper article in which he insisted that no producer had the right to advertise an author's name after having altered his work without his consent.[68]

More than a year passed before Balázs scripted another film. Already persona non grata as far as UFA and other establishment firms were concerned, he denounced capitalist control of Germany's film industry. Indeed, as early as 1922, he had written in *Die Rote Fahne* that "we must create our own film studios that make *our* films."[69] Prometheus, he believed, was a step in the right direction, but the firm could not, by itself, revolutionize the German film industry. Balázs delivered a particularly incendiary lecture at the initial meeting of the People's League for Film Art in February 1928, identifying himself with the slogan "The enemy is on the right—including the film enemy."[70] The League was chaired by Heinrich Mann and numbered among its members many prominent left-wing intellectuals, including Piscator, Freund, Lania, Käthe Kollwitz, Leonhard Frank, and G. W. Pabst.

Despite capitalist control of the German film industry, however, Balázs still believed that film, as the art of seeing and unveiling, worked for revolutionary change, and in 1929 he wrote a scenario, based on a novella by Stefan Zweig, for the film *Narcosis*. Produced by the outsider firm of G. P. Films, *Narcosis* recalled *The Cabinet of Dr. Caligari* in its dreamlike quality. The images members of the audience saw were those emerging from the unconscious of a young woman lying on an operating table. "The reason for this device," Balázs explained, "was to give the scenes and shots only the emotional reality they acquired in the experience of the girl herself, without having to show the many indifferent and unimportant details of life without which it is impossible to present everyday reality so as to be readily understood."[71] Here again, Balázs experimented with what he liked to call "objective subjectivism"—the presentation of a subjective vision as objective reality. In time he hoped to see communism's subjective utopia become objective reality.

This sort of expressionism was something of an anomaly by 1929, when *Neue Sachlichkeit* was the rage in avant-garde circles. Balázs despised the

4. Béla and Anna Balázs in Berlin, late 1920s. Courtesy of the Petőfi Irodalmi Múzeum (Petőfi Museum of Literature), Budapest. Photo by Csaba Gál.

movement and complained publicly when critics cited the famous Walter Ruttman/Karl Freund/Carl Mayer film, *Berlin, Symphony of a Great City*, as an example of the new objectivity. The creative artists who made the film were not, he contended, so naive as to believe that a sterile presentation of "objects" devoid of human significance, constituted art. Art had always to be humanly meaningful, Balázs observed quite rightly, and objects had always to be seen from a particular, subjectively-colored, soul-filled, point of view. Indeed, there was no "objective" reality "without human beings, without their feelings, moods, and dreams."[72]

Nor in Balázs's judgment could *Neue Sachlichkeit* be reconciled with socialism. In fact, it was precisely the reification of man—making him an inhuman object among other objects—that defined the soulless capitalist society that Marx hated. In such a society, one could no longer perceive that which was essential, the "relationships between men." Only the class-conscious proletariat could see through reified "reality" to true, soul-filled reality. It alone knew that men and women were not simply objects, but beings who possessed souls. It alone recognized that even inanimate objects were constituted in part by the inner attitudes and perspective of the observer. In the Soviet Union, for example, a factory machine wore a different, friendlier, "face" than the same machine in capitalist Germany.[73]

Balázs arrived at this dubious notion after viewing the Soviet films he publicly championed. Supported by "the people," Russian filmmakers presented the world through the eyes of proletarian class consciousness. Not only could they portray "Comrade Machine" with a friendly face, but they could also help filmgoers to see that the Soviet masses possessed a "group-physiognomy like /an individual human/ face"—a face, moreover, that reflected a unified revolutionary soul. Balázs had in mind the mutinous sailors on board the Battleship Potemkin and the demonstrators in Vsevolod Pudovkin's *Mother*.[74]

Prometheus imported and distributed most of the Soviet films that Germans saw and Münzenberg regularly engaged Balázs to compose the German intertitles that, in silent films, conveyed minimal dialogue and other narrative information. He performed this task for Viktor Turin's *Turksib* (1929), an account of the building of the Turkistan-Siberian Railway that won international acclaim. More important, he wrote intertitles for Eisenstein's *The General Line* (1929)—the Communist party line, that is. Subsequently retitled *Old and New*, Eisenstein set out to produce a lyrical celebration of the collectivization of Soviet agriculture, pathetically unaware that Stalin was about to declare a war on the peasantry that would claim millions of lives. Balázs wrote to tell Eisenstein that he regarded the responsibility as a great honor and looked forward to becoming better acquainted the next time the Russian was in Berlin.[75]

The two men met for the first time in September 1929, when both attended the initial meeting of the "International League of Independent Film" at the Chateau of La Sarraz near Lausanne, the estate of the cinema enthusiast Hélène de Mandrot, who financed the endeavor. Organized by Robert Aron and Janine Bouissounouse, the League aspired to bring together isolated groups of radical filmmakers with an eye toward coordinating efforts and exchanging information. Ultimately, members purposed to form an international union for production and distribution free of commercial fetters. Representatives came from England, Holland, Belgium, Italy, Spain, France, the United States, Japan, and Germany.

Balázs traveled with the German delegation that included G. W. Pabst, Lupu Pick, Hans Richter, and Walter Ruttman. All of the Western representatives welcomed the Russian delegation with the greatest show of deference.

Accompanying Eisenstein were Grigory Alexandrov, his coscenarist for *October* (*Ten Days That Shook the World*; 1928) and Eduard Tisse, his cinematographer. They maintained that no independent film culture could exist in capitalist states and insisted that their colleagues in the West attach themselves to the revolutionary movement. Balázs assured the Russians that right-(or rather, left-)thinking people admired films such as *Potemkin* and *Mother*, even though conservative German critics thought them one-sided politically. Eisenstein professed indifference to the political charge, but complained that the quality of Russian films had declined and argued that the time had come to shift the focus from revolutionary events to the creation of Socialist man.[76]

The problem of promoting Russian films in Germany was as nothing for Balázs compared to the problems posed by the advent of sound film. The idea of combining sound with film was as old as film itself, but for technical, economic, and artistic reasons, it was not until Warner Brothers in Hollywood gambled on "Vitaphone," a sophisticated sound-on-disk system, that matters came to a head. In 1927, the company released *The Jazz Singer* starring Al Jolson, a film that most regard as the first to employ synchronized dialogue in a realistic way. After the film's success, there was no turning back; by the end of 1929, when Balázs was getting to know Eisenstein, Hollywood's conversion to sound (ultimately sound-on-film) was all but complete. Europe did not lag far behind.

There were many technical problems attendant upon sound recording, not the least of which was the necessary immobility of the actors. More important, however, were the creative problems. Would film degenerate into poor man's theater? Would the visual character of film be prejudiced? Balázs was among those who were most skeptical about sound film, though he acknowledged the futility of blind rejection. He warned against reducing film to theatrical reproduction by subordinating vision to dialogue. That would, in effect, destroy the visual culture he had championed for so long. Thus, he preferred to speak of "sound film" rather than "the talkies."

Sound film too presented difficulties, chief among them its inability to alter *the same sound* creatively in the way that different camera setups could alter perspective on the same object. Nevertheless, Balázs did his best to be optimistic. One had, he suggested, to understand sound film as a completely new art, rather than as a modification of the existing silent film. Like silent film in its infancy, sound film began unimpressively, but it possessed great possibilities, for, properly employed, it could open up an entire world of sound that was as foreign as the world of sight had once been. Sound film would unveil an acoustical environment and teach human beings to *hear* for the first time the language of objects and nature—from the factory din to the melody of an autumn shower on a darkened windowpane and the creaking noise of footsteps on the floor of a lonely room. In a word, sound film could uncover the very soul of an unexplored world of sound.[77]

Clearly, Balázs continued to espouse an expressionist aesthetic, in which sounds would serve as counterpoint to sights and at the same time invest the objective world with human sensibility. Yet he could not allay his fear of talking pictures and he had constantly to screw up his courage. "I believe in the art of the sound film," he wrote early in 1930. "Despite everything. *Credo, quia absurdum est.*" And he continued to hold out hope that silent film would survive as a distinct art.[78]

Those and other themes swirled around in his head when, in 1930, Balázs published *The Spirit of Film,* the most important work of his Berlin years and a testimony to his continued faith in visual culture and in communism as the final solution to his own and society's alienation problem. He began that work by acknowledging that the development of silent film, about which he had written with such enthusiasm in *The Visible Man,* had been interrupted by the coming of sound. He did not attempt to conceal his disappointment at that turn of events, but he refused to counsel despair. In the final analysis, he observed, the human condition, and not the survival of a particular artistic genre, mattered most.[79]

Nevertheless, Balázs devoted many pages of his book to a summary of the camera's ability to create, rather than simply reproduce, new perspectives on man and the world by means of close-ups, montage, and camera setups (*Einstellungen*). He was particularly fervent about the latter because the angle of vision was, unlike close-ups and montage, a *necessary* ingredient in the very constitution of an object. "Every view of the world includes a world view. Therefore every camera standpoint implies an inner human standpoint. For there is nothing more subjective than objectivity." That was particularly true when it came to objects of art, since the creative artist looked always for meaning. He or she chose that standpoint which would yield the most symbolic significance. Once again, Balázs identified himself with expressionist film, even while criticizing films such as *Caligari,* in which expression was achieved by means of décor rather than creative camera use. The idea, once again, was to express what was already there but had never been *seen.*[80]

With respect to montage, which Eisenstein championed, Balázs remained cautious. His own preference was for what he described as "montage without cutting," by which he meant fading from one place, or time, into another. He had, he reminded his readers, experimented with that kind of montage in *Narcosis.* In one of the film's scenes, the hero is about to go on a journey and the camera focuses close-up on the suitcase in his room. As the room begins to fade, the suitcase begins to bounce in a luggage net—the diaphragm opens to reveal a train car. In another scene, the heroine stands alone on the street and the camera focuses on her hands, which hold a white handkerchief. Soon, the handkerchief shades into one, then many white roses, and as the diaphragm opens a bit more, the girl stands working in a flower shop.[81]

Employing close-ups, camera setups, and montage, the makers of the silent film created a visual culture that, with the help of a Communist social/economic transformation, could end human alienation. That project was now endangered. Yet Balázs insisted that history knew no tragedies, but only crises. History had overcome the crises of the past and it would overcome the crisis of visual culture. Sound film was an immature art form, but it too would one day come into its own, and in so doing, would not simply help silent film realize its full potential. On the contrary, it would open up an entirely new sphere of human experience by uncovering the surrounding acoustical world. "The voices of things, the intimate language of nature." Just as silent film had taught men and women to *see* the world, so sound film would teach them to *hear* it. In this way, it would also teach them to "hear" silence, which existed only where sound was possible.[82]

But Balázs's rather forced optimism concerning the sound film did not extend to screen dialogue. With respect to what was to come, he was extremely critical, in large part because he believed that the visual power of silent film would be hopelessly compromised. Art would be taken from the hands—or rather the faces—of Asta Nielsen, Lillian Gish, and Charlie Chaplin and placed in the hands of script writers. And only gifted writers could hope to match the art of the silent era's geniuses.[83] Moreover, the likely tendency to focus on dialogue would cause facial and body language once again to atrophy and film to become no more than photographed theater.

Because film luminaries such as Chaplin and Eisenstein shared these fears, *The Spirit of Film* confirmed Balázs's reputation as Germany and Europe's leading film theorist. He could therefore afford to ignore *Die Linkskurve*, which criticized him for failing to work out a "historical-materialistic foundation" for his ideas. Less easy to dismiss was Rudolf Arnheim, a young student of Gestalt psychology who also preferred silent films and was working on a film theory of his own. Arnheim recommended Balázs's new study, but maintained that it raised more questions than it answered.[84] At the same time, he directed attention to the fact that as a theorist the Hungarian possessed the decided advantage of having written film scripts.

Indeed, it was as a scenarist that "the red" G. W. Pabst approached Balázs with regard to a film version of Brecht and Weill's *Threepenny Opera*, a very hot property at the time. From the first, the mercurial Brecht and his friend Leo Lania had been unable to agree with Pabst's plans for adaptation, and when, by the fall of 1930, it had become clear that no agreement was possible, Brecht and Weill brought a suit against the production company, Nero Films, in a doomed effort to jettison the entire project. The court judge split the common suit into separate actions and, in the end, Brecht lost and Weill won on a minor point. Meanwhile, Pabst had asked his favorite scenarist, Ladislaus Vajda, to rewrite the script. Brecht affected outrage and so, in a last effort at compromise, Pabst called in Balázs to produce yet another rewrite. The Hungarian accepted the challenge in the belief that he might be able to make a film more radical even than the stage version.

Balázs's hand in the film was unmistakable, even though he later claimed that his contribution was limited to technical revisions. For one thing, the dialogue was "often condensed almost to silent screen standards." For another, he clearly contributed to what one reviewer described as Pabst's "uncanny instinct for selection of camera angles."[85] Finally, he influenced the director, who made his reputation with the realist film *The Joyless Street* (1925), to make a *Threepenny Opera* that was far more expressionistic and "fabulous" than the hard-bitten stage version. Lotte Eisner has described a scene that only Balázs could have written: "Mackie Messer, filmed through panes of glass, tries to seduce Polly and asks her to go away with him; we see him talking but can only guess what he is saying. The image gives the sound a background and this, at the beginning of the sound film, is captivating."[86]

Indeed, the entire film was bathed in a fantastic, dreamlike glow. In his fury, Brecht castigated Balázs as "a man of letters of inferior rank," and the leftist critic Herbert Jhering accused him of being a tool of the film industry and an enemy of authors,[87] an indictment that infuriated Balázs, who had turned down a lucrative offer from UFA when first he arrived in Berlin. Nor was he happy about Alfred Durus's scathing attack in *Die Rote Fahne*.[88] What comfort he could, he took from the film's general artistic and commercial success.

It was undoubtedly due in part to Balázs's most recent triumph that Leni Riefenstahl, the beautiful dancer and actress, approached him to ask for his help with a film entitled *The Blue Light* that she wished to star in and direct. Despite the fact that she had little money and would have to defer payment of his salary, he readily agreed to write the scenario because he knew that she was a protegé of Dr. Arnold Fanck, creator of the mountain film genre.

Originally a geologist infatuated with mountain climbing, Fanck made a series of films during the 1920s that bore such titles as *The Wonder of Skis*, *Struggle With the Mountains*, and *The Mountain of Destiny*. A master of the breathtaking view, he was not overly interested in story lines. Kracauer believed that his films reflected a mentality that was "kindred to /the/Nazi spirit," despite the fact that Fanck collaborated with the left-leaning Pabst on the 1929 film *The White Hell of Pitz Palü*. Balázs did not share Kracauer's judgment and even wrote a laudatory forward to Fanck's published scenario for *Storms Over Mont Blanc* (1931). In the German's films he saw not Nazism, but that poetic human union with nature concerning which he had written in "On Lyric Sensibility." "Dr. Fanck," he said, "is the great filmmaker of nature." In his work "the snow storm becomes a terrible destiny, because it meshes together with the destiny of men."[89]

Balázs meant that to be taken in a very specific sense. He pointed out that Germany was locked in a great social struggle and suggested that Fanck's portrayal of heroic encounter with nature's elements could stiffen revolutionary resolve. That was why, he argued, advocates of the *Neue Sachlichkeit* attacked Fanck's films; they were always made uncomfortable by those who demanded devotion, sacrifice, and fanaticism.[90]

With that evaluation of Fanck's work as a background, it is not surprising that Riefenstahl remembered her collaboration with Balázs as "an ideal co-operation, and we had a wonderful and good relationship."[91] Both of them were pleased also to be working with Fanck's cameraman, whose name, appropriately enough, was Hans Schneeberger. The story of the blue light was pure Balázs. On nights when the moon is full, Mount Cristallo radiates a blue light that lures young villagers, who then fall to their death among the rocks. Only Junta (played by Riefenstahl) reaches the light safely and the townsfolk therefore consider her to be a witch.

A young Viennese painter, on a visit, is attracted to the girl and joins her in her mountain retreat. One night, he follows her to the peak and discovers that the mysterious light emanates from precious crystals. The promise of wealth is too great a temptation and he and the villagers remove the treasure. Next full moon, Junta loses her way and falls to her death; the painter, too late to help, bends over the shining face of the dead girl, another sacrifice to the god of calculating and avaricious rationality. "What remains is nostalgia for her realm and sadness over a disenchanted world in which the miraculous becomes merchandise."[92] For Balázs at least, the blue light was the symbol of utopia.

In view of her subsequent work as director of the pro-Nazi *Triumph of the Will*, it is worth noting that Riefenstahl was vaguely left-wing in her sympathies at the time she collaborated with Balázs. According to her secretary, "she was very much under his /Balázs's/ influence." Indeed, she trusted him to tutor her in the art of direction. "I was very lucky that he could control the most important scenes in which I acted."[93] Before the film was released in 1932, however, Balázs had accepted an invitation from Soviet officials to help in the film adaptation of Béla Illés's novel about the Hungarian Soviet Republic—*The Burning Tisza River*. It is by no means certain that he intended originally to leave Germany for good, but in April 1932, word reached the troubled Republic that the Moscow Academy of Film had appointed him a permanent member of its faculty.

Berlin: At One with the Party

In 1930, the year that *The Spirit of Film* appeared, Balázs also published *Impossible People*, a confessional novel in which he recreated imaginatively his journey from existential loneliness to proletarian solidarity. And not his only. He announced publicly that he intended to relate the inner history of the "last prewar generation of unpolitical, inward-looking intellectuals."[94] In the aftermath of war, bolshevism, Americanization, and new economic/political realities, he concluded, he and others who had come of age before 1914 could only appear as Don Quixotes and negative revolutionaries, oblivious to social reality. Some members of his generation had never changed, but he and others had found their way to the revolutionary barricades. In order to present their tragedies and triumphs, he had had recourse to the techniques of the modern film, employing verbal "close-ups" of the world from his characters' angles of vision.[95]

As early as 1910, Balázs had begun to play with the idea of a roman à clef that would dramatize the struggles and longings that he, Lukács, and other contemporaries had been experiencing. Only, however, after he helped to organize the Sunday Circle in 1915 did he begin to write, inspired by his friends' extraordinary personalities and ideas. In the summer of 1919, when he was one of the Soviet Republic's cultural leaders, he published two chapters in *Nyugat* under the title "In the Palm of God's Hand." Three years later he permitted a slightly altered version to be published in book form, although he let it be known that it should be regarded as a work in progress. In view of his many commitments, Balázs worked slowly during his last years in Vienna and first years in Berlin. By the time he completed the task, he had reworked *In the Palm of God's Hand* as part one, written a second part, and constructed an entirely new framework for the novel.

The "impossible people" of Balázs's new title are artistic, hypersensitive men and women who feel themselves to be homeless in the world, alienated from others and from the conventions of fin de siècle bourgeois society. Like Balázs and Lukács, they wish to be free to follow their own inclinations, regardless of society's standards and expectations, to live as "naked souls" in a world far removed from that of those who wear the masks of inauthenticity. In general, their strategy is one of withdrawal into a microcosmic utopia in which the creative imagination, or in some cases eroticism, replaces social conventionality. In that utopian world, they seek to end their isolation and join others in a genuine community of souls.

That, in broad outline, is the burden of *In the Palm of God's Hand*. At the time he began the novel, Balázs identified himself with his characters, but after his conversion to communism he began to see his past from a different angle. In the light of his newly-acquired faith, he still affirmed their (and his) rejection of the world as it was, but he had come to believe that they would remain isolated, romantic rebels unless they made contact with objective reality and joined the working class in the concrete effort to create a *macrocosmic* utopia by means of a practical, communist revolution. Failing that, they would end as suicides, decadents, or, in the best case, dwellers in a dream world of their own creation. Thus, *Impossible People* served as Balázs's personal credo, a Dostoevskian novel designed to convert sensitive rebels not to Christianity, as in the Russian writer's case, but to the new religion of communism.

Impossible People opens with a Budapest newspaper report dated May 5, 1917. Police have arrested Johannes Szegedi, a former professor at the Academy of Music, and his wife, for distributing revolutionary handbills to workers and soldiers. Balázs then shifted the scene to 1914, when war is about to engulf Europe. He introduced his readers to Szegedi, who in most essentials is Balázs himself, but also, to some degree, Béla Bartók, with whom Balázs collaborated on *Duke Bluebeard's Castle* (1911) and *The Wooden Prince* (1914–16). We also meet Klara Almady, wife of a psychiatrist named Kálmán Lorx and mother of a child. Although she and Szegedi have only recently met, they have decided to run off together in search of a freer life. In their first hours alone, they exchange accounts of their respective roads to loneliness and alienation.

Klara begins by telling of her father's suicide and having come of age in a world of books and fictional naked souls. She lived in a fairy-tale world that her imaginative mother created for her. As a result, she was particularly shaken when she finally encountered the "real" world. She gained the courage to rebel against that world from her mother's public proclamation that she and a recently-deceased married man had been lovers. In the aftermath of that dramatic revelation, Klara's mother suffered from what Lorx, her doctor, characterized as a severe mental/emotional malady. But Klara preferred to believe that her mother was perfectly normal and that society was sick. Nevertheless, being no more than eighteen years of age, she agreed to marry the "well-adjusted" Lorx.[96]

In his turn, Johannes tells Klara of his youth in the Great Plains town of Tiszavásárhely. Sensitive and talented, he fell in with a school-boy clique presided over by Arpad Zucker, a clever but cynical fellow who was at odds with all social conventions. At Zucker's insistence, Johannes and the others agreed to participate in an "experiment": they would always conduct themselves in ways contrary to accepted behavior. Johannes even derived a certain pleasure from his resulting sense of isolation. In that spiritual state, he went on to Budapest to accept a position at the Music Academy.[97]

In the first day and a half that Klara and Johannes are together, they encounter other impossible people, who, like themselves, seek a community of souls and long for self-realization. The philosopher Heinrich Schneider (modeled in part on the pre-Marxist Lukács) tells them that their escape constitutes a "negative revolution" and that the subjective world alone is real and suitable for the soul. That is why he lives only in the world of his work. He always maintains some distance from other people and, indeed, contracted a marriage to a widow with the understanding that they would live together as independent souls, without intimacy. When the arrangement began to torture him, he left his wife without so much as a word of explanation.[98]

Schneider takes Klara and Johannes to a nearby manor house where they meet Klara's old friend Ilona Nyári, who is married to the wealthy Count

Szentgyörgyi. Ilona, too, longs to live an authentic life, though she holds out little hope. In the diary she gives Klara to read, she tells of her love for the poet Béla Barna, whose real name was Sternberg (Balázs-Bauer). Barna had taught her that people wear masks to disguise their true selves and that soul and body are always estranged. Convinced that he did not love *her*, but rather a poetic idealization, she broke off the relationship and gave herself up to drink and cocaine. In despair, the poet shot himself and she married the count.[99]

From Szentgyörgyi, Johannes first learns of a revolution that is not moral or spiritual in character. The count is a parlor liberal whose political criticisms inspired a teacher by the name of Matthias Szlavek to take revolutionary action, in the course of which he lost his life. Stricken with guilt, Szentgyörgyi began to back away from his former opinions. Disgusted by such a lack of steadfastness, Klara decides to test Johannes by telling him that her husband has committed suicide. He is devastated and Klara, convinced that her lover cannot face up to the consequences of his unconventional behavior, bids him farewell.[100]

In part two, Klara travels to a remote manor house in the Carpathians, there to visit Alice Ránky, a painter and poet modeled after Anna Lesznai. Alice too feels alienated from the world as it is and finds peace only by living in her own world of dreams and fairy tales. She loves Klara, whom she knew in Budapest, but describes her as a "little incorporeal, naked soul." In vain, she advises her friend to return to her roots and relates the story of her own decision to leave her husband and child in Budapest.[101]

In the meantime, Johannes travels toward the town of Szabadka, near Tiszavásárhely. There he hopes to visit his childhood friend Zucker. In the train compartment with him are two workers, one of whom is perusing the Socialist newspaper *Népszava*. In due course the two men begin to discuss the murder of Franz Ferdinand, the sort of subject that had never interested Johannes. Indeed, the musician is suddenly and painfully aware that he lives in a different and more rarified world than that inhabited by the roughhewn men seated across from him. He is, moreover, intrigued by one worker's suggestion that what is impossible in the present social order might come to seem self-evident in another.

On arriving in Szabadka, Johannes locates Zucker and finds that he presides over a decadent circle of drunkards and prostitutes. They seek to end their loneliness and to forge a "religious" community by means of erotic "experimentation" and common possession of a young woman named Esther Tomola. Johannes is attracted to Esti, but not out of lust; rather, he sees in her a soulless sexuality that is at the opposite pole from his disembodied spirituality. Indeed, Zucker cautions him not to introduce the girl to spiritual matters because they would only confuse and undermine her purely sexual identity and thus lower her market value as a prostitute. But the warning comes too late, for Esti now knows that she cannot elevate herself to Johannes's spiritual *niveau*. She drowns herself, just as Lukács's love, Irma Seidler, drowned herself after the brief affair with Balázs.

This is the pivotal moment in Balázs's novel, just as it was in his and Lukács's life. When Johannes receives word of Esti's suicide, he looks into a mirror and examines his face—à la Lillian Gish. On it he reads suffering and anguish, but he knows that he feels nothing. "It was merely a mask, behind which, deep inside, something remained untouched." That something was foreign and alone—it was his very soul. At last he recognizes the terrible truth. "Not one feeling bound him to other men. He felt himself to be forsaken. He was alone in the world." In his own way, he was as decadent as Esti and Zucker; excessive spirituality and eroticism were simply two sides of the same coin. Both were negative rebellions that left the world unchanged.[102]

In his despair and desperation, Johannes seeks out the locally famous "teacher" of whom Esti had spoken. When he tells of his torment, the teacher, who is modeled after Ervin Szabó, is unmoved. "This soul of which you speak is itself an affliction. It is already the sickness itself."[103] In an observation that contains the core of Balázs's film theory, the teacher goes on to say that he is very much interested in the story of Johannes's love affair with Klara because "in the most insignificant love story one can deduce, as if by spectral analysis, the nature of the entire social structure."[104] "Souls" such as Johannes and others were symptoms of a social order that was no longer viable.

And yet, the teacher continues, Johannes and his friends were "negative rebels. Emigrés. You could not and did not want to continue to live in this bourgeois society." Only instead of fighting against it, they simply withdrew. For them, unresolvable moral questions were like empty stomachs; they constituted the tragedies of an intellectual élite. But the teacher assures Johannes that human history knows no tragedies, but only crises, through which it advances in a progressive direction. History and reality had to be seen as totalities in which the only true tragedy is human alienation.[105]

Cut to the quick by the teacher's words, Johannes admits that he is sick and in need of a cure. Luckily for him, the teacher is able to prescribe the remedy, identification with the working-class movement. Unemployed agricultural laborers are on strike and the teacher asks Johannes to help. Johannes agrees and the teacher hands over to him a small package that he is to deliver to an address in Tiszavásárhely. The package contains manifestos and a list of names that must not fall into police hands. As he makes his way out of the teacher's house and into an open field, Johannes hears shots being fired as police attack the peasants; one bullet hits him in the shoulder. But despite the pain, he is filled with an almost mystical joy because "the feelings of body and soul flowed together in this trickle of blood and became indistinguishably one."[106] Like Balázs, Johannes had finally been able to unite body and soul, objectivity and subjectivity, in the concrete actions dictated by the Party.

What Johannes does not know is that Klara is on her way to Tiszavásárhely to rejoin him. In a long letter to Alice Ránky—in reality, Balázs's farewell to Anna Lesznai—she expresses appreciation for the quiet life in a self-created world of fairy tales and paintings. But she says that she must look elsewhere for the way out of her loneliness. She cannot return to her roots but must go on to a new world. And she can do so only in Johannes's company. Together they will complete the unfinished journey and thus find each other as Balázs had begun truly to find his wife Anna. He dedicated *Impossible People* to her as his "co-worker, companion, and comrade."

When Johannes arrives with the package entrusted to him, he tells Klara that he believes he has embarked on the road which they must both travel. "Something completely different had begun, a different life in a different world. They had come among people of the sort they had not before known." Soon they would find themselves in the midst of the revolutionary movement, never again to be alone.[107]

Three years later, waiting to be arrested, they speak of their past and the fate of other "impossible people." Zucker died in the war. Schneider lectures in defense of a vague moral revolution and in opposition to materialistic socialism. Alice writes Christian-mystical verse. All had arrived at a cul-de-sac and all had disappeared from Johannes and Klara's lives. Like Balázs and Anna, the two lovers had acquired new friends. "I believe," Klara says just before their arrest, "that we have been very fortunate."[108]

Needless to say, not every reviewer expressed satisfaction with this ending. Writing in *Nyugat*, the critic Aladár Komlós maintained that the second half of *Impossible People* was too contrived to be convincing. It was all too pat, too sudden, too inexplicable. And well it might have been had Balázs, Lukács, and others not provided living proof. Thomas Mann, an "unpolitical" man himself prior to and during the war, was more perceptive; he described Balázs's work as "a novel that eventually had to be written." And *Die Weltbühne*'s reviewer, Wilhelm Michel, pointed out that at the turn of the century, "spirit" stood in protest against contemporary reality.[109]

Indeed, although modernists adopted many strategies, they did wage unrelenting war against liberal, bourgeois civilization. For them, there came to seem only two possible roads: one to nihilism and one to "religion," broadly defined. Like Lukács, Balázs chose the religion of communism. But communism did not win its first historical victory until October 1917, and thus *Impossible People* suffers from a fundamental anachronism. Johannes and Klara would never have converted, as Balázs did not, to the socialism of 1914. Hungarian socialism, like European socialism in general, was then anything but religious and apocalyptic in character. It was in fact to bolshevism—the socialism that was not yet born—that the two lovers converted and to which Balázs had pledged his soul. *That* conversion is not at all an incomprehensible outcome of the total and transpolitical rejection of bourgeois society that preceded it.

Balázs hoped that his clarion call to homeless intellectual rebels would prompt many to follow his lead, but he did not rest content with the testimony he gave in *Impossible People*. He continued his missionary efforts in the pages of *Die Weltbühne*, one of Weimar Germany' most distinguished reviews. Edited successively by Siegfried Jacobsohn, Kurt Tucholsky, and Carl von Ossietzky, *Die Weltbühne* was the principal organ of the so-called *"linke Intellektuelle"* ("left-wing intellectuals"), radicals who stood to the left of German social democracy but who could not quite bring themselves to join the KPD, however much they sympathized with the Communists' bourgeoisie baiting and revolutionary intransigency. Working from within, Balázs was determined to persuade the discontents who wrote for and read *Die Weltbühne* to surrender their independence and unite with the Party of the proletariat.

Not long after he left for the Soviet Union, Balázs published in *Die Weltbühne* a four-part essay entitled "The Intellectuals' Fear of Socialism,"[110] by which of course he meant communism. In it, he delivered himself of an unusually programmatic political statement, beginning with the observation that left-wing intellectuals had long ago rejected capitalism and social democratic reformism, but continued to ignore the logic of that rejection and refused to take their places alongside revolutionary workers. As a consequence of that hesitation, they found themselves mired in an ideological crisis.

One of the principal reasons for the left-wing intellectuals' reluctance to commit themselves, according to Balázs, was their moral concern. They rejected capitalist society on moral grounds, but recoiled from class struggle, violent revolution, and proletarian dictatorship. Rather lamely, Balázs assured them that the Russian dictatorship was a temporary expedient. And to those who scrupled at the fanning of hatreds, he offered a "dialectical" explanation: The proletariat's hatred was "only the reverse side of an active love." Balázs wrote those words in 1931, at a time when Stalin was murdering millions of peasants during what one survivor has called, without exaggeration, "the hidden holocaust."

In addition to moral reservations, left-wing intellectuals feared the vulgarization of culture that communism might occasion. In general, they disliked the idea of mass culture, convinced that *Kultur* could only be the work of promethean individuals working in heroic solitude. In that, Balázs wrote, they were mistaken, for it was precisely the atomized concept of individualism that had signaled the beginning of bourgeois culture's decline. "For culture is in fact spiritual/intellectual community. It is that which accumulates and develops through generations, because it possesses a transpersonal continuity. Solitude is the opposite of culture." Echoing *Impossible People*, Balázs explained that writers such as George, Rilke, and Rudolf Kassner had consciously isolated themselves in order to escape from bourgeois society. Their flight into solitude was a way of standing against contemporary reality; "it was a negative rebellion." The time had come for intellectuals to engage in an affirmative struggle and to create a broader, not a more circumscribed, culture.

Many who withdrew from bourgeois society did so because of its ever-increasing mechanization and "reification." It was ironic therefore, Balázs pointed out, for intellectuals to fear that communism would produce a mechanized society. After all, Marx had insisted that the revolutionary proletariat was fighting *against* reification. Returning to his favorite theme, Balázs added that the soul's flight into unreality was simply the consequence of capitalist reality's loss of soul. Hence it was a mistake to contrast spiritual inwardness to mechanized objective reality; the two were merely "manifestations of the same process." The task, then, was to reunite subjectivity and objectivity, soul and social reality.

Having made that point, Balázs offered his solution to the problem of alienation. Following Lukács closely, he defended Marxism as the dialectical unity of subject and object, consciousness and being, soul and body. He took notice of the fact that many left-wing intellectuals rejected Marxism precisely because they missed its dialectical character and believed it to be nothing more than "an unspiritual materialism" focused exclusively on the economic determinants of human society and history. That, Balázs insisted, was a misunderstanding of Marx's teachings. To be sure, the master had proclaimed the primacy of Being (*Sein*) over consciousness (*Bewusstsein*), but he had been careful to say that material being and spiritual consciousness were aspects of a *single* dialectical process. Indeed, he assigned to class consciousness, and hence to spirit/mind (*Geist*), "a decisive historical role."

Balázs concluded his appeal to left-wing intellectuals by warning them that by themselves they would lose their way in the subjective dreamworld of bourgeois thought. If they wished to surmount the ideological crisis in which they were floundering, they would have to take their intellectual/spiritual bearings from the proletariat's class consciousness—or, to be more specific, from the custodian of that consciousness, the Communist party. Had he chosen to do so, he might have mentioned his own tireless efforts to serve the KPD, for during his last years in Berlin, Balázs seemed to be everywhere at once—lecturing at Radványi's MASCH, working with the League of Proletarian-Revolutionary Writers, helping to found the People's League for Film Art, reviewing books and theater for *Die Weltbühne*, giving time to the School of the Piscator-Bühne.

His association with Piscator brought Balázs back to the theater, one of his first loves. By then the German directed the Theater am Nollendorfplatz in the West End of Berlin, not far from the Kurfürstendamm. He had recruited a politically committed "dramaturgical collective," the task of which was "to rework texts in the light of our political standpoint and to work out new scenes to suit my ideas for the production, and to help to shape the script."[111]

In addition to its head, Felix Gasbarra, the collective included Balázs, Leo Lania, Johannes R. Becher, Brecht, Alfred Döblin, Erich Mühsam, Ernst Toller, and Kurt Tucholsky.

Balázs wished to do more than serve as an adviser. For the 1927–28 season, therefore, he wrote *Men on the Barricades*, a three-act play that takes place during the Russian Civil War and centers on the question of ends and means. Its tone may be suggested by a line that Balázs put in the mouth of one Comrade Smirnow: "With the honor code of the gentleman, we will not be able to liberate the proletariat."[112] Like Lukács, Balázs had arrived at the place where he would countenance any act that served the religion to which he had given himself. For him, there were no longer any moral imperatives not dictated by the Party.

Piscator did not produce *Men on the Barricades* and Balázs gave it to Max Reichard, who staged it in Freiburg. Nevertheless, he continued his association with the Piscator-Bühne, above all because he believed that its major achievement was "the joining of theater and film."[113] Beginning with the 1925 production of *In Spite of Everything*, a documentary play about the German Revolution of 1918–19 that he and Gasbarra assembled in three weeks, Piscator regularly used film sequences in the plays he staged. Despite criticism, he was convinced that film clips "were not only right for presenting political and social mechanisms, that is, from the point of view of content, but also in a higher sense, right from the formal point of view."[114]

Balázs agreed. For one thing, the silent film so dear to his heart might gain a new lease on life. For another, film, together with new and more imaginative sets, would be able to create a sense of the social whole, the totality upon which Marxist theory rested. He praised, in that respect, Piscator's productions of Ernst Toller's *Hoppla, Such is Life!* (1927) and Alexei Tolstoi's *Rasputin* (1927). Above all, however, he believed that the symbolic power of film could add a new dimension to the theater. "When it becomes a platform for active intellectual/spiritual struggles, the theater will offer as many attractions and sensations as the most modern sound film." In other words, Balázs had come to view the theater as a revolutionary substitute for the disappearing silent film.[115]

For that reason, he did not restrict himself to work with the Piscator-Bühne. In the spring of 1928, he accepted an appointment as artistic director of the KPD-dominated German Workers' Theater Alliance, which sponsored small agitprop groups that performed plays, songs, dances, and pantomimes in major German cities. In addition to his overall artistic leadership, Balázs also directed a troupe called "the Heretics" and helped to target areas, often in and around factories and on busy streetcorners, to which troups were sent. Most of the brief agitprop plays he wrote were collaborative efforts because it was the theater's policy to discourage individuality. In 1929, for example, he wrote a comic drama for children based upon some ideas suggested to him by one Lisa

Tetzner. On November 13, the Group of Young Actors performed *Hans Urian Goes in Search of Bread*, a witty and imaginative piece that was at the same time a veritable compendium of Communist clichés.

Hans Urian lives with his mother, a poor widow who is ill and without food. From her the boy learns that there is enough food in the world for all, if only it were justly distributed. With that in mind, he goes out to ask the local baker for bread, only to discover that the poor man can barely make ends meet because he pays so much for flour. The resigned baker is the first of many to assure the disappointed Hans that the world will one day be more just.[116] He suggests that the boy seek help from a peasant who grows grain. Hans then sets out, accompanied by a hungry hare named Trillewipp, who can speak and fly.

The new friends are disappointed once again when they find out that peasants are also poor because they are obliged to give much of their grain to the landowners. They therefore seize on one peasant's belief that bread is plentiful in the United States. Hans mounts Trillewipp and they fly out over the Atlantic; after several socially instructive adventures en route, they land in New York. To their chagrin, they quickly discover that the rich exploit the poor in the new world as well. Hans obtains a factory job but he is horrified when told that he is expected to make cannons. His father having been killed in the war, he will have none of it. Instead, he incites his coworkers to strike and, as a result, he and the hare must hide in the mouths of cannons, which are about to be shipped to Africa.[117]

Balázs's depiction of the African natives would not pass muster in contemporary progressive circles, but Whites are properly arrogant and criminal. They steal land and food while their missionary piously preaches love and nonresistance to the Blacks. After some hilarious shenanigans, Hans and Trillewipp travel on to China, where Hans is to work in a silk factory. But in the Far East as everywhere else in the world, capitalist exploitation is the order of the day; the factory managers brutalize the child laborers. By now an experienced organizer, Hans calls for a strike, which puts the capitalists to rout. He then challenges the Chinese children to move on to other factories in order to end injustice and exploitation. He, however, returns home with money Trillewipp has earned as a street performer. Once back in Germany, Hans tells the Director of his old school how much he has learned about the various ways the rich exploit the poor around the world. As he proclaims that a more just world must be created, the school children send up a cheer.[118]

Like the converted Balázs, Hans Urian was a wanderer who found his true "home" in the struggle for a new, Communist, world. Indeed, the play was an almost perfectly executed agitprop piece for children—the propaganda is straightforward and presented within the context of a young boy and a talking hare's humorous adventures. Still, Balázs generally preferred to encourage improvization; "it was," he later recalled, "commedia dell'arte in Wedding or in Neukölln, anno 1931."[119] He was particularly proud of the fact that the worker-actors created their own plays, spontaneously. Most of the men and women were amateurs who worked during the day, although some were among the unemployed. According to Balázs, they performed well because they had experienced at first hand the evils of the capitalist system; for them, "revolutionary art /was/ a form of proletarian class consciousness."[120]

So carried away had the Hungarian become that he claimed that the "workers' theater /was/ the folk poetry of the class-conscious proletariat."[121] In his captive mind, he had come to equate crass propaganda with the study and classical assimilation of folk music that his quondam friends, Bartók and Kodály, accomplished earlier in the century. Even someone as sympathetic with Weimar radicalism as John Willett concedes that "such songs and other texts of theirs /the workers' theaters'/ as have survived are not very impressive."[122] Having sacrificed his talent and judgment on communism's altar, Balázs joined the German Communist Party in 1931.

PART TWO

THE AVANT-GARDE

THREE

LAJOS KASSÁK:

THE MA CIRCLE

The Prophet

SOON AFTER Gyula Peidl formed a caretaker government in Budapest, the new authorities in Keszthely took Lajos Kassák into custody. They detained him there for several days before sending him on to the capital with an armed escort. In his autobiography, the pugnacious leader of the Hungarian avant-garde did not complain of his treatment, but he did testify to his mounting apprehension. As always, he took what courage he could from his faithful wife, the self-sacrificing Jolán Simon. Whenever he sank into despair, she appeared with food and news of fast-paced events in the outer world. "They have arrested Ottó Korvin," she whispered one day. Without thinking how his guards might react, Kassák replied: "Now comes a fearful world."[1]

That conviction only deepened in the Budapest cell where Kassák and others were confined. With little to occupy him, he began, for the first time, to fear for his life and to mull over the reasons for the revolution's failure. It was not, he concluded, external enemies, but internal weakness that doomed the Soviet Republic. In general, there had not been enough preparation. More specifically, "he sought the reasons not in the objective, but the subjective factors, in those who made the revolution."[2] Imagine his vengeful delight, then, when the police placed Pál Kéri in his cell. Still angry about Kéri's splenetic attack on him and the Ma Circle in Ferenc Göndör's Az Ember, Kassák snarled that "you and Göndör and the rest were the revolution's first traitors."[3] He could not bring himself to wish Kéri well when, thanks to Jolán's importunities, the authorities transferred him to a prison hospital.

After several weeks during which Kassák thought he would lose his mind, the indefatigable Jolán finally found someone who could help. Alleging that the prisoner suffered from a serious case of gastric tuberculosis, a young doctor recommended that he be transferred to a civilian hospital or sanitarium. Two days later, Kassák walked out of the prison hospital, free to seek private treatment. It was December 1919, almost five months since the police had pounded on his door in Keszthely. His hair reached to his shoulders and he wore an untrimmed beard; his mother and Jolán's three children—Eti, Piri, and Rudi—scarcely recognized him.

Although free for the time being, Kassák knew he was still in danger. Moreover, he quickly discovered that he had no prospect whatever of resuscitating *Ma* or publishing his work elsewhere. There was no other choice, he and Jolán concluded, but exile. His brother-in-law, Béla Uitz, had already fled to Vienna and the *Nyugat* writers Ernő Osvát, Milán Füst, and Zsigmond Móricz had signaled their readiness to help. He had only to find a Danube boat captain willing, for a price, to smuggle him into Austria. By March, a young Communist woman had made all the necessary arrangements. Jolán cut Kassák's hair and he, who always wore a black shirt, dressed in white. Once on board, he hid in a large metal trunk in the lower portion of the smokestack. Six hours later, filthy and exhausted, he was in Vienna.

Soon after his arrival, Jolán and the children emigrated and took up residence with him in a small sublet room on the second floor of a building on Amalien Strasse. Located in District 13 on the outskirts of the city, the room was run down and far too cramped for five people. Without having to be told, Rudi, who did not get on well with Kassák, secured employment as a textile worker and rented a small room of his own, while Eti and Piri accepted temporary accommodations from a charitable organization. Jolán, who sacrificed her career as an actress to follow Kassák into exile, worked like a slave. In addition to watching over her children, she did the cooking and washing. To support her husband, she took in work as a seamstress.

For his part, Kassák could think of nothing but reviving *Ma* and reentering the cultural, if not the political, wars. Joining him in the old imperial capital were such veteran *Ma*-ists as Uitz, his sister (the poet Erzsi Ujvári), her husband Sándor Barta, and the painter Sándor Bortnyik, who in 1922 portrayed Kassák as *The Prophet*, surrounded by followers. And a prophet he surely was, preaching the gospel of the "new man" to those with whom he met regularly at the Schloss-Café, a coffeehouse near Schönbrunn Castle, the Habsburgs' former summer residence. Against all odds, he and they[4] brought out the first number of the Vienna *Ma* on Labor Day, May 1, 1920; on the cover was a sorrowful, abstract expressionist print by János Máttis Teutsch.

Kassák seized the occasion to issue an updated programmatic statement and a call to arms—in Hungarian and German—"to artists of every country." With the collapse of the Hungarian Soviet Republic burning in his memory, he declared that revolutionary artists ought not to serve any class, even the proletariat. Not class rule, but the community of all men should be their aim. And that aim could not be realized by political means or the transformation of material conditions. With unmistakable, but implicit, reference to Kun and Lukács, he cried, "Down with the politics that calculates in human blood! Down with the leader prima donnas who cling to prestige! Down with the Talmudists of the revolution!"[5]

What the times demanded, Kassák insisted, was not the dictatorship of a class, but of the idea. The true revolution was that of human consciousness

5. Sándor Bortnyik. *The Prophet* (1922). Oil on canvas, 31 ½ × 27 ½ in. (80 × 70 cm.).
Courtesy of the Magyar Nemzeti Galéria (Hungarian National Gallery), Budapest.

and it could be won only if artists became the moral and cultural teachers of
humankind. "Hence culture! And again culture!" Disillusioned with the Soviet Republic's politics and without political prospects of his own, Kassák
aspired to lead a permanent revolution of human consciousness and thus to
create not a new political order, but new men, "collective individuals." He
proclaimed that message in a prose poem first entitled "1919 Epic" and later
"Funeral Pyres Sing." In that heroic account of the Soviet Republic's rise and
fall, Kassák played the hero—the "bearded man"—off against Kun, a failed
newspaperman and would-be Napoleon, and other political leaders. He char-

acterized the latter as prima donnas hungry for power and more than willing to resort to terror.[6]

In contrast to such unsavory politicians, the bearded man/Kassák appeared as a "prophet" and authentic spokesman for the people. He warns the leaders that the revolution was premature because changed human beings must always precede a changed economic order. That being the case, they must work not for new laws but new men. His "brothers" and "sisters," he says, need politics less than they do a deeper understanding of their own souls. "It is not necessary to form a /political/ dictatorship around them, as Marxist intellectuals repeat like parrots, but rather to revive in them the dictatorship of the idea."[7] In uncorrupted children he sees hope for the future.

Despite the bearded man's warnings, however, the politicians pursue policies that virtually ensure the victory of the counterrevolution. The hero emigrates from Hungary, but as reaction takes its revenge in Budapest and the countryside, an "activist poet" sits in his jail cell, thinking himself into a future in which the bearded man's prescriptions are followed and the people find the revolution deep within themselves.[8]

The Dadaist Moment

With the lyrical requiem for the Soviet Republic and the manifesto that preceded it, Kassák served notice to the emigré Communists that he would have nothing more to do with politics, the Party, or any art form that the Party might prescribe. Indeed, in his depression over the failed revolution, he looked with no little favor on the artistic attitude represented by postwar dadaism. Not, to be sure, because the world was irredeemably absurd, but because he believed it to be temporarily out of control. That was why he had to endure the pain of defeat and the isolation of exile.

Although dada had been born serendipitously in Zürich in 1916 (the date is the subject of much mock controversy), Richard Huelsenbeck brought the movement to Berlin the following year. There, after the war, it hit its stride. The Berlin dadaists included Communists such as Wieland Herzfelde, John Heartfield (Johann Herzfelde), and George Grosz, as well as anarchists such as Huelsenbeck, Johannes Baader, and Raoul Hausmann. Together those men mounted a ferocious assault on everybody and everything, very much including the various "isms"—Italian futurism, French cubism, and especially German expressionism. They even fell out among themselves, as all good dadaists must.

And always the dadaists contrived to say a great deal about nothing, witness the *Dada Almanach* that Huelsenbeck edited in 1920. In his introduction, which later appeared in *Ma*, RH (Huelsenbeck—though as dada chance would have it, Hausmann's initials as well) hurled insults at logic, but managed to remain unambiguous concerning one point: "Dada is the most direct and active expression of its era; it turns against everything that appears to it to be obsolete, mummified, or attached."[9] Such a sweeping rejection of culture and the past, Balázs charged, was pure nihilism. Thus, it was to their shame "that our activists have greeted the dadaists as their brothers."[10]

Kassák did not deny that the dadaists were "the most desperate enemies of every past," but he insisted that they wanted "to destroy root and branch all 'modern' art because they firmly believe that only after its destruction can the new culture be rebuilt /sic/."[11] That may not have been every dadaist's view, but it was certainly Kassák's own. He wished to wipe the slate clean *so as to* begin anew from scratch; to liberate people from the burden of the past so that they could see and experience the world in fresh and unexpected ways. Only when they learned, for example, to juxtapose words and sentences in unfamiliar patterns, to infer meaning from apparent nonsense, could they revolutionize their consciousness and in that very process create a totally new social order.

Beginning with the second or third number, one member of Kassák's inner circle later recalled, the Vienna *Ma* "openly and emphatically abandoned all intelligible talk and, in general, everything that normal people considered, until then, to be beautiful."[12] Kassák published translations of verse by Huelsenbeck and Hans Arp, along with essays by Hausmann, Tristan Tzara, and Hans Richter. He was particularly captivated, though, by Kurt Schwitters, whom Robert Hughes has called "the great lyric artist of Dadaism."[13] Schwitters, who was independently wealthy, worked in Hanover because Huelsenbeck could not abide his "bourgeois face" and refused to admit him to the dada circle in Berlin.

At one of the first "*Ma* Evenings" in Vienna, Jolán Simon recited a Hungarian translation of Schwitters's most famous poem, "Anna Blume." The effect was as disconcerting as it was mesmerizing. To begin with, there was Jolán's magical, reedy voice, which left an indelible impression. "Decades later," one former *Ma*-ist recalled, "if I read the lines /of "Anna Blume"/, they come back to me in Jolán's musical rendition."[14] And then there was the poem itself, the flavor of which can perhaps be suggested by the following lines:

> Prize question: 1.) Anna Blume has a bird.
> 2.) Anna Blume is red.
> 3.) What color is the bird?
> Blue is the color of your yellow hair.
> Red is the cooing of your green bird.[15]

In the spirit of dada Kassák agreed to coedit, with Andor Németh, a new emigré magazine. Németh, whom Arthur Koestler described as the most "baroque personality" he had ever known,[16] had spent the war years in a French internment camp. Unable to reach Budapest during the time that Kun ruled, he served briefly on the staff of the Hungarian Chargé d'Affairs in Vienna. After the Soviet Republic's collapse, he found himself in the role of a political exile. In need of work, he joined the staff of the *Bécsi Magyar Újság*, which put up the money for *2X2: The Magazine of New Artists*. Németh and Kassák quickly arrived at a curious editorial decision: one would assume responsibility for the first half of each number, the other for the last. Each would act in complete independence of the other, even if that should produce strange juxtapositions.

Only one number of *2X2* appeared, in December 1922. In his section, Kassák published his now famous autobiographical poem: "The Horse Dies, the Birds Take Wing." This is a lyrical account, replete with dadaist images, of the poet's *Wanderjahre*, the years before the war when he walked across Europe to Paris. In Brussels, he and his traveling companion attend a meeting of Russian revolutionaries and feel themselves to be "relatives of Dostoevski's possessed" because "we want to destroy everything." And yet the poet never embraces destruction as an end in itself: "Without doubt the Astrakhan baker's daughter or the Petersburg whore will one day give birth to the new man."[17]

On reaching his destination, the poet sees the city on the Seine, and yet sees nothing. When he returns home, however, he possesses greater self-consciousness of his creative responsibilities. The trip heralded the beginning of his literary career and Kassák conjured it up in the hope of creating in himself a fresh readiness to begin again, to build anew on the ruins of the past. The poem's closing lines, one critic has written, represent the "most expressive and most vivid memorial to Kassák's dadaist moment."[18] "Birds have swallowed the sound/but the trees go on singing/this is already a sign of old age/but it does not mean anything/I am LAJOS KASSÁK/ and above our heads flies the nickel samovar."[19]

The careful reader—and *seer*—of "The Horse Dies" will notice the pictorial effect Kassák achieved by eschewing punctuation, altering the length of the poetic lines, capitalizing letters, and inserting numbers. These were favorite dadaist strategies. Hausmann and Baader, for example, constructed the cover of the first issue of *Der Dada* almost entirely from numbers and letters of varying sizes, moving in different directions. And Schwitters composed a poem entirely of numbers.

According to Hans Richter, the dadaists created "a new typography which gave to the individual letter, word or sentence a freedom it had never possessed (outside the Futurist and Zürich Dada movements) since Gutenberg. An inspired dip into the compositor's type-case, and school orthography was replaced by heterography. Large and small letters joined in new combinations and danced up and down; vertical and horizontal words arranged themselves to carry the meaning, and gave new life to the printed page, so that it not only described the new freedom to the reader, but allowed him to see and feel it for himself."[20]

What to some was the "new freedom" was to others, Kassák included, the new disorder and moral anarchy as well. In attempting to convey something about that disorder and the past's failures, the exiled Hungarian began to rely more and more on visual media, which required no translation. He wanted the Vienna *Ma* to be an international forum and he knew that he was, and would always be, a willing prisoner in his own language house, for unlike most of his fellow exiles, he did not have command of a foreign language.

With the exception of a few pen and ink sketches from the war years, Kassák's earliest visual achievements were his "sketched" or "pictorial poems" inspired by dadaism, as well as cubism and futurism. The first appeared on the January 1, 1921 cover of *Ma*. On New Year's Day the following year, he published one of the most spectacular pictorial poems ever to appear in *Ma's* pages: "Evening Under the Trees." Readers might have found the verbal meaning opaque, but they could not but have been struck by the riot of words and letters—vertical, horizontal, diagonal, upside down, thick, thin, twisting, turning—that formed intriguing pictures. Curiously, the text becomes clearer when one attends to the spatial location of certain sentences and words. In the lower right-hand corner of the second, and last, page, Kassák placed a large black ball under a slanted line that created the visual composition's center of gravity. Directly under the ball, in large and thick capital letters, he wrote the word "*sír*" ("weeps"), which conveys the poem's conceptual essence.

Despite their dadaist pedigree, however, Kassák's pictorial poems contained a hidden, and sometimes not so hidden, constructive element. Out of the seeming anarchy, the Hungarian strove to craft a new unity. Nowhere was that striving more evident than in the brief, visually constructed, poem he published in the October 15, 1922 issue of *Ma*: "ROMboljatok HOGY épithessetek ÉS ÉPITSETEK hogy GYŐZHESSETEK" ("Demolish so that you can build and build so that you can triumph").

From pictorial poems it was but a short step to collages—pieces of paper, cloth, or other material pasted on a surface. Kassák admired Schwitters as the master of dada collage. Having once discovered a torn piece of paper advertising the Kommerz-und Privat-Bank, the German adopted "Merz" as his trademark. He wandered the streets in search of useless articles and scraps of newsprint from which he crafted his collages. At Kassák's request, he contributed a short statement to *Ma* entitled "In What Way Am I Dissatisfied with Oil Painting?" He believed, Schwitters wrote with uncharacteristic sobriety, that artists concentrated too much on oil painting, to the exclusion of the whole world of material at their disposal. "The use in *Merz* painting of precisely those previously uncommon materials in previously uncommon ways demonstrates how inessential the material used is from the point of view of the work."[21]

In his own collages, Kassák restricted himself to paper, usually written or printed material. Where he differed most from Schwitters was in his strong predisposition to compose and arrange in a conscious manner. He gave to his work only the appearance of randomness and chance. Nevertheless, Kassák's association with dadaism offended Hungarian exiles other than Balázs and Lukács. In 1922, Uitz left the Ma Circle to coedit Egység (Unity) with Aladár Komját. The emigré review described itself as "a communist cultural organ" committed to the Proletcult, and in its second number, Andor Réz criticized Ma for disavowing "every order" including the "proletarian order."[22] Never one to suffer insult in silence, Kassák replied immediately, accusing Egység's editors and contributors of being renegades who distorted his and Ma's writings and revolutionary record.[23]

As if one brother-in-law's defection were not enough, Sándor Barta and Erzsi Ujvári also broke ranks in 1922. Together they launched Akasztott Ember (Hanged Man; the title of a Barta poem), which aspired "to bring the class struggle to the cultural sphere."[24] To be sure, Barta was more of a dadaist than Kassák, but he modeled himself after the dada Communists—Herzfelde, Heartfield, and Grosz. He had come to believe that his brother-in-law had moved too far away from political reality, and in 1923 he joined forces with the Egység circle to publish the Communist review Ék (Spike).

Kassák responded in the pages of Ma by speaking of "the tragedy of a generation"[25] whose members had once guided, but latterly had begun to follow, politicians. Worse, at the very moment when progressive Russians had come to recognize the Proletcult as a gigantic failure, Hungarian Communists wanted to champion it. They failed to understand that that which was truly revolutionary in Russian art stood in sharp opposition to the Proletcult. Authentic revolutionary artists worked with superhuman energy to express themselves, and thus the revolution, through their creations.

As these controversies indicate, Kassák remained a proud and difficult man who could not tolerate opinions at variance with his own. New members of his circle learned quickly not to mention the names of Uitz or Barta, or even Bortnyik, who broke away because he could no longer endure Kassák's imperious manner. Sitting in one of his favorite coffeehouses, such as the Colosseum on Nussdorfer Strasse, the prophet declaimed his message of salvation to those who remained loyal.

Always, of course, there was Jolán, who toted newly printed numbers of Ma to the Communist party's bookstore on Alser Strasse, made regular visits to Hungary to organize illegal "Ma Evenings," and sacrificed much of her meager income to keep the magazine afloat. Andor Németh contrived to remain on good terms with Kassák despite many cultural disagreements. And Endre Gáspár, a gifted linguist who did many of Ma's translations, was utterly devoted. He and his wife lived in Döbling, where they welcomed Hungarian emigrés and permitted Kassák to entertain avant-gardists visiting from other countries.

The Berlin Connection: Moholy and Kállai

There were other Hungarian emigrés who found it possible to work with Kassák, though only because they did not reside in Vienna. Chief among them was László Moholy-Nagy, who had been too occupied with his independent study of painting to play a role in the Soviet Republic. We know that that dedication to art troubled him, for on May 15, 1919, two months after Kun seized the reins of power, he made a long entry in his notebook: "During the war, but more strongly even now, I feel my responsibility toward society. My conscience asks incessantly: is it right to become a painter in times of social revolution?" The answer, he concluded, was yes.

> I have had many talks with men and women on my long train trips. I have seen what is needed beyond food. I have finally learned to grasp what is biological happiness in its complete meaning. And I know now that if I unfold my best talents in the way suited best to them—if I try to grasp the meaning of this, my life, sincerely and thoroughly—then I'm doing right in becoming a painter. It is my gift to project my vitality, my building power, through light, color, form. I can give *life* as a painter.[26]

Cognizant of the fact that he was in no personal danger and did not have to leave Hungary, Moholy cooperated with a friend, the sculptor Sándor Gergely, to organize a joint exhibition of their work in Szeged. After visiting the exhibit in November 1919, Gyula Juhász reported that the two men expressed a new artistic faith because they possessed "a new social and cultural world view," one related to that which informed Bartók's music and Walt Whitman's free verse. Taken together, Juhász enthused, such cultural manifestations heralded the coming of a new age of Pericles or a new Renaissance.[27]

Juhász's was, however, a solo voice. Convinced that they could look ahead to only limited opportunities in postwar Hungary, Moholy and Gergely emigrated to Vienna late in November. Soon after their arrival in the once gay city, Moholy forged a close friendship with Lajos Tihanyi, one of the finest of Hungarian portrait painters, who inspired him to paint a series of portraits, including a striking likeness of Jolán Simon. With bold lines, Moholy captured the strength of character Jolán needed to live with Kassák, while at the same time he learned "that the manner in which lines are related, not objects as such, carry the richer message."[28]

But although he was maturing rapidly an an artist, Moholy was restless, and after only six weeks decided to move on. "Coming from a farm in the agricultural center of Hungary, I was less intrigued with the baroque pompousness of the Austrian capital than with the highly developed technology of industrial Germany. I went to Berlin."[29]

6. László Moholy-Nagy. *Jolán Simon*, Vienna (1919–20). Lithographic crayon, 16⅝ × 12 3/4 in. Collection, The Museum of Modern Art, New York. Abby Aldrich Rockefeller Fund (by exchange).

Determined to make a name for himself in that postwar mecca for modernists, Moholy worked his way north as a letterer and sign painter. When he arrived late in the winter of 1920, he was suffering from a severe case of the flu. Thanks to the care that Dr. Reinhold Schairer and his wife Gerda, both Quakers, gave him, Moholy recovered and in due course took a furnished room in Berlin-Charlottenburg. With him was Lucia Schultz, a talented photographer from Prague whom he had met in April. On January 18, 1921, Moholy married Lucia and a year later the couple rented a studio flat on Lützow Strasse in Berlin.

"Many of my paintings of that period," Moholy later recalled, "show the influence of the industrial 'landscape' of Berlin."[30] Like a child on his first visit to an amusement park, the Hungarian from a rustic village began to *see* bridges, railway stations, signs, and machines for the first time. Machines, symbols of the industrial world, especially pleased and fascinated him. Indeed, he warned against intellectual Luddites. It was "dangerously shortsighted to will the elimination, along with dreadnoughts and skyscrapers, of the grandeur of machines and the power over nature that they place in our hands. We need the machine. Without any romanticism. The skyscraper is truly an unhealthy construction that we ought not to copy, but we can accept funiculars, cranes, and water towers, which are inspired creations of the same constructive spirit. Let us not depreciate the absolute value of creations because of the corrupt uses to which particular societies put them. What is bad is not the machine, but the structure of contemporary society."[31]

Moholy's infatuation with machines and mechanics paralleled that of the dadaists. Although, like Kassák, he rejected the more nihilistic and "accidental" aspects of dadaism, he did breathe more easily in the atmosphere of freedom and unlimited possibility that the movement's leaders created. And if at first he took a dim view of Schwitters's work, he learned much from the Cuban Francis Picabia, especially from such compositions as *The Girl Born Without a Mother*, in which a large spoked wheel connects with an imposing axle, and *Alarm-Clock* with its many interlocking wheels.

Moholy drew inspiration also from lesser-known dadaists such as Johannes Mohlzahn, who attempted to portray a "Post-Fantastic" world that witnessed to man's constructive power, Walter Dexel, with whom he exhibited at the Fritz Gurlitt Gallery in 1920, and Robert Michel. The stronger constructive element in those three artists' work appealed to Moholy, who did not approve of Picabia and Marcel Duchamp's playful, ironic attitude, much less their effort to emphasize the eroticism of mechanical forms.

Above all, Moholy wanted his work to project a new vision and fresh opportunities which men and women could seize to construct a world far better than that which had died in the trenches. In his compositions—drawings, paintings, collages—of 1920–21, he placed wheels, transmission belts, and axles, together with letters and numbers. At first glance, the location of the various elements appeared to be arbitrary, but on closer inspection one could often discern the underlying organization. That was true, for example, of *Bridges* (1920), an industrial landscape in which bridges, railway stations, and train cars seem to have been propelled in every direction by an explosion at the center. Yet Moholy built into the landscape two semicircles and, at the center, an inverted human figure pointing a finger at himself (as a constructor?).

Moholy may have hit upon the idea for his famous *Big Wheel* (or *Big Emotional Machine*) of 1920–21 after seeing the Prater's huge ferris wheel. Within and without the large, centrally located wheel, paradigm of the tools man uses, he placed numbers, letters (including his initials, MN), and smaller wheels. By reminding men that they had once invented the wheel, he undoubtedly intended to encourage in them confident and affirmative emotions. "We have it in our power," he seemed to say, "to redesign the wheel, to rebuild a broken world." That, in fact, is what he did say, quite explicitly, in a drawing on which he repeatedly wrote the Hungarian word "*Épits*" ("Build!"). He made that drawing, dated 1919, while in a state of ecstasy. "There were no objects, only lines, straight and curved. Wheels and bridges scattered on the sheet were the only shapes derived from nature."[32]

Moholy dedicated a "bridge" collage of 1920 to Ernő Kállai, "with friendly affection." Few now remember Kállai, but he was one of Weimar Germany's most important and influential art critics. Born in Szakálháza on November 9, 1890, Kállai was the scion of a German father and a Serbian mother.[33] When he was eight, his parents Magyarized the family name, Kannengiesser, to "Kállai," but continued to raise their son bilingually. From 1910 to 1913, young Kállai prepared for a secondary school career at a Budapest teachers' college, and upon completion of his studies, traveled to England, Scandinavia, and the United States. When war broke out, he rushed home to follow the colors. Sent to the Carpathian front, he was severely wounded and reassigned to garrison duty before being permitted to return to civilian life.

Toward the end of the conflict, Kállai visited *Ma*'s exhibition hall on Váci Street in Pest. There he met Kassák, who admired his obvious love of art and recognized his potential as a critic. After the war he taught in Nagymarton and Budapest, but in 1920 requested and received permission to study in Germany. The same year he settled in Berlin, where, with brief interruptions, he made his home until he returned to Hungary in 1935.

Fluent in German as well as Hungarian, Kállai began to write for German magazines almost immediately. He assigned himself the task of introducing the Weimar public to the Hungarian Postimpressionists. Modern Hungarian painting, he maintained, was expressive in character, yet far removed from German expressionism. While the latter cultivated a transcendental sense, the former possessed an almost tangible feeling for this world. The difference in spiritual worlds was that between Oscar Kokoschka's over-refinement, as expressed in his nervous convulsions, and Moholy's intelligent and powerfully-willed affirmations of life and the objective world.[34]

But while the Hungarian artists focused their attention on the physical world, they did not all explore the same landscape. Although they had fled to the great cities of the West, some carried with them their Eastern feeling for nature and the Hungarian plains. Like Lajos Tihanyi, they held themselves aloof from politics or at most dreamed of the day when Hungary would be a peasant democracy. Others, however, embraced the industrial and technological world without so much as a backward glance. At the center of their creations they placed visions of social revolution that would produce a better future for all peoples, regardless of race or nation. Among members of the latter group, Kállai numbered Uitz, Bortnyik, Kassák, and "before all others, Moholy-Nagy, who transvalues the dadaist impulses of chaotic Western culture into radiantly victorious and monumental—yet nimble, airy, and dancing—affirmations of life and beauty."[35]

In the spring of 1921, at almost precisely the same moment, Kállai and Moholy offered their services to Ma. Beginning with the April 25, 1921 issue, Kassák informed readers that "our representative in Germany is László Moholy-Nagy, Berlin-Charlottenburg, Witzlebenstrasse 3." Moreover, he devoted much of the September 15 number to Moholy's work. On the cover was a machine drawing, while inside subscribers could judge a number of drawings and oil reproductions including the Big Emotional Machine. Kállai, signing himself "Péter Mátyás," contributed the lead article: "Moholy-Nagy."

In a brilliant and convincing single-page analysis, Kállai argued that Moholy had combined the insights of dadaism and cubism to celebrate the contemporary world's mastery of machines. In his drawings and paintings, he presented a world that, at first glance, appeared to be chaotic. Yet unlike other dadaists, he had not adopted a negative and pessimistic attitude, nor attempted to make of art an instrument of savage social and moral criticism. Far from having succumbed to despair or nihilism, he viewed the modern industrial world of the great metropolises through the eyes of a wonder-struck Urchild. He loved and affirmed the new world he had discovered in Berlin, and thus, underneath the surface anarchy, he constructed a fundamental, if more or less hidden, order and meaning.[36] Because Moholy and Kállai shared Kassák's faith in the possibility of building a meaningful order, they joined the Ma Circle, while remaining at a comfortable distance from Vienna.

From Dadaism to Constructivism

Why did Kassák remain in Vienna when so much was happening in Berlin? Why was he content to publish Ma in a city that was almost completely indifferent to the international avant-garde? Money was a consideration, but more important was the fact that Kassák wished to maintain contact with Hungarian communities in Austria, Hungary, and the successor states. To have left Austria would have been to cut his last ties to his homeland and resign himself to permanent exile. Moreover, in Berlin or Paris he would have had to learn another language and to cease being a Hungarian writer.

7. László Moholy-Nagy. *Composition 19*, oil on canvas, 111.8 × 92.7 cm. Courtesy of the Busch-Reisinger Museum, Harvard University, Cambridge, Massachusetts. Gift of Sibyl Moholy-Nagy. Appeared in Moholy-Nagy number of *Ma*, September 15, 1921.

In Vienna on the other hand, Kassák could continue to expound his internationalist ideas in his mother tongue. And he could make of *Ma* a meeting place for Western and Eastern European avant-gardists. Indeed, in addition to connections in Germany (*Der Sturm; Merz; Der Dada*), France (*L'Esprit Nouveau*), Holland (*De Stijl*), and the United States (*The Little Review*), he established working relationships with modernist reviews in Zagreb (*Zenit*), Bucharest (*Contimporanul*), Warsaw (*Blok; Praesens*), and Prague (*Pasmo*).

But although he elected to stay in Vienna until such time as he might return home, Kassák knew that his Berlin connection was crucial. Without *Der Sturm* and its Gallery he could never hope to reach a wider German and European public. Although, for example, he had organized an exhibition of Uitz's work in November 1920, he had not been able to do the same for other members of the Ma Circle. *Sturm*'s director Herwarth Walden (Georg Lewin), on the other hand, possessed the financial means and progressive reputation to promote successfully little-known Hungarians. In 1922, the multi-talented entrepreneur, who shared many of Kassák's interests,[37] arranged shows for Moholy, Bortnyik, and László Péri, a geometric and architectonic painter who led him from nonparty radicalism to communism. He showcased Moholy, Péri, Máttis Teutsch, and Béla Kádár in 1923; and Hugo Scheiber, Aurél Bernáth, Béni Ferenczy, Kádár, Moholy, and Kassák in 1924. In addition, Walden's magazine featured many Hungarian illustrations and reproductions and his Sturm Press published the *Ma-Buch* (1923), a collection of Kassák's poetry, translated into German by Endre Gáspár, that included "The Horse Dies, the Birds Take Wing."

Despite the fact that he maintained a close working relationship with Walden, Kassák had lost all interest in expressionism. And so had his Berlin representatives. Shortly after arriving in the German capital, Moholy reported to Hevesy that expressionism had failed, and Walden had become a millionaire whom one could approach only through his secretary. "As one dadaist review says," Moholy wrote, "art is for him /Walden/ only a cover for making money." As a result, Moholy formed a poor opinion of Sturm shows—at least until he himself began to exhibit.[38]

Kállai spoke in greater critical detail about expressionism in the first piece he wrote for Ma (June 1, 1921). After having viewed Berlin exhibitions of work by Vasili Kandinsky, Franz Marc, Karl Schmitt-Rottluf, Robert Delaunay, and Emil Nolde, he concluded that they, like bourgeois intellectuals in general, were trying to escape from a social and natural reality that they viewed in negative terms. As representatives of a declining culture, they had succumbed to an extreme subjectivism; one could detect nothing of objective reality in their work. "Nothing of building, of logic, of construction. Everything is personal experience, again and again only 'personal experience.' "[39] By thus turning art away from life and reality, expressionism had signed its own death warrant.

Kállai did, however, find something to recommend in Walden's vast collection: Marc Chagall's paintings. "Chagall," he informed Ma's readers, "is the only one whose mysteriousness is not a romantic excursion into subjective and psychological curiosities, but rather objective reality raised to the level of myth."[40] More than anything else, it was Walden's growing interest in Chagall and other Russian artists that made it possible for Kállai, Moholy, and Kassák to cooperate with him. Convinced that expressionism was spent as a creative force, the German connoisseur began to promote and encourage constructivism. "In my whole life," Chagall later recalled, "I've never seen so many wonderful rabbis or so many Constructivists as in Berlin in 1922."[41]

The vogue of Russian constructivism in postwar Germany was part of a more encompassing cultural and political affinity between two great powers. This is not the place to rehearse Bismarck's good relations with Tsarist Russia, the affectionate Willy-Nicky letters, or the stunning Rapallo Treaty of 1922. But one should bear in mind that Thomas Mann had good historical reasons for insisting that Russian and German cultures were closely related. The Russian Westernizers of the early nineteenth century admired Schiller and Hegel, while Leibniz and Herder were fascinated by Russia. During and after the war, Mann and other Germans, including Arthur Moeller van den Bruck and Oswald Spengler, read Dostoevski and Tolstoi with a sense of awe.

If anything, the October Revolution lent to Russian culture an even greater aura. Russians and non-Russians alike came to associate Russian literature and art with titanic social transformation, the building of a new and far better world. Had not the bolsheviks promised a world turned upside down by the machine and industrialization? Lenin and his collaborators understood better than most that "for the Russian, the machine came as a liberating force, liberating man from the tyranny of nature and giving him the possibility to create an entirely man-made world, of which he will finally be the master."[42] It was hardly surprising, then, that the dada Communists, John Heartfield and George Grosz, were photographed in 1920 with a placard that read: "Art is dead; long live Tatlin's new machine-art."

Heartfield and Grosz referred to Vladimir Tatlin, the founder of constructivism. A Ukrainian born in 1885, Tatlin learned much from Russian icon painting and had already become a member of the avant-garde before he accompanied a Russian exhibition of folk art to Berlin in the autumn of 1913. From there he set out for Paris, where he met Picasso. The master's sculptures of wood, cardboard, and bent tin awakened the Russian to fresh possibilities, especially the novel notion that sculpture could be conceived of not only as solid mass (modeled clay, cast bronze, carved stone or wood), but as open assembly. After he returned to Russia, Tatlin set to work with common materials such as iron and glass, viewing the resulting sculptures "as icons, transmitters of social truth; and he placed them where Russians put their icons, in corners."[43]

In 1919, with the Civil War raging and bolshevism's fate hanging in the balance, the People's Commissariat for Education commissioned Tatlin to design a *Monument to the Third International* that could be erected in the center of Moscow. All during that year and the next, the great constructor labored in his studio with three assistants. He built several models in metal and wood, one of which, 15 1/2 feet in height, he unveiled at the Eighth Congress of the

Soviets in December 1920. Tatlin characterized his work as "a union of purely artistic forms (painting, sculpture and architecture) for a utilitarian purpose."[44] It immediately became the symbol of the utopian world he and other constructivists planned to build.

There is no doubt, at any rate, that one had to be a utopian to believe that the monument could actually be constructed. Tatlin expected to execute it in iron and glass and to have it reach three hundred feet beyond the Eiffel Tower. A spiral iron framework that soared diagonally upward was to support a glass cube that would accommodate meetings of the International and complete one revolution each year; a glass pyramid that would provide space for executive work and rotate once a month; and a glass cylinder, designed to be an information center and revolve once a day. "Special machinery" would keep all three levels in motion. Or so Nikolai Punin, Tatlin's champion, described it in, among other places, the pages of *Ma*.[45]

Tatlin and his principal rival, Kazimir Malevich, the founder of nonobjective suprematism, did not get along personally, in part because one was materialistic and practical in outlook while the other viewed the world in spiritual terms and believed art to be nonsocial and nonutilitarian. Both, however, modeled themselves after Cézanne, who advised artists to "treat nature by the cylinder, the sphere, the cone," and were therefore more interested in geometric patterns than identifiable objects. That is why El (Lazar Markovich) Lissitzky, artistically the most representative and historically the most important constructivist, believed he could synthesize their work.

Born to Jewish parents, Lissitzky studied engineering in Germany. During the war he trained as an architect in Moscow and in 1917, the year of revolution, he began to collaborate with Chagall and other Jewish artists on book illustration. He soon combined his interest in lettering with the knowledge of nonobjectivist art he gained from a Moscow exhibit of abstract painting. In 1919 he painted his first "Proun," a contraction of a Russian phrase meaning "projects for affirming the new." From the first, Lissitzky's Prouns combined suprematist and constructivist ideas. Precisely painted, austere, and objectless, they were rationally constructed, "architectural" models for a utopian society.

Early in 1922, Lissitzky went to Berlin to help mount a major exhibition of Russian art. With him, Moholy later recalled, he "brought news of Malevich, /Aleksandr/ Rodchenko and the movement called suprematism."[46] The impact of Malevich's work on the Hungarian was immediate and profound. In suprematist abstractions he believed he could sense the human desire for freedom and autonomous creation, and *see* ideas cast into geometric form. At the time, to be sure, he knew nothing of Malevich's theoretical ideas. Those that he did entertain he borrowed from two German utopians: Adolf Behne and Paul Scheerbart.

In the February 15, 1921 issue of *Ma*, Moholy could, and undoubtedly did, read a long excerpt from Behne's *The Return of Art* (1920). Although the radical architectural critic did not display much rigor in argument, he made his central thesis clear: Capitalist society and culture had entered a period of decline. In order to build a new culture and society, artists had to rivet their attention on architecture. "It is a very profound truth," Behne wrote, "that everything else is unimportant next to construction. Architecture, as the primary activity, can transform human beings."[47]

According to Paul Scheerbart, Behne said, artists bear responsibility for creating in the masses a common faith in the new world being constructed. They could do that best by using glass. Robert Hughes has explained why:

> The supreme Utopian material . . . was sheet glass. For hundreds of years, stained glass had enjoyed a more or less sacramental reputation, because stained-glass windows were the great decorative feature—and source of religious instruction— in Gothic cathedrals. Sheet glass acquired a different aura of meaning. It was the face of the Crystal, the Pure Prism. It meant lightness, transparency, structural daring. It was the diametric opposite of stone or brick. It suggested a responsive skin, like the sensitive membrane of the eye, whereas brick and stone were impervious, a crust against the world.[48]

"Glass Architecture," Behne concluded, "brings with it a spiritual/intellectual revolution in Europe; it transforms the restrained, vain, creature of custom into an alert, simple, refined person."[49] Glass architecture, in other words, would revolutionize the modern mass consciousness, create New Men, and thereby revolutionize society. Kassák knew what he was doing when he titled the *Ma* excerpt "Art and Revolution."

And so did the *Ma* dramatist János Mácza, when he wrote from Moscow in 1926 that the meaning of Scheerbart's project "is bound up with the spiritual/ intellectual revolution, as a result of which a complete transformation of the social psyche and ideology ensued." In 1914, the year before Scheerbart died, the Sturm Press brought out his influential *Glass Architecture*. "If we wish to raise our culture to a higher level," he wrote in that utopian work, "we are obliged, willy-nilly, to transform our architecture."[50] The new architecture, he insisted, had to be glass, braced by metal and featuring colored panes. The elimination of stone or brick walls would produce remarkable effects, for natural light from the sun, moon, and stars would irradiate rooms, while the double-paned colored glass would serve in much the same way that it had in Gothic cathedrals. "It would be," Scheerbart concluded, "as if the Earth clothed itself in jewellery of brilliants and enamel. The splendour is absolutely unimaginable . . . and then we should have on earth more exquisite things than the gardens of the Arabian Nights. Then we should have a paradise on earth and would not need to gaze yearningly at the paradise in the sky."[51]

The concept of glass architecture recommended itself to Moholy for more than one reason. For years he had been fascinated by light, because as he put it in a poem of 1917, "Light, total Light creates the total man."[52] Then too, he wanted to emphasize art's constructive powers. And finally, he viewed with optimism the possibilities of building a new society and world. As he saw it, the work of art could serve as a microcosm of the larger world; by properly ordering one, the artist might create in human consciousness a disposition to order the other. The work of art, in sum, could be a micro-utopia. On the cover of the May 1, 1922 issue of Ma, Kassák reproduced Moholy's Glass Architecture, an abstract painting in primary colors and black. It stood out as a utopian model of the kind Behne and Scheerbart recommended.

Two months prior to the appearance of that Labor Day issue, Moholy sent a letter to Kassák. "I am enclosing some Russian photographs," he said. "We'll send the article soon. First it has to be translated from Russian into Hungarian. Ilya Ehrenburg wrote it. A Russian book has just been published by Helikon Press. It is interesting and I will soon send it as well."[53] He knew that Ma's editor shared his excitement about Russian culture—excitement that could be traced back at least to 1920. For in that year, Béla Uitz traveled to the Soviet Union and, upon his return to Vienna, organized a "Russian Evening" (November 13, 1920) for the Ma Circle.

As guest speaker, Uitz invited the Russian critic Konstantin Umanskij, who had recently published, in German, New Art in Russia, 1914–1919. Umanskij brought with him reproductions and photographs of work by Malevich, Tatlin, Rodchenko, Chagall, Kandinsky, Archipenko, and many others. The effect, especially on Kassák and Bortnyik, was electrifying and transformative. Commencing with the March 15, 1921 issue, Kassák replaced the expressionistic lettering he had always used for his magazine's title with large, geometric forms of "M" and "A." Expressionism, Uitz wrote in his summary report of the evening's festivities, was the bourgeoisie's idea of art; the Russians offered something better and more truly revolutionary. With considerable pride, therefore, he recorded the fact that "in Europe to date, only the Ma group has organized a public lecture on Russian art."[54]

As we have already seen, Kassák never succumbed to the temptation simply to destroy. Always he searched for a way to build. Dadaism had cleared the path for a new burst of human creativity. Might not Russian constructivism point the way beyond mere destruction? Kassák believed that it did. Moreover, like Moholy, he had listened carefully to Behne and Scheerbart and judged architecture to be the ideal symbol for a new society. Thus, he christened the geometric abstractions he soon began to paint "pictorial architectures." Because of his position as the undisputed leader of the Hungarian avant-garde, pictorial architecture became, overnight, the peculiarly Hungarian form of constructivism.

Pictorial architecture was social theory—or more precisely, a theory of social revolution—in visual form. Kassák knew that hope for radical change in Hungary, and Europe generally, was fading fast, and he therefore made a virtue

8. Lajos Kassák. *Composition* (1921). 10 × 21 in. gouache. Courtesy of the Paul Kovesdy Collection, New York, N.Y.

of necessity by arguing that "to rely solely on instruments of oppression, solely on economic revolution, makes it impossible to solve the problem of contemporary life." Before the world could be made anew, the masses of people would have to acquire a new revolutionary Weltanschauung, something other than

9. Sándor Bortnyik. *Pictorial Architecture* (1922). Gouache, 23 × 30 in. Courtesy of the Paul Kovesdy Gallery, New York.

Marxian socialism, which was merely a scientific theory. A person might grasp such a theory intellectually, but not *feel* it experientially. "Only art can be the standard setter and revolutionizing agent of our feelings." After men and women experienced psychical liberation, they could remake the world. Or as Kassák summed matters up: "Art transforms us and we become capable of transforming our surroundings."[55]

For Kassák, pictorial architecture was *the* revolutionary form of art because it enabled people to experience emotionally a closed, rationally-ordered world, one in which 2×2 always equaled 4. It stripped away everything accidental. It did not imitate fallen nature, but was itself a second, more perfect, nature; a microcosmic utopia that stood over against the chaotic existing reality. It was a geometric harmony that symbolized harmonious social relations. "Pictorial architecture believes that it is the beginning of a new world," Kassák wrote.[56]

Hungary's social revolution failed because it had not first been prepared for at the affective center of the people's psyche. Pictorial architecture would provide that preparation and thereby guarantee eventual success, without again having to resort to coercion. Kállai could not have agreed more. Every inch the utopian, he enthused that "in Kassák's pictorial architecture, collective civilization's humanity manifests itself with unsparing power. High above the contemporary chaos of unrestrained individual emotions, simple and pure relations of space and form preserve the future." Again and again, he returned to the anarchy of bourgeois capitalist society. For him, as for Kassák, Moholy, and Bortnyik, art could not properly be evaluated apart from its social relevance. That is why he praised his three countrymen's commitment to social revolution and why he insisted that "architecture is the first and most fundamental sine qua non of every future artistic evolution, insofar as it strives for social significance."[57]

Eager to point out that significance, Kassák proposed to Moholy that they coedit a book of reproductions that would introduce an often uncomprehending public to the major currents within modern art. He had in mind something similar to the famous *Blauer Reiter Almanach* that Franz Marc and Vasili Kandinsky edited in 1912. Although informed by the spirit of expressionism, the *Almanach* had attempted to bring together spheres of intellectual life that had formerly been segregated. In it, one could examine musical scores by Arnold Schönberg and Anton Webern, as well as reproductions of art. The *Almanach*'s principal weakness, Kassák believed, was its lack of an organizing principle. In his and Moholy's book, he proposed to delineate a logical progression that culminated with constructivism—or to be specific, pictorial architecture. More important, he wanted that progression to be understood as arising not from the internal logic of art history but the external logic of social revolution. He chose for his title, *Book of New Artists*.

Moholy, because he was in Berlin and had wider access to sources, selected the work to be included, while Kassák wrote the introduction. The two men cooperated at the task of editing. They completed their work early in 1922, and in September the Verlag Julius Fischer (Vienna) published the book in Hungarian and German editions. (Kassák later claimed that there had been an American edition, but no copy has ever been found.) In his introduction, Kassák wasted no time in defining his and Moholy's principle of inclusion. "Here are the most energetic of the destroyers, and here are the most fanatical of the builders."[58] He meant not only the destroyers and builders of art, but of human beings and society as well. As a theoretical framework, he posited a historical dialectic that advanced from religious collectivism to romantic individualism to collective individualism. The collective individual, or New Man, would be free from the shackles of religious belief and filled with both a consciousness of responsibility for others and a desire to create a new social world.

The will to destroy the old and create the new social world first manifested itself, Kassák suggested, in the dialectical development of avant-garde art. Italian futurism helped to destroy classical aesthetics, but lacked a sense of direction and ended by welcoming the world war. German expressionism reacted against futurism, but in its affirmations it represented little more than the petit bourgeois soul's last flowering. Turning to French cubism, which reacted against expressionism, Kassák offered a more generous appraisal, for like Kállai, he admired that movement as the immediate precursor of constructivism. Yet he also shared his colleague's judgment that cubism "did not draw the social-revolutionary and artistic conclusions that flow from /the constructive/ consciousness and that summon us to a world view and action." Cubism, Kassák concluded, merited credit for inspiring a quest for the new and a longing for purity, but it overlooked the fact "that the fields are still strewn with yesterday's ruins."[59]

It was dadaism, according to Kassák, "the tragic scream of our entire social existence," that "with the simultaneous collapse of the entire 'order,' gave meaning to cubism's failure." What modern men and women affirmed in dadaism, he maintained, was its destructive fanaticism. The dadaists sacrificed themselves by turning their creative energies inside out, and thereby paving the way for the modern technological world's towering achievements. The new, post-dada, age was born under the sign of construction, and architecture was the purest of constructive forms. "Art, science, and technology touch at one point. It is necessary to change! It is necessary to create, because that is movement. Movement must be brought into equilibrium because in that way we seize the form. The new form is architecture."[60]

Kassák clearly wished to order the reproductions that followed his introduction so as to provide visual confirmation of his historical scenario, and to some extent he succeeded. Thanks to Moholy, however, the selection and arrangement were not nearly as schematic or tendentious as Kassák would have liked. Throughout, for example, the coeditor interspersed photographs of high voltage wires, a movie projector, a racing car, a dynamo, power stations, silos, a water tower, a railway station, an airplane hanger, and a bird's-eye view of Manhattan.

In accord with the thesis that art, science, and technology came together in their commitment to change and re-creation, the Hungarians provided reproductions of work by leading representatives of the various art isms: futurism (Boccioni), expressionism (Kandinsky; Marc), cubism (Picasso; Braque), dadaism (Grosz; Picabia), constructivism (Tatlin; Lissitzky), neoplasticism (Mondrian; Doesburg; Huszár), suprematism (Malevich). Toward the end of the book, they reproduced three of Moholy's constructions and two of Kassák's pictorial architectures—purportedly the pinnacle of historical evolution.

Like pictorial architecture, the *Book of New Artists* was a theory of social revolution in visual form. That is why Kassák continued to describe *Ma* as an "activist" rather than a "constructivist" publication. In attempting to interpret the movement of the Hungarian activists to readers of *Der Sturm*, Endre Gáspár wrote that Kassák and his followers "have the element of building in common with the constructivists, without, however, falling into machine romanticism."[61] Above all, they wanted to build a new society, one peopled by New Men. As an outstanding student of Kassák's work once observed, pictorial architecture depicted Kassák—the paradigmatic New Man. That, surely, was the import of the famous line from "The Horse Dies": "I am LAJOS KASSÁK."[62]

International Constructivism

Nineteen twenty-two was the annus mirabilis of twentieth-century cultural history. It witnessed the publication of *Ulysses*, *Remembrance of Things Past*, and "The Wasteland." In Nashville, Tennessee, a group of writers that included John Crowe Ransom, Allen Tate, and Robert Penn Warren founded *The Fugitive*, the literary review that launched the Southern Renaissance. The year also marked the apogee of international constructivism. As we have just seen, Kassák and Moholy published their *Book of New Artists* in the fall. Earlier, during the final days of May, avant-gardists from all corners of Europe convened a Congress of International Progressive Artists in Düsseldorf. Their purpose was to rebuild the international community of artists that war had destroyed.

In the event, the Congress proved to be a continuation of war by other means. On the first day, several French and German groups proposed a "Founding Proclamation of the Union of Progressive International Artists" that concluded with the following words: "Forgetting questions of nationality, without political bias or self-seeking intention, our slogan must now be: 'Artists of all nationalities unite.' Art must become international or it will perish."[63] Signatories to the document included Theodor Däubler, Else Lasker-Schüler, Oskar Kokoschka, Romain Rolland, and Vasili Kandinsky.

Hans Richter, El Lissitzky, and other members of the "International Faction of Constructivists" refused to add their names to the list of adherents and took serious issue with the Unionists' plans to underwrite exhibitions and a periodical. On the basis of the minority "Statement" that they issued, it is clear that they objected to the vague and pious language and that they wanted to organize along strictly constructivist lines. Unlike the Unionists, they demanded an art that would summon a new society into being.[64] Failing to gain the upper hand, they stormed out of the meeting place.

In order to add emphasis to the general statement, Lissitzky and Ilya Ehrenburg issued a "Declaration" of their own.[65] They recalled their struggles for the new art in Russia, from which they had learned that artistic progress was possible only in a society developing completely new organizational forms. New art, they asserted, was constructive in character and imperfectly understood even by those who called themselves progressive artists. It was that lamentable situation that they wished to remedy.

The Russians identified themselves as editors of Veshch—Objet—Gegenstand, a polyglot "International Review of Modern Art" they had launched in Berlin. In the first issue, published in 1922, they announced it as their intention to familiarize Russian artists with the newest artistic currents in Western Europe, and to bring Western Europeans up to date concerning Russian art and literature. In particular, they wished to propagate constructivism. "The negative tactics of the 'dadaists,' who are as like the first futurists of the prewar period as two peas in a pod, appear anachronistic to us. Now is the time to build on ground that has been cleared."[66] Among their contributors were Kassák, Uitz, and a third Hungarian—Vilmos Huszár.

Although Kassák reproduced some of Huszár's work in Ma and the Book of New Artists, the artist was not a member of the Ma Circle. Born in Budapest, he studied in Munich and came under Van Gogh's spell. In 1905, he settled in the Dutch genius's homeland, and in 1917, he helped to found the De Stijl ("The Style") movement that included such notables as Theo van Doesburg and Piet Mondrian. Never a political activist, Huszár designed furniture and theaters, and painted in the geometric manner. Yet like his associates, he held out a utopian vision of a world in which perfect and universal harmony would reign. "Art," as Mondrian once put it, "is only a substitute while the beauty of life is still deficient. It will disappear in proportion as life gains in equilibrium."[67]

The movement of which Mondrian was the greatest representative centered around the magazine De Stijl. Kassák respected De Stijl's editor, the indefatigable van Doesburg, who, like him, had been sickened by the war and the social order that he held responsible for it. Van Doesburg aspired to be an internationalist. He agreed, for a time at least, with Mondrian's philosophy of "Neo-

Plasticism," according to which impersonal and austere—one might almost say Calvinist—geometric abstractions, constructed by horizontal and vertical lines and employing primary colors (plus black, white, and grey), were alone acceptable. Those grids and forms, not political action, would remake the world. "A new Europe has already begun to grow within us," van Doesburg wrote in 1921. "The ridiculous, socialistic 1-2-3 internationals were only external; they existed in words. The international of the spirit is internal, unspoken. It does not exist in words, but in visual deeds and inner strength. With that the new world scheme is being formed."[68]

Like Kassák, van Doesburg was a writer as well as a painter. Usually, however, he hid his verbal self behind a pseudonym, or more precisely a new persona: "Aldo Camini" or "I. K. Bonset." In the beginning, only the De Stijl architect J.J.P. Oud knew Bonset's true identity, because van Doesburg's plan was to keep the fictitious alter ego separate from himself. Bonset was to be van Doesburg's other, his dada, face. The dadaist, he wrote in 1923, "places opposites directly next to one another."[69] For van Doesburg, the creative tension between dadaism and constructivism, destruction and reconstruction, was symbolized by the tension between horizontal and vertical lines.

In 1922, "Bonset" founded Mécano, an "international periodical for spiritual hygiene, machine aesthetics, and Neo-Dada." Van Doesburg listed himself coeditor and designated each of the five numbers that appeared by a color: 1—yellow, 2—blue, 3—red, and 4/5—white. On the magazine's cover, he arranged the letters "M," "E," "C," "A," "N," and "O" in a 2.3.2.3. vertical-horizontal sequence. The cogwheel at the center seemed to drive them. The "coeditors" published work by dadaists such as Hausmann, Picabia, Schwitters, and Tzara. In an essay on "constructive poetry," Bonset stated his conviction that "the reconstruction of poetry is impossible without destruction." The constructivist poet, like the Neo-Plasticist painter, had to devise a new language that located the point of equilibrium for horizontal and vertical tensions. In sum: "The new poet constructs his language out of the ruins of the past, and since everything derives from language, he creates with it, in spite of the 'abstraction désintéressée,' a world and a new man."[70]

Not long after he reached the decision to discontinue Mécano, van Doesburg announced that "the epoch of destruction has ended. A new epoch begins: The great epoch of construction."[71] Inspired by his own words, he began experimenting with diagonal lines, in disregard of Mondrian's insistence upon orthogonal (right angle) relationships. Mondrian, who was never a dadaist (though he sometimes signed letters "dada Piet"), reacted by breaking off relations: "After your arbitrary correction of Neo-Plasticism," he wrote, "any collaboration of no matter what kind has become impossible for me."[72]

It was Mondrian, we now know, who went on to earn the greater reputation, but it was van Doesburg who remained the driving force behind De Stijl.

In the magazine's name he issued a statement at the Congress of International Progressive Artists emphasizing the importance of construction and his group's determination to overcome subjectivity. He then published his statement, together with other Congress declarations, in *De Stijl*. On the basis of that valuable record, Kassák, who had been unable to attend, issued a statement of his own, in which he allied the *Ma* Circle with *De Stijl* and *Veshch— Objet—Gegenstand*. Instead of a "Union of Progressive Artists," he proposed the creation of an "International Organization of Constructors Who Possess a Revolutionary Weltanschauung." Not only artists but constructors of every kind—scholars, engineers, and others—would belong. Each group, in its own field of endeavor, would attend to the age's objective demands.[73]

Although, however, the Vienna *Ma*-ists did not attend the Congress, Moholy did. Along with van Doesburg, Richter, Lissitzky, and others, he suggested that the anti-Unionists organize a constructivist congress in Weimar in September. On their arrival, they were amazed to find that van Doesburg— acting as Bonset—had also invited a dadaist contingent composed of Tzara, Arp, and Schwitters. The constructivists expressed their indignation because "at the time," Moholy recalled, "we felt in dadaism a destructive and obsolete force in comparison with the new outlook of the constructivists."[74] Van Doesburg—as opposed to Bonset—managed to calm the protesters, who eventually withdrew, leaving the field to the dadaists.

That same fall, on November 22, the First Exhibition of Russian Art opened at the Galerie van Diemen on Berlin's Unter den Linden. The commissar in charge of that epoch-making exhibition of 594 works was David Shterenberg, himself an artist and author of the catalogue's foreword. He pointed out with pride that visitors to the gallery would discover not only suprematists and constructivists, but artists from older schools such as "World of Art" and "Jack of Diamonds."[75] Kassák made the trip to Berlin, where he met Lissitzky; in the Christmas 1922 issue of *Ma*, he filed his report.

Kassák recalled the influence Russian writers had exercised on Hungarian leftists during the war. There had been in Tolstoi, Dostoevski, and Gorki a "profoundly constructive faith" that could not be found in other contemporary writers. By 1922, however, the constructive spirit had passed from Russia's writers to her visual artists. It could be felt not so much in the work of cubists such as Ivan Puni or expressionists such as Chagall, as in that of suprematists like Malevich and constructivists like Tatlin and Lissitzky. Among the constructivists, Kassák expressed particular admiration for Shterenberg, whose paintings pointed the way toward the ideal of the new man's constructive life.[76]

For one group of constructivists, however, Kassák could not muster any sympathy: the "Society of Young Artists" (Obmokhu Group). Members of the group, pupils of Tatlin and Rodchenko, included Kasimir Medunetsky,

K. Joganson, and the brothers Georg and Vladimir Stenberg. They experimented with open, spatial constructions distinguished by a dynamic, kinetic urge, often expressed by spiral forms. In that, they harked back to the futurists. Umberto Boccioni, the only futurist sculptor, once insisted that "sculpture should bring life to the object by making visible its prolongation into space. The circumscribed lines of the ordinary enclosed statue should be abolished. The figure must be opened up and fused in space."[77] In due course, he developed the idea of "architectonic constructions" based upon the spiral rather than the static pyramid. Thus, he anticipated Tatlin's glass tower.

Tatlin's tower exerted a more immediate influence upon the members of the Obmokhu Group, as did the famous "Realistic Manifesto"[78] that Naum Gabo and his brother Antoine Pevsner promulgated in 1920. The authors spoke there of the "kinetic rhythms" of space and time, "the only forms on which life is built and hence art must be constructed." In place of mass in sculpture, they insisted upon openness; in place of stasis, they lobbied for movement; in place of passive reception, they urged active involvement. "Life does not know rationally abstracted truths as a measure of cognizance, deed is the highest and surest of truths."

Kassák remained skeptical. Having viewed several examples of the Obmokhu Group's work, he concluded that "the spatial constructions presented in the exhibitions are naive and unambitious works. Today, when we have trains that travel at 120 kilometers per hour, heavy-weight cranes, and immense bridges, these things impress one as completely superfluous games, poor in intuition and learning."[79]

Somewhat surprisingly, Kállai disagreed with virtually every one of Kassák's judgments. In a review of the Russian exhibition that he published in Barta's *Akasztott Ember*, he complained because the organizers had arranged the various artistic movements in a causal order while neglecting to call attention to the revolutionary will that defined it. "It seems," he scoffed, "that Lunacharski and his friends did not wish to scare off bourgeois visitors to the exhibition. Hence, they stayed clear of every revolutionary emphasis."[80] As a useful corrective, he commended to his readers the constructive *and* revolutionary theory then being propounded by Moholy and Alfréd Kemény, a theory that was profoundly indebted to the Society of Young Artists' spatial constructions.

In December 1922, *Der Sturm* published a manifesto signed by Moholy and Kemény and entitled "Dynamic-Constructive Energy System."[81] According to the Hungarians, construction, as an organizational principle of human striving, had led, in contemporary art, from technology to a static form that had degenerated into either technological naturalism or formal simplifications confined to horizontals, verticals, and diagonals. "Therefore," they wrote, "we must replace the static principle of classical art with the dynamic principle of universal life."

Instead of static material construction, Moholy and Kemény believed that artists should organize dynamic constructions in which the material functioned only as a conveyor of energy. Such constructions would together constitute a "dynamic-constructive energy-system" in which the observer, having hitherto been receptive (passive) in his contemplation of art works, became an active factor in the play of forces. The system of energy involved problems of freely-moving sculpture, and of film as projected spatial movement. The first models for such an energy system, Moholy and Kemény concluded, could only be demonstrational devices for testing the connections between matter, energy, and space. On the basis of experimental results, art works could be created that would be self-moving, free of machine and technological movement.

Moholy had already provided an experimental model late in 1921, when he welded together his *Nickel Construction*, 14⅛ inches in height and featuring a spiral made from nickel-plated iron that appeared to be weightless. The *Nickel Construction* resembled Boccioni's *Development of a Bottle in Space* (1912), Tatlin's model for the *Monument to the Third International*, and Medunetzsky's metal *Composition* (1919). It did not actually move, but Moholy meant his *Nickel Construction* to be kinetic by stimulating a sense of movement in the imagination of those who beheld it. In that way, they became active collaborators, cocreators of a collective work of art.

Both Moholy and Kállai arrived at their new, dynamic conception of constructivism after coming into contact with Kemény, who studied law, aesthetics, and cultural history at the University of Budapest, where he joined the Galileo Circle. During the months of Kun's rule, Kemény became a peripheral member of the Ma Circle, publishing an essay on Bortnyik's work in which he emphasized his countryman's revolutionary use of "active," rather than "passive" colors. Whether a color was active or passive was relative, because it depended upon its spatial relationship to other colors, but Kemény's main point was that active colors produce in us troubling, provocative feelings, while passive colors encourage reassuring emotions. Active colors incite revolutionary deeds, passive colors promote complacency.[82]

After the fall of the Soviet Republic, Kemény emigrated to Berlin. His closest friend there was László Péri, an actor turned artist who exhibited with Moholy at the Sturm Gallery and made a solid reputation for himself with a series of *Spatial Constructions*. Like Péri, Kemény was a Communist and radical revolutionary who viewed art as a means to advance social goals. Late in 1921, he went to Moscow as a delegate from the Communist Youth International to the Comintern Congress. While there, he delivered two lectures at Inkhuk ("Institute for Artistic Culture") on the relationship between the first and second generations of the Russian avant-garde.[83] He began by comparing expressionism (including suprematism) with constructivism, to the lat-

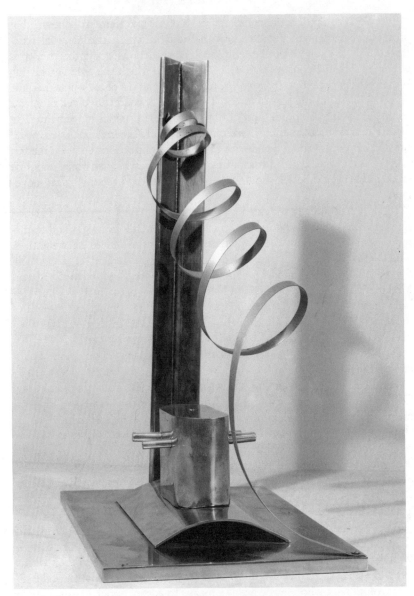

10. László Moholy-Nagy. *Nickel Construction* (1921). Nickel-plated iron, welded, 14⅛ × 6⅞ × 9⅜ in. Collection, The Museum of Modern Art, New York. Gift of Mrs. Sibyl Moholy-Nagy.

ter's considerable advantage. After saluting Tatlin, who was in the audience, as the father of Russian Material-Construction, he identified himself with the members of the Society of Young Artists and their three-dimensional spatial constructions.

Kemény entitled his second lecture "On the Constructive Works of the Obmokhu Group." With Tatlin again in attendance, he criticized the famous constructivist, as well as Aleksandr Rodchenko, for their "naturalistic tendencies," by which he meant their construction of already existing technological equipment in somewhat modified form. Constructivism, he argued, had developed dialectically: Kandinsky versus Malevich and Tatlin; Malevich versus Tatlin; Tatlin and Rodchenko versus the Obmokhu Group. Against the judgment of the critic Osip Brik and of Kassák, Kemény defended members of the latter for their determination to give form to space and identified them as the most forward-looking representatives of the constructivist tradition.

Kemény returned to Berlin in 1922 and worked overtime to spread the dynamic, or kinetic, gospel. In all his writing, he endeavored to suggest the parallels between revolutionary politics and kinetic art. Repeatedly he portrayed the social world and the people who occupy it as constructions that were never static, but always in the process of development, driven by antitheses (read: the struggle of classes). The most significant constructive art works were also the products of antitheses. With Moholy's *Nickel Construction* clearly in mind, he observed that it was "through the strict union of the greatest tensions that the potential energy of the static art work is generated. Despite the physical immobility of the art work, that energy transforms itself into an intensive movement within the observer's psycho-physical being." In other words, dynamic constructivism created in people a new physical makeup and revolutionary "consciousness," as a result of which the world was experienced as the creation of a "dynamic dialectic" of fundamental antitheses rather than of an imperceptible series of numberless changes. Those who attained that consciousness, according to Kemény, would no longer be passively receptive, but actively creative, prepared to act to reconstruct the world.[84]

Kemény maintained that the leading Hungarian constructivists, Moholy and Péri, had advanced beyond the dynamic constructivism of even the best Russian artists. "The art works of the Russian constructivists," he wrote in his review of the Galerie van Diemen exhibition, "are only placed in physical space, without also attempting to define that space."[85] They were interested in producing objects rather than new *relationships*, which to the Hungarians prefigured new social relationships. The idea of spatial constructions, that is, was at the same time a utopian vision of society. It was also, according to Kállai, a product of the Hungarian temperament, which longed "for open space and unlimited freedom of movement in order to be able to form things in accord with its experience. We have in fact no single constructivist in whose work the third dimension is not of decisive significance."[86]

Because Kassák remained closer in spirit to *De Stijl* and *Veshch*, Moholy, Péri, Kállai, and Kemény published a declaration of independence from the *Ma* Circle in the pages of Uitz and Komját's *Egység*. They did not, to be sure, mention Kassák by name. Instead, they attacked the members of De Stijl for their "bourgeois aestheticism," and the Russians for their "technological naturalism."[87] In opposition to both, they proclaimed that their version of constructivism was rooted in Communist ideology. It expressed itself both as a dynamic-constructive energy-system and, in more directly practical terms, as dynamic architecture. Ultimately they concluded, they were working with the proletariat for the creation of a Communist society. They therefore asked to be admitted to the *Egység* circle and announced their readiness to work with the Communist party.

That declaration signaled a fundamental break with Kassák's constructivism. Although Komját refused to admit to his circle any of the manifesto's signers, all of whom had written for the "bourgeois" press, Péri and Kemény joined the Communist party in 1923. Moholy did not, but he had resigned as *Ma*'s Berlin editor in July 1922, and never again cooperated with Kassák. Kállai neither joined the Party nor broke with Kassák, but in a 1925 book on Hungarian art, he wrote that the latter's "efforts as a painter frequently touch on the dilettantish."[88] And after 1923, he rarely published in *Ma*. Worse, in one of his last pieces for the magazine he again singled out De Stijl constructivism for its "exclusivity," charging it with sins of which Kassák's constructivism could equally have been said to be guilty.

The greatest of those sins according to Kállai, was the effort to create intellectualized, objective, static, and harmonious works of art, completely divorced from reality and out of the reach of subjective human consciousness and will. "The society of exclusive constructivism's utopia," he wrote, "floats freely in timeless space, without economic, political, or human ties." Constructivism, rightly understood, was dynamic and dialectical; hence it paralleled the temporal social world in which change occurred only as a consequence of the struggle of antithetical human wills. "History's constructions" he concluded, "are born in a bed of fast-moving time, contingencies, doubts, and catastrophes."[89]

It should be obvious from the foregoing that Kállai, Moholy, Kemény, and Péri rejected what they took to be Kassák's passive utopianism, his unwillingness to be the activist that readers of a publication entitled *Today: Activist Magazine* had every reason to expect. They believed too that his pictorial architectures were too static, too soothing an influence to inspire an activist consciousness in others. But Kassák had already broken with too many of his one-time followers to succumb to self-doubt. Always there was the ego-building Jolán and his own steadfast conviction that he was indeed a prophet. Thus, he continued to promote the idea of pictorial architecture and to open the pages of *Ma* to any artist or group of artists willing to cooperate with him in the struggle for a new art and a new world. Invariably, his collaborators were radicals or "Communists" who remained uncommitted to the Party.

In the July 1, 1922 issue, for example, Kassák showcased the work of Theo van Doesburg. He continued to publish essays, poems, and artwork by dadaists and Russian constructivists, and introduced readers to the "purism" of Charles Edouart Jeanneret (Le Corbusier) and Amédée Ozenfant. As proof of his international commitments, he published special issues of *Ma* in German (March 15, 1923), and in German, Italian, French, and Hungarian (September 15, 1924). Having received an admiring letter from Marinetti in 1924, he penned a critical tribute to the futurist leader—and fascist sympathizer. Marinetti, he wrote, was "a Bakunin of art," a man who freed modern artists from the dead hand of the past. For that he deserved thanks, even if he was not the hoped-for new creator.[90]

At the same time that he opened *Ma* to various avant-garde movements, Kassák contributed work of his own to *De Stijl*, *Der Sturm*, *Veshch*, and other non-Hungarian reviews. Yet for all of his devotion to internationalism, he continued to dream of the day when he might return to Hungary. Unlike Moholy, he refused to accept—much less welcome—as permanent a life outside the national community. In part that was because, in his heart of hearts, he loved the word more than he did the visual image. Behind every modern artistic movement, he later observed, there was a poet: Apollinaire (cubism); Marinetti (futurism); Mayakovsky (the Russians); Breton (the surrealists); Ady (the Hungarian "Eight"); and Kassák himself (Hungarian activism).[91]

Kassák's Return

Defections from the *Ma* Circle could not but embitter a man as defiantly proud as Kassák was. Certainly he never allowed himself to forget that almost from the moment he founded his magazine he began to lose disciples to the Communist party, and thus to "partisan art." To his considerable annoyance, he could not convince them, any more than he could Béla Kun, that artists, even when they were Communists, could accomplish their mission only by retaining their autonomy, because that mission was educative, not political, in nature. "From our point of view," he wrote in the summer of 1923, "art is a productive, politics an unproductive, field of work. The artist creates (produces), the politician only expropriates. It is foolish therefore to want to govern any creative work by means of political (that is external) discipline."[92]

The postwar revolutions in Hungary and elsewhere had failed, Kassák always insisted, not because the opposition was too powerful, but because the proletariat and its leaders were too dictatorial and unprepared. Not, in other words, because of objective, but because of subjective factors. And it was naive to believe that much had changed by the early 1920s. Kassák argued that he and his contemporaries lived in a new period of revolutionary preparation, during which the battle had to be fought with *emotionally-charged* ideas rather than with weapons. I emphasize "emotionally-charged" because as John E. Bowlt has wisely observed, "the best works of Russian (and Hungarian) Constructivism, exemplified by Lissitzky, Kassák and Moholy-Nagy, are distinguished by this very element of *irrationality*."[93] By reaching men and women's deepest emotions, constructive artists could remold their psyche in such a way that they became "collective individuals" capable of living in a *Gemeinschaft* of shared dispositions.

Due largely to Jolán's unflagging loyalty, Kassák did not succumb to despair as one after another of his followers left the *Ma* community. Indeed, he spoke with increasing confidence concerning the creation of a true *Gemeinschaft*. Between 1922 and 1926, he published a series of essays on the "new art" which, in rather disjointed and piecemeal fashion, outlined not only his philosophy of art, but his understanding of history and theory of society.

Kassák's overall argument in those essays bore some resemblance to that of the utopian Socialist, Henri de St. Simon. For both men, history alternated between what the Frenchman called "organic" and "critical" ages. An organic or, as Kassák preferred, a classical/synthetic age, was one in which there existed an "equilibrium." Since they constituted an ideological *and* an affective *Gemeinschaft*, those who lived in a classical age experienced life as stable and balanced. They understood and appreciated the great art of their time because they shared the artists' feelings and Weltanschauung.[94]

Such mutual understanding demonstrated, according to Kassák, that the aim of art was not to "represent" something, but to express the artist's inner being. The true artist recognized instinctively that he was not called to express religious or political beliefs, racial or national aspirations, right- or left-wing party programs—but simply himself. He presented himself as a human ideal not because he was "better" than his fellows, but because he was more self-conscious and able to give objective expression to their essential oneness.[95]

Unfortunately, in Kassák's view, the bourgeois age had been one of decline. The community of feelings and ideas that had once existed was shattered, and with it the equilibrium that distinguished classical art. The world presented itself to men and women of the late nineteenth century as chaotic and unstable. As a result, they themselves became individualistic and selfish, indifferent and insensitive to others. The artist, as a person of the time, was nervous and capricious, concerned only with shifting and superficial moods; in a word, he or she was an impressionist.[96]

The war and the revolutions that succeeded it served to deepen the crisis, while at the same time ushering in an age of transition. Even before the guns of August sounded, Kassák maintained, there were signs of renewal, opposition to the bourgeois age and to impressionism. A new chapter in the history of human community was written when Cézanne triumphed over impressionism and prepared the way for abstract art, the history of which could be traced through the four great avant-garde isms: futurism, expressionism, cubism, and constructivism. Abstract art signaled the triumph of man over nature. It witnessed to man's power to construct his own, autonomous, universe.

Significantly, Kassák identified 1909 as the pivotal year. It was then that Marinetti proclaimed the futurist program, but also, we recall, when Kassák set out on foot for Paris. This is worth remembering, since in all of the essays we are presently considering, one can sense the importance that Kassák attached to his own existence. No one, in his view, was so much a man of his age. No one understood better than he what it meant to live in the twentieth century and what was required to create a new equilibrium and *Gemeinschaft*. No one carried within himself more human possibilities. "I am LAJOS KASSÁK."

The history of the artistic isms was, in microcosm, the history of the present age of transition and preparation. To defend that proposition, Kassák argued that the futurists rebelled against the impressionists. To a certain extent, they expressed new and more vital life forces, but only indirectly, in relation to representations of objects outside of the self. In turn, the expressionists reacted against the futurists. Indeed, they seemed, at first glance, to be close to Kassák's own position. Yet the Hungarian, like the American Alfred H. Barr, Jr., after him, pointed to the fact that many expressionist works were only "near abstractions" in which natural objects continued to appear in nonrealistic form.[97]

Kassák reserved his kindest words for cubism. The cubist was an analyst who tried to discover a formal language with which to express new values. That is why the Hungarian identified his own pictorial architecture as the summit of cubist achievement and the point at which cubism metamorphosed into constructivism, the synthesis and completion of the historic isms. The constructivist was a new type of social person, a collective individualist. He did not represent, he created; his language was geometric. With his appearance there "began the new era of art, the era of construction."[98]

Constructivism, Kassák maintained, held out the promise of a new classical age, one of equilibrium and human community. That age had not yet arrived and that was why many could not comprehend abstract art. They did not share the ideas and feelings of the constructors, who had attained consciousness of themselves as those living in the *present* period of rebuilding. It was therefore incumbent upon the latter, including himself, Kassák wrote, to proceed "from construction to composition—or differently put—from knowledge of ourselves to expression of our will and our stability." With the coming of that new composition, the world would see the most social type of human being, "replete with the tendencies of collective life."[99]

The "new composition" that Kassák envisioned was not an imitation of something already in existence, but a formation "from that which was heretofore unknown, a shaping into a unified body and law." Such an artwork would express the artist's internal harmony and equilibrium, the constructive unity of his being; it would not express a political dogma or any "technical romanticism." The constructivist movement, he said, had reached a crossroads: if its leaders—Kassák had Moholy and Kemény in mind—continued on the road they were currently traveling, they would arrive at "an engineering, speculative dilettantism." If, on the other hand, they discovered the road that led to themselves, they would again be able to express their creative, revolutionary character.[100]

Authentic Communist revolutionaries, Kassák concluded, had overcome their infantile disorder, their putchist mentality. They knew that the creation of new men and a new social order required lengthy preparation. They knew too that they were not all called to perform the same task. Some were engineers, some scholars, some workers, some politicians—and some artists. Each group had its own task, and that of the artists was the transformation of the human mind and spirit.

But there was, Kassák believed, a further specialization: each Communist artist bore a particular responsibility for his own people. "Why, after all, did I wish to create *Ma*," he asked himself years later. "This again I wanted to do for Hungary. I wanted to hold open the gate that led toward life beyond the Hungarian border. Through that magazine, modernism entered Hungary." He had managed, from Vienna, to speak to his countrymen, but with increasing difficulty. "It was my view, as someone active in the socialist movement," he told an interviewer, "that as soon as possible I would return home. As a socialist that was my place, and there I had to carry out educational work."[101]

With a return to his homeland in mind, Kassák began, in 1923, to compile *The Book of Purity* that he eventually sent to a Budapest publisher. An anthology of poems, stories, essays, and artwork, the book was designed to familiarize his countrymen with his life and work in Vienna. Indeed, like the pictorial architectures, the prose poems that Kassák first published in the November 15, 1923 issue of *Ma*, were "about" the artist himself, and hence about the New Man. Lacking titles or even numbers, those six austere, restrained glimpses of life in exile communicated a profound sense of loneliness and sadness.

As witnesses, we see Kassák alone with Jolán, and very bitter. "I am lonely and forsaken, and rapidly becoming bald. My epigones write doltish articles against me. My shoes are worn at the heels." She leaves the flat to do some sewing for a Bulgarian diplomat and returns home with dinner. Only because of her are they able to eat at all. At night she is too tired and too concerned about the children to make love. He pretends to be indifferent, but secretly longs for her.[102]

And yet, as we have seen, Kassák did not give in to despair. Instead, he transcended the melancholy *content* of his daily existence by expressing it in the concise, rectangular *form* of the prose verse. Human tragedy might be inescapable, but when placed within a new context of order and rationality, it could be seen to be potentially useful, an essential part of the world's, and hence the self's, construction. "For whatever is outside us," Kassák wrote, "is also inside us." And then he added, "like a circle in a square or vice versa."[103]

The image was not chosen at random. In an essay of 1925, Kassák observed that "Mondrian in Holland and Malevich in Russia—plainly inspired by cubism—arrived at the quadrilateral as the formal embodiment of the collective world view." Just as the gothic world view, man's longing for God, expressed itself artistically in the pointed arch, so "the collective world view discovered its artistic expression in a quadrilateral—especially in its pure, unsubtle colors and unadorned flatness—that suggests stability, lacks any hierarchical connotation, and seeks to be as inclusive as possible. Instead of the spire and the aesthetically decorative, there is concision on every hand."[104]

Sharing that world view, Kassák and other constructors wanted "rationally and concisely to build around us a world in which we can move more easily and rest more tranquilly." They sought, as he put it in one of his prose poems, "equilibrium! purity of life." The Book of Purity was to be, then, the book of Kassák's simple, yet profound and commutarian soul as well as his prescription for a society in conformity with that soul.[105]

Consider, for example, the twenty-five new, "constructive," verses that Kassák also included in the book. All of them are brief, well-formed, and titleless. Kassák simply numbered them, 41–65. They speak of honorable work and brotherhood, of poverty and loneliness, of living in one's own era, and of building a new world.[106] Consider as well the book's short essays, such as "On Books," wherein Kassák observed that there had been times when books existed solely to satisfy the aristocrat's passion for collection or the bourgeois's aesthetic tastes. In the contemporary world, however, they were necessary and useful to any person's everyday life. Publishers should therefore produce inexpensive editions distinguished by modern forms of typography. They ought to obey "the concise laws /rather than the decorative impulses/ of composition."[107]

In the best-known essay, "The Advertisement," Kassák defended the importance and relevance of ads in the contemporary world. Aestheticians might view them with scorn, but that was because they failed to understand that something was "beautiful" when it was perfect in itself, equal to its task. Sociologists might complain that ads served vulgar commerce, but they forgot that the Russians transformed them from antisocial powers to propagandists for community. In the Soviet Union, ads manifested their authentic character: "simple, concise, and demonstrative." By their "elemental simplicity and purity" they alerted us to important realities of modern life. Truly, Kassák concluded, "the advertisement is applied art, the advertisement artist a socially-relevant constructor."[108] He himself produced a number of strikingly inventive ads.

The Book of Purity put Kassák's many talents on display for those in Hungary who had forgotten, or had never known, him. In addition to the prose poems, the twenty-five new poems, poems in German, English, French, and Czech translation, essays, small sculptures, art work (ads, space constructions, a pictorial architecture), and "The Horse Dies, the Birds Take Wing," the avant-garde leader included seven short, almost surrealistic, "stories" that related some tragedy of everyday life or absurd situation.[109] After sending the anthology to Budapest, he made ready to return home, knowing full well that life there would not be easy.

The return home was for Kassák part of a larger return to the simple, concise, laws of art and life. However much he reveled in the dynamism and excitement of the international avant-garde, he could not, as Moholy could, cut himself off from his roots. Indeed, in an effort consciously to reestablish those roots, he began in 1924 to write his autobiography, *One Man's Life*. And although he completed the work in Hungary, he chose to end the story at the point at which he fled Budapest in 1919. "Outside of Hungary there is no life; and if there is, it is unlike it."

In the same year that Kassák began his autobiography, Jolán made frequent trips to Budapest, where she established contact with various literary and artistic forums. And after a trip to Paris in the spring of 1926, Kassák sent his editorial secretary Aladár Tamás to Budapest to create a "new" journal—*Ma* could not be published in Hungary—under the name *365*. In the fall, he and Jolán crossed the Hungarian frontier. They did not then know that their most fruitful creative years lay behind them.

FOUR

LÁSZLÓ MOHOLY-NAGY:

THE BAUHAUS

Walter Gropius

I WAS VERY PLEASED by the creation of the Bauhaus," Kassák recalled in 1963, "in part because I saw in it the confirmation of my own principles, in part because colleagues of mine were among its leaders." Why then, his interviewer inquired, did he not join, or work more closely with, the German school? "Because," the Hungarian replied, "I was completely occupied, and anyway Moholy-Nagy, Kállai, and Farkas Molnár were *Ma* insiders. My connection was therefore as intimate as if I had personally been there. Had I been there, however, I would not have been able to keep *Ma* going."[1]

For several members of the *Ma* Circle who chose neither to stay in Vienna nor return to Hungary, the Bauhaus became a second home. There, instead of Kassák, they worked with the more congenial Walter Gropius, who studied architecture in Berlin and Munich before joining Peter Behren's practice in 1907. The decision was a wise one, for that same year Behrens accepted appointment as chief designer for AEG (*Allgemeine Elektricitäts Gesellschaft*), Germany's general electricity company. Moreover, his conviction that traditional craftsmanship and mechanized production had somehow to be reconciled influenced Gropius's thinking.

After three years in Behren's employ, Gropius and Adolf Meyer established their own practice in the Imperial capital. Almost immediately the Fagus Shoe-Last Company commissioned the new partners to design a factory at Alfeld-an-der-Leine. The imaginative architects' striking use of glass and steel brought them instant recognition and increased influence in the *Werkbund*, an alliance founded by artists, architects, designers, tradesmen, and manufacturers in 1907. The *Werkbund* sought to promote the "best in art, industry, craftsmanship and trade," and thus to make German goods more competitive internationally. On the eve of war, Hermann Muthesius, the *Werkbund*'s most prominent member, provoked a controversy by arguing in favor of standardized designs. In response, the Belgian-born Henry van de Velde insisted that "so long as there are artists in the *Werkbund*, and so long as they are influenced by its fate, they will protest against the imposition of orders or standardization."[2] Gropius sided with van de Velde, then the director of a Weimar *Kunstgewerbeschule* (arts and crafts school).

Despite the controversy, the *Werkbund* opened a large exhibition in Cologne. Gropius and Meyer designed its Administrative Office-Building, as well as a model factory with a glass facade. Within weeks of completing the projects, war broke out and Gropius exchanged his architect's hat for a cavalry officer's cap. He saw combat on the Western Front, suffered a severe wound, and won the Iron Cross twice. Demobilized on November 18, 1918, he emerged from battle a changed man, committed to a radical restructuring of society.

As a consequence of that commitment, Gropius joined the November Group (*Novembergruppe*) shortly after Max Pechstein, César Klein, Georg Tappert, Heinrich Richter, and Moritz Melzer organized it in December 1918. "We stand on the fertile ground of revolution," the Group's manifesto proclaimed. "Our motto is Liberty, Equality, Fraternity." That was vague enough to attract radical artists of virtually every political and aesthetic stripe, but too vague to unite them for an extended period of time. Indeed, despite the political impulse behind its organization, the Group was never very political in character. Rather than party action, its members contented themselves with exhibitions, concerts, lectures, and film showings.[3]

The November Group's lack of focus, rather than its apolitical character, prompted Gropius, Adolf Behne, and the utopian architect Bruno Taut to found the Working Council for Art (*Arbeitsrat für Kunst*) in December 1919. According to its manifesto, which Taut wrote, "art and the people must build a unity. Art must no longer be the pleasure of a few, but the happiness and life of the masses. The unification of the arts under the wing of a great architecture is the goal."[4] As we shall see, Gropius worked to achieve that unification at the Bauhaus, while activist members of the *Arbeitsrat* disbanded the organization in May 1921.

"The founding of the *Novembergruppe*, the *Arbeitsrat für Kunst*, and the Bauhaus were programmatically and personally very closely linked," one student of the period has written. "The Bauhaus was the only one of the three institutions whose program could be further worked out and whose architectural/applied artistic ideas and pedagogical plans could partially be realized in a practical sense."[5] That partial success owed much to Gropius, whom the departing van de Velde had recommended in 1915 as his successor at the Weimar *Kunstgewerbeschule*. At war's end, Gropius traveled frequently to the city of Goethe and Schiller to discuss the position with leaders of the Social-Democratic government of Saxe-Weimar. In April 1919, the latter appointed the already famous architect to direct both the *Kunstgewerbeschule* and the Academy of Fine Art. "I amalgamated these institutions," he later recalled, "into a *Hochschule für Gestaltung*, or High School for Design, under the name of *Das Staatliche Bauhaus in Weimar*."[6] He did so knowing that the word "*Bauhaus*"—literally "House for Building"—recalled "*Bauhütten*," medieval lodges that housed masons and designers at work on cathedrals.

That same month, Gropius published the new school's program, accompanied by his utopian introduction and the German-American Lyonel Feininger's expressionist woodcut (*Cathedral*). "The ultimate aim of all creative activity," Gropius declared, "is the building!"[7] By that he meant not only literal buildings, but the edifice of society as well. Just as a community of craftsmen-artists would work to create a new architecture—a freedom cathedral of the future—so the members of a wider community had to work to build a new society. "Let us therefore fashion a new guild of artisans without the class-divisive arrogance that seeks to erect a proud wall between artisans and artists! Together let us will, devise, and create the new building of the future, which will unite architecture, sculpture, and painting in one form, and which, from the hands of millions of artisans, will rise toward heaven like a crystal symbol of a new and coming faith."[8]

None of this had anything to do with politics. In a letter to Behne dated January 31, 1920, Gropius spoke categorically: "Every party is dirt; it engenders hate and more hate. We must destroy the parties. I want here to found an unpolitical *Gemeinschaft*."[9] In that spirit, Gropius set forth the Bauhaus "Program" proper. He placed great emphasis on craft training, which comprised six categories: sculpture (including stone masons, stucco-workers, wood carvers, ceramic workers, and plaster casters); metal work (blacksmiths, locksmiths, founders, metal turners); cabinet making; painting and decorating (glass painters, mosaic workers, enamelers); printing (etchers, wood engravers, lithographers, art printers, enchasers); and weaving. To each workshop he assigned an artist (Master of Form) and an artisan (Workshop Master), guides to theory and practice respectively.

Gropius also prescribed training in drawing, painting, and art history. From the beginning, in fact, he found it easier to recruit artists than artisans. Of the first three men he appointed Masters of Form, two were painters and one a sculptor: Johannes Itten, Lyonel Feininger, and Gerhard Marcks. Itten, a Swiss by birth, quickly emerged as the most important figure. He had set up a private school in Vienna during the war and met Schönberg, Berg, Adolf Loos, and Mahler's widow Alma, the beautiful adventuress whom Gropius married in 1915. It was she who recommended him to her husband.

Itten was, to put it mildly, a strange character. He proselytized for Mazdaznan, a cult related to Zoroastrianism that a German-American typographer named Hanish dreamed up. In his personal search for a "higher reality," he shaved his head, wore a robe, practiced vegetarianism and deep-breathing, and purified himself by fasting and using purgatives. Amidst the postwar period's confusions and uncertainties, he persuaded some that he offered a way of life far removed from older, discredited ways.

More important, Itten initiated the so-called preliminary course (*Vorkurs*). Required of every entering student, the *Vorkurs* was six months in length and consisted of elementary instruction in form and materials. Itten later described the three tasks that he set for himself as follows: to free students from "dead conventions"; to help them choose a career by familiarizing them with basic materials; and to disclose to them "the laws of form and color."[10]

Between 1920 and 1922, Gropius appointed five more Masters of Form, all of whom were painters. One, Oskar Schlemmer, helped to guide the sculpture workshop before finding his true niche in that of the theater. He was to become one of the Bauhaus's most important teachers, for the theater held a special attraction for students and faculty alike. It combined media and thus provided a parallel to architecture and, in a broader sense, to society; within the confines of the theater, the artist could rationally organize life. As theater Master, Schlemmer replaced Lothar Schreyer, an expressionist painter who proposed fantastic stagings that included precise instructions concerning the quality, pitch, volume, and rhythm of the actors' voices. Still, if Schreyer was as peculiar as Itten, Gropius's hiring of Georg Muche, Paul Klee, and Vasili Kandinsky was impressive.

Despite such appointments, however, the Bauhaus was in serious trouble by 1922. Itten's idiosyncracies were a problem not only for students, but for the puzzled citizens of Weimar as well. Moreover, the new conservative government of Thuringia took an increasingly jaundiced view of a school that harbored unorthodox—if unpolitical—teachers and students and that evidenced little concrete interest in industrial production. In the fall, the government called upon Gropius to justify its work by organizing a major exhibition for 1923. That request alone was enough to alert Gropius to the need for a change of direction, a turn toward a more sober and sublimated utopianism. But he was also aware of the presence in Weimar of Theo van Doesburg, who taught private courses and delivered public lectures promoting the machine and mass production of well-designed goods. "This is by no means to say," the Dutchman cautioned, "that mechanical production is the only requirement for creative perfection. A prerequisite for the correct use of machines is not quantity alone, but above all, quality. To serve these ends the use of machines must be governed by artistic consciousness."[11]

Van Doesburg boasted at the time that he had "turned everything radically upside down" in Weimar, and certainly, as the late Hans W. Wingler observed, he acted as a catalyst.[12] Gropius regarded the De Stijl leader with undisguised loathing, but he knew that fundamental changes were necessary. On February 3, 1922, he circulated a revealing memorandum to the Masters of Form: "Master Itten recently demanded that one must decide *either* to produce work as an individual in complete opposition to the economic world outside *or* to search for an understanding with industry. . . . I look for unity in the *combination* not the division of these forms of life."[13] Or as he put it in a lecture the following year: "Art and Technology—A New Unity."

Gropius amplified that theme in an essay he timed to coincide with the 1923 exhibition. "The Bauhaus," he wrote, "does not pretend to be a crafts school. Contact with industry is consciously sought, for old trades are no longer very vital and a turning back to them would therefore be an atavistic mistake. . . . The teaching of a craft is meant to prepare for designing for mass production."[14] Informed by that point of view, the exhibition that ran from August 15 to September 30 was a public relations triumph. The Bauhaus's glory years lay just ahead, thanks not least to Gropius's far-sighted decision to appoint László Moholy-Nagy to the faculty.

Subconsciousness and Society

"It was in Berlin in 1922," Gropius subsequently recalled, "that I first met Moholy-Nagy. Impressed by the character and direction of his work, I offered him a professorship at the 'Bauhaus.' "[15] When the energetic Hungarian assumed his post early in 1923, he was only twenty-seven, the youngest Master of Form on the Bauhaus faculty. Yet despite his youth and relative inexperience, he was just the right man to take the school in the new direction Gropius had begun to chart. Over the next five years, the Bauhaus's heyday, he was the commanding figure, in some ways eclipsing the director himself.

When Moholy moved to Weimar he already possessed a utopian theory of society that he was never to forswear. That theory, unsystematic and sometimes self-contradictory, became the informing principle for a series of brilliant avant-garde experiments almost without parallel in the history of modern art. It was based on the assumption that war and the dadaists had swept away the old world in which men were alienated not only from the environment and one another, but from themselves as well. The products of a verbal culture, they had developed their intellect at the expense of their intuition, the biological sense for which was vision. As Moholy later observed, "the deeper meanings so often ascribed to the intuitive more properly belong to sensory apprehension. Here resides the ineffable."[16]

Moholy believed that the destructive imbalance between intellect and intuition had to be redressed, not merely because men and women would reach their fullest potential only when they became "whole," but because visual experiences worked directly on their subconscious, which in turn shaped their conscious life. "Optical configuration /Gestaltung/," he told a Cologne audience in 1931, "is one of the unconscious, unintended means of education that we adopt in order to prepare the form of consciousness that is suitable for a future society." He did not, he insisted, refer to propaganda art, which those involved in the day-to-day class struggle often championed. Revolutionary art as he understood it worked indirectly, but no less effectively, for a new social order and a new man. "Art is the unconscious preparation, the subconscious education of man."[17]

In the "Abstract of an Artist" that he wrote shortly before his death in 1946, Moholy explained how that education worked. Abstract art, he said, "creates new types of spatial relationships, new inventions of forms, new visual laws—

basic and simple—as the visual counterpart to a more purposeful, cooperative human society."[18] Abstract art could accomplish Moholy's purposes because it alone focused on universal forms and relationships. It spoke in a language that was truly international and democratic, free from national and individual particularities and from the elitest cult of the "I."

Unlike its predecessors, including cubism, abstract art had cut itself completely loose from nature. Instead of the natural world of Moholy's Hungarian youth, a world that was static, conservative, and provincial, abstract art presented a uniform, international, and man-made world, corresponding to dynamic metropolises like Berlin. Free of nature, it had also liberated itself from history and tradition; it heralded a new beginning for a new world. Like Moholy, abstract art always looked to the future, never the past.

During Moholy's Bauhaus years, he worked with a burning sense of purpose to create a universal visual order of shifting but harmonious relationships, in the conviction that the long-term subconscious effect of such an order on masses of people would, in time, bring about conscious efforts to make a society in which human beings could live together free of alienation, in harmony with themselves, others, and the industrial/technical environment they had created.

One of the most important steps in the visual, and hence social, education of the masses, was the education of artist/teachers, and Moholy devoted considerable energy to that task. Gropius assigned him to the metal workshop, where the able Christian Dell served as Workshop Master, and more important, to the preliminary course that Itten had formerly taught. On the latter, he collaborated with Josef Albers, who had come to the Bauhaus as a student and was also committed to a new visual education. But from the first it was the Hungarian who dominated the *Vorkurs*. Whereas Itten had dressed like a monk and espoused eastern mysticism, Moholy wore workman's overalls and embraced the modern, rational, technological world of the West. Whereas Itten had stressed the students' subjective response to materials, Moholy emphasized objective knowledge of the properties distinctive to metal, wire, glass, wood, paper, and plastics.

Once students had familiarized themselves with materials, Moholy assigned them exercises in three-dimensional constructions so that they might progress to the problems presented by open space, understood as the relative positions of bodies. He also directed them to construct "studies in equilibrium"—in which, of course, balance and harmony were essential to success—as preparation for studying motion in space by creating kinetic sculptures.[19]

It was a demanding course, but Moholy instilled confidence in his charges by assuring them that everyone was talented and communicating his own optimism and enthusiasm. So charismatic a figure did he become, in fact, that older and more conservative members of the faculty began to express concern. In a letter to his wife, Lyonel Feininger asked in frustration "why attach the

11. Lucia Moholy. *Portrait of Moholy-Nagy* (1925–26). Gelatin silver photograph, 11 × 8 in. (27.9 × 20.3 cm.). Collection, The Museum of Fine Arts, Houston. Museum purchase with funds provided by the Bernstein Development Foundation.

name of art to this mechanization of all visual things, why call it the only art of our age and, moreover, of the future? Is this the atmosphere in which painters like Klee and others among us can develop further? Klee was very uneasy yesterday when he spoke of Moholy."[20]

Three days later, on March 12, 1925, Feininger again wrote to his wife complaining of Moholy. "And then the question of Moholy and his influential opinions; these would never bother me were they not considered by Gropi to be the most important at the Bauhaus."[21] Indeed, as a sign of his approval, Gropius named Moholy coeditor—and as it turned out, guiding genius—of a projected series of Bauhaus Books that he hoped would do for the early twentieth century what the Enlightenment *Encyclopédie* did for the late eighteenth: define for the educated public the new world view.

Shortly before Christmas of 1923, Moholy wrote to Aleksandr Rodchenko, who directed the preliminary course and metal workshop at Moscow's VKHUTEMAS, a school similar to the Bauhaus where Kandinsky had worked before leaving the Soviet Union. He informed the Russian of his plan to edit a series of thirty "brochures" covering a wide range of subjects in the natural and humanistic sciences, and culminating with a study of utopia. To launch the series, he asked Rodchenko to prepare a concise introduction to Russian constructivism.[22] We do not have Rodchenko's reply, if he sent one, and Moholy's plan soon gave place to the series of books that the Munich house of Albert Langen contracted to publish.

With Gropius's full approval, Moholy planned a series of fifty volumes on a range of subjects as broad as that which he had proposed for the series of brochures. In the event, only fourteen titles appeared, but thanks to a publisher's notice we know much about the plan's high quality. Among studies that never made it into print were *Merz-Buch* by Kurt Schwitters, *Futurismus* by F. T. Marinetti and Enrico Prampolini, *Dadaismus* by Tristan Tzara, *Die Stijlgruppe* by Theo van Doesburg, and *Die Ma-Gruppe* by Kassák and Kállai.

Yet despite the fact that Moholy had to scale the plan down, he succeeded in enlisting some of the greatest names in modern art in a collaborative venture of lasting significance. Contributors to the series included van Doesburg, Mondrian, and Oud, Malevich and Albert Gleizes, Klee, Kandinsky, Gropius—and Moholy himself, who thereby added theoretical work to his many other accomplishments. Eventually he wrote two seminal books, but he first appeared in the series as coauthor, with Oskar Schlemmer and Farkas Molnár, of *Die Bühne im Bauhaus* (*The Theater at the Bauhaus*). Of the three authors, only Schlemmer was German.

Along with Moholy, Farkas Molnár was one of a large contingent of talented and influential Hungarians who worked at the Bauhaus. He came from the southern city of Pécs, a cultural center in Baranya county that in prewar days some Hungarians described as a "nest of reds" because it was a stronghold of the trade union and Socialist movements. When the war ended, Pécs was under Yugoslav occupation, and it was to remain so for the next three years. Hoping to forestall its incorporation into counterrevolutionary Hungary, local Socialists, led by Péter Dobrovits, declared the "Hungarian-Serbian Baranya Republic" on August 14, 1921.[23] Six days later, under Allied pressure, the Yugoslavs began to withdraw their troops, thereby sealing the "Republic's" fate.

Dobrovits's *Lamentation Over the Dead Christ*, we recall, had prompted the wartime censors to take action against Kassák's *A Tett*. The radical artist, a Hungarian of Serbian origin, exerted a modernist influence on young artists who had gathered around Molnár. He could not, however, persuade them that Pécs-Baranya would maintain its semi-independence. Thus it was that in the spring of 1921, Molnár, Henrik Stefán, and Hugo Johann set out for Italy, where they painted landscapes in the manner of Cézanne and the early cubists.[24] When the Baranya Republic collapsed in August, they decided not to return.

About that time, Molnár chanced upon some Bauhäusler in Fiesole. Intrigued, he immediately wrote to his friend Alfréd (Fréd) Forbát, a Hungarian from Pécs who had been working for about a year as an architect in Gropius's office. He told Forbát that he and his friends wanted to study at the Bauhaus. After receiving encouragement, he set out for Weimar with Stefán, Johann, Andor Weininger, and Ludwig Čačinovič, arriving in time to begin the winter semester. The new arrivals took the obligatory *Vorkurs* under Itten and, in the spring of 1922, entered one or another of the workshops. At the same time, Molnár attended van Doesburg's wildcat courses, which reinforced his predilection for constructivism.

Convinced that the Bauhaus had gotten off to a false—expressionist—start, Molnár organized the KURI Group. According to Kurt Schmidt, a member, "the KURIs wanted to be free from the zigzag ornamentation, the chaotic disorder and increasing ecstasy of expressionism."[25] Taking their cue from van Doesburg, Mondrian, Lissitzky, and Malevich, they sought, before Gropius announced his own *Kehre*, to unite "the achievements of technology with art." In place of the decorative and expressive, they called for the *Konstruktive, Utilitäre, Rationale*, and *Internationale*—hence KURI.[26]

Joining Molnár in his call for a new direction at the Bauhaus were Stefán, Johann, Weininger, Čačinovič, Schmidt, Otto Umbehr (UMBO, as he was known when he became a photographer), Paul Heberer, Walter Menzel, Walter Herzger, Franz Hessler, Otto Kähler (Peter Keler), H. Koch, R. Kossnik, Georg Teltscher, Rudolf Paris, and Semich Rüstem. In keeping with their commitment to abstraction, those students made of KURI "a completely abstract alliance. KURI was nothing more or less than a certain conception, a common wish."[27] They did not hold meetings and were never together in one place at one time. When Gropius appointed Moholy to the faculty, Molnár followed the simple expedient of declaring KURI's dissolution.

By that time, Molnár had succeeded Forbát in Gropius's office. He had studied architecture in Hungary and when his countryman began working for "Bauhaus Housing Settlement, Inc.," he had the inside track. Like Forbát and Gropius, he viewed architecture as the best means to create a truly human Gemeinschaft. Although the Bauhaus did not then boast a department of architecture, Molnár worked unofficially on many projects dear to his own and Gropius's heart: single-family homes, studio-buildings, skyscrapers, and theaters.[28]

Molnár's contribution to Die Bühne im Bauhaus was his architectural design for the "U-Theater."[29] He did not there take up theoretical questions, but we know from a brief piece he published in Ma that he assigned particular importance to designing stages in such a way that actors and actresses could achieve harmony and equilibrium with their surrounding environment. Space and color, he argued, should not serve simply as background, but as equally important factors in a total, constructed world. If the architectonic idea were properly applied to the theater, Molnár wrote in KURI accents, the constructive, utilitarian, rational man would emerge.[30]

In his contribution, Schlemmer made it clear that theater at the Bauhaus was a visual/spatial, rather than a verbal/temporal, art. Not the power of the word (as opposed to sound), but the utopian effect of visual order was his subject. That order could be achieved only when a stage performer obeyed the laws of space as well as of his body; only, that is, when he was a dancer. Schlemmer drew costume designs for his dancers that symbolized their adherence to spatial laws: "ambulatory architecture" (the laws of surrounding cubical space); "marionette" (the functional laws of the human body in relationship to space); "technical organism" (the laws of motion of the human body in space); and "dematerialization" (the metaphysical forms of expression symbolizing various members of the human body).[31] Ultimately, Schlemmer concluded, only the art (or artificial) figure could achieve complete freedom of movement.

Like Schlemmer, Moholy regarded the theater as a visual art. The war in which he had fought convinced him that the so-called rationality of verbal discourse camouflaged a profound irrationality. Only by reconstituting the subconscious through direct visual means was there any hope of producing a truly rational consciousness. This belief only deepened in Moholy as he learned of others, including theorists of the theater, who shared his distrust of the literary. In 1924, he traveled to Vienna to visit his friend Friedrich Kiesler's "International Exhibition of New Theater Technology," on the basis of which, as he knew, Kassák issued a special "Music and Theater Number" of Ma.

Kassák introduced the number with an essay, "On the New Art of the Theater," that would have fit comfortably into Die Bühne im Bauhaus. He praised Alexander Tairov, who, with his beautiful wife Alice Koonen, founded the Moscow Kamerny (Chamber) Theater in 1914, for understanding the spatial nature of the theater, but complained because the Russian insisted upon the centrality of the actors. Kassák did not mention, but Moholy certainly knew, that Tairov had enlisted the talents of Medunetsky and the Stenberg brothers, members of the Obmokhu Group.

The new art, according to Kassák, had to free the theater from every hierarchy, to place every theatrical element on an equal footing. What was needed above all was an "organizer who possesses the will to create an emotional, visual, and collective order." By "organizer," he did not mean the contemporary producer, who had somehow to accommodate a playwright's text. "The organizer that we have in mind is, like the writer or the architect, a creator." He would not translate literature into theater, but instead would recognize that the theater was a completely new kind of art that could express the emotional and thought world of contemporary man in space and time.[32]

Ideas such as these were in the air, at least in that breathed by leaders of the avant-garde. Kassák included in his special number pieces by Schwitters, Lissitzky, and Tairov himself. In a short manifesto, Herwarth Walden demanded that theater be freed from literature as well as from affected actors. "The material of the theater," he concluded, "is color, form, intonation, and sound in motion. Theater as a work of art grows out of the formation /Gestaltung/ of these elements into an artistic unity."[33]

It is within this avant-garde tradition, if one can be forgiven an oxymoron, that Moholy's "Theater, Circus, Variety" should be read. The dynamic Bauhaus Master allied himself with all those who were working to free the theater from the "literary burden," the logical-conceptual approach to language, and by extension, to the world. Futurists, expressionists, and dadaists had been right to discern the greater theatrical significance of pure sound relationships, a breakthrough comparable to the recognition by abstract painters that it was not the delineated objects, but the relationship of colors to one another that was essential.[34]

With that insight as a starting point, Moholy argued, the theater of the future would be a "theater of totality," in which the "new producer"—Kassák's "organizer"—would exercise mastery over "all formative media /Gestaltungsmittel/, combined so as to create a unified effect, built into an organism of total equilibrium." Among those media was man himself—the actors and actresses. "Of course, he is no longer central, as in the traditional theater, but is to be employed ON AN EQUAL FOOTING WITH THE OTHER FORMATIVE MEDIA," the light, space, planes, form, sound, movement, and spectators that comprised the total environment, the total system of relationships.[35] The visual effect of the resulting balance and order would, Moholy believed, impress itself upon the human subconscious, and thus pave the way for a balanced and ordered society.

Moholy could have included his theater essay in the study he worked on throughout the summer of 1924: *Painting, Photography, Film.* Originally to be titled *Film and Photography,* the book appeared the following year as no. 8 in the Bauhaus series, and again in 1927, in a second, somewhat expanded, edition. It is famous as one of the first, and certainly one of the best, defenses of photography and film as valid and important forms of art. But it is also something more: a utopian theory of society advanced in an artistic idiom.

On almost every page, Moholy signaled his opposition to representational art. He did not deny, of course, that the history of art provided many stunning examples of representational works, but he did insist that their greatness did not lie in the success with which they imitated nature. If they were great, it was because they presented new and harmonic relationships between colors, light values, and forms. Indeed, such paintings would be no less exemplary were they to be turned upside down.[36] That only showed, Moholy maintained, that abstract art alone was valid, particularly in view of photography's superior representational possibilities.

From the standpoint of social change, the danger of representation (or reproduction), Moholy believed, was that it left existing relationships undisturbed. Worse, by meditating on such static relationships, men became passive, resigned to the world as it was. True art, by which Moholy always meant socially transforming art, produced new relationships. Whether in painting, photography, or film, "we want *to produce* systematically, since it is important for life that we create new relationships."[37]

In painting, Moholy emphasized "the production of new, colored harmonies in a state of equilibrium,"[38] but he was more interested in exploring the young arts of photography and film. After only a century of the former and two decades of the latter, men and women had already begun to see the world through different eyes. Yet Moholy was far from satisfied. He pointed out that the camera had been used almost exclusively to reproduce nature. Like any visual art form worthy of the name, photography and film had to strive to produce new and unexpected relationships, to eschew "objects" in favor of the pure elements of vision.

In his own photographs, Moholy preferred to shoot from unorthodox angles and vantage points in order to shift attention away from likenesses to formal and light/shadow relationships. The subject of his work, in short, was vision itself. Yet he was clearly not satisfied with his results either. Perhaps because the word "photograph," both in German and in Hungarian, literally meant "light picture," he wanted to eliminate any temptation to "see" a representation. To that end, he and his wife Lucia hit upon the "photogram" or "cameraless photograph," an "abstraction" with which the dadaists Man Ray and Christian Shad had also experimented.

Perhaps the art historian and critic Franz Roh provided the best description of the photogram:

> The photogram . . . is taken without a camera. The objects are put on sensitive paper. They are left a short or long space of time, held close or at a distance, exposed to intense or subdued light, to a mobile or a fixed light: the results at-

12. László Moholy-Nagy. Untitled (looking down from the Radio Tower, Berlin), silver gelatin print, 1932, 36.2 × 25.6 cm. Special Photography Acquisitions Fund, The Julien Levy Collection, 1979.84. © 1990, The Art Institute of Chicago. All Rights Reserved.

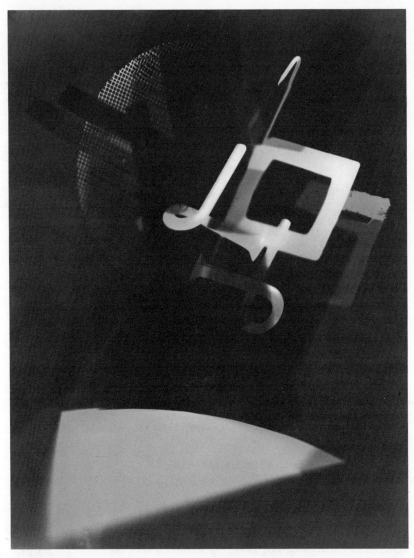

13. László Moholy-Nagy. *Photogram* (1926). Gelatin-silver print, 9 5/16 × 7 in. Collection, The Museum of Modern Art, New York. Anonymous gift. Also courtesy of Ms. Hattula Moholy-Nagy.

tained appear like weird spheres of light, often of marvelous transparency, that seem to penetrate space. Sublime gradations, from gleaming white through a thousand shades of grey down to the deepest black, can be produced thus.[39]

In the photogram, Moholy exalted, light played a role parallel to that of color (pigment) in painting. The newly created relationships between light and darkness, striving as they were for harmony and equilibrium, would also help to constitute a new vision, one that was in motion, because as Moholy once put it, the photogram recorded the "actions of light over a period of time, that is, the motion of light in space. It no longer has anything to do with the record of an existing space (or space-time) structure."[40] It literally *produced* space.

Yet however proud he was of his photograms, Moholy recognized that film offered the greatest possibilities of ever-new light—and in time, color—relationships that would end the domination of old and static relationships, the social correlates of which denied men the opportunity to build a new and harmonious world. In his view, filmmakers had erred by restricting the camera's use to the reproduction of dramatic action. He therefore called upon them to free the medium from nature and to explore the elements of film itself: the tensions of form, chiaroscuro relationships, movement, and tempo.

At the conclusion of *Painting, Photography, Film*, following a collection of photographs and photograms, Moholy placed the "Dynamic of the Metropolis," a film sketch that he wrote in 1921–22 and published in *Ma*'s special music and theater number. Presumably it was to serve as an example of the kind of film for which he had argued in the text. In his words, the aim of the film was "to exploit the camera, its own optical action, optical arrangement of tempo—instead of literary, theatrical action: dynamic of the optical."[41] The "text" itself is a riot of light and dark, of frantic movement, of sensory experience of the sort one finds only in cities that never sleep, or even rest. It is not, however, strictly abstract, but a montage that triggers associations for the viewer.

That "Dynamic of the Metropolis" could nevertheless serve utopian social ends, Moholy never doubted. Even in 1932, in the midst of the Weimar Republic's death agony, he maintained that his, and films like it, were more profoundly relevant to the times than naturalistic and propaganda films. That was so because they were "rooted in the subconscious, and thus present a part of the unconscious means of education that is necessary in order to prepare the appropriate form of consciousness for the future society."[42]

In Moholy's view, abstract compositions, kinetic or not, uncovered universal regularities that were independent of climate, race, temperament, and education—independent, that is, of the alienating particulars of history. Those particulars led inevitably to conflict and disharmony in national and international affairs. The only way to escape from history and to make human beings conscious of biologically rooted relationships was to focus attention on biological being which, unlike historical being, was common to all members of the human community. The most direct avenue to biological being was vision, which Moholy naively believed to be universal in a way that speech (in different languages) was not. It followed from his thesis that visual education prepared the way for utopia, understood as an international *Gemeinschaft*.

Dessau

In 1925, the year that *Painting, Photography, Film* first appeared, the Bauhaus quit Weimar for Dessau, capital of Anhalt. There was little else to be done. The previous fall the Thuringian Minister of Education had informed Gropius that, for reasons of economy, the state could no longer provide the funds necessary to support the school. Cognizant that politics had played an important role in the decision, the Masters took it upon themselves to announce that the Bauhaus would shut its doors on March 31, 1925. By then, however, Gropius had begun to receive offers from other cities—Breslau, Darmstadt, Frankfurt, and Dessau among them. Thanks largely to the determined efforts of its liberal mayor, Fritz Hesse, Dessau entered the winning bid.

Like Weimar, the city by the Elbe enjoyed a well-deserved reputation for liberalism and cultivation. Unlike Weimar, it had become an industrial center, no more than two hours by train from Berlin. Just as important from the Bauhaus's point of view, the Social Democrats had governed the city for years. Hesse, who maintained cordial relations with the Socialists, gained generous appropriations not only for a Bauhaus building, but for faculty housing as well. With such a show of support, Gropius set enthusiastically to work designing the massive complex that was to become one of Weimar Germany's most famous landmarks and symbols. With characteristic imagination, he contrived to forge a union of workshops, administrative offices, lecture theater and stage, canteen, student accommodations, and separate premises for the city's technical school. Particularly striking were the studio apartment balconies, the glass curtain-wall on the workshop side, and the enclosed bridge that spanned a road and housed both the administration and Gropius's private practice. Incredibly, the building was ready for occupancy late in 1926.

While laborers constructed the main building, Gropius designed faculty dwellings that would guarantee a maximum of freedom and independence. In all, the city set aside monies for four houses on Bergkühnauer Allee, about ten walking minutes from the school. Gropius's severely functional residence, with its large windows, flat roof, and balconies, was the model for the three "double houses" built for Klee and Kandinsky, Muche and Schlemmer, Moholy and Feininger. It also served to inspire, on a far less grand scale, 316 single-family dwellings that comprised the Dessau-Törten estate, a planned community for local workers.

Once the physical facilities were ready, Gropius turned his attention to the school's work. In 1926, he began to publish a magazine, *bauhaus*, which he and

Moholy edited jointly. The latter did the lion's share of the work, and in the spirit of uniformity and democracy, he printed every letter in lower case, a practice that was far more radical in German than it would have been in English. During the Hungarian's watch, which came to an end with the first number in 1928, five issues appeared.

Of more far-reaching importance than the launching of bauhaus was Gropius's decision to confer the academic title of "Professor" on those who had been "Masters of Form" in Weimar. There were no longer to be Workshop Masters. Instead, younger, Bauhaus-trained, people (unofficially known as "Young Masters") complemented the faculty. In addition to Albers, those selected for the honor were Herbert Bayer, Hinnerk Scheper, Joost Schmidt, Gunta Stölzl (the only woman), and Marcel Breuer—like Forbát and Molnár, a Hungarian from Pécs.

In 1920, at the tender age of eighteen, Breuer accepted a scholarship to study art in Vienna. Disappointed by his experience in the Austrian capital, he contacted Forbát, who urged him to come to Weimar. "This was the beginning," Forbát later recalled, "of a wonderful career, that in a short time placed him among the foremost of our profession."[43] During his four years of study at the Bauhaus, spent largely in the carpentry workshop, Breuer joined Molnár and Muche in pressing for the establishment of a department of architecture. And no wonder, for he had already mapped out his future: he would begin by mastering smaller objects of furniture such as chairs, then move on to individual components of buildings such as windows, doors, and lights. From there he would proceed to small houses, and finally to large buildings.[44]

Gropius placed Breuer in charge of the furniture (cabinetmaking; formerly carpentry) workshop, and it was during his tenure there—which lasted until 1928—that the young Hungarian began to experiment with tubular steel chairs. The idea, suggested to him by his bicycle, appealed because he wished to allow the occupants of houses freedom to rearrange their environment to suit their changing needs. "The room," he wrote in 1927, "is no longer a self-bounded composition, a closed box, for its dimensions and different elements can be varied in many ways." Moreover, leather or cloth supports were, he argued, more comfortable "in a biological sense."[45] Whether or not that was so, Breuer's chairs became veritable symbols of avant-garde design.

For all his brilliance and success, however, Breuer did not supplant Moholy as the Bauhaus's most illustrious Hungarian. When the latter was not attending to his teaching and editing responsibilities or writing for publication, he could usually be found producing "new relationships," especially those made possible by light. "The capacities of one man seldom allow the handling of more than one problem area," he modestly observed toward the end of his life. "I suspect this is why my work since those days /i.e., the early 1920s/ has been only a paraphrase of the original problem, light."[46]

Most of the time, Moholy explored the possibilities offered by photography, which was not officially taught at the Bauhaus until 1929, when Walter Peterhans arrived on the scene. He did so because, in his view, photography was "configuration of light /Lichtgestaltung/." The photographer was a "modeler of light /Lichtbildner; the German word meaning "photographer"/." If that were not so, Moholy wrote in bauhaus, if it were simply a matter of capturing nature, any photograph would be "good" in which one could discern the object. Proceeding on the stated assumption that "the essential tool of photographic process is not the camera, but the light-sensitive plate or paper," Moholy identified three types of photographic experiment.[47]

The first was the "photogram," which produced effects that he described as sublime. The photogram presented possibilities for working with light that were incomparably greater than any that painting offered. The proof that Moholy provided was in keeping with his theory of personal and social change. "The contrasting relationships of the various graded values of gray— from deepest black to brightest white—that flow into one another, create a penetrating light effect which is without objectlike significance, but which can be appropriated by everyone as a direct optical experience."[48] The photogram's superiority to a camera photograph derived from the fact that the artist could exercise active, sovereign control over the light effect. He, or in many cases she, could create independently of the limitations and chance nature of objects.

The second type of photographic experiment was that in which one used a camera. Drawing upon his own experience, Moholy recommended that objects be "distorted" in some way so as to provide an unprejudiced optical view of the sort that our eyes, bound by conventional laws of association, could not give. He concluded his discussion with a widely quoted proposition: "The illiterate of the future will not be someone who cannot write, but someone who is ignorant of photography."[49]

The third type of photographic experiment was photomontage, or what Moholy preferred to call "photosculpture." He was enthusiastic about the creative possibilities of that art form because it required that photographers abandon mere imitation of nature. Here the task was to paste different photographs together in order to present some idea in its visual immediacy. In that way, artists could bring out unities and associations that might otherwise be overlooked. Moholy conceded, however, that such "sculptures" as his own "Jealousy" were culturally specific in a way that a nonobjective picture, rooted in "biological laws of purely optical experiences," was not.[50]

With reflections such as these, Moholy established his reputation as the leading theorist, as well as practitioner, of the "new photography." Yet he did not stand alone. In Russia, his friend Rodchenko had also taken up photography and he too disdained orthodox angles, or what he called "belly-button shots." The most interesting photographs, he argued, were those shot "down from above" or "up from below."[51] More important, Weimar Germany, the interwar mecca for cultural experimentation, was home to the new photography.

There were certainly more photography exhibitions held in Germany than in any other country. In 1925 the "Film and Photography Exhibition" opened in Berlin. The following year, Frankfurt hosted the "German Photographic Exhibition," where Moholy figured as an "amateur." In 1928, Walter Dexel selected Jena as the site for his exhibition, "New Paths in Photography." Among the eight photographers whose work was represented were Moholy, his wife Lucia, Walter Peterhans, UMBO (Otto Umbehr), and Albert Renger-Patzsch, about whom more will need to be said.[52]

In 1929, the *Werkbund* organized a large international exhibition—*Film und Foto*—in Stuttgart. "Fifo" documented the importance of photographs to art, advertising, and journalism. At the organizers' request, Moholy set up an introductory gallery through which all visitors had to pass, thereby gaining some knowledge of photographic history. He also exhibited ninety-seven of his own photographs, photograms, and photo sculptures. So great was the exhibition's success that it inspired several books, including Werner Gräff's *Es kommt der neue Fotograf* (*Here Comes the New Photographer*; 1929), Franz Roh and Jan Tschichold's *Foto Auge* (*Photo Eye*; 1930), and Roh's *Moholy-Nagy: 60 Fotos* (1930). These, together with the *Werkbund*-sponsored magazine *Die Form*, spread the photographic gospel.

One might also mention Hans Windisch's *Das Deutsche Lichtbild*, a yearbook that aimed to find out whether, and to what extent, it was possible to regard photography as an artistic means of expression. In its pages Moholy published an important article entitled "The Unprecedented Photography." Thrilled by the new art's growing popularity, he proclaimed that its development had been guided by the culture of light. "This century," he wrote, "belongs to light. Photography is the first form of light configuration, if in transposed and—perhaps directly because of that—almost abstract form." He quickly added, however, that film went even further; indeed he insisted that photography reached its apex in film.[53]

Although *Das Deutsche Lichtbild* welcomed contributions from Moholy, it also opened its pages to Albert Renger-Patzsch, Moholy's most serious rival for preeminence among new photographers. The secret of a good photograph, according to Renger-Patzsch, was its "realism." Indeed, the German was one of the greatest practitioners of what Beaumont Newhall has called "straight photography."[54] His pictures were strong and direct, almost clinically objective: extreme close-ups of plants, bold forms of industrial buildings, details of machinery. As a result of his success, the appearance in 1928 of his *Die Welt ist schön* (*The World is Beautiful*) constituted a major event in the history of Weimar culture.

Kállai, who found himself increasingly at theoretical odds with Moholy, published an admiring review of *The World is Beautiful* in *bauhaus*. Without mentioning his old friend and ally by name, he compared Renger-Patzsch's love and reverence for things, his ability to render reality visible, with those who spoke of photography as configuration of light, "the black-white aesthetes, with and without camera, who employ photography as a comfortable vehicle for an intellectual agility that is unburdened by any humanistic concern."[55]

Kállai leveled an even stronger attack on Moholy in a controversial essay published in i10, a Dutch review for which the latter acted as film and photography editor. Just as he praised Renger-Patzsch's photographs for their reverential attitude toward reality, so Kállai challenged abstract painting in the name of that which displayed a "devout admiration to even the most modest expressions of nature."[56] At the same time, he contested Moholy's view that photography would one day render painting obsolete. Because of a painting's "facture"—its material surface—the artist had constantly to refine his compositional techniques in a way that the photographer, working with paper, did not.

Moreover, it was in Kállai's view precisely a painting's materiality—its undeniable physicality—that bound even the most spiritual of artistic visions to quotidian human existence. By contrast, "the lack of facture removes even the clearest photographic representation of nature from our sense of material reality. It may simulate the appearance of reality ever so convincingly, yet this appearance remains incorporeal, without weight, like reflections in a mirror or in water."[57]

In his reply, Moholy labeled it a mistake to think of facture only as palpable surface. The way that something had been produced always showed itself in the finished product; facture referred only to the *manner* in which it showed itself. Hence, by exploring the possibilities inherent in the interplay of light and shadow, photography allowed "a facture of light" to emerge. Painting, at least abstract painting, might not be doomed, but Moholy warned Kállai that "the fanatical zeal with which photography is pursued in all circles today indicates that those with no knowledge of it will be the illiterates of the future."[58]

"Fanatical zeal" was not an exaggeration. We have already mentioned some of those who made photography the cultural rage: Rodchenko, Renger-Patzsch, Peterhans, UMBO. But there were many others, including the dadaists Hans Richter and Raoul Hausmann. Women such as Lotte Jacobi, Elli Marcus, Marianne Breslauer, Florence Henri, and Grete Stern also made names for themselves. Henri and Stern studied at the Bauhaus, where, even before 1929, photographic zeal was unflagging. Herbert Bayer and his wife Irene took it up, and so did T. Lux Feininger, Lyonel's son. The elder Feininger, Georg Muche, Josef Albers, Joost Schmidt, and even Walter Gropius could often be seen with a camera in hand. And Lucia Moholy established a reputation that did not depend upon that of her famous husband. She shot remarkable close-ups in which eyes, noses, and lips doubled as geometric shapes. In addition, she photographed the Bauhaus building from above and below, much to the irritation of Gropius, who preferred straightforward documents made at ground level.

Moholy must have been encouraged by the enthusiasm for photography that he witnessed at the Bauhaus and throughout Weimar Germany. Still, he continued to make it clear that he assigned even greater significance to film, light in motion. It is all the more surprising, therefore, that he attempted, and achieved, so little as a filmmaker. Perhaps as one student of his work has speculated, the enormous expense and lengthy process of refinement account for his failure.[59] Perhaps too he became discouraged when he failed to stir any interest in "Dynamic of the Metropolis."

In 1926, Moholy produced his first film, *Berliner Stilleben* (*Berlin Still Life*). Composed of short takes, the film attempted to measure the pulse of a great, modern capital. Less self-consciously "avant-garde" than his theoretical writings, it actually belonged to the social-realist genre. Three years later he made *Marseille vieux port* (*Marseille Old Port*), another social-realist film that contained seemingly random shots of lower-class life. Neither of these films, then, followed their creator's prescription for pure visual explorations of light in motion. Though not narratives, they were no more abstract than "Dynamic of the Metropolis" had been.

Not until 1930 did Moholy make the kind of film he recommended to others; he called it *Lichtspiel schwarz-weiss-grau* (*Lightplay Black-White-Gray*). The brief film's "star," as the only section of Moholy's "script" to be produced indicates, was his famous *Lichtrequisit* (Light prop; more commonly known as the *Light-Space Modulator*), which, one might say, sent blood surging through the veins of his photograms.

> The shadow of the rotating Light Prop. The superimposition of metal details with the shadows. The shadow revolving; slowly the shadow of a ball surrounded by strong light moving up and down over the original shadow. The Light Prop turns; it is seen from above, below, frontwards, backwards; in normal, accelerated, retarded, reversed motion. Close-up of details. A big black shiny ball rolls from left to right. From right to left. Over again. Positive, negative pictures, fades, prisms; dissolving. Movements, queerly shifting grills. "Drunken" screens, lattices. Views through small openings; through automatically changing diaphragms. Distortion of reflections. Pendulum. Blinding moving light flashes. Revolving spiral, reappearing, again and again. Rotation increases; all concrete shapes dissolve in light.[60]

The Light-Space Modulator was Moholy's greatest and most stunningly original creation. More than any other, that work of genius lent form to his personal artistic/social theory, while at the same time synthesizing many trends within the avant-garde as a whole. For eight years, from 1922 to 1930, Moholy worked on it with the help of his countryman István Sebök, an architect in Gropius's office, and Otto Ball, a technician. Truly, as a leading Hungarian authority has observed, Moholy, like Pygmalion, fell in love with his own creation.[61] And having by then separated from Lucia, he also fell in love with the woman who recognized its worth: Sibyl Pietzsch. Soon to be the second Mrs. Moholy-Nagy, she has given us a description of her first impression:

> In the center of a workshop stood a construction—half sculpture and half machine—a combination of chromium, glass, wire, and rods, in which I recognized the forms of the light-display film. As it turned slowly, invisible lights flared up and turned off, producing gigantic shadows on the walls and the ceiling. "This is beautiful," I gasped. "It's magnificent. It is—" and suddenly I saw the difference between concept and reality, "it is almost as beautiful as the film."[62]

As far as Moholy was concerned, Sibyl had gotten it exactly right.

About four feet in height, the *Light-Space Modulator* possessed a dual identity. It was, to begin with, a kinetic sculpture. Unlike Moholy's earlier *Nickel Construction*, which merely suggested motion, it was a mobile structure driven by an electric motor and composed of a revolving base, a vertical frame and spines, a moving glass spiral and glass base, a tilted chromium grill, large and small perforated metal disks, a moving balance ball, and visible gears. Moholy described its action in this way: "On a circular base through three transparent frames, three motion areas were created. In the one, metal flats moved with an irregular, wavy motion. In the second space cell, perforated metal discs moved up and down releasing a little ball on the top which flashed across the area from the right to the left and back again. In the third cell, a glass spiral revolved producing a virtual cone."[63]

But while Moholy delighted in the *Modulator*'s movement, he was far more enthusiastic about the shifting patterns of (colored and white) light and shadows that the mounted electric bulbs and the rotating, highly polished, reflectors produced. Later he remarked that "the mobile was so startling in its coordinated motions and space articulations of light and shadow sequences that I almost believed in magic." At last he could "paint" with light and others too could see an almost infinite variety of light relationships, ever changing, but always maintained in a state of harmony and equilibrium. Moholy firmly believed that those who viewed these patterns of light in motion would achieve an inner sense of peace and harmony that would eventually translate into a new and far better social order. His disappointment was all the more keen, therefore, when "almost no one could grasp the technical wit or the future promise of the experiment."[64]

To aid others in understanding his vision of a new world, Moholy worked simultaneously on a book that appeared in 1929 as the fourteenth and final volume in the Bauhaus series. Reyner Banham has described the work as a "*summa aesthetica*" of what the Bauhaus taught,[65] and he was right to do so. But it was something else as well: the most complete statement of Moholy's utopian social theory. Originally, he planned to title the book *von kunst zu leben* (*from art to life*; as he did with *bauhaus*, Moholy eschewed capital letters). He

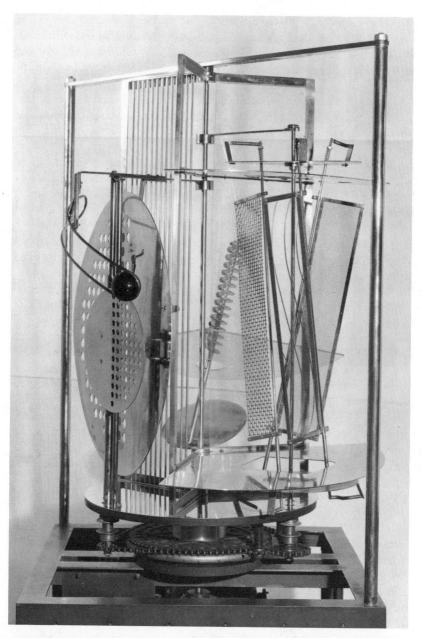

14. László Moholy-Nagy. *Light-Space Modulator* (1923–30). Kinetic sculpture of steel, plastic, wood, and other materials with electric motor. 151.1 × 69.9 × 69.9 cm. Courtesy of the Busch-Reisinger Museum, Harvard University, Cambridge, Massachusetts. Gift of Sibyl Moholy-Nagy.

would have done better to have followed that plan for he wanted above all to show how mankind was beginning to progress from an art that was individualistic and limited to museums and elite audiences, to a life that was suffused with artistic values, values that could be experienced and shared by all members of an integral *Gemeinschaft*.

In the event, however, he chose to call his study *von material zu architektur* (*from material to architecture*). Although that title rendered his purpose somewhat less obvious, Moholy retained the "from . . . to" structure and thus the idea of progress toward a better future. Moreover, the general argument remained unchanged: art was advancing from materials (planes; painting) to volumes (sculpture) to volumes in motion (kinetic sculpture) to bodies in living space (architecture), and finally to shifting patterns of light in space. What the *Light-Space Modulator* achieved in a circumscribed room, night lights could create in the vastnesses of a great city. "The night life of a large city can no longer be imagined without the varied play of electric light advertisements, or air traffic without light signals from towers. The reflectors and neon tubes of advertising lights, the giddy illuminated letters of store fronts, the rotating colored bulbs, and the wide band of moving news bulletins are all elements of a new field of expression that will probably not have to wait much longer for its creative artists."[66] By creating new relationships of light and shadow, as well as of volumes and materials, such artists—or better, formers of life—could create a "new reality" in the world's growing metropolises.[67]

Moholy based his book on lectures he gave at the Bauhaus and he therefore began with some reflections on the importance of education. In the contemporary world, he noted, men and women trained as "specialists," and thus felt themselves to be fragmented and incomplete human beings. And so they were, not only because they had failed to develop all of their abilities and senses, but because they had isolated themselves from their fellows. The future demanded men and women who were "whole" and members of a true *Gemeinschaft*.[68]

Technology could aid in the effort to create "total men." As never before it could satisfy every biological need of every human being. Furthermore, because it was a means and not an end in itself, technology was subject to human control and did not need to occasion suspicion or fear. Still, it had always to be united with art, mankind's greatest, if indirect, teacher. Moholy insisted that it was a mistake to think that art was only for the few, and hence of limited social value; "everyone is talented," he proclaimed, because everyone could share in the joys of sense experience. The true revolution was therefore not material but aesthetic, not a change in the means of production but a recognition of "the right to a satisfying occupation, work that is inwardly fulfilling, a healthy way of life, and a release of energies."[69]

Moholy quickly added, however, that the total, or fully realized, man could only come into being as part of a *Gemeinschaft*. Art was indispensable to society as a whole because it was "the language most closely bound to the senses, a direct linking of man to man."[70] It worked to construct a community, at least when personal expression flowed from the objective and hence universal ground of biologically conditioned experiences.

The move "from" *Gesellschaft* "to" *Gemeinschaft* constituted a break with the static world of individualism and isolation, with the cramped order of unchanging relationships. If it was to ready men for that move, art had to progress from painting and immovable sculpture to kinetics, and from color to light. In that way it would break the spell of tradition and create new and inspiring relationships, new harmonies. And not simply in artists' studios and museums, but in the outer world that everyone inhabited. When Moholy spoke of architecture, he meant the reforming of outdoor *space* and the relative positions of objects within it. When he dreamed of ultimate freedom, he envisioned ever-shifting patterns of light cascading through and reflecting off of transparent buildings in the great cities of the present and the future.

Kállai and Hannes Meyer

By the time *von material zu architektur* appeared, Moholy had left the Bauhaus and returned to Berlin. "I can no longer keep up with the stronger and stronger tendency toward trade specialization in the workshops," he said in an explanatory letter to the school's *Meisterrat* (Board of Masters). "We are now in danger of becoming what we as revolutionaries opposed: a vocational training school which evaluates only the final achievement and overlooks the development of the whole man."[71] His resignation took effect on January 17, 1928, two months before Gropius himself resigned with two years remaining on his contract.

The founding director also had his reasons for wanting to leave. For one thing, he had grown increasingly weary of administration and of having to answer the Bauhaus's many critics, particularly those who possessed bureaucratic authority. "Ninety percent of my work," he complained, "has been devoted to the defense of the school."[72] Then too he wished to devote more time to his architectural practice. Once having made the decision to step down, he moved quickly—too quickly as things turned out—to name Hannes Meyer as his successor. The controversial Meyer, a Swiss-born architect, had arrived on the Dessau scene only in 1927. After first approaching Mart Stam in Holland, Gropius had chosen him to be the first director of the Bauhaus's long-anticipated department of architecture.

Only thirty-eight years old, Meyer could boast of thorough preparation. As a youth, he had worked as a stonemason and carpenter. Subsequently, he made study tours of England, France, Germany, Scandinavia, and Belgium, and gained valuable experience working for Georg Metzendorf, architect for the Krupps. From the first, too, he had been interested in the social implications of architecture, particularly with reference to town-planning and mass housing projects. In 1918 he set up practice in Switzerland, where, eight years later, he entered partnership with Hans Wittwer.

By that time Meyer had developed uncompromising and radical social views, which he made no effort to conceal. No one, certainly, could say that he had dissembled while negotiating with Gropius. In a letter to the latter of February 16, 1927, he stated categorically that "the fundamental tendency of my work will be functional—collectivist and constructive."[73] Faithful to his word, Meyer soon alienated Moholy, Breuer, Bayer, Muche, Kandinsky, and others. Nor did he improve matters by publicizing his Communist sympathies, sympathies that could only make the Bauhaus an even greater object of public suspicion. With his assumption of directorial power, therefore, the stage was set for the Bauhaus's most severe crisis to that time.

As one of his first official acts as Bauhaus director, Meyer invited Ernst Kállai to replace Moholy as working editor of *bauhaus*. For the next two years, the Hungarian, who sometimes changed his theoretical mind with breathtaking abruptness, was his most loyal lieutenant and articulate spokesman. In his initial statement as editor, "the bauhaus lives!,"[74] Kállai attempted to head off any suspicion that the change of leadership signaled the beginning of the school's end. What it did do was to herald a fresh departure, a necessary corrective to the past and to what he and Meyer regarded as an obsession with style.

Kállai did not mention Moholy by name, but elsewhere in the same issue (no. 2/3, 1928) he criticized those who spoke of new "configurations" and wished always to proclaim their aesthetic demands from the lofty reaches ascended by technology. Such theorists would do well, Kállai concluded, to remember that human beings were still earthbound and daily confronted with serious and immediate social problems.[75]

Moholy and Gropius might have believed that they worked for a new and better society, but Kállai and Meyer were not in the least impressed. In their view, the Bauhaus's former leaders had been too remote from social realities, too visionary to see the concrete problems before their eyes. They had made of the Bauhaus an art school for an elite, not an institution actively working for radical social change. "Building and designing are one and the same thing," Meyer declared, "and they are social in character. As an 'advanced school of design' the Bauhaus-Dessau is not an artistic, but a social phenomenon."[76]

Like Moholy, Meyer wanted to build a harmonious society, or *Gemeinschaft*, but he had no use for the Hungarian's aesthetic utopia. He and Kállai both believed that Moholy had traveled too far from material to immaterial; it was time to reverse directions. Geometric and stereometric forms he denounced as "ill-equipped for life and hostile to function." He recoiled at the very suggestion of a "Bauhaus style," and defined "art" as nothing more than a means by which one might search for a collective social order.[77]

Recklessly indifferent to the possible consequences of his actions, Meyer encouraged *Bauhäusler* to take sides on political issues and to form a Communist cell. He appointed the Socialist Ludwig Hilberseimer as head of the architecture department and invited left-wing figures such as Stam, Ernst Toller, the Russian filmmaker Dziga Vertov, and the Czech architect Karel Teige to lecture. At the same time, Kállai praised Stam for his cautious approach to technological refinements, his indifference to beauty, and his emphasis on the simple and functional. Not only religion and art, according to the Hungarian, but houses too could be the opium of the people. Ultimately, he concluded, "good building is not possible without complete economic order and a unified society."[78]

Such single-minded emphasis on society dictated the exclusion of art. In their rejection, Kállai and Meyer differed from Moholy, who wanted to transform life itself into a work of art. Unless the Bauhaus was to become something vastly different from what Gropius and Moholy had intended, the new director was headed for a fall. Indeed, it was not long before the Dessau press seized upon the issue of communism at the Bauhaus, all but compelling Mayor Hesse to ask Meyer for his resignation. When he refused to comply with the request, Hesse dismissed him. Combative to the end, Meyer insisted upon arbitration, only to face charges that he had contributed to a Communist-sponsored fund for the support of striking miners in Mansfield, England.

Meyer chose the magazine *Das Tagebuch* as the place to publish an open letter to Hesse. The letter is fascinating because it summed up the beleaguered director's views and revealed his unmitigated contempt for Gropius, Moholy, and their Bauhaus.[79] When he took the reins of power into his hands, Meyer wrote defiantly, he discovered that students and faculty at the Bauhaus were alike engaged in trivial pursuits without relevance to the real world. "Art stifled life everywhere." Determined to effect dramatic changes, he rolled up his sleeves and set to work.

Meyer boasted that he had brought in teachers such as Hilberseimer and Peterhans, as well as guest lecturers such as Rudolf Carnap, Otto Neurath, and Herbert Feigl. He then proceeded to detail his accomplishments. During his watch, he said, the number of students increased from 160 to 197. A traveling Bauhaus exhibit promoted his conception of materialistic design in Basel, Breslau, Essen, Mannheim, and Zürich. The aircraft, chocolate, and canned goods industries provided the school with commissions to design exhibition displays. His private commission for the construction of the Union School of the General Federation of German Trade Unions in Bernau indirectly involved Bauhaus students. After years of elitist daydreams, "production to fill popular demand became the dominant theme."

As for the political charges leveled against him, Meyer protested that he opposed any institutional involvement in politics. That, he said, was why he ordered the dissolution of the student Communist cell—in March 1930. But he did not deny that he was a nonparty Marxist and he confirmed that "the advancing proletarianization of the Institute seemed to us to be in accordance with our times." For that he would make no apology. Nor would he do anything to appease his enemies. He described Gropius as a vulture who "swooped down from the Eiffel Tower and pecked at my directorial corpse" and he denounced Kandinsky, who had worked against him, for his treachery. To his designated successor, the architect Ludwig Mies van der Rohe, he bequeathed nothing but derision:

> Herr Oberbürgermeister! You are now attempting to rid the Bauhaus, so heavily infected by me, of the spirit of Marxism. Morality, propriety, manners, and order are now to return once more hand in hand with the Muses. As my successor you have had Mies van der Rohe prescribed for you by Gropius and not—according to the statutes—on the advice of the Masters. My colleague, poor fellow, is no doubt expected to take his pickax and demolish my work in blissful commemoration of the Moholyan past of the Bauhaus. It looks as if this atrocious materialism is to be fought with the sharpest weapons and hence the very life to be beaten out of the innocently white Bauhaus box.

In the midst of the arbitration proceedings Meyer abruptly resigned. In October he and several of his students emigrated to the Soviet Union, where he took up a post as professor at Moscow's Higher Institute for Architecture and Building. "I am going to the USSR," he said, "in order to work where a truly proletarian culture is being forged, where socialism is coming into being, where that society already exists for which we here under capitalism have been fighting."[80] For his part, Kállai elected to remain in the German capital.

Berlin

By the time of Meyer's departure from the Bauhaus, Weimar Germany was in the midst of its final crisis. Millions were unemployed and the Nazis seemed poised to seize power. Arrogant and aggressive, Hitler and his followers raised the specter of a new and more terrible war. Such unpropitious circumstances forced Kállai to continue the process of rethinking that he had begun during the mid-1920s. No longer could he entertain the revolutionary illusions of the immediate postwar period. He had always, to be sure, rejected expressionism's extravagant hopes for a new world, but gradually he had come to believe that constructivism too had excited unrealistic expectations.

In particular, Kállai had come to recognize that technology was not the unmixed blessing that Moholy and many other constructivists believed it to be. In the pages of *Die Weltbühne*, to which he regularly contributed, he wrote of technology's limits, its complicity in economic imperialism, its social problematic—in sum, its dark or "shadow," side. There was no doubt in his mind that technology had achieved much that was praiseworthy, but it had also rationalized nature and human relationships to a dangerous, even an irrational, degree.[81]

Indeed, the notions of "rational man" and of a rational utopia that had once seemed so compelling, no longer appeared credible to Kállai. Contemporary events, above all Nazism's emergence as a major political force, testified to the existence of a darker and irreducibly irrational side to human nature. It was with intense fascination, therefore, that he read C. G. Jung's influential speculations. The Swiss psychologist rejected Western rationalism and called attention to a more profound, because more primordial, world of images, or "archetypes," deeply rooted in humankind's "collective unconscious." It was, according to Jung, the *unconscious* rather than the conscious, the irrational image rather than logical reasoning, that was primary. Along with a more or less rational "persona," every human being harbored a more "real" or "shadow" self not subject to reason. To ignore the existence of the shadow self was to be at its mercy.

Kállai, of course, was not a psychologist, but an art critic, and he searched in art for parallels to Jung's insights. Despite its much vaunted realism, he did not find any in *Neue Sachlichkeit*. Otto Dix and other adepts had moved painting away from utopian visions toward nature and reality, but their conception of "reality" was shallow and jaundiced.[82] Nor did Kállai have much use for photography and film. They surpassed *Neue Sachlichkeit* paintings in their realism, but were every bit as superficial and dangerous. In fact, according to Kállai, film was the most subversive of the contemporary arts. He condemned it as an undemanding form of amusement that lured people away from serious art exhibits. Unlike painting, which boasted a static and profound essence, film gloried in continuous and superficial change, or "tempo." And tempo was nothing more than the manifestation of capitalistic anarchy and the chaotic disorganization of modern life.[83]

One could perhaps say that Kállai wished to play Parmenides to Moholy's Heraclitus. He was searching for an eternal and universal foundation, a world of form (*formavilág*), upon which to erect a new and stable human community. Such a foundation could only be rooted in unchanging nature. A great art would therefore be one that dared to delve below the surface of things, to explore nature's deepest structures. Photography and film, along with their predecessors realism and impressionism, knew only the superficial view of nature propounded by nineteenth-century science.[84] Kállai rejected that view and accepted Jung's argument that all attempts to deny the autonomous power of the human mind or psyche were doomed to fail. Science, rightly understood, looked behind the surface physiognomy and consciousness to primordial reality, the collective unconscious and the archetypical ideas shared by all members of the human race, across ages and cultures. "If it were permissible to personify the unconscious," Jung wrote in 1931, "we might call it a collective human being combining the characteristics of both sexes, transcending youth and age, birth and death, and, from having at his command a human experience of one or two million years, almost immortal."[85]

Here at last, Kállai concluded, was Kassák's "collective individual." If it was true that men and women of every culture and historical age possessed a common unconscious, and if that unconscious was human nature's basic reality, then hopes for a worldwide Gemeinschaft were not doomed to fail. All the more eagerly, then, did Kállai seek painters who could convey to others something about the collective unconscious, or what he later called "the hidden face of nature." He found them among the abstract surrealists: Hans Arp, Max Ernst, Joan Miró, Salvador Dali, and by co-optation Paul Klee. Kállai also included the sculptors Constantin Brancusi, Jacques Lipchitz, and Henry Moore.

Surrealism, Kállai argued, was the polar opposite of constructivism. Constructivists were optimistic rationalists in love with technology and inspired by a vision of an ideal society. Surrealists were irrationalists given to metaphysical-existential Angst and driven by a longing to reach the "biological depths."[86] There, in the collective unconscious, the latter believed they could discover a world of eternal images or forms. For that reason, Kállai coined the term "Bioromanticism" to characterize their strivings.

The Bioromantics obeyed Jung's injunction to turn away from the rationalistic-materialistic-utilitarian world, and explored the irrational, unconscious core of Being. Aware of the primal forces—symbolized by the "primal mother"—in human nature, they wanted to construct a new Gemeinschaft on that universal foundation.[87] "While modern art creates visions and symbols of this irrational reality," Kállai wrote in the Sozialistische Monatshefte, "it puts out its feelers toward a new order that can control the murderous growth of mechanistic-quantitative forces in technology and the economy, and lead men to psychical-spiritual self-consciousness."[88]

True realists, the Bioromantics did not shrink from the shadow aspect of human existence. Indeed, they foresaw new catastrophes, at least as terrible as those prophesied by some prewar painters. And yet as Jung urged, they did not conclude that the recognition of dark forces had to lead to despair. Acknowledged and accepted, the shadow could be held in check. Or as Kállai put it, the Bioromantics who painted the devil did so in order to bring him under God's sway. Nature was not only a hellish quagmire, but a place of deepest peace.[89] After the Nazis came to power, however, Germany knew little of such peace, and Kállai returned to Hungary in 1935.

While Kállai reformulated his ideas, Moholy put his into practice. Having resigned at the Bauhaus, he returned to Berlin in the fall of 1928. By then, his marriage to Lucia was coming unraveled; the following year they separated and he fled to the arms of Ellen Frank, an actress whom he photographed often and with evident delight. Faced with the necessity of earning a living, he turned to stage design. The prospect did not at all displease him for he viewed the physical theater as a microcosm of the metropolis, a circumscribed place wherein he could conduct controlled experiments to test some of his ideas concerning the shaping of space. Indeed, in *from material to architecture*, he had characterized the theater as a place where one could literally form space from light and shadows.[90]

Moholy did not lack experience as a stage designer. Shortly after arriving in Berlin in 1920, Lajos Barta had introduced him to Piscator, for whom he then designed sets for a production of Upton Sinclair's *Prince Hagen*. Eight years later he reported directly to the newly created Kroll Opera, where Otto Klemperer, Ernst Legal, and Hans Curjel had combined their talents to challenge the more staid Unter den Linden Opera. Delighted to welcome someone of Moholy's stature, the trio gave him responsibility for a new production of Jacques Offenbach's *The Tales of Hoffmann*.

Of his work on *Hoffmann* Moholy observed that "it was an attempt to create spaces out of light and shadow. Among other things, flats and backdrops turn into tools for the interplay of shadow effects. Everything is transparent, and all these transparencies combine into a rich yet still perceivable space articulation."[91] Curjel added that "for the first time in the history of the theater, steel chairs were used as furniture on stage, Marcel Breuer's early Bauhaus models, whose chrome lustre shone magically in colored light."[92]

Piscator entrusted Moholy with his next major assignment, designing the sets for the 1929 production of Walter Mehring's *The Merchant of Berlin*, a political drama about a Jewish speculator at the time of the 1923 inflation. Taking his cue from the famous director's class-conscious outlook, Moholy essayed a bold experiment. "The tragic proletarian level, the tragicomic middle-class level, and the grotesque militaristic-capitalistic level were represented by three platforms, moving vertically on the stage. The different levels merged and separated, rose and fell, while endless conveyor belts carried men and objects in incessant motion."[93] His guiding principle, Moholy wrote in the program notes, was that "when the optical, acoustical and kinetic elements are given as much space as literary ones, we draw nearer to the essence of theater."[94]

Not every critic agreed. Nor did every theatergoer. Socialists and Nationalists who argued about everything else were united in opposition to what they regarded as intellectual decadence and technological mania. Yet Moholy remained convinced that stage design, or "stage architecture" as he preferred to call it, offered the most immediate possibility for realizing his goal of reshaping space and thus creating ever-changing visual harmonies. In 1931, therefore, he accepted the Kroll Opera's invitation to design sets for Giacomo Puccini's *Madame Butterfly*. Working with him was the talented György Kepes, recently arrived from Budapest.

The collaborative endeavor was a resounding success, especially from Moholy's point of view. According to Curjel, "a rotating scaffolding created constantly new space-effects through light and color projections on the stage horizon. . . . During the entr'acte between /the/ second and third act/s/, which prepares for the final catastrophe, the leading part is transformed through shadow movement into an alienated, hovering, only virtual shape—transposition of the human actor into an apparition behind the gray veil of the night."[95]

It was not long after *Butterfly* opened that Moholy met Sibyl Pietzsch, who seemed to understand the *Light-Space Modulator* as no one else, or at least as no other woman. Like many men, Moholy believed that no woman could fully understand him or satisfy his complicated needs. Lucia had taught him how to think, but she had left him "alone" with his emotions. Ellen Frank was beautiful, but affairs were like drinking, he said; they lasted only as long as the intoxication. "No woman," he told the understanding Sibyl, "understands totality in a man."[96] However that may be, the two soon became lovers.

Moholy's newly found personal happiness contrasted sharply with the sadness he felt about political events in Germany. When Hitler came to power he knew that his life there was nearing an end. Shortly after a deranged Dutchman burned the Reichstag building in February 1933, Moholy and Sibyl attended a speech by Carl von Ossietzky, a defiant opponent of the new regime. On the way home they stopped off at a small café, where they ran into Moholy's quondam friend Alfréd Kemény, who was then writing for *Die Rote Fahne* under the name "Durus." Slavishly faithful to the Communist party, Kemény had long since broken off relations with Moholy, whom he did not scruple to denounce publicly and vituperatively.

When Moholy spoke of fighting the Nazis with his art, Kemény only sneered: "Art for the dandies or art for the people?" Speechless with rage, Moholy and Sibyl returned to his studio, where he began to draw on typewriter paper. He worked all through the night in order to answer Kemény in the only way he knew. "By dawn," Sibyl later recalled, "a pattern of ordered spheres had been created, related to each other by beams of light and fields of tension, a moving universe whose motion was sustained by the interdependence of all its worlds."[97] That vision of harmony, simultaneously artistic and social, was his final word to his adopted country; early in 1934, he emigrated to Holland, where Sibyl and their infant daughter Hattula later joined him.

Before he left Germany, Moholy had had to look on helplessly as the Nazis suppressed the Bauhaus, directed in its last years by Mies van der Rohe. In hopes of saving the school, Mies had imposed a ban on political activity, which did not prevent the Hungarian photographers Irena Blühová and Judith Kárász from joining the Faction of Communist Students.[98] This fact and others made it easier for the Nazis, who gained control of the Dessau city parliament in 1931, to charge the school with *Kulturbolschewismus*. To no one's surprise, the parliament soon rescinded its support of the Bauhaus and terminated all staff contracts.

In a desperate final attempt to save the Bauhaus, Mies rented an unused telephone factory in the Steglitz suburb of Berlin. Soon after the school reopened, however, Hindenburg named Hitler Chancellor. "The end came on 11 April 1933 during the first days of the summer term. Early in the morning police arrived with trucks and closed the Bauhaus. Bauhaus members without proper identification (and who had this?) were loaded on the trucks and taken away."[99] The Nazis held out the prospect of another reopening, but only after unacceptable conditions had been met. On July 20, 1933, therefore, the faculty voted to terminate the Bauhaus.

PART THREE

THE LIBERALS

FIVE

AUREL KOLNAI:

THE PATH TO ROME

Oszkár Jászi

OSZKÁR JÁSZI quit Budapest for Vienna on May 1, 1919. He traveled without his wife, Anna Lesznai, who stayed behind to complete plans for the reform of arts and crafts education in Hungary. Although not a Communist, she remained on friendly terms with Lukács and Balázs and supported their efforts to revolutionize Hungarian culture. Just as important, she no longer believed that her marriage to Jászi could be saved. He had arrived at the same conclusion and almost as soon as he reached Austria, he notified her that he wished to end their union. In a thirty-page letter of reply, she told him that she would not stand in his way. Like Kierkegaard, she said, he was the kind of man for whom a woman was an impediment to work. Besides, she could not share his traditional views concerning the role of women and the relationship between the sexes. Nor, finally, was she altogether comfortable with his strict concept of personal morality. She preferred to judge human actions by the less legalistic standard of love.[1]

By November, when Lesznai arrived in Vienna, only the details of the divorce remained to be worked out. She and Jászi parted friends, but they were both too sensitive and self-reflective not to feel the pain. As was his habit at such times, Jászi threw himself into his work. There was, he knew, much to be done. No sooner had the Horthy regime replaced the Soviet Republic than news began to reach Vienna of an officially tolerated White Terror. So appalling were conditions, that Jászi concluded that the new government could not long survive; international opinion would recoil from the terror and open talk of *revanche*.

In place of the counterrevolutionary regime, Jászi hoped to see a government headed by Mihály Károlyi. Almost as soon as the October Revolution's leader left Hungary for Prague on July 5, 1919, Jászi reestablished contact with him. "Only you," he told his friend, "can be the leader of the country once it regains consciousness and rids itself of its hangmen and usurious leeches."[2] Matters could not, of course, revert to what they had been in 1918. Jászi still favored a Danubian confederation, but he no longer envisioned any possibility of preserving the country's territorial integrity. He was resigned to a *Mitteleuropa* of nation-states. In fact, he claimed to be relieved that his homeland would no longer be burdened with explosive nationality problems. For the first time, the peoples of Danubia had an opportunity to organize on a basis of equality and mutual respect. Each nation could maintain its political independence while entering into regional cooperation to promote economic development.

Jászi could not, as he had before 1918, recommend such a scheme to Hungary's political leaders, and he therefore pinned his hopes on the successor states, especially Czechoslovakia, where his friend, Thomas Masaryk, served as President. He adopted, in short, a "Little Entente orientation." That decision entailed personal risk, for it exposed Jászi to the charge of treasonable disloyalty to his country. Even some of his friends were uneasy; whatever the regime in Hungary, Fr. János Hock preferred its leaders to those who had seized Hungarian territory. And in reaction to Jászi's efforts to persuade the Yugoslavs not to return Pécs-Baranya to Horthy's Hungary, Arnold Dániel complained that "one cannot conduct Hungarian politics supported by the greatest enemies of Hungarian concerns."[3]

It was not long before Jászi conceded Dániel's point. The efforts of Béla Linder, Mayor of Pécs, notwithstanding, the Yugoslav government, under pressure from the Allies, ordered the evacuation of Baranya in August 1921. The preceding fall, the Czechs had expelled Károlyi, apparently because of his contacts with Bohumir Šmeral, who preferred a "United Socialist Europe" to an independent Czechoslovakia. In a letter of March 21, 1922, Jászi told Károlyi that Eduard Beneš did not see any "essential difference between Horthy's and the emigration's foreign policy, because he believes that if the emigration returns home, it will not be able to pursue any but a policy of /territorial/ integrity." In the same sober mood, Pál Szende observed that "the Horthy regime owes its existence to the open sympathy of the Entente and the secret sympathy of influential politicians in the successor states."[4]

But while Jászi came to expect less and less of the Little Entente countries, he refused to entertain the idea of an Eastern, Russian, orientation, even as Károlyi was doing precisely that. The moral revulsion that he felt for the Communists was, if anything, greater than that for Hungary's counterrevolutionaries. In that respect, there is a revealing entry in his diary wherein he commented on his wife's unbroken friendship with Communist converts. Such a friendship testified to an existential gulf that could not be bridged. "In view of such profound moral and aesthetic differences, one cannot speak of a common, a true, home."[5]

Jászi's rejection of communism was not based solely, or even principally, on his experience of bolshevik rule. Instead, it flowed from his uncompromising opposition to Marxism as a theory that denied human freedom and hence undermined moral responsibility. In a letter to Károlyi, he insisted that it was Marxism, not socialism, that was driving a wedge between them. "Do not forget that Marxism is only one of the forms of socialism; I am as much a socialist as you, but I regard Marxism as a bloody *deadlock* which ruins the working class movement."[6]

Throughout his life, Jászi considered ideas—consciousness—to be more important to social change than material factors. He acknowledged that the latter had always to be taken into account, but insisted that the modern crisis could not be understood and overcome until men recognized that, in the deepest sense, it was a test of the human soul. That test had begun when the Enlightenment and French Revolution shook the foundations of religion, and hence of traditional values. In place of Christianity, eighteenth-century thinkers set reason, which soon proved unable to sustain moral conviction; by the middle of the nineteenth century, more scientific, and cynical, thinkers called morality itself into question.

Not moral imperatives, they proclaimed knowingly, but unchanging laws of nature determined human history. It remained for Marx to codify the expulsion of divine and ethical purposes from the social world, substituting for them the "scientific" logic of economic determinism.[7] In view of the consequences which faith in that logic had produced, Jászi proposed that Christianity's moral values be again recognized. Some Socialists were doing just that, because they had concluded that the Christian world view was revolutionary in the true sense of the word: It proclaimed the validity of absolute moral imperatives and the moral responsibility of all men. In a union of Christianity and socialism they saw Europe's best hope.[8] As a result of conversations with Karl Polányi, Jászi came to identify that hope with guild socialism.

Now largely forgotten, guild socialism drew inspiration from Ruskin and William Morris, from Robert Owen, the Chartists, and the Christian-Socialist followers of John F. D. Maurice. It dated to the publication, in 1906, of Arthur J. Penty's *The Restoration of the Gild System*. Architect and Anglican, Penty despised modern industrialism and advocated a return to the medieval system of guilds. Before long, A. R. Orage and S. G. Hobson took up his theories, adjusted to fit modern conditions. Together they popularized guild Socialist ideas in the pages of the journal *New Age*.

In the *Bécsi Magyar Újság*, Jászi wrote enthusiastically about political decentralization and industrial self-management. For some reason, he identified Eugen Dühring as one of the unselfconscious and unknown fathers of the guild Socialist movement. When first he took notice of the blind and misanthropic philosopher in 1919, he had labeled him a "liberal Socialist" and an enemy of Marxism. Indeed, it was Engels's *Herrn Eugen Dührings Umwälzung der Wissenschaft*, commonly known as *Anti-Dühring*, that suggested to Jászi the title *Anti-Marx* for a book that he worked on sporadically between 1919 and 1921.[9]

Published for the first time in 1983 as *Marxism, or Liberal Socialism*, the book represents Jászi's first postrevolutionary effort to affix a name to a non-Marxist form of socialism. In it he called attention to the fact that Marx had had only contempt for the peasantry. Capitalism prepared the way for socialism and was thus a progressive force during its time, but peasants represented reaction. In their heart of hearts, Communists knew, Jászi observed, that peasants were the bearers of the most subversive of ideas: freedom, individualism, spontaneity, continuity. An assimilated Jew, Jászi attributed Marx and the Marxists' hatred of the peasantry to the fact that so many of them were Jews. 'To be a peasant or a Jew is more," he wrote revealingly, "than to be a town or a city dweller; this difference signifies the two extreme poles of human sensibility."[10]

Above all else, though, Jászi assailed Marx for his determinism and consequent failure to recognize the importance and independence of human consciousness. Consciousness was not, as Marx had taught, determined by social existence. However limited by social conditions, it remained history's most creative and dynamic force. That was particularly true of man's moral consciousness, without which no social progress was possible. "However unrealistic, however utopian these /religious-moral ideologies/ might sometimes be, the soul of a new world shines forth from them."[11]

Unlike Marx and his followers, the "liberal Socialists"—thinkers as diverse and quixotic as Dühring, Henry George, and Franz Oppenheimer—emphasized the power that creative ideas alone possessed to promote social progress. It followed from that recognition, according to Jászi, that intellectuals who elevated themselves above classes, parties, and nations—free-floating intellectuals as Mannheim would later call them—had a crucial role to play in the history of mankind. Jászi likened them to Plato's philosopher kings, without, of course, antidemocratic sympathies. And he called for the creation of an international organization of "Knights of the Spirit."[12]

As an example of what such an organization might accomplish, Jászi outlined three fundamental reforms that would free socialism from its Marxist shackles. The most important was the adoption of a new ethic based upon the old consensus between religious and natural law. Next was the elaboration of a new theory that would revolve around mutual aid and free trade. On the basis of the ethic and theoretical work, he proposed a program of action aimed at moral regeneration and economic reorganization, the latter to be characterized by decentralization, self-management, and cooperation. Most important, the program called for the breaking up of large landed estates and the creation of small peasant holdings.[13]

At the time that he sketched it out, Jászi's liberal Socialist program was not as utopian as it later came to seem. Moreover, his emphasis on the generative capacity of human consciousness and the transforming potential of moral renewal exerted a powerful influence on Hungarian thinkers of his own and subsequent generations. Critical of Marx's optimistic determinism, he refused to give in to Spengler's pessimistic determinism.[14] A man of the highest character, he was a conservative liberal devoted to the slow but steady improvement of the human condition and opposed to any idea, such as class struggle, that was informed by hatred and an appetite for violence. He was very far from being the greatest thinker of his generation of Hungarians, but he was the greatest man. When finally, in 1924, he concluded that contemporary circumstances left "no room for the democratic, liberal, and confederative politics for which I have fought for three decades," he accepted an offer to join the faculty at Oberlin College, near Cleveland.[15] In the late summer of 1925, therefore, he left his beloved Europe and sailed for the United States. Although he could not know it at the time, the college town in the American Midwest was to be his final destination.

Ilona Duczynska and Karl Polányi

Almost as soon, we recall, as King Karl appointed Károlyi Minister President, soldiers and workers released Ilona Duczynska and Tivadar Sugár from their prison cells. The two revolutionaries married on November 17, 1918, but separated within weeks, undoubtedly because both were young and headstrong. During the months that Károlyi retained power, Sugár worked closely with Béla Kun, while Duczynska had all she could do to survive the spanish influenza, a virulent strain that claimed twenty million lives worldwide. When, however, she heard the news that Kun had proclaimed a Soviet Republic, she departed immediately from the clinic where she was receiving treatment.

Still weak, she volunteered for service in the Commissariat of Foreign Affairs' propaganda office. Toward the end of May, however, the government sent her to Zürich, where, because she had numerous contacts, she was to explain Kun's policies to newspaper editors and others in a position to influence Swiss public opinion. This she did until the Republic fell, when her Swiss friends moved her to a peasant cottage in order to evade the police. In the spring of 1920, she, along with several Russians who had emigrated after the revolution of 1905, set out for Moscow, a trip that a Soviet Red Cross mission organized. On arrival in late May, she proceeded immediately to the Hungarian House, where Hungarian emigrés had gathered. Over the next four months, she worked alongside Karl Radek, preparing for the Comintern's Second World Congress.[16] Impressed by her devotion to the cause, Comintern leaders decided in September to send Duczynska on to Vienna, where she was to work for the Hungarian Communist party. To head off trouble at the Czech-Austrian frontier, smugglers helped her and the German Communist Paul Frölich enter the country illegally.

Like many other Hungarian emigrés, Duczynska made her way to Hinterbrühl, near Vienna, where Genia Schwarzwald operated a free guest house called Helmstreitmühle. Balázs, who had also taken advantage of the Austrian woman's hospitality, described the new arrival to his diary as "God's most affecting creature" and worried—or rather, hoped—that she might fall in love with him.[17] To his surprise and disappointment, however, she had eyes only for Karl Polányi, whom she met there for the first time. At thirty-three, Polányi was eleven years her senior and anything but a Communist; he was, however, Ervin Szabó's cousin and a man mature enough to occupy the place in Duczynska's life once filled by her beloved father. Before long, their friendship turned to love.

Polányi had emigrated from Hungary on June 8, 1919, ill and out of sympathy with Kun's regime. As Jászi's loyal follower, he had strained every nerve to defend Károlyi's democratic republic. Almost instinctively, he recognized the danger to the new government from the left, and in a public lecture delivered late in 1918, he set Hungarian Radicalism apart from Marxism:

> Marxism views the world *from without*; for it, social development is a pure automatism, propelled by the machinery of the class struggle. Radicalism, on the other hand, views the world *from within* and recognizes in human progress its own work. Intellectual and spiritual labor must become conscious of itself in order to take over the direction of society in accordance with the prerogatives of the intellect and the spirit, which at all times have been society's hidden guides.[18]

For the better part of Károlyi's rule, Polányi was confined to a hospital bed, recuperating from the physical afflictions that were the outward marks of his military service. He did, however, address the Galileo Circle in February 1919. The occasion was a memorial service for Ady, whom Polányi eulogized for his ability to communicate to Hungarians a sense of moral responsibility and a belief that men were not the helpless victims of impersonal forces, but masters of their own destiny.[19] Perhaps it was for that reason that he did not emigrate the moment Kun assumed power. Instead, he accepted an official position in the hope that he might find a way to serve his country; for three months, he labored for the People's Commissariat of Social Production.

It must have been a trying experience. Called by Sándor Varjas and Jenő Varga to lecture at the Agitators' Training School late in April, he made little effort to disguise his disagreement with the regime's economic policies. Not, of course, that he had anything good to say about those of the past. He denounced the prewar monopolistic control of the Hungarian economy by capitalists who were forever proclaiming the virtues of competition, and he insisted that wartime centralization meant only that the state acted as a front for cartels and special interests; it did not make a real effort to socialize commerce. Polányi emphasized this because he wished to refute those "very few" Socialists who favored a similar economic centralization. What the Soviet authorities ought to do was to place economic power in the workers' hands and to organize the socialization of *consumption*, so that those in real need could be supplied with the available goods. He made it clear that he favored the elimination of any state organization that interfered with the flow of goods from the places of production to "cooperatives or groups or socialized stores" located in close proximity to working-class residential areas.[20]

In the end, Polányi could not support a government that based itself on Marxist principles and attempted to control every aspect, including the economic, of its citizens' lives. Lonely, depressed, and in poor health, he emigrated to Austria, where he met the irrepressible Duczynska. Just as she discovered important qualities in him, so he recognized traits in her that he admired. Of Polish descent, she came from a cultural world similar to that of his Russian mother. For that reason alone, he was convinced, his beloved father would have approved the match.[21] What is more, the fiery young woman possessed an instinct for political action that he lacked. In their union, they were to find their completion as human beings. After Duczynska's divorce from Sugár became final in the spring of 1922, she and Polányi married and moved into an apartment in a workers' section of Vienna; early in 1923, Duczynska gave birth to their daughter, Kári.

But she did more than that. She worked a miracle in Polányi, who had been in a severe depression ever since his father died in 1905. Service in the war had only aggravated his condition, as he recalled in the psychologically revealing essay on *Hamlet* that he published in *The Yale Review* in 1954. As an officer on the Eastern Front, he read and reread Shakespeare's tragedy until he came to associate his own predilection for "inaction" with that of the Dane. Hamlet, he argued, "is unable to decide to live."[22] When his father's spirit orders him to kill the King, he cannot obey, because to do so would involve him in the world. "His refusal to set the world aright springs from his dread of becoming part of a world that he has learned to detest with all his being." But with that refusal came guilt and melancholy.

From his own father, Polányi had learned the meaning of responsibility. When, for example, a business venture of his failed, Mihály Pollacsek insisted that every shareholder be paid to the last penny, even though to do so spelled his own financial ruin. The longer Polányi lived, the more certain he became that he had failed to obey his father's implied injunction to live in and improve society; he had preferred to withdraw, to maintain his independence from a society he detested. As one of the consequences of that withdrawal, the Galileo Circle that he led remained politically impotent. "Mea maxima culpa," he wrote subsequently in that regard.[23]

How would it be possible, he asked himself after meeting Duczynska, to be free *and* to live in society? The answer, he concluded, was to achieve a clear understanding of society, on the basis of which men could summon something better into being. "The real condition for action," he wrote to Jászi on January 7, 1920, "is that *we have an image of society*. Without such an *image*, we are helpless because we do not have a thorough 'knowledge' of that which we are confronting. . . . I contend that today we do not possess such an image of society."[24] Even the most distorted image, he continued, was better than none at all. The theory of class struggle, however crude, vouchsafed to its champions an advantage over those who offered no convincing alternative.

In this way, Polányi established to his satisfaction the interdependence of social analysis and praxis, of himself and his wife. Complementing each other, they might one day bring about the *gradual* creation of a new and better society, one in which he could fulfill his responsibilities to his fellowmen and, the demands of his conscience met, still be free. It was with that ambition—to be free *in* society—in mind that he resolved to focus his attention on concrete social reality and thus to honor his father's example of responsibility toward others.

Of course the influence did not all move in one direction. Thanks to Polányi, Duczynska began to adopt a somewhat more critical attitude toward the Communists, if not necessarily to communism. Never sympathetic with the Landler faction, she came to share the opinion of Paul Levi, one-time leader of the German Communist Party, that Kun was an irresponsible adventurer, the "mastermind" behind the ill-fated March Action, a quixotic and abortive effort to manufacture a revolution in Prussian Saxony. Thus it was that she published "On the Decomposition of the Hungarian Communist Party" in the March 1, 1922 number of *Unser Weg*, a renegade journal that Levi edited. There she protested the Party's centralized, militaristic organization, rejected Lukács's claim that Communists must act immorally to achieve moral ends, and attacked Kun's corrupt financial manipulations.[25]

As a predictable result, the Party, under instructions from Moscow, charged her with "Luxemburgist deviations" and pronounced her excommunication. She and Polányi then joined the Austrian Social Democratic Party, the members of which prided themselves on their principled position between reformist socialism and bolshevism. Within the emigré community, they allied themselves with Jászi, who praised Duczynska, "the courageous and noble revolutionary,"[26] for her love of truth and effort to uncover the sources of Hungarian communism's moral and political bankruptcy. After he assumed editorial direction of the *Bécsi Magyar Újság* in June 1921, he invited the Polányis to work with him.

Polányi and the Bécsi Magyar Újság

Like Jászi, Polányi believed that the Hungarian Soviet Republic had confirmed his initial, and negative, judgment of Marxism. He had not, however, abandoned all hope that another, more democratic and realistic, form of socialism might summon a new world into being. Marxism was an ephemeral ideology, economically fanciful and politically immoral. Socialism, on the other hand, was eternal, the slow, realistic, and moral path to human brotherhood. True socialists knew that they had to solve concrete economic problems without resorting to violence.[27]

In a letter to his brother Michael, Polányi reiterated that the desire of men was "to live together, by one another and for one another. To love one another boundlessly and in an immediate way." Social dislocations, he continued, helped to create much of contemporary dissatisfaction in that regard; that was why he was a Socialist. And yet, one could not simply cry out against the abuse of state power and the possession of capital. "We are the state, *we* are capital—but in what way? We shall remain servants until we understand this. It will, however, be possible to understand only if we create forms of life from which we can see beyond these symbols. But how do we create them? That is the question! I would say by means of a Christian-spirited gild life."[28]

Polányi had become a proponent of guild socialism, a movement, as we have seen, for which Jászi also felt an affinity. In the person of G.D.H. Cole he discovered a brilliant spokesman for the cause. Cole challenged the orthodox Marxist thesis according to which economic factors determined the character of noneconomic forms of human association. "Whatever fine theories other people may spin," he wrote, defenders of the "materialist" or "economic" conception of history "continue to proclaim the hard fact that the human race marches upon its belly, and that the economic order of Society determines everything else." That so many had come to accept such a view of history and society was a consequence, according to the Englishman, of capitalist arrangements. "Our preoccupation with economics occurs only because the economic system is diseased."[29]

Like Jászi, Cole never wavered in his conviction that human volition determined the direction of social development. He insisted therefore that "Guild Socialism was fundamentally an ethical and not a materialist doctrine."[30] It was truly *social*, rather than economic, in character. The quondam Fabian defined "society" very precisely as "the complex of organized associations and institutions within the community."[31] By "associations" he meant groups of individuals pursuing a common purpose or aggregate of purposes by means of cooperative action. Those purposes defined an association's function within the social whole. The good society was that in which functional associations worked together cooperatively and coherently.

Cole shared with the syndicalists a distrust of the Leviathan state, but he did not call for its complete destruction—at least not at first. Instead, he identified the state as an association that possessed legitimate, if limited, social functions; it was only on the basis of its widespread modern activities that men had concluded that its functions were "practically universal and unlimited."[32] In fact, the state's function was to deal with those matters, and those only, that affected each of its members more or less equally and in the same way. Thus, the state was justified in regulating the consumption of vital commodities and services. It was not justified, however, in arrogating to itself the right to coordinate the activities of all other associations; it was not sovereign. The responsibility for social coordination, Cole argued, could be invested only in a body that represented all essential associations and hence all essential functions within society. He called that body the "Commune."[33]

Clearly, Cole reprobated the unlimited state not only in its contemporary forms but in the forms that centralizing Socialists proposed to give it. He wished to transfer most of the powers of the state, and of capital, to self-governing workers' associations, or "guilds," because he believed that they alone could encourage a communal spirit reminiscent of that which informed medieval life. Each guild would comprise all workers in a particular industry or service. Thus, for example, "the Railway Guild would include all the workers of every type—from general managers and technicians to porters and engine cleaners required for the conduct of the railways as a public service."[34]

Cole conceded that such a guild society was a utopia, but denied that it was naively unrealistic; it could be built, he insisted, by redirecting trade union development. If existing trade unions were reorganized along industrial lines, they would become guilds. Having accomplished that, trade unionists might pursue a policy of modified "direct action" that Cole called "encroachment," wresting power bit by bit from capitalists and, ultimately, from state officials who had laid claim to far more jurisdiction than was their due.

In the pages of the *Bécsi Magyar Újság*, Polányi introduced Cole and his ideas to Hungarian emigrés, many of whom had good reason to distrust the bolshevik interpretation of socialism. He lavished praise on the Englishman for having provided guild socialism with a scientific basis by discovering in the structure of existing society those elements that were already making for industrial self-government. Workers had only to transform their unions by trade into associations by industry in order to create modern guilds. They would then be in a position to press their demands for self-government and a new organization of society in which the state would be no less, but no more, than one of the essential guilds.

The state would defend the interests of consumers, while the industrial guilds defended those of producers. Harmony would be assured because as functional associations, guilds represented *the same persons* in their various social functions. By this brilliant theoretical breakthrough, according to Polányi, Cole had liberated socialism from bondage to collectivist-Communist nationalization. At a stroke he had discredited centralization, with its attendant threat of bureaucratization, and reaffirmed socialism's commitment to human freedom.[35]

Under Cole's influence, Polányi concluded that those whom Marx had labeled "utopian Socialists" had been far more realistic than he. It was not the "Realpolitiker of the class struggle, but rather Robert Owen, the 'utopian,' who became the spiritual father of the world's most realistic proletarian movement."[36] It was he who established practical socialism for workers at his New Lanark factory. For the remainder of his life, Polányi revered Owen because, having internalized Christianity's emphasis on the uniqueness of each person, he had proclaimed the final revelation: the reality of society and of man as a social being. In his most famous work, *The Great Transformation*, Polányi wrote that Owen believed "that only in a cooperative commonwealth could 'all that is truly valuable in Christianity' cease to be separated from man."[37]

Polányi too believed this. Although he never credited the historic Faith's dogmatic claims, he always insisted that its moral principles, rightly understood, had prepared the way for socialism's communal morality. As early as 1913, he had observed that "the New Testament revelation possessed a socialist flavor."[38] And in the *Bécsi Magyar Újság* he restated the familiar argument of theological liberalism: the Church's risen savior had been in reality a revolutionary humanist, champion of freedom, equality, and solidarity, the prophet of modern socialism.[39] Polányi never abjured this confession of faith.

The Polányi Debate

In an effort to stimulate fuller discussion of guild socialism on the continent, Polányi published a lengthy article entitled "Socialist Accounting" in a 1922 issue of the *Archiv für Sozialwissenschaft und Sozialpolitik*. There he took it for granted that socialism was superior to capitalism and that the transition from the latter to the former had already begun. He wished to argue instead that guild socialism was preferable to centralized state socialism because it alone could solve the "key problem" of a Socialist economy, that of accounting. Men would never, he maintained, be free to pursue their highest ideals until such time as they understood the economic costs and thus came to recognize that the realization of those ideals depended on them alone.[40]

Throughout his essay, Polányi reminded readers that under socialism the standpoint of society took precedence over that of individuals. As a result, the goals of a Socialist economy were quite distinct from those that a capitalist economy pursued. Socialist economists projected two principal demands: the maximum productivity of goods that promised the greatest public benefit, and the securing of social justice in the form of an equitable distribution of those goods.[41] Unlike the defenders of the free market, they concerned themselves with the community's spiritual, cultural, and moral aims, insofar as they depended upon material means for their achievement. At the same time, according to Polányi, Socialists had to make public the production costs that attended the decision to serve social justice.

That was where Socialist accounting came in. To make it possible, Polányi pointed to the need to distinguish between "natural costs" that were intrinsic to the very process of production and "social costs" that, in the pursuit of social justice, constituted an additional burden. Such a distinction was possible only in a "functionally-organized socialist transition economy," because production and social aims were functionally distinct and corresponded to different human motives. To merge those motives in a single organization such as the centralized state was to blur the economy's distinctively *social* component and thus to weaken men's consciousness of their moral will.[42]

Having said that, Polányi set forth his plan for a functionally organized society. He envisioned two principal associations: the "Commune" and the "Guild Congress." The Commune, though less extensive than the contemporary state, was to be the political organ, the owner of the means of production, and the bearer of the community's higher aims. With respect to common needs such as water, gas, and electricity, it would represent consumers who would otherwise be represented by consumer cooperatives. The Guild Congress would comprise the industrial and service guilds and be equal in status to the Commune, together with which it would constitute the highest authority in society. Polányi assumed that the Commune and Guild Congress would never lock in irreconcilable conflict, since they were *functional* representatives of one and the same person. By mutual agreement, they would set "just" wages *and* prices.[43]

Under the system he sketched out, Polányi suggested that natural costs of production, such as the price of tools and buildings, be charged to the Guild Congress's account, social costs to the Commune. In that way, men could *see* clearly the consequences of their will to a better world. In a centralized economy, on the other hand, they could never learn to discriminate properly between their economic and moral wills.[44] Thus, Polányi designed his entire argument to dramatize men's capacity and responsibility for building a new social order. Indeed, in an unpublished manuscript entitled *Behemoth* that he wrote at that time, he insisted that "there never existed a more absurd superstition than the belief that the history of man is governed by laws which are independent of his will and action."[45]

Polányi knew of course that he would not go unchallenged. First to respond was Ludwig von Mises, one of the most brilliant defenders of (neo-) classical liberal economics.[46] Mises congratulated Polányi for having conceded that the problem of economic calculation could not be solved in a centrally administered economy, and for having set forth in detail the system of guild socialism. Moreover, he granted that the Hungarian had taken proper care to propose a relationship of reciprocal exchange between the Commune and the Guild Congress. They were to receive and to give as if they were owners; "thus a market and market prices are formed." Mises maintained, however, that Polányi's system was fatally flawed because its basic character was shrouded in mystery. Was he advocating syndicalism or state socialism? One could not be certain and there could be no viable compromise system. Polányi assigned to the Commune the ownership of the means of production; at the same time, however, he reserved to the guilds the right of disposal. This constituted a fundamental confusion, for Mises insisted that ownership *meant* the right of disposal.

Nor did Mises accept Polányi's account of how Commune and Guild Congress would work together harmoniously. Having been elected in different manners, the two principal associations could indeed arrive at conflicting points of view, which could then be resolved only if one or the other possessed the final word. If the Commune was ultimately supreme, Polányi was defending the very centralized system he wished to oppose. If the Guild Congress predominated, he was espousing syndicalism, a naive system that "presupposes without any further ado a stationary condition of society and does not trouble itself about how the system accommodates itself to changes in the economic data."[47]

Having exposed this apparent contradiction, Mises did not elect to extend his critique. Yet however informed his argument, he did not provide an altogether convincing refutation of Polányi's claim that Commune-Guild Congress cooperation was ensured by the fact that they both represented human functions rather than whole persons. Nor did he take note of the emphasis on moral responsibility that was the principal burden of Polányi's essay.

It remained for Felix Weil to level further charges at Polányi. The wealthy Marxist who dreamed up Frankfurt's Institute for Social Research maintained that the Hungarian and all other guild socialists were hopelessly naive and confused. To begin with, he argued that Socialist economies were centrally administered by definition—by Marx and Engels's definition that is. As proof, he pointed out that centrally administered economies had played the decisive roles in the only two historical attempts to realize socialism, in Russia and Hungary. What he did not say, evidently because it did not occur to him, was that Polányi opposed economic centralization precisely because of his experience in Hungary.[48]

Weil heaped scorn on Polányi's crucial distinction between natural and social costs. Neither, he wrote, possessed any objective meaning; moreover, "these completely imaginary 'cost groups' cannot be separated in reality by objective criteria of any kind." They must remain nothing more than vague estimates. Nor in a Socialist economy could Polányi or anyone else calculate prices with any degree of exactitude, since they were arbitrary and subject to nonmarket change; "an accounting on the basis of such unreal prices is a worthless pastime," he sneered. Polányi's Socialist accounting, Weil concluded, was neither socialist nor an authentic accounting. The Hungarian's real problems—and Weil was still being critical here—were actually moral in nature.[49] In this he was more right than he knew.

In his calm, and on the whole judicious, rejoinder, Polányi emphasized the fact that he had presented a *social* theory first and an economic theory only second. In his view, economics could and should depend upon society, not vice versa as in classical and Marxist theory. With Cole, he might well have said that he wished to treat "the influence of economic factors upon noneconomic forms of association as a form of *perversion*, leading to a failure of the association so affected to fulfil its proper function in Society."[50] As a Marxist who assumed the priority of economics, Weil, Polányi wrote, took the opposite view and thus he mistakenly equated the functional organization of society with the guild Socialist means of production.[51] This led him to overlook the primary importance of social organization and thus to make a series of unwarranted charges, such as that Polányi held that there could be no conflict of interest between Commune and Guild Congress.

This was a mistake that the more perceptive Mises did not make. The Austrian economist was quick to perceive that Polányi's case rested on the viability of a functional social order. He was wrong, Polányi argued, to think that a constitutional system was viable only if a single body possessed power to make final decisions. On the contrary, the equilibrium of power mandated by the functional principle necessitated the replacement of coercion by cooperation. Mises was right, Polányi pointed out, to see that Commune and Guild Congress could experience conflict—but conflict between diverse interests within the same human group, *not* between the same interests of distinct groups, as was the case in a class society. In the confrontation of functional representatives, men confronted themselves. "The necessity of a compromise of functional interests rests then upon the psychic and physical unity of the individual and requires no further proof, even if none is available."[52]

Taken all in all, Polányi acquitted himself well in debate. Friedrich von Hayek, Mises's most brilliant disciple, believed the *direction* of Polányi's thinking to be more promising from a Socialist point of view than futile attempts to defend centralized management.[53] And if the Hungarian's functional theory of society now seems excessively optimistic with respect to human possibility, it seemed far less so in postwar Central Europe, where most believed that a new economic order would accompany the new political order. Certainly it was Polányi's intent to substitute realism for utopianism. Just as certainly, he performed an important service by rekindling a sense of moral responsibility and combating the economistic prejudice that man is driven by his nature to sacrifice every human value on the altar of mammon. Classical liberals and Marxists were alike mistaken, he believed, in their assumption that economic instincts and forces must determine the character of man and society. Already he could have written what he did write many years later: "Aristotle was right: man is not an economic, but a social being."[54]

Red Vienna

It would be a mistake to imagine that Polányi attained his outlook on economics and society by intellection alone. We have seen that he inherited his sensitivity to moral issues and belief in personal responsibility from his father. And he opposed bolshevism not only because he rejected its theoretical assumptions, but because he had witnessed its political practice in soviet Hungary. By the same token, he placed his faith in democratic socialism because he admired G.D.H. Cole's writings, *and* because he lived in "Red Vienna." The wide-ranging experiment the Austrian Social Democrats performed in the beleaguered postwar capital was, he often remarked, "one of the high points of western civilization."[55] In *The Great Transformation*, he made his debt to the city explicit: "Here, in a purely capitalistic surrounding, a socialist municipality established a regime which was bitterly attacked by economic liberals. No doubt some of the interventionist policies practiced by the municipality were incompatible with the mechanism of a market economy. But purely economic arguments did not exhaust an issue which was primarily social, not economic."[56]

Polányi, Duczynska, their daughter, and, before long, his mother-in-law occupied a flat on the Vorgartenstrasse, near the Danube and the Prater. Peter Drucker remembers that the flat was in an "old and grimy five-story tenement, the lower floors of which were boarded up."[57] The building stood in the midst of tumbledown shacks, abandoned-car lots, and city dumps. From such proletarian surroundings, the Polányis gazed out with hope at the city's rapidly changing face. Before their eyes the Social Democrats continued and expanded the work of socialization that Karl Lueger and the Christian Socials began prior to 1914.

The Social Democrats won the municipal elections of May 4, 1919, capturing 100 of the 165 seats in the city council. As they hoped to make Vienna an autonomous Federal State independent of Lower Austria, they were pleased to discover that the country's other states also supported the plan. The latter feared that together with Lower Austria, Vienna might wield power in Austria akin to that of Prussia in Germany. With that evolving consensus as a background, the 1920 constitution provided for separate diets, as well as a common diet that would consider matters of common concern. Article 114 provided that a separate state of Vienna could be formed "by concurrent laws of the city council of Vienna and the state /diet/ of Lower Austria."[58] In pursuance of that article, the responsible bodies proclaimed Vienna to be an autonomous state on December 29, 1921, the action to take effect on January 1, 1922.

The ruling Social Democrats, who had lost Federal power to the Christian Socials in 1920, wasted no time in attempting to make of Vienna a Socialist showplace and of the Viennese "*neue Menschen*." Under the direction of Hugo Breitner, the Socialist banker who controlled the city council's office of finances, they implemented an extensive program of tax reform in an effort to secure the necessary financial base for a sweeping program of welfare. Determined to place the greatest burden of taxation on the more affluent, Breitner and his assistant Robert Danneberg resolved to assess direct rather than indirect taxes, set steeply progressive rates, and tax luxuries of every conceivable kind.

By 1923, they had put the new tax system in place. Viennese paid taxes on automobiles, saddle and carriage horses, dogs, household servants in excess of one, entertainment, and food and drink served to patrons of "bars, cabarets, varieties, concert *cafés*, concert restaurants, *Heurigen und Buschenschenken*, liquor and breakfast rooms, and further in public houses which—in the light of the prices asked, the social position of the customers, the equipment, favorable situation or comfort offered—may be considered as luxury establishments."[59] With the income generated by these measures, which critics labeled "tax Bolshevism," the Social Democrats carried out their ambitious plans. Julius Tandler, Vienna's crusading welfare director, acted as their principal agent.

From the first, Tandler placed considerable emphasis on the well-being of young people. The city's Office of Youth worked to reduce the alarming rate of infant mortality and constructed nursery schools and kindergartens, particularly in workers' districts, that shepherded children all day so that both parents could work. The office also established day-care centers for children of school age who would otherwise have been alone after school hours. Education director Otto Glöckel prescribed a thoroughgoing school reform that provided free materials and lunches and inculcated in students a spirit of community, or what Tandler called a "consciousness of social responsibility."[60]

That was only the beginning. Tandler was committed to the idea of cradle-to-grave provision and, among many other programs, organized a relief for the indigent and all who were unable to provide an elementary livelihood for themselves and their dependents. Turning to health problems, he declared war on tuberculosis—called by some "the Vienna sickness" because of its high incidence in the city. On the grounds of its Lainz Hospital, the city erected a building specifically for those who suffered from the dread disease. It also maintained sanitariums and recuperative homes.

The city's most ambitious and controversial initiative was its housing program, which became the symbol of the Socialist transformation. Faced with a critical housing shortage after the war, authorities began to purchase land, particularly that which was available for immediate construction. At the same time, they bought or acquired an interest in enterprises that produced important building materials. Finally, in September 1923, the city council passed a resolution authorizing the construction of twenty-five thousand apartments over a period of five years. Working with strict instructions, builders reserved at least 50 percent of the allotted space for courtyards and playgrounds. The more than sixty thousand apartments they built by 1933 were cramped, but sunny and clean. The city selected residents on the basis of a complicated formula and held rents to a legal minimum that for most workers amounted to less than 5 percent of income.

Of the city's various properties, the gigantic Karl-Marx-Hof in Heiligenstadt was the most famous. Virtually self-sufficient, it comprised 1325 apartments. In addition, the planners provided two laundries, two kindergartens, a youth center, a library, a dental clinic, a health insurance office, a pharmacy, a post office, twenty-five shops, and two bathing establishments. Critics complained of the expense and noted that a tenement of such proportions might serve as a fortress in the event of civil war. But the Polányis viewed it and the entire program of reform as irrefutable evidence that peaceful, democratic socialism was more than a utopian dream. All the more so because the city council supported the modest but real efforts of the Consumers' Cooperative Society of Vienna which, in 1909, the Social Democratic Party had recognized as a component of the workers' movement equal in status to trade unions and the Party itself.

Inspired by Red Vienna's achievements, Polányi heralded Socialist municipalities as paradigms and portents of a democratic socialism already evolving. He did not underestimate, however, the challenge presented by the Austrian School of economics, the members of which maintained that since Socialist parties had come to power in parts of postwar Central and Eastern Europe, Socialists had to address the practical problem of organizing production along radically different lines. That was especially true in Austria, where the slower pace of social revolution permitted calm reflection. As Hayek later observed, "Whatever one may think about the importance of the actual experiments made in Austria, there can be little doubt that the theoretical contributions made there to the understanding of the problems will prove to be a considerable force in the intellectual history of our time." He listed Polányi's *Archiv* essay among the most important contributions from the Socialist side.[61]

For their part, the members of the Austrian School looked back to Carl Menger's pathbreaking book of 1871, *Grundsätze der Volkswirtschaftslehre*. Against the German historical school, Menger maintained that economic theorems were valid for all times and places. In particular, he defended what has come to be called the principle of marginal utility, according to which each additional unit of a given commodity increases an individual consumer's satisfaction by a decreasing magnitude. It followed that value resided *not* in the commodity itself, but in fluctuating human wants. This "subjectivist" theory soon claimed the allegiance of two other distinguished economists: Eugen Böhm-Bawerk and Friedrich von Wieser.

By the time Polányi arrived in Vienna, however, Mises had emerged as the Austrian School's most influential spokesman. A mere *Privatdozent* at the university—he was a Jew—Mises earned his living as Secretary of the Vienna Chamber of Commerce. But in his famous *Privatseminar* and book *Die Gemeinwirtschaft: Untersuchungen über den Sozialismus* (1922), he challenged socialization in theory and practice. Like Menger, Mises was a liberal, convinced that economics was a science based upon universally valid principles. Thus, he contended that private ownership of the means of production and the free market alone conduced to economic rationality. Indeed, according to him, the very expression "economic rationality" was tautological, for "all rational action is economic, all economic activity is rational action."[62]

That being the case, Mises insisted that socialism was not simply economically undesirable; it was impossible, an unfortunate choice of words that he subsequently regretted. What he meant to say was that under socialism, no one could make calculations about the most rational (efficient) means of producing goods, because such calculations could be made only on the basis of money prices established by a free market. "Where there is no market there is no price control; without price control there is no economic calculation." But if that was true, how could Mises account for Red Vienna's relative success? His answer was that such municipal undertakings were only oases in larger systems that were fundamentally capitalistic. Hence, municipal socialists based their economic calculations on those made by the greater, free-market, society.[63]

Despite his problematic insistence on the existence of natural economic laws, Mises offered some penetrating criticisms of socialism, understood as a system of central planning. Yet for all his lofty contempt, he shared the Marxist view of man as an economic being. Indeed, while Marxists projected hope of creating neue Menschen, Mises held to the liberal view that man was rational (and hence economic) by his very nature. To the extent that society was not dependent upon economic laws, it was not rational. Polányi was not nearly so pessimistic about the possibilities of socialism, at least of the guild variety, but he was prepared to concede that economic intervention might not always be defensible in strictly technical terms. He understood—and in this at least he was Mises's superior—that beginning with Adam Smith (Professor of Moral Philosophy), every serious economic theorist had been a moral philosopher. Economics was not in essence a science; it was an ethic.

Der Österreichische Volkswirt

Faced with insurmountable financial difficulties, Jászi shut down the Bécsi Magyar Újság in December 1923. To his friend, Polányi expressed his regret that the newspaper was folding at a time when it was most needed. Although he was thinking of the struggle against counterrevolutionary Hungary, he also knew that he had lost his only regular source of income. With a family to feed and Austrian inflation veering out of control, he had little time to secure regular employment. It was with a profound sense of relief, therefore, that he received and quickly accepted an offer from Walther Federn to become a staff writer for Der Österreichische Volkswirt, a left-leaning weekly modeled on England's Economist. He wrote immediately to his brother Michael to report the good news: "I shall probably be able to live on the salary. There will be no editorial work. I will work, read, study, and write everything at home. The magazine is a serious economic weekly, however far it lags behind its great English models."[64]

Federn, who founded the *Volkswirt* in 1908, maintained editorial offices in his flat at Porzellangasse 27, near the Liechtenstein Gallery. There the magazine's staff gathered every Tuesday morning to discuss current national and international events, formulate the magazine's editorial position, and select specific subjects for commentary. Its members, seven or eight in number, often argued fiercely, but they maintained a mutual respect and profited from their disagreements. Participants in those editorial shootouts remembered that Polányi was the dominant personality and that he invariably brought with him an enormous mass of magazines, books, and newspaper clippings.[65]

As the *Volkswirt*'s principal commentator on international affairs, Polányi scrutinized a vast number of sources—*The Times* of London, *Le Temps*, the *Frankfurter Allgemeine Zeitung*, and many others. He provided readers with thoughtful and well-informed analyses of such timely topics as inflation, reparations, Franco-German relations, the League of Nations, the Locarno Treaties, and the Kellogg-Briand Pact. He devoted his most sustained attention to the persistent economic crisis in postwar Europe. In particular, he followed events in England, commenting on the historical importance of the general strike of 1926 and the emergence of "Neoliberal" economics. Neoliberals such as John Maynard Keynes and *Economist* editor W. T. Layton had not, he regretted, abandoned capitalism, but they did display a willingness to venture beyond its frontiers.[66] Moreover, they recognized, in Keynes's words, "that the fiercest contests and the most deeply felt divisions of opinion are likely to be waged in the coming years not round technical questions, where the arguments on either side are mainly economic, but round those which, for want of better words, may be called psychological or, perhaps, moral."[67]

Polányi looked to England not only because it was the home of Neoliberal economics, but because it constituted the world's greatest democracy. With the rise of the Labour party, he foresaw the possibility of a new and more democratic socialism. The economic solutions the English worked out would possess the greatest significance "for the future shape of democracy and socialism on the continent."[68] Apropos of which he wrote in praise of the Labour and Socialist International that forty-one parties from thirty countries organized in Hamburg in 1923. The Second International, he observed, had been dominated by parties that had emerged under absolutist or semiabsolutist governments in Russia, Prussia, and Austria-Hungary. As a result, they themselves had acquired antidemocratic habits. The LSI, on the other hand, took its bearings from "the most progressive democracy, England."[69]

But although Polányi hoped that the English example would encourage the growth of democratic socialism on the continent, he feared that communism and, still worse, fascism might gain the upper hand. Having listened attentively to Duczynska's report of her trip to Italy in the mid-twenties, he came increasingly to identify fascism with crisis-ridden capitalism. This idea eventually crystallized into a full-blown theory, which Polányi outlined for his brother Michael late in 1932. Modern Western societies he explained, were characterized by the interplay of economy and democracy. Between the two, however, a chasm had opened up. Too often ignorant of economics, the Left rallied around democracy; disdainful of democratic politics, the Right championed a free economy at any cost. In order to reunite the two spheres, those—like Polányi—who possessed a knowledge of economics and love for democracy would have to provide guidance. Here he echoed Keynes, who in 1926 had written that "the next step forward must come, not from political agitation or premature experiments, but from thought."[70]

Polányi worked his idea out in greater detail in a *Volkswirt* article entitled "Economy and Democracy." This was the most important of his many pieces for the magazine, not only because it extended his functional theory of society, but because it demonstrated that that theory was, *au fond*, a theory of alienation. Economy and politics were by nature, he argued, vital functions within that union of persons that is society. Yet in the contemporary world they had become divorced to such an extent that they warred against each other. The right attacked the Left in the name of the economy; democracy, it charged, had caused inflation, trade unionism, and mishandling of the currency. Even workers blamed democracy for their economic woes and looked with increasing favor on fascism and communism. With less success, the Left counterattacked in the name of politics or, more strictly, of democracy. As if, Polányi complained, those two basic functions of society could properly be embodied in rival interest groups.[71]

This antagonism within society could only lead to catastrophe, witness the fact that bolsheviks, fascists, and military dictators were destroying democracy throughout the European continent. "Nothing," Polányi maintained, "can save democracy today but a new mass culture formed by economic and political education /Bildung/. That alone can protect it from suicide."[72] The making of such a culture would be an arduous task because the postwar world had produced entirely new economic and political constellations and problems. One could no longer rely upon what one had learned prior to 1914. That, indeed, was why so many failed to understand the nature of the fascist threat.

Yet however dark the future might seem, Polányi reaffirmed his lifelong faith in moral freedom and the efficacy of man's moral will. In the mirror of knowledge, he believed that men and women would ultimately see that economics and politics were merely different functions of their communal existence and that the gulf between them was the societal manifestation of an unnecessary self-alienation. Once again, Polányi held England up as an example for the rest of Europe. "For Englishmen, Free Trade /in English/ does not merely mean free trade /Freihandel/ in the continental sense of the word, but also peace, freedom, and the rights of the people."[73] This served as an illustration of the symbiotic relationship that could exist between economics and Christian ethics, a subject that was of vital and continuing interest to Polányi.[74] It was that relationship which he hoped to see developed in a functionally organized society.

It should be clear from all of this that Duczynska went too far when, in later years, she described this period of her husband's life as theoretically "unproductive."[75] In fact, Polányi had begun to formulate ideas, particularly those that related to the economic history of England, that he later worked out in full in *The Great Transformation*. Partly in order to study that history at first-hand and partly because the *Volkswirt* faced critical financial problems, Polányi left Austria for England late in 1933. His daughter joined him there the following summer and Duczynska, who initially stayed behind in Vienna to continue work on her doctoral dissertation in physics, followed in 1936. With her she brought an eye-witness account of Austria's brief civil war of 1934, in the wake of which she worked for the proscribed social democratic *Schutzbund* and joined the illegal Austrian Communist party.[76]

Aurel Kolnai's "Crimes against Psychoanalysis"[77]

Polányi practiced the altruism he preached, going so far as to share his salary with fellow exiles. Often too he arranged for publication, in the *Volkswirt* and *Bécsi Magyar Újság*, of work by Hungarian writers, among whom was Aurel Kolnai. Born in 1900 to a liberal Jewish family, the intellectually precocious Kolnai read with avid interest each number of *Huszadik Század*; an atheist from his twelfth year, he looked upon Jászi as his "personal deity."[78] Under the latter's influence, he joined the Galileo Circle, and at one meeting listened with rapt attention as Sándor Ferenczi unveiled the mysteries of psychoanalysis. He was especially intrigued by the learned physician's insistence that the new science could be a means for transforming *society* as well as individuals. Thus, at the beginning of his intellectual/spiritual odyssey, Kolnai adhered to what historians now refer to as the Freudian Left.

Not that he was a Freudian Marxist in the manner of Wilhelm Reich or Herbert Marcuse. Quite the contrary. As an admirer of Jászi and a self-styled "liberal Socialist," he preferred progressive evolution to what he described disparagingly as regressive revolution. He rallied in support of Károlyi, but joined the silenced opposition when Kun came to power. A fortnight before the Soviet Republic collapsed, he and his parents made their way first to Czechoslovakia and then to Austria. "It was in these days," he later recalled, "that the emigré mentality became fixed in me, that in some essential sense, I ceased to be a Hungarian and started to accustom myself to the idea that wherever I might live I should live in exile."[79]

Kolnai quickly succumbed "altogether to the incomparable charm, un-national and de-nationalizing, of Vienna as a city."[80] Early in 1920, he and his parents ventured back to Hungary, only to find the White Terror still raging. Knowing he could not live in such a world, he retreated to Vienna, where he made his home until 1937. Only twenty, he managed to eke out a living as a contributor (signing himself "István Lenz") to *Bécsi Magyar Újság* and an editor of *Tűz,* a literary weekly. In possession of a good command of German, he also contributed to German-language publications.

Indeed, he had been giving thought to writing, in German, a psychoanalytic critique of Marxism and bolshevism. Not only had he experienced at firsthand Hungary's bolshevik experiment, but he had read Paul Federn's *Zur Psychologie der Revolution: Die vaterlose Gesellschaft* (1919). A Social Democrat, Federn derived his inspiration from *Totem and Tabu*, in which Freud postulated a primeval act of parricide. Sexually-deprived sons who desired their mother had once banded together in revolt against their father, whom they then murdered and devoured. In the aftermath, however, the brothers discovered that they harbored ambivalent feelings for their father and, out of a profound sense of remorse, relinquished their sexual claims to his woman. By thus outlawing incest, they made possible a cohesive and relatively peaceful clan life, a civilized society.

Federn argued that the father-son relationship constituted the basis for every system of authority. Thus, the Kaiser's fall represented a repetition of the original rebellion of the "sons" against their "father." Germans had then to create a fatherless society, a community of brothers. According to Federn, who supported the Independent Socialists, they could do that only by organizing a true soviet (council) system and rejecting a dictatorship of the proletariat, which would merely reinstate the father-son relationship in altered form. Indeed, they would find it necessary to resist strenuously the psychological disposition to submit themselves to a new father.[81]

After reading Federn's work, Kolnai proposed to Ferenczi that he write for the International Psychoanalytical Library a psychoanalytical critique of communism. Working rapidly, he completed *Psychoanalysis and Sociology* within a year. With good reason, he later described this book as "the silliest rubbish I ever concocted."[82] Like so many Freudian works, it overflowed with fantastic speculations and rigid theoretical constructions. Perhaps the best that one can say for it is that it evidenced a serious interest in the psychology of revolution, a subject that Dostoevski treated with unsurpassed brilliance.

In the final analysis, Kolnai argued in that youthful work, both anarchism and communism aimed at the complete destruction of society and the consequent release of the libido. The anarchists, however, hoped to accomplish this immediately. In the jargon of psychoanalysis, they wished to kill the father (society) and reenter the mother (community). Instead of disciplined cooperation, therefore, they sought an unmediated fusion of souls.[83] Without saying so, Kolnai based this analysis on Lukács's Leninism. Indeed, he cited Lenin's *State and Revolution* as evidence in support of his claim that communism was simply a more methodical and realistic version of anarchism. Less hostile to the father, Communists did not scruple to establish a dictatorship and thereby postpone the day when they too would return to the mother. And even if that dictatorship was over, rather than by, the proletariat, the members of that class, having lost all contact with the soil (symbol of the mother), longed to regress and "possess" the mother. Like the anarchists, then, they moved in a reactionary direction.[84]

Writing in *Imago: Zeitschrift für Anwendung der Psychoanalyse auf die Geistes-wissenschaften*, Theodor Reik praised Kolnai for having called attention to the role that psychoanalysis could play in extending understanding of the psychical side of sociological problems;[85] thereafter, the journal's editors—Freud, Otto Rank, and Hanns Sachs—welcomed articles and reviews from Kolnai's pen. What is more, the London publishing house of George Allen and Unwin commissioned and quickly released an English translation of the German text. To no one's surprise, the Russian Communists took a far dimmer view of Kolnai's book. Both V. Iurinets, who rejected Freud, and M. A. Reisner, who sympathized, subjected it to criticism.[86]

Such international attention might well have turned Kolnai's head had he not been so intensely serious about life and his work. However well read he was for someone of tender age, he recognized that he "knew scandalously little."[87] He aspired especially to make a systematic study of ethics, a subject that he had ignored in *Psychoanalysis and Sociology* for a reason that one is tempted to describe as a form of repression: that it was irrelevant to his project. In November 1922, therefore, he enrolled as a student of philosophy at the University of Vienna.

From Psychoanalysis to Phenomenology

As he began his years of university study, philosophy interested Kolnai "chiefly in view of its ethical and cultural implications and its dovetailing with political preferences." From the first, he was drawn to phenomenology, "that glorious movement of a new realism, the most important departure in philosophy since Socrates and Aristotle"[88]—not so much the phenomenology of Edmund Husserl as that of Max Scheler, the tortured and brilliant thinker who essayed to establish the objective and absolute character of ethical values without having to adopt Kant's formalism and thereby miss the richness and diversity of the concrete, content-filled, moral life. For too long, Scheler had written, ethics had been "constituted either as absolute and a priori, and therefore rational, or as relative, empirical, and emotional. That ethics can and must be both absolute *and* emotional has rarely even been considered."[89]

Even those who reject Scheler's position will concede that he possessed a bold and powerful mind. Taking Pascal's famous *"logique du coeur"* literally, he maintained that it was not reason, but feeling—when it "intended" an object—that disclosed universal values. Feeling, that is, exercised a cognitive function; it produced knowledge of values that were a priori and "material" (content-filled). Love and hate, in particular, presented to men's consciousness ethical values that could be discovered in no other way. It followed from Scheler's argument not only that values were such as could be *discovered*, but that they could not be revealed in their totality to a single person or even a single culture. Fresh experiences of love and hate could produce previously unknown moral insights.

By pursuing this line of argument, Scheler accomplished something remarkable: he turned ethical relativism against itself, insisting that the observable variety of "moral value-estimations" constituted evidence for an absolute order of values. "Because moral value-estimations and their systems are more manifold and richer in their qualities than the diversity of mere natural dispositions and realities of peoples would allow one reasonably to expect, one must assume an objective realm of values which our experiencing can enter only gradually and according to definite structures of the selection of values."[90] Ironically, it had been the attempt to identify absolute morality with that of one particular culture and time that had engendered suspicion and finally ethical relativism.

There was, of course, more to Scheler's ethics than that. He also posited a hierarchical typology of values and endeavored to show that men could discern a common value *essence* in value estimations that appeared at first glance to be contradictory. He maintained, for example, that men had always and everywhere held murder to be immoral. In order to support that claim, he provided a phenomenological account of murder that identified and separated out all historically particular excrescences. And in what may have been his best book, *The Nature of Sympathy*, he offered a more detailed phenomenology of love and hatred that was as dazzling as it was profound. Having identified those feelings as phenomenologically "given" and hence irreducible, he attempted to refute theories of a naturalistic and reductive kind, especially Freud's "ontogenetic theory."[91]

During the spring of 1924, Kolnai read *The Nature of Sympathy* and *Formalism in Ethics*, on the basis of which he concluded that Scheler was the greatest moral thinker since Kant. Because, therefore, of his interest in psychoanalysis, he considered very carefully the phenomenologist's critique of Freud's libido theory, recommending it to Freudians in his final contribution to *Imago*. Against the founder of psychoanalysis, Scheler insisted that no one could derive the various kinds of love from the "libido," for they inhered in the very structure of man's being. Since in his view love disclosed moral values, Scheler saw in Freud's theory a formidable threat. How, he asked, could true moral ideas be possible on Freudian premises? "There is an obvious *circularity* in Freud's explanation here: All higher moral feelings and activities, and hence, presumably, all moral motives as such, are allegedly due to the 'sublimation of libido.' But in order to account for the 'sublimation' itself, Freud proceeds to postulate the existence of a 'morality' *at the behest* of which the repression of libido can be effected, and its diversion to 'higher activities' take place!"[92]

In his *Imago* article, Kolnai challenged Freudians to consider seriously Scheler's critique, though he continued to believe that the psychoanalytic account of the adaptability of instinctual impulses contributed to a morality that endeavored to create, and not merely behold, ethical values. If Scheler feared that Freud might lead men to confuse good and evil (the valuable and the worthless), Kolnai worried that Scheler, in his concern to protect values from contamination, might encourage men to withdraw from imperfect reality. Such a withdrawal, he maintained, was inconsistent with the Christianity Scheler professed.[93]

To that Christianity Kolnai was more and more attracted. Yet despite the power of Scheler's writings, he was won to Catholicism primarily by G. K. Chesterton. Having read Hungarian translations of *Orthodoxy, Heretics,* and *What's Wrong With the World,* he had arrived at the conclusion that one might be Catholic without being a political reactionary. No idea informed his mind so strongly and enduringly as Chesterton's "conservative conception of Reform." That conception served as the basis for Kolnai's evolving social theory and deserves to be cited in full.

> That change cannot be evaluated, nor, consequently, valued, except in the framework of permanent standards; that progress, in the sense connoting improvement, not only demands a setting of conservation historically but presupposes it logically; that an active work of reform, as distinct from aimless destruction and likewise ... from a mere passive mood of anarchy, depends less on intellectual innovations than on intellectual constancy; that discontent sustained enough to be operative requires patience, which is to say, content at a deeper level; that without a background of love, just anger itself is pointless; that insistence upon what ought to be is meaningless and self-contradictory unless it is based on a primal affirmation of what is; that there can be no pith in our criticism of realities unless we are "optimists" about Reality; that we can only aim at a more perfect order if we first accept Order.[94]

Kolnai made an initial attempt to apply his conservative conception of reform in his doctoral dissertation, published in 1927 as *Ethical Value and Reality.* The title derived from his conviction that ethical value was so embedded in reality that one could not properly be studied without constant reference to the other. Like Scheler, that is, Kolnai rejected any rigid separation of Is from Ought. Values, he maintained, were phenomenologically given in reality. Men and women were already *in* a value-laden world prior to the moment when they first reflected upon moral questions. Indeed, they discovered new values only in close conjunction with values that already existed; hence the *fundamental* value of the world as it was given to them. The world as a whole, as a background of ethical significance, was worthy of their affirmation. To be sure, they should seek to reform those discrete constituents of reality that were valueless or insufficiently valuable. Always, however, they had to remember that *"genuine reform requires the permanence of the background."*[95] Or as Chesterton once put it, Christians insist upon the "need for a first loyalty to things, and then for a ruinous reform of things."[96]

Since *Ethical Value and Reality* was his doctoral dissertation, Kolnai did not work out his social theory in detail. Instead, he focused on ethical reform in a more general sense, insisting that it was not a matter of imposing values, conceived of as "laws," on reality. Ethical intention, in the phenomenological sense of intending an object, strove for existing values, as they related to, and were borne by, persons. Following Scheler, Kolnai identified ethical intention as a manifestation of love. When we love another person, he argued, we affirm not only that one's objective values, but also the plentitude of his or her essential worth. Such love is grounded in our love for God as the highest bearer of value and the paradigmatic unity of the good and the real. Indeed, that we are able to love imperfect persons at all is a consequence of our awareness of God's love for them and a finite world.[97]

In his focus on love, Kolnai did not rely on Scheler alone. He pointed out that Franz Brentano defended "the immediate intentional character of love over against the view that the good would first be apprehended without love and then be loved on the basis of that knowledge (Aristotle). He cited Hume: 'How ought one to understand that something is to be loved without practical experience of love?' "[98] He remembered too that Chesterton had said that love presupposed the separate identity of persons. Rejecting "the doctrine that we are really all one person; that there are no real walls of individuality between man and man," Chesterton defined the Christian position: "I want to love my neighbor not because he is I, but precisely because he is not I. I want to adore the world, not as one likes a looking-glass, because it is one's self, but as one loves a woman, because she is entirely different. If souls are separate love is possible. If souls are united love is obviously impossible."[99]

Chesterton taught him, Kolnai later recalled, "that 'Christian love' meant, not an equivalent but the extreme anti-thesis of a vital 'merging' into an indistinct 'community-soul' or a 'loss of identity' and riddance from responsibility."[100] Marxists such as Lukács, on the other hand, refused to concede that there existed a domain of persons that could not and should not be co-opted by society as an undifferentiated totality. As a result, they attempted to force individuals into an ersatz unity. "The 'conscious self-regulation of the *Gemeinschaft*' means in general, as Polányi characterized it admirably, 'apparent collective consciousness and real foreign domination.' "[101]

His dissertation in good order, Kolnai completed his university studies in 1926. Having settled accounts with psychoanalysis and steeped himself in the writings of Catholic thinkers such as Chesterton, Scheler, Brentano, and Dietrich von Hildebrand, he was that same year received into the Church of Rome. In his memoirs, he explained his decision:

> Sound reason aware of its limitations but trustful of its applications to objects outside the mind, reverence for the manifoldness of reality, open-minded acceptance of the order of the universe and the realm of values as *"given"* in our world-experience—to maintain or safeguard any of these, it was by no means necessary to embrace Catholicism; but the historical linkage between these principles and the Catholic intellectual tradition, the dominant general propensity of mankind to turn against the former in proportion as it deserted the latter, seemed to bear witness, if not to the truth of Catholicism, at least to a deep enduring concordance of Catholicism with the spirit of Truth. Sanity, morality, and the full experience of a world undeprived of its wealth of meaning, dimension, colour, savour and weight were undoubtedly possible without the Faith; but they were all of greater intrinsic perfection and endowed with greater security under the Faith. Above all, the Faith alone would guarantee their status and effective presence on the vast scale of our common civilization. Entering the Church not only placed me in the supernatural presence of God and offered me access to the Communion of Saints; it also made me feel as if I were firmly lodged in the one valid, universal and imperishable medium of communication with my fellow man.[102]

Shortly after he converted, Kolnai began work on *Sexual Ethics*, a masterful examination of nonformal, or material, sexual ethics that opens with the matter-of-fact observation that human beings always assign value judgments to sexual conduct. As a consequence, no one genuinely concerned with ethical questions relating to sex could afford to ignore reality; indeed, Kolnai insisted that any moral ideal that stood altogether in opposition to reality was certain to be false. As he had argued in *Ethical Value and Reality*, ethics and ethical reform presupposed a fundamental acceptance of the world as it was. The values of a particular society might be "relative," but they were nonetheless authoritative. Rightly understood, relativity meant "incomplete, imperfectly comprehended absolutism, not senselessness, fancy, or caprice." Indeed, it was precisely men's awareness of their finite perspective that encouraged in them a belief in absolute good; given values pointed them toward the absolute and vouchsafed their union with it.[103]

Nor were finite historical perspectives as contradictory as one might think. However much they differed with respect to the details of their indictment, for example, all societies rejected lasciviousness and uncontrolled sexuality. And it was that rejection, according to Kolnai, that formed the basis for all nonformal sexual ethics. It reflected a universal recognition that sexual congress, while by no means evil in itself, posed a significant threat to human community. Divorced from a loving relationship between spiritual persons, sex possessed the power to destroy personhood by treating the partner as a mere object; instead of creating or reinforcing a community of lives, it "intended" the total amalgamation of one person with another. In this, Kolnai was convinced, it resembled the attempt of contemporary political tyrannies to destroy the integrity of human personality and force every citizen into the inhuman "Totality" of a Lukács or an Othmar Spann.[104]

Kolnai made the connection between depersonalizing lasciviousness and depersonalizing totalitarianism quite explicit when he denounced "the fiction of an absolute, all-surveying social consciousness" as a "chimera." Both bolshevism, despite its talk of the proletariat's struggle for freedom, and fascism, despite its "corporative" facade and tactical support of traditional social powers, were attempting to deify society as a "totality" that dissolved persons into an undifferentiated mass governed by a will that purported to be its own but was in fact that of the state. In that way, they were destroying the true community of persons that had its foundation in such intimate, independent, and timeless communal institutions as marriage and the family. "The family," he wrote, "is *something more timeless, something more deeply 'social,'* than society itself in the form of the all-embracing state."[105]

At the core of the family was the institution of marriage, the form of an abiding sexual *and* personal community and thus an indispensable element in the structure of society. As such it was never merely a private matter. Marriage tamed the sexual instinct by enlisting it in the service of higher things—love and mutual responsibility between two spiritual persons. In that way, and in that way only, sex could contribute to the making and sustaining of a community of lives. That was why, Kolnai argued, no society opposed marriage as something immoral; even the Soviet Union had decided not to wage war on the venerable institution.[106]

It should be clear from this brief summary that Kolnai was interested in sexual ethics primarily because of its relationship to social theory. He wished, in fact, to project a vision of society that was concrete, rooted in the world as it is given to us, and at odds with the contemporary visions of bolshevism, fascism, *and* American capitalism. He called his vision "socialism," but insisted that the society he was defending was perfectly compatible "with the Christian, monogamous family, understood as a community of lives."[107] It was a society suffused with family values, a society where single-family homes replaced municipal housing of the sort preferred by the rulers of Red Vienna. It was, finally, the "distributist" society of Chesterton's imagination. In *What's Wrong With the World*, the Englishman observed that "the idea of private property universal but private, the idea of families free but still families, of domesticity democratic but still domestic, of one man one house—this remains the real vision and magnet of mankind."[108]

In Defense of Christian Europe

Although he had demonstrated a talent for formal philosophy, Kolnai did not seek an academic appointment. He knew that his chances were slim and that, in any case, a teaching career would yield no income for several years. Even more important, he could not persuade himself to withdraw into an ivory tower at a time when Europe was in the throes of a gathering spiritual and political crisis. Thus, he worked as a free-lance editor and writer with a mission: "to preserve and strengthen Christian civilization, with constitutional democracy as the régime proper to it, by raising some of its motifs, values or axioms to a higher level of consciousness, thus rendering their status more secure and invulnerable; and by providing an essential criticism of its inner and outer enemies, meant to strike at their very nerve, not merely their accidental and topical defects."[109] Criticism would prepare the way for preservation and renewal.

With obvious and pained regret, Kolnai identified psychoanalysis as one of Christian Europe's principal enemies. New to Catholicism, he was not surprised to discover that his coreligionists frowned upon Freud and his theories. From Friedrich Wilhelm Foerster, a Protestant with Catholic leanings, they borrowed the critical terms: pansexualism, materialism, false intellectualism, disavowal of the higher world, inadmissible inference from pathological to normal spiritual life.[110] Although Foerster taught in Vienna from 1912 to 1914, he soon moved on to Germany, from whence came most of the Catholic critiques of psychoanalysis.

Indeed, despite Freud's repeated complaint that he was a prophet without honor in his own country, Austrian Catholics began a concerted counterattack only during the early 1920s. It was then that organizations such as the Leo-Society for Art and Science and the Logos Academic Union began to sponsor lectures by critics of psychoanalysis, the most trenchant of whom was Rudolf Allers, a Jewish-born convert and member of the circle around Dietrich von Hildebrand. In his writings and lectures Allers accused psychoanalysis of being an enemy of the Christian family and hence of Christian civilization.

Among Austrian Catholics, matters came to a head in 1927, when Freud published *The Future of an Illusion*, an open apology for atheism. Because of his Hobbesian view of the state of nature, the aging patriarch had once insisted that civilization was necessary for order and any sense of human community. But was religion still required for the maintenance of civilization? That was the fundamental question, for Freud took it to be axiomatic that on their own merits, religious claims could not withstand the light of reason. Religious faith was an illusion, the fulfillment of a primordial wish for protection from a hostile environment.

By way of reply to his own question, Freud asserted without hesitation that civilization ran a far greater risk if men maintained their belief than if they surrendered it. Already, in fact, science had undermined religious faith to such an extent that it no longer exerted a significant influence. There was little cause to keep up the pretense and good reason to believe that men and women would more willingly reconcile themselves to instinctual restraint if they admitted "the purely human origin of all the regulations and precepts of civilization."[111]

In a chapter that was especially offensive to Catholics, Freud characterized religion as "the universal obsessional neurosis of humanity," and thus, like individual neurosis, a phase in the growth to maturity. "If this view is right," Freud concluded, "it is to be supposed that a turning-away from religion is bound to occur with the fatal inevitability of a process of growth, and that we find ourselves at this very juncture in the middle of that phase of development. Our behaviour should therefore be modelled on that of a sensible teacher who does not oppose an impending new development but seeks to ease its path and mitigate the violence of its irruption."[112] The time had come to replace repression with the operation of intellect.

With The Future of an Illusion, Freud initiated a series of writings in which he grappled with the cultural questions that had long fascinated him. In his last years, he wrote two of his most imaginative and controversial works, Civilization and Its Discontents and Moses and Monotheism. He cannot have been surprised that those books prompted numerous protests, especially from Catholics. In the pages of Volkswohl, the theoretical organ of the Christian Social Party, Allers registered the obvious objection that psychology was not competent to make claims that transcended the restricted field of psychical phenomena. More important, he challenged the question-begging naturalistic assumptions upon which Freud's theories rested. Atheism, he concluded, was an unrealizable "illusion of the future" because it projected an impoverished reality.

Taking his cue from Allers, Kolnai entitled his Volkswohl critique of Freud "An Illusion of the Future." His principal objection flowed naturally from his gradual conversion from psychoanalysis to phenomenology, from the unconscious to the conscious. Freud, he observed, was once again true to himself and the "science" he invented when he reduced the healthy to the sick, the higher values to the contemptible. Just why one should make that reduction was not clear. And if, Kolnai continued mischievously, mankind's religious phase had been one of immaturity, it had produced wondrous "children's games" like Greek philosophy, Roman law, medieval cathedrals, and the theories of Newton and Descartes. He concluded that Freud's way of thinking was but a modern version of that ancient illusion of men who thought they no longer needed God, the illusion symbolized by the Tower of Babel.[113]

That such an illusion could produce dangerous consequences, Kolnai did not doubt. He was therefore disturbed when he encountered Thomas Mann's celebrated essay, "Freud's Position in the History of Modern Thought." In essence, Mann argued that Freud was the authentic heir of the nineteenth-century romantics, the greatest contemporary explorer of the human heart's darker regions. But that did not mean, Mann hastened to add, that the Austrian genius reprobated reason and enlightenment. Quite the contrary, for like his romantic predecessors, Freud was a revolutionary who understood that genuine enlightenment could best be served by exposing to the light of reason those powers of darkness, those irrational instincts, that had to be recognized before they could be tamed. Psychoanalysis's "profoundest expertise in morbid states," Mann wrote, "is unmistakably at work not ultimately for the sake of disease and the depths, not, that is, with an interest hostile to reason; but first and last, armed with all the advantages that have accrued from exploring the dark abysses, in the interest of healing and redemption, of 'enlightenment' in the most humane sense of the word."[114]

There was undoubtedly an element of truth in this idea, to which, as we recall, Mann had given fictional expression in The Magic Mountain. But Kolnai questioned whether a preoccupation with the darker side of human nature would in fact lead men and women to higher things. Deeper reflection would show, he believed, that immersion in the erotic experiences of childhood served only to divert attention from important questions, including those that pertained to society and political institutions. Despite Mann's praise, Freud had not solved the complex problem of the relationship between instinct and morality, between the dark imprisonments of the soul and the luminous aims of the person. Catholic Christianity was alone in its ability to give all aspects of human nature their due without falling into the trap of subordinating the higher to the lower.[115]

The main reason that Mann failed to appreciate the dangers of psychoanalysis was that he, like Freud, retained an overall faith in progress. That faith blinded him to the problem of bolshevism, an ideology that pretended to be the culmination of the progressive movement. In fact, Kolnai argued, it was more satanic and murderous than the fascism Mann rightly feared precisely because it was more novel, less governed by the past. Because bolshevism claimed to fix its eyes on a historically determined future and to embody the people's will, it could justify a more all-encompassing tyranny. "In bolshevism," according to Kolnai, "there is a great deal more nobility and positive good—but also more ominous malice and unlimited arrogance—than in fascism. It stands at once closer to God and to Satan. For that reason it is, despite many shared characteristics, a far more diabolical force and a more immediate danger for those who seek God."[116]

Kolnai's comparison of bolshevism and fascism appeared in Der Deutsche Volkswirt, a well-paying review that Gustav Stolper edited. It outraged Duczynska, whom Kolnai once described as "the most impressive and inexorable revolutionary fanatic I have ever met."[117] Not long before his article appeared, Duczynska had made a brief visit to Mussolini's Italy, and she quickly forwarded to Stolper two essays designed, among other things, to serve as public responses to Kolnai. In each she provided an intelligent and well-informed analysis of fascist *praxis* and the problem of consolidating a revolutionary regime. At the same time, however, she offered her customary apology for Russian communism. The bolsheviks, she insisted, had succeeded in establishing the Soviet state's independence from the Communist party, even if the latter did set the general line for governmental action. What was more, they had eliminated extra-legal organizations such as the Red Guards, unlike Mussolini, who continued to employ the fascist militia to terrorize the old state apparatus.[118]

Kolnai did not publish an explicit rejoinder, but he undoubtedly extended the debate with Duczynska at the Polányis' apartment, to which he regularly repaired.[119] He also continued to indict the bolsheviks for acting on the assumption that progress was mechanical and hence that they had created a better society by virtue of their recent appearance on the scene. Indeed, by their historical performance, bolsheviks demonstrated that such a conception of progress could lead to barbarism. By subordinating men and women to an all-encompassing state masquerading as a *Gemeinschaft*, they had denied one of Christianity's most important doctrines: that of the free spiritual personality and the communal order appropriate to it.[120]

It was evident from his antibolshevik broadsides that Kolnai regarded communism as the greatest long-term threat to Christian Europe. It advanced a consistent ideology, appealed to men's longing for community, and presented itself as the historical heir of the progressive movement. Convinced of its own legitimacy, it had established in Russia, and in Hungary, brutal dictatorships that operated with clear consciences. Its ambition was nothing less than the creation of a Communist Europe, indeed a Communist world. Kolnai took that ambition seriously, but he also viewed with growing alarm the aims of those in Hungary, Austria, and elsewhere in Europe who were working for the counterrevolution. These activists presented a more immediate if less deeply rooted challenge to Christian Europe.

Drawing upon his knowledge of the Horthy regime in Hungary, Kolnai recognized that counterrevolution had at least as much in common with revolution as it had with traditional conservatism. For one thing, it never envisioned a restitution of the prerevolutionary period pure and simple, but sought instead to incorporate elements of the revolutionary order.[121] Horthy's Hungary, for example, had mitigated the landowners' domination of the peasantry and made improvements in public education. In nineteenth-century France, Napoleon had completed the bourgeois law code, the Restoration kings had worked out constitutional life, and Napoleon III had introduced universal suffrage.[122]

For another thing, the counterrevolution was more dictatorial than traditional conservatism, more interested in state power than in social supremacy. In part, that was because it did not draw its support from the upper classes alone. Horthy appealed to certain of the lower classes, particularly the peasantry, which had suffered so much in 1919 at the hands of Kun and the Budapest proletariat. Just so, Kolnai observed, Austria's paramilitary *Heimwehr*, organized in 1919 to defend the country's frontiers, did not draw primarily upon the conservative peasant masses, but upon a minority of workers from the heavy industries of Styria, many of whom were former Communists. All in all, Kolnai concluded, the evidence showed that the counterrevolution could not be identified with any particular class; its appeal was to isolated, déclassé individuals.[123]

In this, of course, counterrevolutionary regimes differed from revolutionary bolshevism, which made of the proletariat the redemptive class. They differed also in that they lacked clear-cut ideologies. They were churches founded upon many and contradictory heresies, despotisms of the will in search of legitimizing ideas. Theorists, all of whom rejected liberal individualism and longed for a renewed sense of community, stood ready and able to provide such ideas. Kolnai was particularly concerned to take on Austrian proponents of the so-called "corporative state." The theory of corporatism harked back to the nineteenth-century romantics Adam Müller and Karl von Vogelsang, both of whom hoped to re-create what they took to be the harmonious social order of the Middle Ages, one uncontaminated by democracy and capitalism.

After 1918, Othmar Spann, professor of economics and sociology at Vienna, updated and popularized Müller and Vogelsang's ideas. He opposed democracy and capitalism because both were rooted in "individualism." According to his "neoromantic universalism," society was "a totality /Ganzheit/ whose parts are not independent, but are members of this totality."[124] True individuality always presupposed a pairing /Gezweiung/—of artist and public, mother and child, teacher and pupil. It developed only in relationship to another. Spann regarded that relationship as a model for the relationship between society as a totality and its members.

Spann condemned capitalism as the economic system proper to individualism. It had emerged as a result of "the shattering of the corporative spirit, of the corporative harmony of the Middle Ages, as it found expression in guild, church, fief, cooperative and fraternal organs of all kinds."[125] As the economic system proper to universalism, he recommended corporatism. His system was detailed and so complicated that he himself sometimes seemed unaware of its statist logic. The basic components of his new society were not to be individuals but *Gemeinschaften* called *Stände* (estates), organized hierarchically. Although the system was designed to be highly decentralized, a superior *Stand* could always issue binding orders to one inferior. Thus, the political *Stand*, which could alone speak for the nation as a whole, would have effective control of the entire hierarchy of *Stände*.

On a December evening in 1928, Kolnai attended a lecture that Spann delivered to an appreciative gathering of the Leo-Society. Incensed by what he heard, he set down some reflections on the anti-Catholic character of the famous sociologist's ideas.[126] He did not deny that there were points of convergence between Catholicism and Spann's universalism, including a rejection of individual autonomy and a recognition of the importance of community. But he pointed out that Catholics could never sanction Spann's deification of the social totality. From the church's point of view, God was the ultimate reality to which the Gemeinschaften, as well as the individuals comprising them, were subordinate. To ignore that authority and discount the primary significance of persons, as Spann did, was to fall into the trap of a "universalism" that was merely a euphemism for a centralized state tyranny.

Kolnai obtained added ammunition for his Spann critique from Dietrich von Hildebrand's Metaphysik der Gemeinschaft (1930), which contained "the most devastating critique of Othmar Spann's totalitarian fascist philosophy of the state,"[127] and from discussions with Polányi, who devoted much of a 1930 essay on fascism to a critical examination of Spann's work. The counterrevolutionary theorist was right, Kolnai's friend argued, to attack individualism, but only that which was atheistic in inspiration. The individualism of Dostoevski's atheists—Kirilov, Raskolnikov, Stavrogin, and Ivan Karamazov—recognized no responsibility to God or to men. It was the creed of Übermenschen who believed themselves to be fully autonomous—to be, in effect, gods.[128]

But, Polányi observed, there was also a Christian understanding of individualism, and Spann was prepared to sacrifice that too on the altar of a coercive and dehumanizing totality. According to the Christian view of individualism, a completely autonomous being—if such were conceivable—would not be a "person." Personhood derived from a relationship with God and one's fellow men; it was not real outside of community. "The reality of community," according to Polányi, "is the relationship of persons." Any conception of community that undermined personhood in an effort to achieve an undifferentiated oneness was fundamentally anti-Christian. "The battle is engaged," he concluded, "between the representatives of the religion which has discovered the human person and those who have made the determination to abolish the idea of the person the centre of their new religion."[129]

Because he was not a Catholic, Polányi was less angered than Kolnai about Austrian Catholicism's growing attachment to the corporative scheme. The split within the Catholic camp between those who favored Sozialpolitik—work for gradual change within the existing socio-economic framework—and those who held out for Sozialreform—a radical reconstruction of society along corporative lines—continued to exist. But during the late 1920s and early 1930s, the balance shifted decisively away from the former toward the latter. There were a number of reasons for the shift, including long-standing Catholic dissatisfaction with the modern state and capitalist economy. In addition, fear of the social democrats increased after the Social Democratic Party raised the specter of dictatorship in its Linz Program of 1926. Worse, on July 15, 1927, workers burned the Palace of Justice after a jury acquitted members of the right-wing *Frontkämpfer* who, in a Burgenland clash with the *Schutzbund*, had shot and killed a war veteran and a seven-year-old boy. Staring civil war in the face, police killed eighty-nine demonstrators and wounded hundreds more. As a result, the *Heimwehr* agitated even more for fundamental change.

Most important, perhaps, was the publication in 1931 of Pope Pius XI's encyclical letter *Quadragesimo anno*, "Reconstructing the Social Order and Perfecting it Conformably to the Precepts of the Gospel." In it, the pontiff attempted to update Leo XIII's *Rerum novarum*, generally thought to have marked the victory of *Sozialpolitik*. Although he said much that could be interpreted as continued support for that position, he did advocate the reconstruction of the social order along corporative lines. Social harmony could best be assured, he proclaimed, by replacing classes with vocational groups, by "binding men together not according to the position they occupy in the labor market, but according to the diverse functions which they exercise in society."[130] It was to be the state's responsibility to implement that fundamental reform.

Clearly, the Pope's encyclical signaled the Church's reversion to the premises of *Sozialreform*. It was rumored at the time that Ignaz Seipel, priest and former chancellor, had been one of the drafters of the document. In any event, there is no doubt that the Christian Social leader had abandoned his earlier *Sozialpolitik* position and begun to lobby for the corporative state. Indeed, soon after having resigned as chancellor in April 1929, Seipel had announced his support for the *Heimwehr* private army. At about the same time, he sought out Spann, about whom he had once harbored profoundly ambivalent feelings, and proposed an intellectual alliance.[131] "We have before us," Kolnai lamented, a "portrait of the aging Seipel: the fascist interpretation of the papal encyclical *Quadragesimo anno*, . . . the adoption of Spann's 'doctrine of totality,' that pseudo-Christian, pagan ideology of authority that wears the masks of science and Catholicism."[132]

In 1932, the year of Seipel's death, the diminutive Engelbert Dollfuss assumed the Austrian chancellorship. When, the following year, Hindenburg appointed Hitler Chancellor, the Austrian Catholic *Lager* became even more impatient to draw up a new constitution that would create the "*Quadragesimo anno* state." In March 1933, Dollfuss suspended parliament, and in September he spoke at a mass rally of the incipient *Vaterländische Front*. "The day of the capitalist system, the era of the capitalist-liberal economic order is past," he declared. "We demand a social, Christian, German Austria, on a corporative basis and under strong authoritarian leadership."[133]

Fearing the worst, Kolnai made an eleventh-hour effort to alert Austrians to the impending danger. Corporatists, he said, used the catchword "*Stand*" in order to cloak their real intentions. Their talk of the "*Quadragesimo anno* State" was meaningless, for Pius XI had not prescribed a particular constitutional form; he had recommended an economic organization. The vocational estates (*Berufsstände*) of which he spoke were to be organs of economic self-government, not administrative arms of the state; strictly speaking, a *Stände Staat* was a contradiction in terms. *Quadragesimo anno* could not, therefore, be reconciled with Spann's theories, according to which the political estate (*Herrschaftsstand*) was merely one of the vocational estates; its task was to direct affairs of state. In practice that would mean that the fascist party would exercise state power, while the other estates followed orders.[134]

Just how right Kolnai was, events soon demonstrated. In February 1934, the Socialists, with their backs to the wall, organized a general strike. Dollfuss was in Budapest at the time and Emil Fey, state secretary for security affairs, called upon the *Heimwehr* to do battle with the *Schutzbund*; the ensuing civil war was brief. Unequal to the task, the members of the *Schutzbund* barricaded themselves in the huge, fortresslike tenements that the Socialist government had constructed ten years earlier. There they held out for twenty-four hours before surrendering. With the end of the civil war, Red Vienna passed into history.

Concrete Conservatism

As the Catholic hierarchy and the Christian Social Party embraced the corporative state, Kolnai gave in to "fits of anti-clericalism" and, late in 1930, transferred his allegiance to the Social Democratic Party.[135] Yet he remained a convinced and practicing Catholic, thanks not least to Fr. Georg Bichlmair, S. J., the remarkable man who had instructed him in the Faith and baptized him into the Roman Catholic Church. Rigorously orthodox and well connected in Rome, Fr. Bichlmair worked tirelessly to stem the mass defection of industrial workers from the church. He deplored the fact that so many of the alienated regarded the Bride of Christ as an uncritical defender of capitalism and he called upon Catholics to work for economic reform.[136] Grateful for allies, he maintained close relations with "The League of Austrian Religious Socialists."

An interconfessional, though largely Catholic, group of Christians organized the League in 1926. From the beginning, their leader was Otto Bauer, not to be confused with Austro-Marxism's leading theoretician. Bauer was a metal worker, a Catholic, and a self-styled Marxist who hoped to enlist Christians in the day-to-day struggle for socialism. With that in mind, he allied the League with the Social Democratic Party, while retaining for it complete freedom of action. On January 15, 1927, he coedited the first number of *Menschheitskämpfer: Blatt der religiösen Sozialisten Österreichs*, in the programmatic statement for which he denounced capitalism and invited Christians to join the proletarian class struggle.

Bauer scheduled the League's first Vienna Conference for the following November, amid rumors that Catholic bishops were about to condemn membership in the Social Democratic Party. In an effort to forestall such a declaration, the League's most important theoretician, Karl Polányi, proposed that a resolution be drafted and addressed to the bishops. Entitled "Church and Proletariat," the resolution maintained that by identifying itself with the Christian Social Party, the Catholic Church had become an instrument of capitalism and an opponent of the working class. It asked, therefore, that the Church sever its ties to capital's political representative and set believers free to obey their political conscience.[137]

Without waiting for a reply, the Religious Socialists organized a series of conferences in 1928, culminating with a two-day "Convention for Christianity and Socialism" in November. Kolnai was one of the fifteen hundred who attended in the hope of finding an answer to a question he had posed in *Der Österreichische Volkswirt*: "Church and socialism, the only two hopes of our disillusioned age, are groping for each other. Who ought first to offer the hand of union?"[138] After the Convention, he had his answer. Eager to spread the word, he filed an enthusiastic report for the *Volkswirt*. "The movement proceeds," he wrote, "from a denial of the alleged opposition between socialism and religion, particularly the Christian religion, and most especially the Catholic religion (Austria being a Catholic country); it endeavors to transcend the historically conditioned antithesis between the socialist workers' movement and the Catholic Church, and to elucidate the ultimate mutuality of both's ideals."[139]

Few Catholics were impressed. Most believed that the Religious Socialists' conception of Christianity owed more to socialism than their conception of socialism owed to Christianity. But the League was undeterred. On Whit Saturday, 1930, Bauer opened a conference in the small town of Berndorf with a charge to all members: "We need for our conference an inner as well as an outer relationship to Whitsuntide. Something of the miracle of *Gemeinschaft* in the original pentecostal community must also be alive in us. We want to create the new social and economic order in the likeness of *Gemeinschaft* and for *Gemeinschaft*."[140] With that in mind, the members of the conference drafted the League's "Berndorf Program," which proclaimed that capitalism would be replaced by a new social and economic order informed by democratic principles. State ownership would be held to a minimum and cooperatives encouraged. Once in control of the means of production, workers would develop as *persons* and no longer be degraded into commodities.

The program's drafters discouraged the formation of separatist parties and advocated work within the larger Socialist movement. At the same time, they counseled the Social Democratic Party to permit individual freedom in matters of Weltanschauung. The Party was to be a political and economic organization of the working people, neutral with respect to ideology. In that way, freethinking and Christian Socialists could obey their conscience in cultural matters.[141]

Having studied the Berndorf Program carefully, Kolnai joined the League. He was hopeful when, through Fr. Bichlmair's good offices, Bauer forwarded a copy of the Program to Rome. More than likely, he was in the overflowing Kirche am Hof on April 26, 1931; on that day, League members came to hear Fr. Bichlmair preach. Full of confidence, the charismatic priest predicted that the papal encyclical, soon to be promulgated, would emphasize the compatibility of Catholic social doctrine with Socialist programs. He was therefore shocked and disappointed when, on May 24, the *Reichspost* published the German version of *Quadragesimo anno*. There he read Pius XI's uncompromising declaration: " 'Religious Socialism,' 'Christian Socialism' are expressions implying a contradiction in terms. No one can be at the same time a sincere Catholic and a true Socialist."[142]

Kolnai was every bit as disappointed. Publicly, he stressed that the Pope knew the difference between communism and social democracy and did not condemn socialism as a social-economic system. Anyway, he wrote in exasperation, "It is absolutely not obvious, even to a believing and ecclesiastically loyal Catholic, that one should decide the concrete questions of political and social-economic order on the basis of papal encyclicals."[143] Together with Polányi, he continued to work for the League. In the pages of the *Menschheitskämpfer*, he maintained that only a socialism rooted in faith could defeat the political religion of fascism. But time was running out. After Dollfuss assumed power, the government looked upon the journal with mounting disapproval. Officials confiscated the issue of October 1933 and soon thereafter forced the editors to cease publication and the League to disband.

Unlike "the little" Otto Bauer, who was more Socialist than Catholic, Kolnai placed his faith first. Even before his conversion, he had been impressed by Hilaire Belloc's statement that "Europe will return to the Faith, or her civilization will fail." As he put it in his memoirs: "That Europe could only be herself, or even her best self, in her mediaeval shape seemed no more than an arbitrary paradox; but that her life was somehow bound up with the survival of her religious matrix, that her life-sap was ultimately Catholic and that her crisis had to do with her having departed too far from that religious basis seemed fairly reasonable suggestions."[144]

As a consequence of that conviction, Kolnai's social theories were fundamentally conservative. In retrospect, he remembered the interwar years as a time when he fell short of anything like "essential conservatism," but opined that his outlook "was not precisely un-conservative."[145] By 1934, in fact, he had accepted the main outlines of what he characterized as "concrete conservatism."[146] Conservatives, as well as thinkers on the left, were alive to modern society's loss of community and placed much of the blame on the atomizing effects of capitalist economic arrangements. Exploitation, poverty, class hatred, and the destruction of every *Gemeinschaft* were due, Kolnai believed, to the workings of economic liberalism. Thus, a religious and moral critique of capitalism was necessary.

All the more so, according to Kolnai, because capitalism's destruction of *Gemeinschaft* had produced revolutionary communism and counterrevolutionary fascism. What lent each its seductive attraction was the promise of *Gemeinschaft* restored. Instead, each attempted to destroy the primacy of spiritual persons by forcing them into an impersonal and ersatz unity that refused to tolerate differences. Therein lay the source of a satanic dehumanization. "As a matter of fact," Kolnai wrote in his memoirs, "the more I thought about the 'final goal' of Communism, the less I liked it; before long, I decided that the 'love-community' of Communist society proper, which by supposition would be past all dictatorship and indeed all State compulsion, was even *more* execrable than the 'transitional' present reality of the Communist Terror State itself. Far from the end 'justifying' the means, the immorality of the end was what really accounted for, and surpassed, the immorality of the means. For the specific and gigantic evilness of Communism lay, not in the unrestrained use of violence as such, but in the negation of man's individual personality—taken in its juridical, economic and intellectual distinctness from all 'community.'"[147]

In opposition to the all-powerful state "communities" of communism and fascism, Kolnai defended the dignity of the human person and his self-determination within the context of hierarchically ordered small communities. "The path to freedom and self-government," he wrote, "leads through intimate communities. And that is the Christian, the Catholic principle: to defend the living community of familiar . . . spheres against the omnipotence of an Enlightened or other form of state absolutism, against the atomized isolation of individuals."[148] The contemporary political system most consistent with that principle, he argued, was democracy, understood in a decidedly conservative sense.

The democracy that Kolnai defended was not that of Rousseau, in whose conception of the General Will he espied the seed of tyranny and the certain destruction of *Gemeinschaften* intermediately situated between individuals and the state. Nor was it that of naive optimists, the believers in inevitable progress. Nor, finally, that of fanatical egalitarians. "Equality means here equal right (not equal competency), equal human dignity (not equal social rank for all men); and insofar as a certain compromise with respect to position in life is demanded, this in no way means that all should think, act, and look alike, but that all should have an equal right and opportunity to be 'unequal' in conformity with their personal particularity."[149]

But if Kolnai's program of political democracy was largely one of preservation, that of economic democracy entailed fundamental changes. In his search for an alternative to large-scale capitalism, he looked to guild socialism. "How inextricably intertwined," he enthused, "are England's guild socialist (functionalist) currents with Christian-medieval ideas."[150] The guild socialists were endeavoring to re-create the communal atmosphere of the precapitalist era by replacing classes with vocational estates that would be self-governing *Gemein-*

schaften. Kolnai knew that the plan could not be implemented overnight, but like Polányi, he believed that society already contained elements, such as trade unions and cooperatives, that might lead to industrial self-government.

Kolnai's understanding of guild socialism was colored and modified by Distributism, the socio-economic theory championed by Chesterton and Belloc. In the latter's *The Servile State* he read that a medieval guild "was a society partly co-operative, but in the main composed of private owners of capital whose corporation was self-governing, and was designed to check competition between its members: to prevent the growth of one at the expense of the other. Above all, most jealously did the Guild safeguard the division of property, so that there should be formed within its ranks no proletariat upon the one side, and no monopolising capitalist upon the other."[151]

In the spirit of those guilds, Belloc recommended that a Distributive State replace the Capitalist State before the Collectivist/Socialist State instituted a new and more frightening form of servility. In the Distributive State, property and economic power would be widely distributed among citizens. Those who favored such a state of affairs were "Conservatives or Traditionalists. They are men who respect and would, if possible, preserve the old forms of Christian European life."[152] Kolnai agreed that the restoration of widely distributed private property was more important than mitigation of misery.[153]

Chesterton too emphasized the importance of property as "the art of the democracy. It means that every man should have something that he can shape in his own image, as he is shaped in the image of heaven. But because he is not God, but only a graven image of God, his self-expression must deal with limits; properly with limits that are strict and even small." The great capitalist, Chesterton argued in his most mischievous manner, were enemies of property because they were enemies of their own limitations. "They do not want their own land; but other people's."[154]

Kolnai recognized the dogmatic and utopian aspects of Distributism. Belloc, he could not help but notice, was very vague when it came to explaining just *how* property would be redistributed. Nevertheless, the theory reminded him of Jászi's prewar call for the partition of Hungary's great estates (*latifundia*) and the creation of a free class of small proprietary farmers. It also evidenced a respect for the Christian idea of the free spiritual person. Unlike state socialism and the *Ständestaat*, it stood out as an improvement on monopolistic capitalism. Much later in his life, Kolnai still held "that a wholesome fabric of society requires the *predominance* of the peasant and, in general, the small-owner type among its citizens."[155]

But what was to be done in an immediate and concrete way to overcome capitalism? In answer to that question, Kolnai praised Christian trade unions. In particular, he admired Leopold Kunschak, a saddler journeyman who had been instrumental in launching the Catholic trade union movement in 1892, and quickly became its most articulate spokesman. Like Kunschak, Kolnai insisted that a workers' movement founded upon Christianity was superior to its secular rivals, "for it is a better struggle that is born from love and not from hate; it is a better struggle for justice that is sustained not by blind faith in a 'law' of class struggle, but by faith in moral laws and the free will of men."[156]

In the act of common struggle, Christian workers could transform themselves from members of a class into members of an estate (*Stand*). That would not mean the proletarianization of all men, but the extension to workers of personal property. Only in that way could workers/owners create a new culture, but one still rooted in *bourgeois* values and Christian moral truths. Kolnai recognized that this conservative project faced almost insurmountable obstacles in the contemporary age. But as a devout Catholic, he took comfort from his faith. "Always," he wrote, "when one era is in decline, the Church appears to die; but the era withdraws from the world's stage and the Church reappears. 'Heaven and earth shall pass away, but my words shall not pass away.'"[157]

SIX

KARL MANNHEIM:

THE SOCIOLOGY OF KNOWLEDGE

Paul Szende

O N MAY 2, 1919, Paul Szende boarded a Danube boat headed for Vienna. He had recently celebrated his fortieth birthday, and as he took a long last look at his native land, he dwelled more on the past than on the future. As so often in his life, he was alone, not because he lacked fot friends or was unpopular with the ladies, but because he placed a premium on independence. And yet like many such men he experienced bouts of loneliness. Jászi, who knew him as well as any man, observed that Szende "was usually the last to leave a gathering, and one could see that he did not willingly return to his seclusion."[1]

This sensitive and intelligent man first gazed out at the world on February 7, 1879, from the town of Nyírbátor, located in Szabolcs county in eastern Hungary. His family was Jewish. The father, Adolf Schwarcz, had studied in Vienna and earned his living as the town physician. The mother was from a landowning family and by all accounts possessed a forceful personality. In addition to Paul (Pál), she gave birth to Emil and Mária. For the sake of the children, the Schwarczs chose to Magyarize their name to "Szende" in 1895.

At the time, Paul was enrolled at the Evangelical Gymnasium in nearby Nyíregyháza, where he displayed a particular aptitude for historical studies. His uncle, the historian Ignác Acsády, had much to do with that, but Szende seems always to have believed that Hungarian historians had too often conspired to shore up an economic, social, and political order in which the nation's landowning classes enjoyed supremacy. He resolved to do something about that, but not before he completed his studies at the University of Budapest. After taking degrees in political science (1900) and law (1902), he prepared for his bar examination, which he passed without difficulty in 1904.

For the next four years, Szende practiced law without being able to muster much enthusiasm. Thus, he was quick to accept an offer to serve as General Secretary of the National Association of Commerce (*Országos Magyar Kereskedelmi Egyesülés*, or OMKE), a newly formed organization that represented the interests of small businessmen. Subsequently named a Vice President, Szende worked for OMKE until October 31, 1918, the day of the Károlyi Revolution. Although critics wondered out loud how a man of the left could identify with such an organization, Szende was unapologetic. In his judgment, the class enemy in backward Hungary was the landed nobility; against semi-feudalism, he championed bourgeois democracy.

This sympathy for small businessmen and peasants, together with a recognition of the importance of the nationality question, militated against Szende's joining the Social Democratic Party. Instead, he gravitated toward Jászi and "bourgeois radicalism." Indeed, the friendship he forged with Jászi around 1905 remained a—perhaps the—fixed point of his life and work. Anna Lesznai spoke without exaggeration of Szende's "hero worship" of her ex-husband.[2] The warm feelings were certainly mutual, witness the moving tribute Jászi paid when Szende died of a heart attack before his time.[3] Together the two men worked on *Huszadik Század*, lectured to the Sociological Society and its Free School, and engaged in seemingly endless political controversies. And like virtually every member of their generation, they drew a common inspiration from Ady's poetry.

Szende was therefore flattered when he read, in a 1913 issue of *Világ*, Ady's "Sit in Judgment, Werbőczi!,"[4] a poetic lament for backward Hungary and an attack on landowners. The poet had inscribed the poem to him. "My dear Bandi /a familiar form of 'Endre'/," Szende wrote to his friend, "I finally found your address and now hasten to congratulate you for the wonderful poem that appeared last week in *Világ*. It only goes to show that you are not only Hungary's foremost poet, but her best politician as well."[5]

Ady had made his dedication for a good reason. The young Szende's most famous piece of writing was a historical essay on István Werbőczi (1458–1541), a statesman and jurist who had become a national saint after seeking to exclude foreigners from the Hungarian throne and promoting the interests of the gentry (lower nobility). In 1514, the year that György Dózsa led an abortive but bloody peasant uprising, Werbőczi published the *Tripartitum*, a codification of Hungarian law according to which the rights of the gentry were identical to those of the magnates (upper nobility).[6] Naturally then, the gentry revered his memory.

Just as naturally, Ady and the Hungarian left regarded Werbőczi as the symbol of the Hungary they wished to change. For them, the enigmatic, Christ-like figure of Dózsa represented not only a new and better Hungary, but the sinfulness of the gentry. For when that awe-inspiring leader was captured, he was executed in a brutal and symbolic manner. His tormentors placed him on a red-hot throne, a red-hot crown on his head and a red-hot scepter in his hand. While life was still in him, they compelled six of his lieutenants to eat his body and drink his blood.

Szende's study of Werbőczi was not an antiquarian investigation written for scholars. It constituted a challenge to the gentry's worldview and to contemporary Hungary's social, economic, and political order. In a more immediate sense, it was a response to *The Life of István Werbőczi* (1899) by Vilmos

Fraknói, an outstanding historian and Roman Catholic Bishop of Jewish origin. As Szende acknowledged, Fraknói had done his homework. But while not completely uncritical, he had painted a flattering portrait of the jurist and the gentry, which, he pointed out, had always been more purely Magyar than the class of magnates and the relatively small bourgeoisie. If the gentry had not played a leading role in modern Hungarian history, Fraknói argued, the country might be economically richer and culturally more advanced, but it would be less independent and less Magyar.[7]

In a clever opening move, Szende announced that he would base his argument solely on information that Fraknói provided. He then proceeded to cast doubt on Werbőczi's motives by showing how much he profited from his support of national leaders. Indeed, the modestly born jurist ended life as one of Hungary's greatest landowners.[8] To those who protested that, after all, it was Werbőczi's *Tripartitum* that mattered, Szende had a ready rejoinder; Werbőczi had plagiarized from the *Summa legum*, a fourteenth-century Austrian law book. Worse, when one examined the *Tripartitum*'s guiding principles, one noticed how precisely they corresponded to the class interests of the magnates and the gentry. Both were confirmed in their control of the land and their freedom from the necessity of productive work. As a consequence, Szende concluded, Hungary fell behind Western Europe in economic and political development and—contra Fraknói—lost its independence to the Turks and the Habsburgs.[9]

Such a radical rethinking of the past served the cause of progress, Szende believed, because it exposed ideologies designed to buttress existing social, economic, and political arrangements. Early on he concluded that class consciousness was every bit as vital to progress as economic reform. Indeed, in reply to a questionnaire that *Huszadik Század* circulated in 1912, Szende foreshadowed much of his later work:

> The existing economic organization and power factors are no greater obstacles to the development of a better social order than those traditions and ideologies that the schools, churches, sciences, and newspapers instill in our souls and that persuade blue- and white-collar workers, as well as the better part of the bourgeoisie, that the preservation of existing power relations is in their best interest; indeed that it is their human and patriotic obligation. Thus the common goal of the radical bourgeois and social democratic workers' movements is enlightenment, the *awakening of class consciousness*. On the other hand, those whose interests coincide with contemporary class rule attempt to obscure class consciousness.[10]

On June 6, 1914, Szende helped Jászi organize The National Citizens' Radical Party, but when the war began, he reported as an artilleryman and saw service in Galicia. At OMKE's request, he was soon released from duty and permitted to return to Budapest, where he studied the effects of war on the economy and defended the Radical Party's program. To those who confused radicals and bolsheviks he wrote that the former *favored* capitalism and private property, while opposing the unrestricted political and economic rule of finance capital and the landowning class. They did not disguise their view that state intervention would be required to carry out a much-needed land reform.[11]

A few months after Szende made that statement, the war ended and Károlyi assumed power. The new leader immediately named Szende "state secretary" in charge of the Ministry of Finance. Officially, he himself took the Finance portfolio because he thought it unwise to have more than one Jew among the new government's ministers and he had already named Zsigmond Kunfi Minister of Culture. On November 25, however, he relented and elevated Szende to ministerial rank.

The conservative historian Gusztáv Gratz subsequently described Károlyi's hard-working Finance Minister as "learned, undoubtedly serious, and familiar with economic questions."[12] And yet Szende quickly became one of the government's most controversial figures, for in an interview he granted to a Dutch newspaper, he made the mistake of saying that "we are going to carry out a transferral of wealth, the likes of which has never been seen in the history of Hungary or indeed of the world."[13] Even colleagues opposed such radical plans, but in the end it did not matter. The proposals could not be written into law before March 21, the day Kun established the Soviet Republic and Szende resigned. Lacking any sympathy for the Communists, he followed Jászi to Vienna.

Szende in Vienna

Szende maintained a lonely and spartan existence in Vienna. He lived in modest flats on Alser Strasse, behind the university, and on Neuer Markt near the Hofburg. His family forwarded small sums of money, but in the main he supported himself by commenting on current affairs for Hungarian- and German-language newspapers such as the *Bécsi Magyar Újság*, *Kassai Napló* (*Kassa Journal*), *Aradi Hírlap* (*Arad Daily*), *Erdélyi Hírlap* (*Transylvanian Daily*), *Arbeiter Zeitung* and *Leipziger Volkszeitung*. Even with such outlets as these for his work, he barely managed to make ends meet. Thus, although he was a connoisseur of fine food, he found it necessary to take virtually all of his meals at the *Gemeinschaftsküche*, a vegetarian soup-kitchen. To a friend he boasted that he had trained himself to live without money.[14]

During his first years in exile, it is true, Szende believed that he would soon be returning to Hungary. To hasten the coming of that day, he worked closely with Jászi to discredit the Horthy government and prepare for a resurrected democratic republic. For bolshevism he felt nothing but loathing. He spoke disparagingly of "the religious roots of communism, its simplicity and chiliastic character." He thundered against a doctrine that represented "a mixture of the messianism and simplicity of primitive Christianity and the intolerance and orthodoxy of Catholicism." Under the hypnotic spell of the Russian Revolution, he charged, Central European communists had ignored Marx's teachings about revolutionary preparedness and sought to impose their "mystical" vision of a new world by force. Few of them had previously established any contact with the workers' movement, and war and political collapse had bequeathed to them an obsession with power.[15]

For Szende, communism was an aberration produced by the shattering blows of war and defeat. It was not a—much less the—authentic interpretation of Marxism. That honor belonged to European social democracy. With all of its faults, it remained the greatest organized force for progress, the greatest champion of economic reform and education. For that reason, he became a charter member of the Világosság (Clarity) Group of Hungarian Social Democrats in Viennese exile.

The leader of that small but energetic Group was Szende's old friend Kunfi, who, like the Austro-Marxists, wished to stake out ground between bolshevism and the conservatism of Germany's Majority Socialists. Indeed, he joined the Austro-Marxist editorial staffs of Arbeiter-Zeitung and Der Kampf and invited members of the Világosság Group to contribute. As a consequence, Szende came into contact with such Socialist luminaries as Karl Renner, Otto Bauer, Karl Grünberg, Karl Seitz, Karl Kautsky, and Rudolf Goldscheid. "In his exile," Jászi wrote of him, "Western socialism's great organization became the home into which his idealistic and thirsty soul entered."[16]

Szende certainly admired the Austro-Marxists' achievements in Red Vienna, attributing them to their ability to judge the complicated postwar situation not "with credulous and dogmatic simplicity, but with proper sobriety." They knew, that is, that historical transformations required time, that before the bourgeois democracy projected by the French Revolution could fully be realized, France had to pass through three more revolutions—in 1830, 1848, and 1870. With that in mind, Szende urged continued patience, attention to economic processes, and ideological confrontation.

The latter was particularly germane, according to Szende, because the bourgeoisie sought to escape, or at least to delay, its destiny by propagating its Weltanschauung in schools, churches, the press, and the scholarly community.[17] As a consequence, the masses found themselves baffled and constrained by "traditional ideologies, authoritarian principles; they are pupils of confessional schools, capable only by degrees of independent thinking."[18] It was the responsibility of the Socialist movement to end the educational monopoly of the ruling classes and introduce the working class to the latest advances in modern thought, especially with respect to the social determinants of knowledge and theory.[19]

Szende practiced what he preached. In Hungary he had been one of the Free School of the Sociological Society's most popular lecturers. In Vienna, he spoke regularly, in Hungarian and German, to Socialist audiences. Moreover, beginning in 1925 he made annual trips to Paris, where he delivered lectures, in French, to the *Collège libre des sciences sociales* and organizations of the French Socialist Party. In due course he met and established working relationships with Party leaders such as Léon Blum and Jean Longuet. As a member of the League of Human Rights, he worked with the historian Alphonse Aulard, and as a welcome guest at Mme. Menard-Dorian's salon, he came to know Aristide Briand, Eduard Herriot, Emile Vandervelde—and Albert Einstein.[20]

In the French capital Szende lectured on a range of topics, including the sociology of ideas. But in the late 1920s and early 1930s, he found it ever more urgent to address the problem of fascism because he feared that the working class might be seduced by counterrevolutionary demagogues. "In resisting fascism," he wrote in 1929, "combatting its ideology is just as necessary as creating proletarian defense organizations."[21] He was especially concerned to warn against what he regarded as the pernicious influence of Henri Bergson's "mystical" philosophy. It was no accident, according to Szende, that Bergson had stimulated Georges Sorel's feverish imagination. Through Sorel, Bergson was the "spiritual grandfather" of both fascism and communism.[22]

Szende conceded that Bergson's link to bolshevism was more difficult to establish, but he insisted that Sorel had influenced Lenin and, though he never mentioned him by name, Lukács. "The category of totality—whereby the proletariat is represented as the bearer and history as the self-realization of human social consciousness (in essence the proletariat's class consciousness)—that is zealously propagated by some Communist philosophers, does not derive from Hegel, despite all the idealist jargon. Its true source is Sorel, or rather Bergson. It is not a category, but a vision of totality."[23]

In 1918–19, Szende had looked on helplessly as Hungarian Communists undermined Károlyi's democratic revolution and co-opted the Social Democratic Party. Now fascists too sought to bring social democracy to its knees. Like bolshevism, the new ideology was counterrevolutionary, a "Marxist anti-Marxism" that, more often than not, was led by men who had once been revolutionary Socialists. This conviction, that bolshevism had bred fascism, that the two ideologies were two sides of the same counterrevolutionary coin, informed all of Szende's publicistic writings of the late 1920s and early 1930s. Bolshevism, he wrote, was a "functional," while fascism was an "intentional" counterrevolution. Yet both movements hated democracy and both employed similar mass psychological methods.[24]

At the same time that he campaigned in print against fascism and communism, Szende was preparing a major study of mysticism, as a mode of thought and a corrupting influence on the psychology of the masses. Although he did not live to complete the book, he left behind an abstract, on the basis of which one can see that he planned the first section to be a relatively straightforward description of religious mysticism as a form of irrationalism that, translated into secular terms, had invaded and deformed the social and political consciousness of the masses in such a way that communism and fascism were able to achieve otherwise inexplicable victories. "Redemption through Dictatorship" was to have been one of the topics in the book's second section: a sociological critique of mysticism.[25]

Mysticism, Szende argued, was a kind of thinking and knowledge based upon "experience" (*Erlebnis*) of an altogether different sort than the practical experience (*Erfahrung*) of everyday life, which all men shared. The quintessential mystical experience was that of becoming one with the Absolute, and often with a community (*Gemeinschaft*) of believers as well. The mystic experienced his entry into the community as a return from exile, a restoration of a prior condition of unity. For him, the distinction between self and other (or others), subject and object, was thereby overcome.[26]

Such was the mystical experience from the point of view of an individual. As a mass, *social*, phenomenon, mysticism took the form, according to Szende, of "the doctrine of redemption, messianism, the doctrine of the world's end, of eschatology." Without saying so, he was taking Lukács's Marxism as his model. For political mystics, he wrote, good and evil were to a certain extent identical, different sides of the same process; they therefore had to be viewed dialectically. "Mystical thinking moves by contradictions and aims at totality." Despite, or rather because of, contradictions, the mystic entertained no doubt that he possessed total and absolute truth. Echoing the young Lukács's description of Marxism on the eve of his conversion, Szende wrote that "the *Credo quia absurdum* is for the mystic not only a precept of religious dogma, but also a spiritual pleasure."[27]

One cannot read Szende's work-in-progress on mysticism without sensing that he had formed a profoundly pessimistic view of his time. Louis Eisenmann, the distinguished French student of Central European history, remembered him as a lonely man, fighting for the distant future.[28] Indeed, Szende came increasingly to believe that the deterioration of his own health paralleled that of Europe. After the Austrian civil war, he left Vienna for Prague, where he hoped to rededicate himself to serious theoretical work. No sooner had he arrived in that beautiful city, however, than he suffered a heart attack. Seriously ill, he managed to join his mother and sister in Seini, Romania, shortly before he died on July 15, 1934.

Szende's Ideologiekritik

During his last years, Szende complained often and bitterly because he could not find time to pursue his theoretical interests. "I have a great many plans," he wrote to a friend in 1930. "I could now write ten books if I could find a publisher who would pay enough. There is, unfortunately, little prospect of that. If you should have a child, my dear Drusza, do not allow him to make his living from scholarly work. I have seen many hopeless occupations in my day, but never one like that."[29] After 1923, when he had to accept even more publicistic work to make ends meet, he exploited fugitive moments in his 10–12-hour workday to advance the systematic studies of mathematics, physics, philosophy, and psychology that he had begun with such determination during the years immediately following the war. It was then that he had managed to read widely, especially in the positivist tradition.

Already conversant with the work of Comte and Spencer, Szende devoted much of his attention to Mill's *System of Logic*, which argued that the principles of logic were generalizations of empirical data. He also acquainted himself with the ideas of Ernst Haeckel and Wilhelm Wundt, while mastering the critical positivism of Ernst Mach and Joseph Petzoldt. From there he turned to the French mathematician and philosopher Jules Henri Poincaré, who emphasized the "conventional" elements in mathematics and the physical sciences and made a great impression on Einstein, whose epoch-making work Szende wished above all else to understand. Guided by the Viennese physicist W. Misar, he immersed himself in the Special and General Theories of Relativity.[30]

It had been less than a month after Szende arrived in Vienna that photographs of a solar eclipse had validated Einstein's theories. To the young Karl Popper—a frequent caller at the Polányis' flat—that dramatic event "was a great experience . . . , and one which had a lasting influence on my intellectual development."[31] Szende could have said much the same thing, for he sensed almost immediately that the contradictory reception of the General Theory could shed light on the slow pace of the democratic revolution in Central Europe.

Just as the war, with its accompanying transvaluation of all values, had made possible the revolutions of 1917–19, so had it prepared a sympathetic reception for a revolutionary theory of the physical world. During more than four years of unprecedented destruction, men had come to trust concrete experience more than abstract principles. In *A Farewell to Arms* Frederic Henry says that "abstract words such as glory, honor, courage, or hallow were obscene beside the concrete names of villages, the numbers of roads, the names of rivers, the numbers of regiments and the dates." He, like most of those who survived, suspected all absolutes, including those of time and space. In Szende's judgment, they were right to do so, but at the same time he observed that they had not been able to incorporate either the Theory of Relativity or the everyday notion of relativity into their thought processes in an organic way. Much of the time, indeed, they fell back on old, absolutist, habits of mind, just as political communities fell back on traditional beliefs and modes of behavior.[32]

The reasons for this anomaly, according to Szende, were fundamentally cultural and hence social, since the dominant social class placed its imprint on every aspect of collective life and every area of human investigation. If, he concluded, "one analyzes all . . . cultural fields, one comes to the conclusion that their combined effect is to create a mentality which places almost insurmountable obstacles in the way of . . . the ascendancy of the relativistic conception. In almost all of these fields, the absolutist turn of mind prevails." Churches, schools, and the press conspired together to force nearly everyone, against the abundant evidence experience and common sense provided, to think in absolute moral, economic, and legal categories. That so many embraced absolutes was not a consequence of their desire to place themselves at the service of the ruling class, but of their ties to the past. The very language they spoke carried within it the absolutist prejudice. It therefore masked the truth.[33]

Even so, Szende was thrilled to be alive. No previous time in human history, he wrote, had provided a better occasion "to explore the tendencies of historical development than our period of collapse and revolution."[34] His most significant contribution to that task appeared in a 1922 number of Grünberg's *Archiv* and was entitled "Masking and Unmasking: The Struggle of Ideologies in History."[35]

"Masking and Unmasking" was a work in the Marxist tradition, but like virtually all of the Hungarian emigrés' writings, it emphasized the power of ideas, of consciousness, to summon a new social order into being. To say, Szende wrote, that a historical event or series of events is necessary is not to say that no acts of the will are required to bring them about. "Conscious collaboration in the bringing about /of historical events/ constitutes an ingredient of necessity and is calculated in as a causal factor."[36] The struggle that propelled history forward was above all a struggle for men's hearts and minds. The principal means of advancing that struggle was therefore education, the bringing of enlightenment to the masses, without whose active involvement "revolution" simply replaced one ruling elite with another.

Writing as a social theorist and philosopher of history, Szende focused his attention on "ideology," a word that can be traced back to 1796, the year that Destutt de Tracy, the reform-minded leader of the French *Idéologues*, coined it. But even before the *Idéologues* appeared on the scene, Condillac had singled out Francis Bacon's criticism of the "idols" as the starting point for a reformation of consciousness. Bacon, he knew, had distinguished four species of idols, or mental distortions, that prevented men from seeing nature as it is in itself. Condillac called these distortions "prejudices." And so did Helvétius, who developed the notion into a rudimentary sociology of knowledge. "Our ideas" he wrote in 1758, "are the necessary consequence of the societies in which we live."[37] Nevertheless, he believed, like Szende after him, that education could expose and eliminate prejudice.

In a sense Marx agreed, but as Lukács had pointed out, he always held that "education" could only be gained by active participation in the revolutionary movement. In any event, Marx, and with him Nietzsche and Freud, took additional steps along the "road to suspicion."[38] He did stop short, however, of a thoroughgoing relativism and in that respect Szende was more radical. Indeed, the Hungarian arrived at a relativism so complete that it threatened his own theoretical position.

Szende began with the unexceptional observation that the distinguishing characteristic of all known social orders was the rule of a minority over a majority. What he thought striking, however, was the fact that so many members of the majority, few of whom benefited from existing arrangements, supported their preservation. Why was that so? The answer, he suggested, was not simply that they were the victims of coercion or the threat of coercion; it was that their consciousness, the ways in which they thought, predisposed them to do so. He therefore proposed to reexamine the nature of human thought.

For Szende, "ideology" was not necessarily a pejorative term, a mere product of false consciousness. All thinking, he maintained, was ideological because ideologies were necessary *interpretations* of experience, which was given to us directly in the form of simple, undistorted sensations and observations.[39] It was in the act of interpretation that distortion and falsification crept in. To be sure, interpretations did, sometimes, promote the alteration of the existing social order. But far more often they worked to preserve that order by masking the historical, contingent, *relative* character of social structures, structures that accorded with a tiny minority's interests.

Masking ideologies imprinted an authoritarian disposition on the human mind. They did so in a myriad ways, though chiefly by insisting upon the existence of absolutes—in religion, ethics, metaphysics, politics, and society. Absolutes, being timeless, were by their very nature not subject to change and any effort to modify or replace them was therefore not only perverse, but senseless. Similarly, so-called a priori truths, those prior to experience, admitted of no change; reliance on them only reinforced the conviction that the most fundamental truths were eternally valid. By extension, men came to believe that existing social arrangements were unchangeable, not subject to correction by experience or the will of the people. "Absolutes" such as God, the State, and the Nation were arrived at by a process of abstraction that removed them so far from experience that they could more easily lay claim to general validity. Over time, they became hypostatized or reified into autonomous, supernatural essences.[40]

So historically dominant had masking ideologies been, Szende argued, that the burden of the past weighed heavily on the present. Recalling how regularly the Hungarian nobility appealed to history to justify its leading role in society, he took a dim view of "the cult of tradition."[41] "The older an understanding, an idea, is," he once complained, "the more one believes it."[42] Particularly exasperating, in his view, was the traditional, and hence conservative, influence of language. Built into the words with which we formed our thoughts were the legacies of an earlier, and more religious, time. "Language," Szende observed, "is more popish than the Pope."[43]

If language itself was in the masking ideologies' service, was not resignation and hopelessness the proper attitude? Szende professed not to think so because he had confidence in the unmasking ideologies that not only undermined the influence of their opposites, but promoted the cause of a new social order, one that served the interests of the majority. Those unmasking ideologies never lost sight of concrete experience and thus they possessed the power to drive home to human consciousness the fact that there are no absolutes. Informed by Einstein's theory, they could show that all truths and values were relative to particular historical circumstances.[44]

It was the historic responsibility of those, like Szende himself, who had been enlightened by the unmasking ideologies to teach others the ways of critical positivism. "A new education," the Hungarian wrote, "a pedagogy that systematically unmasks, must everywhere supplant the old." In addition to the teachings of Einstein and Marx, such an education would emphasize certain aspects of Nietzsche's work, such as the genetic method—according to Szende the unmasking method par excellence—employed in *The Genealogy of Morals*. It would also draw upon Freud's ideas because they revealed how the sublimation of sexual drives encouraged religiosity and hence lent support to the status quo.[45] At the same time, however, Szende cautioned Freudians that dogmatism only strengthened the absolutist tendency in human thought.

The new education and the habits of mind that it would promote would in time—and Szende emphasized that—reduce the authoritarian bent of the human intellect and thereby prepare the ground for a new social order based upon human solidarity and cooperation. Prospects were good, according to Szende, because the historical dialectic of masking and unmasking had reached a new age of unmasking. The war and postwar revolutions had provided an opportunity to win a more lasting victory for enlightenment and social change. In the past, unmasking ideologies and the revolutions they precipitated had achieved only temporary successes, in part because the human nervous system seeks ever new equilibria in the form of settled social conditions, in part because previous revolutions and social movements had themselves exhibited the same kind of ideas that the old regimes nurtured, ideas that were absolutist and a priori in character.[46]

In a telling critique of violent revolution that bore some resemblance to Edmund Burke's, Szende charged that the bourgeois and national revolutions of the modern age had relied too exclusively on metaphysical abstractions such as Freedom, Equality, and Human Rights. Even the great French Revolution exhibited that flaw. Although it began a process of unmasking, it soon passed over into a new form of authoritarianism. Robespierre's Cult of Reason was the first step on the way to the Directory's autocracy and thus to Napoleon.[47] As disillusion with the revolution set in, the old ideologies reasserted themselves. Men preferred the authority they knew to that which they did not.

The revolutions that followed in the wake of the world war presented the same spectacle. Far from relying upon self-discipline and self-sacrifice, revolutionary leaders were intoxicated by power. It was enough, in their view, to turn the ideology of power against the old ruling classes, who had lost their power and authority as a result of the military and economic collapse. That was notably true of the Russian Revolution. In the name of the proletariat—a mystical, reified essence, an abstraction—the bolsheviks established a dictatorship over the population. The entire system breathed the spirit of dogmatic absolutism.[48] Communism and reaction, revolution and counterrevolution, revealed themselves to be two sides of the same coin.

Clearly, Szende concluded, the mental process of abstraction constituted the *mechanism* by which the bias in favor of absolutes was planted deeply in human consciousness. That process had its origins in the medieval social order, which possessed a predominantly absolutist character. Those, especially churchmen, who were responsible for the cultivation of the sciences, were either members or servants of the ruling class. They therefore made it their business either to keep knowledge from the masses or, what was just as effective, to dispense it in disinfected, abstract, form.[49] Under the guise, conscious or not, of the need for exactitude, they pushed the sciences in the direction of abstractness, thereby cutting them off from their origins in experience. In that way, they lent them an increasingly absolutist, a priori, character while at the same time insulating them from criticism.

Szende's theoretical essays did not go unnoticed. In a review of them that appeared in the *Revue Internationale de Sociologie*, the French sociologist Achille Ouy argued that the burden of Szende's work was the role that ideas, even those that seemed most removed from action, played in social evolution.[50] That, certainly, was one of Szende's principal interests. Just as important, however, was his claim that the categories of human thought were socially determined. It was that argument which caught the attention of the American philosopher Arthur Child, who observed that Szende had "attempted to describe not simply the result of social determination but also the mechanism, the mental process, through which social determination is effected." By thus attempting to "analyze mind as basically a social structure and process," the Hungarian had made a major contribution, even if his work was overly schematic and sometimes naive.[51]

More recently, the Hungarian-born French scholar, Joseph Gabel, has hailed Szende as "the real pioneer of the sociology of ideologies, as distinct from (although related to) the sociology of knowledge."[52] He has, moreover, rightly called attention to the influence that Szende's writings exerted on Karl Mannheim, a countryman with whom he had little, if any, personal contact. Mannheim recognized that on Szende's showing the status of Szende's *own* theory was problematic. Was it "true?" If so, what did that mean? Were there grounds for preferring his theory of knowledge to, say, Kant's? Szende appealed, as Nietzsche did, to "life."[53] That is a pragmatic criterion; "truth" is that which best serves life. In Szende's case, of course, it was the life of the many, not the few. But what reason could the Hungarian give for making that value discrimination, when, according to him, all value judgments were relative? Was it best for a particular historical era? Then why complain about *past* arrangements? Clearly, before the sociology of knowledge could be taken seriously, it would have to solve the thorny problem of relativism.

Karl Mannheim's Quest for Synthesis and Community

Before setting out for Vienna in the autumn of 1919, Karl Mannheim did what he could to help Lukács and other communist friends escape from Hungary. Although innocent of Communist affiliation, he chose to follow them into exile because he had compromised himself in the eyes of Hungary's new authorities by accepting a university appointment during the time Kun wielded power. As far as the Horthy government was concerned, Mannheim was "a flag-bearer of the criminal regime."[54] The absurdity of that charge may be measured by the fact that, as we have seen, the Communist members of the reconstituted Sunday Circle refused to readmit him. That was a painful rejection because in the Circle Mannheim had discovered a model for a community in which intellectuals with differing points of view could achieve a synthesis.

Mannheim would always look back with gratitude on those Sunday gatherings in Balázs's apartment, and during the years he lived in Germany he devoted all of his energy to the creation of a new and larger community of intellectuals, one in which varying perspectives on life could first be understood and then made to harmonize. "I belong," he wrote to a friend, "to those intellectuals who represent a new type of human stratum. This stratum stands closer to me than those people who, on a class basis, chase a romantic dream and want to make it come true."[55]

After the war and revolutions, intellectuals were anything but of one mind and Mannheim therefore experienced exile as loneliness and isolation. The problem of alienation, which had long perplexed him, suddenly seemed very concrete. All the more so when, early in 1920, he decided to leave Vienna, where for several weeks he lived in a refugee camp, for Freiburg. He made the move at the urging of Vilmos Szilasi, and having arrived, set to work on a one-act tragedy (never published) entitled "The Lady from Biarritz" (Christmas, 1920). This was not a sudden inspiration, for nine years earlier he had spoken to Lukács about his literary ambitions. "I had tried various forms in the past, verse and *Kleine Dramen*, but now thought that the only suitable form was the tragedy, because the others were all either based on remembering or else on desiring, while tragedy, if one halted its tremendous speed with a strong hand, created a unique association between stage and audience, which were then suddenly and truthfully faced with the frightening uncertainty of the ultimate questions."[56]

In the play, Mannheim explored the problem of human understanding and the impossibility of achieving a direct, mystical, union with others. He did so by dramatizing the troubled relationship between a painter, Klaus Döring, and his wife Ruth. Although she loves him, he believes that marriage, as a cultural form, will never conquer alienation and make possible the union of two souls. Despite her impassioned pleas, he refuses to declare his love. Worse, he asks her to pack his bags in preparation for his annual journey to Biarritz, to meet the woman he truly loves. Unable to endure the pain of betrayal any longer, Ruth resolves to learn more about her rival, and then to plead with her to release Klaus. To that end she recruits a friend, Martin Eis, to follow her husband to Biarritz. She can scarcely believe it when Eis reports that the "lady" in question is a figment of her husband's imagination.

When confronted, Klaus confesses that as a young man he patronized a bordello where he encountered another way of life, one that stood outside all conventional forms. For him, the imaginary lover personified such a life. "Since this time," he declares, "I have not been free; my soul is anchored there. I flee from everything that constrains me, no longer a citizen of your world, only an unsettled stranger, always ready to move on."[57] Ruth had been his last connection with the world of forms. In future he would live wholly in a direct, unmediated world.

We know from "Soul and Culture," his Free School lecture, that Mannheim rejected Klaus Döring's brand of worldly denial. The contemporary soul might well require new cultural forms in which to find expression, but it could never achieve self-knowledge or union with another *directly*, in the manner claimed by the mystics. As early as 1912, in letters to Lukács, he had insisted that men could only overcome alienation, from themselves and others, through the media of cultural forms. In a passage that presaged his play, he summoned Dostoevski as his witness: "The error of those who retired into themselves was that they believed that the further they remove themselves from earthly things, the closer they get to heaven, but it was precisely Dostoevski who demonstrated that the more tenaciously we stick to the earth the closer we have come to the heavens."[58]

In his lecture, Mannheim enlarged on the point, arguing that mystics had been wrong to believe that they could achieve knowledge of the soul through withdrawal from life and immersion in the self. Men and women ought not to take up a position outside of events because it was only through the manifestations of their life that they could chart their soul's path. Hence, what had to be inquired into was the relation of the soul to its *Werk* (a favorite word of the mystics). A privileged modality of the soul that was prior to culture, each work necessarily became a "cultural object" as it entered the flow of time, and, for that reason, the mystics "wanted to cast off the *Werk*; they felt that it could not bring forth fulfillment, because it stands out against the soul, draws toward itself, becomes an end in itself, falsifies. Nevertheless, they later acknowledged its inevitability. Meister Eckhart, in his sermon 'Mary and Martha,' proclaimed the necessity of the *Werk*."[59]

In the sermon to which Mannheim referred, Eckhart stood the biblical account in St. Luke 10: 38–42 on its head. According to the gospel version, Jesus defended Mary, who sat at his feet, against the censure of her sister Martha, who was busy preparing the evening meal. Eckhart, however, praised Martha because she sacrificed pure, spiritual pleasure in order to draw near to God through work. "Martha, and with her all the friends of God, are careful or troubled, . . . a state in which temporal work is as good as any communing with God, for it joins us as straitly to God as the best that can happen to us barring the vision of God in his naked nature."[60]

According to Mannheim, then, it was through works (culture) that men and women confronted their own souls. But work had yet another mission: to serve as a temporary bridge between human beings, to cast light upon the shared possibilities of human existence. Inevitably, however, cultural forms began to take on lives of their own, increasingly alienated from the soul content that inspired their creation. Culture became a "Golem," more and more divorced from the soul, and when alienation became complete, there arose what Mannheim, following Lukács, called "aesthetic cultures." Because he and his friends were confronted by an aesthetic culture, Mannheim explained, they had undertaken the task of cultural criticism, the analysis of the structure of cultural forms, which, he allowed, bore some relationship, still obscure, to social forms.[61]

That task, Mannheim had long been convinced, was broadly philosophic in character. Philosophy differed from other cultural forms in that it could achieve knowledge of the soul through a "synthesis" of its manifestations in time. Hence, as the soul progressed along its path of self-manifestation, philosophy had to alter its form in order to provide an ever-more-encompassing synthesis. To that end, philosophy, as form, had to be subjected to criticism lest it ossify at one stage of the soul's journey. And just as the path of philosophy was synthesis, so the path of criticism was "analysis." Of course, Mannheim told Lukács, "the process of synthesis and analysis run parallel all the time, complementing each other in order to fulfill each other."[62]

No sooner had Mannheim arrived in Germany than he prepared a German translation of the dissertation he had written to win his doctorate in philosophy at the University of Budapest in 1918; in 1922, the prestigious *Kant-Studien* published it as "The Structural Analysis of Epistemology." The study represented Mannheim's first significant contribution to the task of cultural criticism he had outlined in "Soul and Culture." That he chose to analyze the theory of knowledge was not surprising, for the principal ambition of modern philosophy since Descartes had been to discover truth and avoid error. The time had come, Mannheim believed, to subject the epistemological center of modern philosophy to critical analysis.

As Paul Kecskemeti[63] observed, the burden of Mannheim's argument was that epistemology could not achieve its stated objectives unaided.[64] Those objectives, according to Mannheim, were to identify the ultimate presuppositions of any possible knowledge and evaluate them. The problem, as he saw it, was that epistemology itself was dependent upon those presuppositions, which could be defined in logical, psychological, or ontological terms without it being possible to identify one set as "true"; every epistemology had simply to accept the assumptions of one of these three "pure systematizations." Hence, *"instead of being a critique of value, it /epistemology/ becomes a theory concerning a value's attainability or realizability."*[65]

That was why Mannheim began by stating his main contention: "We concede primacy among logical forms to systematization. The simpler forms must, in our opinion, be understood in terms of this 'all-embracing,' 'highest' form." Epistemology could be comprehended only with reference to the systematization—logical, psychological, or ontological—of which it formed a part. Hence, philosophy had taken a wrong turn with Descartes. We ought not "to explain, in atomizing fashion as it were, 'complex structures' in terms of simple elements, but rather the opposite—the simpler in terms of the 'more complex.'"[66]

Mannheim's essay owed an enormous debt to the work of Béla Zalai, especially "The Problem of Philosophic Systematization" (1911). In that difficult piece of writing, Zalai insisted that the "truth" of a philosophic system could not be demonstrated within its own terms; "it is impossible to resolve the question of the 'truth' of Euclidean or non-Euclidean geometry within the framework of Euclidean or non-Euclidean geometry." Each system was structured by a postulate or ultimate assumption and had necessarily to perceive the "object" of its ambitions within the terms of its structure. "As regards the structure of the epistemological system itself, it will be evident that the 'object' or the 'stuff' ... is radically different from the 'object' of the metaphysical philosophic system."[67]

Thus, one could not say that one system explained the universe "better" than another; each was relative to the determinants of its own structure. Was one left then with a cosmic relativism? The answer, according to Zalai, was no, for our recognition that systems could not account for themselves forced us to seek a transcendental vantage point beyond systems and hence unrestricted by systematic limitations. To be sure, in seeking a solution to the problem of philosophic systematization beyond systems one was driven into terra incognita.

Zalai's transcendental philosophy sought a harmony of the forms of the various systems—a form of forms, or what he called the "Absolute." Of course, the Absolute could not be grasped in terms of the categories of any one system ("truth," "existence," and such) because it lay in a region beyond systems. "We cannot proceed to the Absolute; we proceed from it. It will not become our possession; it was our possession. . . . We cannot reach reality, the harmony of the forms, the idea; the philosophic act is the imitation of the attainment—the possession—just as the imitation of the figure is the artistic act."[68] Of particular importance to Mannheim's essay and his subsequent sociology of knowledge was Zalai's insistence on the necessarily partial, one might say "relational," perspectives attainable by philosophic systems and his attempt to secure a place for the Absolute beyond such limited perspectives—indeed as their source.

At the same time that Mannheim was exploring the implications of these ideas, he drew new inspiration from Martin Heidegger. While still in Hungary, he had read "Der Zeitbegriff in der Geschichtswissenschaft," a penetrating essay in which Heidegger showed how the meaning of time depended upon its function within specific modes of inquiry such as natural science and history.[69] No doubt Mannheim sensed that the argument bore a resemblance to Zalai's. On his arrival in Freiburg, he discussed the matter with Szilasi, whom he visited regularly. Szilasi had dedicated an early work to Zalai's memory and, through Husserl, had met and befriended Heidegger. If Mannheim did not meet Heidegger at his friend's home, he did attend the German's lectures for two semesters. And with good reason. Heidegger was already working out a "fundamental ontology" as the ground for any knowledge whatsoever.

During the postwar years, Heidegger reflected deeply on Europe's cultural crisis without giving in to despair. In an effort to overcome nihilistic tendencies, he was prepared to rethink the entire history of Western thought. Mannheim responded enthusiastically to that determination because he too wished to face reality and *work* for a better world. He rejected those, such as the mystics, who withdrew from life and those, such as Lukács and Balázs, who dreamed of creating a utopia in which men might meet as "naked souls," free of form. Unlike Klaus Döring, he chose to seek union with a woman within the bonds of matrimony. On March 22, 1921, shortly after he took up residence in Heidelberg, he married Júlia Láng, the erudite psychologist who had reviewed the published version of "Soul and Culture." Their marriage wrote *finis* to Mannheim's love-affair with Zalai's widow, Olga Máté.[70]

Although few in Germany had heard of him, Mannheim received a welcome in Heidelberg from Emil Lederer, the social theorist and husband of Emma Seidler, sister of Lukács's first love. The Lederers informed those whom they knew that the new arrival had been a member of Lukács's inner circle, an impressive credential in the eyes of all who remembered what an imposing presence Lukács had been during his years in the city on the Neckar. Chief

15. The young Karl Mannheim. Courtesy of the Petőfi Irodalmi Múzeum (Petőfi Museum of Literature), Budapest. Photo by Csaba Gál.

among Lukács's admirers was Marianne Weber, Max's widow, who continued her husband's practice of opening the family home to local scholars and students. Mannheim became a frequent caller, and years later Adolf Löwe remembered that he and other regular visitors sensed immediately Lukács's profound influence on the Hungarian newcomer.[71]

Although he still longed to return to Hungary, Mannheim was comfortable enough, thanks to his parents, and could not but marvel at Heidelberg's charm, climate, and vibrant intellectual life. Certainly he shared the idea held by most German thinkers he met that cultural issues were of more vital concern than scientific problems. On the other hand, he found intellectuals to be, if anything, more uncertain and confused than they were in his native land. That confusion, he wrote in the "Heidelberg Letters" he published in *Tűz*, was exacerbated by the decentralization of German intellectual life. "The general loss of direction that is characteristic of our entire age coincides with the multiplicity that originates in the German cultural decentralization, and plunges the individual into the swirling maelstrom of intellectual currents. Today, most cultivated Germans are covert sectarians, adherents of some iso- lated movement. They view the world in the spirit of some 'ism' and they attempt to find their bearings in the chaos that surrounds them on the basis of a couple of not very sharply contured principles. There is not 'one thing' either here or elsewhere in the world that everyone could hold to be true, and they therefore place their trust in the redeeming power of partial truths."[72]

Heidelberg's most famous "sectarian" was Stefan George, the esoteric poet who presided over a small but dedicated community of disciples. George's little sect held no attraction for Mannheim because its members drew in- ward, separating themselves from the world. He wished to acclimatize himself to the world and to build a new community and culture, or shared context of meaning.

As Mannheim saw it, the initial step in that project was to devise a method by which sectarians and partisans of various isms could come to understand, and thus cease to talk past, one another. Before one could arrive at the truth, Mannheim reasoned, one had first to know what those who were participating in the discussion *meant* by what they said.[73] This hermeneutical propaedeutic could not be carried out as effortlessly as many assumed. Or so Mannheim argued in "Contributions Towards a Theory of Interpreting World Views."

Leaning heavily on Wilhelm Dilthey's work, Mannheim addressed the problem of intersubjective communication, on the possibility of which hinged the likelihood of establishing genuine human community. Recalling what he had learned from Zalai, he argued that the meaning of a cultural product could not be exhausted, or even specified, unless one placed it in larger contexts of meaning which he designated "expressive" and "documentary."[74] A "work"— an act or a word—was rarely, if ever, immediately intelligible; it had to be interpreted. The task of interpretation required knowledge that was extrinsic to the cultural object itself. The more we know about the contexts of meaning into which an object fits, the less likely we are to misunderstand. That is why, for example, we are more apt to comprehend the utterance of a friend than a translation of *The Republic*.

By "expressive meaning," Mannheim meant that intended by the creator of the cultural object. To ask what Plato intended to say in *The Republic* was, he knew, not the same as to ask what readings the text permits. If we wish to argue with Plato in an effort to arrive at truth, we must first understand what he said, and that can be done only on the basis of historical investigation and biographical insight.

Even a detailed knowledge of a person's life and personality is not, however, sufficient to make the meaning of expressive acts reasonably certain—and that is the best we can ever attain. Precisely here, according to Mannheim, docu- mentary meaning entered in. It too pointed beyond the work to a larger con- text, even if the creator was not consciously aware of it. That context Mannheim called the Weltanschauung, the mediately given, atheoretical systematization which the creator took for granted. Documentary meaning was not personal, but cultural in extent.[75] It operated within what Schleiermacher and Dilthey called the "hermeneutical circle": we come to know a Weltanschauung through cultural objectifications, and we come to understand cultural objectifications through the Weltanschauung. This contradicts logic and constitutes a paradox. Yet we know that the circle yields meaning, for we understand words with reference to the sentence, while we understand the sentence by reference to the meaning of the words that comprise it.[76]

Mannheim's reflections on interpreting the meaning of cultural objects constituted a remarkably mature contribution to a scholarly debate that has continued to rage. But it was more than that, for the Hungarian wanted above all to dispel the confusion of his own time. By endeavoring to understand the Weltanschauung of an earlier age, he argued, we can come to understand our own. In attempting to understand, say, the Age of Pericles, each successive age possesses a unique, but partial, perspective. That is why there is no such thing as a "definitive" history—one that is final and complete. Yet not all histories and perspectives are equal in worth, because some ages have a closer affinity for the Periclean Age than others. And because they are closer in historical experience and spirit to the object of study, their interpretations are more insightful. They increase our understanding more than those of other, spiritually less similar, ages.[77] By the same token, when a past age lights up with special clarity, we are entitled to assume that it speaks to our own more directly than others.

When he wrote "Contributions" in 1920–21, Mannheim was only beginning to develop an interest in sociology. Prior to that time, he had identified the new "science" with the Huszadik Század circle, and with Comte and Spencer. In short, he thought of it as a pseudo-branch of the natural sciences, an offspring of positivism. In Heidelberg however, he met and came to admire Alfred Weber, who championed a "cultural sociology" that rejected positivism in the name of history and the philosophy of history. In most of the essays he wrote in the early 1920s, Mannheim cited with approval Weber's "Principles of Cultural Sociology: Social Process, the Process of Civilization, and Cultural Movement."

Like Mannheim, Weber attempted to answer troubling questions concerning the contemporary world. To that end, he distinguished between "civilization" and "culture." Both were embedded in the social process of historical entities, but they were governed by distinct laws of development. Civilization created nothing, but discovered truths of universal, and hence communicable, validity; truths of mathematics, the natural sciences, and technology. It constituted a single process in which one could trace progress.[78]

But whereas the truths of civilization were universal and communicable, those of culture were unique and incommunicable. Unlike science and mathematics, cultural values could not be separated from the historical era to which they belonged. The culture of the Greek Golden Age could not be repeated because Greek society of the fifth century B.C. could not be reconstituted. All "renaissances" were, when closely observed, new creations. There is no "progress" nor necessary process of development, only strivings to express the contents of a unique historical soul. To understand cultures, therefore, we require a historical, not a scientific, method.

Weber defined the task of cultural sociology as the exploration of the dynamic relationship between civilization and culture, and between each and the social process. While warning against any attempt to impose an evolutionary or morphological (Spenglerian) schema on *both* civilization and culture, he suggested that periods of great cultural productivity might be the result of fresh understandings of the soul, which were, in turn, results of new social experiences triggered by scientific advances.[79] He concluded by lamenting the fact that the modern soul had not yet taken appropriate cultural form.

If *that* was "sociology," Mannheim was interested. He attended Weber's seminars and organized a private one of his own, to which he gave the title "What is Sociology?" Among those who attended were members of the city's intellectual elite: the Lederers, Alfred and Marianne Weber, Heinrich Rickert, Karl Jaspers, Martin Buber, László Radványi, and Anna Seghers. In the fall of 1922, Mannheim committed his thoughts on the subject of cultural sociology to paper. Published only in 1980, they witness to Zalai's lasting influence and support A. P. Simonds's contention that Mannheim opposed any form of reductionism, any attempt to demonstrate that a simpler, meaningless, factor *caused* a certain spiritual (cultural) creation.

There was a time, Mannheim observed, when the meaning of cultural formations was functionally related to that of more comprehensive spiritual totalities, for example the political state to the system of theology. In such cases, meaning spread downward from above. In more recent times, however, influential attempts had been made to reverse that direction by reducing meaningful formations to simpler, meaningless, and seemingly unrelated elements. Vulgar Marxists were guilty of that error, and so were Freudians, who sought to explain spiritual processes that produce cultural formations by scientific methods of a purely causal character. In that way, they applied methods appropriate to civilization to culture. They confused the search for causes with the interpretation of meaning.[80]

The time had come, Mannheim insisted, to jettison such reductive enterprises and to revive that which was methodologically sound in the old metaphysics, namely the effort to elucidate meaning by referring to a larger and more comprehensive context of meaning. Precisely that was cultural sociology's aim. Cultural sociologists attempted to understand the meaning of a cultural creation by broadening the investigation to include those comprehensive totalities called Weltanschauungen—whether of a creative individual, a group, or a historical period. In that way, meaningful entities were functionally—not causally—related to other, more encompassing meaningful entities.[81]

The Weltanschauung, Mannheim urged, mediated between spiritual creations and social life. Thus, in addition to cultural formations, cultural sociologists interrogated social forms in order to discern in them the same Weltanschauung rooted in the same experiential contexts (*Erlebniszusammenhänge*).[82]

> One employs the categories of *the whole and the part* and of *correspondence* when one sees neither in the cultural formations nor in the social, but rather in the *Weltanschauung* the ultimate *self-developing* factor, and when one sees in the forms of socialization as well as in the spiritual formations only the emanation of the same substance. The correspondence and the categories of the whole and the part then signify an ultimate anchoring of the forms of socialization and of culture in the totality that exists in and through them.[83]

Mannheim concluded by cautioning that while each historical age was dominated by a particular Weltanschauung, other worldviews existed side by side with it. "Or, as one says, the people of an age do not live in the same time."[84]

Like Ernst Troeltsch, whose lectures he had attended in Berlin, Mannheim maintained that "historicism," the recognition of man's essential historicity and the affirmation of an infinite variety of truths and cultural forms immersed in the flow of time, was the dominant contemporary Weltanschauung.[85] It informed not only the cultural sciences, but everyday thinking as well. The disposition to view every aspect of life in historical terms was not wholly new, for it had roots in Romanticism and represented, like that earlier movement, a reaction against the Enlightenment. Living in a historicist age, Mannheim rejected the Enlightenment's claim to have discovered a supratemporal rationality that was universally and timelessly valid and that provided the only kind of truth, that modeled after mathematics and natural science. In Alfred Weber's terms, the Enlightenment and the bearer of its Weltanschauung, the bourgeoisie, confused civilization with culture and attempted to apply a methodology appropriate for the former to the latter as well.

Worse, the Enlightenment's insistence on a truth that could be detached from any historical setting and communicated to all men in all times and places had contributed mightily to the dissolution of *Gemeinschaft* and the creation of impersonal, generalized, *Gesellschaft*. Historicism made it possible to recognize that in addition to, and in many ways greater than, the communicable knowledge of the natural sciences, there existed a conjunctive knowledge that was perspectivistic because it was generated within a restricted community of those who shared an experiential context of meaning. It did not have as its object the universally valid facts of nature, but the unique and specific meanings of culture.[86]

There is nothing at all strange about Mannheim's argument. He was merely describing a commonplace situation, in which shared historical experiences are the prerequisites for proper understanding. As an example, he pointed out that revolutionary speeches, read long after the event, lacked the meaning and power we know they possessed for those who shared with the speakers a common experiential context.[87] One must first believe, and thus become a member of the Christian community, St. Augustine famously observed, *before* one can begin truly to understand the Faith.

We are all aware that our close friends understand us better than strangers and casual acquaintances do. But Mannheim made an even bolder claim: that we come to understand *ourselves* better when we enter into "existential relationships" with others. Each person who belongs to our community (*Gemeinschaft*) brings out a different side of us, one we may not previously have recognized. Moreover, close friends make it possible for us to see ourselves through different eyes.[88] This is not factual knowledge about our physical being, but meaningful knowledge about our souls or essential selves. It is not absolute in that it is complete and terminal, but it is a form of knowledge. Only those who take the positivist approach to truth to be the only approach will deny it. But that is what the debate is all about.

And there is, as Mannheim was keenly aware, a debate. Critics of historicism routinely charge that it is a form of relativism. That charge, Mannheim knew, had to be confronted head on, without flinching. In one sense, to be sure, he believed the criticism to be misguided because it assumed the doctrine of the supratemporality of all valid knowledge, on the basis of which it then proceeded to dismiss all competing forms of knowledge. Still, historicism did imply a relativism of sorts, one that held that nonscientific truths were available only from within history, from a unique perspective. They were therefore never more than partial. But not all perspectives were equal in worth, any more than every angle of vision afforded equal access to a visual object.

"It is a fact," Mannheim wrote, "that historicism . . . is as much the cause of our utter dissolution, our relativism, as it is the only means capable of leading us beyond this state." By pursuing analyses of a historical era's primary and secondary Weltanschauungen, we will quickly observe the limits they impose and begin to search for a synthesis of partial perspectives, a "totality" which while never final, yet establishes a new and more comprehensive center of orientation. From each new center the same objects are reorganized and thus can be seen to yield new meaning.[89]

This too is a common experience. "An event or experience can so alter our lives that what was formerly meaningful becomes meaningless and an apparently unimportant past experience may take on meaning in retrospect."[90] Meaning changes with time and perspective because it resides in a relationship that is historical. That relationship is, however, real, not imaginary and subjective, and it is made possible by an existing context. Without that context of meaning, there could be no authentic understanding, any more than someone who knows no English or history could understand an English sentence by looking up each word in a foreign-language dictionary.

Syntheses, we see, can be constructed not only from the various perspectives *within* a given historical epoch, but also from the various epochs themselves. Unlike the linear, progressive development of the natural sciences and technology, however, the evolution of culture is "dialectical," not in the logical and teleological Hegelian sense, but in that each successive structure preserves earlier structures in the form of a new system with a new center of systematization.[91] This was Mannheim's way of saying that truth in the cultural sciences does not consist of terminal answers, but of deeper understanding. Insights available to any one epoch or to perspectives within an epoch are limited and in that sense relative, but that does not mean that nothing is true or that anything may be true. Some perspectives yield clearer insights than others.

This raises another question: Who is to judge whether or not a particular perspective enlarges our understanding? Mannheim's reply was that those who were most deeply rooted in the culture, art connoisseurs for example, are best able to make those judgments. Their judgments of art cannot, in the nature of the case, be infallible, but they are authoritative, and others in the tradition-bound experiential (cultural) community recognize them to be so.[92]

From the History of Ideas to the Sociology of Knowledge

In 1925–26, Mannheim published interlocking essays in which he announced his abandonment, or rather his deeper penetration, of the interpretive project known as the history of ideas (*Ideengeschichte*): "The Problem of a Sociology of Knowledge" and "Ideological and Sociological Interpretation of Intellectual Creations." He had always rejected every effort to provide a purely immanent account of intellectual history. Understanding, he had argued, required an extrinsic interpretation, because one had to place ideas in larger contexts of meaning called Weltanschauungen. But that, he had come to think, was not the end of it, for worldviews were themselves embedded in still more fundamental contexts of meaning that were not ideational at all. Once that context had been religious Being (*Sein*), but in the modern world, it had become social Being. Thus, the contemporary hermeneutical discipline was not the history of ideas, but the "sociology of knowledge."

Mannheim arrived at that conclusion as a result of several influences. Among the most important was the "unmasking consciousness" of modern *Ideologiekritik*. Although he did not yet refer to Szende's work directly, Mannheim had learned much from his fellow exile's "Masking and Unmasking: The Struggle of Ideologies in History." The aim of unmasking, Mannheim observed, was not so much to refute ideas, as to destroy their *extra-theoretical* or practical efficacy in the class struggle.[93] Rising classes in particular considered ideas to be servants of the ruling class's "real"—social, economic, and political—interests. And not individual ideas alone, but the entire Weltanschauung which they expressed.

The adepts of *Ideologiekritik*, according to Mannheim, were on the right track, particularly when they insisted upon the experiential centrality of the social and signaled their reverence for the empirical. And yet, they were not radical enough. Having grasped the fact that their opponents' ideologies were "functions" of their social positions, they refused to say the same about their own.[94] The sociology of knowledge faced up to that necessary recognition. However, and this was Mannheim's second point, the latter's purpose was not to provide causal explanations, but interpretive understanding.

Mannheim insisted on this point because he did not want anyone to confuse the sociology of knowledge with the critique of ideology. He believed the latter to be vulnerable to the charge of having committed the genetic fallacy, while the former was not. The sociology of knowledge did not attempt to reduce a meaningful structure to some meaningless—blind, natural—cause. It placed each meaningful structure in a more comprehensive context of meaning, that of ever-changing social Being, in order to grasp the presuppositions that accompany *every* idea and theoretical construct. The sociology of knowledge was, in sum, "a specific, novel interpretation of meaning given by Being."[95]

But critics of ideology such as Szende were not the only thinkers who contributed to the emergence of the sociology of knowledge. In a pathbreaking study of 1924, Max Scheler provided the new discipline with its name. He had begun to turn away from Catholicism, but continued to insist that men could catch sight, however dimly, of timeless essences. The content and validity of their thinking was not determined by the real factors of social life, but such factors did *select* certain ideas in accord with social interests. The function of real factors, that is, was to make a selection from among the possibilities made available by mind. Timeless truth could not, therefore, be apprehended fully by any one nation, culture, or cultural era, but only by taking all historically selected perspectives together.[96]

Mannheim commended Scheler for advancing beyond the notion that one epoch or culture had a corner on truth, but he criticized him for continuing to insist upon the reality of timeless essences. In Scheler's view, according to Mannheim, certain essences proved to be accessible to one cultural group, others to another. "Synthesis" consisted of adding together the essential contents as they became visible.[97] For Mannheim, such an additive synthesis was possible only for the natural sciences. Synthesis in the cultural sciences always entailed viewing old and new elements from the standpoint of new centers of systematization. And with each new center, or "totality," every part's relationship to other parts and to the whole was altered; as a result, each assumed new meaning.

Mannheim's argument bore a striking resemblance to T. S. Eliot's in "Tradition and the Individual Talent." With respect to the appearance of a new and genuine work of art, Eliot had observed that the existing order of artistic monuments "is complete before the new work arrives; for order to persist after the supervention of novelty, the *whole* existing order must be, if ever so slightly, altered; and so the relations, proportions, values of each work of art toward the whole are readjusted; and this is conformity between the old and the new. Whoever has approved this idea of order . . . will not find it preposterous that the past should be altered by the present as much as the present is directed by the past."

"The essential point," Mannheim wrote, "is that /in the cultural sphere/, man *always thinks from new centers*, and even if he 'preserves' (in the Hegelian sense of the word) previous concepts in the new system, these concepts exhibit a *change of meaning, because of which an additive synthesis* of the concepts that had hitherto been lodged in different systems becomes impossible."[98] If that was so, cultural thinking could lead to deeper understanding, but it could never, even in principle, reach a final terminus, a total truth. It had for its objects not eternal essences, but historical configurations.

Mannheim was far less critical of Lukács, who was the greatest influence on his turn to the sociology of knowledge. Like so many other Central European intellectuals, he recognized the epoch-making significance of his former mentor's *History and Class Consciousness*, and he reflected deeply on its claims. Lukács understood not only that Weltanschauungen were closely identified with social classes, but that changes in Weltanschauungen were preceded by changes in social reality brought about by an aspiring class. Moreover, he responded sympathetically to modern historicism.[99] Indeed, in "The Changing Function of Historical Materialism," Lukács had, as we have seen, relativized historical materialism itself by insisting that changing historical reality dictated the abandonment of economic determinism and the affirmation of class-conscious acts of will.

Mannheim was especially impressed by that essay because it demonstrated that Lukács had not rejected historicism on grounds that it had once been identified with conservatism. To be sure, by the time the left had adopted it, historicism had undergone a change of function; placed within a new—sociopolitical—context of meaning, it itself assumed new meaning. Thus, according to Mannheim, "if we want to achieve something more than a history of ideas, we must include in our way of thinking this central concept of every sociology of thought and culture: the concept of *change of function*."[100]

On the basis of that insight, suggested to him by Lukács's book, Mannheim prepared the *Habilitationsschrift* that he hoped would win him the right to lecture as a *Privatdozent* in the Philosophical Faculty of Heidelberg's Ruprecht-Karls-University. Published in its entirety only in 1984, Mannheim titled his work "Old Conservatism: A Contribution to the Sociology of Knowledge."

This brilliant study, part of which Mannheim subsequently (1927) published in the *Archiv für Sozialwissenschaft und Sozialpolitik*, was much more than an academic exercise: it was above all a coming to grips with *History and Class Consciousness*, one in which Mannheim saluted Lukács's contribution and clarified his own, quite distinct, position.

A historical study, Mannheim's thesis dealt primarily with the postwar crisis. The Hungarian exile examined early nineteenth-century German conservatism because he wished to isolate the moment when historical thinking, or historicism, emerged to challenge the Enlightenment's rationalist, natural scientific thinking. Just as in "The Problem of a Sociology of Knowledge," he insisted in his methodological remarks that an examination that restricted itself to the immanent logic of ideas was not enough. In order truly to understand, one had to look beyond the ideational antithesis of nature and history to the more radical opposition between two different ways of thinking rooted in different Weltanschauungen. Having done that, Mannheim continued, one had to enter a still more encompassing context of meaning: the social world with its contests between political forces.[101] The movement of ideas, he argued, could only be grasped as part of a much more comprehensive movement of social strata pursuing political objectives.

Mannheim accepted the Marxists' contention that the French Revolution signaled the triumph of the bourgeoisie, and he relied heavily on Lukács's "Reification and the Consciousness of the Proletariat" for his analysis of bourgeois thought. In addition to being revolutionary and wed to the natural sciences, such thought, he maintained, reflected capitalist economic arrangements; bourgeois thinkers inevitably conceived of human relationships in abstract, reified, terms.[102]

The Romantics rebelled against such thinking, not simply or even primarily because of some immanent development of ideas, but because certain social strata—the peasantry, the petit-bourgeoisie, and the nobility—refused to be drawn into the bourgeois-capitalist processes of rationalization and reification. They struggled to keep concrete, historical, antirationalist thinking alive in the form of Romanticism because they wanted to defend the old prerevolutionary social, economic, and political world against the capitalist bourgeoisie's imperial encroachments. Historicism, in short, "originated everywhere as a political argument against the revolutionary break with the past."[103]

In general, Mannheim observed, men "ascribed the critique of capitalism to the proletarian-socialist movement, which emerged only later. There are many indications, however, that this critique was initiated by the rightist opposition and only from there passed over to the designs of the 'leftist opposition.' " Only later did historicism undergo a change of function. No longer did it entail experiencing the present as the latest stage of the past, but rather as the beginning of the future.[104] When it came to opposing the bourgeois capitalist world and abstract, rational thinking, Lukács's Marxism manifested the latter experience, but it nevertheless retained an affinity for Romantic conservatism. Both embraced historical thinking and both rejected the scientific worldview. Moreover, Lukács, like Marx before him, borrowed the idea of dialectical development from the conservative Hegel. Both Hegelian Marxism and conservatism were "irrational" when compared with Enlightenment thinking.

It might appear from Mannheim's analysis that he wished, however indirectly, to identify himself with Lukács's historicist version of Marxism, but such was not the case. Despite the affinities between Marxism and conservatism, Mannheim pointed out that the former had emerged during the bourgeois rationalist epoch, and thus even as it accepted certain strands of irrationalism, it remained firmly within the world of rationalism, unable to shake free of the positivist tendency in bourgeois philosophy.[105] That was clear not only when one examined the Marxism of the Second International, but also when one looked carefully at the Hegelian Marxism that Lukács espoused. Hegel's dialectical reason was not that of the positivists, but it possessed a powerful logic of its own. It did not so much destroy the Enlightenment's faith in reason, as it modified it. The trouble with Hegel, Marx, and Lukács, in Mannheim's view, was that their thinking was not sufficiently historical and irrational.

In the historical (as opposed to theoretical) section of his thesis, Mannheim characterized conservatism in early nineteenth-century Prussia as the result of a union of Romanticism (the ideational reaction to the Enlightenment) with the nobility's socio-political (estates-oriented) opposition to the French Revolution abroad and bureaucratic-absolutist rationalism at home. That conservatism was historicist through and through, but it was *articulated* less by members of the nobility than by "socially unattached intellectuals," a concept Mannheim borrowed from Alfred Weber.[106]

The Hungarian's characterization of such intellectuals was at the same time a self-characterization. So circumscribed with difficulties was their life as critics, that they, like Mannheim, sought a career in officialdom and a necessarily loose attachment to a particular social stratum. That union provided them with a standpoint from which to view history, without completely depriving them of the ability to understand other standpoints, especially if they had had any experience of exile. "Distance from one's own former existence, imposed by fate, makes one clearsighted about history and sociology."[107]

Mannheim's discussion of conservative historicism and its spokesmen reflected his preoccupation with contemporary issues and controversies. One has only to consider, for example, his portrait of Adam Müller, whom he linked explicity with Hegel, and who served unmistakably as a stand-in for Lukács. According to Mannheim, Müller countered the static natural law thinking of the Enlightenment with a thinking characterized by movement; he followed a path from antithetical thinking to dynamic thinking to dialectical thinking.[108]

Mannheim's Müller resembles Lukács too in that he emphasizes the concept of "mediation," which "already contains *a breaking-through of the contemplative habit of conduct.*"[109] He sees, that is, that the subject of knowledge stands within the flow of time and participates in the creation of the object that he simultaneously grasps. Mannheim clearly formulated the relationship between theory and practice with Lukács in mind:

> *Thought is here a function of life* and praxis, and not the reverse—as though praxis were a mere application of theory to that which is immediately given. It is not the case that the theoretical subject decides and the practical subject carries out the decision, but rather that comprehension of the concrete is the decision, mediation by the practical subject who participates in the life of what is to be comprehended. *Knowledge is action* and simultaneously knowledge that grows out of action.[110]

Müller, then, belonged to the same dynamic, dialectical tradition of thinking as his greater countryman Hegel. But in his commitment to the politics of counterrevolution he stood closer in a structural sense to Marx and Lukács, who, belonging to the progressive rather than the conservative camp, yet employed the same kind of thinking in the service of a new, revolutionary function. Their version carried more weight in the 1920s not because it was necessarily superior to Müller's, but because the social stratum that bore the latter—the nobility—could no longer hope realistically to achieve its purposes.[111] The proletariat as bearer of Hegelian Marxism was, on the other hand, very much a part of the contemporary constellation of viable social forces.

As has already been suggested, Mannheim rejected Lukács's Marxism as an exclusive position because it represented a rationality that was different, but if anything more imperious, than that of the Enlightenment. In refusing to recognize any validity for other standpoints, it revealed itself to be insufficiently radical and historical. But one could not say the same of that tradition of thought, also deriving from Müller and early nineteenth-century conservatism, that culminated in the work of Dilthey and the "school" of *Lebensphilosophie.*

Mannheim retained a good bit of sympathy for this more thoroughgoing variety of historicism, but he did not believe that it would ultimately prevail against rationalism in the world of ideas because it could not prevail in the socio-political world. Sprung from conservatism and the social bearers of conservatism, it had not attached itself to another, still viable social stratum; its champions had become politically indifferent. And because they were depoliticized, they could not find a direction for change; inwardly they had given up on the evolving, rationalized world.[112] This de facto abandonment of the world could not, as we know, satisfy Mannheim. Thus, he looked for a tertium datur, a historicist tradition that preserved the dynamic thinking of Hegelian Marxism and *Lebensphilosophie*, but offered some nonrevolutionary hope for a changed world and hence a victory over bourgeois rationalism and a way out of the intellectual crisis. He discovered it in the so-called "Historical School" of jurisprudence and its leading spokesman, Friedrich Karl von Savigny.

Mannheim's concluding chapter on the Historical School was the most important section of his thesis, for in it he used his historical research to define his own position and to explain how it differed from the positions maintained by Max Weber and Georg Lukács. As the principal member of the Historical School, Savigny *was* Mannheim. Let us see, therefore, how Mannheim described Savigny/himself. The German, he began, was a historical thinker who opposed bourgeois natural law theory and the rationalization of life that sponsored it. At the same time, he rejected any attempt to impose upon historical life a rationality of a higher—dialectical—order. For him, the task of thinking was not to *create* something new, but to *clarify* what already existed and what was beginning to emerge.[113] Interest in emerging ideas and emerging historical reality (the "political") distinguished Savigny from the politically indifferent proponents of *Lebensphilosophie*.

In order to clarify new and emerging historical reality, however, Savigny insisted that a thinker had to be existentially rooted in a specific community (*Gemeinschaft*); his thought had to be "existentially connected" ("*seinsverbundenes Denken*"). That was an insight he owed to Justus Möser, who limited the "community" to individual estates. "For Möser, every estate is a distinct sphere of life, a distinct existentially connected *Gemeinschaft*."[114] According to Savigny, on the other hand, the modern world compelled an enlargement of the community to include the people of the nation (the *Volk*) as a whole. That was Mannheim's way of saying that Lukács's class/*Gemeinschaft* was unnecessarily limited in scope.

How did this standpoint differ from Max Weber's? Mannheim, after all, accepted the German sociologist's view that rationalization, the "disenchantment of the world," was the greatest contemporary problem. To answer this question the Hungarian contrasted the work of Gustav Hugo (read: Max Weber) with that of Savigny. According to Mannheim, Hugo (1764–1844) had exercised an influence on Savigny (1779–1861), especially with respect to the importance of achieving a synthesis of socio-political and ideational opponents. A representative of the ancien régime, Hugo worked into that standpoint something of the bourgeois critique of the ancien régime. In like manner, "Max Weber, without doubt the most important representative of 'late bourgeois' thinking, assimilated into his own position the socialist critique."[115]

Despite the worth of Hugo and Weber's efforts at synthesis, however, Mannheim criticized both for giving in to a "realism of disillusionment"—and cited the reason. Living in an age when two or more social strata/Weltanschauungen of approximately equal weight confronted one another, they satisfied their desire for realism by pitting one perspective against another, and vice versa. Unhappily, that project drove them to a despairing insistence upon value freedom (*Normfreiheit*) and a cynical rejection of utopian projections, and thus of hope.[116]

Savigny/Mannheim, on the other hand, rejected resignation and disillusionment, trusting in the "silently operating powers" of the people and the positive emerging experiences of history. Savigny's admittedly cautious optimism, according to Mannheim, had much to do with the fact that he belonged to a different generation than Hugo did. That difference in generations offered him what it denied Hugo: a greater appreciation of the complete transformation of thought and experience then taking place.[117] Max Weber's resignation, Mannheim intended to say, was a result of his place in time; he was born too soon to see any possibility of a way out, a possibility of which Mannheim believed he had caught sight.

Mannheim could not bring his thesis to a conclusion without returning a final time to Lukács (Adam Müller). In his last pages he described in detail the similarities and differences between "Savigny" and "Müller." In a striking, but unacknowledged, reference to the Sunday Circle that had meant so much to him during the war, Mannheim pointed out that Müller and Savigny had both belonged to the "Christian-German Dining Society" from which "dull philistines" were forever excluded.[118] (Shades of Balázs on the Sunday Circle: "Only *serious* people who are metaphysically disposed are invited.")

Just as striking, and revelatory, were the comparative portraits that Mannheim drew of the two men. "Savigny was no politician." He was "not excessive like the ambitious Müller." His program was "a subdued evolutionary one." Summing up the differences between Müller/Lukács and Savigny/Mannheim, Mannheim wrote:

> There there is conflict, here unfolding. There extending the reach of rationalization, here far-reaching irrationalization of thinking itself. The one road—out of Müller's position—leads, as we saw, to the dialectic. Out of Savigny's 'method of clarification' came the splendidly developed method of 'clarifying *interpretation*' of cultural forms that sustains all of today's historicized cultural sciences. . . . Savigny represented a *quiet opposition* of the estate element while Müller stood for a radical and more straightforward rebellion of the spirit.[119]

In the end, Savigny chose to become a professor and thus to search for a synthesis of his estates-romantic mentality and that of the bourgeois bureaucracy. Unlike Müller, he understood that such a synthesis "paralyzed the movement toward separation of the originally distinct mentalities and turned them in a new, autonomous, and progressive direction." In his view, the mentality of state officials was reactionary only in exceptional cases; thanks to its peculiar center of gravity it was moderately progressive. If it never sought to change the entire system, it was always prepared to correct it from within.[120]

With Savigny's example in mind, Mannheim submitted his thesis to the Heidelberg Faculty of Philosophy in December 1925. Emil Lederer was the chief reader on a committee that also included Alfred Weber and Carl Brinkman. On the basis of the committee's enthusiastic endorsement, the Faculty quickly forwarded a favorable recommendation to the University Senate. When the Senate expressed some reservation because Mannheim had not secured German citizenship, the Faculty replied that his application was pending, his mother had been a "*Reichsdeutsche*," and some of his relatives had been German officials, judges, and officers. Moreover, Lederer and Weber testified to the fact that Mannheim had never been politically active and was not disposed to become so. After further deliberation, the Senate licensed him as a *Privatdozent* in May 1925; the vote was six to four.[121] Thus where Lukács had failed, Mannheim succeeded.

Lukácskritik

Those familiar with Mannheim's *Habilitationsschrift* must have been surprised when his abbreviated *Archiv* version, "Conservative Thought," appeared in 1927. Although the freshly minted *Privatdozent* alluded to the Historical School in several places, he omitted the vital section devoted entirely to it and Savigny. We do not know why he chose not to include the analysis that was most personal in character and that dwelled at length on his differences with Lukács. It is possible that he worried lest Lukács recognize himself as "Müller," and that he wished publicly to emphasize his agreements with his quondam friend. Mannheim's personal loyalty to members of the Sunday Circle was very great, and he always strove for synthesis and reconciliation rather than antithesis and alienation.

Mannheim's fidelity to Lukács was balanced, to be sure, by his determination to clarify his own position and its relationship to the Marxism of *History and Class Consciousness*. To do that, he knew, he would have to show in detail how his concept of dialectical development differed from that of Lukács. Unlike the latter, who emphasized the polarization of classes and the total victory of the proletariat and its conception of reality, Mannheim wanted to lay stress on the possibilities for a synthesis of competing social and intellectual forces. His was not a dialectic of uncompromising conflict and violently imposed pseudo-synthesis, but rather of genuine reconciliation and mutual understanding; one that proceeded on the assumption that all social groups were finite and hence limited in their understanding of the world.

Just at the time that he was preparing to provide a more satisfactory account of dialectical evolution, Mannheim read the most electrifying work of philosophy published during the Weimar years: Heidegger's *Sein und Zeit*. As we have seen, he had long admired the German thinker and he shared Szilasi's view that the new book proved that the postwar era was not sick unto death. "Our age," Szilasi had written with Heidegger in mind, "is healthy and young, far from death and full of future promise."[122] As if to second Szilasi, Mannheim drafted a special conclusion for "Conservative Thought" in which he characterized his own enterprise as a complement to Heidegger's: "It is the duty of the sociology of knowledge . . . on one side, and of the phenomenological analysis of meaning on the other, so to refine themselves that the evolution of political-historical thinking, and of historical consciousness generally, becomes a thoroughly and accurately researched problem."[123]

In the course of reading *Being and Time*, Mannheim marked a passage in which Heidegger, following Dilthey, called attention to the importance of generations:

> Destiny /*Das Geschick*/ does not compose itself out of individual fates /*aus einzelnen Schicksalen*/, any more than Being-with-one-another can be grasped as an appearing together of various subjects. Fates have already been guided in advance, in Being-with-one-another in the same world and in resolution for specific possibilities. In communication and struggle, the power of destiny first becomes free. The fateful destiny of Dasein in and with its 'generation' constitutes the full authentic historizing of Dasein.[124]

Mannheim cited this passage in "The Problem of Generations," the first of two related, and closely argued, essays in which he provided a critique of Lukács.

Mannheim had always been conscious of his own generational identity. He might, indeed, have written what Jászi did write after Ady died in 1919: "With his new cadences, symbols, and accents, /Ady/ forged a spiritual unity out of all those who /wanted a new Hungary but who/ would never have been capable of uniting on the basis of economic interest, class affinity, or political conviction."[125] Thanks to the great poet, the sociologist of knowledge was far more aware of belonging to a generation than he was to a social class. That circumstance led him to reflect that like some classes during certain eras, some "generation units" /*Generationeinheiten*/ were capable of winning a hearing for their worldview from individuals who were older and younger.[126] Mannheim was undoubtedly thinking here of the young people who attended the lectures of the Free School of the Humanistic Sciences, and older scholars such as Bernát Alexander and Géza Révész, who expressed varying degrees of sympathy for the Sunday Circle's orientation.

A "generation unit," according to Mannheim, was similar in structure to a *conscious* class. It was not simply a biological generation, any more than a class in Lukács's sense was merely an aggregate of people with a like relationship to the means of production; in both of those cases, the "location" only defined possibilities. Nor was the generation unit a "coherent generation," one whose members were born in the same historical and social area and thus participated in a common destiny. A generation unit was "a much more concrete association than that brought about by a mere coherent generation." Its members responded in distinct, often polarized and antagonistic, ways to the latter's shared life experiences.[127]

Although a unit included many individuals who had no personal contacts, it always formulated its aims within concrete groups that made possible vital interpersonal relationships. Only in a genuine community (*Lebensgemeinschaft*) did members of a generation unit give expression to the new life impulses they experienced. Not by chance, Mannheim cited as an example of what he meant the Christian-German Dining Society—the same community that he used in his *Habilitationsschrift* as a pseudonym for the Sunday Circle. From that Society, he wrote, the set of ideas comprising modern German conservatism emerged.[128]

From this it is clear that Mannheim intended to challenge Lukács's claim that class and class consciousness alone propelled history forward. "At what stage of development, and under what conditions, class consciousness arises out of a class's situation," he wrote, "can be the subject of historical and sociological research. A similar historical and sociological problem emerges when a new generation becomes conscious of its generational location and makes this knowledge the basis of its Being-united."[129]

Both a conscious class and a conscious generation unit were, according to Mannheim, restricted in their experience and hence in their thinking. But the latter had at least one advantage: it continuously encountered new lives that brought into the culture "new accesses" or insights. Those insights might unsettle accumulated cultural possessions, but they also offered new choices and revisions. They taught men to forget what was no longer useful and to long for that which had not yet been achieved. Unlike classes, which were often rigid and unwilling to compromise, "the generations are in a state of constant reciprocity."[130] Thus, they were more likely to seek and to create a new synthesis, a new center of systematization, that could assimilate emerging historical realities. It was, in sum, in the dialectic of generations (generation units), rather than of classes, that the hope of synthesis rested.

Synthesis, the creation of a more comprehensive standpoint from which to interpret evolving historical meanings, was always the result of dialectical advance. And that advance, according to Mannheim, was made possible not only by the existence of generations, but also by competition in intellectual life.[131] Mannheim identified this second factor in a splendid lecture he delivered to the Sixth Conference of German Sociologists, which met in Zürich in September 1928. Entitled "The Significance of Competition in the Intellectual Field," the lecture served to advance his career dramatically. A mere *Privatdozent* at the time, Mannheim was a last minute choice to be one of the two principal speakers, the other being the senior scholar Leopold von Wiese.

Competition, Mannheim told the members of his audience, had to be re-garded as a feature not only of economic and social life, but of intellectual life as well. Social groups sought ascendancy and power, and as an integral part of their struggle they strove to make their own interpretation of existence what Heidegger called "the public interpretation of existence." That is important because men and women were not born into, nor did they live in, a world in general, but in a world that was *already* interpreted in a certain way. Heideg-ger, Mannheim pointed out, had called the subject which provided this public interpretation "*das Man*"—the "they."[132] This "they" was not a collection of individuals, but a body of presuppositions that exercised a dictatorship over the "authentic" self. The self in an inauthentic mode of being thought and acted only in ways that "they" approved.

Mannheim accepted Heidegger's justly famous analysis, but he proposed to go beyond phenomenological description to a sociological account of how a particular public interpretation of the world achieved preeminence. As a pre-liminary step, he noted that "the interpretation of the world is for the most part a correlate of the power struggles of particular groups."[133] By way of elab-oration, he identified four types of social process, the first two of which—consensus, or the spontaneous cooperation of individuals and groups, and monopoly, the domination of one group—were able to produce a public inter-pretation of existence because they were characteristic of societies in which social relationships were static. Consensus, for example, was common in prim-itive or archaic societies, while monopoly was achieved in medieval Europe and China.

Mannheim called the third type of social process "atomized competition." This emerged in the wake of a breakdown in consensus or monopoly control; new social groups arose and sought to promote their own peculiar interpreta-tion of existence. In the West, this process was typical of the early modern era and culminated in Descartes's decision to doubt everything and bring every-thing before the bar of Reason. Before long, it was clear to all that people did not think in the same way. Someone in Manchester, for example, approached an object of thought very differently from someone who moved in German-Pietist circles. Likewise, members of French salons viewed things from a differ-ent angle than those who attended German universities.[134]

Intellectual fragmentation was the result. Yet out of the disappearance of a universally accepted interpretation of the world and the consequent experi-ence of radical polarization, there had emerged, in the contemporary period, a fourth type of social process: the concentration of competing standpoints.[135] This occurred when weak and isolated groups sought allies in their political struggle to gain preeminence and thus to change the world. As a new concen-tration grew in strength, it became more recalcitrant and extreme in its atti-tude toward its competitors. That was why the great contemporary concentrations (or polarizations)—liberalism, conservatism, and socialism—refused to seek some accommodation and interpretive synthesis.

The fact of the matter was, Mannheim went on, that no one standpoint was able to achieve monopoly power. But even though competition had produced polarization, it also worked in favor of synthesis. It was a mistake to absolut-ize class and theoretical differences as Lukács had done. Instead, one had to keep in mind that polarization was itself the result of synthesis; socialists, for example, tolerated wide differences of opinion in order to present a united front against their opponents. Mutual accommodation and borrowing was an empirically verifiable occurrence, and as such heralded future and greater syntheses.[136]

As a prime example of a successful large-scale synthesis, Mannheim cited Hegel's reconciliation of Reason and History, but he made it clear at the same time that he did not believe that the great dialectician's solution was the only one possible. There ought to be no doubt, Mannheim emphasized, "that we believe in no absolute synthesis, that is a synthesis that transcends the histori-cal process and that could, with God's eyes so to speak, directly comprehend the 'meaning of history.' We must not open ourselves to self-deception, to which Hegel completely succumbed, even if we regard synthesis as the best that thinking is capable of bringing forth from the standpoint of the socializa-tion of knowledge."[137]

What all of this meant was that Mannheim believed the contemporary crisis and polarization of intellectual competitors to be pregnant with possibil-ities. His declaration of faith deserves to be cited in full:

> In the course of modern development there arise phases, periods of time, in which the dominant generation becomes free to achieve a synthesis. Such generations initiate something new insofar as they are capable of seeing, from a synthetic point, those alternatives and tensions that their fathers still absolutized. For them, unresolved problems shift into a completely different existential location, and the old oppositions lose their sharpness. The possibility arises of finding a more encompassing perspective from which partial configurations are discerned in their one-sidedness and simultaneously overcome. (It seems to me, by the way, that precisely the sociology of knowledge provides such a broader perspective, from which purely theoretical-philosophical differences that cannot be recon-ciled immanently can be viewed in their one-sidedness and thus comprehended from a vantage point provided by synthesis.)[138]

Ferdinand Tönnies, President of the German Society for Sociology, pre-sided over the discussion that followed von Wiese and Mannheim's presenta-tions. That discussion launched "the sociology of knowledge dispute" that occupies such a prominent place in the history of Weimar culture.[139] In dis-putes of that kind Mannheim was clearly in his element, though he was disappointed that so many of the discussants chose to focus on the issue of his alleged "materialism." He was neither a materialist nor an idealist, he said; indeed, he rejected every "either/or" in the hope of "clarifying the situation, and at the same time annulling the absolutized antinomies."[140] It was with that hope in mind that he had turned to the sociology of knowledge.

Ideology and Utopia

We know that Mannheim was acutely aware that he lived in an age of crisis, one in which old certainties had disappeared and the twin specters of relativism and nihilism haunted the minds of men and women everywhere in Europe. We know too that, early on, he had overcome the temptation to withdraw from the world in order to find some private haven in the midst of the storm. Every inch the intellectual, he had no desire to enter an ivory tower from which to contemplate events disinterestedly. Indeed, he had been deeply wounded when Lukács and Balázs turned him away from the reconstituted Sunday Circle in 1921 for failing to decide in favor of a Communist movement prepared to act in order to transform the world.

In reply to his former friends' rejection, and in support of his conviction that intellectual problems could be resolved only within the wider context of a political resolution, Mannheim published, in 1929, his most celebrated work: *Ideology and Utopia*. Profoundly influenced by *History and Class Consciousness*, *Being and Time*, Szende's "Masking and Unmasking," and Gestalt psychology, the book comprised three related, but independent, essays: "Ideology and Utopia"; "Is Politics as a Science Possible?"; and "The Utopian Consciousness." The sociology of knowledge was, Mannheim told his readers, too new and undeveloped to permit a more systematic work. Taken together, however, he hoped the essays would clarify the problematic contemporary situation, not as a mere academic exercise, but as a necessary preparation for responsible political action.[141]

Mannheim wanted *Ideology and Utopia* to be read as a sociological history of the structure of modern consciousness.[142] By "sociological," he meant that he would seek to relate succeeding stages of consciousness to the political activity of social groups. By "structure" he meant that each stage of consciousness constituted a *Gestalt*, the elements of which derived their meaning from their relationship to one another and to the whole.

There had been a time, prior to the evolution of the modern world, when men had not been conscious of their capacity to make their own history. They were therefore still ruled by unconscious forces, or what appeared to be blind fate. Submission to higher powers had then seemed to be the surest path, an "ethic of fate" (*Schicksalsethik*) the appropriate guide to conduct.[143] That life of resignation began to disappear only when, in the course of socio-political rebellions against the status quo, men and women became increasingly conscious of those "ideologies" that, by failing to keep pace with changing reality, served the interests of those social groups which traditionally dominated social and political life.

More specifically, Mannheim traced the origins of modernity to the rise of the bourgeoisie and its struggle against the aristocracy. Unwilling to accept the world as an immutable given, an objective unity before which men must meekly submit, Enlightened bourgeois thinkers maintained that the unity of the world (the object) was not inherent, but was instead created by the active subject, human consciousness. That was a momentous shift because it signaled a growing awareness that men had it within their power to make history, to change what is (*Sein*) in the direction of what ought to be (*Sollen*). No longer bound by the "ethic of fate," men were free to act in accord with an "ethic of conviction" (*Gesinnungsethik*).[144]

As important as this breakthrough in the direction of reality was, however, it did not go far enough. Convinced of the universal validity of their own prescriptions for change, Enlightened thinkers never developed a historical sense and always spoke of "consciousness in general." Ironically enough, the move toward a *historicized* consciousness came about as a result of the bourgeoisie's success during the French Revolution. It was in reaction to that victory that conservative groups became aware that they too had it within their power to effect historical change. The intellectual fruit of that reaction was the historical thought of the Historical School and of Hegel. "Consciousness in general" was now replaced by a far more concrete subject: the "spirit of the Volk" (*Volksgeist*) or the higher unity of the "World Spirit" (*Weltgeist*).[145]

But although the conservatives discovered more concrete historical subjects, it remained for the proletariat to uncover an even less encompassing form of consciousness—that of classes. Marx and his followers, while affirming the validity of the proletariat's consciousness—its congruence with reality—described the consciousness of every other class as "false," a form of "ideology." What the Marxists failed to grasp, according to Mannheim, was that the concept of ideology could not long remain the privilege of one class. It was only a matter of time before political exigencies *and* logic turned the critique of ideology against Marxism itself. When that happened, "ideology" took on new meaning.[146]

Marxism's genius, Mannheim believed, was to have recognized that the "particular" concept of ideology—that which focused on specific ideas that individual members of rival classes propounded in a more or less conscious effort to mask reality—did not get at the source of things. Marxists therefore formulated a more radical, or "total," concept of ideology that had reference to the total structure of a whole class's consciousness. They were right to make this move but wrong in believing that the total concept, like the particular, described a *causal* relationship between interest and the masking of reality.

It did not. Unlike the particular concept, which referred only to the content of ideas, the total concept referred to the whole form, the very categorical apparatus, of a collective subject's mind. This form or way of thinking was not *determined* by the group's way of life because the two could not be separated, even in principle. Ways of thinking and ways of living were inextricably interrelated, two sides of the same coin; they might best be described, therefore, as corresponding to one another.[147]

The Marxists erred as well by insisting upon the "special" form of the total concept of ideology, which restricts its application to enemy classes. By failing to recognize their own standpoint as an ideology, they could not arrive at the "general," all-inclusive, form of the total concept, with the emergence of which *Ideologiekritik* metamorphosed into the sociology of knowledge.[148] Once that had occurred, "ideological consciousness" achieved a far greater congruence with historical reality.

At the same time, however, recognition of the ideological character of all thinking had generated a profound crisis of confidence. If all thinking was bound to a particular social location (*Standortsgebunden*), was not relativism the inescapable consequence? That depended, according to Mannheim, on whether or not one accepted static, scientific thinking as the paradigm for all thinking whatsoever. To do so was in his judgment to beg the question of whether or not there were other, equally valid, forms of thinking. Once one recognized, with the aid of the sociology of knowledge, that the old epistemology was itself historical in character and hence limited in extent, one was free to explore ways of thinking that sought knowledge that could not, by its very historical nature, be absolute and universal.[149]

Consciousness of the fact that nonscientific thought was ideological (in the general, total sense) did not, Mannheim insisted, lead to relativism, but to "relationism," which held that all historical (nonscientific) truths derived their validity from their reciprocal interrelationship in a given totality, or system of thought. Here Mannheim drew freely from the insights of Gestalt psychology, with which his wife had familiarized him. When, that is, he spoke of "totality," he did not mean an immediate and eternally valid vision of reality such as God might attain, but the greatest possible expansion of our necessarily limited visual horizon.[150]

Such an expansion could only be achieved by synthesizing contemporary standpoints—liberalism, conservatism, socialism-communism—all of which were aspects of competing social-political movements. The crisis in which Europe found itself was not the result of recognizing the limits of every standpoint, but of continuing to assert the absolute validity of one of them—which was the same as to seek the supremacy of one political group. Of intellectuals who made such assertions and sought such supremacy, particularly on behalf of a class to which they were not themselves born, Mannheim was especially critical. In a clear reference to Lukács, he spoke of the "casuistry" and "fanaticism" of radicalized intellectuals who were attempting to overcome the mistrust with which their new allegiance had been greeted.[151]

The true mission of intellectuals, Mannheim argued, was to be the bearers of as broad a synthesis as the historical moment would allow. They were uniquely qualified to assume that identity because they were relatively unattached socially. In the modern world, they were recruited from various social groups, and the farther they removed themselves from direct involvement in the social process of production, the more they were inclined to rely on the new unifying social bond of education. That education provided them with a broader frame of reference and hence a greater awareness of conflicting viewpoints.[152]

Still feeling the sting of Lukács and Balázs's criticism of his failure to join the Communist movement, Mannheim pointed out that many critics described the intellectuals' unattachedness in negative terms. In particular, political extremists who insisted upon definite "decisions" judged more circumspect intellectuals to be "without character." They failed to consider, Mannheim protested, "whether in the political sphere the decision in favor of dynamic mediation is not every bit as much a decision as the relentless advocacy of past principles or the one-sided emphasis on the future."[153]

By mediating between standpoints, intellectuals could extend the context in which more direct decisions might be taken. They freed themselves and others from the narrow range of choices available to party faithful. Concerned first of all to clarify the historical situation, they remained *oriented* toward action, not contemplation. But unlike the uncompromising party radicals who acted in accord with the "ethic of conviction," they adopted the "ethic of responsibility" (*Verantwortungsethik*). Such an ethic enjoined a consideration of the possible consequences of actions insofar as they could be foreseen. It held, moreover, that conviction itself should be subjected to examination.[154]

As Mannheim pointed out, Max Weber had first provided a clear description of a politics based upon the ethic of responsibility. He did not say, though he undoubtedly knew, that Weber had Lukács in mind when he described and criticized implicitly the politics based upon the ethic of conviction.[155] Weber's researches, he concluded, reflected a stage in politics and ethics at which blind fate was at least partially disappearing as a factor in the social process, and knowledge of the knowable was the duty of all acting persons. That knowledge was not a product of idle contemplation, but of a self-clarification that prepared the way for political action.[156]

Up to this point in *Ideology and Utopia*, much of what Mannheim had to say he had said, somewhat differently, in his earlier work. However, in the third essay, "The Utopian Consciousness," he broke new and important ground.

Like the ideological consciousness, he argued there, the utopian was incongruent with existing reality. But instead of being behind the advance of time, it was ahead of it. Instead of being directed toward the preservation of obsolete ways, it intended the shattering of the existing order and the creation of new ways. Instead of viewing the surrounding reality as "reality as such," it recognized it as a time-bound historical form.

Mannheim made it clear that when he spoke of "utopias" he did not mean ideas that were unrealizable in principle. Rather, he referred to those which appeared to be unrealizable in one social order, but might very well be realized in another.[157] They were best thought of, therefore, as "relative utopias." We know that there are such because some so-called utopias of the past subsequently became realities. In the main body of his essay, Mannheim traced the historical careers of four forms (Gestalten) of the modern utopian consciousness, and correlated them with social strata that attempted to transform existing reality.

The first form of the modern utopian consciousness was the chiliasm of the militant Anabaptists. This was a subject to which Mannheim had been guided by his fellow exile, László Radványi. Then a student at the University of Heidelberg, Radványi frequently visited the Mannheims, and in 1923 completed a fascinating doctoral dissertation on chiliasm in which he pointed out that the Elect purposed to destroy not the Rejected as individuals, but the principle of evil that resided in political and ecclesiastical institutions. Against such formidable forces, they could proceed only in their collective might. That was why "chiliastic action was always a *social* action; the chiliastic movement is always a *social* movement."[158]

Taking his cue from Radványi's study, Mannheim argued that the origin of modern utopianism could be traced to the moment when chiliasm united with the active wills of oppressed social strata.[159] At that early and primitive stage the utopian consciousness was ahistorical in character; for it, there was no past and no future, but only an "absolute present." The same, however, could not be said of the succeeding form of the utopian consciousness, the liberal-humanitarian idea. Though it distanced itself from chiliasm, that "utopia" also emerged in a struggle, this time the bourgeoisie's, against the existing order.

Over against "bad" reality, the bourgeoisie set a "correct," "regulative" idea that was to be realized in this world, albeit slowly and in the distant future. Unlike the chiliastic utopia, that of liberal-humanitarianism was bound up, however incompletely, with historical becoming. "This greater proximity to the historical," Mannheim observed, "reveals that /here/ the *historical conception of time*—the certain characteristic of a structure of consciousness—is more definite than in the chiliastic consciousness. The chiliastic consciousness had, as we saw, no organ for the process of becoming; it knew only the abrupt moment, the meaning-filled now."[160]

Like the chiliasts, however, the liberals emphasized the efficacy of free will and hence the essentially indeterminate character of human action. The third, conservative, form of the utopian consciousness, on the other hand, emphasized the determinate character of human action. Mannheim recognized that members of conservative social groups did not, originally, have a utopia. Only when confronted with opposition did their own dominant role in the existing order become problematic, leading in due course to self-defense and the creation of a counter utopia.[161]

Quite understandably, given their long-established loyalty to the existing order, they conceived of utopia as an idea concretely embedded in contemporary reality. "Reality /Sein/, the 'here and now,' is no longer experienced as 'wretched reality,' but as the bearer of the plentitude of meaning." Man, on such a view, was not completely free at any moment to remake the world at the command of some ought (Sollen); rather, the structure (Sein) of the existing order unfolded like a flower in accord with some inner imperative or logic determined by the past. "If for liberals the future was everything and the past nothing, for conservatives the most important confirmation of the experience of determinateness was to be found in the disclosure of the meaning of the past, in the discovery of time as the creator of values."[162]

Thanks to the conservative version of utopia, modern consciousness had become *historical*. It was this, above all, that the fourth form of utopian consciousness, that of the Socialists and Communists, borrowed from the conservative form. Socialists embraced determinateness and the embedding of utopia in reality, but unlike the conservatives, who oriented themselves toward the past and identified utopia with the present stage of reality, they joined an orientation toward the past with one toward the future, synthesizing conservatism and liberalism. "Not only the past, but also the future is virtually present."[163] This idea, that the present could only be understood fully in the light of its concrete fulfillment in a future that was in the process of becoming, was, as Mannheim recognized, extraordinary and distinctive.[164]

In conclusion, Mannheim reemphasized the fact that each successive form of utopia moved closer to the historical-social process, and hence away from chiliasm. By involving themselves more and more in reality, utopias, even for all practical purposes the Socialist-Communist variety, destroyed themselves. But, Mannheim cautioned, a world without a utopian consciousness that pointed out a *direction* for historical change actively chosen, corresponded, in the world of art, to the Neue Sachlichkeit, which was devoid of anything but brute, hopeless reality. "The complete destruction of reality-transcending elements in our world will lead to a Sachlichkeit /objectivity/, in the face of which human will will run aground."[165]

This, then, was Mannheim's political credo. He defended what might best be described as a program of conservative reform, conscious of the limiting character of the past and the dangers of an ethic of conviction, but open to change guided by human will. It was in most ways a restatement of Jászi's views. It was clearly a repudiation of Lukács's politics. Mannheim looked toward the future not as a preconceived *actuality*, but as a meaningful *possibility*. "For the only form," he concluded, "in which the future presents itself, is that of possibility."[166]

The Mannheim Debate

Like the Lukács debate that preceded it, the Mannheim debate was a major event in the history of modern social thought. Of the some thirty participants in the controversy, I propose to consider only those who focused most perceptively, or revealingly, on *Ideology and Utopia*'s relationship to philosophy (especially Heidegger's) and to Marxism.

In October 1929, the *Neue Schweizer Rundschau* published a review of Mannheim's book by Ernst Robert Curtius, the distinguished, conservatively inclined, literary historian. Curtius accused Mannheim of "sociologism," the attempt to place sociology on the throne that belonged by right to philosophy. By doing so, the Hungarian had undermined confidence in an autonomous, self-validating, realm of ideas, values, and meanings. "He does not recognize an autonomy of mind /Geist/. Thinking is 'never an end in itself.'" Such a view, Curtius maintained, was nothing more than a variant form of that European nihilism that Nietzsche had so presciently described.[167]

In the November issue of the same periodical, Mannheim denied that the "dynamic relationism" for which he stood had anything to do with nihilism. The fact that he believed that the existing crisis of existence and thought could be resolved was enough to demonstrate that he had not succumbed to despair. He had called attention to the modern crisis in order to comprehend and overcome it. He had not sought to replace philosophy with sociology. In fact, in the effort to widen the contemporary view of the world, he had found it necessary to go beyond the older conception of sociology as a specialized discipline by reaching out in the seemingly rival directions of political action and philosophy. In the former case he acknowledged his debt to Marxism and its instinct for acting in the world, but he chose to dwell at greater length on the latter case, and on his indebtedness to *Lebensphilosophie* and the philosophy of consciousness.[168]

Yes, he conceded, he did oppose the absolutizing of particular points of view, but he was not only not against, but expressly *for* a properly formulated metaphysics/ontology, one that would analyze historical being as the most fundamental and encompassing context for action and thought; in fact, he wrote, "I even teach its absolute necessity for an existentially related kind of empiricism." At the same time, the sociology of knowledge's relationizing accomplished for philosophical ontology the revision of those particulars of being (*Sein*) that had formerly posed as absolutes. "In this connection, the struggle for an ontology, such as Heidegger advocates, is actually one of the most decisive achievements of contemporary philosophy."[169]

Despite Mannheim's sincere words of praise for Heidegger, however, Hannah Arendt argued that the sociologist and the philosopher were engaged in distinct, and ultimately irreconcilable, enterprises. Arendt was Heidegger's student and, as we now know, his lover. In a dense but brilliant review for *Die Gesellschaft*, she maintained that "in philosophical terms, the problem that lies at the heart of Mannheim's sociology is the questionable nature of the relationship of the ontic to the ontological."[170] Whereas philosophy, by which she meant Heidegger's thinking, inquired after the Being (or the "to be") of beings (*Sein des Seienden*), sociology inquired after beings themselves.

In order to understand Arendt's point, one must remember that Heidegger maintained an important distinction between ontic and ontological inquiries. The former he associated with substance metaphysics; they were investigations concerning the nature of things, including human beings insofar as they too were objects in the world. This was, according to Heidegger, a perfectly legitimate enterprise, but it was not *fundamental* because it necessarily presupposed an ontological understanding of the meaning of human existence, which was at the same time an understanding of what it means to be at all. *Being and Time* is devoted, in its entirety, to spelling out why, and analyzing how, ways of Being (existentials) make possible every kind of inquiry.

In this, existentials bear a structural resemblance to Kant's categories. Kant, it will be recalled, argued that cause and effect were a priori categories of the mind that made experience possible. Similarly, when Heidegger identified Being-in-the-World as the most general of existentials, he did not refer to the world as a specific historical entity (*Seiende*). "Ontologically," he wrote, "'world' is not a way of characterizing those entities which Dasein essentially is *not*; it is rather a characteristic of Dasein itself."[171] Similarly, and in a brilliant challenge to the ontic thinking that he believed led to nihilism, Heidegger showed how "time" was possible because of Dasein's temporality, rather than vice versa.[172]

Like Mannheim, Heidegger was a historical thinker indebted to Dilthey's pioneering work. But he was not concerned with particular moments in time, or with the truth of a particular age and socio-political system. He attempted to provide nothing less than a universally valid description of the structure of Dasein as the fundamental ground for considerations of any kind whatever. According to Arendt, however, "the sociologist does not inquire after 'Being-in-the-World' /*In-der-Welt-sein*/ as Dasein's formal structure in general, but after the momentary and historically specific world in which man momentarily lives. This delineation of sociology appears to be harmless, since the discipline is only laying out the limits of its competence. It first poses a threat to philosophy when it asserts that the world cannot in principle be uncovered as a formal structure of human existence /*Sein*/, but only as a momentary substantive, and specific world of a specific life. In that way the possibility of an understanding of Being as *ontology* is denied. . . . In every attempt to render an account of our own existence, we are referred back to the ever-changing ontic element, which stands as true *reality* over against the 'theories' of philosophers."[173]

Arendt was correct in her analysis, for although Mannheim thought he was working out a social ontology of sorts, he did focus his attention on the ontical reality of a historical world, not the ontological structure of human existence. Reality, for him, was in a constant state of flux, an eternal becoming. For Heidegger, on the other hand, the existential-ontological structure of Dasein lay a priori and was valid for all men in all historical times and places. Specific historical worlds did not concern him, since they were all made possible—that is, *meaningful*—by the a priori structure of Dasein's existence.

Philosophically difficult distinctions such as these did not discomfit Paul Tillich, the religious Socialist who was also profoundly impressed by Heidegger's work, if not by his personality. In the review of *Ideology and Utopia* that he wrote for *Die Gesellschaft*, he charged Mannheim, quite without justification, with having ascribed to the intelligentsia an *"absolute standpoint."* Socialism, he insisted, rightly reserved the privileged contemporary standpoint for the proletariat. More perceptively, he noticed that Mannheim's discussion of ideology was more negative in the essay on utopia than it was in the introductory essay, and he questioned the notion of a "conservative utopia."[174]

Tillich's piece was relatively straightforward in comparison with that which Herbert Marcuse published in the same place. Like Arendt, Marcuse had been one of Heidegger's protégés, but he was also a Marxist appalled not only by Soviet Marxism-Leninism, but also by revisionism and Neo-Kantian Marxism. Not yet associated with the Frankfurt Institut für Sozialforschung, he had been much taken with the work of Lukács and Korsch. His interest in *Ideology and Utopia* was thus primarily directed toward its relevance to Hegelian Marxism. That relevance, he believed, was very great because of Mannheim's recognition of "the universal historicity of human Dasein."[175]

Indeed, Marcuse made it clear throughout his essay that he respected Mannheim. Nevertheless, he was eager to engage the Hungarian in debate concerning one fundamental problem: "the truth of historical being */Sein/.*" What disturbed him most was what he took to be Mannheim's suggestion that, at any moment, the existing historical order of life presented an exhaustive inventory of real possibilities with respect to value and truth. On the contrary, Marcuse wrote, "the historical stage of being is not a final one; in its very historicity it points beyond itself." For to be historical *meant* to be in perpetual flux.[176]

Mannheim, of course, never disputed the inevitability of change, and he had emphasized the importance of relative utopias in mapping out new directions. Nevertheless, he regarded such utopias as possibilities that might become realities if men and women recognized limits and moved ahead in a responsible manner, one step at a time. Such a reformist view could never satisfy Marcuse, who did not see history and truth as things men made by acts of will without a clear blueprint for the distant future, without, that is, a final destination. Like Lukács and Révai, he thought he knew where history was headed and where future truth lay. "It is not simply the value-neutral necessity of historical development that lends 'truth' to the revolutionary deed of the proletariat, which completes the overthrow of capitalist society and begins the building of socialist society. Rather, it is the evident superiority of the socialist 'order of life' vis-à-vis the capitalist one."[177]

"Evident," according to Marcuse, because socialism corresponded to certain "fundamental structures" (Grundstrukturen) that underlay all historical realizations. Marxism revealed to Marcuse the character of those fundamental structures, but Heidegger provided him with the notion of universally experienced ways to be. This is clear from the example he gave. "The mode of the realization of human living together [Miteinanderleben) in capitalist society, for example, is a quite specific realization of the fundamental structure of human living together in general—not of any formal and abstract, but of a highly concrete, fundamental structure."[178] An order of life was "true," therefore, when it uncovered such fundamental structures, and "false" when it covered them up.

Despite Marcuse's criticism of Mannheim, however, his overall attitude was one of sympathy and appreciation. For Max Horkheimer, the new director of the Institut für Sozialforschung, such an attitude on the part of a Marxist was ill-considered. In a review essay that he wrote for the Grünberg Archiv, Horkheimer did his utmost to prevent other Marxists from making the same mistake. He began with a competent summary of Mannheim's views and then turned to his principal charge, which was precisely the opposite of that leveled by Curtius. "In the context of the sociology of knowledge," he wrote, "the modern concept of ideology is placed in the service of a task that runs counter to the theory in which it originated. Marx wanted to transform philosophy into positive science and praxis; the ultimate intention of the sociology of knowledge is a philosophical one. It is troubled by the problem of absolute truth, its form and its content; in that problem's clarification it sees its mission."[179]

More specifically, Horkheimer took vigorous exception to Mannheim's expansion of the particular and special concept of ideology into one that was total and general. By doing so, he argued, the Hungarian had removed from Marx's concept of ideology the last vestiges of its accusatory meaning and completed its naturalization by speculative philosophy (Geistesphilosophie). Instead of being a critique of existing social and political arrangements, it had become a problem related to eternal truth.[180] It was no longer, in sum, a weapon in the struggle for a new world, an unmasker of interests and of the causal determination of ideas.

Mannheim did not reply to Horkheimer or to any of his other critics, with the already noted exception of Curtius. He must have been struck, however, by the feeble prospects for intellectual synthesis and socio-political community. Even those to whom he had once, in Budapest, felt close, had deserted him. Mercifully, from Mannheim's point of view, Lukács remained publicly silent about *Ideology and Utopia*, in large measure because he had fallen into disgrace, a result of the Blum Theses debacle and of Moscow's rejection of *History and Class Consciousness*. But in his place Béla Fogarasi launched an all-out attack in the tightly controlled Communist review *Unter dem Banner des Marxismus*.

Mannheim was quite mistaken, Fogarasi sneered, to think that he could overthrow Marx's theory of ideology by turning it against Marxism itself. The idea of turning a theory against itself was an old logical ploy that Mannheim had learned from his "masters," Lukács and Zalai, and that he had first employed in his critique of epistemology. Such a philosophical game would not work against Marxism, because in historical reality praxis, not formal logical categories, held sway. And praxis demonstrated that Marxism was not simply another ideology, but "the objective knowledge of social reality." By the same token, the bourgeoisie's Weltanschauung *was* ideological, not because it was determined by a class standpoint, but because it derived from the *specific*, capitalist, class standpoint.[181]

This was more of a pronouncement than an argument, but Fogarasi had long since placed party fidelity before philosophy—and before old friendships. He tarred the fallen Zalai and the disgraced Lukács with the same brush that he used on Mannheim. He heaped scorn on the latter for his "eclecticism," his longing for synthesis, and his optimistic views concerning the intelligentsia. The sociological intelligentsia, whose ideologue Mannheim was said to be, was composed of those who either belonged to the bourgeoisie from the beginning or had been bought off. In the latter case, they were indistinguishable from social democratic intellectuals.[182]

Fogarasi insisted upon this latter identity because he wished to accuse Mannheim of what, for the German Communist Party in 1930, was the sin of sins: social fascism. As a former friend, Mannheim must have been profoundly saddened as he read Fogarasi's lamentable conclusion: "So it is not surprising that the social fascists prepared an enthusiastic reception for Mannheim's work. Hilferding's *Die Gesellschaft* publishes one essay after another on the 'sociology of knowledge,' and Prussia's new social democratic Minister of Education hastened to appoint the author Professor at Frankfurt University."[183]

Frankfurt

On the strength of *Ideology and Utopia* and a considerable reputation as a teacher, Frankfurt's Goethe University did invite Mannheim to succeed the retiring Franz Oppenheimer as Professor of Sociology. The appointment, which Lederer and Hans Kelsen had turned down, took effect in 1930, the year that the depression hit Germany. In February, Mannheim, still settling his affairs in Heidelberg, took time to write Balázs in order to thank him for his congratulatory note and a copy of *The Spirit of Film*.[184] In a reflective mood, he registered his regret that, after having received so much from life, he continued to miss the "old-style friendships." As the years passed, he had discovered that "the soul is scarcely capable any longer of assimilating the other to itself with the same openness." He expressed his wish that they might spend an evening together, recalling the past and the difficult struggles they had known in exile. For although, as *Ideology and Utopia* made clear, he had revised many of his former ideas, "the core of the 'Sunday Circle'" was still very much alive in him. Perhaps after all, Mannheim concluded, differences of opinion were honest expressions of changing experiences and a changing subject. What he could never agree to, however, was the sort of "one-sided" view of the world to which Balázs and Lukács were committed.

It was, then, a rather melancholy Mannheim who took up residence in Frankfurt later that year. Fortunately, the University allowed him to bring young Norbert Elias as his assistant and assigned him an office proximate to that of Adolph Löwe. Both were on the first floor of the building that housed the Institut für Sozialforschung.[185] Mannheim found it difficult to be anything more than correct in his dealings with Horkheimer, but both men attended meetings of a discussion group known as the *Kränzchen* ("small gathering") that included among its members Löwe, Leo Löwenthal, Kurt Riezler, Friedrich Pollack, Karl Mennicke, and Paul Tillich. Mannheim also participated in a group interested in dialectical theology and Christian socialism; members included Horkheimer, Theodor Adorno (who was passed over for the sociology professorship), Riezler, Emil Brunner, and Martin Dibelius.[186]

Mannheim's primary academic interest at Frankfurt was a postgraduate, interdisciplinary seminar on early German liberalism, a topic that ran parallel to his previous work on conservatism. At the same time, he prepared the entry on "Sociology of Knowledge" for Alfred Vierkandt's *Hand Dictionary of Sociology* (1931). That article was a briefer and more schematic version of *Ideology and Utopia*, although it contained some fresh ideas and emphases. For example, Mannheim's reply to the charge that the sociology of knowledge was a form of determinism depended upon a verbal distinction he had not made in his book. There he had used the terms *Seinsverbundenheit* ("relatedness to being") and *Seinsgebundenheit* ("subjection to being") more or less interchangeably. In the article, he maintained that the discovery of the *Seinsverbundenheit* of all views constituted a first step toward the overcoming of their *Seinsgebundenheit*.[187] In other words, consciousness of limits conduced to a greater freedom from determination.

As far as the complicated issue of ontology was concerned, Mannheim protested that he had not the space to discuss the issue at sufficient length. Nevertheless, he was obviously irritated by Hannah Arendt's Heideggerian critique of *Ideology and Utopia*. However justified, he wrote, the attempt to work out a fundamental ontology was, to do so without benefit of the sociology of knowledge invited danger; one might mistake for a truly *fundamental* ontology one that was merely accidental and historical.[188]

It was a point to which he returned in a lecture delivered to German university teachers of sociology on February 28, 1932. "When one understands aright the significance the sociology of knowledge has for philosophy," he observed, "one prepares the way for a cooperation between ontology and sociology." Mannheim conceded that primacy belonged to ontology, but he warned again of the danger of hypostatizing a particular, historical ontology and insisted that the sociology of knowledge could help prevent such an eventuality by providing the indispensable critique.[189]

Despite his continued championship of the sociology of knowledge, however, Mannheim displayed a new awareness of the method's potential for mischief. Having emphasized the importance of collective will in the process of knowing, he trembled at the thought that his words might help pave the way for a triumph of the will. Two months before Mannheim spoke, unemployment in Germany had passed the five-million mark and Hitler's stock continued to rise. In two weeks a presidential election would be held, and no one could be certain that the aged Hindenburg would turn back the Nazi challenge. If, Mannheim told his audience, one were to conclude that "a true will lays the foundation for true knowledge," one might well open the door to anyone who presented himself as the personification of that "true will." Such an appropriation of the insight into thought's relatedness to being would be intolerable; that insight's proper use was in aiding the process of self-criticism and overcoming subjection to being, *not* in legitimizing some partisan party.[190]

Just as the sociology of knowledge was subject to improper use, so, Mannheim reflected, was political democracy. Contemporary events had revealed, he said, that modern dictatorships were themselves democratic because they too had to be supported by the masses. It was imperative, therefore, that democratic states educate and enlighten their citizens. With people who thought in a rational manner, Mannheim elaborated, one could reckon. When they had conflicts of interest, they could work out some sort of compromise. But "with masses and hordes who are ruled only by moods and 'myths,' compromises can be arrived at only as blind natural events, only—as with certain barbaric primitives—by exterminating the opposing parties."[191] He did not then know just how tragically right he was.

Mannheim's recognition of the Nazi threat did nothing to increase his interest in communist politics, though he continued to respect Lukács's powerful intellect. This was evident when, on January 26 and 27, 1933, less than a week before Hindenburg appointed Hitler Chancellor, his former mentor arrived in Frankfurt to deliver a lecture on the young Hegel to the local Kant Society. Mannheim attended the lecture, and a more informal talk on dialectical materialism as well. According to one contemporary, he sided with Lukács during the ensuing discussions; on a personal level, however, the two men displayed a decided coolness toward each other.[192]

On the very day that Lukács arrived in the city on the Main, Mannheim had written a cordial letter to Jászi, to whose political views he was drawn ever more consciously. In reply to Jászi's request for advice concerning his son, who planned to attend a German university, Mannheim recommended Frankfurt because "the atmosphere is much freer than anywhere else." He then closed with a salute: "I continue to regard you with the same esteem as of old. The example that you gave to our generation exerts an influence even now."[193] In the end, as three of the best informed students of his work have argued, "Mannheim's model in political thinking was Jászi."[194]

Three months after Hitler assumed power, Mannheim wrote again to Jászi, this time about Germany's tragedy—and his own. As a recently naturalized citizen and a Jew, he had been "suspended" from his position. "This is the second time," he sighed, "that I have experienced something like this, but I always have the strength to begin anew, unbroken."[195] He never received Jászi's reply, perhaps because he hurriedly left Germany for Holland, where he and Júlia stayed with their old friend and teacher Géza Révész, then a professor of psychology in Amsterdam. After a brief sojourn there, the Mannheims moved on to England, their final destination.

CONCLUSION

COMMUNITY AND CONSCIOUSNESS

PERHAPS the dispersed members of the /cultural/ community, having again gone their separate ways after existential contact, live to the end different tendencies from among the possibilities and seeds they appropriated. They bear them, individually, to distinctive conclusions along the lines of their particular intentions, but they nevertheless continue to form a unity at this stage, because they have developed the *same*, if also different, seeds."[1] Mannheim committed these words to paper in 1924, with his generation of Hungarian exiles in mind. His preoccupation with syntheses enabled him to see that despite their differences, the Communists, avant-gardists, and liberals were united in a common quest for community.

Even before they emigrated they had been particularly alive to the fragmentation that characterizes modern and, still more, modernizing societies. As we have seen, Hungarian intellectuals of both sexes had individual reasons for feeling isolated, but they struggled to overcome a collective estrangement as well. With the exceptions of Kassák, Kállai, and perhaps Moholy, all of the major figures in this study were assimilated Jews.[2] As such, "they were almost completely alienated from their Jewish past; and as Hungarian nationals they were increasingly shut out of an inward-looking and increasingly anti-Semitic national community."[3]

Understandably, then, these men and women sought a place of refuge in one or another of the circles gathered around Lukács, Kassák, and Jászi. Together they challenged the liberalism of their fathers, the liberalism that had disappointed them. When, after the war, the democratic and soviet republics collapsed and a counterrevolutionary government openly described itself as "Christian" and "National"—as opposed to "alien" (Jewish)—they chose exile, an experience which added a new dimension to their felt marginality. Cast out of their homeland and cut off from their Budapest circle, or "life-community" (Mannheim), they attached themselves to larger families: international communism, the international avant-garde, the Bauhaus, the Austrian Social Democratic Party, the Roman Catholic Church, the free-floating intelligentsia. From within these redoubts they summoned others to join in the creation of a wider world of shared values and goals, one from which fragmentation, alienation, and loneliness would forever be banished. Among themselves, they argued vociferously concerning the nature of the future community and the fate of the individual. Would persons be preserved and realized as the liberals desired, preserved but collectivized as the avant-gardists believed, or merged in undifferentiated union as the Communists hoped?

In any case, the failure of the postwar revolutions and the constraints of exile taught the Hungarians a lesson they never forgot: *Gemeinschaft* was neither inevitable nor imminent. Their dreams of instant regeneration shattered and their political prospects bleak, they concluded that more was required than political, social, and economic change. Revolution and fundamental reform alike demanded greater preparation and a more profound reconstruction. Nothing less than the transformation of human consciousness by means of education—variously understood—would do.

Thus, they arrived at a position remarkably similar to that of the Italian Marxist Antonio Gramsci, who produced an impressive body of work while living out his life in Mussolini's prisons between 1926 and 1937. Gramsci projected a "long historical period" before the final victory of socialism. Intellectuals, he concluded, had important work to do, for the workers could not win political power before they achieved cultural "hegemony," or control of society's intellectual life. Right thinking would eventually produce men and women who possessed the moral will to build a new world on unshakable foundations. If, like Gramsci, the Hungarian emigrés have gained a hearing, it is not only because this has been the century of the exile, but because even those with very different commitments recognize that the future of Western civilization will be decided only after a protracted *Kulturkampf*.

NOTES

INTRODUCTION

1. Gábor Vermes, "Leap into the Dark: The Issue of Suffrage in Hungary during World War I," in Robert A. Kann et al. (eds.), *The Habsburg Empire in World War I* (Boulder: East European Quarterly, 1977), p. 31.

2. István Tisza, "Nemzet és társadalom," *Magyar Figyelő*, 1, 22 (1911), p. 291.

3. See Norman Stone, "Hungary and the Crisis of July 1914," *Journal of Contemporary History*, 1, 3 (1966).

4. Ferenc Herczeg, "A szent háboru," *Magyar Figyelő*, 4, 16 (1914), p. 241.

5. József Galántai, "Magyarország az első világháborúban," in Péter Hanák (ed.), *Magyarország története, 1890–1918*, 2 (Budapest: Akadémiai Kiadó, 1978), p. 1099; Gusztáv Gratz, *A dualizmus kora: Magyarország története, 1867–1918*, 2 (Budapest: Magyar Szemle Társaság, 1934), pp. 312–13.

6. On this whole question see the outstanding work of Roland N. Stromberg, *Redemption by War: The Intellectuals and 1914* (Lawrence: The Regents Press of Kansas, 1982).

7. Georg Lukács, "Die deutschen Intellektuellen und der Krieg," *Text und Kritik*, 39/40 (1973), pp. 65–69.

8. Marianne Weber, *Max Weber: A Biography*, trans. Harry Zohn (New York: John Wiley, 1975), pp. 518–19.

9. Georg Lukács, *Die Theorie des Romans: Ein geschichtsphilosophischer Versuch über die Formen der grossen Epik* (Neuwied: Hermann Luchterhand Verlag, 1971), p. 5.

10. See Eva S. Balogh, "The Turning of the World: Hungarian Progressive Writers on the War," in Kann et al., *The Habsburg Empire in World War I*, pp. 185–201.

11. See Oszkár Jászi, "Háború és kultura," *Huszadik Század*, 15 (1914), pp. 249–63, and Erzsébet Vezér, "Ady és a radikálisok," *Irodalomtörténet*, 9, 4 (1977), pp. 848, 850.

12. Béla Balázs, "Paris-e vagy Weimar?" *Nyugat*, 7 (1914), pp. 200–203.

13. Béla Balázs, Diaries, MTAK:K, MS 5023/19, pp. 6–7. April 9, 1915.

14. Béla Balázs, *A vándor énekel*, ed. Sándor Radnóti (Budapest: Magyar Helikon, 1975), p. 312.

15. *Irodalmi Muzeum: Emlékezések* (Budapest, 1967), p. 34.

16. See István Gál, "A Hungarian at King's," *The New Hungarian Quarterly*, 12, 41 (1971), pp. 188–91, and "'Rosti Magdolna,' a Nyugat rejtélyes angol szakértője," *Irodalomtörténet*, 8, 4 (1976), pp. 942–51.

17. Gyula Szekfű, *Három nemzedék és ami utána következik* (Budapest: A Királyi Magyar Egyetemi Nyomda, 1934), p. 367.

18. Endre Ady, *Jóslások magyarországról*, ed. Géza Féja (Budapest: Athenaeum Irodalmi és Nyomdairt. Kiadása, 1936), p. 39.

19. Cited in József Varga, *Ady és kora* (Budapest: Kossuth Könyvkiadó, 1977), p. 398.

20. Endre Ady, *Összes versei* (Budapest: Szépirodalmi Könyvkiadó, 1967), pp. 763–64.

21. Gunther E. Rothenberg, "The Habsburg Army in the First World War: 1914–1918," in Kann et al., *The Habsburg Empire in World War I*, p. 74.

22. Ibid., p. 77; Norman Stone, *The Eastern Front, 1914–1917* (New York: Charles Scribner's Sons, 1975), pp. 80–91.

23. Vermes, "Leap into the Dark," p. 32.

24. Cited in Lajos Pók, *Babits Mihály* (Budapest: Szépirodalmi Könyvkiadó, 1970), p. 80.

25. Karl August Kutzbach (ed.), *Paul Ernst und Georg Lukács: Dokumente einer Freundschaft* (Emsdetten: Verlag Lechte, 1974), pp. 81–82.

26. Éva Karádi and Erzsébet Vezér (eds.), *A Vasárnapi Kör* (Budapest: Gondolat, 1980), p. 72.

27. See Lee Congdon, *The Young Lukács* (Chapel Hill: The University of North Carolina Press, 1983), pp. 118–19, and Éva Karádi, "Lukács, Fülep és a magyar szellem-tudományi iskola," *Magyar Filozófiai Szemle*, 29, 1–2 (1985), p. 38.

28. *Irodalmi Muzeum: Emlékezések*, p. 12.

29. Interview with Arnold Hauser in London, August 28, 1971.

30. Lukács, *Die Theorie des Romans*, pp. 5–6.

31. Ibid., p. 5, and *Gelebtes Denken*, ed. István Eörsi (Frankfurt am Main: Suhrkamp Verlag, 1981), pp. 69–70.

32. On Szittya, see Ferenc Bodri, " 'Az út, amin haladtunk, alámerült . . . ,' " *Új Írás*, no. 9 (1988), pp. 117–28; no. 10 (1988), pp. 111–22.

33. Cited in György Rónay, *Kassák Lajos* (Budapest: Szépirodalmi Könyvkiadó, 1971), p. 121.

34. Cited in Júlia Szabó, *A magyar aktivizmus története* (Budapest: Akadémiai Kiadó, 1971), p. 15.

35. See Kálmán Vargha et al. (eds.), *Program és hivatás* (Budapest: Gondolat Kiadó, 1978), pp. 434–38.

36. Gratz, *A dualizmus kora*, 2, p. 337.

37. Lajos Sipos, *Babits Mihály és a forradalmak kora* (Budapest: Akadémiai Kiadó, 1976), pp. 9–10, and István Gál, *Bartóktól Radnótiig* (Budapest: Magvető Kiadó, 1973), pp. 96–97.

38. Lajos Kassák, *Egy ember élete*, 2 (Budapest: Magvető Kiadó, 1983), p. 308.

39. Ibid., p. 332.

40. Cited in Galántai, "Magyarország az első világháborúban," p. 1145.

41. Gratz, *A dualizmus kora*, 2, pp. 348–49.

42. Ady called her *csacsi* ("little silly"), then "Csacsika" or "Csacsinszka," and finally "Csinszka."

43. Ady, *Összes versei*, p. 805.

44. Vermes, "Leap into the Dark," p. 38.

45. Cited in ibid., pp. 41–42.

46. Galántai, "Magyarország az első világháborúban," p. 1168.

47. Ibid., p. 1172, and Bernadotte E. Schmitt and Harold C. Vedeler, *The World in the Crucible, 1914–1919* (New York: Harper & Row, 1984), pp. 195–96.

48. Rothenberg, "The Habsburg Army in the First World War," p. 81; Galántai, "Magyarország az első világháborúban," p. 1185; Schmitt and Vedeler, *The World in the Crucible*, p. 262.

49. Galántai, "Magyarország az első világháborúban," p. 1221.

50. Michael Károlyi, *Fighting the World: The Struggle for Peace*, trans. E. W. Dickes (London: Kegan Paul, Trench, Trubner & Co., 1924), p. 264.

51. See Lee Congdon, "The Moralist as Social Thinker: Oszkár Jászi in Hungary,

1900–1919," in Walter Laqueur and George L. Mosse (eds.), *Historians in Politics* (London: Sage Publications, 1974), p. 301.

52. Károlyi, *Fighting the World*, p. 264.

53. See Lee Congdon, "Karl Polanyi in Hungary, 1900–19," *Journal of Contemporary History*, 11, 1 (1976), p. 176.

54. "Mohol" was the village from which he came.

55. Moholy's letter to Babits, December 18, 1918. Babits Papers, OSZK:K, Fond 3/904.

56. Jászi in Ervin Szabó, *Társadalmi és pártharcok a 48–49-es magyar forradalomban* (Bécs: Bécsi Magyar Kiadó, 1921), p. 29.

57. Cited in Gábor Kemény, *Szabó Ervin és a magyar társadalomszemlélet* (Budapest: Magvető Kiadó, 1977), pp. 94–95.

58. Jászi in Szabó, *Társadalmi és pártharcok*, p. 27.

59. Ilona Duczynska, "Korán reggel," *Új Írás*, 13, 3 (1973), p. 13.

60. György Dalos, *A cselekvés szerelmese: Duczynska Ilona élete* (Budapest: Kossuth Könyvkiadó, 1984), p. 17.

61. Cited in Duczynska, "Korán reggel," p. 19.

62. Both cited in Dalos, *A cselekvés szerelmese*, p. 21.

63. "Beszélgetés Duczynska Ilonával," *Valóság*, 17, 7 (1974), p. 51.

64. Ilona Duczynska, "A cselekvés boldogtalan szerelmese," *Valóság*, 21, 5 (1978), p. 13.

65. Ibid., p. 14.

66. György Litván, "A Moralist Revolutionary's Dilemma: In Memory of Ervin Szabó," *Radical History Review*, no. 24 (1980), p. 90.

67. Dalos, *A cselekvés szerelmese*, pp. 68, 82.

68. "Ady forradalmi hatása: Filminterjú Lukács Györggyel," *Élet és Irodalom*, January 29, 1977, p. 6.

69. Karádi and Vezér, *A Vasárnapi Kör*, pp. 83, 85.

70. Károly Mannheim, *Lélek és kultura* (Budapest: Benkő Gyula Cs. és Kir. Udvari Könyvkereskedése, 1918), pp. 10–11.

71. Here Mannheim allowed that there was some kind of relationship, still problematic, between cultural and social forms. Though he credited Marx with this discovery, he hastened to add that he and his colleagues rejected the *"Überbau"* theory. Ibid., p. 24.

72. Ibid., p. 20.

73. Károly Mannheim, "A háború bölcseletéhez," *Huszadik Század*, 18 (1917), p. 417.

74. Károly Tolnai, *Ferenczy Noémi* (Budapest: Bisztrai Farkas Ferencz Kiadása, 1934), p. 10.

75. Oszkár Jászi, "Mannheim Károly: *Lélek és kultura,*" *Huszadik Század*, 19 (1918), p. 192.

76. Béla Fogarasi, "Konzervativ és progressziv idealizmus," *Huszadik Század*, 19 (1918), pp. 193–206.

77. György Lukács, *Ifjúkori művek, 1902–1918*, ed. Árpád Tímár (Budapest: Magvető Kiadó, 1977), pp. 837–44.

78. Ibid., pp. 843–44.

79. Ervin Szabó, "A konzervativ és progressziv idealizmus vitája," *Huszadik Század*, 19 (1918), pp. 376–78.

80. Béla Fogarasi, "Záróbeszéd," Huszadik Század, 19 (1918), p. 94.

81. József Lengyel, Visegrádi utca (Budapest: Szépirodalmi Könyvkiadó, 1962), p. 34.

82. Vargha, Program és hivatás, pp. 451–53.

83. Ady, Összes versei, pp. 949–50.

84. Loránt Hegedüs, Ady és Tisza (Budapest: Nyugat, 1940), p. 91. See St. Matthew 27:46: "And about the ninth hour Jesus cried with a loud voice, saying, Eli, Eli lama sabachthani? that is to say, My God, my God, why hast thou forsaken me?"

85. Ferenc Pölöskei, "Szemben az árral: Tisza István utolsó évei," Valóság, 26, 5 (1983), p. 95; Gábor Vermes, István Tisza (New York: East European Monographs, 1985), p. 453.

86. Anna Lesznai, Kezdetben volt a kert, 2 (Budapest: Szépirodalmi Könyvkiadó, 1966), p. 430.

87. So called because demonstrators wore asters in their lapels for All Saints' Day.

88. Cited in Lesznai, Kezdetben, 2, p. 450.

89. In accordance with a secret treaty of August 17, 1916, the Allies had already promised to hand Transylvania over to the Romanians.

90. Oscar Jászi, Revolution and Counter-Revolution in Hungary (New York: Howard Fertig, 1969), p. 58.

91. Oszkár Jászi, "Proletárdiktatura," Szabadgondolat, 8, 10 (1918), pp. 225–26.

92. György Lukács, "A köztársasági propaganda," Világ, November 10, 1918, p. 17.

93. György Lukács, "A bolsevizmus mint erkölcsi problema," Szabadgondolat, 8, 10 (1918), pp. 228–32.

94. György Lukács, Utam Marxhoz, 1, ed. György Márkus (Budapest: Magvető Könyvkiadó, 1971), pp. 187–97.

95. Russian terrorist and author of The Pale Horse.

96. Cited in David Kettler, "Culture and Revolution: Lukács in the Hungarian Revolutions of 1918/19," Telos, no. 10 (1971), p. 69.

97. Lengyel, Visegrádi utca, p. 138.

98. Kassák, Egy ember élete, 2, p. 479.

99. Ibid., p. 473.

100. Sándor Barta, "1918. Szabadulás," Ma, 3, 11 (1918), p. 135.

101. Árpád Szélpál, "Forradalmi művészet—vagy pártművészet," Ma, 4, 1 (1919), pp. 4, 9–10.

102. Kassák, Egy ember élete, 2, p. 415.

103. Ibid., p. 428.

104. Lajos Kassák, "Ady Endre, 1877–1919," Ma, 4, 2 (1919), pp. 14–15.

105. Congdon, "The Moralist as Social Thinker," pp. 310–11.

106. Peter Pastor, Hungary between Wilson and Lenin: The Hungarian Revolution of 1918–1919 and the Big Three (Boulder: East European Quarterly, 1976), pp. 46–47; Gábor Vermes, "The October Revolution in Hungary: From Károlyi to Kun," in Iván Völgyes (ed.), Hungary in Revolution, 1918–19 (Lincoln: University of Nebraska Press, 1971), pp. 52–53.

107. See Lajos Kassák, "Aktivizmus," Ma, 4, 4 (1919), pp. 46–51.

108. Pastor, Hungary between Wilson and Lenin, p. 119.

109. Jászi, Revolution and Counter-Revolution, p. 92.

110. Whether or not Károlyi signed the resignation is still a matter of controversy.

111. Sándor Garbai, cited in Pastor, Hungary between Wilson and Lenin, p. 142.

112. For the text of "The Documents of Unity," see Rudolf L. Tőkés, *Béla Kun and the Hungarian Soviet Republic* (New York: Frederick A. Praeger, 1967), p. 247.

113. Kunfi was not, however, the cipher some historians have made him out to be.

114. Peter Gay, *Weimar Culture: The Outsider as Insider* (New York: Harper and Row, 1968), p. xiv.

115. Farkas József (ed.), *"Mindenki újakra készül . . . "*: *Az 1918/19-es forradalmak irodalma*, 4 (Budapest: Akadémiai Kiadó, 1967), pp. 930–31.

116. Ibid., pp. 284–86.

117. Ibid., pp. 84, 336–37, 750, 771, 1094.

118. György Lukács, *Magyar irodalom—Magyar kultúra*, ed. Ferenc Fehér and Zoltán Kenyeres (Budapest: Gondolat Kiadó, 1970), pp. 646, 648.

119. Cited in Congdon, *The Young Lukács*, p. 159.

120. Jászi, *Revolution and Counter-Revolution*, p. 146.

121. József, *"Mindenki,"* 4, p. 197.

122. Ibid., pp. 913–14.

123. Ibid., pp. 101–3, 971.

124. Ibid., p. 187.

125. Ibid., pp. 339–41.

126. For the controversy, see ibid., pp. 170–74, 186–88, 196–98, 955–56.

127. Farkas József, *Értelmiség és forradalom* (Budapest: Kossuth Könyvkiadó, 1984), plate between pp. 224 and 225; Krisztina Passuth, *Moholy-Nagy* (Budapest: Corvina, 1982), p. 15.

128. Cited in Krisztina Passuth, "Debut of László Moholy-Nagy," *Acta Historiae Artium*, 19 (1973), p. 125.

129. Lajos Kassák, "A plakát és az új festészet," *Ma*, 1, 1 (1916), pp. 2–4.

130. Cited in Jászi, *Revolution and Counter-Revolution*, pp. 138–39.

131. Károly Urbán, *Lukács György és a magyar munkásmozgalom* (Budapest: Kossuth Könyvkiadó, 1985), pp. 38–39.

132. Rózsa Borus (ed.), *A század nagy tanúi* (Budapest: RTV. Minerva, 1978), p. 189.

133. Cited in Alfred D. Low, "Soviet Hungary and the Paris Peace Conference," in Völgyes, *Hungary in Revolution*, p. 149.

134. József, *"Mindenki,"* 4, pp. 460–61.

135. See ibid., pp. 461–63.

136. Lajos Kassák, "Levél Kun Bélához a művészet nevében," *Ma*, 4, 7 (1919), pp. 146–48.

137. Renato Poggioli, *The Theory of the Avant-Garde*, trans. Gerald Fitzgerald (New York: Harper and Row, 1971), p. 25.

138. Cited In Low, "Soviet Hungary and the Paris Peace Conference," p. 149.

139. Zsuzsa L. Nagy, "Problems of Foreign Policy before the Revolutionary Governing Council," in Völgyes, *Hungary in Revolution*, p. 135. Balázs was one who saw action against the Romanians.

140. Borus, *A század nagy tanúi*, pp. 191–94.

CHAPTER ONE
THE ROAD TO LENIN

1. Victor Serge, *Memoirs of a Revolutionary, 1901–1941*, trans. Peter Sedgwick (London: Oxford University Press, 1963), pp. 187–88.

2. Baumgarten was a German writer, born in Hungary. Steinbach was a neurotic pianist of Viennese birth, and Lukács's first wife's lover.

3. Kutzbach, *Paul Ernst und Georg Lukács*, pp. 154–56.

4. Ernst Bloch, "Zur Rettung von Georg Lukács," *Die weissen Blätter*, 6 (1919), pp. 529–30.

5. Éva Karádi, "Lukács fordulatának heidelbergi fogadtatása," *Magyar Filozófiai Szemle*, 31, 4 (1987), p. 688.

6. Karádi and Vezér, *A Vasárnapi Kör*, p. 93. This description is in Balázs's diary.

7. Ibid., pp. 93–94.

8. Ibid., p. 93.

9. Kutzbach, *Paul Ernst und Georg Lukács*, p. 157.

10. István Mészáros, *Lukács' Concept of Dialectic* (London: Merlin Press, 1972), pp. 130–31.

11. Lukács, *Gelebtes Denken*, p. 258.

12. Cited in Congdon, *The Young Lukács*, p. 149.

13. Lukács, *Gelebtes Denken*, pp. 263–64.

14. Lukács, *Utam Marxhoz*, 1, pp. 20–21.

15. Serge, *Memoirs*, p. 187.

16. György Borsányi, *Kun Béla* (Budapest: Kossuth Könyvkiadó, 1979), pp. 201–3.

17. Georg Lukács, *Taktik und Ethik: Politische Aufsätze, I, 1918–1920*, ed. Jörg Kammler and Frank Benseler (Neuwied: Hermann Luchterhand Verlag, 1975), p. 220.

18. Georg Lukács, *Revolution und Gegenrevolution: Politische Aufsätze, II, 1920–1921*, ed. Jörg Kammler and Frank Benseler (Neuwied: Hermann Luchterhand Verlag, 1976) p. 243.

19. Lukács, *Taktik und Ethik*, pp. 175–87.

20. Cited in Georg Lukács, *Tactics and Ethics: Political Essays, 1919–1929*, trans. Michael McColgan, ed. Rodney Livingstone (New York: Harper and Row, 1975), pp. xvi–xvii.

21. Robert C. Tucker (ed.), *The Lenin Anthology* (New York: W. W. Norton, 1975), p. 582.

22. Lukács, *Taktik und Ethik*, pp. 189, 222–23; *Tactics and Ethics*, p. 120.

23. Lukács, *Taktik und Ethik*, p. 223; *Revolution und Gegenrevolution*, p. 49.

24. Lukács, *Taktik und Ethik*, pp. 225–26.

25. Lukács, *Revolution und Gegenrevolution*, pp. 24–25.

26. Balázs in Karádi and Vezér, *A Vasárnapi Kör*, pp. 96–97.

27. Ibid., pp. 99–100.

28. Ibid., p. 99.

29. Cited in Éva Karádi, "A Lukács-kör Bécsben," *Magyar Filozófiai Szemle*, 31, 3 (1987), p. 605.

30. György Lukács, *A modern dráma fejlődésének története*, 1 (Budapest: Franklin-Társulat, 1911), p. 58.

31. Georg Lukács, *Organisation und Illusion: Politische Aufsätze, III, 1921–1924*, ed. Jörg Kammler and Frank Benseler (Neuwied: Hermann Luchterhand Verlag, 1977), pp. 114–17.

32. Georg Lukács, "Stawrogins Beichte," *Die Rote Fahne*, July 16, 1922, n.p.

33. Lukács, *Organisation und Illusion*, p. 124.

34. Cited in Isaiah Berlin, *Russian Thinkers* (New York: Penguin Books, 1979), p. 167.

35. Vissarion Belinski, *Selected Philosophical Works* (Moscow: Foreign Languages Publishing House, 1956), p. 305.

36. Georg Lukács, *Studies in European Realism* (New York: Grosset and Dunlap, 1964), pp. 99, 123.

37. Lukács, *Organisation und Illusion*, pp. 124–25.

38. György Lukács, *Történelem és osztálytudat*, ed. Mihály Vajda (Budapest: Magvető Kiadó, 1971), pp. 64–68.

39. Gábor used the pseudonym "Ladislaus Sas."

40. Erwin Piscator, *The Political Theatre*, trans. Hugh Rorrison (New York: Avon Books, 1978), p. 45.

41. András Diószegi, *Gábor Andor* (Budapest: Gondolat, 1966), p. 71.

42. See György Fukász, *A magyarországi polgári radikalizmus történetéhez 1900–1918: Jászi Oszkár ideológiájának bírálata* (Budapest: Gondolat, 1960), p. 316n.

43. See Karádi and Vezér, *A Vasárnapi Kör*, pp. 158–60.

44. Béla Fogarasi, "Bevezetés a marxi filozófiába," in Kristóf Nyíri (ed.), *A magyar marxista filozófia a két világháború között* (Budapest: Kossuth Könyvkiadó, 1979), pp. 35–65.

45. Georg Lukács, *Geschichte und Klassenbewusstsein: Studien über marxistische Dialektik* (Neuwied: Hermann Luchterhand Verlag, 1970), p. 23.

46. Ibid., p. 56.

47. Ibid., p. 63n.

48. Ibid., pp. 58–93.

49. Ibid., pp. 356–400.

50. Ibid., p. 126.

51. Ibid., p. 18.

52. Ibid., pp. 94–118.

53. Ibid., p. 115.

54. Ibid., pp. 170–355.

55. Ibid., p. 27.

56. Ibid., p. 194.

57. Ibid., p. 209.

58. Ibid., p. 244.

59. Leszek Kolakowski, *Main Currents of Marxism*, 3, trans. P. S. Falla (Oxford: Clarendon Press, 1978), p. 298.

60. Albert Camus, *The Rebel*, trans. Anthony Bower (New York: Vintage Books, 1956), p. 234.

61. Morris Watnick, "Georg Lukács: An Intellectual Biography," *Soviet Survey*, January-March 1959, p. 80.

62. Karl Korsch, "Marxismus und Philosophie," *Archiv für die Geschichte des Sozialismus und der Arbeiterbewegung*, 2 (1923), p. 121.

63. Ibid., pp. 67–68.

64. Béla Fogarasi, "Karl Korsch: Marxismus und Philosophie," *Die Internationale*, June 15, 1924, pp. 414–16.

65. Karl Korsch, "The Present State of the Problem of 'Marxism and Philosophy'—An Anti-Critique," in *Marxism and Philosophy*, trans. Fred Halliday (New York: Monthly Review Press, 1970), p. 99n.

66. László Radványi, "Korsch, Karl: Marxismus und Philosophie," *Archiv für Sozialwissenschaft und Sozialpolitik*, 53 (1925), pp. 528–35.

67. Miklós Mesterházi and Tamás Krausz (eds.), *Filozófiai Figyelő Évkönyve: A "történelem és osztálytudat" a 20-as évek vitáiban*, 4 (Budapest: Lukács Archívum és Könyvtár, 1981), p. 141.

68. Josef Révai, "Georg Lukács: *Geschichte und Klassenbewusstsein. Studien über marxistische Dialektik*," *Archiv für die Geschichte des Sozialismus und der Arbeiterbewegung*, 11 (1923), pp. 227–36.

69. Ernst Bloch, "Aktualität und Utopie: Zu Lukács' 'Geschichte und Klassenbewusstsein,' " in *Philosophische Aufsätze zur Objektiven Phantasie* (Frankfurt am Main: Suhrkamp Verlag, 1969), pp. 598–621.

70. Éva Karádi (ed.), "Dokumentumok Lukács György heidelbergi korszakából," *Valóság*, 17, 11 (1974), p. 28.

71. Bloch, "Aktualität und Utopie," p. 621.

72. Ibid., p. 601.

73. Mesterházi and Krausz, *Filozófiai Figyelő Évkönyve*, 1, p. 304.

74. A. Deborin, "Lukács und seine Kritik des Marxismus," *Arbeiter-Literatur*, 1, 2 (1924), pp. 615–40.

75. Ibid., pp. 618, 622, 627.

76. I follow here the abbreviated Hungarian translation in Nyíri, A *magyar marxista filozófia a két világháború között*, pp. 75–86.

77. Lukács, *Gelebtes Denken*, p. 123.

78. Cited in Paul Breines and Andrew Arato, *The Young Lukács and the Origins of Western Marxism* (New York: The Seabury Press, 1979), p. 180.

79. Watnick, "Georg Lukács: An Intellectual Biography," *Soviet Survey*, April-June 1958, p. 53.

80. Cited in Martin Jay, *The Dialectical Imagination: A History of the Frankfurt School and the Institute of Social Research, 1923–1950* (Boston: Little, Brown and Company, 1973), p. 5.

81. Martin Jay, "The Frankfurt School's Critique of Marxist Humanism," *Social Research*, 39, 2 (1972), p. 287.

82. István Gál (ed.), *Babits-Szilasi levelezés* (Budapest: Irodalmi Múzeum, n.d.), p. 113.

83. Siegfried Marck, "Neukritizistische und neuhegelsche Auffassung der marxistischen Dialektik," *Die Gesellschaft*, 1, 6 (1924), pp. 573–78.

84. Siegfried Marck, *Die Dialektik in der Philosophie der Gegenwart*, 1 (Tübingen: Verlag von J.C.B. Mohr /Paul Siebeck/, 1929), pp. 123–24, 128.

85. Martin Heidegger, *Being and Time*, trans. John Macquarrie and Edward Robinson (New York: Harper and Row, 1962), p. 427.

86. Marck, *Die Dialektik in der Philosophie der Gegenwart*, 1, pp. 129, 131.

87. Judith Marcus-Tar, *Thomas Mann und Georg Lukács* (Budapest: Corvina Kiadó, 1982), p. 25.

88. Thomas Mann, "Brief an Dr. Seipel," in *Gesammelte Werke*, 11 (Frankfurt am Main: S. Fischer Verlag, 1974), p. 782.

89. Katia Mann, *Unwritten Memories*, trans. Hunter and Hildegarde Hannum (New York: Alfred A. Knopf, 1975), p. 73.

90. See Judith Marcus-Tar, "Georg Lukács, Thomas Mann und 'Der Tod in Venedig,' " *Die Weltwoche*, July 2, 1971, p. 31.

91. See the excellent analysis in Marcus-Tar, *Thomas Mann und Georg Lukács*.

92. Cited in ibid., p. 70.

93. Thomas Mann, *Der Zauberberg*, 2 (Frankfurt am Main: Fischer Bücherei, 1967), p. 426.

94. Ibid., p. 419.

95. Georg Lukács, *Lenin: Studie über den Zusammenhang seiner Gedanken* (Neuwied: Hermann Luchterhand Verlag, 1967), pp. 11, 16, 18.

96. Ibid., p. 46.

97. György Lukács, *Curriculum vitae*, ed. János Ambrus (Budapest: Magvető Kiadó, 1982), pp. 177–78.

98. Szabó, *Társadalmi és pártharcok*, p. 81.

99. Aladár Tamás (ed.), *A 100%: A KMP legális folyóirata, 1927–1930* (Budapest: Akadémiai Kiadó, 1977), p. 193.

100. See Miklós Lackó, *Szerep és mű* (Budapest: Gondolat, 1981), pp. 54–55, 93–94.

101. Tamás, *A 100%*, p. 191.

102. M. H. Abrams, *Natural Supernaturalism* (New York: W. W. Norton, 1971), p. 182.

103. Georg Lukács, "Die neue Ausgabe von Lassalles Briefen," *Archiv für die Geschichte des Sozialismus und der Arbeiterbewegung*, 11 (1925), pp. 403–5.

104. Ibid., pp. 414–15, 423.

105. Georg Lukács, "Moses Hess und die Probleme der idealistischen Dialektik," *Archiv für die Geschichte des Sozialismus und der Arbeiterbewegung*, 12 (1926), pp. 113, 116–17, 125–26, 138.

106. Ibid., p. 145.

107. Ibid., pp. 148–52.

108. Tamás, *A 100%*, p. 298.

109. Cited in Marcus-Tar, *Thomas Mann und Georg Lukács*, p. 20.

110. Thomas Mann, *Essays*, trans. H. T. Lowe-Porter (New York: Vintage Books, 1957), p. 177.

111. Kutzbach, *Paul Ernst und Georg Lukács*, pp. 177–79.

112. See Lukács, *Ifjúkori művek*, pp. 90–105.

113. Mann, *Der Zauberberg*, 2, p. 523. See also Thomas Mann, *Order of the Day*, trans. H. T. Lowe-Porter, et al. (Freeport, New York: Books for Libraries Press, 1969), pp. 43–44.

114. Cited in Lackó, *Szerep és mű*, pp. 83–84.

115. Kutzbach, *Paul Ernst und Georg Lukács*, p. 179.

116. Jane Degras (ed.), *The Communist International, Documents. II, 1923–1928* (London: Oxford University Press, 1960), pp. 505–6.

117. Lukács, *Történelem és osztálytudat*, pp. 675–76.

118. See Károly Urbán, "A Blum-tézisek 'utóélete,' " *Magyar Filozófiai Szemle*, 29, 1–2 (1985), pp. 126–28.

119. Lukács, *Curriculum vitae*, p. 455.

120. Lukács, *Gelebtes Denken*, p. 143.

121. Lukács, *Geschichte und Klassenbewusstsein*, p. 25.

122. Karl Marx, *Ökonomisch-philosophische Manuskripte* (Leipzig: Verlag Philipp Reclam jun., 1970), pp. 157–59.

123. Ibid., p. 159.

124. Lukács, *Geschichte und Klassenbewusstsein*, p. 26.

125. See Marx, *Ökonomisch-philosophische Manuskripte*, p. 235, and Richard Schacht, *Alienation* (Garden City, New York: Anchor Books, 1970), p. 64.

126. Marx, *Ökonomisch-philosophische Manuskripte*, p. 236.

127. Lukács, *Geschichte und Klassenbewusstsein*, pp. 25, 42–43.

128. Ágnes Heller (ed.), *Lukács Reappraised* (New York: Columbia University Press, 1983), pp. 177–78.

129. Georg Lukács, "Mein Weg zu Marx," in *Marxismus und Stalinismus* (Reinbek: Rowohlt Taschenbuch Verlag, 1970), p. 11; Marija Hevesi, *"Baloldaliság" a filozófiában: Az 1920-as évek filozófiai vitáinak történetéből*, trans. István Csibra (Budapest: Kossuth Könyvkiadó, 1979), pp. 268–69.

130. Lukács, *Gelebtes Denken*, p. 140.

131. László Sziklai, *Lukács és a fasizmus kora* (Budapest: Magvető Kiadó, 1985), p. 121.

132. László Sziklai, "Szellemi közösségben: Lukács György és Mihail Lifsic," *Világosság*, 25, 2 (1984), pp. 81, 88.

133. Lukács, *Gelebtes Denken*, p. 142.

134. David Pike argues that Lukács was hustled out of Moscow in order to save his life. David Ryazanov was already in serious trouble. See Pike, *Lukács and Brecht* (Chapel Hill: The University of North Carolina Press, 1985), p. 53.

135. Éva Gábor, "Egy 'elfelejtett' vasárnapos emlékeiből," *Világosság*, 21, 7 (1980), p. 452.

136. In 1931 he reported four thousand for Berlin, eight thousand for Berlin and its environs. See A., "Die Marxistische Arbeiterschule (MASCH): Aus einem Gespräch mit ihrem Leiter," *Die Linkskurve*, 3, 6 (1931), pp. 19–20.

137. Henry Pachter, *Weimar Etudes* (New York: Columbia University Press, 1982), p. 37.

138. Gábor, "Egy 'elfelejtett' vasárnapos emlékeiből," p. 452; Sziklai, *Lukács és a fasizmus kora*, p. 124.

139. Helga Gallas, *Marxistische Literaturtheorie: Kontroversen im Bund proletarisch-revolutionärer Schriftsteller* (Neuwied: Hermann Luchterhand Verlag, 1971), p. 29.

140. Andor Gábor, "Die bunte Welt des Genossen Barbusse," *Die Linkskurve*, 1, 5 (1929), p. 5.

141. Andor Gábor "Über proletarisch-revolutionäre Literatur," *Die Linkskurve*, 1, 3 (1929), pp. 3, 6.

142. Edward J. Brown, *The Proletarian Episode in Russian Literature, 1928–1932* (New York: Columbia University Press, 1953), p. 9.

143. Gallas, *Marxistische Literaturtheorie*, pp. 51–52, 211n.

144. Cited in Brown, *The Proletarian Episode*, p. 63.

145. Ibid., pp. 66, 73.

146. K. A. Wittfogel, "Zur Frage der marxistischen Aesthetik," *Die Linkskurve*, 2, 6 (1930), p. 11.

147. Andreas Réz, "Hauptrichtungen in der neueren ungarischen revolutionären Literatur," *Arbeiter-Literatur*, 1, 9 (1924), p. 482.

148. Gallas, *Marxistische Literaturtheorie*, pp. 60–61.

149. Georg Lukács, "Willi Bredels Romane," *Die Linkskurve*, 3, 11 (1931), pp. 23–27.

150. Cited in Brown, *The Proletarian Episode*, p. 79.

151. Ibid., p. 78.

152. Georg Lukács, "Gegen die Spontaneitätstheorie in der Literatur," *Die Links-kurve*, 4, 4 (1932), pp. 30–33.

153. Georg Lukács, "Tendenz oder Parteilichkeit?" *Die Linkskurve*, 4, 6 (1932), pp. 13–21.

154. Georg Lukács, "Reportage oder Gestaltung," *Die Linkskurve*, 4, 7 (1932), pp. 23–30; 4, 8 (1932), pp. 26–31.

155. On LEF, see Herman Ermolaev, *Soviet Literary Theories, 1917–1934: The Genesis of Socialist Realism* (Berkeley: University of California Press, 1963), pp. 73–75.

156. Ernst Ottwalt, " 'Tatsachenroman' u. Formexperiment: Eine Entgegnung an Georg Lukács," *Die Linkskurve*, 4, 10 (1932), pp. 22–23.

157. Georg Lukács, "Aus der Not eine Tugend," *Die Linkskurve*, 4, 11/12 (1932), pp. 15–24.

158. Bertolt Brecht, *On Theatre: The Development of an Aesthetic*, ed. and trans. John Willett (New York: Hill and Wang, 1964), p. 23.

159. Lukács, "Aus der Not eine Tugend," p. 20.

160. Julius Hay, *Born 1900: Memoirs*, trans. J. A. Underwood (La Salle, Illinois: Open Court, 1975), pp. 100–102.

161. Julius Hay, *Gott, Kaiser und Bauer* (Zürich: Verlag Oprecht & Helbling, 1935), pp. 15–17.

162. Ibid., p. 53.

163. Ibid., p. 54.

164. Ibid., pp. 60–61.

165. Ibid., p. 93.

166. Hay, *Born 1900*, p. 107.

167. Lukács, *Magyar irodalom—Magyar kultúra*, pp. 219–20, 222. Written in 1940.

168. In Hay, *Born 1900*, p. 17.

169. Georg Lukács, "Shaws Bekenntnis zur Sowjetunion," *Die Linkskurve*, 3, 9 (1931), p. 7.

170. Georg Lukács, "Goethe und die Dialektik," *Der Marxist*, 2, 5 (1932), pp. 13–24.

171. Georg Lukács, *Goethe and His Age*, trans. Robert Anchor (London: Merlin Press, 1968), pp. 138–39.

172. Cited in Brown, *The Proletarian Episode*, p. 231.

173. Lukács, *Curriculum vitae*, pp. 227, 466.

174. Ibid., pp. 104, 106.

175. Ibid., p. 111.

176. See, for example, Lukács, *Gelebtes Denken*, p. 140.

CHAPTER TWO
THE ROAD TO THE PARTY

1. Béla Balázs, *Napló, 1914–1922*, ed. Anna Fábri (Budapest: Magvető Könyvkiadó, 1982), p. 348.

2. Lukács's letter to Martin Buber, November 21, 1921. LAK.

3. Balázs, *Napló*, pp. 518–19.

4. Petőfi was of Slovak descent.

5. Balázs, *Napló*, pp. 358–59.

6. Balázs, A vándor énekel, p. 213.

7. Béla Balázs, Álmodó ifjúság (Budapest: Magvető és Szépirodalmi Könyvkiadó, 1976), p. 86.

8. Balázs cited in Joseph Zsuffa, Béla Balázs: The Man and the Artist (Berkeley: University of California Press, 1987), p. 93.

9. Magda K. Nagy, Balázs Béla világa (Budapest: Kossuth Könyvkiadó, 1973), p. 277. I was unable to locate a copy of the book.

10. Balázs, Napló, p. 350.

11. Ibid., pp. 419, 453.

12. Ibid., pp. 500, 511–12; Balázs, Válogatott cikkek, pp. 101–2.

13. Béla Balázs, Halálesztetika (Budapest: Deutsch Zsigmond és Társa Könyvkereskedése, n.d.), pp. 12–13.

14. Ibid., pp. 36–37.

15. Béla Balázs, A szinjáték elmélete (Wien: Europa Ismeretterjesztő Könyvtár, 1922), pp. 58–59.

16. Balázs, Válogatott cikkek, pp. 103–5.

17. Balázs, Napló, p. 416.

18. Béla Balázs, Der Mantel der Träume (München: Verlagsanstalt D. & R. Bischoff, 1922), pp. 1–6.

19. Ibid., pp. 12–18.

20. Ibid., pp. 106–11.

21. Ibid., pp. 25–29.

22. Thomas Mann, "Ein schönes Buch," Gesammelte Werke, 10 (Frankfurt am Main: S. Fischer Verlag, 1960), pp. 624–26.

23. Balázs, Napló, p. 518.

24. Lukács, Magyar irodalom—Magyar kultúra, pp. 78–80.

25. Béla Balázs, Der Phantasie-Reiseführer: Das ist ein Baedeker der Seele für Sommerfrischler (Wien: Paul Zsolnay Verlag, 1925), p. 25.

26. Ibid., p. 43.

27. Ibid., p. 54.

28. Cited in Abrams, Natural Supernaturalism, p. 181.

29. Balázs, Der Phantasie-Reiseführer, p. 60.

30. Ibid., pp. 86–87, 94.

31. Balázs, A vándor énekel, p. 234.

32. See Béla Balázs, Levelei Lukács Györgyhöz, ed. Júlia Lenkei (Budapest: MTA Filozófiai Intézet, 1982), p. 181, and Hilda Bauer, Emlékeim. Levelek Lukácshoz, ed. Júlia Lenkei (Budapest: MTA Filozófiai Intézet, 1985), pp. 24–25.

33. Béla Balázs, Halálos fiatalság, ed. Ferenc Fehér and Sándor Radnóti (Budapest: Magyar Helikon, 1974), pp. 336–39, 342.

34. Ibid., p. 348.

35. Ibid., pp. 348–49.

36. Ibid., pp. 352–53.

37. István Nemeskürty, Word and Image: History of the Hungarian Cinema, trans. Zsuzsanna Horn (Budapest: Corvina Press, 1968), pp. 19, 25, 32.

38. Ibid., p. 21, and Michael Korda, Charmed Lives: A Family Romance (New York: Random House, 1979), pp. 46, 49.

39. Korda, Charmed Lives, pp. 70–73.

40. Balázs, Napló, p. 521.

41. Ibid., pp. 496–97.

42. Cited in Béla Balázs, Schriften zum Film, 1, ed. Helmut H. Diederichs, Wolfgang Gersch, and Magda Nagy (München: Carl Hanser Verlag, 1982), p. 26.

43. Ibid., p. 149.

44. Ibid., pp. 150–51.

45. Béla Balázs, Schriften zum Film, 2, ed. Helmut H. Diederichs and Wolfgang Gersch (München: Carl Hanser Verlag, 1984), p. 216.

46. Balázs, Schriften, 1, pp. 186, 194, 244.

47. Ibid., pp. 205–8.

48. J. Huizinga, The Waning of the Middle Ages (Garden City, New York: Anchor Books, 1954), p. 284.

49. Balázs, Schriften, 1, pp. 52–58.

50. Ibid., p. 136.

51. Ibid., pp. 66, 341, 354.

52. Ibid., pp. 60–62, 77.

53. Ibid., p. 80.

54. Cited in Siegfried Kracauer, From Caligari to Hitler: A Psychological History of the German Film (Princeton: Princeton University Press, 1947), p. 7.

55. Balázs, Schriften, 1, p. 91.

56. Ibid., pp. 92, 101–2, 137–38.

57. Robert Musil, "Ansätze zu neuer Ästhetik: Bemerkungen über eine Dramaturgie des Films," Der Neue Merkur, 8, 6 (1925), p. 489; Balázs, Schriften, 2, p. 33.

58. Balázs, Schriften, 1, pp. 269–70.

59. Anna Balázs in Balázs's Diary, MTAK:K, Ms 5024/1, p. 1.

60. Balázs, Schriften, 2, pp. 209–12.

61. Ibid., pp. 34–35; Sergei Eisenstein, Film Form: Essays in Film Theory, ed. and trans. Jay Leyda (New York: Harcourt, Brace and World, 1949), p. 49.

62. Balázs, Schriften, 2, p. 22.

63. Gertraude Kühn, Karl Tümmler, and Walter Wimmer (eds.), Film und revolutionäre Arbeiterbewegung in Deutschland, 1918–1932, 1 (Berlin: Henschelverlag, 1975), pp. 180–81.

64. Béla Balázs, Theory of the Film, trans. Edith Bone (New York: Dover Publications, 1970), p. 160.

65. Balázs, Schriften, 2, pp. 212–14, 298–99n.

66. Ibid., p. 21; Kühn et al., Film und revolutionäre Arbeiterbewegung, 1, p. 209.

67. Balázs, Schriften, 2, p. 23.

68. Ibid., pp. 11, 226–28, 340.

69. Balázs, Schriften, 1, p. 147.

70. Balázs, Schriften, 2, p. 28.

71. Balázs, Theory of the Film, p. 150.

72. Balázs, Schriften, 2, pp. 219–21, 233.

73. Ibid., pp. 221, 236–39.

74. Ibid., pp. 221, 338–39.

75. Ibid., p. 261.

76. Ibid., pp. 258–60, 318n.

77. Ibid., pp. 246, 252–56, 266–68.

78. Ibid., p. 268.
79. Ibid., pp. 51–52.
80. Ibid., pp. 71, 81.
81. Ibid., p. 97.
82. Ibid., pp. 152, 159.
83. Ibid., pp. 174–75.
84. T. K. Fodor, "Der Geist des Films," *Die Linkskurve*, 4, 2 (1932), pp. 34–35; Rudolf Arnheim, "Der Geist des Films," *Die Weltbühne*, 26, 2 (1930), p. 724.
85. *The Threepenny Opera* (London: Lorrimer Publishing, 1984), pp. 12, 101.
86. Lotte H. Eisner, *The Haunted Screen* (Berkeley: University of California Press, 1973), p. 318.
87. Balázs, *Schriften*, 2, pp. 17, 353–58.
88. See Kühn et al., *Film und revolutionäre Arbeiterbewegung*, 1, p. 245.
89. Balázs, *Schriften*, 2, pp. 287–88.
90. Ibid., p. 290.
91. Cited in John Ralmon, "Béla Balázs in German Exile," *Film Quarterly*, 30, 3 (1977), p. 17. Novelist Josef Skvorecky suggests they were lovers. *The Engineer of Human Souls* (New York: Washington Square Press, 1985), p. 108.
92. Kracauer, *From Caligari to Hitler*, pp. 258–59.
93. Both cited in Ralmon, "Béla Balázs in German Exile," p. 18.
94. Béla Balázs, "Selbstanzeige," *Die Literarische Welt*, November 22, 1929, p. 8.
95. Béla Balázs, "Unmögliche Menschen," *Die Weltbühne*, 25, 11 (1929), pp. 734–35.
96. Béla Balázs, *Unmögliche Menschen* (Frankfurt am Main: Rütten & Loening Verlag, 1930), pp. 9–10, 36–54.
97. Ibid., pp. 54–95.
98. Ibid., pp. 111–32.
99. Ibid., pp. 146–200.
100. Ibid., pp. 220–28.
101. Ibid., pp. 228–59.
102. Ibid., pp. 397–99.
103. Ibid., p. 405.
104. Ibid., p. 419.
105. Ibid., pp. 420–21.
106. Ibid., p. 432.
107. Ibid., p. 445.
108. Ibid., p. 447.
109. Aladár Komlós, *Kritikus számadás* (Budapest: Szépirodalmi Könyvkiadó, 1977), p. 257; Balázs, *Schriften*, 2, p. 14; Wilhelm Michel, "Unmögliche Menschen," *Die Weltbühne*, 26, 1 (1930), p. 359.
110. Béla Balázs, "Die Furcht der Intellektuellen vor dem Sozialismus," *Die Weltbühne*, 28, 1 (1932), pp. 93–96, 131–34, 166–68, 207–10.
111. Piscator, *The Political Theatre*, p. 194.
112. Béla Balázs, "Menschen auf der Barrikade," *Die Weltbühne*, 25, 2 (1929), p. 94.
113. Balázs, *Schriften*, 2, p. 340.
114. Piscator, *The Political Theatre*, p. 97.
115. Balázs, *Schriften*, 2, pp. 107, 225–26, 275.

116. Béla Balázs, *Hans Urian geht nach Brot* (Freiburg im Breisgau: Max Reichard Verlag, n.d.), p. 11.

117. Ibid., pp. 22, 43.

118. Ibid., pp. 48–49, 57–58, 60–61, 73–74.

119. Ludwig Hoffmann and Daniel Hoffmann-Ostwald (eds.), *Deutsches Arbeitertheater, 1918–1933*, 2 (München: Verlag Rogner & Bernhard, 1973), p. 456.

120. Balázs, *Schriften*, 2, p. 245.

121. Hoffmann and Hoffmann-Ostwald, *Deutsches Arbeitertheater*, 2, p. 120.

122. John Willett, *Art and Politics in the Weimar Period: The New Sobriety, 1917–1933* (New York: Pantheon Books, 1978), p. 156.

CHAPTER THREE
THE MA CIRCLE

1. Kassák, *Egy ember élete*, 2, p. 640.

2. Imre Bori and Éva Körner, *Kassák irodalma és festészete* (Budapest: Magvető, 1967), p. 116.

3. Kassák, *Egy ember élete*, 2, p. 646.

4. In accordance with Austrian law, the aesthetician Fritz Brügel served as "responsible editor."

5. Ludwig Kassák, "An die Künstler aller Länder!" *Ma*, 5, 1–2 (1920), pp. 2–4.

6. Lajos Kassák, "1919 Eposz," *Ma*, 5, 4 (1920), pp. 43–44, 48.

7. Ibid., 5, 3 (1920), pp. 28, 31–32; 5, 4 (1920), pp. 41, 46.

8. Lajos Kassák, "Máglyák énekelnek," *Ma*, 6, 1–2 (1920), p. 16.

9. Richard Huelsenbeck (ed.), *Dada Almanach* (Berlin: Erich Reiss Verlag, 1920), p. 4.

10. Béla Balázs, "Dada," in Hubertus Gassner (ed.), *Wechsel Wirkungen: Ungarische Avantgarde in der Weimarer Republik* (Marburg: Jonas Verlag, 1986), p. 537.

11. Cited in Mary Gluck, "Toward a Historical Definition of Modernism: Georg Lukács and the Avant-Garde," *The Journal of Modern History*, 58, 4 (1986), p. 876.

12. Andor Németh, *A szélén behajtva* (Budapest: Magvető Könyvkiadó, 1973), p. 603.

13. Robert Hughes, *The Shock of the New* (New York: Alfred A. Knopf, 1981), p. 63.

14. Sándor Vajda in Ilona Illés and Ernő Taxner (eds.), *Kortársak Kassák Lajosról* (Budapest: Petőfi Irodalmi Múzeum, n.d.), p. 38.

15. Cited in Hans Richter, *Dada: Art and Anti-Art* (New York: Oxford University Press, 1965), p. 140.

16. Arthur Koestler, *The Invisible Writing* (New York: The Macmillan Company, 1954), p. 168.

17. Lajos Kassák, *A ló meghal, a madarak kirepülnek* (Budapest: Magyar Helikon, 1967), p. 34.

18. Imre Bori, *A szecessziótól a dadáig* (Újvidék: Forum Könyvkiadó, 1969), p. 287.

19. Kassák, *A ló meghal*, p. 49.

20. Richter, *Dada*, p. 116.

21. Kurt Schwitters, "Miképen vagyok elégedetlen az olajfestészettel," *Ma*, 6, 3 (1921), pp. 29–30.

22. Vargha, *Program és hivatás*, pp. 471–72; Emőke G. Komoróczy, *Kassák az emi-*

grációban 1920–1926 (Budapest: Csepeli Munkásotthon Olvasó Munkás Klub, 1987), p. 90.

23. Lajos Kassák, "Válasz sokfelé és álláspont," *Ma*, 8, 8 (1922), p. 54.

24. Cited in Komoróczy, *Kassák az emigrációban*, p. 92.

25. Lajos Kassák, "Egy generáció tragédiája," *Ma*, 8, 7–8 (1923), n.p.

26. Cited in Sibyl Moholy-Nagy, *Moholy-Nagy: Experiment in Totality* (Cambridge, Massachusetts: The M.I.T. Press, 1969), p. 12.

27. Gyula Juhász, *Összes művei*, 6, ed. László Péter (Budapest: Akadémiai Kiadó, 1969), pp. 260–61.

28. László Moholy-Nagy, *The New Vision* (New York: George Wittenborn, 1947), p. 68.

29. Ibid., p. 72.

30. Ibid.

31. Moholy-Nagy, "Vita az új tartalom és az új forma problemájáról," *Akasztott Ember*, December 20, 1922, p. 3.

32. Moholy-Nagy, *The New Vision*, p. 71.

33. I follow here Éva Forgács's introduction to Ernő Kállai, *Művészet veszélyes csillagzat alatt: Válogatott cikkek, tanulmányok*, ed. Éva Forgács (Budapest: Corvina Kiadó, 1981), especially p. 10.

34. Ernő Kállai, "Zur nachimpressionistischen Malerei in Ungarn," in Gassner, *Wechsel Wirkungen*, pp. 101–3.

35. Ernő Kállai, "Jungungarische Malerei," in ibid., pp. 103–4.

36. Péter Mátyás, "Moholy-Nagy," *Ma*, 6, 9 (1921), p. 119.

37. See Ildiko Hajnal-Neukäter, "Herwarth Walden und Lajos Kassák—ein Porträt," in Gassner, *Wechsel Wirkungen*, pp. 61–67.

38. Moholy-Nagy's letter to Iván Hevesy, April 5, 1920, in Krisztina Passuth, *Moholy-Nagy* (Budapest: Corvina, 1982), p. 360.

39. Péter Mátyás /Ernő Kállai/, "Új művészet, I," *Ma*, 6, 7 (1921), p. 99.

40. Ibid.

41. Cited in John E. Bowlt, "Art in Exile: The Russian Avant-Garde and the Emigration," *Art Journal*, 41, 3 (1981), p. 218.

42. Camilla Gray, *The Russian Experiment in Art, 1863–1922*, rev. Marian Burleigh-Motley (London: Thames and Hudson, 1986), p. 200.

43. Hughes, *The Shock of the New*, p. 89.

44. Cited in Gray, *The Russian Experiment in Art*, p. 255.

45. N. Punin, "Tatlin üvegtornya," *Ma*, 7, 5–6 (1922), p. 31.

46. Moholy-Nagy, *The New Vision*, p. 80.

47. Adolf Behne, "Művészet és forradalom," *Ma*, 6, 4 (1921), p. 44.

48. Hughes, *The Shock of the New*, pp. 175–77.

49. Behne, "Művészet és forradalom," p. 44.

50. Both cited in János Brendel, "Der deutsche Einfluss von Scheerbart und Wilhelm Ostwald auf die ungarische Konstruktivisten-theorie," in Gassner, *Wechsel Wirkungen*, pp. 173, 175.

51. Cited in Hughes, *The Shock of the New*, p. 177.

52. Cited in Sibyl Moholy-Nagy, *Moholy-Nagy*, p. 12.

53. Moholy-Nagy to Kassák, February 22, 1922, in Passuth, *Moholy-Nagy*, p. 361.

54. Béla Uitz, "Jegyzetek a *Ma* orosz estélyéhez," *Ma*, 6, 4 (1921), p. 52.

55. Lajos Kassák, "Képarchitektura," *Ma*, 7, 4 (1922), p. 53.

56. Ibid., p. 54.

57. Péter Mátyás /Ernő Kállai/, "Kassák Lajos," *Ma*, 7, 1 (1921), p. 139; "A kubizmus és a jövendő művészet," *Ma*, 7, 2 (1922), p. 31.

58. Introduction to Lajos Kassák and László Moholy-Nagy (eds.), *Új művészek könyve* (Budapest: Európa Könyvkiadó and Corvina Kiadó, 1977), n.p. This is a facsimile of the first edition: (Wien: Verlag Julius Fischer, 1922).

59. Ibid., and Kállai "A kubizmus és a jövendő művészet," p. 31.

60. Introduction to Kassák and Moholy-Nagy, *Új művészek könyve*, n.p.

61. Andreas Gáspár, "Die Bewegung der ungarischen Aktivisten," in Gassner, *Wechsel Wirkungen*, p. 34.

62. György Rónay, *Kassák Lajos* (Budapest: Szépirodalmi Könyvkiadó, 1971), p. 185.

63. Stephen Bann (ed.), *The Tradition of Constructivism* (London: Thames and Hudson 1974), p. 59.

64. Ibid., pp. 68–69.

65. I follow here the texts in ibid., pp. 63–64, and in "A haladó művészek első nemzetközi kongresszusa," *Ma*, 8, 8 (1922), p. 62.

66. Bann, *The Tradition of Constructivism*, p. 55.

67. Cited in Mildred Friedman's foreword to *De Stijl: 1917–1931: Visions of Utopia*, ed. Mildred Friedman (New York: Abbeville Press, 1982), p. 9.

68. Cited in ibid., p. 105.

69. Cited in Jane Beckett, "Dada, Van Doesburg and De Stijl," *Journal of European Studies*, 9, 33/34 (1979), p. 22.

70. Bann, *The Tradition of Constructivism*, pp. 109, 112.

71. Cited in Beckett, "Dada, Van Doesburg and De Stijl," p. 23. My translation from the French.

72. Cited in George Rickey, *Constructivism: Origins and Evolution* (New York: George Braziller, 1967), p. 36.

73. "A haladó művészek első nemzetközi kongresszusa," pp. 63–64.

74. László Moholy-Nagy, *Vision in Motion* (Chicago: Paul Theobald and Company, 1956), p. 315.

75. Bann, *The Tradition of Constructivism*, p. 71.

76. Lajos Kassák, "A berlini orosz kiállitáshoz," *Ma*, 8, 2–3 (1922), n.pp.

77. Cited in Alfred H. Barr, Jr., *Cubism and Abstract Art* (Cambridge: Harvard University Press, 1986), p. 60.

78. See Bann, *The Tradition of Constructivism*, pp. 3–11.

79. Kassák, "A berlini orosz kiállitáshoz," n.p.

80. Kállai, *Művészet veszélyes csillagzat alatt*, p. 71.

81. László Moholy-Nagy and Alfréd Kemény, "Dynamisch-konstruktives Kraftsystem," *Der Sturm*, 13 (1922), p. 186.

82. Alfréd Kemény, "Bortnyik képei és grafikája," *Ma*, 4, 7 (1919), pp. 172–74.

83. Alfréd Kemény, "Vorträge und Diskussionen am 'Institut für Künstlerische Kultur,'" in Gassner, *Wechsel Wirkungen*, pp. 226–30.

84. Alfréd Kemény, "Das dynamische Prinzip," *Der Sturm*, 14 (1923), p. 64.

85. Alfréd Kemény, "Bemerkungen zur Ausstellung der russischen Künstler in Berlin," in Gassner, *Wechsel Wirkungen*, p. 233.

86. Ernst Kállai, *Neue Malerei in Ungarn* (Leipzig: Klinkhardt & Biermann Verlag, 1925), p. 115.

87. László Moholy-Nagy et al., "Nyilatkozat," in Júlia Szabó, *A magyar aktivizmus művészete, 1915–1927* (Budapest: Corvina, 1981), p. 195.

88. Kállai, *Neue Malerei in Ungarn*, p. 116.

89. Ernő Kállai, "Korrekturát," *Ma*, 8, 9–10 (1923), n.p.

90. Ludwig Kassák, "F. T. Marinetti," *Ma*, 10, 1 (1925), n.p.

91. Lajos Kassák, *Az izmusok története* (Budapest: Magvető Könyvkiadó, 1972), p. 163.

92. Lajos Kassák, "Vissza a kaptafához," *Ma*, 9, 1 (1923), n.p.

93. John E. Bowlt, "The Art of Construction," in *Die 20er Jahre in Osteuropa* (Köln: Galerie Gmurzynska, n.d.), p. 15.

94. Lajos Kassák, *Éljünk a mi időnkben: Írások a képzőművészetről*, ed. Zsuzsa Ferencz (Budapest: Magvető Könyvkiadó, 1978), p. 70.

95. Ibid., p. 80.

96. Ibid., p. 85.

97. Ibid., p. 77; Kassák, *Az izmusok története*, pp. 11, 20–21; Barr, *Cubism and Abstract Art*, pp. 12–13.

98. Kassák, *Az izmusok története*, pp. 22–23; *Éljünk a mi időnkben*, pp. 86–87; "Rechenschaft," *Ma*, 8, 5–6 (1923), n.p.

99. Lajos Kassák, "Konstrukciótól a kompozicióig," *Ma*, 8, 9–10 (1923), n.p.

100. Kassák, "Vissza a kaptafához," n.p.

101. Kassák, *Éljünk a mi időnkben*, pp. 462–63.

102. Lajos Kassák, "A Tisztaság könyvéből," *Ma*, 9, 2 (1923), n.pp.

103. Ibid.

104. Kassák, *Az izmusok története*, p. 26.

105. Ibid; "A Tisztaság könyvéből," n.p.

106. See especially "49," in Lajos Kassák, "Versei," *Ma*, 9, 8–9 (1925), n.p.

107. Kassák, *Éljünk a mi időnkben*, pp. 94–96.

108. Ibid., pp. 102–4.

109. See Lajos Kassák, *A fal mögött áll és énekel* (Budapest: Magvető Könyvkiadó, 1974), pp. 401–20.

CHAPTER FOUR
THE BAUHAUS

1. Kassák, *Éljünk a mi időnkben*, pp. 462–63, 465.

2. Gillian Naylor, *The Bauhaus Reassessed* (New York: E. P. Dutton, 1985), pp. 40, 43.

3. Ida Katherine Rigby, *An alle Künstler! War—Revolution—Weimar* (San Diego: San Diego State University Press, 1983), p. 69; Helga Kliemann, *Die Novembergruppe* (Berlin: Gebr. Mann Verlag, 1969), p. 48.

4. Cited in Rigby, *An alle Künstler!*, p. 78.

5. Kliemann, *Die Novembergruppe*, p. 14.

6. Walter Gropius, *The New Architecture and the Bauhaus* (Cambridge, Massachusetts: The M.I.T. Press, 1965), p. 52.

7. Hans M. Wingler (ed.), *The Bauhaus: Weimar, Dessau, Berlin, Chicago* (Cambridge, Massachusetts: The M.I.T. Press, 1969), p. 31. My translation from the German on accompanying plates.

8. Ibid.

9. Cited in Marcel Franciscono, *Walter Gropius and the Creation of the Bauhaus in Weimar: The Ideals and Artistic Theories of Its Founding Years* (Urbana: University of Illinois Press, 1971), p. 148n. My translation from the German.

10. Cited in Naylor, *The Bauhaus Reassessed*, p. 76.

11. Cited in ibid., p. 94.

12. Ibid., p. 95; Wingler, *The Bauhaus*, p. 5.

13. Cited in Frank Whitford, *Bauhaus* (London: Thames and Hudson, 1984), p. 120.

14. Walter Gropius, Ise Gropius, and Herbert Bayer (eds.), *Bauhaus, 1919–1928* (New York: The Museum of Modern Art, 1938), p. 25.

15. Gropius in Moholy-Nagy, *The New Vision*, p. 5.

16. Ibid., p. 68n.

17. In Andreas Haus, *Moholy-Nagy: Fotos und Fotogramme* (München: Schirmer/Mosel, 1978), p. 78.

18. Moholy-Nagy, *The New Vision*, p. 76.

19. Rainer Wick, "László Moholy-Nagy als Kunstpädagoge," in Gassner, *Wechsel Wirkungen*, pp. 278–79.

20. Feininger to Julia Feininger, March 9, 1925, in Wingler, *The Bauhaus*, p. 97.

21. Ibid.

22. Passuth, *Moholy-Nagy*, p. 44.

23. See Leslie C. Tihany, "The Baranya Republic and the Treaty of Trianon," in Béla K. Király, Peter Pastor, and Ivan Sanders (eds.), *Total War and Peacemaking: A Case Study on Trianon* (Brooklyn: Brooklyn College Press, 1982), pp. 297–98, 313.

24. Éva Bajkay-Rosch, "Die KURI-Gruppe," in Gassner, *Wechsel Wirkungen*, p. 261.

25. Kurt Schmidt, "Der Vorkurs von Johannes Itten und die Kuris am Bauhaus," in Gassner, *Wechsel Wirkungen*, p. 268.

26. Farkas Molnár, "KURI Manifest," in Gassner, *Wechsel Wirkungen*, pp. 266–68.

27. Schmidt, "Der Vorkurs von Johannes Itten und die Kuris am Bauhaus," p. 269.

28. See Otto Mezei, "Ungarische Architekten am Bauhaus," in Gassner, *Wechsel Wirkungen*, pp. 342–44.

29. Oskar Schlemmer, László Moholy-Nagy, and Farkas Molnár, *Die Bühne im Bauhaus* (Mainz: Florian Kupferberg Verlag, 1965), pp. 57–62.

30. Farkas Molnár, "A mechanikus színpad," *Ma*, 8, 9–10 (1923), n.p.

31. Schlemmer et al., *Die Bühne im Bauhaus*, pp. 15–17.

32. Ludwig Kassák, "Über neue Theaterkunst," *Ma*, 9, 8–9 (1924), n.p.

33. Herwarth Walden, "Das Theater als künstlerisches Phänomen," *Ma*, 9, 8–9 (1924), n.p.

34. Schlemmer et al., *Die Bühne im Bauhaus*, pp. 46–47.

35. Ibid., pp. 49–50, 54, 56.

36. László Moholy-Nagy, *Malerei, Fotografie, Film* (Mainz: Florian Kupferberg Verlag, 1967), p. 11.

37. Ibid., pp. 21–22, 27–28.

38. Ibid., p. 21.

39. Franz Roh in Richard Kostelanetz (ed.), *Moholy-Nagy* (New York: Praeger Publishers, 1970), p. 49.

40. Cited in Joseph Harris Caton, *The Utopian Vision of Moholy-Nagy: Technology, Society, and the Avant-Garde. An Analysis of the Writings of Moholy-Nagy on the Visual Arts.* Dissertation, Princeton University, 1980.

41. Moholy-Nagy, *Malerei, Fotografie, Film*, p. 121.

42. In Uwe M. Schneede (ed.), *Die zwanziger Jahre: Manifeste und Dokumente deutscher Künstler* (Köln: DuMont Buchverlag, 1979), p. 265.

43. Fréd Forbát, "Erinnerungen," in Gassner, *Wechsel Wirkungen*, p. 347.

44. Hubertus Gassner, "Zwischen den Stühlen sitzend sich im Kreise drehen," in Gassner, *Wechsel Wirkungen*, p. 326.

45. Gropius, et al., *Bauhaus, 1919–1928*, p. 126; Naylor, *The Bauhaus Reassessed*, p. 151.

46. Moholy-Nagy, *The New Vision*, p. 75.

47. L. Moholy-Nagy, "fotografie ist lichtgestaltung," *bauhaus*, 2, 1 (1928), p. 2.

48. Ibid.

49. Ibid., p. 7.

50. Ibid., pp. 8–9.

51. In Beaumont Newhall, *The History of Photography* (New York: The Museum of Modern Art, 1982), p. 201.

52. Van Deren Coke, *Avant-Garde Photography in Germany, 1919–1939* (New York: Pantheon Books, 1982), pp. 10–11.

53. László Moholy-Nagy, "Das beispiellose Fotographie," in Schneede, *Die zwanziger Jahre*, p. 245.

54. Newhall, *The History of Photography*, p. 192.

55. Ernő Kállai, "Die Welt ist schön!" in Gassner, *Wechsel Wirkungen*, p. 496.

56. Ernst Kállai, "Painting and Photography," in Harvey L. Mendelsohn (ed.), *Bauhaus Photography* (Cambridge, Massachusetts: The M.I.T. Press, 1985), p. 132.

57. Ibid.

58. László Moholy-Nagy in ibid., p. 136.

59. Andrea Kaliski Miller, "Films," in Eleanor M. Hight et al., *Moholy-Nagy: Photography and Film in Weimar Germany* (Wellesley: Wellesley College Museum, 1985), p. 122.

60. László Moholy-Nagy, "Light Display, Black and White and Gray," in Kostelanetz, *Moholy-Nagy*, p. 150.

61. Passuth, *Moholy-Nagy*, p. 56.

62. Sibyl Moholy-Nagy, *Moholy-Nagy*, p. 64.

63. Cited in Diane Kirkpatrick, "Light in the Work of László Moholy-Nagy," *Cross Currents*, 7 (1988), p. 301.

64. Moholy-Nagy, *The New Vision*, pp. 80, 83.

65. Reyner Banham, *Theory and Design in the First Machine Age*, second ed. (New York: Praeger, 1967), p. 285.

66. László Moholy-Nagy, *von material zu architektur* (Mainz: Florian Kupferberg Verlag, 1968), p. 166.

67. Ibid., p. 188.

68. Ibid., pp. 10–11.

69. Ibid., pp. 14, 16.

70. Ibid., p. 73.

71. Cited in Sibyl Moholy-Nagy, Moholy-Nagy, p. 46.

72. Cited in Whitford, Bauhaus, p. 185.

73. Cited in Naylor, The Bauhaus Reassessed, p. 143.

74. Ernst Kállai, "das bauhaus lebt!," bauhaus, 2, 2/3 (1928), pp. 1–2.

75. Ernst Kállai, "ein bild, ein mensch," bauhaus, 2, 2/3 (1928), p. 30.

76. Hannes Meyer, "bauhaus und gesellschaft," bauhaus, 3, 1 (1929), p. 2.

77. Ibid.

78. Ernst Kállai, "wir leben nicht, um zu wohnen," bauhaus, 3, 1 (1929), p. 10; "forgó pál: új építészet," bauhaus, 2, 4 (1928), p. 27.

79. Wingler, The Bauhaus, pp. 163–65.

80. Cited in Whitford, Bauhaus, p. 191.

81. See Ernst Kállai, "Grenzen der Technik," Die Weltbühne, 27 (1931), pp. 503–5; "Kunst und Technik," Sozialistische Monatshefte, 37 (1931), p. 1102.

82. See Ernst Kállai, "Burgfriede in der Kunst," Die Weltbühne, 26 (1930), pp. 463–65.

83. Ernst Kállai, "Malerei und Film," Die Weltbühne, 27 (1931), pp. 805–7.

84. Kállai, Művészet veszélyes csillagzat alatt, pp. 151–52.

85. C. G. Jung, Modern Man in Search of a Soul, trans. W. S. Dell and Cary F. Baynes (New York: Harcourt, Brace and World, 1933), p. 186.

86. Kállai, "Kunst und Technik," p. 1103.

87. See Kállai, Művészet veszélyes csillagzat alatt, p. 148; "Malerei und Film," p. 808.

88. Ernst Kállai, "Kunst und Wirklichkeit," Sozialistische Monatshefte, 37 (1931), p. 1005.

89. Kállai, Művészet veszélyes csillagzat alatt, pp. 148, 151.

90. Moholy-Nagy, von material zu architektur, pp. 215–19.

91. Cited in Kostelanetz, Moholy-Nagy, p. 95.

92. Cited in Bernd Vogelsang, "Erläuterungen zur Bühnenausstattung von Moholy-Nagy für die Inszenierung von 'Hoffmanns Erzählungen' in der Kroll-Oper, Berlin 1929," in Gassner, Wechsel Wirkungen, p. 447.

93. Sibyl Moholy-Nagy, Moholy-Nagy, p. 51.

94. Cited in Caton, The Utopian Vision of Moholy-Nagy, p. 178.

95. Kostelanetz, Moholy-Nagy, p. 96.

96. Sibyl Moholy-Nagy, Moholy-Nagy, p. 74.

97. Ibid., p. 89.

98. Andreas Haus, "Die Präsenz des Materials—Ungarische Fotografen aus dem Bauhaus-Kreis," in Gassner, Wechsel Wirkungen, p. 482.

99. Pius Pahl, student at the Berlin Bauhaus, cited in Whitford, Bauhaus, p. 196.

CHAPTER FIVE
THE PATH TO ROME

1. Erzsébet Vezér, Lesznai Anna élete (Budapest: Kossuth Könyvkiadó, 1979), pp. 80–81.

2. Cited in György Litván, "Documents of a Friendship: From the Correspondence of Michael Károlyi and Oscar Jászi," East Central Europe, 4, 2 (1977), p. 123.

3. Cited in Lee Congdon, "Trianon and the Emigré Intellectuals," in Király et al., *Total War and Peacemaking*, p. 392.

4. Both cited in ibid., p. 393.

5. Cited in Vezér, *Lesznai Anna élete*, pp. 81–82.

6. Litván, "Documents of a Friendship," p. 130.

7. Oszkár Jászi, "Az elgáncsolt megváltás," *Századvég*, no. 1 (1985), pp. 149–54.

8. Oszkár Jászi, "Keresztény szocializmus és szocialista kereszténység," *Századvég*, no. 1 (1985), pp. 154–59.

9. "A kiadó jegyzete," in Oszkár Jászi, *Marxizmus, vagy liberális szocializmus*, ed. Péter Kende (Malakoff: Dialogues Européens, 1983), p. 138.

10. Ibid., pp. 55, 82.

11. Ibid., pp. 40–42.

12. Ibid., pp. 71, 137.

13. Ibid., pp. 119–21.

14. Oszkár Jászi, "A nyugati kultura pusztulásának filozófusa Oswald Spengler megmérése," *Századvég*, no. 1 (1985), pp. 196–201.

15. Péter Hanák, *Jászi Oszkár dunai patriotizmusa* (Budapest: Magvető Könyvkiadó, 1985), p. 108.

16. Ilona Duczynska, "Önéletrajza," *Kritika*, no. 8 (1978), p. 21.

17. Balázs, *Napló*, p. 452.

18. Károly Polányi, *A radikalizmus programmja és célja* (Szeged: A Szegedi Polgári Radikális Párt, n.d.), p. 11.

19. Zoltán Horváth (ed.), "A Galilei Körre vonatkozó ismeretlen dokumentumok," *Századok*, 105, 1 (1971), pp. 96–98.

20. Károly Polányi, "Előadása 1919. április 28-án a kereskedelem szocializálásáról," *Magyar Filozófiai Szemle*, 23, 5 (1979), pp. 717–19, 721–23.

21. Polányi's letter to Kári Polányi-Levitt, cited in Károly Polányi, *Fasizmus, demokrácia, ipari társadalom: Társadalomfilozófiai írások*, ed. Kári Polányi-Levitt and Marguerite Mendell (Budapest: Gondolat, 1986), pp. 18–19.

22. Karl Polanyi, "Hamlet," *The Yale Review*, 43, 3 (1954), p. 339.

23. Horváth, "A Galilei Körre vonatkozó ismeretlen dokumentumok," p. 100.

24. Polányi's letter to Jászi, January 7, 1920, cited by János Gyurgyák in Gyurgyák (ed.), *Polányi Károly, 1886–1964* (Budapest: Fővárosi Szabó Ervin Könyvtár, 1986), p. 34.

25. Ilona Duczynska, "Zum Zerfall der K.P.U.," *Unser Weg*, March 1, 1922, pp. 97–105.

26. Jászi, *Marxizmus, vagy liberális szocializmus*, p. 147.

27. Károly Polányi, *Egy gazdaságelmélet küszöbén: Cikkek a Bécsi Magyar Újságban, 1921–1923*, ed. János Gyurgyák (Budapest: Az Eötvös Loránd Tudományegyetem, 1985), pp. 109–10, 398.

28. Polányi's letter to Michael Polányi, 1923. Michael Polányi Papers.

29. G.D.H. Cole, *Social Theory* (London: Methuen and Co., 1920), pp. 146, 154.

30. G.D.H. Cole, *The Second International, 1889–1914*, 1 (London: Macmillan and Co., 1956), p. 246.

31. Cole, *Social Theory*, p. 29.

32. Ibid., p. 83.

33. G.D.H. Cole, *Guild Socialism Restated* (New Brunswick: Transaction Books, 1980), p. 125.

34. Ibid., p. 47.

35. János Gyurgyák (ed.), "Polányi Károly a Bécsi Magyar Újságnál," *Medvetánc*, nos. 2–3 (1981), pp. 191–92.

36. Ibid., p. 187.

37. Karl Polanyi, *The Great Transformation: The Political and Economic Origins of Our Time* (Boston: Beacon Press, 1957), p. 258A.

38. p./olányi/, k./ároly/, "Az ó-testamentomi kinyilatkoztatás . . . ," *Szabadgondolat*, 3, 3 (1913), p. 99.

39. Gyurgyák, "Polányi Károly a Bécsi Magyar Újságnál," pp. 199–200.

40. Karl Polányi, "Sozialistische Rechnungslegung," *Archiv für Sozialwissenschaft und Sozialpolitik*, 49 (1922), pp. 382, 416.

41. Ibid., pp. 385, 388, 414.

42. Ibid., pp. 397, 403, 416.

43. Ibid., pp. 403, 403n, 404, 404n, 405.

44. Ibid., pp. 408–9, 417.

45. Cited in the introduction to Polányi, *Fasizmus, demokrácia, ipari társadalom*, p. 27.

46. Ludwig Mises, "Neue Beiträge zum Problem der sozialistischen Wirtschaftsrechnung," *Archiv für Sozialwissenschaft und Sozialpolitik*, 51 (1924), pp. 488–500.

47. Ludwig von Mises, *Die Gemeinwirtschaft: Untersuchungen über den Sozialismus* (München: Philosophia Verlag, 1981), pp. 245–46.

48. See Felix Weil, "Gildensozialistische Rechnungslegung: Kritische Bemerkungen zu Karl Polányi: 'Sozialistische Rechnungslegung,'" *Archiv für Sozialwissenschaft und Sozialpolitik*, 52 (1924), pp. 203, 213.

49. Ibid., pp. 213n, 214, 216–17.

50. Cole, *Social Theory*, p. 145.

51. Karl Polányi, "Die funktionelle Theorie der Gesellschaft und das Problem der sozialistischen Rechnungslegung (Eine Erwiderung an Prof. Mises und Dr. Felix Weil)," *Archiv für Sozialwissenschaft und Sozialpolitik*, 52 (1924), p. 226.

52. Ibid., pp. 224–25.

53. F. A. Hayek (ed.), *Collectivist Economic Planning* (London: Routledge and Kegan Paul, 1935), p. 38.

54. Karl Polanyi, *Primitive, Archaic and Modern Economies: Essays*, ed. George Dalton (Garden City, New York: Anchor Books, 1968), p. 65.

55. Hans Zeisel, "Polanyi, Karl," *International Encyclopedia of the Social Sciences*, 12 (New York: The Macmillan Company and The Free Press, 1968), p. 172.

56. Polanyi, *The Great Transformation*, pp. 286–87.

57. Peter F. Drucker, *Adventures of a Bystander* (New York: Harper and Row, 1978), p. 126.

58. Cited in Charles A. Gulick, *Austria from Habsburg to Hitler*, 1 (Berkeley: University of California Press, 1948), p. 108.

59. Cited in ibid., p. 366.

60. Cited in Ernst Glaser, *Im Umfeld des Austromarxismus* (Wien: Europaverlag, 1981), p. 137. See also Peter Csendes, *Geschichte Wiens* (München: R. Oldenbourg Verlag, 1981), p. 147.

61. Hayek, *Collectivist Economic Planning*, pp. 30, 291.

62. Mises, *Die Gemeinwirtschaft*, p. 90.

63. Ibid., pp. 98, 111.

64. Polányi to Michael Polányi, May 20, 1924. Michael Polányi Papers.

65. Walther Federn (ed.), *Sonderausgabe zur Zwanzigjahrfeier des "Österreichischen Volkswirts"* (Wien: Verlag "Der Österreichische Volkswirt", 1928), p. 20; Drucker, *Adventures of a Bystander*, p. 124.

66. Karl Polanyi, "Liberale Wirtschaftsreformen in England," *Der Österreichische Volkswirt*, 20, 1 (1928), p. 544.

67. John Maynard Keynes, *Essays in Persuasion* (New York: W. W. Norton and Company, 1963), p. 319.

68. Karl Polanyi, "Probleme des englischen Generalstreiks," *Der Österreichische Volkswirt*, 18, 2 (1926), p. 974.

69. Karl Polanyi, "Die neue Internationale," *Der Österreichische Volkswirt*, 17, 2 (1925), p. 1379.

70. Polányi to Michael Polányi, November 21, 1932. Michael Polányi Papers; Keynes, *Essays in Persuasion*, p. 321.

71. Karl Polanyi, "Wirtschaft und Demokratie," *Der Österreichische Volkswirt*, 25, 1 (1933), p. 301.

72. Ibid.

73. Ibid., pp. 302–3.

74. See Polányi to Michael Polányi, September 30, 1933, and to Irene Grant, October 13, 1933. Michael Polányi Papers.

75. Ilona Duczynska, "Polányi Károly (1886–1964)," *Századok*, 105, 1 (1971), p. 94.

76. Duczynska, "Önéletrajza," p. 21.

77. Aurel Kolnai, *Twentieth-Century Memoirs*, unpublished manuscript, chapter 3, p. 33.

78. Ibid., chapter 2, p. 42.

79. Aurel Kolnai, "Chesterton and Catholicism: Excerpts from *Twentieth-Century Memoirs*," *The Chesterton Review*, 8, 2 (1982), p. 136.

80. Kolnai, *Twentieth-Century Memoirs*, chapter 3, p. 13.

81. See Helmut Dahmer, *Libido und Gesellschaft: Studien über Freud und die Freudsche Linke* (Frankfurt am Main: Suhrkamp Verlag, 1973), pp. 279–82; Johannes Reichmayr and Elisabeth Wiesbauer, "Das Verhältnis von Sozialdemokratie und Psychoanalyse in Österreich zwischen 1900 und 1938," in Wolfgang Huber (ed.), *Beiträge zur Geschichte der Psychoanalyse in Österreich* (Wien: Geyer-Edition, 1978), pp. 39–40.

82. Kolnai, *Twentieth-Century Memoirs*, chapter 3, p. 34.

83. Aurel Kolnai, *Psychoanalyse und Soziologie: Zur Psychologie von Masse und Gesellschaft* (Leipzig: Internationaler Psychoanalytischer Verlag, 1920), p. 89.

84. Ibid., pp. 106–7, 115–18, 130, 149.

85. Theodor Reik, "Internationale Psychoanalytische Bibliothek," *Imago*, 7, 2 (1921), p. 196.

86. Dahmer, *Libido und Gesellschaft*, p. 290; See also Martin A. Miller, "Freudian Theory Under Bolshevik Rule: The Theoretical Controversy During the 1920s," *Slavic Review*, 44, 4 (1985), p. 633.

87. Kolnai, "Chesterton and Catholicism," p. 139.

88. Kolnai, *Twentieth-Century Memoirs*, chapter 6, pp. 3, 32.

89. Max Scheler, *Formalism in Ethics and Non-Formal Ethics of Values*, trans. Manfred S. Frings and Roger L. Funk (Evanston: Northwestern University Press, 1973), p. 254.

90. Ibid., p. 304.

91. See Max Scheler, *The Nature of Sympathy*, trans. Peter Heath (Hamden, Connecticut: Archon Books, 1970), pp. 196–209.

92. Ibid., p. 206.

93. Aurel Kolnai, "Max Schelers Kritik und Würdigung der Freudschen Libidolehre," *Imago*, 11, 1/2 (1925), pp. 144–45.

94. Kolnai, "Chesterton and Catholicism," p. 154.

95. Aurel Kolnai, *Der ethische Wert und die Wirklichkeit* (Freiburg im Breisgau: Herder & Co. G.M.B.H. Verlagsbuchhandlung, 1927), pp. 30, 47.

96. Gilbert K. Chesterton, *Orthodoxy* (Garden City, New York: Image Books, 1959), pp. 66, 74.

97. Kolnai, *Der ethische Wert und die Wirklichkeit*, pp. 77–79, 138.

98. Ibid., pp. 141–42.

99. Chesterton, *Orthodoxy*, p. 131.

100. Kolnai, "Chesterton and Catholicism," pp. 157–58.

101. Kolnai, *Der ethische Wert und die Wirklichkeit*, pp. 101–5.

102. Kolnai, "Chesterton and Catholicism," p. 160.

103. Aurel Kolnai, *Sexualethik: Sinn und Grundlagen der Geschlechtsmoral* (Paderborn: Ferdinand Schöningh Verlag, 1930), pp. 12, 32, 34, 46, 338.

104. Ibid., pp. 58–59, 66–67.

105. Ibid., pp. 369, 371.

106. Ibid., pp. 93, 168.

107. Ibid., p. 436.

108. Gilbert K. Chesterton, *What's Wrong With the World* (New York: Dodd, Mead and Company, 1910), p. 97.

109. Kolnai, *Twentieth-Century Memoirs*, chapter 6, pp. 33–34.

110. Wolfgang Huber, "Katholiken und Psychoanalyse in Österreich bis zum Ständestaat," in Huber, *Beiträge zur Geschichte der Psychoanalyse in Österreich*, pp. 70–71.

111. Sigmund Freud, *The Future of an Illusion*, trans. James Strachey (New York: W. W. Norton and Company, 1961), p. 41.

112. Ibid., p. 43.

113. Aurel Kolnai, "Eine Illusion der Zukunft," *Volkswohl*, 19, 2 (1928), pp. 53–56.

114. Thomas Mann, *Past Masters and Other Papers*, trans. H. T. Lowe-Porter (New York: Alfred A. Knopf, 1933), p. 191.

115. Aurel Kolnai, "Thomas Mann, Freud und der Fortschritt," *Volkswohl*, 20, 9 (1929), pp. 326–27.

116. Aurel Kolnai, "Fascismus und Bolschewismus," *Der Deutsche Volkswirt*, 1, 7 (1926), p. 213.

117. Kolnai, *Twentieth-Century Memoirs*, chapter 2, p. 34.

118. Helene Duczynska-Polanyi, "Fascismus und Miliz," *Der Deutsche Volkswirt*, 1, 19 (1927), pp. 572–73.

119. Conversation with Kári Polányi-Levitt in Budapest, October 1986.

120. Aurel Kolnai, "René Fülöp-Miller: Geist und Gesicht des Bolschewismus," *Das Neue Reich*, 9, 38 (1927), p. 794; see also "Die Ideologie des sozialen Fortschritts," *Der Deutsche Volkswirt*, 1, 30 (1927), pp. 933–36, and "Kritik des sozialen Fortschritts," *Der Deutsche Volkswirt*, 1, 31 (1927), pp. 965–69.

121. Aurel Kolnai, "Gegenrevolution," *Kölner Vierteljahrshefte für Soziologie*, 10, 2 (1931), p. 172.

122. Ibid., 10, 3 (1932), p. 299.

123. Ibid., 10, 2 (1931), pp. 187, 189; 10, 3 (1932), p. 312.

124. Cited in Alfred Diamant, *Austrian Catholics and the First Republic: Democracy, Capitalism, and the Social Order, 1918–1934* (Princeton: Princeton University Press, 1960), p. 132.

125. Cited in ibid., p. 136.

126. Aurel Kolnai, "Ist O. Spanns 'Universalismus' mit katholischem Denken vereinbar?," *Volkswohl*, 20, 3 (1929), pp. 81–85, 126–31.

127. Aurel Kolnai, "Katholizismus und Demokratie," *Der Österreichische Volkswirt*, 26, 1 (1933–34), pp. 319–20.

128. Karl Polanyi, "The Essence of Fascism," in John Lewis, Karl Polanyi, and Donald K. Kitchin (eds.), *Christianity and the Social Revolution* (Freeport: Books for Libraries Press, 1972), pp. 368–69.

129. Ibid., pp. 370, 390.

130. Cited in Diamant, *Austrian Catholics and the First Republic*, p. 177.

131. Klemens von Klemperer, *Ignaz Seipel: Christian Statesman in a Time of Crisis* (Princeton: Princeton University Press, 1972), p. 363.

132. Aurel Kolnai, "Das Seipel-Bild," *Der Österreichische Volkswirt*, 24, 2 (1932), p. 1102.

133. Cited in Diamant, *Austrian Catholics and the First Republic*, p. 194.

134. Aurel Kolnai, "Die Ideologie des Ständestaates," *Der Kampf*, 27, 1 (1934), pp. 13–14, 21.

135. Kolnai, *Twentieth-Century Memoirs*, chapter 6, pp. 37–38.

136. See P. Georg Bichlmair, S. J., *Das proletarische Freidenkertum* (Wien: Der Seelsorger, 1925).

137. Josef Aussermair, *Kirche und Sozialdemokratie: Der Bund der religiösen Sozialisten, 1926–1934* (Wien: Europaverlag, 1979), p. 40.

138. Aurel Kolnai, "Das Weihnachtsmanifest der österreichischen Bischöfe," *Der Österreichische Volkswirt*, 18, 1 (1925–26), p. 392.

139. Aurel Kolnai, "Religiöse Sozialisten," *Der Österreichische Volkswirt*, 21, 1 (1928–29), p. 190.

140. Cited in Aussermair, *Kirche und Sozialdemokratie*, p. 70.

141. See ibid., pp. 205, 207, 210–12, 214.

142. Cited in Diamant, *Austrian Catholics and the First Republic*, p. 181n.

143. Kolnai, "Die Ideologie des Ständestaates," pp. 14, 20; "Quadragesimo anno," *Der Österreichische Volkswirt*, 23, 2 (1931), p. 892.

144. Kolnai, "Chesterton and Catholicism," p. 140.

145. Kolnai, *Twentieth-Century Memoirs*, chapter 6, p. 37.

146. Aurel Kolnai, "Die Aufgabe des Konservativismus," *Der Österreichische Volkswirt*, 26, 2 (1934), p. 946.

147. Kolnai, "Chesterton and Catholicism," p. 136.

148. Kolnai, "Das Weihnachtsmanifest der österreichischen Bischöfe," p. 390.

149. See Aurel Kolnai, "Autorität und Demokratie," *Volkswohl*, 20, 10 (1929), p. 364; "Tote und lebendige Demokratie," *Der Deutsche Volkswirt*, 2, 26 (1928), p. 855; "Persönlichkeit und Massenherrschaft," *Der Österreichische Volkswirt*, 26, 1 (1933–34), pp. 442–43.

150. Kolnai, "Das Weihnachtsmanifest der österreichischen Bischöfe," p. 392.

151. Hilaire Belloc, *The Servile State* (New York: Henry Holt and Company, 1946), p. 49.

152. Ibid., pp. 105–6.

153. Aurel Kolnai, "Bellocs Vision vom Sklavenstaat," *Schönere Zukunft*, November 1928, p. 117.

154. Chesterton, *What's Wrong With the World*, pp. 58–59.

155. Kolnai, "Chesterton and Catholicism," p. 137.

156. Aurel Kolnai, "Die christlichen Gewerkschaften im Kampfe gegen den Kapitalismus," *Volkswohl*, 20, 11 (1929), p. 410.

157. Aurel Kolnai, "Chestertons Religionsphilosophie," *Das Neue Reich*, 9, 40 (1927), p. 823.

CHAPTER SIX
THE SOCIOLOGY OF KNOWLEDGE

1. Oszkár Jászi, "Szende Pál, az ember, a munkás és a harcos," *Századunk*, 9 (1934), p. 313.

2. Lesznai, *Kezdetben volt a kert*, 2, p. 336.

3. See Jászi, "Szende Pál, az ember, a munkás és a harcos."

4. Ady, *Összes versei*, pp. 670, 673.

5. Cited in Géza Szabó, "Adalékok Szende Pál adópolitikájához," *Acta Academiae Paedagogicae Nyíregyháziensis*, 5 (1973), 51n.

6. See István Werbőczy, *Hármaskönyve*, trans. Sándor Kolosvári and Kelemen Ovári (Budapest: Franklin-Társulat, 1897), p. 55.

7. Vilmos Fraknói, *Werbőczi István életrajza* (Budapest: A Magyar Történelmi Társulat Kiadása, 1899), p. 348.

8. Pál Szende, "Werbőczi," *Huszadik Század*, 8, 10 (1907), p. 831.

9. Ibid., pp. 834–36.

10. Cited in János Gyurgyák (ed.), *Szende Pál, 1879–1934* (Budapest: Fővárosi Szabó Ervin Könyvtár, 1985), p. 27.

11. Pál Szende, "A polgári radikálizmus," *Világ*, 9, 42 (1918), p. 1.

12. Gusztáv Gratz, *A forradalmak kora: Magyarország története, 1918–1920* (Budapest: Magyar Szemle Társaság, 1935), p. 10.

13. Cited in Tibor Hajdu, *Az 1918-as magyarországi polgári demokratikus forradalom* (Budapest: Kossuth Könyvkiadó, 1968), p. 371.

14. Béla Halasi, "Emlékezés Szende Pálról," *Századunk*, 9, 8–9 (1934), p. 329.

15. Paul Szende, "Oscar Jászi, *Magyar kálvária. Magyar feltámadás*," *Archiv für die Geschichte des Sozialismus und der Arbeiterbewegung*, 10 (1922), p. 104; "Die Krise der mitteleuropäischen Revolution. Ein massenpsychologischer Versuch," *Archiv für Sozialwissenschaft und Sozialpolitik*, 47 (1920/1921), pp. 357, 360, 367.

16. Jászi, "Szende Pál, az ember, a munkás és a harcos," p. 319.

17. Paul Szende, "Zur Soziologie der Revolution," *Der Kampf*, 16, 9/10 (1923), pp. 333–34.

18. Paul Szende, "Robert Michels. Zur Soziologie des Parteiwesens in der modernen Demokratie," *Der Kampf*, 19, 2 (1926), p. 90.

19. See Paul Szende, "Philosophie und soziales Leben," *Der Kampf*, 23, 6/7 (1930), pp. 296–300.

20. István Varró, "Szende Pál. 1879–1934," Századunk, 9, 8–9 (1934), p. 341; Artur Székely, "Szende Pál emlékezete," A Kereskedelmi Élet, no. 44 (1947), p. 5.

21. Paul Szende, "Der Faschismus in Europa," Der Kampf, 22, 4 (1929), p. 200.

22. Paul Szende, "Bergson, der Metaphysiker der Gegenrevolution," Die Gesellschaft (1930), 2, pp. 552, 558, 564–65.

23. Ibid., p. 566.

24. Ibid.; Paul Szende, "Das Zeitalter der Denkfaulheit," Der Kampf, 26, 11 (1933), pp. 453–55.

25. Paul Szende, Mystik, ed. Fritz Guttmann (Wien: Thalia, 1936), p. 10.

26. Ibid., pp. 17–18, 23.

27. Ibid., pp. 57, 62, 64.

28. Louis Eisenmann, "Souvenirs," Századunk, 9, 8–9 (1934), pp. 323–24.

29. Cited in Gyurgyák, Szende Pál, p. 43.

30. Horváth, Irodalom és történelem, p. 32; Emil Goldmann, "Szende, der Polyhistor," Századunk, 9, 8–9 (1934), p. 324.

31. Cited in Paul Johnson, Modern Times: The World from the Twenties to the Eighties (New York: Harper and Row, 1983), p. 3.

32. Paul Szende, "Soziologische Gedanken zur Relativitätstheorie," Die neue Rundschau, 2 (1921), p. 1093.

33. Ibid., pp. 1089–91; "Az Einstein-féle elmélet történeti jelentősége," Nyugat, 15, 2 (1922), p. 121.

34. Paul Szende, Demaskierung: Die Rolle der Ideologien in der Geschichte (Wien: Europa Verlag, 1970), pp. 17–18.

35. Here I follow Demaskierung, a republication, in book form, of the original article.

36. Szende, Demaskierung, p. 21.

37. Cited in George Lichtheim, The Concept of Ideology and Other Essays (New York: Vintage Books, 1967), p. 9.

38. See Gunter W. Remmling, Road to Suspicion: A Study of Modern Mentality and the Sociology of Knowledge (New York: Appleton-Century-Crofts, 1967).

39. Szende, Demaskierung, pp. 22, 43, 93.

40. Ibid., pp. 36, 56–58; see also Paul Szende, "Das System der Wissenschaften und die Gesellschaftsordnung," Kölner Vierteljahrshefte für Sozialwissenschaften, 2, 4 (1922), p. 7.

41. Szende, Demaskierung, p. 71.

42. Paul Szende, "Wissenschaft und Autorität," Der Kampf, 15, 9/10 (1922), p. 302.

43. Szende, Demaskierung, p. 69.

44. Ibid., p. 84.

45. Ibid., pp. 53–54, 75, 89, 91.

46. Ibid., pp. 95, 102.

47. Ibid., p. 96.

48. Ibid., pp. 98–99.

49. Paul Szende, "Eine soziologische Theorie der Abstraktion," Archiv für Sozialwissenschaft und Sozialpolitik, 50 (1923), pp. 424, 469.

50. Achille Ouy, "Paul Szende," Revue Internationale de Sociologie, 1925, p. 79.

51. Arthur Child, "The Theoretical Possibility of the Sociology of Knowledge," Ethics, 51, 4 (1941), pp. 411, 413, 415.

52. Joseph Gabel, "Hungarian Marxism," Telos, no. 25 (1975), p. 188n.

53. See Szende, "Eine soziologische Theorie der Abstraktion," p. 462.

54. Cited in Lee Congdon, "Karl Mannheim as Philosopher," *Journal of European Studies*, 7, 1 (1977), p. 12.

55. Cited in Éva Gábor, "Mannheim Károly a két világháború között," in István Hermann et al. (eds.), *A magyar filozófiai gondolkodás a két világháború között* (Budapest: Kossuth Könyvkiadó, 1983), p. 83.

56. Mannheim's Diary, cited in Mátyás Sárközi, "The Influence of Georg Lukács on the Young Karl Mannheim in the Light of a Newly Discovered Diary," *The Slavonic and East European Review*, 64, 3 (1986), p. 438.

57. Karl Mannheim, *Die Dame aus Biarritz. Ein Spiel in vier Szenen*, 1920. MTA Kézirattár, Ms. 5084/72–85.

58. Cited in Congdon, "Karl Mannheim as Philosopher," p. 6.

59. Mannheim, *Lélek és kultura*, p. 10.

60. Cited in Congdon, *The Young Lukács*, p. 124.

61. Mannheim, *Lélek és kultura*, p. 24.

62. Cited in Congdon, "Karl Mannheim as Philosopher," p. 6.

63. Kecskemeti married Erzsébet Láng, Júlia's sister; he was close to Mannheim.

64. Paul Kecskemeti, "Introduction," in Karl Mannheim, *Essays on the Sociology of Knowledge* (New York: Oxford University Press, 1952), p. 11.

65. Karl Mannheim, *Wissenssoziologie*, ed. Kurt H. Wolff (Neuwied: Hermann Luchterhand Verlag, 1964), p. 239.

66. Ibid., pp. 168–69.

67. Béla Zalai, "A filozófiai rendszerezés problémája," *A Szellem*, 1, 2 (1911), pp. 166–67.

68. Ibid., pp. 182–85.

69. See Martin Heidegger, *Frühe Schriften* (Frankfurt am Main: Vittorio Klostermann, 1978), pp. 413–33.

70. I am indebted for this information to Professor Árpád Kadárkay.

71. See Gábor, "Mannheim Károly a két világháború között," p. 84.

72. Károly Mannheim, "Heidelbergi levél," *Tűz*, 1, 1–2 (1921), pp. 49–50.

73. On Mannheim's work as hermeneutical in intent, see the outstanding study by A. P. Simonds, *Karl Mannheim's Sociology of Knowledge* (Oxford: Clarendon Press, 1978).

74. Mannheim, *Wissenssoziologie*, p. 104.

75. Ibid., pp. 118–19.

76. For an excellent discussion of this point, see Richard E. Palmer, *Hermeneutics* (Evanston: Northwestern University Press, 1969), pp. 87–88, 118–21.

77. Mannheim, *Wissenssoziologie*, pp. 126, 129.

78. Alfred Weber, "Prinzipielles zur Kultursoziologie," *Archiv für Sozialwissenschaft und Sozialpolitik*, 47, 1 (1920), pp. 11–16, 21.

79. Ibid., pp. 22, 31–32, 43.

80. Karl Mannheim, *Strukturen des Denkens*, ed. David Kettler, Volker Meja, and Nico Stehr (Frankfurt am Main: Suhrkamp, 1980), pp. 52–53, 87, 149n.

81. Ibid., pp. 53, 88.

82. Ibid., pp. 101, 105.

83. Ibid., p. 108.

84. Ibid., p. 147.

85. Mannheim, *Wissenssoziologie*, pp. 246–47.

86. Mannheim, *Strukturen des Denkens*, pp. 223–27.
87. Ibid., p. 219.
88. Ibid., p. 213.
89. Ibid., pp. 189, 197–98.
90. Palmer, *Hermeneutics*, p. 118.
91. Mannheim, *Wissenssoziologie*, p. 283.
92. Mannheim, *Strukturen des Denkens*, p. 240.
93. Mannheim, *Wissenssoziologie*, pp. 315, 317.
94. Ibid., pp. 321, 330.
95. Ibid., p. 396.
96. Max Scheler, "Probleme einer Soziologie des Wissens," in Scheler (ed.), *Versuche zu einer Soziologie des Wissens* (München: Verlag von Duncker & Humblot, 1924), pp. 14, 44–45.
97. Mannheim, *Wissenssoziologie*, pp. 351–52.
98. Ibid., p. 356.
99. Ibid., p. 328.
100. Ibid., p. 383.
101. Karl Mannheim, *Konservatismus: Ein Beitrag zur Soziologie des Wissens*, ed. David Kettler, Volker Meja, and Nico Stehr (Frankfurt am Main: Suhrkamp Verlag, 1984), p. 51.
102. Ibid., p. 82.
103. Ibid., pp. 83, 156.
104. Ibid., pp. 87, 121.
105. Ibid., p. 91.
106. Ibid., pp. 138–41, 144, 250n.
107. Ibid., p. 157.
108. Ibid., p. 170.
109. Ibid., p. 177. In this connection, Mannheim specifically mentions Lukács, p. 262n.
110. Ibid., p. 180.
111. Ibid., p. 184.
112. Ibid., pp. 182–83.
113. Ibid., pp. 186, 215, 266n.
114. Ibid., pp. 192, 195.
115. Ibid., pp. 200, 211.
116. Ibid., p. 210.
117. Ibid., p. 214.
118. Ibid., p. 217.
119. Ibid., pp. 218–20.
120. Ibid., pp. 221–22.
121. Introduction to ibid., pp. 17–18; Henk E. S. Woldring, *Karl Mannheim: The Development of his Thought*, trans. Stanley M. Wiersma (Assen: Van Gorcum, 1986), pp. 26–27.
122. Cited in Lee Congdon, "Szilasi Vilmos és a magyar kultúra," *Filozófiai Figyelő*, 2, 3–4 (1980), p. 38.
123. Mannheim, *Wissenssoziologie*, p. 508.
124. Cited in ibid., p. 517; Heidegger, *Being and Time*, p. 436.
125. Oszkár Jászi, "Ady és a magyar jövő," *Huszadik Század*, August 1919, p. 2.

126. Mannheim, *Wissenssoziologie*, p. 549.

127. Ibid., pp. 542, 544, 547.

128. Ibid., pp. 547–48.

129. Ibid., p. 526n.

130. Ibid., pp. 532, 540.

131. Ibid., p. 569.

132. Ibid., pp. 573–74.

133. Ibid., p. 575.

134. Ibid., pp. 583–84.

135. Ibid., p. 586.

136. Ibid., pp. 604, 609.

137. Ibid., p. 608.

138. Ibid., p. 607.

139. See Volker Meja and Nico Stehr (eds.), *Der Streit um die Wissenssoziologie*, 1–2 (Frankfurt am Main: Suhrkamp Verlag, 1982).

140. Ibid., 1, p. 397.

141. Karl Mannheim, *Ideologie und Utopie* (Frankfurt am Main: Vittorio Klostermann, 1985), pp. 49, 51, 167.

142. Ibid., pp. 179n, 224.

143. Ibid., p. 167.

144. Ibid., pp. 61–62, 167.

145. Ibid., p. 62.

146. Ibid., pp. 68–69.

147. Ibid., pp. 53–55.

148. Ibid., pp. 70–71. Note Mannheim's use of Einstein's terms: "special" and "general."

149. Ibid., pp. 71–72.

150. Ibid., pp. 77, 92–93.

151. Ibid., p. 138.

152. Ibid., pp. 134–36.

153. Ibid., pp. 137–38.

154. Ibid., p. 167.

155. See Weber's famous essay, "Politics as a Vocation," in *From Max Weber: Essays in Sociology*, trans. and ed. by H. H. Gerth and C. Wright Mills (New York: Oxford University Press, 1946), pp. 77–128.

156. Mannheim, *Ideologie und Utopie*, p. 167.

157. Ibid., pp. 172–73.

158. Ladislaus Radványi, *Der Chiliasmus* (Budapest: MTA Filozófiai Intézet Lukács Archívum, 1985), p. 69.

159. Mannheim, *Ideologie und Utopie*, p. 184.

160. Ibid., pp. 191, 195.

161. Ibid., p. 199.

162. Ibid., pp. 202–3.

163. Ibid., p. 212.

164. He had been struck by an article in *Kommunismus* in which Révai had written that "the present only exists because the past and the future exist; the present is the form of the unnecessary past and the unrealized future. Tactics are the future appearing as the present." Cited in ibid., p. 212n.

165. Ibid., pp. 214, 220, 224–25.

166. Ibid., p. 223.

167. Meja and Stehr, *Der Streit um die Wissenssoziologie*, 2, pp. 419, 423–25.

168. Ibid., pp. 428, 432.

169. Ibid., p. 434.

170. Ibid., p. 516.

171. Heidegger, *Being and Time*, p. 92.

172. Ibid., p. 468.

173. Meja and Stehr, *Der Streit um die Wissenssoziologie*, 2, p. 519.

174. Ibid., pp. 453–55.

175. Ibid., p. 459.

176. Ibid., pp. 460, 465, 470.

177. Ibid., pp. 470–71.

178. Ibid., p. 472.

179. Ibid., p. 479.

180. Ibid., p. 491.

181. Adalbert Fogarasi, "Die Soziologie der Intelligenz und die Intelligenz der Soziologie," *Unter dem Banner des Marxismus*, 4 (1930), pp. 362–63, 366.

182. Ibid., pp. 368, 373.

183. Ibid., p. 374.

184. Mannheim to Balázs, February 15, 1930. In Gassner, *Wechsel Wirkungen*, pp. 539–40.

185. Martin Jay, "The Frankfurt School's Critique of Karl Mannheim and the Sociology of Knowledge," *Telos*, no. 20 (1974), p. 72.

186. Woldring, *Karl Mannheim*, p. 33.

187. Mannheim, *Ideologie und Utopie*, p. 259; see also David Kettler, Volker Meja, and Nico Stehr, *Karl Mannheim* (Chichester: Ellis Horwood, 1984), pp. 64–65.

188. Mannheim, *Ideologie und Utopie*, p. 239.

189. Karl Mannheim, *Die Gegenwartsaufgaben der Soziologie* (Tübingen: Verlag von J.C.B. Mohr /Paul Siebeck/, 1932), p. 55.

190. Ibid., p. 40.

191. Ibid., pp. 36–38.

192. See Gábor, "Mannheim Károly a két világháború között," p. 108n.

193. Cited in ibid., p. 99.

194. Kettler, Meja, and Stehr, *Karl Mannheim*, p. 38.

195. Cited in the introduction to Mannheim, *Konservatismus*, p. 37.

CONCLUSION
COMMUNITY AND CONSCIOUSNESS

1. Mannheim, *Strukturen des Denkens*, p. 263.

2. Moholy's father's name was Weisz, which may or may not have been Jewish.

3. Mary Gluck, *Georg Lukács and His Generation, 1900–1918* (Cambridge: Harvard University Press, 1985), pp. 8–9.

BIBLIOGRAPHY

UNPUBLISHED SOURCES

Babits, Mihály. Papers. Országos Széchenyi Könyvtára: Kézirattár. Budapest, Hungary.

Balázs, Béla. Diaries. Magyar Tudományos Akadémia Könyvtára: Kézirattár. Budapest, Hungary.

Caton, Joseph Harris. *The Utopian Vision of Moholy-Nagy: Technology, Society, and the Avant-Garde. An Analysis of the Writings of Moholy-Nagy on the Visual Arts.* Doctoral Dissertation, Princeton University, 1980.

Hauser, Arnold. Conversation. London, August 28, 1971.

Ignotus, Paul. Conversation. London, June 1975.

Kolnai, Aurel. *Twentieth-Century Memoirs.*

Lukács, György. Manuscripts, Correspondence. Magyar Tudományos Akadémia Filozófiai Intézet Lukács Archívum és Könyvtár. Budapest, Hungary.

Mannheim, Karl. *Die Dame aus Biarritz. Ein Spiel in vier Szenen.* Magyar Tudományos Akadémia Könyvtára: Kézirattár. Budapest, Hungary.

Polányi, Károly. Letters to Oszkár Jászi. Országos Széchenyi Könyvtára: Kézirattár. Budapest, Hungary.

Polányi, Michael. Papers. Joseph Regenstein Library, The University of Chicago.

Polányi-Levitt, Kári. Conversation. Budapest, October 1986.

PRIMARY SOURCES

A., "Die Marxistische Arbeiterschule (MASCH): Aus einem Gespräch mit ihrem Leiter." *Die Linkskurve* 3, no. 6 (1931): 19–20.

"A haladó művészek első nemzetközi kongresszusa" /The First International Congress of Progressive Artists/. *Ma* 8, no. 8 (1922): 61–64.

Ady, Endre. *Jóslások magyarországról* /Prophecies Concerning Hungary/. Edited by Géza Féja. Budapest: Athenaeum Irodalmi és Nyomdairt. Kiadása, 1936.

―――. *Költészet és forradalom* /Poetry and Revolution/. Edited by József Varga. Budapest: Kossuth Könyvkiadó, 1969.

―――. *Összes versei* /Collected Poems/. Budapest: Szépirodalmi Könyvkiadó, 1967.

"Ady forradalmi hatása: Filminterjú Lukács Györggyel" /The Revolutionary Influence of Ady: Film Interview with György Lukács/. *Élet és Irodalom.* January 29, 1977, p. 6.

Arnheim, Rudolf. "Der Geist des Films." *Die Weltbühne* 26, no. 2 (1930): 723–24.

―――. *Film as Art.* Berkeley: University of California Press, 1957.

Balázs, Béla. *A szinjáték elmélete* /Theory of the Drama/. Wien: Europa Ismeretterjesztő Könyvtár, 1922.

―――. *A vándor énekel* /The Wanderer Sings/. Edited by Sándor Radnóti. Budapest: Magyar Helikon, 1975.

―――. *Álmodó ifjúság* /Dreaming Youth/. Budapest: Magvető és Szépirodalmi Könyvkiadó, 1976.

―――. *Az álmok köntöse* /Mantle of Dreams/. Edited by Ferenc Fehér and Sándor Radnóti. Budapest: Magyar Helikon, 1973.

Balázs, Béla. "Das indirekte Wien." *Die Literarische Welt*, May 21, 1926, p. 9.

———. *Das richtige Himmelblau: Drei Märchen*. München: Drei Masken Verlag, 1925.

———. *Der Mantel der Träume*. München: Verlagsanstalt D. & R. Bischoff, 1922.

———. *Der Phantasie-Reiseführer: Das ist ein Baedeker der Seele für Sommerfrischler*. Wien: Paul Zsolnay Verlag, 1925.

———. "Die Furcht der Intellektuellen vor dem Sozialismus." *Die Weltbühne* 28, no. 1 (1932): 93–96, 131–34, 166–68, 207–10.

———. *Halálesztetika* /Death Aesthetics/. Budapest: Deutsch Zsigmond és Társa Könyvkereskedése, n.d.

———. *Halálos fiatalság* /Mortal Youth/. Edited by Ferenc Fehér and Sándor Radnóti. Budapest: Magyar Helikon, 1974.

———. *Hans Urian geht nach Brot*. Freiburg im Breisgau: Max Reichard Verlag, n.d.

———. "Hungarian Letter." *The Dial* 74, no. 4 (1923): 387–94.

———. *Levelei Lukács Györgyhöz* /Letters to György Lukács/. Edited by Julia Lenkei. Budapest: MTA Filozófiai Intézet, 1982.

———. "Menschen auf der Barrikade." *Die Weltbühne* 25, no. 2 (1929): 91–94.

———. *Napló, 1914–1922* /Diary, 1914–1922/. Edited by Anna Fábri. Budapest: Magvető Könyvkiadó, 1982.

———. "Paris-e vagy Weimar?" /Paris or Weimar?/ *Nyugat* 7 (1914): 200–203.

———. *Schriften zum Film*, 1. Edited by Helmut H. Diederichs, Wolfgang Gersch, and Magda Nagy. München: Carl Hanser Verlag, 1982.

———. *Schriften zum Film*, 2. Edited by Helmut H. Diederichs and Wolfgang Gersch. München: Carl Hanser Verlag, 1984.

———. "Selbstanzeige." *Die Literarische Welt*, November 22, 1929, p. 8.

———. *Theory of the Film*. Translated by Edith Bone. New York: Dover Publications, 1970.

———. *Unmögliche Menschen*. Frankfurt am Main: Rütten & Loening Verlag, 1930.

———. "Unmögliche Menschen." *Die Weltbühne* 25, no. 2 (1929): 734–35.

———. *Válogatott cikkek és tanulmányok* /Selected Articles and Studies/. Edited by Magda K. Nagy. Budapest: Kossuth Könyvkiadó, 1968.

Barta, Sándor. "1918. Szabadulás" /1918. Liberation/. *Ma* 3, no. 11 (1918): 135.

Becher, Johannes R. "Unsere Front." *Die Linkskurve* 1, no. 1 (1929), 1–3.

Behne, Adolf. "Művészet és forradalom" /Art and Revolution/. *Ma* 6, no. 4 (1921): 43–49.

Belinski, Vissarion. *Selected Philosophical Works*. Moscow: Foreign Languages Publishing House, 1956.

Belloc, Hilaire. *The Servile State*. New York: Henry Holt and Company, 1946.

"Beszélgetés Bortnyik Sándorral" /Conversation with Sándor Bortnyik/. *Kritika*, no. 8 (1976): 16–20.

"Beszélgetés Duczynska Ilonával" /Conversation with Ilona Duczynska/. *Valóság* 17 no. 7 (1974): 50–60.

Bichlmair, P. Georg, S. J. *Das proletarische Freidenkertum*. Wien: Der Seelsorger, 1925.

Bloch, Ernst. "Aktualität und Utopie: Zu Lukács' 'Geschichte und Klassenbewusstsein.'" *Philosophische Aufsätze zur Objektiven Phantasie*. Frankfurt am Main: Suhrkamp Verlag, 1969, pp. 598–621.

———. *Thomas Münzer als Theologe der Revolution*. Frankfurt am Main: Suhrkamp Verlag, 1969.

————. "Zur Rettung von Georg Lukács." *Die weissen Blätter* 6 (1919): 529–30.

Borus, Rózsa (ed.). *A század nagy tanúi* /Great Witnesses of the Century/. Budapest: RTV. Minerva, 1978.

Brauneck, Manfred (ed.). *Die Rote Fahne: Kritik, Theorie, Feuilleton, 1918–1933.* München: Wilhelm Fink Verlag, 1973.

Brecht, Bertolt. *Die Dreigroschenoper.* Reinbek bei Hamburg: Rowohlt Taschenbuch Verlag, 1963.

————. *On Theatre: The Development of an Aesthetic.* Edited and translated by John Willett. New York: Hill and Wang, 1964.

Chesterton, Gilbert K. *Orthodoxy.* Garden City, New York: Image Books, 1959.

————. *The Everlasting Man.* Garden City, New York: Image Books, 1955.

————. *What's Wrong With the World.* New York: Dodd, Mead and Company, 1910.

Cole, G.D.H. *Guild Socialism Restated.* New Brunswick: Transaction Books, 1980.

————. *Social Theory.* London: Methuen and Co., 1920.

Das Deutsche Lichtbild. Berlin: Verlag Robert & Bruno Schultz, 1927.

Deborin, A. "Lukács und seine Kritik des Marxismus." *Arbeiter-Literatur* 1, no. 2 (1924): 615–40.

Degras, Jane (ed.). *The Communist International, Documents. Vol. II, 1923–1928.* London: Oxford University Press, 1960.

Dilthey, Wilhelm. *Gesammelte Schriften,* 7. Stuttgart: B. G. Teubner, 1973.

Drucker, Peter F. *Adventures of a Bystander.* New York: Harper and Row, 1978. ✗

Duczynska, Ilona. "A cselekvés boldogtalan szerelmese" /The Unhappy Lover of Action/. *Valóság* 21 no. 5 (1978): 8–19.

————. "Der Fascismus zwischen Revolution und Normalisierung." *Der Deutsche Volkswirt* 1, no. 20 (1927): 601–5.

————. "Fascismus und Miliz." *Der Deutsche Volkswirt* 1, no. 19 (1927): 572–75.

————. "Korán reggel" /Early in the Morning/. *Új Írás* 13, no. 3 (1973): 7–25.

————. "Mesterünk: Szabó Ervin" /Our Teacher: Ervin Szabó/. *Kortárs* 12, no. 10 (1968): 1619–26.

————. "Önéletrajza" /Autobiography/. *Kritika*, no. 8 (1978): 20–21.

————. "Polányi Károly (1886–1964)." *Századok* 105, no. 1 (1971): 89–95.

————. "Polányi Károly. Jegyzetek az életútról" /Karl Polányi. Notes on His Life's Path/. *Magyar Filozófiai Szemle*, nos. 5–6 (1971): 763–67.

————. "Zum Zerfall der K.P.U." *Unser Weg*, March 1, 1922, 97–105.

Eisenmann, Louis. "Souvenirs." *Századunk* 9, nos. 8–9 (1934): 323–24.

Eisenstein, Sergei. *Film Form: Essays in Film Theory.* Edited and translated by Jay Leyda. New York: Harcourt, Brace and World, 1949.

Federn, Walther (ed.). *Sonderausgabe zur Zwanzigjahrfeier des "Österreichischen Volkswirts".* Wien: Verlag "Der Österreichische Volkswirt," 1928.

Fekete, Éva, and Karádi, Éva (eds.). *Lukács György élete képekben és dokumentumokban* /The Life of György Lukács in Photographs and Documents/. Budapest: Corvina Kiadó, 1980.

Fodor, T. K. "Der Geist des Films." *Die Linkskurve* 4, no. 2 (1932): 34–35.

Fogarasi, Béla. "Die Soziologie der Intelligenz und die Intelligenz der Soziologie." *Unter dem Banner des Marxismus* 4 (1930): 359–75.

————. "Karl Korsch: Marxismus und Philosophie." *Die Internationale* 7, no. 12 (1924): 414–16.

Fogarasi, Béla. "Konzervativ és progressziv idealizmus" /Conservative and Progressive Idealism/. *Huszadik Század* 19 (1918): 193–206.

―――. "Zalai Béla." *Athenaeum* 1 (1915): 428–41.

―――. "Záróbeszéd" /Closing Address/. *Huszadik Század* 19 (1918): 92–95.

Fraknói, Vilmos. *Werbőczi István életrajza* /Biography of István Werbőczi/. Budapest: A Magyar Történelmi Társulat Kiadása, 1899.

Freud, Sigmund. *The Future of an Illusion*. Translated by James Strachey. New York: W. W. Norton and Company, 1961.

Gábor, Andor. "Die bunte Welt des Genossen Barbusse." *Die Linkskurve* 1, no. 5 (1929): 5–6.

―――. *Gespenster bei Sonnenlicht*. Edited by Harri Günther. Halle-Leipzig: Mitteldeutscher Verlag, 1979.

―――. "Über proletarisch-revolutionäre Literatur." *Die Linkskurve* 1, no. 3 (1929): 3–6.

―――. "Zwei Bühnenereignisse." *Die Linkskurve* 4, nos. 11/12 (1932): 27–32.

Gál, István (ed.). "Babits béke-írásaiból" /From Babits's Writings on Peace/. *Irodalomtörténeti Közlemények* 80, no. 4 (1976): 520–33.

―――. (ed.). *Babits-Szilasi levelezés* /The Babits-Szilasi Correspondence/. Budapest: Irodalmi Múzeum, n.d.

Gáspár, Endre. "Kassák Lajos, az ember és munkája" /Lajos Kassák: The Man and His Work/. *Ma* 8, nos. 7–8 (1923): n.pp.

Goldmann, Emil. "Szende, der Polyhistor." *Századunk* 9, nos. 8–9 (1934): 324.

Gropius, Walter. *The New Architecture and the Bauhaus*. Cambridge, Massachusetts: The M.I.T. Press, 1965.

―――, Gropius, Ise, and Bayer, Herbert (eds.). *Bauhaus, 1919–1928*. New York: The Museum of Modern Art, 1938.

Guttmann, Fritz. "Szende Pál tudományos munkássága 1919-től 1934-ig" /Paul Szende's Scholarly Work from 1919 to 1934/. *Századunk* 9, nos. 8–9 (1934): 345–59.

Halasi, Béla. "Emlékezés Szende Pálról" /Recollection of Paul Szende/. *Századunk* 9, nos. 8–9 (1934): 328–29.

Hatvany, Lajos. *Ady*, 1. Budapest: Szépirodalmi Könyvkiadó, 1959.

―――. *Das verwundete Land*. Leipzig: E. P. Tal & Co. Verlag, 1921.

Hay, Julius. *Born 1900: Memoirs*. Translated by J. A. Underwood. La Salle, Illinois: Open Court, 1975.

―――. *Gott, Kaiser und Bauer*. Zürich: Verlag Oprecht & Helbling, 1935.

Hayek, F. A. (ed.). *Collectivist Economic Planning*. London: Routledge & Kegan Paul, 1935.

Heidegger, Martin. *Being and Time*. Translated by John Macquarrie and Edward Robinson. New York: Harper and Row, 1962.

―――. *Frühe Schriften*. Frankfurt am Main: Vittorio Klostermann, 1978.

Herczeg, Ferenc. "A szent háboru" /The Holy War/. *Magyar Figyelő* 4, no. 16 (1914): 241–43.

Hevesy, Iván. "Az új plakát" /The New Poster/. *Ma* 4, no. 5 (1919): 106–7.

―――. "Tömegkultura—tömegművészet" /Mass Culture—Mass Art/. *Ma* 4, no. 4 (1919): 70–71.

―――. "Túl az impresszionizmuson" /Beyond Impressionism/. *Ma* 4, no. 3 (1919): 31–34, 39–40.

Hildebrand, Dietrich von. *Metaphysik der Gemeinschaft.* Regensburg: Verlag Josef Habbel, 1975.

Hoffmann, Ludwig, and Hoffmann-Ostwald, Daniel (eds.). *Deutsches Arbeitertheater, 1918–1933,* 1–2. München: Verlag Rogner & Bernhard, 1973.

Horváth, Zoltán (ed.). "A Galilei Körre vonatkozó ismeretlen dokumentumok" /Unknown Documents Concerning the Galileo Circle/. *Századok* 105, no. 1 (1971): 95–104.

Huelsenbeck, Richard (ed.). *Dada Almanach.* Berlin: Erich Reiss Verlag, 1920.

Illés, Ilona, and Taxner, Ernő (eds.). *Kortársak Kassák Lajosról* /Contemporaries on Lajos Kassák/. Budapest: Petőfi Irodalmi Múzeum, n.d.

Irodalmi Múzeum: Emlékezések /Literary Museum: Recollections/. Budapest, 1967.

Jászi, Oszkár. "A nyugati kultura pusztulásának filozófusa Oswald Spengler megmérése" /Measuring Oswald Spengler, the Philosopher of Western Civilization's Decline/. *Századvég,* no. 1 (1985): 196–201.

————. "Ady és a magyar jövő" /Ady and the Hungarian Future/. *Huszadik Század,* August 1919, p. 2.

————. "Az elgáncsolt megváltás" /Thwarted Redemption/. *Századvég,* no. 1 (1985): 149–54.

————. "Eugen Dühring." *Századvég,* no. 1 (1985): 185–91.

————. "Háború és kultura" /War and Culture/. *Huszadik Század* 15 (1914): 249–63.

————. "Keresztény szocializmus és szocialista kereszténység" /Christian Socialism and Socialistic Christianity/. *Századvég,* no. 1 (1985): 154–59.

————. *Magyarország jövője és a Dunai egyesült államok* /Hungary's Future and the United States of Danubia/. Budapest: Az Új Magyarország Részvénytársaság, 1918.

————. "Mannheim Károly: *Lélek és kultura*" /Karl Mannheim: *Soul and Culture*/. *Huszadik Század* 19 (1918): 192.

————. *Marxizmus, vagy liberális szocializmus* /Marxism, or Liberal Socialism/. Edited by Péter Kende. Malakoff: Dialogues Européens, 1983.

————. *Mult és jövő határán* /On the Border Between Past and Future/. Budapest: Pallas Irodalmi és Nyomdai Részv.-Társ. Kiadása, 1918.

————. "Proletárdiktatura" /Proletarian Dictatorship/. *Szabadgondolat* 8, no. 10 (1918): 225–26.

————. *Revolution and Counter-Revolution in Hungary.* New York: Howard Fertig, 1969.

————. "Szende Pál, az ember, a munkás és a harcos" /Paul Szende: The Man, the Worker, and the Fighter/. *Századunk* 9 (1934): 313–20.

József, Farkas (ed.). "*Mindenki újakra készül . . .*": *Az 1918/19–es forradalmak irodalma* /Everyone is Preparing for New Things: The Literature of the 1918/19 Revolutions/. 4. Budapest: Akadémiai Kiadó, 1967.

Juhász, Gyula. "A Ma útja és célja" /Ma's Path and Goal/. *Ma* 4, no. 1 (1919): 10–11.

————. *Összes művei* /Collected Works/. 6. Edited by László Péter. Budapest: Akadémiai Kiadó, 1969.

Jung, C. G. *Modern Man in Search of a Soul.* Translated by W. S. Dell and Cary F. Baynes. New York: Harcourt, Brace and World, 1933.

Kaes, Anton (ed.). *Kino-Debatte.* Tübingen: Max Niemeyer Verlag, 1978.

Kállai, Ernő. "A konstruktiv művészet társadalmi és szellemi távlatai" /Constructivism's Social and Intellectual Perspectives/. *Ma* 8, no. 8 (1922): 55–56, 58–59.

Kállai, Ernő. "A kubizmus es a jövendő művészet" /Cubism and the Coming Art/. *Ma* 7, no. 2 (1922): 26–28, 30–32.

———. "bescheidene malerei." *bauhaus* 2, no. 4 (1928): 1–2.

———. "Burgfriede in der Kunst." *Die Weltbühne* 26 (1930): 463–65.

———. "das bauhaus lebt!" *bauhaus* 2, nos. 2/3 (1928): 1–2.

———. "Die Wohnung." *Sozialistische Monatshefte* 32 (1926): 322–26.

———. "ein beliebter vorwurf gegen das bauhaus." *bauhaus* 2, no. 4 (1928): 15.

———. "ein bild, ein mensch." *bauhaus* 2, nos. 2/3 (1928): 30.

———. "E-t-i-k-a-?" /E-t-h-i-c-s?/ *Ma* 9, no. 2 (1923): n.p.

———. "forgó pál: új építészet" /pál forgó: new architecture/. *bauhaus* 2, no. 4 (1928): 27.

———. "Grenzen der Technik." *Die Weltbühne* 27 (1931): 503–5.

———. "Kassák Lajos." *Ma* 7, no. 1 (1921): 139.

———. "Konstruktivizmus" /Constructivism/. *Ma* 8, nos. 7–8 (1923): n.p.

———. "Korrekturát" /Proofread/. *Ma* 8, nos. 9–10 (1923): n.pp.

———. "Kunst und Technik." *Sozialistische Monatshefte* 37 (1931): 1095–1103.

———. "Kunst und Wirklichkeit." *Sozialistische Monatshefte* 37 (1931): 998–1005.

———. "Malerei und Film." *Die Weltbühne* 27 (1931): 805–8.

———. "Moholy-Nagy." *Ma* 6, no. 9 (1921): 119.

———. *Művészet veszélyes csillagzat alatt: Válogatott cikkek, tanulmányok* /Art Under a Dangerous Constellation: Selected Articles and Studies/. Edited by Éva Forgács. Budapest: Corvina Kiadó, 1981.

———. *Neue Malerei in Ungarn.* Leipzig: Klinkhardt & Biermann Verlag, 1925.

———. "Technika és konstruktiv művészet" /Technology and Constructivism/. *Ma* 7, nos. 5–6 (1922): 7–9.

———. "Trübsinnbilder." *Die Weltbühne* 28 (1932): 291–93.

———. "Új művészet, I" /New Art/. *Ma* 6, no. 7 (1921): 99.

———. "Új művészet, II" /New Art/. *Ma* 6, no. 8 (1921): 114–15.

———. "wir leben nicht, um zu wohnen." *bauhaus* 3, no. 1 (1929): 10.

Karádi, Éva (ed.). "Dokumentumok Lukács György heidelbergi korszakából" /Documents from György Lukács's Heidelberg Period/. *Valóság* 17, no. 11 (1974): 28–44.

———, and Vezér, Erzsébet (eds.). *A Vasárnapi Kör* /The Sunday Circle/. Budapest: Gondolat, 1980.

Károlyi, Michael. *Fighting the World: The Struggle for Peace.* Translated by E. W. Dickes. London: Kegan Paul, Trench, Trubner & Co., 1924.

———. *Memoirs: Faith Without Illusion.* New York: E. P. Dutton & Co., 1957.

Kassák, Lajos. "A berlini orosz kiállitáshoz" /On the Russian Exhibition in Berlin/. *Ma* 8, nos. 2–3 (1922): n.pp.

———. *A fal mögött áll és énekel* /He Stands Behind the Wall and Sings/. Budapest: Magvető Könyvkiadó, 1974.

———. *A ló meghal, a madarak kirepülnek* /The Horse Dies, the Birds Take Wing/. Budapest: Magyar Helikon, 1967.

———. "A plakát és az új festészet" /The Poster and the New Painting/. *Ma* 1, no. 1 (1916): 2–4.

———. "A Tisztaság könyvéből" /From The Book of Purity/. *Ma* 9, no. 2 (1923): n.pp.

———. "Ady Endre 1877–1919." *Ma* 4, no. 2 (1919): 14–15.

———. "Aktivizmus" /Activism/. *Ma* 4, no. 4 (1919): 46–51.

———. "An die Künstler aller Länder!" *Ma* 5, nos. 1–2 (1920): 2–4.

———. *Az izmusok története* /History of the Isms/. Budapest: Magvető Könyvkiadó, 1972.

———. "Bildarchitektur." *Ma* 8, no. 1 (1922): n.p.

———. *Egy ember élete* /One Man's Life/, 2. Budapest: Magvető Kiadó, 1983.

———. "Egy generáció tragédiája" /Tragedy of a Generation/. *Ma* 8, nos. 7–8 (1923): n.p.

———. *Éljünk a mi időnkben: Írások a képzőművészetről* /Let Us Live in Our Time: Writings on Visual Art/. Edited by Zsuzsa Ferencz. Budapest: Magvető Könyvkiadó, 1978.

———. "1919 Eposz" /1919 Epic/. *Ma* 5, no. 3 (1920): 27–36; 5, no. 4 (1920): 41–52.

———. "F. T. Marinetti." *Ma* 10, no. 1 (1925): n.p.

———. "Képarchitektura" /Pictorial Architecture/. *Ma* 7, no. 4 (1922): 52–54.

———. "Konstrukciótól a kompozicióig" /From Construction to Composition/. *Ma* 8, nos. 9–10 (1923): n.p.

———. "Levél Kun Bélához a művészet nevében" /Letter to Béla Kun in the Name of Art/. *Ma* 4, no. 7 (1919): 146–48.

———. "Máglyák énekelnek" /Funeral Pyres Sing/. *Ma* 6, nos. 1–2 (1920): 15–16.

———. "Rechenschaft." *Ma* 8, nos. 5–6 (1923): n.p.

———. "Tovább a magunk utján" /Onward on Our Path/. *Ma* 3, no. 12 (1918): 138–39.

———. "Über neue Theaterkunst." *Ma* 9, nos. 8–9 (1924): n.p.

———. "Válasz sokfelé és álláspont" /Viewpoint and Reply in Many Parts/. *Ma* 8, no. 8 (1922): 50–54.

———. "Versei" /Poems/. *Ma* 9, nos. 8–9 (1925): n.p.

———. "Vissza a kaptafához" /Back to the Same Pattern/. *Ma* 9, no. 1 (1923): n.p.

———, and Moholy-Nagy, László (eds.). *Új művészek könyve* /Book of New Artists/. Budapest: Európa Könyvkiadó and Corvina Kiadó, 1977. Facsimile of the first edition: Wien: Verlag Julius Fischer, 1922.

Kecskeméti, Pál. "A szociológia történetfilozófiai megalapozása: Mannheim Károly" /Sociology's Historico-Philosophical Foundation: Karl Mannheim/. *Századunk* 1 (1926): 447–57.

———. "Introduction," in Karl Mannheim, *Essays on the Sociology of Knowledge*. New York: Oxford University Press, 1952, 1–32.

Kemény, Alfréd. "Bortnyik képei és grafikája" /Bortnyik's Paintings and Graphics/. *Ma* 4, no. 7 (1919): 172–74.

———. "Das dynamische Prinzip." *Der Sturm* 14 (1923): 62–64.

Keynes, John Maynard. *Essays in Persuasion*. New York: W. W. Norton and Company, 1963.

Koestler, Arthur. *The Invisible Writing*. New York: The Macmillan Company, 1954.

Kolnai, Aurel. "Autorität und Demokratie." *Volkswohl* 20, no. 10 (1929): 361–71.

———. "Bellocs Vision vom Sklavenstaat." *Schönere Zukunft*, November 1928, 116–18.

———. "Chesterton and Catholicism: Excerpts from *Twentieth-Century Memoirs*." *The Chesterton Review* 8, no. 2 (1982): 127–61.

———. "Chestertons Religionsphilosophie." *Das Neue Reich* 9, no. 40 (1927): 821–23.

Kolnai, Aurel. "Das Problem des Konservativismus." *Der Österreichische Volkswirt* 26, no. 2 (1934): 903–6.

———. "Das Seipel-Bild." *Der Österreichische Volkswirt* 24, no. 2 (1932): 1102.

———. "Das Weihnachtsmanifest der österreichischen Bischöfe." *Der Österreichische Volkswirt* 18, no. 1 (1925–26): 389–92.

———. "Der Abbau des Kapitalismus: Die Soziallehren G. K. Chestertons." *Der Deutsche Volkswirt* 1, no. 44 (1927): 1382–86.

———. *Der ethische Wert und die Wirklichkeit.* Freiburg im Breisgau: Herder & Co. G.M.B.H. Verlagsbuchhandlung, 1927.

———. "Der Inhalt der Politik." *Zeitschrift für die gesamte Staatswissenschaft* 94 (1933): 1–38.

———. "Die Aufgabe des Konservativismus." *Der Österreichische Volkswirt* 26, no. 2 (1934): 943–46.

———. "Die christlichen Gewerkschaften im Kampfe gegen den Kapitalismus." *Volkswohl* 20, no. 11 (1929): 405–15.

———. "Die Ideologie des sozialen Fortschritts." *Der Deutsche Volkswirt* 1, no. 30 (1927): 933–36.

———. "Die Ideologie des Ständestaates." *Der Kampf* 27, no. 1 (1934): 13–23.

———. "Die Machtideen der Klassen." *Archiv für Sozialwissenschaft und Sozialpolitik* 62 (1929): 67–110.

———. "Eine Illusion der Zukunft." *Volkswohl* 19, no. 2 (1928): 53–56.

———. "Fascismus und Bolschewismus." *Der Deutsche Volkswirt* 1, no. 7 (1926): 206–13.

———. "Gegenrevolution." *Kölner Vierteljahrshefte für Soziologie* 10, no. 2 (1931): 171–99; 10, no. 3 (1932): 295–319.

———. "Ist O. Spanns 'Universalismus' mit katholischem Denken vereinbar?" *Volkswohl* 20, no. 3 (1929): 81–85, 126–31.

———. "Katholizismus und Demokratie." *Der Österreichische Volkswirt* 26, no. 1 (1933–34): 318–21.

———. "Kritik des sozialen Fortschritts." *Der Deutsche Volkswirt* 1, no. 31 (1927): 965–69.

———. "Max Scheler als Sozialphilosoph." *Der Deutsche Volkswirt* 2, no. 38 (1928): 1300–3.

———. "Max Schelers Kritik und Würdigung der Freudschen Libidolehre." *Imago* 11, nos. 1/2 (1925): 135–46.

———. "Persönlichkeit und Massenherrschaft." *Der Österreichische Volkswirt* 26, no. 1 (1933–34): 442–44.

———. *Psychoanalyse und Soziologie: Zur Psychologie von Masse und Gesellschaft.* Leipzig: Internationaler Psychoanalytischer Verlag, 1920.

———. *Psychoanalysis and Sociology.* Translated by Eden and Cedar Paul. London: George Allen & Unwin, 1921.

———. "Quadragesimo anno." *Der Österreichische Volkswirt* 23, no. 2, (1931): 892.

———. "Rechts und Links in der Politik." *Der Deutsche Volkswirt* 1, no. 22 (1927): 665–71.

———. "Religiöse Sozialisten." *Der Österreichische Volkswirt* 21, no. 1 (1928–29): 190.

————. "René Fülöp-Miller: Geist und Gesicht des Bolschewismus." *Das Neue Reich* 9, no. 38 (1927): 793–94.

————. *Sexualethik: Sinn und Grundlagen der Geschlechtsmoral.* Paderborn: Ferdinand Schöningh Verlag, 1930.

————. "Thomas Mann, Freud und der Fortschritt." *Volkswohl* 20, no. 9 (1929): 321–27.

————. "Tote und lebendige Demokratie." *Der Deutsche Volkswirt* 2, no. 26 (1928): 854–57.

Korsch, Karl. "Georg Lukács: Lenin, Studie über den Zusammenhang seiner Gedanken." *Die Internationale* 7, no. 12 (1924): 413–14.

————. "Marxismus und Philosophie." *Archiv für die Geschichte des Sozialismus und der Arbeiterbewegung* 2 (1923): 74–121.

————. "The Present State of the Problem of 'Marxism and Philosophy'—An Anti-Critique," *Marxism and Philosophy*, translated by Fred Halliday. New York: Monthly Review Press, 1970, 98–144.

Kühn, Gertraude, Tümmler, Karl, and Wimmer, Walter (eds.). *Film und revolutionäre Arbeiterbewegung in Deutschland, 1918–1932,* 1–2. Berlin: Henschelverlag, 1975.

Kutzbach, Karl August (ed.). *Paul Ernst und Georg Lukács: Dokumente einer Freundschaft.* Emsdetten: Verlag Lechte, 1974.

Láng, Juliska. *"Lélek és kultura" /Soul and Culture/.* *Athenaeum* 4 (1918): 159–61.

Lengyel, József. *Visegrádi utca* /Visegrád Street/. Budapest: Szépirodalmi Könyvkiadó, 1962.

Lenin, V. I. *Materialism and Empirio-Criticism.* Moscow: Foreign Languages Publishing House, n.d.

————. *Two Tactics of Social-Democracy in the Democratic Revolution.* New York: International Publishers, 1935.

Lesznai, Anna. *Kezdetben volt a kert* /In the Beginning Was the Garden/. 1–2. Budapest: Szépirodalmi Könyvkiadó, 1966.

Lieber, Hans-Joachim (ed.). *Ideologienlehre und Wissenssoziologie.* Darmstadt: Wissenschaftliche Buchgesellschaft, 1974.

Lifshitz, Mikhail. *The Philosophy of Art of Karl Marx.* Translated by Ralph B. Winn. London: Pluto Press, 1973.

Lindsay, Vachel. *The Art of the Moving Picture.* New York: The Macmillan Company, 1915.

Lissitzky, El, and Arp, Hans. *Die Kunstismen.* Erlenbach-Zürich: Eugen Rentsch Verlag, 1925.

Lukács, György. "A bolsevizmus mint erkölcsi problema" /Bolshevism as a Moral Problem/. *Szabadgondolat* 8, no. 10 (1918): 228–32.

————. "A köztársasági propaganda" /Republican Propaganda/. *Világ,* November 10, 1918, p. 17.

————. *A modern dráma fejlődésének története* /History of the Evolution of the Modern Drama/. 1–2. Budapest: Franklin-Társulat, 1911.

————. "Aus der Not eine Tugend." *Die Linkskurve* 4, nos. 11/12 (1932): 15–24.

————. *Curriculum vitae.* Edited by János Ambrus. Budapest: Magvető Kiadó, 1982.

————. "Die deutschen Intellektuellen und der Krieg." *Text und Kritik* 39/40 (1973): 65–69.

Lukács, György. "Die neue Ausgabe von Lassalles Briefen." *Archiv für die Geschichte des Sozialismus und der Arbeiterbewegung* 11 (1925): 401–23.

————. *Die Theorie des Romans: Ein geschichtsphilosophischer Versuch über die Formen der grossen Epik.* Neuwied: Hermann Luchterhand Verlag, 1971.

————. "Gegen die Spontaneitätstheorie in der Literatur." *Die Linkskurve* 4, no. 4 (1932): 30–33.

————. *Gelebtes Denken.* Edited by István Eörsi. Frankfurt am Main: Suhrkamp Verlag, 1981.

————. "Gerhart Hauptmann." *Die Linkskurve* 4, no. 10 (1932): 5–12.

————. *Geschichte und Klassenbewusstsein: Studien über marxistische Dialektik.* Neuwied: Hermann Luchterhand Verlag, 1970.

————. *Goethe and His Age.* Translated by Robert Anchor. London: Merlin Press, 1968.

————. "Goethe und die Dialektik." *Der Marxist* 2, no. 5 (1932): 13–24.

————. *Ifjúkori művek, 1902–1918* /Youthful Works, 1902–1918/. Edited by Árpád Tímár. Budapest: Magvető Kiadó, 1977.

————. *Karl Marx und Friedrich Engels als Literaturhistoriker.* Berlin: Aufbau-Verlag, 1948.

————. *Lenin: Studie über den Zusammenhang seiner Gedanken.* Neuwied: Hermann Luchterhand Verlag, 1967.

————. *Magyar irodalom—Magyar kultúra* /Hungarian Literature—Hungarian Culture/. Edited by Ferenc Fehér and Zoltán Kenyeres. Budapest: Gondolat Kiadó, 1970.

————. "Moses Hess und die Probleme der idealistischen Dialektik." *Archiv für die Geschichte des Sozialismus und der Arbeiterbewegung* 12 (1926): 105–55.

————. *Organisation und Illusion: Politische Aufsätze, III, 1921–1924.* Edited by Jörg Kammler and Frank Benseler. Neuwied: Hermann Luchterhand Verlag, 1977.

————. "Reportage oder Gestaltung." *Die Linkskurve* 4, no. 7 (1932): 23–30; 4, no. 8 (1932): 26–31.

————. *Revolution und Gegenrevolution: Politische Aufsätze, II, 1920–1921.* Edited by Jörg Kammler and Frank Benseler. Neuwied: Hermann Luchterhand Verlag, 1976.

————. *Selected Correspondence, 1902–1920.* Edited and translated by Judith Marcus and Zoltán Tar. New York: Columbia University Press, 1986.

————. "Shaws Bekenntnis zur Sowjetunion." *Die Linkskurve* 3, no. 9 (1931): 5–8.

————. "Stawrogins Beichte." *Die Rote Fahne*, July 16, 1922, n.p.

————. *Studies in European Realism.* New York: Grosset & Dunlap, 1964.

————. *Tactics and Ethics: Political Essays, 1919–1929.* Translated by Michael McColgan, edited by Rodney Livingstone. New York: Harper and Row, 1975.

————. *Taktik und Ethik: Politische Aufsätze, I, 1918–1920.* Edited by Jörg Kammler and Frank Benseler. Neuwied: Hermann Luchterhand Verlag, 1975.

————. "Tendenz oder Parteilichkeit?" *Die Linkskurve* 4, no. 6 (1932): 13–21.

————. *Történelem és osztálytudat* /History and Class Consciousness/. Edited by Mihály Vajda. Budapest: Magvető Kiadó, 1971.

————. *Utam Marxhoz* /My Road to Marx/, 1. Edited by György Márkus. Budapest: Magvető Könyvkiadó, 1971.

————. "Willi Bredels Romane." *Die Linkskurve* 3, no. 11 (1931): 23–27.

Mann, Katia. *Unwritten Memories.* Translated by Hunter and Hildegarde Hannum. New York: Alfred A. Knopf, 1975.

Mann, Thomas. "Brief an Dr. Seipel." *Gesammelte Werke*, 11. Frankfurt am Main: S. Fischer Verlag, 1974, 780–82.

———. *Der Zauberberg*, 1–2. Frankfurt am Main: Fischer Bücherei, 1967.

———. "Ein schönes Buch." *Gesammelte Werke*, 10. Frankfurt am Main: S. Fischer Verlag, 1960, 624–26.

———. *Order of the Day*. Translated by H. T. Lowe-Porter, et al. Freeport, New York: Books for Libraries Press, 1969.

———. *Past Masters and Other Papers*. Translated by H. T. Lowe-Porter. New York: Alfred A. Knopf, 1933.

Mannheim, Károly. "A háború bölcseletéhez" /Toward a Philosophy of the War/. *Huszadik Század* 18 (1917): 416–18.

———. *Die Gegenwartsaufgaben der Soziologie*. Tübingen: Verlag von J. C. B. Mohr (Paul Siebeck): 1932.

———. "Ernst Bloch: Geist der Utopie." *Athenaeum* 5, nos. 5–6 (1919): 207–11.

———. "Heidelbergi levél" /Heidelberg Letter./ *Tűz* 1, nos. 1–2 (1921): 46–50.

———. "Heidelbergi levelek /Heidelberg Letters/, II." *Tűz* 2, nos. 1–3 (1922): 91–95.

———. *Ideologie und Utopie*. Frankfurt am Main: Vittorio Klostermann, 1985.

———. *Konservatismus: Ein Beitrag zur Soziologie des Wissens*. Edited by David Kettler, Volker Meja, and Nico Stehr. Frankfurt am Main: Suhrkamp Verlag, 1984.

———. *Lélek és kultura* /Soul and Culture/. Budapest: Benkő Gyula Cs. és Kir. Udvari Könyvkereskedése, 1918.

———. "Letters to Lukács, 1910–1916." Edited by Éva Gábor. *The New Hungarian Quarterly* 16, no. 57 (1975): 93–105.

———. *Strukturen des Denkens*. Edited by David Kettler, Volker Meja, and Nico Stehr. Frankfurt am Main: Suhrkamp, 1980.

———. *Wissenssoziologie*. Edited by Kurt H. Wolff. Neuwied: Hermann Luchterhand Verlag, 1964.

Marck, Siegfried. *Die Dialektik in der Philosophie der Gegenwart*, 1. Tübingen: Verlag von J.C.B. Mohr (Paul Siebeck): 1929.

———. "Neukritizistische und neuhegelsche Auffassung der marxistischen Dialektik." *Die Gesellschaft* 1, no. 6 (1924): 573–78.

Marx, Karl. *Ökonomisch-philosophische Manuskripte*. Leipzig: Verlag Philipp Reclam jun., 1970.

Matlaw, Ralph E. (ed.). *Belinsky, Chernyshevsky, and Dobrolyubov: Selected Criticism*. New York: E. P. Dutton & Co., 1962.

Meja, Volker, and Stehr, Nico (eds.). *Der Streit um die Wissenssoziologie*, 1–2. Frankfurt am Main: Suhrkamp Verlag, 1982.

Mendelsohn, Harvey L. *Bauhaus Photography*. Cambridge, Massachusetts: The M.I.T. Press, 1985.

Mesterházi, Miklós, and Krausz, Tamás (eds.). A *"történelem és osztálytudat"* a 20-as évek vitáiban /History and Class Consciousness in the Debates of the 1920s/, 1–4. Budapest: Lukács Archívum és Könyvtár, 1981.

Meyer, Hannes. "bauen." *bauhaus* 2, no. 4 (1928): 12–13.

———. "bauhaus und gesellschaft." *bauhaus*, 3, no. 1 (1929): 2.

Michel, Wilhelm. "Unmögliche Menschen." *Die Weltbühne* 26 (1930): 359–62.

Mises, Ludwig von. *Die Gemeinwirtschaft: Untersuchungen über den Sozialismus*. München: Philosophia Verlag, 1981.

Mises, Ludwig von. "Neue Beiträge zum Problem der sozialistischen Wirtschaftsrechnung." *Archiv für Sozialwissenschaft und Sozialpolitik* 51 (1924): 488–500.

Moholy, Lucia. *Moholy-Nagy, Marginal Notes.* Krefeld: Scherpe Verlag, 1972.

Moholy-Nagy, László. "Die beispiellose Fotografie." *Das Deutsche Lichtbild.* Berlin: Verlag Robert & Bruno Schultz, 1927, x–xi.

———. "fotografie ist lichtgestaltung." *bauhaus* 2, no. 1 (1928): 2–9.

———. "geradlinigkeit des geistes—umwege der technik." *bauhaus*, no. 1 (1926): 5.

———. "Levelei Babits Mihályhoz" /Letters to Mihály Babits/. *Tiszatáj* 26, no. 8 (1972): 29–34.

———. *Malerei, Fotografie, Film.* Mainz: Florian Kupferberg Verlag, 1967.

———. "Neue Gestaltung in der Musik." *Der Sturm* 14 (1923): 102–6.

———. *60 Fotos.* Edited by Franz Roh. Berlin: Klinkhardt & Biermann Verlag, 1930.

———. *The New Vision.* New York: George Wittenborn, 1947.

———. "Versei" /Poems/. *Tiszatáj* 26, no. 8 (1972): 25–27.

———. *Vision in Motion.* Chicago: Paul Theobald and Company, 1956.

———. "Vita az új tartalom és az új forma problémájáról" /Debate Concerning the Problem of New Content and New Form/. *Akasztott Ember*, December 20, 1922, p. 3.

———. *von material zu architektur.* Mainz: Florian Kupferberg Verlag, 1968.

———, and Kemény, Alfréd. "Dynamisch-konstruktives Kraftsystem." *Der Sturm* 13 (1922): 186.

Molnár, Farkas. "A mechanikus szinpad" /The Mechanical Stage/. *Ma* 8, nos. 9–10 (1923): n.p.

Mozetič, Gerald (ed.). *Austromarxistische Positionen.* Wien: Hermann Böhlaus Nachf., 1983.

Musil, Robert. "Ansätze zu neuer Ästhetik: Bemerkungen über eine Dramaturgie des Films." *Der Neue Merkur* 8, no. 6 (1925): 488–506.

Németh, Andor. *A szélén behajtva* /Folded at the Margin/. Budapest: Magvető Könyvkiadó, 1973.

Nyíri, Kristóf (ed.). *A magyar marxista filozófia a két világháború között* /Hungarian Marxist Philosophy between the Two World Wars/. Budapest: Kossuth Könyvkiadó, 1979.

Ottwalt, Ernst. " 'Tatsachenroman' u. Formexperiment: Eine Entgegnung an Georg Lukács." *Die Linkskurve* 4, no. 10 (1932): 21–26.

Ouy, Achille. "Paul Szende." *Revue Internationale de Sociologie* (1925): 79–82.

Pachter, Henry. *Weimar Etudes.* New York: Columbia University Press, 1982.

Piscator, Erwin. *The Political Theatre.* Translated by Hugh Rorrison. New York: Avon Books, 1978.

Polányi, Károly. *A radikalizmus programmja és célja* /Radicalism's Program and Goal/. Szeged: A Szegedi Polgári Radikális Párt, n.d.

———. "Az ó-testamentomi kinyilatkoztatás . . . " /The Old Testament's Revelation . . . /. *Szabadgondolat* 3, no. 3 (1913): 99.

———. "Der englische Generalstreik." *Der Österreichische Volkswirt* 18, no. 2 (1926): 881–83.

———. "Die funktionelle Theorie der Gesellschaft und das Problem der sozialistischen Rechnungslegung (Eine Erwiderung an Prof. Mises und Dr. Felix Weil)." *Archiv für Sozialwissenschaft und Sozialpolitik* 52 (1924): 218–28.

———. "Die neue Internationale." *Der Österreichische Volkswirt* 17, no. 2 (1925): 1379–81.

———. *Egy gazdaságelmélet küszöbén: Cikkek a Bécsi Magyar Újságban, 1921–1923* /On the Threshold of an Economic Theory: Articles in the *Bécsi Magyar Újság, 1921–1923*/. Edited by János Gyurgyák. Budapest: Az Eötvös Loránd Tudományegyetem, 1985.

———. "Előadása 1919. április 28-án a kereskedelem szozializálásáról" /Lecture on the Socialization of Commerce, April 28, 1919/. *Magyar Filozófiai Szemle* 23, no. 5 (1979): 715–24.

———. "England und die Wahlen." *Der Österreichische Volkswirt* 17, no. 1 (1924–25): 153–54.

———. *Fasizmus, demokrácia, ipari társadalom: Társadalomfilozófiai írások* /Fascism, Democracy, Industrial Society: Writings on Social Philosophy/. Edited by Kári Polányi-Levitt and Marguerite Mendell. Budapest: Gondolat, 1986.

———. "Hamlet." *The Yale Review* 43, no. 3 (1954): 336–50.

———. "Liberale Sozialreformer in England." *Der Österreichische Volkswirt* 20, no. 1 (1927–28): 597–600.

———. "Liberale Wirtschaftsreformen in England." *Der Österreichische Volkswirt* 20, no. 1 (1927–28): 544–45.

———. *Primitive, Archaic and Modern Economies: Essays.* Edited by George Dalton. Garden City, New York: Anchor Books, 1968.

———. "Probleme des englischen Generalstreiks." *Der Österreichische Volkswirt* 18, no. 2 (1926): 971–74.

———. "Sozialistische Rechnungslegung." *Archiv für Sozialwissenschaft und Sozialpolitik* 49 (1922): 377–420.

———. "The Essence of Fascism." *Christianity and the Social Revolution.* Edited by John Lewis, Karl Polanyi, and Donald K. Kitchin. Freeport: Books for Libraries Press, 1972.

———. *The Great Transformation: The Political and Economic Origins of Our Time.* Boston: Beacon Press, 1957.

———. "Wirtschaft und Demokratie." *Der Österreichische Volkswirt* 25, no. 1 (1932–33): 301–3.

Punin, N. "Tatlin üvegtornya" /Tatlin's Glass Tower/. *Ma* 7, nos. 5–6 (1922): 31.

Radványi, László. "A Marxista Munkásiskola 1925–1933" /The Marxist Workers School, 1925–1933/. *Világosság* 21, no. 7 (1980): 453–55.

———. *Der Chiliasmus.* Budapest: MTA Filozófiai Intézet Lukács Archívum, 1985.

———. "Korsch, Karl: Marxismus und Philosophie." *Archiv für Sozialwissenschaft und Sozialpolitik* 53 (1925): 528–35.

Reik, Theodor. "Internationale Psychoanalytische Bibliothek." *Imago* 7, no. 2 (1921): 195–97.

Révai, Josef. "Georg Lukács: *Geschichte und Klassenbewusstsein. Studien über marxistische Dialektik.*" *Archiv für die Geschichte des Sozialismus und der Arbeiterbewegung* 11 (1923): 227–36.

Réz, Andreas. "Hauptrichtungen in der neueren ungarischen revolutionären Literatur." *Arbeiter-Literatur* 1, no. 9 (1924): 478–83.

Rosen, Artur. "Die Abenteuer eines Zehnmarkscheins." *Die Literarische Welt*, November 12, 1926, p. 7.

Scheler, Max. *Formalism in Ethics and Non-Formal Ethics of Values.* Translated by Manfred S. Frings and Roger L. Funk. Evanston: Northwestern University Press, 1973.

———. "Probleme einer Soziologie des Wissens." *Versuche zu einer Soziologie des Wissens.* Edited by Max Scheler. München: Verlag von Duncker & Humblot, 1924, 3–146.

———. *The Nature of Sympathy.* Translated by Peter Heath. Hamden, Connecticut: Archon Books, 1970.

Schlemmer, Oskar, Moholy-Nagy, László, and Molnár, Farkas. *Die Bühne im Bauhaus.* Mainz: Florian Kupferberg Verlag, 1965.

Schneede, Uwe M. (ed.). *Die zwanziger Jahre: Manifeste und Dokumente deutscher Künstler.* Köln: DuMont Buchverlag, 1979.

Schwitters, Kurt. "Miképen vagyok elégedetlen az olajfestészettel" /Why I Am Dissatisfied with Oil Painting/. *Ma* 6, no. 3 (1921): 29–30.

Serge, Victor. *Memoirs of a Revolutionary, 1901–1941.* Translated by Peter Sedgwick. London: Oxford University Press, 1963.

Solomon, Maynard (ed.). *Marxism and Art.* New York: Alfred A. Knopf, 1973.

Szabó, Ervin. "A konzervativ és progressziv idealizmus vitája" /The Conservative and Progressive Idealism Debate/. *Huszadik Század* 19 (1918): 376–78.

———. *Imperializmus és tartós béke* /Imperialism and Lasting Peace/. Budapest: Pallas Irodalmi és Nyomdai Részvénytársaság, 1917.

———. *Társadalmi és pártharcok a 48–49-es magyar forradalomban* /Social and Party Conflicts in the 1848–49 Hungarian Revolution/. Bécs: Bécsi Magyar Kiadó, 1921.

Szélpál, Árpád. "Forradalmi művészet—vagy pártművészet" /Revolutionary Art—or Party Art/. *Ma* 4, no. 1 (1919): 4, 9–10.

Szende, Pál. "A polgári radikálizmus" /Citizens Radicalism/. *Világ* 9, no. 42 (1918): 1–2.

———. "Az Einstein-féle elmélet történeti jelentősége" /The Historical Significance of the Einsteinian Theory/. *Nyugat* 15, no. 2 (1922): 117–25.

———. "Bergson, der Metaphysiker der Gegenrevolution." *Die Gesellschaft* (1930): 542–68.

———. "Christian Hungary and Jewish Capitalism." *The New Europe* 17, no. 211 (1920): 67–72.

———. "Das System der Wissenschaften und die Gesellschaftsordnung." *Kölner Vierteljahrshefte für Sozialwissenschaften* 2, no. 4 (1922): 5–17.

———. "Das Zeitalter der Denkfaulheit." *Der Kampf* 26, no. 11 (1933): 452–57.

———. *Demaskierung: Die Rolle der Ideologien in der Geschichte.* Wien: Europa Verlag, 1970.

———. "Der Faschismus in Europa." *Der Kampf* 22, no. 4 (1929): 198–200.

———. "Die Donauföderation." *Der Kampf* 25, nos. 8/9 (1932): 344–49.

———. "Die Krise der mitteleuropäischen Revolution. Ein massenpsychologischer Versuch." *Archiv für Sozialwissenschaft und Sozialpolitik* 47 (1920/1921): 337–75.

———. "Eine soziologische Theorie der Abstraktion." *Archiv für Sozialwissenschaft und Sozialpolitik* 50 (1923): 407–85.

———. *Mystik.* Edited by Fritz Guttmann. Wien: Thalia, 1936.

———. "Oscar Jászi: *Magyar kálvária. Magyar feltámadás*" /Oszkár Jászi: *Hungarian Calvary. Hungarian Resurrection*/. *Archiv für die Geschichte des Sozialismus und der Arbeiterbewegung* 10 (1922): 99–105.

——— "Philosophie und soziales Leben." *Der Kampf* 23, nos. 6/7 (1930): 296–300.

——— "Soziologische Gedanken zur Relativitätstheorie." *Die neue Rundschau* 2 (1921): 1086–95.

——— *Új október felé* /Toward a New October/. Wien: Bécsi Magyar Kiadó, 1922.

——— "Werbőczi." *Huszadik Század* 8 (1907): 821–38.

——— "Wissenschaft und Autorität." *Der Kampf* 15, nos. 9/10 (1922): 302–7.

——— "Zur Soziologie der Revolution." *Der Kampf* 16, nos. 9/10 (1923): 329–37.

Szilasi, Vilmos. *Platon* /Plato/. Budapest: Franklin-Társulat, 1910.

Tamás, Aladár (ed.). *A 100%: A KMP legális folyóirata, 1927–1930* /100%: The Hungarian Communist Party's Legal Periodical, 1927–1930/. Budapest: Akadémiai Kiadó, 1977.

The Threepenny Opera. Classic Film Scripts. London: Lorrimer Publishing, 1984.

Tisza, István. "A választójogi reform küszöbén" /On the Threshold of Suffrage Reform/. *Magyar Figyelő* 2, no. 17 (1912): 329–52.

——— "Nemzet és társadalom" /Nation and Society/. *Magyar Figyelő* 1, no. 22 (1911): 281–93.

——— "Szabadgondolkodás" /Free Thinking/. *Magyar Figyelő* 1, no. 7 (1911): 3–8.

Tolnai, Károly. *Ferenczy Noémi.* Budapest: Bisztrai Farkas Ferencz Kiadása, 1934.

Tolstoy, Leo. *Resurrection.* Translated by Vera Traill. New York: The New American Library, 1961.

Troeltsch, Ernst. *Der Historismus und seine Probleme.* Darmstadt: Scientia Aalen, 1961.

Tucker, Robert C. (ed.). *The Lenin Anthology.* New York: W. W. Norton and Company, 1975.

Uitz, Béla. "Jegyzetek a *Ma* orosz estélyéhez" /Notes on *Ma's* Russian Evening/. *Ma* 6, no. 4 (1921): 52.

Vandervelde, Emile. "A la mémoire de Paul Szende." *Századunk* 9, nos. 8–9 (1934): 321.

Varga, József (ed.). "Négy Ady-levél Jászi Oszkárhoz" /Four Letters From Ady to Oszkár Jászi/. *Irodalomtörténeti Közlemények* 78, no. 6 (1974): 725–27.

Vargha, Kálmán (ed.). *Program és hivatás* /Program and Mission/. Budapest: Gondolat Kiadó, 1978.

Vezér, Erzsébet (ed.). *Írástudó nemzedékek: A Polányi család története dokumentumokban* /Generations of Intellectuals: The History of the Polányi Family in Documents/. Budapest: MTA Filozófiai Intézet Lukács Archívum, 1986.

Walden, Herwarth. "Das Theater als künstlerisches Phänomen." *Ma* 9, nos. 8–9 (1924): n.p.

Weber, Alfred. "Prinzipielles zur Kultursoziologie." *Archiv für Sozialwissenschaft und Sozialpolitik* 47 (1920): 1–49.

Weber, Marianne. *Max Weber: A Biography.* Translated by Harry Zohn. New York: John Wiley, 1975.

Weber, Max. *From Max Weber: Essays in Sociology.* Translated and edited by H. H. Gerth and C. Wright Mills. New York: Oxford University Press, 1946.

Weil, Felix. "Gildensozialistische Rechnungslegung: Kritische Bemerkungen zu Karl Polányi: 'Sozialistische Rechnungslegung.'" *Archiv für Sozialwissenschaft und Sozialpolitik* 52 (1924): 196–217.

Werbőczy, István. *Hármaskönyve* /Tripartitum/. Translated by Sándor Kolosvári and Kelemen Ovári. Budapest: Franklin-Társulat, 1897.

Wingler, Hans M. (ed.). *The Bauhaus: Weimar, Dessau, Berlin, Chicago.* Translated by Wolfgang Jabs and Basil Gilbert. Cambridge, Massachusetts: The M.I.T. Press, 1969.

Wittfogel, K. A. "Zur Frage der marxistischen Aesthetik." *Die Linkskurve* 2, no. 5 (1930): 6–7; 2, no. 6 (1930): 8–11; 2, no. 7 (1930): 20, 22–24; 2, no. 8 (1930): 15–17; 2, no. 9 (1930): 22–26; 2, no. 10 (1930): 20–23; 2, no. 11 (1930): 8–12.

Zalai, Béla. "A filozófiai rendszerezés problémája" /The Problem of Philosophic Systematization/. *A Szellem* 1, no. 2 (1911): 159–86.

Zeisel, Hans. "Polanyi, Karl." *International Encyclopedia of the Social Sciences*, 12. New York: The Macmillan Company and The Free Press, 1968.

SECONDARY SOURCES

Abrams, M. H. *Natural Supernaturalism.* New York: W. W. Norton and Company, 1971.

Angress, Werner T. "Pegasus and Insurrection: *Die Linkskurve* and Its Heritage." *Central European History* 1, no. 1 (1968): 35–55.

Apitzsch, Ursula. *Gesellschaftstheorie und Ästhetik bei Georg Lukács bis 1933.* Stuttgart: Friedrich Frommann Verlag Günther Holzboog, 1977.

Apró, Ferenc. "Moholy-Nagy László ismeretlen fényképei és elfelejtett versei" /Unknown Photographs and Forgotten Poems of László Moholy-Nagy/. *Tiszatáj* 32, no. 5 (1978): 71–75.

―――. "Újabb Moholy-Nagy-rajzok Szegeden" /Fresh Drawings of Moholy-Nagy in Szeged/. *Tiszatáj* 29, no. 3 (1975): 68–72.

Aron, Raymond. *German Sociology.* Translated by Mary and Thomas Bottomore. New York: The Free Press of Glencoe, 1964.

Aussermair, Josef. *Kirche und Sozialdemokratie: Der Bund der religiösen Sozialisten, 1926–1934.* Wien: Europaverlag, 1979.

Avantgarde Osteuropa, 1910–1930. 1967.

Banham, Reyner. *Theory and Design in the First Machine Age.* New York: Praeger, 1967.

Bann, Stephen (ed.). *The Tradition of Constructivism.* London: Thames and Hudson, 1974.

Barany, George. " 'Magyar Jew or: Jewish Magyar'? (To the Question of Jewish Assimilation in Hungary)," *Canadian-American Slavic Studies* 8, no. 1 (1974): 1–44.

Barnicoat, John. *A Concise History of Posters.* London: Thames and Hudson, 1972.

Barr, Alfred H., Jr. *Cubism and Abstract Art.* Cambridge: Harvard University Press, 1986.

Beckett, Jane. "Dada, Van Doesburg and De Stijl." *Journal of European Studies* 9, nos. 33/34 (1979): 1–25.

Beke, László. "Képzőművészet a Ma tíz évfolyamában" /Visual Art in the Ten Volumes of Ma/. *Kritika* 9, no. 3 (1971): 48–51.

Béládi, Miklós. "A magyar irodalmi avantgarde" /The Hungarian Literary Avant-Garde/. *Jelenkor* 16, no. 10 (1973): 932–36.

―――. "Az avantgarde a forradalomban" /The Avant-Garde in the Revolution/. *Literatura* 7, nos. 2–3 (1979): 162–71.

✗ Berlin, Isaiah. *Russian Thinkers.* New York: Penguin Books, 1979.

Berman, Russell. "Lukács' Critique of Bredel and Ottwalt: A Political Account of an Aesthetic Debate of 1931–32." *New German Critique*, no. 10 (1977): 155–78.

Blake, Peter. *Marcel Breuer: Architect and Designer*. New York: Architectural Record and The Museum of Modern Art, 1949.

Bodri, Ferenc. "'Az út, amin haladtunk, alámerült . . . '" /'The Road We Traveled Became Mired . . . '/ *Új Írás*, no. 9 (1988): 117–28; no. 10 (1988): 111–22.

———. "Moholy-Nagy László fotóművészete" /László Moholy-Nagy's Photographic Art/. *Fotóművészet* 16, no. 2 (1973): 3–11.

Bojtár, Endre. *A kelet-európai avantgarde irodalom* /East European Avant-Garde Literature/. Budapest: Akadémiai Kiadó, 1977.

Bori, Imre. *A szecessziótól a dadáig* /From Secession to Dada/. Újvidék: Forum Könyvkiadó, 1969.

———, and Körner, Éva. *Kassák irodalma és festészete* /Kassák's Writing and Painting/. Budapest: Magvető, 1967.

Borsányi, György. *Kun Béla*. Budapest: Kossuth Könyvkiadó, 1979.

Botar, Oliver A. I. "Ernő Kállai and the Hidden Face of Nature." *The Structurist*, nos. 23–24 (1983–84): 77–82.

Breines, Paul. "Praxis and Its Theorists: The Impact of Lukács and Korsch in the 1920's." *Telos*, no. 11 (1972): 67–103.

———, and Arato, Andrew. *The Young Lukács and the Origins of Western Marxism*. New York: The Seabury Press, 1979.

Bowlt, John E. "Art in Exile: The Russian Avant-Garde and the Emigration." *Art Journal* 41, no. 3 (1981): 215–21.

Brown, Edward J. *The Proletarian Episode in Russian Literature, 1928–1932*. New York: Columbia University Press, 1953.

Camus, Albert. *The Rebel*. Translated by Anthony Bower. New York: Vintage Books, 1956.

Child, Arthur. "The Theoretical Possibility of the Sociology of Knowledge." *Ethics* 51, no. 4 (1941): 392–418.

Churchill, Winston S. *The Unknown War: The Eastern Front*. New York: Charles Scribner's Sons, 1932.

Coke, Van Deren. *Avant-Garde Photography in Germany, 1919–1939*. New York: Pantheon Books, 1982.

Cole, G.D.H. *The Second International, 1889–1914*. London: Macmillan and Co., 1956.

Congdon, Lee. "Aurel Kolnai: In Defense of Christian Europe." *The World and I* 3, no. 9 (1988): 631–45.

———. "Endre Ady's Summons to National Regeneration in Hungary, 1900–1919." *Slavic Review* 33, no. 2 (1974): 302–22.

———. "From 'Geschichte und Klassenbewusstsein' to the Blum Theses." *Georg Lukács—Ersehnte Totalität*. Edited by Gvozden Flego and Wolfdietrich Schmied-Kowarzik. Bochum: Germinal Verlag, 1986.

———. "History and Class Consciousness." *The World and I* 2, no. 6 (1987): 549–61.

———. "Hungary in Crisis: Communism and the Intellectuals—1918." *East European Quarterly* 14, no. 2 (1980): 155–69.

———. "Karl Mannheim as Philosopher." *Journal of European Studies* 7, no. 1 (1977): 1–18.

———. "Karl Polanyi in Hungary, 1900–19." *Journal of Contemporary History* 11, no. 1 (1976): 167–83.

Congdon, Lee. "Szilasi Vilmos és a magyar kultúra" /Vilmos Szilasi and Hungarian Culture/. *Filozófiai Figyelő* 2, nos. 3–4 (1980): 29–51.

———. "The Moralist as Social Thinker: Oszkár Jászi in Hungary, 1900–1919." *Historians in Politics*. Edited by Walter Laqueur and George L. Mosse. London: Sage Publications, 1974, 273–313.

———. *The Young Lukács*. Chapel Hill: The University of North Carolina Press, 1983.

Cook, David A. *A History of Narrative Film*. New York: W. W. Norton and Company, 1981.

Csanak, Dóra F. *Balázs Béla hagyatéka az akadémiai könyvtár kézirattárában (MS 5009–MS 5024)* /Béla Balázs's Literary Remains in the Manuscripts Archive of the Academy Library/. Budapest: Bibliotheca Academiae Scientiarum Hungaricae, 1966.

Csendes, Peter. *Geschichte Wiens*. München: R. Oldenbourg Verlag, 1981.

Czeike, Felix. *Liberale, Christlichsoziale und Sozialdemokratische Kommunalpolitik (1861–1934)*. Wien: Verlag für Geschichte und Politik, 1962.

Dahmer, Helmut. *Libido und Gesellschaft: Studien über Freud und die Freudsche Linke*. Frankfurt am Main: Suhrkamp Verlag, 1973.

Dalos, György. *A cselekvés szerelmese: Duczynska Ilona élete* /The Lover of Action: Life of Ilona Duczynska/. Budapest: Kossuth Könyvkiadó, 1984.

Dautrey, Charles, and Guerlain, Jean-Claude. *L'activisme hongrois*. Paris: Editions Goutal-Darly, 1979.

Deák, István. *Weimar Germany's Left-Wing Intellectuals: A Political History of the Weltbühne and Its Circle*. Berkeley: University of California Press, 1968.

Dénes, Zsófia. "Néhány újabb adat Moholy-Nagy Lászlóról" /Some New Data Concerning László Moholy-Nagy/. *Magyar Nemzet*, August 4, 1974, p. 11.

Diamant, Alfred. *Austrian Catholics and the First Republic: Democracy, Capitalism, and the Social Order, 1918–1934*. Princeton: Princeton University Press, 1960.

Die 20er Jahre in Osteuropa. Köln: Galerie Gmurzynska, n.d.

Diószegi, András. *Gábor Andor*. Budapest: Gondolat, 1966.

Divényi, Mihály. "Szende történetírói egyénisége" /Szende's Individuality as a Historian/. *Századunk* 9 (1934): 342–43.

Eisner, Lotte H. *The Haunted Screen*. Berkeley: University of California Press, 1973.

Elderfield, John. "Dissenting Ideologies and the German Revolution." *Studio International* 180, no. 927 (1970): 180–87.

Ermolaev, Herman. *Soviet Literary Theories, 1917–1934: The Genesis of Socialist Realism*. Berkeley: University of California Press, 1963.

Esslin, Martin. *Brecht: The Man and His Work*. Garden City, New York: Doubleday and Company, 1961.

Fehér, Ferenc. "The Last Phase of Romantic Anti-Capitalism: Lukács' Response to the War." *New German Critique*, no. 10 (1977): 139–54.

Fekete, Éva. "Lukács György az első világháború éveiben" /György Lukács During the Years of the First World War/. *Valóság* 20, no. 2 (1977): 33–44.

Ferenczi, László. *Én Kassák Lajos vagyok* /I Am Lajos Kassák/. Budapest: Kozmosz Könyvek, 1987.

Fogarassy, László. "Kik öltek meg gróf Tisza Istvánt?" /Who Murdered Count István Tisza?/ *Történelmi Szemle*, no. 2 (1980): 338–41.

Forgács, Éva. "A Bauhaus és a művészet új fogalma" /The Bauhaus and the New Conception of Art/. *Valóság* 16, no. 6 (1973): 21–32.

————. "Ernő Kállai: The Art Critic of a Changing Age." *The New Hungarian Quarterly* 17, no. 64 (1976): 174–81.

Franciscono, Marcel. *Walter Gropius and the Creation of the Bauhaus in Weimar: The Ideals and Artistic Theories of Its Founding Years.* Urbana: University of Illinois Press, 1971.

Friedman, Mildred (ed.). *De Stijl: 1917–1931: Visions of Utopia.* New York: Abbeville Press, 1982.

Frisby, David. *The Alienated Mind: The Sociology of Knowledge in Germany 1918–33.* London: Heineman Educational Books, 1983.

Fukász, György. *A magyarországi polgári radikalizmus történetéhez 1900–1918: Jászi Oszkár ideológiájának bírálata* /Toward the History of Citizens Radicalism in Hungary 1900–1918: Critique of Oszkár Jászi's Ideology/. Budapest: Gondolat, 1960.

Gabel, Joseph. "Hungarian Marxism." *Telos,* no. 25 (1975): 185–91.

————. *Mannheim et le marxisme hongrois.* Paris: Méridiens Klincksieck, 1987.

Gábor, Éva. "Egy 'elfelejtett' vasárnapos emlékeiből" /From the Recollections of a 'Forgotten' Member of the Sunday Circle/. *Világosság* 21, no. 7 (1980): 449–52.

————. "Mannheim in Hungary and in Weimar Germany." *International Society for the Sociology of Knowledge Newsletter* 9, nos. 1–2 (1983): 7–14.

Gál, István. "A Hungarian at King's." *The New Hungarian Quarterly* 12, no. 41 (1971): 188–91.

————. *Bartóktól Radnótiig* /From Bartók to Radnóti/. Budapest: Magvető Kiadó, 1973.

————. " 'Rosti Magdolna,' a *Nyugat* rejtélyes angol szakértője" /'Rosti Magdolna,' *Nyugat*'s Mysterious Expert on England/. *Irodalomtörténet* 8, no. 4 (1976): 942–51.

Galántai, József. "Magyarország az első világháborúban" /Hungary in the First World War/. *Magyarország története, 1890–1918.* Edited by Péter Hanák. Budapest: Akadémiai Kiadó, 1978, 1083–1234.

————. "Oszkár Jászi's Conceptions on Federalism During the First World War." *Études historiques hongroises,* 2. Edited by Zs. P. Pach et al. Budapest: Akadémiai Kiadó, 1975, 311–26.

Gallas, Helga. *Marxistische Literaturtheorie: Kontroversen im Bund proletarisch-revolutionärer Schriftsteller.* Neuwied: Hermann Luchterhand Verlag, 1971.

Gassner, Hubertus (ed.). *Wechsel Wirkungen: Ungarische Avantgarde in der Weimarer Republik.* Marburg: Jonas Verlag, 1986.

Gay, Peter. *Weimar Culture: The Outsider as Insider.* New York: Harper and Row, 1968.

Gelven, Michael. *A Commentary on Heidegger's "Being and Time".* New York: Harper and Row, 1970.

Glaser, Ernst. *Im Umfeld des Austromarxismus.* Wien: Europaverlag, 1981.

Gluck, Mary. *Georg Lukács and His Generation, 1900–1918.* Cambridge: Harvard University Press, 1985.

————. "Politics versus Culture: Radicalism and the Lukács Circle in Turn of the Century Hungary." *East European Quarterly* 14, no. 2 (1980): 129–54.

————. "Toward a Historical Definition of Modernism: Georg Lukács and the Avant-Garde." *The Journal of Modern History* 58, no. 4 (1986): 845–82.

Goldmann, Lucien. *Lukács et Heidegger.* Edited by Youssef Ishaghpour. Paris: Denoël/ Gonthier, 1973.

Gratz, Gusztáv. *A dualizmus kora: Magyarország története, 1867–1918* /The Era of Dualism: History of Hungary, 1867–1918/, 2. Budapest: Magyar Szemle Társaság, 1934.

Gratz, Gusztáv. A forradalmak kora: Magyarország története, 1918–1920 /The Era of Revolutions: History of Hungary, 1918–1920/. Budapest: Magyar Szemle Társaság, 1935.

Gray, Camilla. The Russian Experiment in Art, 1863–1922. Revised by Marian Burleigh-Motley. London: Thames and Hudson, 1986.

Gruber, Helmut. "Willi Münzenberg's German Communist Propaganda Empire 1921–1933." The Journal of Modern History 38, no. 3 (1966): 278–97.

Grunenberg, Antonia. Bürger und Revolutionär: Georg Lukács, 1918–1928. Köln: Europäische Verlagsanstalt, 1976.

Gulick, Charles A. Austria from Habsburg to Hitler, 1–2. Berkeley: University of California Press, 1948.

Gyertyán, Ervin. "Béla Balázs and the Film." The New Hungarian Quarterly 2, no. 3 (1961): 189–94.

György, Péter. "Az elsikkasztott forradalom" /The Misappropriated Revolution/. Valóság 29, no. 8 (1986): 66–85.

Gyurgyák, János (ed.). "Polányi Károly a Bécsi Magyar Újságnál" /Karl Polányi at the Bécsi Magyar Újság/. Medvetánc, nos. 2–3 (1981): 173–242.

————— (ed.). Polányi Károly, 1886–1964. Budapest: Fővárosi Szabó Ervin Könyvtár, 1986.

————— (ed.). Szende Pál, 1879–1934. Budapest: Fővárosi Szabó Ervin Könyvtár, 1985.

Hajdu, Tibor. Az 1918–as magyarországi polgári demokratikus forradalom /The 1918 Bourgeois Democratic Revolution in Hungary/. Budapest: Kossuth Könyvkiadó, 1968.

—————. The Hungarian Soviet Republic. Translated by Etelka de Láczay, Rudolph Fischer, and Mária Kovács. Budapest: Akadémiai Kiadó, 1979.

Halperin, S. William. Germany Tried Democracy: A Political History of the Reich from 1918 to 1933. New York: W. W. Norton and Company, 1965.

Hanák, Péter. Jászi Oszkár dunai patriotizmusa /Oszkár Jászi's Danubian Patriotism/. Budapest: Magvető Könyvkiadó, 1985.

—————. "Kastély az ugaron" /Manor-House on the Wasteland/. Élét és Irodalom 21, no. 37 (1977): 7.

Hanák, Tibor. Lukács war anders. Meisenheim am Glan: Verlag Anton Hain, 1973.

Hanisch, Ernst. Die Ideologie des Politischen Katholizismus in Österreich, 1918–1938. Wien: Geyer Edition, 1977.

Haus, Andreas. Moholy-Nagy: Fotos und Fotogramme. München: Schirmer/Mosel, 1978.

Hegedüs, Loránt. Ady és Tisza /Ady and Tisza/. Budapest: Nyugat, 1940.

Heller, Ágnes (ed.). Lukács Reappraised. New York: Columbia University Press, 1983.

Hermann, István. Lukács György élete /Life of György Lukács/. Budapest: Corvina Kiadó, 1985.

—————. et al. (eds.). A magyar filozófiai gondolkodás a két világháború között /Hungarian Philosophic Thought between the Two World Wars/. Budapest: Kossuth Könyvkiadó, 1983.

Hevesi, Marija. "Baloldaliság" a filozófiában: Az 1920-as évek filozófiai vitáinak történetéből /"Left-Wingism" in Philosophy: From the History of the Philosophical Controversies of the 1920s/. Translated by István Csibra. Budapest: Kossuth Könyvkiadó, 1979.

Hight, Eleanor M. et al. *Moholy-Nagy: Photography and Film in Weimar Germany.* Wellesley: Wellesley College Museum, 1985.

Hirschbach, Frank D. et al. (eds.). *Germany in the Twenties: The Artist as Social Critic.* Minneapolis: University of Minnesota, 1980.

Horváth, Zoltán. *Irodalom és történelem* /Literature and History/. Budapest: Szépirodalmi Könyvkiadó, 1968.

Huber, Wolfgang (ed.). *Beiträge zur Geschichte der Psychoanalyse in Österreich.* Wien: Geyer-Edition, 1978.

Hughes, Robert. *The Shock of the New.* New York: Alfred A. Knopf, 1981.

Huizinga, J. *The Waning of the Middle Ages.* Garden City, New York: Anchor Books, 1954.

Humphreys, S. C. "History, Economics, and Anthropology: The Work of Karl Polanyi." *History and Theory* 8, no. 2 (1969): 165–212.

Ignotus, Paul. "Die intellektuelle Linke im Ungarn der Horthy-Zeit." *Südost-Forschungen* 27 (1968): 148–241.

Irinyi, Károly. "Jászi és a közép-európai államszövetség terve" /Jászi and the Plan for a Central-European Confederation/. *Világosság* 23, no. 7 (1982): 418–22.

Janos, Andrew C. *The Politics of Backwardness in Hungary, 1825–1945.* Princeton: Princeton University Press, 1982.

Jay, Martin. *The Dialectical Imagination: A History of the Frankfurt School and the Institute of Social Research, 1923–1950.* Boston: Little, Brown and Company, 1973.

——. "The Frankfurt School's Critique of Karl Mannheim and the Sociology of Knowledge." *Telos,* no. 20 (1974): 72–89.

——. "The Frankfurt School's Critique of Marxist Humanism." *Social Research* 39, no. 2 (1972): 285–305.

Johnson, Paul. *Modern Times: The World from the Twenties to the Eighties.* New York: Harper and Row, 1983.

Jones, Peter d'A. *The Christian Socialist Revival, 1877–1914: Religion, Class, and Social Conscience in Late-Victorian England.* Princeton: Princeton University Press, 1968.

József, Farkas. *Értelmiség és forradalom* /Intelligentsia and Revolution/. Budapest: Kossuth Könyvkiadó, 1984.

——. *"Rohanunk a forradalomba":* A magyar irodalom eszmélése, 1914–1919 /"We Are Rushing Headlong to Revolution": The Consciousness of Hungarian Literature, 1914–1919/. Budapest: Gondolat Kiadó, 1969.

Juhász Nagy, Sándor. *A magyar októberi forradalom története (1918 okt. 31–1919 Márc. 21)* /The History of Hungary's October Revolution (October 31, 1918–March 21, 1919/. Budapest: Cserépfalvi, 1945.

Kammler, Jörg. *Politische Theorie von Georg Lukács: Struktur und historischer Praxisbezug bis 1929.* Neuwied: Hermann Luchterhand Verlag, 1974.

Kann, Robert A.; Király, Béla K.; and Fichtner, Paula S. (eds.). *The Habsburg Empire in World War I.* Boulder: East European Quarterly, 1977.

Karádi, Éva. "A Lukács-kör Bécsben" /The Lukács Circle in Vienna/. *Magyar Filozófiai Szemle* 31, no. 3 (1987): 601–11.

——. "Lukács fordulatának heidelbergi fogadtatása" /The Heidelberg Reception of Lukács's Volte-Face/. *Magyar Filozófiai Szemle* 31, no. 4 (1987): 683–98.

——. "Lukács, Fülep és a magyar szellemtudományi iskola" /Lukács, Fülep and Hungary's School of the Humanistic Sciences/. *Magyar Filozófiai Szemle* 29, nos. 1–2 (1985): 1–55.

Karcsai Kulcsár, István (ed.). *A film költészete: Az útkereső Balázs Béla* /The Poetry of Film: The Path-Seeking Béla Balázs/. Budapest: Múzsák Közművelődési Kiadó, 1984.

Kemény, Gábor. *Szabó Ervin és a magyar társadalomszemlélet* /Ervin Szabó and the Hungarian View of Society/. Budapest: Magvető Kiadó, 1977.

Kettler, David. "Culture and Revolution: Lukács in the Hungarian Revolutions of 1918/19." *Telos*, no. 10 (1971): 35–92.

————. "Sociology of Knowledge and Moral Philosophy: The Place of Traditional Problems in the Formation of Mannheim's Thought." *Political Science Quarterly* 82, no. 3 (1967): 399–426.

————; Meja, Volker; and Stehr, Nico. *Karl Mannheim*. Chichester: Ellis Horwood, 1984.

Király, Béla K.; Pastor, Peter; and Sanders, Ivan (eds.). *Total War and Peacemaking: A Case Study on Trianon*. Brooklyn: Brooklyn College Press, 1982.

Kirkpatrick, Diane. "Light in the Work of László Moholy-Nagy." *Cross Currents*, no. 7 (1988): 295–308.

Klemperer, Klemens von. *Ignaz Seipel: Christian Statesman in a Time of Crisis*. Princeton: Princeton University Press, 1972.

Kliemann, Helga. *Die Novembergruppe*. Berlin: Gebr. Mann Verlag, 1969.

Koch, Gertrud. "Béla Balázs: The Physiognomy of Things." *New German Critique*, no. 40 (1987): 167–77.

Kolakowski, Leszek. *Main Currents of Marxism*, 1–3. Translated by P. S. Falla. Oxford: Clarendon Press, 1978.

Komlós, Aladár. *Kritikus számadás* /Critical Reckoning/. Budapest: Szépirodalmi Könyvkiadó, 1977.

Komoróczy, Emőke G. *Kassák az emigrációban 1920–1926* /Kassák in the Emigration 1920–1926/. Budapest: Csepeli Munkásotthon Olvasó Munkás Klub, 1987.

Korda, Michael. *Charmed Lives: A Family Romance*. New York: Random House, 1979.

Kostelanetz, Richard (ed.). *Moholy-Nagy*. New York: Praeger Publishers, 1970.

Kovesdy, Paul K. (ed.). *Art of the Twenties*. New York: Matignon Gallery, n.d.

———— (ed.). *Béla Bartók and the East European Avant-Garde Art*. New York: Matignon Gallery, n.d.

Kovrig, Bennett. *Communism in Hungary: From Kun to Kádár*. Stanford: Hoover Institution Press, 1979.

Kracauer, Siegfried. *From Caligari to Hitler: A Psychological History of the German Film*. Princeton: Princeton University Press, 1947.

Kurucz, Jenő. *Struktur und Funktion der Intelligenz während der Weimarer Republik*. Köln: Grote, 1967.

Lackó, Miklós. *Szerep és mű* /Role and Work/. Budapest: Gondolat, 1981.

————. *Válságok—választások* /Crises—Choices/. Budapest: Gondolat, 1975.

Lane, Barbara Miller. *Architecture and Politics in Germany, 1918–1945*. Cambridge, Massachusetts: Harvard University Press, 1985.

Laqueur, Walter. *Russia and Germany*. Boston: Little, Brown and Company, 1965.

————. *Weimar: A Cultural History*. New York: G. P. Putnam's Sons, 1974.

Lederer, E. "Die Geschichtsauffassung der bürgerlichen Radikalen: Die historischen

Schriften von Pál Szende." *Études historiques hongroises.* Edited by Zs. P. Pach et al. Budapest: Akadémiai Kiadó, 1975, 239–73.

Lengyel, András. "A fiatal Révai 'etikus' nézeteiről: Adalék Lukács György és Révai József 1919-es kapcsolatához" /On the Young Révai's "Ethical" Views: Data on the Relationship between György Lukács and József Révai in 1919/. *Irodalomtörténet* 5, no. 2 (1973): 281–311.

Lenk, Kurt. *Marx in der Wissenssoziologie: Studien zur Rezeption der Marxschen Ideologiekritik.* Neuwied: Hermann Luchterhand Verlag, 1972.

Leser, Norbert (ed.). *Das geistige Leben Wiens in der Zwischenkriegszeit.* Wien: Österreichischer Bundesverlag, 1981.

———. *Zwischen Reformismus und Bolschewismus: Der Austromarxismus als Theorie und Praxis.* Wien: Europaverlag, 1968.

Lewis, Jill. "Red Vienna: Socialism in One City, 1918–27." *European Studies Review* 13, no. 3 (1983): 335–55.

Leyda, Jay. *Kino: A History of the Russian and Soviet Film.* London: George Allen & Unwin, 1960.

Lichtheim, George. *The Concept of Ideology and Other Essays.* New York: Vintage Books, 1967.

Litván, György. "A Moralist Revolutionary's Dilemma: In Memory of Ervin Szabó." *Radical History Review* no. 24 (1980): 77–90.

———. "Documents of a Friendship: From the Correspondence of Michael Károlyi and Oscar Jászi." *East Central Europe* 4, no. 2 (1977): 111–46.

———. "Irányzatok és viták a bécsi magyar emigrációban" /Tendencies and Controversies in the Hungarian Emigration in Vienna/. *A két világháború közötti Magyarországról* /On Hungary between the Two World Wars/. Edited by Miklós Lackó. Budapest: Kossuth Könyvkiadó, 1984, 183–225.

———. " 'Tragikai vétség'—avagy időszerűtlen program? Jászi Oszkár és a 'Kisantantorientáció' " /"Tragic Offense"—or Untimely Program? Oszkár Jászi and the "Little Entente Orientation"/. *Élet és Irodalom,* May 3, 1980, p. 5.

Loader, Colin. *The Intellectual Development of Karl Mannheim: Culture, Politics, and Planning.* Cambridge: Cambridge University Press, 1985.

Löwy, Michael. *Pour une sociologie des intellectuels révolutionnaires: L'évolution politique de Lukács 1909–1929.* Paris: Presses Universitaires de France, 1976.

Lukacs, John. *Budapest 1900.* New York: Weidenfeld & Nicolson, 1988.

Macartney, C. A. *The Social Revolution in Austria.* Cambridge: Cambridge University Press, 1926.

Mályusz, Elemér. *The Fugitive Bolsheviks.* London: Grant Richards, 1931.

Mansbach, Steven A. *Visions of Totality: László Moholy-Nagy, Theo Van Doesburg, and El Lissitzky.* Ann Arbor: UMI Research Press, 1980.

Marcus-Tar, Judith. "Georg Lukács, Thomas Mann und 'Der Tod in Venedig.'" *Die Weltwoche,* July 2, 1971, p. 31.

———. *Thomas Mann und Georg Lukács.* Budapest: Corvina Kiadó, 1982.

———, and Tarr Zoltán (eds.). *Georg Lukács: Theory, Culture, and Politics.* New Brunswick: Transaction Publishers, 1989.

Markovits, Györgyi. "A bécsi Világosságról" /On the Vienna Világosság/. *Magyar Könyvszemle* 95, no. 3 (1979): 301–7.

Mellor, David (ed.). *Germany: The New Photography, 1927–33*. London: Arts Council of Great Britain, 1978.

Mesterházi, Miklós. *A messianizmus történetfilozófusa—Lukács György munkássága a húszas években* /The Historical Philosopher of Messianism—György Lukács's Work in the 1920s/. Budapest: MTA Filozófiai Intézet Lukács Archívum, 1987.

————. "Rudas László és a húszas évek Lukács-vitája" /László Rudas and the Lukács Debate of the 1920s/. *Magyar Filozófiai Szemle* 28, nos. 1–2 (1984): 93–118.

————, and Krausz, Tamás. *Mű és történelem: Viták Lukács György műveiről a huszas években* /Work and History: Debates on György Lukács's Works in the 1920s/. Budapest: Gondolat, 1985.

Mészáros, István. *Lukács' Concept of Dialectic*. London: The Merlin Press, 1972.

Miller, Martin A. "Freudian Theory Under Bolshevik Rule: The Theoretical Controversy During the 1920s." *Slavic Review* 44, no. 4 (1985): 625–46.

Moholy-Nagy, Sibyl. "Constructivism from Kasimir Malevitch to László Moholy-Nagy." *Arts & Architecture* 83, no. 5 (1966): 24–28.

————. *Moholy-Nagy: Experiment in Totality*. Cambridge, Massachusetts: The M.I.T. Press, 1969.

Nagy, Magda K. *Balázs Béla világa* /Béla Balázs's World/. Budapest: Kossuth Könyvkiadó, 1973.

Naylor, Gillian. *The Bauhaus Reassessed*. New York: E. P. Dutton, 1985.

Nemeskürty, István. *Word and Image: History of the Hungarian Cinema*. Translated by Zsuzsanna Horn. Budapest: Corvina Press, 1968.

Németh, Lajos. *Modern Art in Hungary*. Translated by Lili Halápy and Elizabeth West. Budapest: Corvina Press, 1969.

Newhall, Beaumont. *The History of Photography*. New York: The Museum of Modern Art, 1982.

Novák, Zoltán. *A Vásárnap Társaság* /The Sunday Society/. Budapest: Kossuth Könyvkiadó, 1979.

————. *Thomas Mann és a fiatal Lukács* /Thomas Mann and the Young Lukács/. Budapest: Kossuth Könyvkiadó, 1988.

Nyíri, Kristóf, and Kiss, Endre (eds.). *A magyar filozófiai gondolkodás a századelőn* /Hungarian Philosophic Thought at the Beginning of the Century/. Budapest: Kossuth Könyvkiadó, 1977.

Palmer, Richard E. *Hermeneutics*. Evanston: Northwestern University Press, 1969.

Palmier, Jean-Michel. "Béla Balázs, théoricien marxiste du cinéma." In *Béla Balázs, L'esprit du cinéma*. Paris: Payot, 1977, 7–117.

Passuth, Krisztina. "Debut of László Moholy—Nagy." *Acta Historiae Artium* 19 (1973): 125–42.

————. *Magyar művészek az európai avantgarde-ban: A kubizmustól a konstruktivizmusig 1919–1925* /Hungarian Artists in the European Avant-Garde: From Cubism to Constructivism 1919–1925/. Budapest: Corvina, 1974.

————. *Moholy-Nagy*. Budapest: Corvina, 1982.

Pastor, Peter. *Hungary between Wilson and Lenin: The Hungarian Revolution of 1918–1919 and the Big Three*. Boulder: East European Quarterly, 1976.

Pike, David. *German Writers in Soviet Exile, 1933–1945*. Chapel Hill: The University of North Carolina Press, 1982.

————. *Lukács and Brecht*. Chapel Hill: The University of North Carolina Press, 1985.

Poggioli, Renato. *The Theory of the Avant-Garde*. Translated by Gerald Fitzgerald. New York: Harper and Row, 1971.

Pók, Lajos. *Babits Mihály*. Budapest: Szépirodalmi Könyvkiadó, 1970.

Pölöskei, Ferenc. "Szemben az árral: Tisza István utolsó évei" /Against the Tide: István Tisza's Last Years/. *Valóság* 26, no. 5 (1983): 87–97.

Rabinbach, Anson (ed.). *The Austrian Socialist Experiment: Social Democracy and Austromarxism, 1918–1934*. Boulder: Westview Press, 1985.

————. *The Crisis of Austrian Socialism: From Red Vienna to Civil War, 1927–1934*. Chicago: The University of Chicago Press, 1983.

Racine, Nicole. "The Clarté Movement in France, 1919–21." *The Journal of Contemporary History* 2, no. 2 (1967): 195–208.

Ralmon, John. "Béla Balázs in German Exile." *Film Quarterly* 30, no. 3 (1977): 12–19.

Remmling, Gunter W. *Road to Suspicion: A Study of Modern Mentality and the Sociology of Knowledge*. New York: Appleton-Century-Crofts, 1967.

————. *The Sociology of Karl Mannheim*. Atlantic Highlands, New Jersey: Humanities Press, 1975.

Richter, Hans. *Dada: Art and Anti-Art*. New York: Oxford University Press, 1965.

Rickey, George. *Constructivism: Origins and Evolution*. New York: George Braziller, 1967.

Ridley, Hugh. "Tretjakov in Berlin." *Culture and Society in the Weimar Republic*. Edited by Keith Bullivant. Manchester: Manchester University Press, 1977, 150–65.

Rigby, Ida Katherine. *An alle Künstler! War—Revolution—Weimar*. San Diego: San Diego State University Press, 1983.

Robinson, Paul A. *The Freudian Left*. New York: Harper and Row, 1969.

Rónay, György. *Kassák Lajos*. Budapest: Szépirodalmi Könyvkiadó, 1971.

Rossi, Sirpa. "Über das Problem der Verdinglichung bei Lukács und Heidegger." *Ajatus* 34 (1972): 155–61.

Rucker, R. D. "Abram Moiseevic Deborin: Weltanschauung and Role in the Development of Soviet Philosophy." *Studies in Soviet Thought* 19, no. 3 (1979): 185–207.

Salyámosy, Miklós. *Magyar irodalom Németországban, 1913–1933* /Hungarian Literature in Germany, 1913–1933/. Budapest: Akadémiai Kiadó, 1973.

Sárközi, Mátyás. "The Influence of Georg Lukács on the Young Karl Mannheim in the Light of a Newly Discovered Diary." *The Slavonic and East European Review* 64, no. 3 (1986): 432–39.

Schacht, Richard. *Alienation*. Garden City, New York: Anchor Books, 1970.

Schlett, István. "Szabó Ervin és az 'etikai idealizmus' vitája 1918-ban" /Ervin Szabó and the "Ethical Idealism" Debate in 1918/. *Valóság* 11, no. 10 (1968): 95–101.

Schmitt, Bernadotte E., and Vedeler, Harold C. *The World in the Crucible, 1914–1919*. New York: Harper and Row, 1984.

Shattuck, Roger. *The Banquet Years: The Origins of the Avant-Garde in France—1885 to World War I*. New York: Vintage Books, 1968.

Simonds, A. P. *Karl Mannheim's Sociology of Knowledge*. Oxford: Clarendon Press, 1978.

Sipos, Lajos. *Babits Mihály és a forradalmak kora* /Mihály Babits and the Era of Revolutions/. Budapest: Akadémiai Kiadó, 1976.

Staller, Tamás. "Karl Mannheim és a tudásszociológia" /Karl Mannheim and the Sociology of Knowledge/. *Valóság* 25, no. 12 (1982): 50–60.

Steneberg, Eberhard. *Russische Kunst Berlin, 1919–1932*. Berlin: Gebr. Mann Verlag, 1969.

Stone, Norman. "Hungary and the Crisis of July 1914." *Journal of Contemporary History* 1, no. 3 (1966): 153–70.

———. *The Eastern Front, 1914–1917*. New York: Charles Scribner's Sons, 1975.

Štraus, Tomáš. *Kassák: Ein ungarischer Beitrag zum Konstruktivismus*. Köln: Galerie Gmurzynska, 1975.

Stromberg, Roland N. *Redemption by War: The Intellectuals and 1914*. Lawrence: The Regents Press of Kansas, 1982.

Szabó, Géza. "Adalékok Szende Pál adópolitikájához" /Data Concerning Paul Szende's Politics of Taxation/. *Acta Academiae Paedagogicae Nyíregyháziensis* 5 (1973): 43–51.

Szabó, Júlia. *A magyar aktivizmus művészete, 1915–1927* /The Art of Hungarian Activism, 1915–1927/. Budapest: Corvina, 1981.

———. *A magyar aktivizmus története* /The History of Hungarian Activism/. Budapest: Akadémiai Kiadó, 1971.

Szabolcsi, Miklós. "Előszó: Balázs Béla" /Introduction: Béla Balázs/. In Béla Balázs, *Lehetetlen emberek* /Impossible People/. Budapest: Szépirodalmi Könyvkiadó, 1965, 7–37.

———. "Út a magánytól a közösségig: Balázs Béla" /The Road from Loneliness to Community: Béla Balázs/. *A magyar irodalom története 1919-től napjainkig* /History of Hungarian Literature from 1919 to the Present/. Edited by Miklós Szabolcsi. Budapest: Akadémiai Kiadó, 1966, 245–62.

———; Illés, László, and József, Farkas (eds.). *"Wir kämpften treu für die Revolution": Studien zur Geschichte der ungarischen sozialistischen Literatur*. Budapest: Akadémiai Kiadó, 1979.

Székely, Artur. "Szende Pál emlékezete" /Recollection of Paul Szende/. *A Kereskedelmi Élet*, no. 44 (1947).

Szekfű, Gyula. *Három nemzedék és ami utána következik* /Three Generations and After/. Budapest: A Királyi Magyar Egyetemi Nyomda, 1934.

Szerdahelyi, Edit. "Irodalom és politika 1918–1919-ben" /Literature and Politics in 1918–1919/. *Valóság* 12, no. 6 (1969): 41–47.

Szerdahelyi, István (ed.). *Lukács György és a magyar kultúra* /György Lukács and Hungarian Culture/. Budapest: Kossuth Könyvkiadó, 1982.

Sziklai, László. "A Blum-tézisek 'nagysága és bukása'" /The "Greatness and Defeat" of the Blum Theses/. *Világosság* 25, no. 4 (1984): 230–37.

——— (ed.). *Az élő Lukács* /The Living Lukács/. Budapest: Kossuth Könyvkiadó, 1986.

———. *Lukács és a fasizmus kora* /Lukács and the Fascist Era/. Budapest: Magvető Kiadó, 1985.

———. *Proletárforradalom után: Lukács György marxista fejlődése 1930–1945* /After the Proletarian Revolution: György Lukács's Marxist Evolution 1930–1945/. Budapest: Kossuth Könyvkiadó, 1986.

———. "Szellemi közösségben: Lukács György és Mihail Lifsic" /In Intellectual Community: György Lukács and Mikhail Lifshitz/. *Világosság* 25, no. 2 (1984): 81–89.

Tar, Zoltán. *The Frankfurt School: The Critical Theories of Max Horkheimer and Theodor W. Adorno*. New York: John Wiley & Sons, 1977.

Tasi, József. "Októbrizmus vagy bolsevizmus? Gábor Andor és Jászi Oszkár polémiája"

/Octoberism or Bolshevism? The Controversy between Andor Gábor and Oszkár Jászi/. *Irodalomtörténeti Közlemények* 85, no. 4 (1981): 398–420.

Tőkés, Rudolf L. *Béla Kun and the Hungarian Soviet Republic.* New York: Frederick A. Praeger, 1967.

Ungarische Avantgarde, 1909–1930. Munich: Galleria del Levante, n.d.

Ungvári, Tamás. *Avantgarde vagy realizmus? Brecht és Lukács vitájáról* /Avant-Garde or Realism? On the Brecht-Lukács Debate/. Budapest: Magvető Kiadó, 1979.

―――― "Brecht és Lukács vitája a harmincas években" /Brecht and Lukács's Debate in the 1930s/. *Valóság* 21, no. 9 (1978): 27–41.

Urbán, Károly. "A Blum-tézisek 'utóélete' " /The "Afterlife" of the Blum Theses/. *Magyar Filozófiai Szemle* 29, nos. 1–2 (1985): 125–45.

―――― *Lukács György és a magyar munkásmozgalom* /György Lukács and the Hungarian Working-Class Movement/. Budapest: Kossuth Könyvkiadó, 1985.

Varga, József. *Ady és kora* /Ady and His Age/. Budapest: Kossuth Könyvkiadó, 1977.

Varró, István. "Szende Pál, 1879–1934." *Századunk* 9, nos. 8–9 (1934): 330–41.

Vermes, Gábor. "Count István Tisza and the Preservation of the Old Order." *Canadian-American Review of Hungarian Studies* 2, no. 1 (1975): 33–42.

―――― *István Tisza.* New York: East European Monographs, 1985.

―――― "The Agony of Federalism in Hungary under the Károlyi Regime, 1918/1919." *East European Quarterly* 6, no. 4 (1972): 487–503.

Vezér, Erzsébet. *Lesznai Anna élete* /Life of Anna Lesznai/. Budapest: Kossuth Könyvkiadó, 1979.

Völgyes, Iván (ed.). *Hungary in Revolution, 1918–19.* Lincoln: University of Nebraska Press, 1971.

Watnick, Morris. "Georg Lukács: An Intellectual Biography." *Soviet Survey*, January-March 1958, 60–66; April-June 1958, 51–57; July-September 1958, 61–68; January-March 1959, 75–81.

Weitemeier, Hannah (ed.). *László Moholy-Nagy.* Stuttgart: Verlag Gerd Hatje, 1974.

――――(ed.). *Licht-Visionen: Ein Experiment von Moholy-Nagy.* Berlin: Bauhaus-Archiv, 1972.

Wem gehört die Welt—Kunst und Gesellschaft in der Weimarer Republik. Berlin: Neue Gesellschaft für Bildende Kunst, 1977.

Whitford, Frank. *Bauhaus.* London: Thames and Hudson, 1984.

Willett, John. *Art and Politics in the Weimar Period: The New Sobriety, 1917–1933.* New York: Pantheon Books, 1978.

Williams, Robert C. *Culture in Exile: Russian Emigrés in Germany, 1881–1941.* Ithaca: Cornell University Press, 1972.

Wingler, Hans M. *Kleine Bauhaus-Fibel.* Berlin: Bauhaus-Archiv, 1974.

Woldring, Henk E. S. *Karl Mannheim: The Development of his Thought.* Translated by Stanley M. Wiersma. Assen: Van Gorcum, 1986.

Zalán, Vince. "A rajongó: A 'filmes' Balázs Béláról" /The Devotee: On Béla Balázs as a Film Enthusiast/. *Filmvilág*, no. 8 (1984): 19–22.

Zsuffa, Joseph. *Béla Balázs: The Man and the Artist.* Berkeley: University of California Press, 1987.

INDEX